GENERAL MOTORS | CHEVROLET SPRINT & METRO, GEO METRO/SUZUKI SWIFT 1985-2000 REPAIR MANUAL

Covers all U.S. and Canadian models of Chevrolet Sprint and Metro, Geo Metro, and Suzuki Swift

by **Joseph D'Orazio**, A.S.E.

CHILTON *Automotive Books*

PUBLISHED BY **HAYNES NORTH AMERICA**, Inc.

Manufactured in USA
© 2001 Haynes North America, Inc.
ISBN 1 56392 427 7
Library of Congress Control No. 2001090882

Haynes Publishing Group
Sparkford Nr Yeovil
Somerset BA22 7JJ England

Haynes North America, Inc
861 Lawrence Drive
Newbury Park
California 91320 USA

ABCDE
FGHIJ
KLMNO
PQ

Contents

Contents

DRIVE TRAIN

7

SUSPENSION AND STEERING

8

BRAKES

9

BODY AND TRIM

10

GLOSSARY

APPENDIX

MASTER INDEX

SAFETY NOTICE

Proper service and repair procedures are vital to the safe, reliable operation of all motor vehicles, as well as the personal safety of those performing repairs. This manual outlines procedures for servicing and repairing vehicles using safe, effective methods. The procedures contain many NOTES, CAUTIONS and WARNINGS which should be followed, along with standard procedures to eliminate the possibility of personal injury or improper service which could damage the vehicle or compromise its safety.

It is important to note that repair procedures and techniques, tools and parts for servicing motor vehicles, as well as the skill and experience of the individual performing the work vary widely. It is not possible to anticipate all of the conceivable ways or conditions under which vehicles may be serviced, or to provide cautions as to all possible hazards that may result. Standard and accepted safety precautions and equipment should be used when handling toxic or flammable fluids, and safety goggles or other protection should be used during cutting, grinding, chiseling, prying, or any other process that can cause material removal or projectiles.

Some procedures require the use of tools specially designed for a specific purpose. Before substituting another tool or procedure, you must be completely satisfied that neither your personal safety, nor the performance of the vehicle will be endangered.

Although information in this manual is based on industry sources and is complete as possible at the time of publication, the possibility exists that some car manufacturers made later changes which could not be included here. While striving for total accuracy, the authors or publishers cannot assume responsibility for any errors, changes or omissions that may occur in the compilation of this data.

PART NUMBERS

Part numbers listed in this reference are not recommendations by Haynes North America, Inc. for any product brand name. They are references that can be used with interchange manuals and aftermarket supplier catalogs to locate each brand supplier's discrete part number.

SPECIAL TOOLS

Special tools are recommended by the vehicle manufacturer to perform their specific job. Use has been kept to a minimum, but where absolutely necessary, they are referred to in the text by the part number of the tool manufacturer. These tools can be purchased, under the appropriate part number, from your local dealer or regional distributor, or an equivalent tool can be purchased locally from a tool supplier or parts outlet. Before substituting any tool for the one recommended, read the SAFETY NOTICE at the top of this page.

ACKNOWLEDGMENTS

Portions of materials contained herein have been reprinted with the permission of General Motors Corporation, Service Technology Group.

While every attempt is made to ensure that the information in this manual is correct, no liability can be accepted by the authors or publishers for loss, damage or injury caused by any errors in, or omissions from, the information given.

1

GENERAL INFORMATION AND MAINTENANCE

HOW TO USE THIS BOOK

Chilton's Total Car Care manual for the 1985 - 00 Metro and Sprint is intended to help you learn more about the inner workings of your vehicle while saving you money on its upkeep and operation.

The beginning of the book will likely be referred to the most, since that is where you will find information for maintenance and tune-up. The other sections deal with the more complex systems of your vehicle. Operating systems from engine through brakes are covered to the extent that the average do-it-yourselfer becomes mechanically involved. This book will not explain such things as rebuilding a differential for the simple reason that the expertise required and the investment in special tools make this task uneconomical. It will, however, give you detailed instructions to help you change your own brake pads and shoes, replace spark plugs, and perform many more jobs that can save you money, give you personal satisfaction and help you avoid expensive problems.

A secondary purpose of this book is a reference for owners who want to understand their vehicle and/or their mechanics. In this case, no tools at all are required.

Where to Begin

Before removing any bolts, read through the entire procedure. This will give you the overall view of what tools and supplies will be required. There is nothing more frustrating than having to walk to the bus stop on Monday morning because you were short one bolt on Sunday afternoon. So read ahead and plan ahead. Each operation should be approached logically and all procedures thoroughly understood before attempting any work.

All sections contain adjustments, maintenance, removal and installation procedures, and in some cases, repair or overhaul procedures. When repair is not considered practical, we tell you how to remove the part and then how to install the new or rebuilt replacement. In this way, you at least save labor costs. "Backyard" repair of some components is just not practical.

Avoiding Trouble

Many procedures in this book require you to "label and disconnect . . . " a group of lines, hoses or wires. Don't be lulled into thinking you can remember where everything goes - you won't. If you hook up vacuum or fuel lines incorrectly, the vehicle may run poorly, if at all. If you hook up electrical wiring incorrectly, you may instantly learn a very expensive lesson.

You don't need to know the official or engineering name for each hose or line. A piece of masking tape on the hose and a piece on its fitting will allow you to assign your own label such as the letter A or a short name. As long as you remember your own code, the lines can be reconnected by matching similar letters or names. Do remember that tape will dissolve in gasoline or other fluids; if a component is to be washed or cleaned, use another method of identification. A permanent felt-tipped marker or a metal scribe can be very handy for marking metal parts. Remove any tape or paper labels after assembly.

Maintenance or Repair?

It's necessary to mention the difference between maintenance and repair. Maintenance includes routine inspections, adjustments, and replacement of parts which show signs of normal wear. Maintenance compensates for wear or deterioration. Repair implies that something has broken or is not working. A need for repair is often caused by lack of maintenance. Example: draining and refilling the automatic transmission fluid is maintenance recommended by the manufacturer at specific mileage intervals. Failure to do this can shorten the life of the transmission/transaxle, requiring very expensive repairs. While no maintenance program can prevent items from breaking or wearing out, a general rule can be stated: MAINTENANCE IS CHEAPER THAN REPAIR.

Two basic mechanic's rules should be mentioned here. First, whenever the left side of the vehicle or engine is referred to, it is meant to specify the driver's side. Conversely, the right side of the vehicle means the passenger's side. Second, screws and bolts are removed by turning counterclockwise, and tightened by turning clockwise unless specifically noted.

Safety is always the most important rule. Constantly be aware of the dangers involved in working on an automobile and take the proper precautions. See the information in this section regarding SERVICING YOUR VEHICLE SAFELY and the SAFETY NOTICE on the acknowledgment page.

Avoiding the Most Common Mistakes

Pay attention to the instructions provided. There are 3 common mistakes in mechanical work:

1. Incorrect order of assembly, disassembly or adjustment. When taking something apart or putting it together, performing steps in the wrong order usually just costs you extra time; however, it CAN break something. Read the entire procedure before beginning disassembly. Perform everything in the order in which the instructions say you should, even if you can't immediately see a reason for it. When you're taking apart something that is very intricate, you might want to draw a picture of how it looks when assembled at one point in order to make sure you get everything back in its proper position. We will supply exploded views whenever possible. When making adjustments, perform them in the proper order. One adjustment possibly will affect another.

2. Overtorquing (or undertorquing). While it is more common for overtorquing to cause damage, undertorquing may allow a fastener to vibrate loose causing serious damage. Especially when dealing with aluminum parts, pay attention to torque specifications and utilize a torque wrench in assembly. If a torque figure is not available, remember that if you are using the right tool to perform the job, you will probably not have to strain yourself to get a fastener tight enough. The pitch of most threads is so slight that the tension you put on the wrench will be multiplied many times in actual force on what you are tightening. A good example of how critical torque is can be seen in the case of spark plug installation, especially where you are putting the plug into an aluminum cylinder head. Too little torque can fail to crush the gasket, causing leakage of combustion gases and consequent overheating of the plug and engine parts. Too much torque can damage the threads or distort the plug, changing the spark gap.

There are many commercial products available for ensuring that fasteners won't come loose, even if they are not torqued just right (a very common brand is Loctite,). If you're worried about getting something together tight enough to hold, but loose enough to avoid mechanical damage during assembly, one of these products might offer substantial insurance. Before choosing a threadlocking compound, read the label on the package and make sure the product is compatible with the materials, fluids, etc. involved.

3. Crossthreading. This occurs when a part such as a bolt is screwed into a nut or casting at the wrong angle and forced. Crossthreading is more likely to occur if access is difficult. It helps to clean and lubricate fasteners, then to start threading the bolt, spark plug, etc. with your fingers. If you encounter resistance, unscrew the part and start over again at a different angle until it can be inserted and turned several times without much effort. Keep in mind that many parts, especially spark plugs, have tapered threads, so that gentle turning will automatically bring the part you're threading to the proper angle. Don't put a wrench on the part until it's been tightened a couple of turns by hand. If you suddenly encounter resistance, and the part has not seated fully, don't force it. Pull it back out to make sure it's clean and threading properly.

Be sure to take your time and be patient, and always plan ahead. Allow yourself ample time to perform repairs and maintenance. You may find maintaining your car a satisfying and enjoyable experience.

TOOLS AND EQUIPMENT

See Figures 1, 2, 3, 4, 5, 6, 7, 8, 9, 10, 11, 12, 13, 14 and 15

Naturally, without the proper tools and equipment it is impossible to properly service your vehicle. It would also be virtually impossible to catalog every tool that you would need to perform all of the operations in this book. Of course, it would be unwise for the amateur to rush out and buy an expensive set of tools

on the theory that he/she may need one or more of them at some time.

The best approach is to proceed slowly, gathering a good quality set of those tools that are used most frequently. Don't be misled by the low cost of bargain tools. It is far better to spend a little more for better quality. Forged wrenches, 6 or 12-point sockets and fine tooth ratchets are by far preferable to their less expensive counterparts. As any good mechanic can tell you, there are few worse

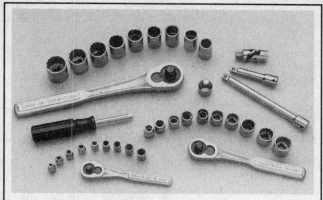

Fig. 1 All but the most basic procedures will require an assortment of ratchets and sockets

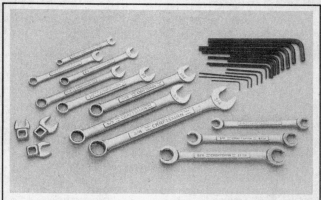

Fig. 2 In addition to ratchets, a good set of wrenches and hex keys will be necessary

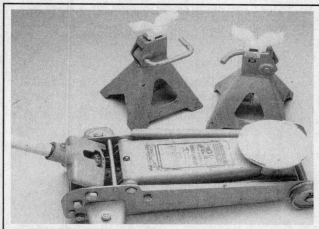

Fig. 3 A hydraulic floor jack and a set of jackstands are essential for lifting and supporting the vehicle

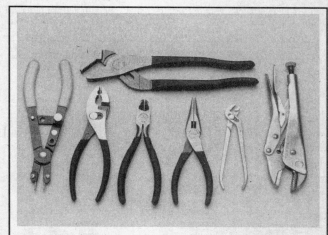

Fig. 4 An assortment of pliers, grippers and cutters will be handy for old rusted parts and stripped bolt heads

experiences than trying to work on a vehicle with bad tools. Your monetary savings will be far outweighed by frustration and mangled knuckles.

Begin accumulating those tools that are used most frequently: those associated with routine maintenance and tune-up. In addition to the normal assortment of screwdrivers and pliers, you should have the following tools:

• Wrenches/sockets and combination open end/box end wrenches in sizes from 1/8 - 3/4 in. or 3 - 19mm, as well as a 13/16 in. or 5/8 in. spark plug socket (depending on plug type).

Note: If possible, buy various length socket drive extensions. Universal-joint and wobble extensions can be extremely useful, but be careful when using them, as they can change the amount of torque applied to the socket.

• Jackstands for support.
• Oil filter wrench.
• Spout or funnel for pouring fluids.
• Grease gun for chassis lubrication (unless your vehicle is not equipped with any grease fittings - for details, please refer to information on Fluids and Lubricants, later in this section).
• Hydrometer for checking the battery (unless equipped with a sealed, maintenance-free battery).

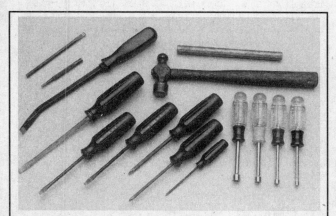

Fig. 5 Various drivers, chisels and prybars are great tools to have in your toolbox

Fig. 6 Many repairs will require the use of a torque wrench to assure the components are properly fastened

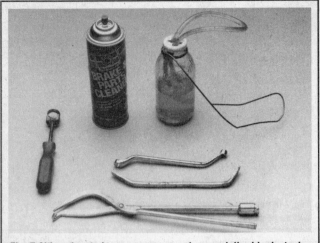

Fig. 7 Although not always necessary, using specialized brake tools will save time

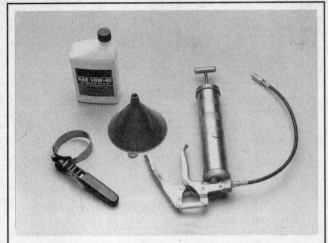

Fig. 8 A few inexpensive lubrication tools will make maintenance easier

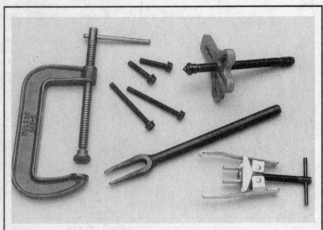

Fig. 9 Various pullers, clamps and separator tools are needed for many larger, more complicated repairs

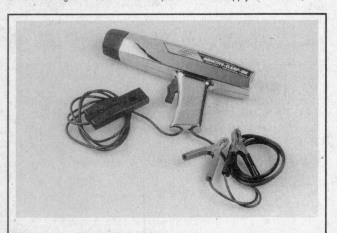

Fig. 10 A variety of tools and gauges should be used for spark plug gapping and installation

- A container for draining oil and other fluids.
- Rags for wiping up the inevitable mess.

In addition to the above items there are several others that are not absolutely necessary, but handy to have around. These include Oil Dry, (or an equivalent oil absorbent gravel - such as cat litter) and the usual supply of lubricants, antifreeze and fluids, although these can be purchased as needed. This is a basic list for routine maintenance, but only your personal needs and desire can accurately determine your list of tools.

After performing a few projects on the vehicle, you'll be amazed at the other tools and non-tools on your workbench. Some useful household items are: a large turkey baster or siphon, empty coffee cans and ice trays (to store parts), ball of twine, electrical tape for wiring, small rolls of colored tape for tagging lines or hoses, markers and pens, a note pad, golf tees (for plugging vacuum lines), metal coat hangers or a roll of mechanic's wire (to hold things out of the way), dental pick or similar long, pointed probe, a strong magnet, and a small mirror (to see into recesses and under manifolds).

A more advanced set of tools, suitable for tune-up work, can be drawn up easily. While the tools are slightly more sophisticated, they need not be outrageously expensive. There are several inexpensive tach/dwell meters on the market that are every bit as good for the average mechanic as a professional model. Just be sure that it goes to a least 1200 - 1500 rpm on the tach scale and that it works on 4, 6 and 8-cylinder engines. The key to these purchases is to make them with an eye towards adaptability and wide range. A basic list of tune-up tools could include:
- Tach/dwell meter.
- Spark plug wrench and gapping tool.
- Feeler gauges for valve adjustment.
- Timing light.

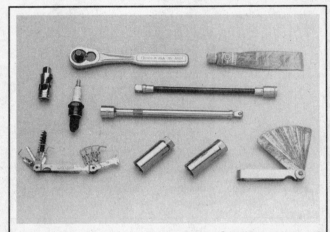

Fig. 11 Inductive type timing light

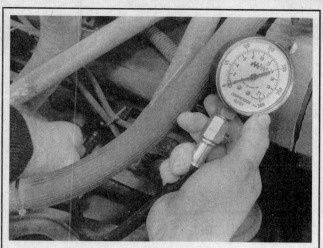

Fig. 12 A screw-in type compression gauge is recommended for compression testing

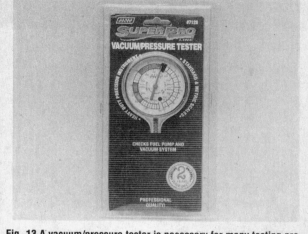

Fig. 13 A vacuum/pressure tester is necessary for many testing procedures

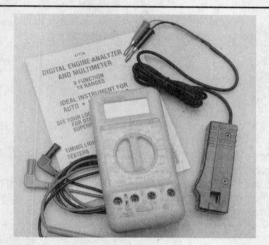

Fig. 14 Most modern automotive multimeters incorporate many helpful features

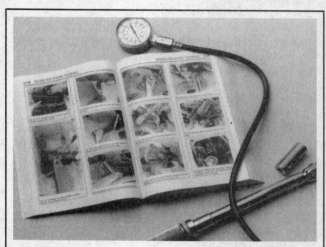

Fig. 15 Proper information is vital, so always have a Chilton Total Car Care manual handy

The choice of a timing light should be made carefully. A light which works on the DC current supplied by the vehicle's battery is the best choice; it should have a xenon tube for brightness. On any vehicle with an electronic ignition system, a timing light with an inductive pickup that clamps around the No. 1 spark plug cable is preferred.

In addition to these basic tools, there are several other tools and gauges you may find useful. These include:

• Compression gauge. The screw-in type is slower to use, but eliminates the possibility of a faulty reading due to escaping pressure.

• Manifold vacuum gauge.

• 12V test light.

• A combination volt/ohmmeter

• Induction Ammeter. This is used for determining whether or not there is current in a wire. These are handy for use if a wire is broken somewhere in a wiring harness.

As a final note, you will probably find a torque wrench necessary for all but the most basic work. The beam type models are perfectly adequate, although the newer click types (breakaway) are easier to use. The click type torque wrenches tend to be more expensive. Also keep in mind that all types of torque wrenches should be periodically checked and/or recalibrated. You will have to decide for yourself which better fits your pocketbook, and purpose.

Special Tools

Normally, the use of special factory tools is avoided for repair procedures, since these are not readily available for the do-it-yourself mechanic. When it is possible to perform the job with more commonly available tools, it will be pointed out, but occasionally, a special tool was designed to perform a specific function and should be used. Before substituting another tool, you should be convinced that neither your safety nor the performance of the vehicle will be compromised.

Special tools can usually be purchased from an automotive parts store or from your dealer. In some cases special tools may be available directly from the tool manufacturer.

DIAGNOSTIC TEST EQUIPMENT

Modern vehicles equipped with computer-controlled fuel, emission and ignition systems require modern electronic tools to diagnose problems. Many of these tools are designed solely for the professional mechanic and are too costly and difficult to use for the average do-it-yourselfer. However, various automotive aftermarket companies have introduced products that address the needs of the average home mechanic, providing sophisticated information at affordable cost. Consult your local auto parts store to determine what is available for your vehicle.

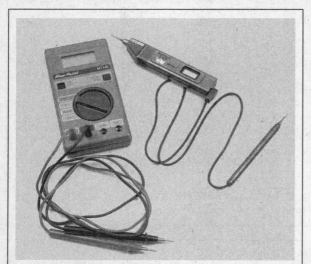

Digital multimeters come in a variety of styles and are a "must-have" for any serious home mechanic. Digital multimeters measure voltage (volts), resistance (ohms) and sometimes current (amperes). These versatile tools are used for checking all types of electrical or electronic components

Trouble code tools allow the home mechanic to extract the "fault code" number from an on-board computer that has sensed a problem (usually indicated by a Check Engine light). Armed with this code, the home mechanic can focus attention on a suspect system or component

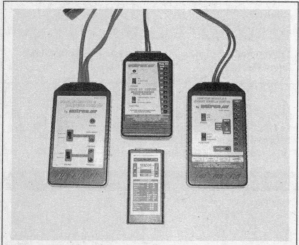

Sensor testers perform specific checks on many of the sensors and actuators used on today's computer-controlled vehicles. These testers can check sensors both on or off the vehicle, as well as test the accompanying electrical circuits

Hand-held scanners represent the most sophisticated of all do-it-yourself diagnostic tools. These tools do more than just access computer codes like the code readers above; they provide the user with an actual interface into the vehicle's computer. Comprehensive data on specific makes and models will come with the tool, either built-in or as a separate cartridge

SERVICING YOUR VEHICLE SAFELY

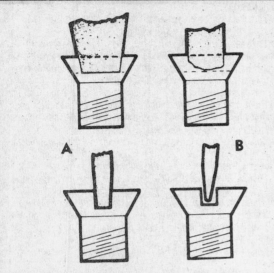

Fig. 16 Screwdrivers should be kept in good condition to prevent injury or damage which could result if the blade slips from the screw

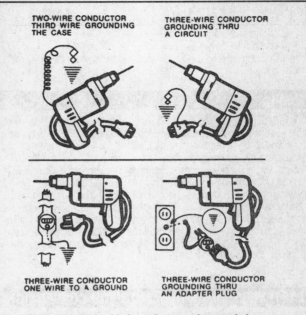

TWO-WIRE CONDUCTOR THIRD WIRE GROUNDING THE CASE

THREE-WIRE CONDUCTOR GROUNDING THRU A CIRCUIT

THREE-WIRE CONDUCTOR ONE WIRE TO A GROUND

THREE-WIRE CONDUCTOR GROUNDING THRU AN ADAPTER PLUG

Fig. 17 Power tools should always be properly grounded

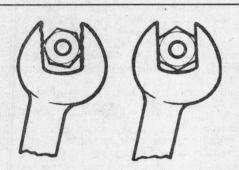

Fig. 18 Using the correct size wrench will help prevent the possibility of rounding off a nut

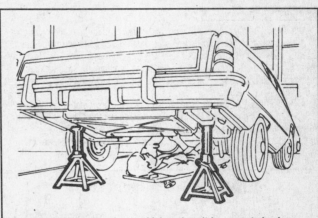

Fig. 19 NEVER work under a vehicle unless it is supported using safety stands (jackstands)

See Figures 16, 17, 18 and 19

It is virtually impossible to anticipate all of the hazards involved with automotive maintenance and service, but care and common sense will prevent most accidents.

The rules of safety for mechanics range from "don't smoke around gasoline," to "use the proper tool(s) for the job." The trick to avoiding injuries is to develop safe work habits and to take every possible precaution.

Do's

• Do keep a fire extinguisher and first aid kit handy.
• Do wear safety glasses or goggles when cutting, drilling, grinding or prying, even if you have 20 - 20 vision. If you wear glasses for the sake of vision, wear safety goggles over your regular glasses.
• Do shield your eyes whenever you work around the battery. Batteries contain sulfuric acid. In case of contact with the eyes or skin, flush the area with water or a mixture of water and baking soda, then seek immediate medical attention.
• Do use safety stands (jackstands) for any undervehicle service. Jacks are for raising vehicles; jackstands are for making sure the vehicle stays raised until you want it to come down. Whenever the vehicle is raised, block the

wheels remaining on the ground and set the parking brake.
• Do use adequate ventilation when working with any chemicals or hazardous materials. Like carbon monoxide, the asbestos dust resulting from some brake lining wear can be hazardous in sufficient quantities.
• Do disconnect the negative battery cable when working on the electrical system. The secondary ignition system contains EXTREMELY HIGH VOLTAGE. In some cases it can even exceed 50,000 volts.
• Do follow manufacturer's directions whenever working with potentially hazardous materials. Most chemicals and fluids are poisonous if taken internally.
• Do properly maintain your tools. Loose hammerheads, mushroomed punches and chisels, frayed or poorly grounded electrical cords, excessively worn screwdrivers, spread wrenches (open end), cracked sockets, slipping ratchets, or faulty droplight sockets can cause accidents.
• Likewise, keep your tools clean; a greasy wrench can slip off a bolt head, ruining the bolt and often harming your knuckles in the process.
• Do use the proper size and type of tool for the job at hand. Do select a

wrench or socket that fits the nut or bolt. The wrench or socket should sit straight, not cocked.

• Do, when possible, pull on a wrench handle rather than push on it, and adjust your stance to prevent a fall.

• Do be sure that adjustable wrenches are tightly closed on the nut or bolt and pulled so that the force is on the side of the fixed jaw.

• Do strike squarely with a hammer; avoid glancing blows.

• Do set the parking brake and block the drive wheels if the work requires a running engine.

Don'ts

• Don't run the engine in a garage or anywhere else without proper ventilation - EVER! Carbon monoxide is poisonous; it takes a long time to leave the human body and you can build up a deadly supply of it in your system by simply breathing in a little every day. You may not realize you are slowly poisoning yourself. Always use power vents, windows, fans and/or open the garage door.

• Don't work around moving parts while wearing loose clothing. Short sleeves are much safer than long, loose sleeves. Hard-toed shoes with neoprene soles protect your toes and give a better grip on slippery surfaces. Jewelry such as watches, fancy belt buckles, beads or body adornment of any kind is not safe working around a vehicle. Long hair should be tied back under a hat or cap.

• Don't use pockets for toolboxes. A fall or bump can drive a screwdriver deep into your body. Even a rag hanging from your back pocket can wrap around a spinning shaft or fan.

• Don't smoke when working around gasoline, cleaning solvent or other flammable material.

• Don't smoke when working around the battery. When the battery is being charged, it gives off explosive hydrogen gas.

• Don't use gasoline to wash your hands; there are excellent soaps available. Gasoline contains dangerous additives which can enter the body through a cut or through your pores. Gasoline also removes all the natural oils from the skin so that bone dry hands will suck up oil and grease.

• Don't service the air conditioning system unless you are equipped with the necessary tools and training. When liquid or compressed gas refrigerant is released to atmospheric pressure it will absorb heat from whatever it contacts. This will chill or freeze anything it touches.

• Don't use screwdrivers for anything other than driving screws! A screwdriver used as an prying tool can snap when you least expect it, causing injuries. At the very least, you'll ruin a good screwdriver.

• Don't use an emergency jack (that little ratchet, scissors, or pantograph jack supplied with the vehicle) for anything other than changing a flat! These jacks are only intended for emergency use out on the road; they are NOT designed as a maintenance tool. If you are serious about maintaining your vehicle yourself, invest in a hydraulic floor jack of at least a 1 1/2 ton capacity, and at least two sturdy jackstands.

FASTENERS, MEASUREMENTS AND CONVERSIONS

Bolts, Nuts and Other Threaded Retainers

See Figures 20, 21, 22 and 23

Although there are a great variety of fasteners found in the modern car or truck, the most commonly used retainer is the threaded fastener (nuts, bolts, screws, studs, etc.). Most threaded retainers may be reused, provided that they are not damaged in use or during the repair. Some retainers (such as stretch bolts or torque prevailing nuts) are designed to deform when tightened or in use and should not be reinstalled.

Whenever possible, we will note any special retainers which should be replaced during a procedure. But you should always inspect the condition of a retainer when it is removed and replace any that show signs of damage. Check all threads for rust or corrosion which can increase the torque necessary to achieve the desired clamp load for which that fastener was originally selected. Additionally, be sure that the driver surface of the fastener has not been compromised by rounding or other damage. In some cases a driver surface may become only partially rounded, allowing the driver to catch in only one direction. In many of these occurrences, a fastener may be installed and tightened, but the driver would not be able to grip and loosen the fastener again. (This could lead to frustration down the line should that component ever need to be disassembled again).

If you must replace a fastener, whether due to design or damage, you must ALWAYS be sure to use the proper replacement. In all cases, a retainer of the same design, material and strength should be used. Markings on the heads of most bolts will help determine the proper strength of the fastener. The same material, thread and pitch must be selected to assure proper installation and safe operation of the vehicle afterwards.

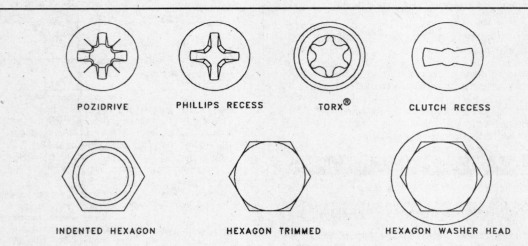

POZIDRIVE   PHILLIPS RECESS   TORX®   CLUTCH RECESS

INDENTED HEXAGON   HEXAGON TRIMMED   HEXAGON WASHER HEAD

Fig. 20 Here are a few of the most common screw/bolt driver styles

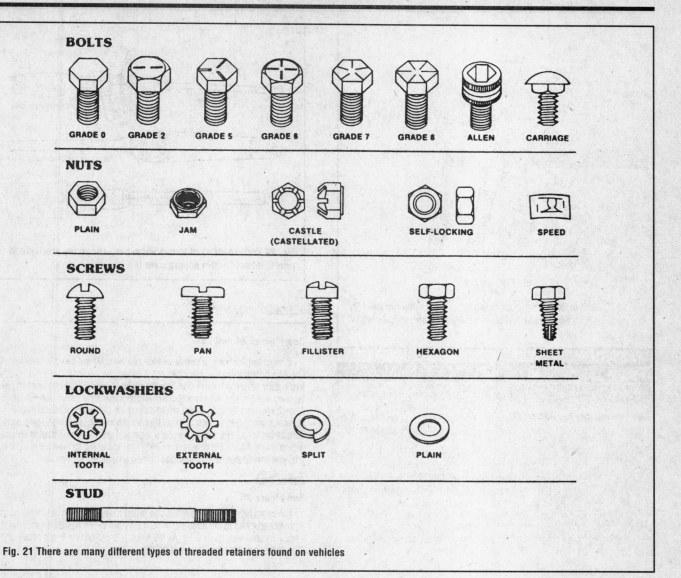

BOLTS

GRADE 0 | GRADE 2 | GRADE 5 | GRADE 6 | GRADE 7 | GRADE 8 | ALLEN | CARRIAGE

NUTS

PLAIN | JAM | CASTLE (CASTELLATED) | SELF-LOCKING | SPEED

SCREWS

ROUND | PAN | FILLISTER | HEXAGON | SHEET METAL

LOCKWASHERS

INTERNAL TOOTH | EXTERNAL TOOTH | SPLIT | PLAIN

STUD

Fig. 21 There are many different types of threaded retainers found on vehicles

Thread gauges are available to help measure a bolt or stud's thread. Most automotive and hardware stores keep gauges available to help you select the proper size. In a pinch, you can use another nut or bolt for a thread gauge. If the bolt you are replacing is not too badly damaged, you can select a match by finding another bolt which will thread in its place. If you find a nut which threads properly onto the damaged bolt, then use that nut to help select the replacement bolt. If however, the bolt you are replacing is so badly damaged (broken or drilled out) that its threads cannot be used as a gauge, you might start by looking for another bolt (from the same assembly or a similar location on your vehicle) which will thread into the damaged bolt's mounting. If so, the other bolt can be used to select a nut; the nut can then be used to select the replacement bolt.

In all cases, be absolutely sure you have selected the proper replacement. Don't be shy, you can always ask the store clerk for help.

❋❋ WARNING:

Be aware that when you find a bolt with damaged threads, you may also find the nut or drilled hole it was threaded into has also been damaged. If this is the case, you may have to drill and tap the hole, replace the nut or otherwise repair the threads. NEVER try to force a replacement bolt to fit into the damaged threads.

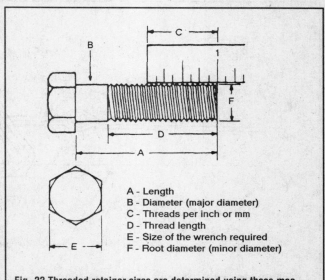

A - Length
B - Diameter (major diameter)
C - Threads per inch or mm
D - Thread length
E - Size of the wrench required
F - Root diameter (minor diameter)

Fig. 22 Threaded retainer sizes are determined using these measurements

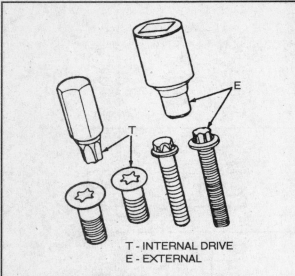

T - INTERNAL DRIVE
E - EXTERNAL

Fig. 23 Special fasteners such as these Torx, head bolts are used by manufacturers to discourage people from working on vehicles without the proper tools

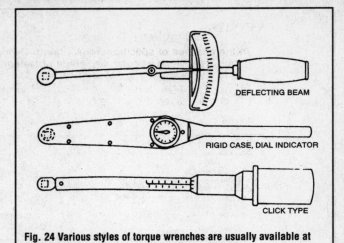

DEFLECTING BEAM

RIGID CASE, DIAL INDICATOR

CLICK TYPE

Fig. 24 Various styles of torque wrenches are usually available at your local automotive supply store

Torque

Torque is defined as the measurement of resistance to turning or rotating. It tends to twist a body about an axis of rotation. A common example of this would be tightening a threaded retainer such as a nut, bolt or screw. Measuring torque is one of the most common ways to help assure that a threaded retainer has been properly fastened.

When tightening a threaded fastener, torque is applied in three distinct areas, the head, the bearing surface and the clamp load. About 50 percent of the measured torque is used in overcoming bearing friction. This is the friction between the bearing surface of the bolt head, screw head or nut face and the base material or washer (the surface on which the fastener is rotating). Approximately 40 percent of the applied torque is used in overcoming thread friction. This leaves only about 10 percent of the applied torque to develop a useful clamp load (the force which holds a joint together). This means that friction can account for as much as 90 percent of the applied torque on a fastener.

TORQUE WRENCHES

See Figures 24 and 25

In most applications, a torque wrench can be used to assure proper installation of a fastener. Torque wrenches come in various designs and most automotive supply stores will carry a variety to suit your needs. A torque wrench should be used any time we supply a specific torque value for a fastener. A torque wrench can also be used if you are following the general guidelines in the accompanying charts. Keep in mind that because there is no worldwide standardization of fasteners, the charts are a general guideline and should be used with caution. Again, the general rule of "if you are using the right tool for the job, you should not have to strain to tighten a fastener" applies here.

Beam Type
See Figure 26

The beam type torque wrench is one of the most popular types. It consists of a pointer attached to the head that runs the length of the flexible beam (shaft) to a scale located near the handle. As the wrench is pulled, the beam bends and the pointer indicates the torque using the scale.

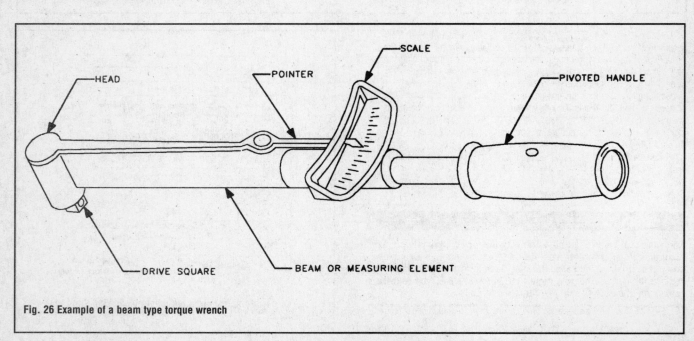

HEAD

POINTER

SCALE

PIVOTED HANDLE

DRIVE SQUARE

BEAM OR MEASURING ELEMENT

Fig. 26 Example of a beam type torque wrench

Standard Torque Specifications and Fastener Markings

In the absence of specific torques, the following chart can be used as a guide to the maximum safe torque of a particular size/grade of fastener.

- There is no torque difference for fine or coarse threads.
- Torque values are based on clean, dry threads. Reduce the value by 10% if threads are oiled prior to assembly.
- The torque required for aluminum components or fasteners is considerably less.

U.S. Bolts

SAE Grade Number	1 or 2			5			6 or 7		
Number of lines always 2 less than the grade number.									
Bolt Size	Maximum Torque			Maximum Torque			Maximum Torque		
(Inches)—(Thread)	Ft./Lbs.	Kgm	Nm	Ft./Lbs.	Kgm	Nm	Ft./Lbs.	Kgm	Nm
¼—20	5	0.7	6.8	8	1.1	10.8	10	1.4	13.5
—28	6	0.8	8.1	10	1.4	13.6			
⁵⁄₁₆—18	11	1.5	14.9	17	2.3	23.0	19	2.6	25.8
—24	13	1.8	17.6	19	2.6	25.7			
⅜—16	18	2.5	24.4	31	4.3	42.0	34	4.7	46.0
—24	20	2.75	27.1	35	4.8	47.5			
⁷⁄₁₆—14	28	3.8	37.0	49	6.8	66.4	55	7.6	74.5
—20	30	4.2	40.7	55	7.6	74.5			
½—13	39	5.4	52.8	75	10.4	101.7	85	11.75	115.2
—20	41	5.7	55.6	85	11.7	115.2			
⁹⁄₁₆—12	51	7.0	69.2	110	15.2	149.1	120	16.6	162.7
—18	55	7.6	74.5	120	16.6	162.7			
⅝—11	83	11.5	112.5	150	20.7	203.3	167	23.0	226.5
—18	95	13.1	128.8	170	23.5	230.5			
¾—10	105	14.5	142.3	270	37.3	366.0	280	38.7	379.6
—16	115	15.9	155.9	295	40.8	400.0			
⅞— 9	160	22.1	216.9	395	54.6	535.5	440	60.9	596.5
—14	175	24.2	237.2	435	60.1	589.7			
1— 8	236	32.5	318.6	590	81.6	799.9	660	91.3	894.8
—14	250	34.6	338.9	660	91.3	849.8			

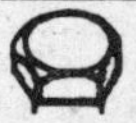

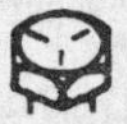

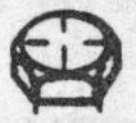

Metric Bolts

Relative Strength Marking	4.6, 4.8			8.8		
Bolt Markings						
Bolt Size	Maximum Torque			Maximum Torque		
Thread Size x Pitch (mm)	Ft./Lbs.	Kgm	Nm	Ft./Lbs.	Kgm	Nm
6 x 1.0	2-3	.2-.4	3-4	3-6	4-.8	5-8
8 x 1.25	6-8	.8-1	8-12	9-14	1.2-1.9	13-19
10 x 1.25	12-17	1.5-2.3	16-23	20-29	2.7-4.0	27-39
12 x 1.25	21-32	2.9-4.4	29-43	35-53	4.8-7.3	47-72
14 x 1.5	35-52	4.8-7.1	48-70	57-85	7.8-11.7	77-110
16 x 1.5	51-77	7.0-10.6	67-100	90-120	12.4-16.5	130-160
18 x 1.5	74-110	10.2-15.1	100-150	130-170	17.9-23.4	180-230
20 x 1.5	110-140	15.1-19.3	150-190	190-240	26.2-46.9	160-320
22 x 1.5	150-190	22.0-26.2	200-260	250-320	34.5-44.1	340-430
24 x 1.5	190-240	26.2-46.9	260-320	310-410	42.7-56.5	420-550

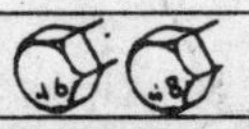

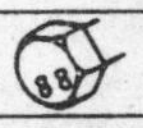

Fig. 25 Standard and metric bolt torque specifications based on bolt strengths - WARNING: use only as a guide

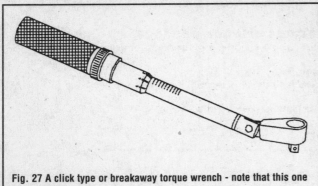

Fig. 27 A click type or breakaway torque wrench - note that this one has a pivoting head

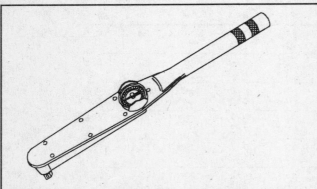

Fig. 29 The rigid case (direct reading) torque wrench uses a dial indicator to show torque

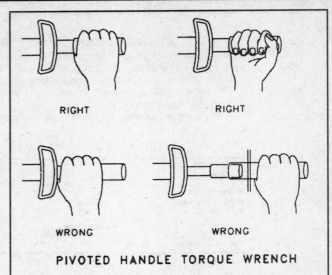

PIVOTED HANDLE TORQUE WRENCH

Fig. 28 Torque wrenches with pivoting heads must be grasped and used properly to prevent an incorrect reading

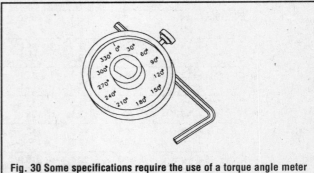

Fig. 30 Some specifications require the use of a torque angle meter (mechanical protractor)

Click (Breakaway) Type
See Figure 27

Another popular design of torque wrench is the click type. To use the click type wrench you pre-adjust it to a torque setting. Once the torque is reached, the wrench has a reflex signaling feature that causes a momentary breakaway of the torque wrench body, sending an impulse to the operator's hand.

Pivot Head Type
See Figure 28

Some torque wrenches (usually of the click type) may be equipped with a pivot head which can allow it to be used in areas of limited access. BUT, it must be used properly. To hold a pivot head wrench, grasp the handle lightly, and as you pull on the handle, it should be floated on the pivot point. If the handle comes in contact with the yoke extension during the process of pulling, there is a very good chance the torque readings will be inaccurate because this could alter the wrench loading point. The design of the handle is usually such as to make it inconvenient to deliberately misuse the wrench.

Note: It should be mentioned that the use of any U-joint, wobble or extension will have an effect on the torque readings, no matter what type of wrench you are using. For the most accurate readings, install the socket directly on the wrench driver. If necessary, straight extensions (which hold a socket directly under the wrench driver) will have the least effect on the torque reading. Avoid any extension that alters the length of the wrench from the handle to the head/driving point (such as a crow's foot). U-joint or wobble extensions can greatly affect the readings; avoid their use at all times.

Rigid Case (Direct Reading)
See Figure 29

A rigid case or direct reading torque wrench is equipped with a dial indicator to show torque values. One advantage of these wrenches is that they can be

held at any position on the wrench without affecting accuracy. These wrenches are often preferred because they tend to be compact, easy to read and have a great degree of accuracy.

TORQUE ANGLE METERS

See Figure 30

Because the frictional characteristics of each fastener or threaded hole will vary, clamp loads which are based strictly on torque will vary as well. In most applications, this variance is not significant enough to cause worry. But, in certain applications, a manufacturer's engineers may determine that more precise clamp loads are necessary (such is the case with many aluminum cylinder heads). In these cases, a torque angle method of installation would be specified. When installing fasteners which are torque angle tightened, a predetermined seating torque and standard torque wrench are usually used first to remove any compliance from the joint. The fastener is then tightened the specified additional portion of a turn measured in degrees. A torque angle gauge (mechanical protractor) is used for these applications.

Standard and Metric Measurements
See Figure 31

Throughout this manual, specifications are given to help you determine the condition of various components on your vehicle, or to assist you in their installation. Some of the most common measurements include length (in. or cm/mm), torque (ft. lbs., inch lbs. or Nm) and pressure (psi, in. Hg, kPa or mm

CONVERSION FACTORS

LENGTH–DISTANCE

Inches (in.)	x 25.4	= Millimeters (mm)	x .0394	= Inches
Feet (ft.)	x .305	= Meters (m)	x 3.281	= Feet
Miles	x 1.609	= Kilometers (km)	x .0621	= Miles

VOLUME

Cubic Inches (in3)	x 16.387	= Cubic Centimeters	x .061	= in3
IMP Pints (IMP pt.)	x .568	= Liters (L)	x 1.76	= IMP pt.
IMP Quarts (IMP qt.)	x 1.137	= Liters (L)	x .88	= IMP qt.
IMP Gallons (IMP gal.)	x 4.546	= Liters (L)	x .22	= IMP gal.
IMP Quarts (IMP qt.)	x 1.201	= US Quarts (US qt.)	x .833	= IMP qt.
IMP Gallons (IMP gal.)	x 1.201	= US Gallons (US gal.)	x .833	= IMP gal.
Fl. Ounces	x 29.573	= Milliliters	x .034	= Ounces
US Pints (US pt.)	x .473	= Liters (L)	x 2.113	= Pints
US Quarts (US qt.)	x .946	= Liters (L)	x 1.057	= Quarts
US Gallons (US gal.)	x 3.785	= Liters (L)	x .264	= Gallons

MASS–WEIGHT

Ounces (oz.)	x 28.35	= Grams (g)	x .035	= Ounces
Pounds (lb.)	x .454	= Kilograms (kg)	x 2.205	= Pounds

PRESSURE

Pounds Per Sq. In. (psi)	x 6.895	= Kilopascals (kPa)	x .145	= psi
Inches of Mercury (Hg)	x .4912	= psi	x 2.036	= Hg
Inches of Mercury (Hg)	x 3.377	= Kilopascals (kPa)	x .2961	= Hg
Inches of Water (H_2O)	x .07355	= Inches of Mercury	x 13.783	= H_2O
Inches of Water (H_2O)	x .03613	= psi	x 27.684	= H_2O
Inches of Water (H_2O)	x .248	= Kilopascals (kPa)	x 4.026	= H_2O

TORQUE

Pounds–Force Inches (in–lb)	x .113	= Newton Meters (N·m)	x 8.85	= in–lb
Pounds–Force Feet (ft–lb)	x 1.356	= Newton Meters (N·m)	x .738	= ft–lb

VELOCITY

Miles Per Hour (MPH)	x 1.609	= Kilometers Per Hour (KPH)	x .621	= MPH

POWER

Horsepower (Hp)	x .745	= Kilowatts	x 1.34	= Horsepower

FUEL CONSUMPTION*

Miles Per Gallon IMP (MPG)	x .354	= Kilometers Per Liter (Km/L)
Kilometers Per Liter (Km/L)	x 2.352	= IMP MPG
Miles Per Gallon US (MPG)	x .425	= Kilometers Per Liter (Km/L)
Kilometers Per Liter (Km/L)	x 2.352	= US MPG

*It is common to covert from miles per gallon (mpg) to liters/100 kilometers (1/100 km), where mpg (IMP) x 1/100 km = 282 and mpg (US) x 1/100 km = 235.

TEMPERATURE

Degree Fahrenheit (°F)	= (°C x 1.8) + 32
Degree Celsius (°C)	= (°F – 32) x .56

Fig. 31 Standard and metric conversion factors chart

Hg). In most cases, we strive to provide the proper measurement as determined by the manufacturer's engineers.

Though, in some cases, that value may not be conveniently measured with what is available in your toolbox. Luckily, many of the measuring devices which are available today will have two scales so the Standard or Metric measurements may easily be taken. If any of the various measuring tools which are available to you do not contain the same scale as listed in the specifications, use the accompanying conversion factors to determine the proper value.

The conversion factor chart is used by taking the given specification and multiplying it by the necessary conversion factor. For instance, looking at the first line, if you have a measurement in inches such as "free-play should be 2 in." but your ruler reads only in millimeters, multiply 2 in. by the conversion factor of 25.4 to get the metric equivalent of 50.8mm. Likewise, if the specification was given only in a Metric measurement, for example in Newton Meters (Nm), then look at the center column first. If the measurement is 100 Nm, multiply it by the conversion factor of 0.738 to get 73.8 ft. lbs.

MODEL IDENTIFICATION

The Chevrolet Sprint (1985 - 88) and the Geo/Chevrolet Metro/Suzuki Swift (1989 - 00) are very similar vehicles. All Sprint models, and Metro models to 1994, were equipped with a 1.0L SOHC 3-cylinder engine backed by either a 5-speed manual or 3-speed automatic transaxle. The Suzuki Swift comes equipped with a 1.3L SOHC 4-cylinder engine as do some 1995 and later Metro models (as an option).

Several variations have been built during the model run. In 1987, a tur-bocharged version of the 1.0L engine was made available. The turbocharged engine provided significant gains in horsepower and torque over the normally aspirated engine, while still providing fuel efficiency and driveability. It also introduced Electronic Fuel Injection (EFI) to the line-up. EFI has been used exclusively since 1988.

The other major variation was the introduction of the convertible in 1990.

SERIAL NUMBER IDENTIFICATION

Vehicle

See Figures 32 and 33

The Vehicle Identification Number (VIN) plate is located on the left upper instrument panel and is visible from the outside of the vehicle. A great deal of information about your vehicle can be extracted by the code numbers that make up this 17 digit number. Model and body style information, along with year of production and engine size are also listed on this plate. The engine code is in the 8th position. The 10th digit indicates the model year.

Engine

See Figure 34

Engines are stamped with an engine identification serial number which iden-tifies the model year, engine displacement and engine type.

Fig. 32 Vehicle identification plate location

Fig. 33 The vehicle identification number is also stamped into the firewall

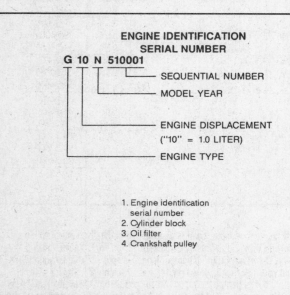

ENGINE IDENTIFICATION SERIAL NUMBER

G 10 N 510001

— SEQUENTIAL NUMBER
— MODEL YEAR
— ENGINE DISPLACEMENT ("10" = 1.0 LITER)
— ENGINE TYPE

1. Engine identification serial number
2. Cylinder block
3. Oil filter
4. Crankshaft pulley

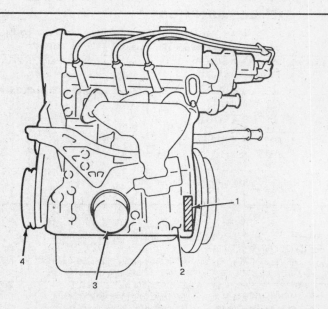

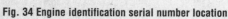
Fig. 34 Engine identification serial number location

ENGINE AND VEHICLE IDENTIFICATION

Engine Code

Code ①	Liters (cc)	Cu. In.	Cyl.	Fuel Sys.	Type	Eng. Mfg.
M	1.0 (1000)	61	3	2bbl	SOHC	Suzuki
2	1.0 (1000)	61	3	EFI③	SOHC	Suzuki
5	1.0 (1000)	61	3	2bbl	SOHC	Suzuki
5	1.0 (1000)	61	3	EFI	SOHC	Suzuki
6	1.0 (1000)	61	3	TFI	SOHC	Suzuki
9	1.3 (1300)	79	4	EFI	SOHC	Suzuki
3	1.3 (1300)	79	4	EFI	DOHC	Suzuki
2	1.3 (1300)	79	4	EFI	SOHC	Suzuki

Model Year

Code ②	Year
F	1985
G	1986
H	1987
J	1988
K	1989
L	1990
M	1991
N	1992
P	1993
R	1994
S	1995
T	1996
U	1997
V	1998
W	1999
Y	2000

2bbl: 2 barrel carburetor
EFI - Electronic Fuel Injection
TFI: Throttle body Fuel Injection
SOHC - Single Over Head Camshaft
DOHC - Dual Over Head Camshaft

① Engine ID / 8th digit of the VIN
② 10th digit of the VIN
③ Turbo

GENERAL ENGINE SPECIFICATIONS

Year	Model	Engine Displacement Liters (cc)	Engine ID/VIN	Engine Type	No. of Cyl.	Fuel System Type	Net Horsepower @ rpm	Net Torque @ rpm (ft. lbs.)	Bore x Stroke (in.)	Compression Ratio	Oil Pressure @ rpm
1985	Sprint	1.0 (1000)	M	SOHC	3	2bbl	48@5100	57@3200	2.91x3.03	9.5:1	54@2000
1986	Sprint	1.0 (1000)	5	SOHC	3	2bbl	48@5100	57@3200	2.91x3.03	9.5:1	54@2000
1987	Sprint	1.0 (1000)	2	SOHC	3	EFI ①	70@5100	107@3200	2.91x3.03	8.3:1	54@2000
	Sprint	1.0 (1000)	5	SOHC	3	2 bbl	48@5100	57@3200	2.91x3.03	9.5:1	54@2000
1988	Sprint	1.0 (1000)	2	SOHC	3	EFI ①	70@5500	107@3500	2.91x3.03	8.3:1	42-60@3000
	Sprint	1.0 (1000)	5	SOHC	3	2 bbl	48@5100	78@3200	2.91x3.03	9.5:1	42-54@3000
1989	Metro	1.0 (1000)	5	SOHC	3	EFI	52@5700	58@3300	2.91x3.03	9.5:1	39@4000
	Swift	1.3 (1300)	3	SOHC	4	EFI	70@5500	74@3000	2.91x3.03	9.5:1	39@4000
	Swift	1.3 (1300)	3	DOHC	4	EFI	100@6500	83@5000	2.91x3.03	9.5:1	39@4000
1990	Metro	1.0 (1000)	5	SOHC	3	EFI	52@5700	58@3300	2.91x3.03	9.5:1	39@4000
	Swift	1.3 (1300)	3	SOHC	4	EFI	70@5500	74@3000	2.91x3.03	9.5:1	39@4000
	Swift	1.3 (1300)	3	DOHC	4	EFI	100@6500	83@5000	2.91x3.03	9.5:1	39@4000
1991	Metro	1.0 (1000)	6	SOHC	3	EFI	52@5700	58@3300	2.91x3.03	9.5:1	39@4000
	Swift	1.3 (1300)	3	SOHC	4	EFI	70@5500	74@3000	2.91x3.03	9.5:1	39@4000
	Swift	1.3 (1300)	3	DOHC	4	EFI	100@6500	83@5000	2.91x3.03	9.5:1	39@4000
1992	Metro	1.0 (1000)	6	SOHC	3	EFI	52@5700	58@3300	2.91x3.03	9.5:1	39@4000
	Swift	1.3 (1300)	3	SOHC	4	EFI	70@5500	74@3000	2.91x3.03	9.5:1	39@4000
	Swift	1.3 (1300)	3	DOHC	4	EFI	100@6500	83@5000	2.91x3.03	9.5:1	39@4000
1993	Metro	1.0 (1000)	6	SOHC	3	EFI	52@5700	58@3300	2.91x3.03	9.5:1	39@4000
	Swift	1.3 (1300)	3	SOHC	4	EFI	70@5500	74@3000	2.91x3.03	9.5:1	39@4000
	Swift	1.3 (1300)	3	DOHC	4	EFI	100@6500	83@5000	2.91x3.03	9.5:1	39@4000
1994	Metro	1.0 (1000)	6	SOHC	3	EFI	52@5700	58@3300	2.91x3.03	9.5:1	54@2000
	Swift	1.3 (1300)	3	SOHC	4	EFI	70@5500	74@3000	2.91x3.03	9.5:1	39@4000
	Swift	1.3 (1300)	3	DOHC	4	EFI	100@6500	83@5000	2.91x3.03	9.5:1	39@4000
1995	Metro	1.0 (1000)	6	SOHC	3	TFI	55@5700	58@3300	2.91x3.03	9.5:1	54@3000
	Metro	1.3 (1300)	9	SOHC	4	TFI	70@5500	74@3000	2.91x3.03	9.5:1	54@3000
	Swift	1.3 (1300)	3	SOHC	4	EFI	70@5500	74@3000	2.91x3.03	9.5:1	39@4000
1996	Metro	1.0 (1000)	6	SOHC	3	TFI	55@5700	58@3300	2.91x3.03	9.5:1	54@3000
	Metro	1.3 (1300)	9	SOHC	4	TFI	70@5500	74@3000	2.91x3.03	9.5:1	54@3000
	Swift	1.3 (1300)	3	SOHC	4	EFI	70@5500	74@3000	2.91x3.03	9.5:1	39@4000
1997	Metro	1.0 (1000)	6	SOHC	3	TFI	55@5700	58@3300	2.91x3.03	9.5:1	54@3000
	Metro	1.3 (1300)	9	SOHC	4	TFI	70@5500	74@3000	2.91x3.03	9.5:1	54@3000
	Swift	1.3 (1300)	3	SOHC	4	EFI	70@5500	74@3000	2.91x3.03	9.5:1	39@4000
1998	Metro	1.0 (1000)	6	SOHC	3	TFI	55@5700	58@3300	2.91x3.03	9.5:1	54@3000
	Metro	1.3 (1300)	9	SOHC	4	TFI	70@5500	74@3000	2.91x3.03	9.5:1	54@3000
	Swift	1.3 (1300)	3	SOHC	4	EFI	70@5500	74@3000	2.91x3.03	9.5:1	39@4000
1999	Metro	1.0 (1000)	6	SOHC	3	TFI	55@5700	58@3300	2.91x3.03	9.5:1	54@3000
	Metro	1.3 (1300)	9	SOHC	4	TFI	70@5500	74@3000	2.91x3.03	9.5:1	54@3000
	Swift	1.3 (1300)	3	SOHC	4	EFI	70@5500	74@3000	2.91x3.03	9.5:1	39@4000
2000	Metro	1.0 (1000)	6	SOHC	3	TFI	55@5700	58@3300	2.91x3.03	9.5:1	54@3000
	Metro	1.3 (1300)	9	SOHC	4	TFI	70@5500	74@3000	2.91x3.03	9.5:1	54@3000
	Swift	1.3 (1300)	3	SOHC	4	EFI	70@5500	74@3000	2.91x3.03	9.5:1	39@4000

2 bbl - Two Barrel Carburetor
SOHC - Single Over Head Camshaft
DOHC - Dual Over Head Camshaft

EFI - Electronic Fuel Injection
TFI - Throttle body Fuel Injection
① Turbo

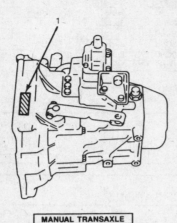
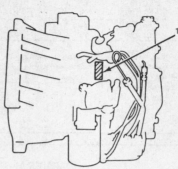

TRANSAXLE IDENTIFICATION NUMBER PLATE LOCATION

N 100001 ——————— (M/T)
N 700001 ——————— (A/T)
└— Serial Number
└— Model Year (Refer to VIN Designation)

MANUAL TRANSAXLE

AUTOMATIC TRANSAXLE

1. Transaxle identification number plate

Fig. 35 Transaxle identification number location

Transaxle

See Figure 35

Transaxles are stamped with a transaxle identification serial number which identifies the model year, transaxle serial number and transaxle type.

ROUTINE MAINTENANCE

Proper maintenance and tune-up is the key to long and trouble-free vehicle life, and the work can yield its own rewards. Studies have shown that a properly tuned and maintained vehicle can achieve better gas mileage than an out-of-tune vehicle. As a conscientious owner and driver, set aside a Saturday morning, say once a month, to check or replace items which could cause major problems later. Keep your own personal log to jot down which services you performed, how much the parts cost you, the date, and the exact odometer reading at the time. Keep all receipts for such items as engine oil and filters, so that they may be referred to in case of related problems or to determine operating expenses. As a do-it-yourselfer, these receipts are the only proof you have that the required maintenance was performed. In the event of a warranty problem, these receipts will be invaluable.

The literature provided with your vehicle when it was originally delivered includes the factory recommended maintenance schedule. If you no longer have this literature, replacement copies are usually available from the dealer. A maintenance schedule is provided later in this section, in case you do not have the factory literature.

Air Cleaner

Replace the cleaner element every 30,000 miles (50,000 km). Replace more often under dusty conditions. Replace the crankcase vent filter if so equipped.

REMOVAL & INSTALLATION

1.0L Engine
See Figures 36, 37, 38, 39 and 40

1. Loosen and remove the air cleaner wing nut.
2. Unlatch the 4 upper air cleaner case clamps, as required.
3. Remove the air cleaner upper case and remove the air cleaner element.

To install:

Inspect all hoses leading to the air cleaner. Replace the hoses if cracked or damaged.

Clean the inside of the air cleaner base of debris and install a new element. Ensure the recess in the air cleaner element fits properly into the air cleaner base.

4. Install the upper air cleaner case.
5. Latch the upper air cleaner case clamps, as required.
6. Install and tighten the air cleaner wing nut.

Fig. 36 Loosen the air cleaner assembly wing nut

Fig. 37 Loosen the air cleaner assembly spring clamps

Fig. 38 Remove the air cleaner upper case

Fig. 39 Air cleaner element in lower case

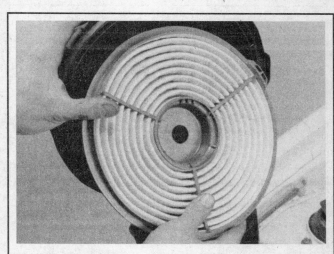

Fig. 40 Removing/installing the air cleaner element

1.3L Engine
See Figure 41

1. Remove the retaining bolt from the air cleaner cover.
2. Unclip the two clips from the air cleaner box to the air cleaner cover.
3. Push the cover to the side in order to gain access to the air filter.

To install

4. Clean the inside of the housing.
5. Install new air filter in the air box.
6. Align the cover to the air box and secure with the two clips.
7. Hand thread the bolt that retains the cover to the fender.
8. Torque to 89 inch lbs. (10 Nm).

Fuel Filter

Replace the fuel filter element every 30,000 miles (50,000 km). Replace more often under dusty conditions. The fuel filter is located in the engine compartment on carburetor and turbocharged models, and at the left side of the fuel tank on fuel injection models.

On 1998 and newer models, the fuel filter is located in the fuel tank. The filter is serviced with the fuel pump.

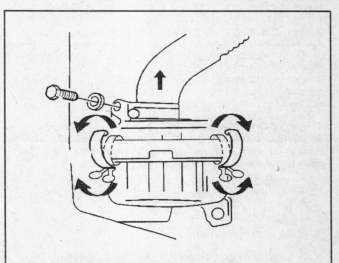

Fig. 41 Air cleaner assembly on the 1.3L engine

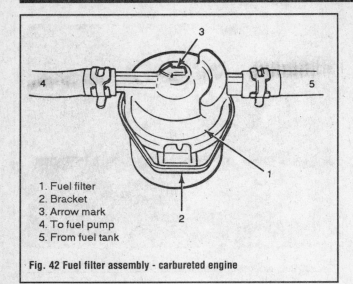

1. Fuel filter
2. Bracket
3. Arrow mark
4. To fuel pump
5. From fuel tank

Fig. 42 Fuel filter assembly - carbureted engine

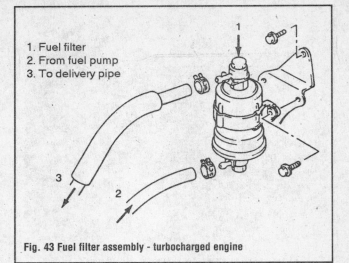

1. Fuel filter
2. From fuel pump
3. To delivery pipe

Fig. 43 Fuel filter assembly - turbocharged engine

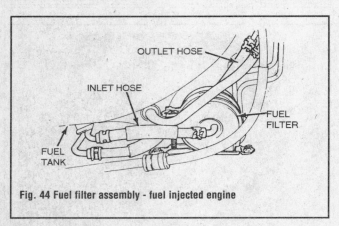

Fig. 44 Fuel filter assembly - fuel injected engine

Fig. 45 Fuel filter assembly as shown from under vehicle - fuel injected engine

FUEL SYSTEM PRESSURE RELIEF

On fuel injected and turbocharged vehicles, it is necessary to relieve the fuel system pressure prior to servicing the fuel filter. If the pressure in the tank is not relieved prior to system service, the fuel in the tank may be forced out through the lines during servicing. Refer to Fuel Systems for fuel pressure release procedures.

FILTER REMOVAL & INSTALLATION

See Figures 42, 43, 44 and 45

1. Relieve the fuel system pressure. Refer to Fuel System, Relieving the fuel System Pressure.
2. Disconnect the negative battery cable.
3. As required, raise and support the vehicle safely.

Note: A small amount of fuel may be released after the fuel hose is disconnected. In order to reduce the chance of personal injury, cover the fitting to be disconnected with a shop rag.

4. Label and disconnect all fuel lines from the fuel filter.
5. Remove the bolts from the fuel filter mounting bracket and remove the fuel filter.

To install:

6. Inspect the fuel lines surrounding the filter and replace as necessary if damaged.
7. Install the new fuel filter and tighten the bracket bolts securely.
8. Install the fuel lines and tighten the clamps securely.
9. Lower the vehicle and connect the negative battery cable.

10. Start the vehicle. It may take a few seconds to prime the fuel system.
11. Check for fuel system leaks and repair as necessary.

PCV System

The Positive Crankcase Ventilation (PCV) helps control the pressure created by the blow-by gases created during combustion. This system allows the engine to reuse some of the gases that are a product of combustion. Inspect the PCV system for proper operation every 30,000 miles (50,000 km). If the engine is idling rough, check for a clogged PCV valve or plugged hose. For more information, please refer to Driveability and Emission Controls, Emission Controls.

REMOVAL & INSTALLATION

See Figures 46, 47, 48, 49 and 50

Models Equipped with Air Cleaner

1. Remove the air cleaner assembly and lay it aside.
2. Locate the PCV valve at the intake manifold between the throttle body/carburetor and the valve cover.
3. Loosen the hose clamps and remove the PCV hose.
4. Loosen and remove the PCV attaching bar.
5. Pull the PCV valve from the intake manifold.
6. Inspect the valve for operation: (1) Shake it to see if the valve is free; (2) Blow through it (air will pass in one direction only).
7. To install, reverse the removal procedures.

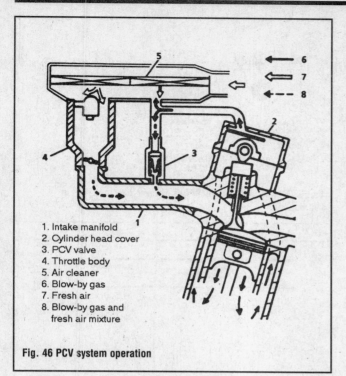

1. Intake manifold
2. Cylinder head cover
3. PCV valve
4. Throttle body
5. Air cleaner
6. Blow-by gas
7. Fresh air
8. Blow-by gas and fresh air mixture

Fig. 46 PCV system operation

Models Equipped With Air Cleaner Box

1. Remove clamp and hose from the PCV valve.
2. Remove the valve from the valve cover.

To install

3. Install the new valve in the valve cover.
4. Install the hose and clamp onto the PCV valve.

Evaporative Emission System

Inspect the evaporative emission system, including the charcoal canister, for proper operation every 30,000 miles (50,000 km). Replace any worn, plugged or collapsed hoses or damaged seals. Clean or replace the canister as needed.

REMOVAL & INSTALLATION

1. Label and disconnect the charcoal canister vent hoses.

Fig. 49 Remove the PCV valve

Fig. 47 Removing the PCV hose

Fig. 48 Remove the PCV attaching bar

2. Remove the canister-to-bracket bolt.
3. Lift the canister from the bracket.
4. To install, reverse the removal procedures.

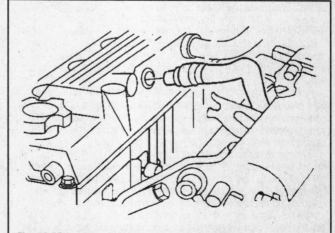

Fig. 50 PCV removal on air box equipped vehicles

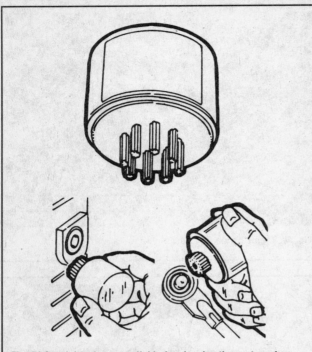

Fig. 51 Special tools are available for cleaning the posts and clamps on side terminal batteries.

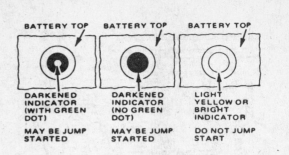

Fig. 52 Maintenance free batteries contain their own built in hydrometer.

Temperature (°F)	Minimum Voltage
70 or above	9.6
60	9.5
50	9.4
40	9.3
30	9.1
20	8.9
10	8.7
0	8.5

Fig. 53 Battery minimum voltage specifications

Battery

All Sprint/Metro/Swift models have a Maintenance Free battery as standard equipment, eliminating the need for fluid level checks and the possibility of specific gravity tests. Never-the-less, the battery does require some attention.

Note: Keep flames or sparks away from the battery. It gives off explosive hydrogen gas. The battery electrolyte contains sulfuric acid. If you should get any on your skin or in your eyes, flush the affected areas with plenty of clear water. If it lands in your eyes, seek medical help immediately.

GENERAL MAINTENANCE

See Figure 51

At least once a year, the battery terminals and the cable clamps should be cleaned. Remove the side terminal bolts and the cables, negative cable first. Clean the cable clamps and the battery terminals with a wire brush until all corrosion, grease, etc. is removed and the metal is shiny. It is especially important to clean the inside of the clamp thoroughly. A small deposit of foreign material or oxidation will prevent a sound electrical connection and inhibit either starting or charging. Special tools are available for cleaning side terminal clamps and terminals.

Before installing the cables, loosen the battery hold-down clamp, remove the battery and check the battery tray. Clear it of any debris and check it for soundness. Rust should be wire brushed away and the metal given a coat of anti-rust paint. Replace the battery and tighten the hold-down clamp securely but be careful not to overtighten, which will crack the battery case.

Surface coatings on battery cases can actually conduct electricity which will cause a slight voltage drain, so make sure the battery case is clean. Batteries can be cleaned using a paste made from mixture of baking soda and water. Spread the paste on any corrosion, wait a few minutes, and rinse with water. Finish the job by cleaning metal parts with a wire brush.

After the clamps and terminals are clean, reinstall the cables, negative cable last. Give the clamps and terminals a thin external coat of nonmetallic grease after installation, to retard corrosion.

Cables

Check the cables at the same time that the terminals are cleaned. If the cable insulation is cracked, broken or the ends are frayed, the cable should be replaced with a new one of the same length and gauge. Cables can be checked for continuity with an ohmmeter.

TESTING

See Figures 52 and 53

Maintenance free batteries, do not require normal attention as far as fluid level checks are concerned. The sealed top battery cannot be checked for charge using a hydrometer, since there is no provision for access to the electrolyte. Check the condition of the battery as follows:

1. If the indicator eye on top of the battery is dark, the battery has enough fluid. If the eye is lit (light yellow or bright), the electrolyte fluid is too low and the battery must be replaced.

2. If a green dot appears in the middle of the eye, the battery is sufficiently charged. If no green dot is visible, charge the battery.

3. It may be necessary to tip the battery from side-to-side to get the green dot to appear after charging.

4. After charging the battery, connect a battery load tester and a voltmeter across the battery terminals (the battery cables should be disconnected from the battery). Apply a load to the battery for 15 seconds to remove the surface charge. Remove the load.

5. Wait 15 seconds to allow the battery to recover. Apply the load again for 15 seconds while reading the voltage. Remove the load.

6. Check the results against the chart. If the battery voltage is at or above the specified voltage for the temperature listed, the battery is good. If the voltage falls below what's listed, the battery should be replaced.

CHARGING OF BATTERY

When it is necessary to charge a battery several cautions should be observed.

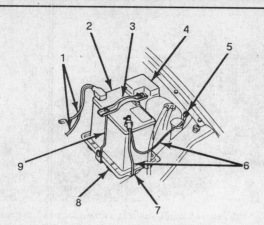

1. Positive battery cable
2. Battery
3. Battery retainer
4. Fuse and relay box
5. Body ground bolt
6. Negative battery cable
7. Harness retainer
8. Battery carrier
9. Battery hold down bracket

Fig. 54 Battery, cables, carrier and hold down brackets

• Do not charge an extremely cold battery. The battery may not accept current for several hours after charging has begun.
• The charging area should be well ventilated.
• If the battery feels hotter than 125-degees F during charging, or if violent gassing or spewing of electrolyte through the vent holes occurs, discontinue charging or reduce the charging rate.
1. Batteries with a built-in hydrometer showing a green dot do not require charging unless they have just been discharged by cranking the engine or leaving the lights on.
2. Connect the battery charger cables to the positive and negative battery terminals. Make sure all charger connections are clean and tight.
3. Charge the battery using the charge setting for 12V DC batteries that gives the highest charge rate to the battery.
4. Charge the battery until the green dot appears in the hydrometer. Check the battery every half-hour. The battery may need to be tipped or gently shaken for the green dot to appear.
5. Test the battery after charging and replace as necessary.

BATTERY REPLACEMENT

See Figure 54

1. Disconnect the negative battery cable from the negative battery terminal.
2. Disconnect the positive battery cable from the positive battery terminal.
3. Remove the hold down nuts and battery retainer from the brackets.
4. Carefully lift the battery from the engine compartment.

To install:
5. Clean the battery tray and terminal ends of all corrosion.
6. Install the battery in the engine compartment and position in the tray.
7. Install the battery retainer and tighten nuts to 71 inch lbs. (8 Nm).
8. Install the positive battery cable on the positive battery terminal and tighten the nut to 11 ft. lbs. (15 Nm).
9. Install the negative battery cable on the negative battery terminal and tighten the nut to 11 ft. lbs. (15 Nm).

Belts

Inspect the belts for signs of glazing or cracking. A glazed belt will be perfectly smooth from slippage, while a good belt will have a slight texture of fabric visible. Cracks will usually start at the inner edge of the belt and run outward. All worn or damaged drive belts should be replaced immediately. It is best to replace all drive belts at one time, as a preventive maintenance measure, during this service operation.

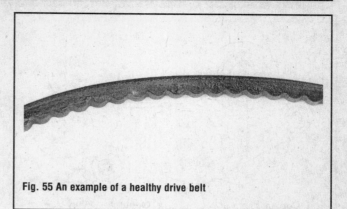

Fig. 55 An example of a healthy drive belt

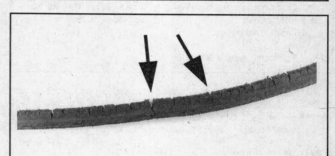

Fig. 56 Deep cracks in this belt will cause flex, building up heat that will eventually lead to belt failure

Fig. 57 The cover of this belt is worn, exposing the critical reinforcing cords to excessive wear

INSPECTION

See Figures 55, 56 and 57

Check the drive belts every 30,000 miles (50,000 km) or 24 months for evidence of cracking, fraying or incorrect tension. Determine the belt tension at a point halfway between the pulleys by using a GM Belt Tension Gauge No. BT-33-95-ACBN or equivalent. If tension is found to be too much or too little, perform the tension adjustments.

ADJUSTMENT

See Figure 58

• It is better to have belts too loose than too tight. Overly tight belts will lead to bearing failure, particularly in the water pump and alternator. However, loose belts place an extremely high impact load on the driven components due to the whipping action of the belt.
• A GM Belt Tension Gauge No. BT-33-95-ACBN or equivalent is required for tensioning accessory drive belts.

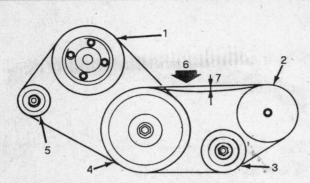

1. Coolant pump pulley
2. Compressor clutch pulley
3. Idler pulley
4. Crankshaft pulley
5. Generator pulley
6. 0.25 - 0.32 in deflection
7. 22 lbs. of pressure

Fig. 58 Checking drive belt tension

1. If the belt is cold, operate the engine (at idle speed) for 15 minutes; the belt will seat itself in the pulleys allowing the belt fibers to relax or stretch. If the belt is hot, allow it to cool, until it is warm to the touch.
2. Loosen the component-to-mounting bracket bolts.
3. Using a GM Belt Tension Gauge or equivalent, place the tension gauge at the center of the belt between the longest span.
4. Applying belt tension pressure on the component, adjust the drive belt tension to the correct specifications.
5. While holding the correct tension on the component, tighten the component-to-mounting bracket bolt.
6. When the belt tension is correct, remove the tension gauge.

REMOVAL & INSTALLATION

Alternator/Water Pump Belt

1. Remove the air cleaner assembly.
2. Remove the air compressor suction pipe bracket, as required.
3. Raise and support the vehicle safely. Remove the right lower splash shield.
4. Remove the air compressor drive belt by releasing the tensioner pulley and removing the belt from the crankshaft and compressor pulleys.
5. Lower the alternator cover plate, then lower the vehicle.
6. Loosen the adjusting bolt on the upper generator mounting bracket and remove the water pump/alternator drive belt from the vehicle.

To install:

7. Install the water pump/alternator drive belt on the pulleys.
8. Raise and support the vehicle safely. Install the lower generator cover plate and tighten bolts to 89 inch lbs. (10 Nm).
9. Install the air compressor drive belt by releasing the tensioner pulley.
10. Install the right lower splash shield and lower the vehicle.
11. Adjust the drive belt tension to 0.25 - 0.35 in. and tighten the upper generator adjustment bolt to 17 ft. lbs. (23 Nm).
12. Install the air compressor suction pipe bracket, as required.
13. Install the air cleaner assembly.

Air Conditioner Compressor Belt

1. Remove the air cleaner assembly.
2. Remove the air compressor suction pipe bracket, as required.
3. Raise and support the vehicle safely. Remove the right lower splash shield.
4. Remove the air compressor drive belt by releasing the tensioner pulley and removing the belt from the crankshaft and compressor pulleys.

To Install:

5. Install the air compressor drive belt by releasing the tensioner pulley.
6. Install the right lower splash shield and lower the vehicle.
7. Adjust the drive belt tension to 0.25 - 0.35 in. and tighten the upper

Fig. 59 A soft spongy hose (identifiable by the swollen section) will eventually burst and should be replaced

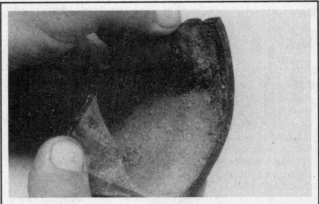

Fig. 60 Hoses are likely to deteriorate from the inside if the cooling system is not periodically flushed

generator adjustment bolt to 17 ft. lbs. (23 Nm).
8. Install the air compressor suction pipe bracket, as required.
9. Install the air cleaner assembly.

Hoses

INSPECTION

See Figures 59 and 60

Upper and lower radiator hoses, along with the heater hoses, should be checked for deterioration, leaks and loose hose clamps at least every 15,000 miles (24,000 km). It is also wise to check the hoses periodically in early spring and at the beginning of the fall or winter when you are performing other maintenance. A quick visual inspection could discover a weakened hose which might have left you stranded if it had remained unrepaired.

Whenever you are checking the hoses, make sure the engine and cooling system are cold. Visually inspect for cracking, rotting or collapsed hoses, and replace as necessary. Run your hand along the length of the hose. If a weak or swollen spot is noted when squeezing the hose wall, the hose should be replaced.

REMOVAL & INSTALLATION

See Figure 61

Radiator Hoses

1. Drain the cooling system.

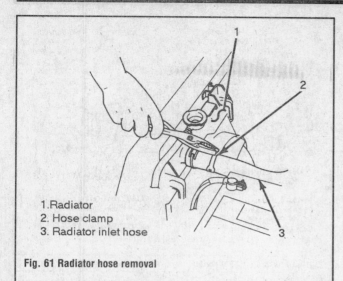

1. Radiator
2. Hose clamp
3. Radiator inlet hose

Fig. 61 Radiator hose removal

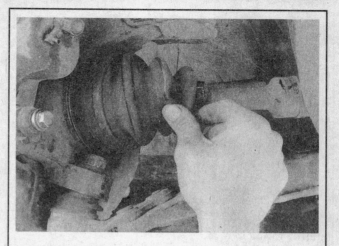

Fig. 62 CV-boots must be inspected periodically for damage

❊❊ CAUTION:

When draining the coolant, keep in mind that cats and dogs are attracted by the ethylene glycol antifreeze, and are quite likely to drink any that is left in an uncovered container or in puddles on the ground. This will prove fatal in sufficient quantity. Always drain the coolant into a sealable container. Coolant should be reused unless it is contaminated or several years old.

2. Remove the upper radiator hose by releasing the hose clamps at the thermostat outlet and radiator.

To install:

3. Install the upper radiator hose and tighten the clamps securely.
4. Fill the cooling system with a 50/50 mixture of antifreeze and water.

Heater Hoses

1. Drain the cooling system.
2. Remove the heater core inlet hose by releasing the hose clamps at the bulkhead and at the intake manifold.
3. Remove the heater core outlet hose by releasing the hose clamps at the bulkhead and the coolant pump inlet pipe running along the top of the transaxle. Remove the hose from the vehicle.

To install:

4. Install the heater core outlet hose to the bulkhead fitting and coolant pump inlet pipe and secure with hose clamps.
5. Install the heater core inlet hose to bulkhead fitting and intake manifold. Secure with hose clamps.
6. Fill the cooling system with a 50/50 mixture of antifreeze and water.

Timing Belt

SERVICING

The 1.0L and 1.3L engines utilize a timing belt to drive the camshaft from the crankshaft's turning motion and to maintain proper valve timing. Some manufacturers schedule periodic timing belt replacement to assure optimum engine performance, to make sure the motorist is never stranded should the belt break (as the engine will stop instantly) and for some (manufacturers with interference motors) to prevent the possibility of severe internal engine damage should the belt break.

Chevrolet recommends replacement intervals anywhere from 60,000 miles (96,500 km) to 100,000 miles (161,000 km). You will have to decide for yourself if the peace of mind offered by a new belt is worth it on higher mileage engines.

Whether or not you decide to replace it, you would be wise to check it peri-

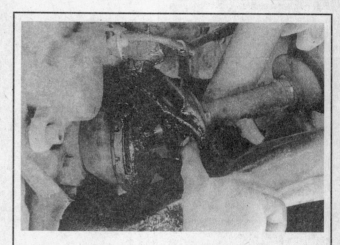

Fig. 63 A torn boot should be replaced immediately

odically to make sure it has not become damaged or worn. Generally speaking, a severely worn belt may cause engine performance to drop dramatically, but a damaged belt (which could give out suddenly) may not give as much warning. In general, any time the engine timing cover is removed you should inspect the belt for premature parting, severe cracks or missing teeth.

CV-Boots

See Figures 62 and 63

The CV (Constant Velocity) boots should be checked for damage each time the oil is changed and any other time the vehicle is raised for service. These boots keep water, grime, dirt and other damaging matter from entering the CV-joints. Any of these could cause early CV-joint failure which can be expensive to repair. Heavy grease thrown around the inside of the front wheel(s) and on the brake caliper/drum can be an indication of a torn boot. Thoroughly check the boots for missing clamps and tears. If the boot is damaged, it should be replaced immediately. Please refer to Drivetrain, Constant Velocity Shafts for more information on the procedures.

Spark Plugs

See Figure 64

A typical spark plug consists of a metal shell surrounding a ceramic insula-

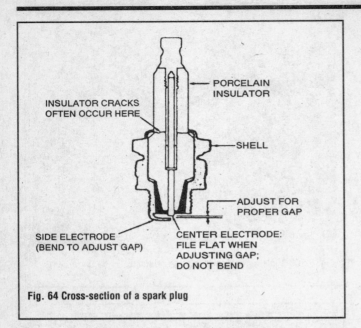

Fig. 64 Cross-section of a spark plug

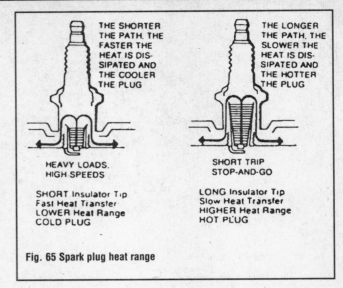

Fig. 65 Spark plug heat range

tor. A metal electrode extends downward through the center of the insulator and protrudes a small distance. Located at the end of the plug and attached to the side of the outer metal shell is the side electrode. The side electrode bends in at a 90-degree angle so that its tip is just past and parallel to the tip of the center electrode. The distance between these two electrodes (measured in thousandths of an inch or hundredths of a millimeter) is called the spark plug gap.

The spark plug does not produce a spark, but instead provides a gap across which the current can arc. The coil produces anywhere from 20,000 to 50,000 volts (depending on the type and application) which travels through the wires to the spark plugs. The current passes along the center electrode and jumps the gap to the side electrode, and in doing so, ignites the air/fuel mixture in the combustion chamber.

SPARK PLUG HEAT RANGE

See Figure 65

Spark plug heat range is the ability of the plug to dissipate heat. The longer the insulator (or the farther it extends into the engine), the hotter the plug will operate; the shorter the insulator (the closer the electrode is to the block's cooling passages) the cooler it will operate. A plug that absorbs little heat and remains too cool will quickly accumulate deposits of oil and carbon since it is not hot enough to burn them off. This leads to plug fouling and consequently to misfiring. A plug that absorbs too much heat will have no deposits but, due to the excessive heat, the electrodes will burn away quickly and might possibly lead to preignition or other ignition problems. Preignition takes place when plug tips get so hot that they glow sufficiently to ignite the air/fuel mixture before the actual spark occurs. This early ignition will usually cause a pinging during low speeds and heavy loads.

The general rule of thumb for choosing the correct heat range when picking a spark plug is: if most of your driving is long distance, high speed travel, use a colder plug; if most of your driving is stop and go, use a hotter plug. Original equipment plugs are generally a good compromise between the 2 styles and most people never have the need to change their plugs from the factory-recommended heat range.

REMOVAL & INSTALLATION

A set of spark plugs usually requires replacement after about 20,000 - 30,000 miles (32,000 - 48,000 km), depending on your style of driving. In normal operation plug gap increases about 0.001 in. (0.025mm) for every 2500 miles (4000 km). As the gap increases, the plug's voltage requirement also increases. It requires a greater voltage to jump the wider gap and about two to three times as much voltage to fire the plug at high speeds than at idle. The improved air/fuel ratio control of modern fuel injection combined with the higher voltage output of modern ignition systems will often allow an engine to

run significantly longer on a set of standard spark plugs, but keep in mind that efficiency will drop as the gap widens (along with fuel economy and power).

When you're removing spark plugs, work on one at a time. Don't start by removing the plug wires all at once, because, unless you number them, they may become mixed up. Take a minute before you begin and number the wires with tape.

1.0L and 1.3L Engine (except 1998 - 00)

1. Disconnect the negative battery cable, and if the vehicle has been run recently, allow the engine to thoroughly cool.

2. Carefully twist the spark plug wire boot to loosen it, then pull upward and remove the boot from the plug. Be sure to pull on the boot and not on the wire, otherwise the connector located inside the boot may become separated.

3. Using compressed air, blow any water or debris from the spark plug well to assure that no harmful contaminants are allowed to enter the combustion chamber when the spark plug is removed. If compressed air is not available, use a rag or a brush to clean the area.

Note: Remove the spark plugs when the engine is cold, if possible, to prevent damage to the threads. If removal of the plugs is difficult, apply a few drops of penetrating oil or silicone spray to the area around the base of the plug, and allow it a few minutes to work.

4. Using a spark plug socket that is equipped with a rubber insert to properly hold the plug, turn the spark plug counterclockwise to loosen and remove the spark plug from the bore.

✺✺ WARNING:

Be sure not to use a flexible extension on the socket. Use of a flexible extension may allow a shear force to be applied to the plug. A shear force could break the plug off in the cylinder head, leading to costly and frustrating repairs.

To install:

5. Inspect the spark plug boot for tears or damage. If a damaged boot is found, the spark plug wire must be replaced.

6. Using a wire feeler gauge, check and adjust the spark plug gap. When using a gauge, the proper size should pass between the electrodes with a slight drag. The next larger size should not be able to pass while the next smaller size should pass freely.

7. Carefully thread the plug into the bore by hand. If resistance is felt before the plug is almost completely threaded, back the plug out and begin threading again. In small, hard to reach areas, an old spark plug wire and boot could be used as a threading tool. The boot will hold the plug while you twist the end of the wire and the wire is supple enough to twist before it would allow the plug to crossthread.

A normally worn spark plug should have light tan or gray deposits on the firing tip.

A carbon fouled plug, identified by soft, sooty, black deposits, may indicate an improperly tuned vehicle. Check the air cleaner, ignition components and engine control system.

This spark plug has been left in the engine too long, as evidenced by the extreme gap- Plugs with such an extreme gap can cause misfiring and stumbling accompanied by a noticeable lack of power.

An oil fouled spark plug indicates an engine with worn piston rings and/or bad valve seals allowing excessive oil to enter the chamber.

A physically damaged spark plug may be evidence of severe detonation in that cylinder. Watch that cylinder carefully between services, as a continued detonation will not only damage the plug, but could also damage the engine.

A bridged or almost bridged spark plug, identified by a build-up between the electrodes caused by excessive carbon or oil build-up on the plug.

Fig. 66 Inspect the spark plug to determine engine running conditions

✸✸ WARNING:

Do not use the spark plug socket to thread the plugs. Always carefully thread the plug by hand or using an old plug wire to prevent the possibility of crossthreading and damaging the cylinder head bore.

8. Carefully tighten the spark plug. If the plug you are installing is equipped with a crush washer, seat the plug, then tighten about 1/4 turn to crush the washer. If you are installing a tapered seat plug, tighten the plug to specifications provided by the vehicle or plug manufacturer.

9. Apply a small amount of silicone dielectric compound to the end of the spark plug lead or inside the spark plug boot to prevent sticking, then install the boot to the spark plug and push until it clicks into place. The click may be felt or heard, then gently pull back on the boot to assure proper contact.

1998 - 00 1.3L Engine

1. Remove the electrical connectors from the coils.
2. The number 1 spark plug wire must be removed from the clip on the 2 - 3 coil.

3. Unbolt the two ignition coils.
4. Disconnect the number 1 plug wire and the 1 - 4 coil from the plugs.
5. Disconnect the number 3 plug wire and the 2 - 3 coil from the plugs.
6. Remove the spark plugs from the head.

To install

7. Gap the spark plugs. 0.039 - 0.043 in. (1.0 - 1.1 mm).
8. Install the plugs into the head. Torquing to 21 ft. lbs. (28 Nm).
9. Install the number 3 plug wire and the 2 - 3 coil to the plugs.
10. Install the number 4 plug wire and the 1 - 4 coil to the plugs.
11. Bolt the coils to the head.
12. Place the number 1 plug wire into the clip on the 2 - 3 coil.
13. Connect the electrical connectors to the coils.

INSPECTION & GAPPING

See Figures 66, 67, 68, 69 and 70

Check the plugs for deposits and wear. If they are not going to be replaced, clean the plugs thoroughly. Remember that any kind of deposit will decrease the

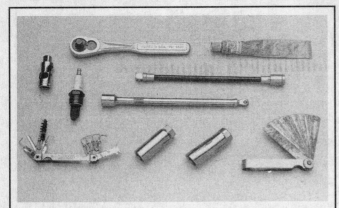

Fig. 67 A variety of tools and gauges are needed for spark plug service

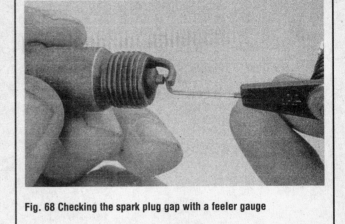

Fig. 68 Checking the spark plug gap with a feeler gauge

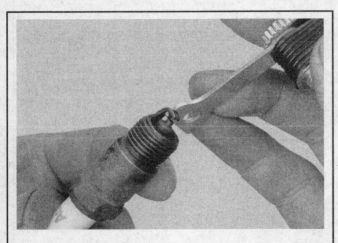

Fig. 69 Adjusting the spark plug gap

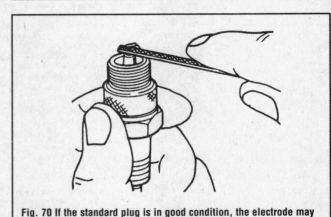

Fig. 70 If the standard plug is in good condition, the electrode may be filed flat - WARNING: do not file platinum plugs

efficiency of the plug. Plugs can be cleaned on a spark plug cleaning machine, which can sometimes be found in service stations, or you can do an acceptable job of cleaning with a stiff brush. If the plugs are cleaned, the electrodes must be filed flat. Use an ignition points file, not an emery board or the like, which will leave deposits. The electrodes must be filed perfectly flat with sharp edges;

rounded edges reduce the spark plug voltage by as much as 50%.

Check spark plug gap before installation. The ground electrode (the L-shaped one connected to the body of the plug) must be parallel to the center electrode and the specified size wire gauge (please refer to the Tune-Up Specifications chart for details) must pass between the electrodes with a slight drag.

Note: NEVER adjust the gap on a used platinum type spark plug.

Always check the gap on new plugs as they are not always set correctly at the factory. Do not use a flat feeler gauge when measuring the gap on a used plug, because the reading may be inaccurate. A round-wire type gapping tool is the best way to check the gap. The correct gauge should pass through the electrode gap with a slight drag. If you're in doubt, try one size smaller and one larger. The smaller gauge should go through easily, while the larger one shouldn't go through at all. Wire gapping tools usually have a bending tool attached. Use that to adjust the side electrode until the proper distance is obtained. Absolutely never attempt to bend the center electrode. Also, be careful not to bend the side electrode too far or too often as it may weaken and break off within the engine, requiring removal of the cylinder head to retrieve it.

Spark Plug Wires

TESTING

See Figure 71

At every tune-up/inspection, visually check the spark plug cables for burns, cuts, or breaks in the insulation. Check the boots and the nipples on the distributor cap and/or coil. Replace any damaged wiring.

Every 50,000 miles (80,000 Km) or 60 months, the resistance of the wires should be checked with an ohmmeter. Wires with excessive resistance will

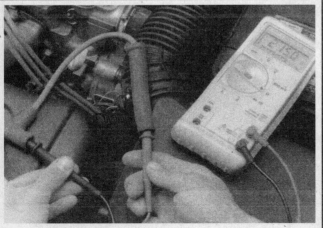

Fig. 71 Checking individual plug wire resistance with a digital ohmmeter

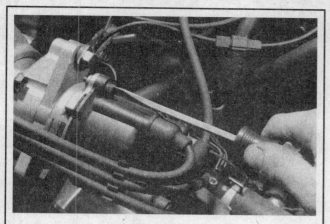

Fig. 72 Loosen the distributor cap attaching screws

Fig. 73 Carefully remove the distributor cap, taking care not to stretch the ignition wires or damage the rotor

Fig. 74 After the distributor cap is removed the rotor is in plain sight

Fig. 75 The rotor is removed by pulling with a slight twist

cause misfiring, and may make the engine difficult to start in damp weather.

To check resistance:
1. Remove one ignition wire.
2. Using a digital multimeter, check the resistance of the wire.
3. The resistance should be 3 - 6.5 ohms per foot.
4. Replace if necessary.
5. Install the ignition wire.
6. Repeat for each ignition wire on the vehicle including the coil wire.

Distributor Cap & Rotor

REMOVAL & INSTALLATION

See Figures 72, 73, 74, 75 and 76

1. Disconnect the negative battery cable.
2. Disconnect the ignition coil high tension wire at the coil.
3. Loosen and remove the 2 distributor cap attaching screws.
4. Carefully remove the distributor cap. Take care not to stretch the high tension spark plug cables or damage the rotor.
5. Remove the rotor by pulling with a slight twist.

To install:

6. Inspect the condition of the distributor cap. If the cap shows signs of cracks, broken pieces, carbon tracking, charred or eroded terminals, or a worn or damaged rotor button, replace it.

7. Inspect the condition of the distributor rotor. If the rotor shows signs of cracks, broken pieces, a charred or eroded tip, physical contact of the tip with

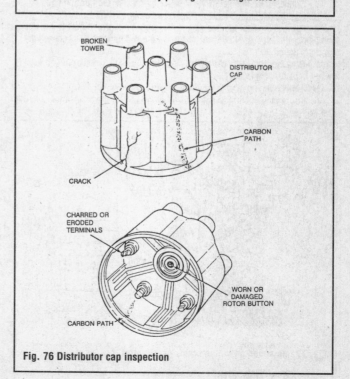

Fig. 76 Distributor cap inspection

the cap or insufficient spring tension, replace it.

8. Apply a light coating of dielectric grease to the distributor cap terminals and rotor tip.

9. Install the rotor by aligning the flat on the rotor and shaft. Push the rotor until it bottoms on the shaft.

10. Check the condition of the distributor cap gasket and replace as necessary.

11. Install the distributor cap and tighten the attaching screws securely.

12. Reinstall the coil high tension wire at the coil.

Ignition Timing

GENERAL INFORMATION

The ignition timing specification is used to determine when the spark plug receives the high voltage charge in relation to the position of the piston. When the piston is at the top of its stroke, it is referred to being at the Top Dead Center (TDC). At the top of the stroke (TDC), the piston is referred to as being at 0-degrees. The timing must be set so that as the piston travels upward, the spark will jump the air gap at the right time in order to give the piston the most power available on its downward, or power stroke. Since the air fuel mix takes time to ignite and burn, the timing must be set Before Top Dead Center (BTDC). If the timing is set too far advanced (BTDC), the flame front will try to stop the piston from traveling upward. This will more than likely cause a pinging or detonation. If the timing is set too far retarded, or After Top Dead Center (ATDC), there will be a lack of power. The effective stroke will be diminished because the piston will be traveling downward before the flame front reaches the piston head. The optimum timing has been determined by the manufacturer and placed on a label under the hood of the vehicle. If the label is missing you can refer to the charts given to you in this book for the correct timing specifications.

INSPECTION & ADJUSTMENT

1985 - 97

1. Run the engine until it reaches operating temperature. Stop the engine, but keep the ignition switch in the **ON** position for approximately 5 seconds.

2. Start and run the engine at 2000 RPM for 5 minutes. After 5 minutes bring the engine down to an idle.

3. Turn OFF all accessories.

4. Connect a tachometer to the negative terminal of the ignition coil.

5. Use the underhood labels for ignition timing specifications.

6. Remove the cap from the diagnostic connector, located next to the ignition coil or the left side strut tower and insert a fused jumper wire between the appropriate terminals.

7. On a four pin connector: jump terminals C and D. On six pin connectors: jump terminals D and E.

8. Aim the timing light at the timing marks.

9. Loosen the distributor hold-down bolt and rotate the distributor until the correct timing is reached.

10. Torque the hold-down bolt to 11 - 15 ft. lbs. (15 - 20 Nm). Confirm the timing advances with engine speed.

11. Remove the jumper wire, the timing light, and the tachometer.

1998 - 00 Models

Periodic adjustment of the ignition timing is not necessary for these engines. If ignition timing is not within specification, there is a fault in the engine control system. Diagnose and repair the problem as necessary.

Valve Lash

In 1989 the Metro moved to hydraulic lifters. These lifters need no adjustments. The valve train maintains zero lash.

ADJUSTMENTS

Note: This procedure is only for 1985 - 1988 Sprint.

1. Remove the air cleaner and the cylinder head cover.

2. Rotate the crankshaft clockwise and align timing notch on crankshaft pulley with the 0 mark on the timing tab.

3. Remove the distributor cap and check if the rotor is positioned correctly (pointing at the number one cylinder terminal on the cap).

4. If the rotor is not pointed to number one, then rotate the engine 360-degrees and align the notch with the 0 mark.

5. Using a feeler gauge check the intake and exhaust valves for the proper clearances: Intake: 0.006 in. (0.15 mm) Exhaust: 0.008 in. (0.20 mm).

6. If the clearances do not meet the specification, back off the lock locknut and turn the adjusting screw. Torque the locknut to 11 - 13 ft. lbs. (15 - 19 Nm).

7. Rotate the engine 240-degrees and align the timing notch with the left attaching bolt of the timing belt outside cover. Check and adjust the valve lash for Number 3 cylinder.

8. Rotate the engine 240-degrees and align the timing notch with the right attaching bolt of the timing belt outside cover. Check and adjust the valve lash for Number 2 cylinder.

9. Install the distributor cap, cylinder head cover and air cleaner. Torque cylinder head cover bolts to 48 inch lbs. (5 Nm).

Idle Speed & Mixture Adjustments

ADJUSTMENT

See Figures 77, 78, 79, 80 and 81

Carbureted Vehicles

The cooling fan runs and stops automatically according to the coolant temperature. For this reason, make sure that the cooling fan is not running before

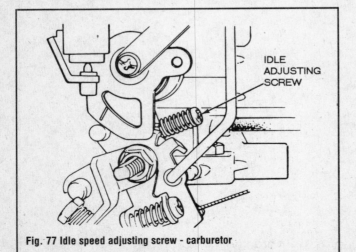

Fig. 77 Idle speed adjusting screw - carburetor

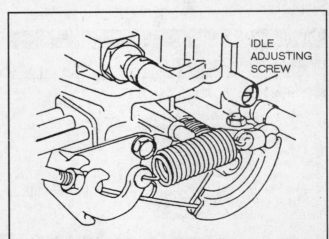

Fig. 78 Idle speed adjusting screw - fuel injection

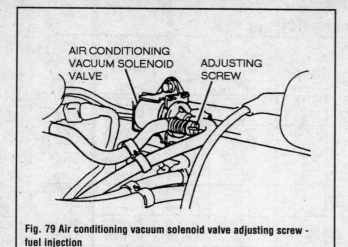

Fig. 79 Air conditioning vacuum solenoid valve adjusting screw - fuel injection

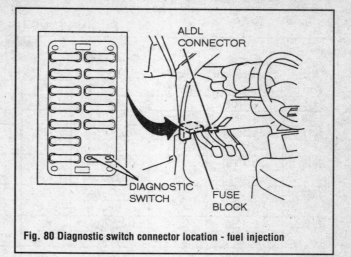

Fig. 80 Diagnostic switch connector location - fuel injection

performing idle speed check and adjustment.
1. Confirm the following prior to checking or adjusting the idle speed.
   a. Check that the lead wires and hoses of the engine emission control system are connected correctly.
   b. Check that the accelerator cable has 0.12 - 0.20 in. (3 - 5 mm) free-play when engine is at operating temperature.
   c. Check that the ignition timing is within specification.
   d. Check that the valve lash is adjusted to specification.
2. Connect a tachometer to the engine according to the manufacturer's instructions.
3. Place transaxle gear shift lever in **N** position and set parking brake.
4. Start engine and warm engine to normal operating temperature.
5. Ensure that the lights, heater fan, rear defogger, cooling fan and air conditioner are **OFF**.
6. Check the idle speed. If not within specifications, adjust by turning the idle adjusting screw on the carburetor.
7. If idle speed can not be adjusted to specification by turning the adjusting screw, it can be due to a faulty return of the throttle valve or some other mechanical reason. Determine the cause and repair.
8. After idle adjustment, check idle-up system for proper operation.
9. Stop engine and check to ensure that accelerator cable has some play. If not, adjust cable.

Fuel Injected Vehicles

1987 - 93

1. Confirm the following prior to checking or adjusting the idle speed.
   a. Check that the lead wires and hoses of the engine emission control system are connected correctly.
   b. Check that the accelerator cable has 0.12 - 0.20 in. (3 - 5 mm) free-play when engine is at operating temperature.
   c. Check that the ignition timing is within specification.
2. Place automatic transaxle gear shift lever in **P** position or manual transaxle gear shift lever in **NEUTRAL** position and set parking brake.
3. Ensure that the lights, heater fan, rear defogger, cooling fan and air conditioner are **OFF**.
4. Ensure that air cleaner is installed correctly.
5. Remove cover on idle speed adjusting screw.
6. Start engine and warm engine to normal operating temperature.
7. Install a spare fuse into the **DIAG SW** connector in the fuse block under the left side of the dash.
8. Check and adjust idle speed to specification. Turn idle speed screw in to decrease idle and out to increase idle.
9. If equipped with air conditioning, check and adjust the air conditioner idle speed vacuum solenoid valve.

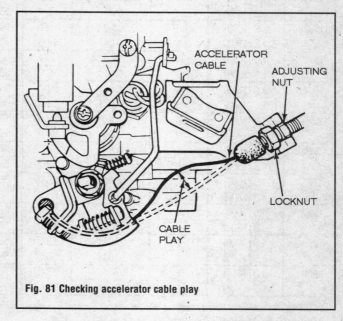

Fig. 81 Checking accelerator cable play

10. With idle speed correct, turn air conditioner **ON**.
11. Check that engine idle is within specification or slightly higher. If not, adjust air conditioner vacuum solenoid valve adjusting screw to obtain correct idle.
12. Turn air conditioner **OFF** and check that idle speed is within specifications.

Note: On some vehicles, a slightly higher idle setting on the vacuum solenoid valve may be needed to maintain proper idle characteristics with the air conditioning system operating.

13. After adjusting idle speed remove the spare fuse from the connector.

1994 - 00

The 1994 - 00 engines covered by this manual utilize sophisticated fuel injection systems in which an engine control computer utilizes information from various sensors to control idle speed and air/fuel mixtures. No periodic adjustments are either necessary or possible on these systems. If a problem is suspected, please refer to Driveability and Emission Controls for more information on electronic engine controls and fuel injection.

ENGINE TUNE-UP SPECIFICATIONS

Year	Engine Displacement Liters (cc)	Engine ID/VIN	Spark Plugs Gap (in.)	Ignition Timing (deg.) MT	AT	Fuel Pump (psi)	Idle Speed (rpm) MT	AT	Valve Clearance In.	Ex.
1985	1.0 (1000)	M	0.039-0.043	10B	6B	3.5	750	850	0.006	0.008
1986	1.0 (1000)	5	0.039-0.043	10B	6B	3.5	800	850	0.006	0.008
1987	1.0 (1000)	2	0.039-0.043	12B	—	25-35	750	—	0.006	0.008
	1.0 (1000)	5	0.039-0.043	10B	6B	3.5	750 ②	850	0.006	0.008
1988	1.0 (1000)	2	0.039-0.043	12B	—	25-35	750	—	0.006	0.008
	1.0 (1000)	5	0.039-0.043	10B	6B	3.5	750 ②	850	0.006	0.008
1989	1.0 (1000)	5	0.039-0.043	6B	6B ①	3.5	800	850	HYD	HYD
	1.3 (1300)	3	0.041	5B ①	5B ①	23-30	800	850	HYD	HYD
1990	1.0 (1000)	5	0.039-0.043	6B	6B ①	25-35	750 ③	850	HYD	HYD
	1.3 (1300)	3	0.041	5B ①	5B ①	23-30	800	850	HYD	HYD
1991	1.0 (1000)	6	0.039-0.043	6B	6B ①	25-31	800 ④	850	HYD	HYD
	1.3 (1300)	3	0.041	5B ①	5B ①	23-30	800	850	HYD	HYD
1992	1.0 (1000)	6	0.039-0.043	5B	5B ①	25-31	800 ④	850	HYD	HYD
	1.3 (1300)	3	0.041	5B ①	5B ①	23-30	800	850	HYD	HYD
1993	1.0 (1000)	6	0.039-0.043	5B	5B ①	23-30	800	850	HYD	HYD
	1.3 (1300)	3	0.041	5B ①	5B ①	23-30	800	850	HYD	HYD
1994	1.0 (1000)	6	0.041	5B ①	5B ①	23-30	800	850	HYD	HYD
	1.3 (1300)	3	0.041	5B ①	5B ①	23-30	800	850	HYD	HYD
1995	1.0 (1000)	6	0.041	5B ①	5B ①	23-30	800	850	HYD	HYD
	1.3 (1300)	9	0.041	5B ①	5B ①	23-30	800	850	HYD	HYD
1996	1.0 (1000)	6	0.041	5B ①	5B ①	23-30	800	850	HYD	HYD
	1.3 (1300)	9	0.041	5B ①	5B ①	23-30	800	850	HYD	HYD
1997	1.0 (1000)	6	0.041	5B ①	5B ①	23-30	800	850	HYD	HYD
	1.3 (1300)	9	0.041	5B ①	5B ①	23-30	800	850	HYD	HYD
1998	1.0 (1000)	6	0.041	5B ①	5B ①	23-30	800	850	HYD	HYD
	1.3 (1300)	9	0.041	5B ①	5B ①	23-30	800	850	HYD	HYD
1999	1.0 (1000)	6	0.041	5B ①	5B ①	23-30	800	850	HYD	HYD
	1.3 (1300)	9	0.041	5B ①	5B ①	23-30	800	850	HYD	HYD
2000	1.0 (1000)	6	0.041	5B ①	5B ①	23-30	800	850	HYD	HYD
	1.3 (1300)	9	0.041	5B ①	5B ①	23-30	800	850	HYD	HYD

NOTE: The Vehicle Emission Control Information label often reflects specification changes made during production. The label figures must be used if they differ from those in this chart.

B - Before Top Dead Center

HYD - Hydraulic

① Connect a fused jumper from Duty Check cavity 4 to cavity 5 for fixed timing (DLC connector located at left strut tower)

② Insert jumper wire between terminals in DLC connector E1 and TE1

Air Conditioning System

SYSTEM SERVICE & REPAIR

Note: It is recommended that the A/C system be serviced by an EPA Section 609 certified automotive technician utilizing a refrigerant recovery/recycling machine.

The do-it-yourselfer should not service his/her own vehicle's A/C system for many reasons, including legal concerns, personal injury, environmental damage and cost. The following are some of the reasons why you may decide not to service your own vehicle's A/C system.

According to the U.S. Clean Air Act, it is a federal crime to service or repair (involving the refrigerant) a Motor Vehicle Air Conditioning (MVAC) system for money without being EPA certified. It is also illegal to vent R-12 and R-134a refrigerants into the atmosphere. Selling or distributing A/C system refrigerant (in a container which contains less than 20 pounds of refrigerant) to any person who is not EPA 609 certified is also not allowed by law.

State and/or local laws may be more strict than the federal regulations, so be sure to check with your state and/or local authorities for further information. For further federal information on the legality of servicing your A/C system, call the EPA Stratospheric Ozone Hotline.

Note: Federal law dictates that a fine of up to $25,000 may be levied on people convicted of venting refrigerant into the atmosphere. Additionally, the EPA may pay up to $10,000 for information or services leading to a criminal conviction of the violation of these laws.

When servicing an A/C system you run the risk of handling or coming in contact with refrigerant, which may result in skin or eye irritation or frostbite. Although low in toxicity (due to chemical stability), inhalation of concentrated refrigerant fumes is dangerous and can result in death; cases of fatal cardiac arrhythmia have been reported in people accidentally subjected to high levels of refrigerant. Some early symptoms include loss of concentration and drowsiness.

Fig. 82 A coolant tester can be used to determine the freezing and boiling levels of the coolant in your vehicle

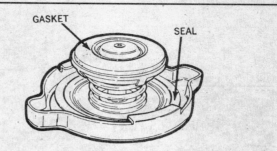

Fig. 83 To ensure efficient cooling system operation, inspect the radiator cap gasket and seal

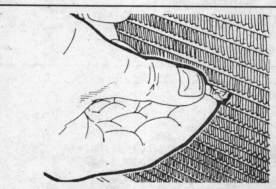

Fig. 84 Periodically remove any debris from the condenser and radiator fins

Note: Generally, the limit for exposure is lower for R-134a than it is for R-12. Exceptional care must be practiced when handling R-134a.

Also, refrigerants can decompose at high temperatures (near gas heaters or open flame), which may result in hydrofluoric acid, hydrochloric acid and phosgene (a fatal nerve gas).

R-12 refrigerant can damage the environment because it is a Chlorofluorocarbon (CFC), which has been proven to add to ozone layer depletion, leading to increasing levels of UV radiation. UV radiation has been linked with an increase in skin cancer, suppression of the human immune system, an increase in cataracts, damage to crops, damage to aquatic organisms, an increase in ground-level ozone, and increased global warming.

R-134a refrigerant is a greenhouse gas which, if allowed to vent into the atmosphere, will contribute to global warming (the Greenhouse Effect).

It is usually more economically feasible to have a certified MVAC automotive technician perform A/C system service on your vehicle. Some possible reasons for this are as follows:

• While it is illegal to service an A/C system without the proper equipment, the home mechanic would have to purchase an expensive refrigerant recovery/recycling machine to service his/her own vehicle.

• Since only a certified person may purchase refrigerant - according to the Clean Air Act, there are specific restrictions on selling or distributing A/C system refrigerant - it is legally impossible (unless certified) for the home mechanic to service his/her own vehicle. Procuring refrigerant in an illegal fashion exposes one to the risk of paying a $25,000 fine to the EPA.

R-12 Refrigerant Conversion

If your vehicle still uses R-12 refrigerant, one way to save A/C system costs down the road is to investigate the possibility of having your system converted to R-134a. The older R-12 systems can be easily converted to R-134a refrigerant by a certified automotive technician by installing a few new components and changing the system oil.

The cost of R-12 is steadily rising and will continue to increase, because it is no longer imported or manufactured in the United States. Therefore, it is often possible to have an R-12 system converted to R-134a and recharged for less than it would cost to just charge the system with R-12.

If you are interested in having your system converted, contact local automotive service stations for more details and information.

PREVENTIVE MAINTENANCE

See Figures 82 and 83

Although the A/C system should not be serviced by the do-it-yourselfer, preventive maintenance can be practiced and A/C system inspections can be performed to help maintain the efficiency of the vehicle's A/C system. For preventive maintenance, perform the following:

• The easiest and most important preventive maintenance for your A/C system is to be sure that it is used on a regular basis. Running the system for five minutes each month (no matter what the season) will help ensure that the seals and all internal components remain lubricated.

Note: Some newer vehicles automatically operate the A/C system compressor whenever the windshield defroster is activated. When running, the compressor lubricates the A/C system components; therefore, the A/C system would not need to be operated each month.

• In order to prevent heater core freeze-up during A/C operation, it is necessary to maintain proper antifreeze protection. Use a hand-held coolant tester (hydrometer) to periodically check the condition of the antifreeze in your engine's cooling system.

Note: Antifreeze should not be used longer than the manufacturer specifies.

• For efficient operation of an air conditioned vehicle's cooling system, the radiator cap should have a holding pressure which meets manufacturer's specifications. A cap which fails to hold these pressures should be replaced.

• Any obstruction of or damage to the condenser configuration will restrict air flow which is essential to its efficient operation. It is, therefore, a good rule to keep this unit clean and in proper physical shape.

Note: Bug screens which are mounted in front of the condenser (unless they are original equipment) are regarded as obstructions.

• The condensation drain tube expels any water which accumulates on the bottom of the evaporator housing into the engine compartment. If this tube is obstructed, the air conditioning performance can be restricted and condensation buildup can spill over onto the vehicle's floor.

SYSTEM INSPECTION

See Figure 84

Although the A/C system should not be serviced by the do-it-yourselfer, pre-

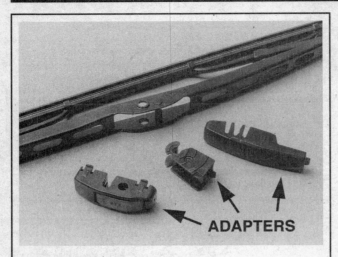
Fig. 85 Bosch® wiper blade and fit kit

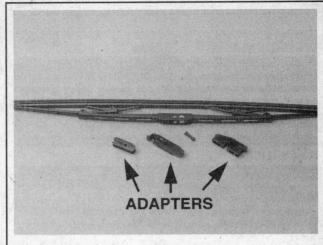
Fig. 86 Lexor® wiper blade and fit kit

Fig. 87 Pylon® wiper blade and adapter

Fig. 88 Trico® wiper blade and fit kit

ventive maintenance can be practiced and A/C system inspections can be performed to help maintain the efficiency of the vehicle's A/C system. For A/C system inspection, perform the following:

The easiest and often most important check for the air conditioning system consists of a visual inspection of the system components. Visually inspect the air conditioning system for refrigerant leaks, damaged compressor clutch, abnormal compressor drive belt tension and/or condition, plugged evaporator drain tube, blocked condenser fins, disconnected or broken wires, blown fuses, corroded connections and poor insulation.

A refrigerant leak will usually appear as an oily residue at the leakage point in the system. The oily residue soon picks up dust or dirt particles from the surrounding air and appears greasy. Through time, this will build up and appear to be a heavy dirt impregnated grease.

For a thorough visual and operational inspection, check the following:
Check the surface of the radiator and condenser for dirt, leaves or other material which might block air flow.
- Check for kinks in hoses and lines. Check the system for leaks.
- Make sure the drive belt is properly tensioned. When the air conditioning is operating, make sure the drive belt is free of noise or slippage.
- Make sure the blower motor operates at all appropriate positions, then check for distribution of the air from all outlets with the blower on **HIGH** or **MAX**.

Note: Keep in mind that under conditions of high humidity, air discharged from the A/C vents may not feel as cold as expected, even if the system is working properly. This is because vaporized moisture in humid air retains heat more effectively than dry air, thereby making humid air more difficult to cool.

- Make sure the air passage selection lever is operating correctly. Start the engine and warm it to normal operating temperature, then make sure the temperature selection lever is operating correctly.

Windshield Wipers

ELEMENT (REFILL) CARE & REPLACEMENT

See Figures 85, 86, 87, 88, 89, 90, 91, 92, 93 and 94

For maximum effectiveness and longest element life, the windshield and wiper blades should be kept clean. Dirt, tree sap, road tar and so on will cause streaking, smearing and blade deterioration if left on the glass. It is advisable to wash the windshield carefully with a commercial glass cleaner at least once a month. Wipe off the rubber blades with the wet rag afterwards. Do not attempt to move wipers across the windshield by hand; damage to the motor and drive mechanism will result.

To inspect and/or replace the wiper blade elements, place the wiper switch in the **LOW** speed position and the ignition switch in the **ACC** position. When the wiper blades are approximately vertical on the windshield, turn the ignition switch to **OFF**.

Examine the wiper blade elements. If they are found to be cracked, broken or torn, they should be replaced immediately. Replacement intervals will vary with usage, although ozone deterioration usually limits element life to about one

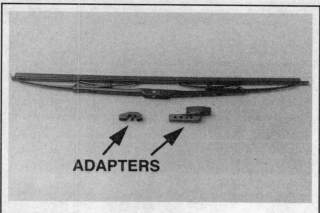

ADAPTERS

Fig. 89 Tripledge® wiper blade and fit kit

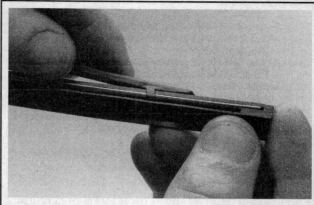

Fig. 90 To remove and install a Lexor® wiper blade refill, slip out the old insert and slide in a new one

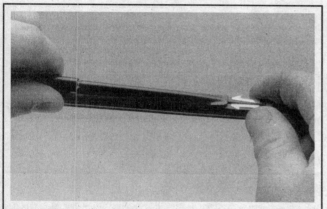

Fig. 91 On Pylon® inserts, the clip at the end has to be removed prior to sliding the insert off

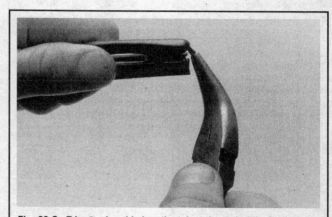

Fig. 92 On Trico® wiper blades, the tab at the end of the blade must be turned up . . .

year. If the wiper pattern is smeared or streaked, or if the blade chatters across the glass, the elements should be replaced. It is easiest and most sensible to replace the elements in pairs.

If your vehicle is equipped with aftermarket blades, there are several different types of refills and your vehicle might have any kind. Aftermarket blades and arms rarely use the exact same type blade or refill as the original equipment. Here are some typical aftermarket blades; not all may be available for your vehicle:

The Anco® type uses a release button that is pushed down to allow the refill

to slide out of the yoke jaws. The new refill slides back into the frame and locks in place.

Some Trico® refills are removed by locating where the metal backing strip or the refill is wider. Insert a small screwdriver blade between the frame and metal backing strip. Press down to release the refill from the retaining tab.

Other types of Trico® refills have two metal tabs which are unlocked by squeezing them together. The rubber filler can then be withdrawn from the frame jaws. A new refill is installed by inserting the refill into the front frame jaws and sliding it rearward to engage the remaining frame jaws. There are usually four

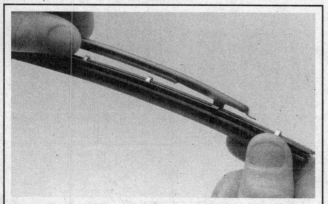

Fig. 93 . . . then the insert can be removed. After installing the replacement insert, bend the tab back

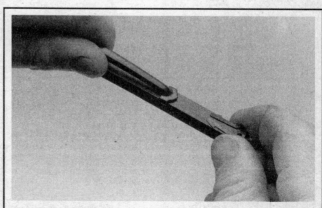

Fig. 94 The Tripledge® wiper blade insert is removed and installed using a securing clip

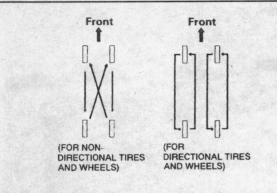

Fig. 95 Compact spare tires must NEVER be used in the rotation pattern

Fig. 96 Unidirectional tires are identifiable by sidewall arrows and/or the word "rotation"

jaws; be certain when installing that the refill is engaged in all of them. At the end of its travel, the tabs will lock into place on the front jaws of the wiper blade frame.

Another type of refill is made from polycarbonate. The refill has a simple locking device at one end which flexes downward out of the groove into which the jaws of the holder fit, allowing easy release. By sliding the new refill through all the jaws and pushing through the slight resistance when it reaches the end of its travel, the refill will lock into position.

To replace the Tridon® refill, it is necessary to remove the wiper blade. This refill has a plastic backing strip with a notch about 1 in. (25mm) from the end. Hold the blade (frame) on a hard surface so that the frame is tightly bowed. Grip the tip of the backing strip and pull up while twisting counterclockwise. The backing strip will snap out of the retaining tab. Do this for the remaining tabs until the refill is free of the blade. The length of these refills is molded into the end and they should be replaced with identical types.

Regardless of the type of refill used, be sure to follow the part manufacturer's instructions closely. Make sure that all of the frame jaws are engaged as the refill is pushed into place and locked. If the metal blade holder and frame are allowed to touch the glass during wiper operation, the glass will be scratched.

Tires and Wheels

Common sense and good driving habits will afford maximum tire life. Fast starts, sudden stops and hard cornering are hard on tires and will shorten their useful life span. Make sure that you don't overload the vehicle or run with incorrect pressure in the tires. Both of these practices will increase tread wear.

Note: For optimum tire life, keep the tires properly inflated, rotate them often and have the wheel alignment checked periodically.

Inspect your tires frequently. Be especially careful to watch for bubbles in the tread or sidewall, deep cuts or underinflation. Replace any tires with bubbles in the sidewall. If cuts are so deep that they penetrate to the cords, discard the tire. Any cut in the sidewall of a radial tire renders it unsafe. Also look for uneven tread wear patterns that may indicate the front end is out of alignment or that the tires are out of balance.

TIRE ROTATION

See Figures 95 and 96

Tires must be rotated periodically to equalize wear patterns that vary with a tire's position on the vehicle. Tires will also wear in an uneven way as the front steering/suspension system wears to the point where the alignment should be reset.

Rotating the tires will ensure maximum life for the tires as a set, so you will not have to discard a tire early due to wear on only part of the tread. Regular rotation is required to equalize wear.

When rotating "unidirectional tires," make sure that they always roll in the same direction. This means that a tire used on the left side of the vehicle must not be switched to the right side and vice-versa. Such tires should only be rotated front-to-rear or rear-to-front, while always remaining on the same side of

the vehicle. These tires are marked on the sidewall as to the direction of rotation; observe the marks when reinstalling the tire(s).

Some styled or "mag" wheels may have different offsets front to rear. In these cases, the rear wheels must not be used up front and vice-versa. Furthermore, if these wheels are equipped with unidirectional tires, they cannot be rotated unless the tire is remounted for the proper direction of rotation.

Note: The compact or space-saver spare is strictly for emergency use. It must never be included in the tire rotation or placed on the vehicle for everyday use.

TIRE DESIGN

See Figure 97

For maximum satisfaction, tires should be used in sets of four. Mixing of different types (radial, bias-belted, fiberglass belted) must be avoided. In most cases, the vehicle manufacturer has designated a type of tire on which the vehicle will perform best. Your first choice when replacing tires should be to use the same type of tire that the manufacturer recommends.

When radial tires are used, tire sizes and wheel diameters should be selected to maintain ground clearance and tire load capacity equivalent to the original specified tire. Radial tires should always be used in sets of four.

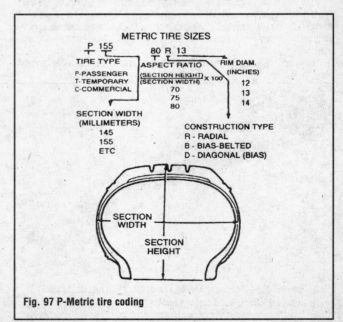

Fig. 97 P-Metric tire coding

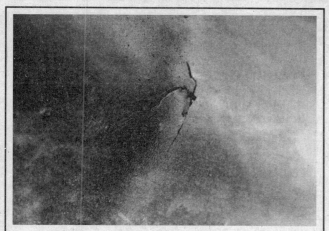

Fig. 98 Tires should be checked frequently for any sign of puncture or damage

Fig. 99 Tires with deep cuts, or cuts which bulge, should be replaced immediately

✳✳ CAUTION:

Radial tires should never be used on only the front axle.

When selecting tires, pay attention to the original size as marked on the tire. Most tires are described using an industry size code sometimes referred to as P-Metric. This allows the exact identification of the tire specifications, regardless of the manufacturer. If selecting a different tire size or brand, remember to check the installed tire for any sign of interference with the body or suspension while the vehicle is stopping, turning sharply or heavily loaded.

Snow Tires

Good radial tires can produce a big advantage in slippery weather, but in snow, a street radial tire does not have sufficient tread to provide traction and control. The small grooves of a street tire quickly pack with snow and the tire behaves like a billiard ball on a marble floor. The more open, chunky tread of a snow tire will self-clean as the tire turns, providing much better grip on snowy surfaces.

To satisfy municipalities requiring snow tires during weather emergencies, most snow tires carry either an M + S designation after the tire size stamped on the sidewall, or the designation "all-season." In general, no change in tire size is necessary when buying snow tires.

Most manufacturers strongly recommend the use of 4 snow tires on their vehicles for reasons of stability. If snow tires are fitted only to the drive wheels, the opposite end of the vehicle may become very unstable when braking or turning on slippery surfaces. This instability can lead to unpleasant endings if the driver can't counteract the slide in time.

Note that snow tires, whether 2 or 4, will affect vehicle handling in all non-snow situations. The stiffer, heavier snow tires will noticeably change the turning and braking characteristics of the vehicle. Once the snow tires are installed, you must re-learn the behavior of the vehicle and drive accordingly.

Note: Consider buying extra wheels on which to mount the snow tires. Once done, the "snow wheels" can be installed and removed as needed. This eliminates the potential damage to tires or wheels from seasonal removal and installation. Even if your vehicle has styled wheels, see if inexpensive steel wheels are available. Although the look of the vehicle will change, the expensive wheels will be protected from salt, curb hits and pothole damage.

TIRE STORAGE

If they are mounted on wheels, store the tires at proper inflation pressure. All tires should be kept in a cool, dry place. If they are stored in the garage or basement, do not let them stand on a concrete floor; set them on strips of wood, a mat or a large stack of newspaper. Keeping them away from direct moisture is of paramount importance. Tires should not be stored upright, but in a flat position.

INFLATION & INSPECTION

See Figures 98, 99, 100, 101, 102, 103, 104 and 105

The importance of proper tire inflation cannot be overemphasized. A tire employs air as part of its structure. It is designed around the supporting strength of the air at a specified pressure. For this reason, improper inflation drastically reduces the tire's ability to perform as intended. A tire will lose some air in day-to-day use; having to add a few pounds of air periodically is not necessarily a sign of a leaking tire.

Two items should be a permanent fixture in every glove compartment: an accurate tire pressure gauge and a tread depth gauge. Check the tire pressure (including the spare) regularly with a pocket type gauge. Too often, the gauge on the end of the air hose at your corner garage is not accurate because it suffers too much abuse. Always check tire pressure when the tires are cold, as pressure increases with temperature. If you must move the vehicle to check the

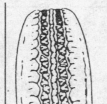

- DRIVE WHEEL HEAVY ACCELERATION
- OVERINFLATION

- HARD CORNERING
- UNDERINFLATION
- LACK OF ROTATION

Fig. 100 Examples of inflation-related tire wear patterns

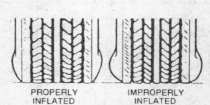

PROPERLY INFLATED   IMPROPERLY INFLATED
RADIAL TIRE

Fig. 101 Radial tires have a characteristic sidewall bulge; don't try to measure pressure by looking at the tire. Use a quality air pressure gauge

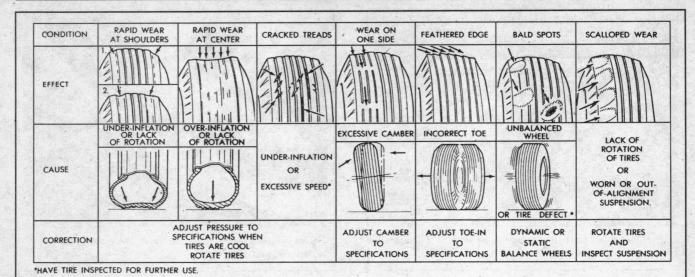

CONDITION	RAPID WEAR AT SHOULDERS	RAPID WEAR AT CENTER	CRACKED TREADS	WEAR ON ONE SIDE	FEATHERED EDGE	BALD SPOTS	SCALLOPED WEAR
EFFECT							
CAUSE	UNDER-INFLATION OR LACK OF ROTATION	OVER-INFLATION OR LACK OF ROTATION	UNDER-INFLATION OR EXCESSIVE SPEED*	EXCESSIVE CAMBER	INCORRECT TOE	UNBALANCED WHEEL OR TIRE DEFECT *	LACK OF ROTATION OF TIRES OR WORN OR OUT-OF-ALIGNMENT SUSPENSION.
CORRECTION	ADJUST PRESSURE TO SPECIFICATIONS WHEN TIRES ARE COOL ROTATE TIRES			ADJUST CAMBER TO SPECIFICATIONS	ADJUST TOE-IN TO SPECIFICATIONS	DYNAMIC OR STATIC BALANCE WHEELS	ROTATE TIRES AND INSPECT SUSPENSION

*HAVE TIRE INSPECTED FOR FURTHER USE.

Fig. 102 Common tire wear patterns and causes

tire inflation, do not drive more than a mile before checking. A cold tire is generally one that has not been driven for more than three hours.

A plate or sticker is normally provided somewhere in the vehicle (door post, hood, tailgate or trunk lid) which shows the proper pressure for the tires. Never counteract excessive pressure build-up by bleeding off air pressure (letting some air out). This will cause the tire to run hotter and wear quicker.

❊❊ CAUTION:

Never exceed the maximum tire pressure embossed on the tire! This is the pressure to be used when the tire is at maximum loading, but it is rarely the correct pressure for everyday driving. Consult the owner's manual or the tire pressure sticker for the correct tire pressure.

Once you've maintained the correct tire pressures for several weeks, you'll be familiar with the vehicle's braking and handling personality. Slight adjustments in tire pressures can fine-tune these characteristics, but never change the cold pressure specification by more than 2 psi. A slightly softer tire pressure will give a softer ride but also yield lower fuel mileage. A slightly harder tire will give crisper dry road handling but can cause skidding on wet surfaces. Unless you're fully attuned to the vehicle, stick to the recommended inflation pressures.

All tires made since 1968 have built-in tread wear indicator bars that show up as 1/2 in. (13mm) wide smooth bands across the tire when 1/16 in. (1.5mm) of tread remains. The appearance of tread wear indicators means that the tires should be replaced. In fact, many states have laws prohibiting the use of tires with less than this amount of tread.

You can check your own tread depth with an inexpensive gauge or by using a Lincoln head penny. Slip the Lincoln penny (with Lincoln's head upside-down)

into several tread grooves. If you can see the top of Lincoln's head in 2 adjacent grooves, the tire has less than 1/16 in. (1.5mm) tread left and should be replaced. You can measure snow tires in the same manner by using the "tails" side of the Lincoln penny. If you can see the top of the Lincoln memorial, it's time to replace the snow tire(s).

CARE OF SPECIAL WHEELS

If you have invested money in magnesium, aluminum alloy or sport wheels, special precautions should be taken to make sure your investment is not wasted and that your special wheels look good for the life of the vehicle.

Special wheels are easily damaged and/or scratched. Occasionally check the rims for cracking, impact damage or air leaks. If any of these are found, replace the wheel. But in order to prevent this type of damage and the costly replacement of a special wheel, observe the following precautions:

- Use extra care not to damage the wheels during removal, installation, balancing, etc. After removal of the wheels from the vehicle, place them on a mat or other protective surface. If they are to be stored for any length of time, support them on strips of wood. Never store tires and wheels upright; the tread may develop flat spots.
- When driving, watch for hazards; it doesn't take much to crack a wheel.
- When washing, use a mild soap or non-abrasive dish detergent (keeping in mind that detergent tends to remove wax). Avoid cleansers with abrasives or the use of hard brushes. There are many cleaners and polishes for special wheels.
- If possible, remove the wheels during the winter. Salt and sand used for snow removal can severely damage the finish of a wheel.
- Make certain the recommended lug nut torque is never exceeded or the wheel may crack. Never use snow chains on special wheels; severe scratching will occur.

Fig. 103 Tread wear indicators will appear when the tire is worn

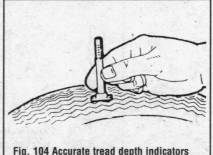

Fig. 104 Accurate tread depth indicators are inexpensive and handy

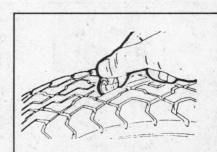

Fig. 105 A penny works well for a quick check of tread depth

FLUIDS AND LUBRICANTS

Fluid Disposal

Used fluids such as engine oil, transmission fluid, antifreeze and brake fluid are hazardous wastes and must be disposed of properly. Before draining any fluids, consult with the local authorities; in many areas, waste oil, etc. is being accepted as a part of recycling programs. A number of service stations and auto parts stores are also accepting waste fluids for recycling.

Be sure of the recycling center's policies before draining any fluids, as many will not accept different fluids that have been mixed together, such as oil and antifreeze.

Fuel and Engine Oil Recommendations

ENGINE OIL

See Figure 106

Use ONLY SJ or SJ/CD rated oils of the recommended viscosity. Under the classification system developed by the American Petroleum Institute, the SG rating designates the highest quality oil for use in passenger vehicles. In addition, oils labeled Energy Conserving or Fuel Saving are recommended due to their superior lubricating qualities (less friction - easier engine operation) and fuel saving characteristics.

Pick oil viscosity with regard to the anticipated temperatures during the period before your next oil change. Using the accompanying chart, choose the oil viscosity for the lowest expected temperature. You will be assured of easy cold starting and sufficient engine protection.

Synthetic Oils

Synthetic oils should not be used on low mileage and high mileage engines. Due to the nature of the synthetic oils, an engine that is still not broken in will have trouble in seating rings if these oils are used. The high mileage engine can experience problems as well. The ability of the synthetic oil to clean deposits is very good. This will remove the deposits that are possibly holding seals and components together. Synthetic oils will also cause a slight leak to turn into a flowing river of oil.

On the other hand, engines past the break in period that are in good condition will benefit from the use of synthetic oils. Although the cost is high, the rewards are very good. Longer oil life, reduced friction, and better fuel economy are just a few of the benefits. These oils are recommended for engines that are used in high heat conditions, such as highway use. You do have to weigh in the cost of the oil into your decision.

FUEL

Your vehicle is designed to operate on unleaded fuel. Fuel should be selected for the brand and octane which performs best with your engine. Judge a gasoline by its ability to prevent spark knock (pinging) and general all-weather performance.

Use of a fuel too low in octane will result in spark knock (pinging). Since many factors affect operating efficiency, such as altitude, terrain, air temperature and humidity, knocking may result even though the recommended fuel is being used. If persistent knocking occurs, it may be necessary to switch to a slightly higher grade of fuel. Continuous or heavy knocking may result in engine damage.

Fuel requirement can change with time, due to carbon buildup in the engine, which changes the compression ratio. If your engine knocks, pings or runs on, switch to a higher grade of fuel and check the ignition timing. Sometimes changing brands of gasoline will cure the problem. If it is necessary to retard the timing from specifications, don't change it more than a few degrees. Retarded timing will reduce the power output and the fuel mileage, plus it will increase the engine temperature.

Engine

OIL LEVEL CHECK

See Figures 107 and 108

The engine oil should be checked on a regular basis, ideally at each fuel stop. When checking the oil level, it is best that the oil be at operating temperature. Checking the level immediately after stopping will give a false reading due to oil left in the upper part of the engine. Be sure that the vehicle is resting on a

Lowest Air Temperature Anticipated	Multiviscosity Engine Oil
Above 40°F	SAE 10W-30, 40, 50 or 20W-40, 50
Above 32°F	SAE 10W-30 or 10W-40
Above 0°F	SAE 10W-30 or 10W-40
Below 0°F	SAE 5W-20 or 5W-30
	Single-Viscosity Engine Oil
Above 40°F	SAE 30 or 40
Above 32°F	SAE 20W-20
Above 0°F	SAE 20
Below 0°F	SAE 10W

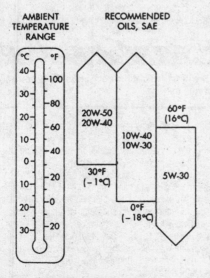

Fig. 106 Recommended viscosity grades

Fig. 107 The correct oil level should be between the "ADD" and "FULL" level on the dipstick

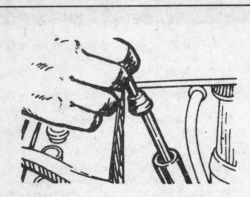

Fig. 108 The oil level is checked with the dipstick. When checking oil level, note the color and smell of the oil. Oil that is black or has a gas smell indicates a need for engine service.

level surface, allowing time for the oil to drain back into the crankcase.

1. Open the hood and locate the dipstick. Remove it from the tube (located on right side of the engine compartment).
2. Wipe the dipstick with a clean rag.
3. Insert the dipstick fully into the tube and remove it again.

Note: When checking oil level, note the color and smell of the oil. Oil that is black or has a gas smell indicates a need for engine service.

4. Hold the dipstick horizontally and read the oil level. The level should be between the FULL and ADD marks.
5. If the oil level is at or below the ADD mark, oil should be added as necessary. Oil is added through the capped opening on the valve cover(s) on gasoline engines. Refer to the "Engine Oil and Fuel Recommendations" in this Section for the proper viscosity oil to use.
6. Replace the dipstick and check the level after adding oil. Be careful not to overfill the crankcase. Approximately one quart of oil will raise the level from ADD to FULL.

OIL AND FILTER CHANGE

See Figures 109 and 110

- Engine oil should be changed every 7,500 miles (12,000 km). The oil change and filter replacement interval should be cut in half under conditions such as:Driving in dusty conditions.Extensive or prolonged idling.
- Extensive short trip operation in freezing temperatures (when the engine

Fig. 110 Adding engine oil through the filler hole in the rocker cover.

Fig. 109 Oil filter location - as seen from under the vehicle.

is not thoroughly warmed-up).
- Frequent long runs at high speed and high ambient temperatures.

To change the oil, the vehicle should be on a level surface and the engine should be at operating temperature. This is to ensure that the foreign matter will be drained away along with the oil and not left in the engine to form sludge. You should have available a container that will hold a minimum of 8 quarts of liquid, a wrench to fit the old drain plug, a spout for pouring in new oil and a rag or two, which you will always need. If the filter is being replaced, you will also need a band wrench or filter wrench to fit the end of the filter.

When you have finished this job, you will notice that you now possess four or five quarts of dirty oil. The best thing to do with it is to pour it into plastic jugs, such as milk or antifreeze containers. Then, locate a service station where you can pour it into their used oil tank for recycling.

❈❈ CAUTION:

Pouring used motor oil into a storm drain not only pollutes the environment, it violates Federal law. Dispose of waste oil properly.

1. Position the vehicle on a level surface, raise and support the vehicle safely. Slide a drain pan under the oil drain plug.
2. From under the vehicle, loosen, but do not remove the oil drain plug. Cover your hand with a rag or glove and slowly unscrew the drain plug.

❈❈ CAUTION:

The engine oil will be HOT. Keep your arms, face and hands clear of the oil as it drains out.

3. Remove the plug and let the oil drain into the pan. Do not drop the plug into the drain pan.
4. When all of the oil has drained, clean off the drain plug and reinstall it into pan. Torque the drain plug to 26 ft.lb. (35 Nm).
5. Using an oil filter wrench, loosen the oil filter.
6. Cover your hand with a rag and spin the filter off by hand; turn it slowly.
7. Coat the rubber gasket on a new filter with a light film of clean engine oil. Screw the filter onto the mounting stud and tighten it according to the directions on the filter (usually hand-tight one turn past the point where the gasket contacts the mounting base); DO NOT overtighten the filter.
8. Refill the engine with the specified amount of clean engine oil.
9. Run the engine for several minutes, checking for leaks. Check the level of the oil and add oil if necessary.

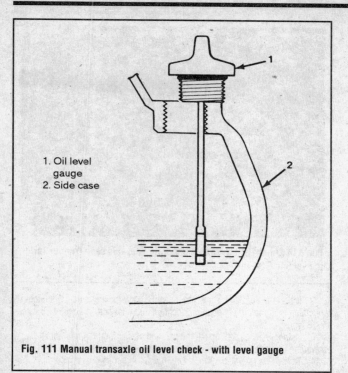

1. Oil level gauge
2. Side case

Fig. 111 Manual transaxle oil level check - with level gauge

Manual Transaxle

FLUID RECOMMENDATIONS

When adding fluid or refilling the manual transaxle always use GL-5, 80W or 80W - 90 weight gear oil.

LEVEL CHECK

With Oil Level Gauge
See Figure 111

1. Drive the vehicle to bring the transmission up to operating temperature.
2. With the engine stopped, remove the oil level gauge front the side case of the transaxle.
3. Check the color and smell of the oil. If it is black in color or smells burnt, further transmission service is needed.
4. Wipe off oil level gauge with clean cloth.

Fig. 113 Automatic transaxle dipstick location

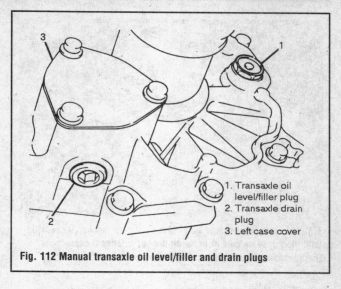

1. Transaxle oil level/filler plug
2. Transaxle drain plug
3. Left case cover

Fig. 112 Manual transaxle oil level/filler and drain plugs

5. Fit the oil level gauge to the transaxle side case so that the threads rest on top of the case.
6. Remove the gauge and check oil level. The level should be between **FULL** and **LOW** level line.
7. If the level is below **LOW** mark, add oil until the proper level is reached.

With Oil Level/Filler Plug

1. Drive the vehicle to bring the transmission up to operating temperature.
2. Raise and support the vehicle safely.
3. Remove the transaxle oil level/filler plug.
4. Check the color and smell of the oil. If it is black in color or smells burnt, further transmission service is needed.
5. Transaxle oil level should be even with the bottom of the plug hole. If oil level is low, adjust oil level accordingly.
6. Install transaxle oil level/filler plug and tighten to 40 ft. lbs. (54 Nm).
7. Lower the vehicle.

DRAIN AND REFILL

See Figure 112

1. Raise and support the vehicle safely.
2. Place a drain pan under transaxle.
3. Remove transaxle oil level/filler plug or oil level gauge.
4. Remove transaxle drain plug using a 10mm hex socket or wrench and drain oil.
5. Check the color and smell of the oil. If it is black in color or smells burnt, further transmission service is be needed.
6. Apply Loctite, pipe sealant, or equivalent to the threaded portion of the transaxle drain plug.
7. Install the transaxle drain plug and tighten to 21 ft. lbs. (28 Nm).
8. Remove drain pan from under transaxle and lower vehicle.
9. Properly dispose of used oil.

Automatic Transaxle

FLUID RECOMMENDATIONS

When adding fluid or refilling the automatic transaxle always use Dexron,III Automatic Transmission Fluid.

LEVEL CHECK

See Figures 113 and 114

1. Drive the vehicle to bring the transmission up to operating temperature.

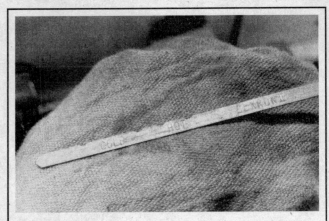

Fig. 114 Fluid level should be between the cold notches if checking with the transaxle cold or between the hot notches if checking with the transaxle at normal operating temperature.

Fig. 115 Automatic transaxle fluid drain plug - as seen from under the vehicle

2. Place vehicle on a level surface.

3. With the engine running at idle, run the selector lever through each range and return to the **P** position.

4. Remove the fluid level indicator from the transmission filler tube and wipe clean.

5. Reinsert fluid level indicator into filler tube making sure it is seated in its original position.

6. Remove the indicator and check the fluid level. The level should be between the **FULL HOT** and **LOW HOT** marks.

7. If the level is below the LOW HOT mark, add fluid as necessary to bring the fluid level to the FULL HOT mark.

8. Check the color and smell of the fluid. If it is brown in color (transmission fluid is usually red) or smells burnt, further transmission service is be needed.

9. Reinsert fluid level indicator into filler tube making sure it is seated in its original position.

DRAIN AND REFILL

See Figure 115

1. Raise and support the vehicle safely.
2. Place a drain pan or suitable container under the transaxle pan.
3. Remove the transaxle drain plug and drain the fluid.
4. Lower the vehicle.
5. Fill the transaxle with fluid and check fluid level.

PAN AND FILTER SERVICE

1. Raise and support the vehicle safely.
2. Place a drain pan or suitable container under the transaxle pan.
3. Remove the transaxle drain plug and drain the fluid.
4. Remove the 15 transaxle pan bolts and carefully lower the pan. Take note of the location of the 2 bolts with cross-recesses in their heads.

Note: Do not attempt to pry the pan away from the transaxle. Doing so will damage the gasket mating surfaces. If the pan is frozen, use a mallet and a wood block to lightly tap it free.

To install:

5. Inspect the bottom of the pan for large pieces of metal or other foreign matter. A small amount of clutch material in the pan is normal. However, if large amounts of clutch material, metal shavings or other foreign matter are present, further transaxle service is necessary.

6. Clean the fluid filter screen with solvent and dry thoroughly. If the screen mesh is damaged, replace it.

7. Clean the transaxle fluid pan magnet and the bottom of the pan.

8. Using a gasket scraper remove the gasket. Install the new transaxle pan gasket.

9. Install the fluid filter screen to the valve body making sure the solenoid wire clamp is in the correct position. Tighten fluid filter screen bolts to 53 inch lbs. (6 Nm).

10. Using a new gasket, install the pan and 15 pan bolts. Apply Loctite,, or equivalent, to the threaded portion of the 2 cross-recess bolts.

11. Tighten pan bolts to 53 inch lbs. (6 Nm) in a criss-cross pattern.

12. Install the transaxle drain plug and tighten to 17 ft. lbs. (23 Nm).

13. Lower the vehicle.

14. Fill the transaxle with fluid and check the fluid level.

Cooling System

FLUID RECOMMENDATIONS

The cooling system should be filled with a 50/50 mixture of good quality ethylene glycol antifreeze and water.

LEVEL CHECK

See Figure 116

The coolant level should be checked at regular intervals, or if the temperature gauge registers abnormally hot. The coolant level should be between the **FULL** and **LOW** marks on the coolant reservoir tank. Add coolant to the reservoir tank as required to maintain proper coolant level.

At 15,000 mile (25,000 km) intervals the cooling system should be checked for leaks or damage. Also the proper level and freeze protection of the antifreeze should be checked. It is important to maintain the proper level of protection

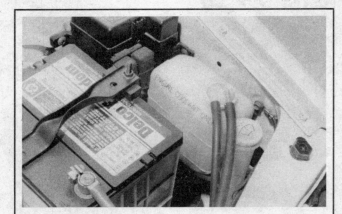

Fig. 116 Engine coolant reservoir tank

Fig. 117 Radiator drain plug - as seen from under the vehicle

against freezing and loss of coolant from boiling. Inexpensive antifreeze testers are available to measure the degree of protection provided by the cooling system.

DRAIN AND REFILL

See Figure 117

1. With the engine cold, remove the radiator cap. Turn the cap slowly to the left until it reaches a stop. Wait until pressure is relieved, then press down on cap and continue to rotate to the left.
2. Open the radiator drain plug to drain the coolant. Drain the coolant into a suitable container.

✳✳ CAUTION:

When draining the coolant, keep in mind that cats and dogs are attracted by the ethylene glycol antifreeze, and are quite likely to drink any that is left in an uncovered container or in puddles on the ground. This will prove fatal in sufficient quantity. Always drain the coolant into a sealable container. Coolant should be reused unless it is contaminated or several years old.

3. Add a 50/50 mixture of good quality ethylene glycol antifreeze and water to the radiator and reservoir tank. Fill the radiator to the base of the filler neck and the reservoir tank to the **FULL** mark.
4. Run the engine, with the radiator cap removed, until the upper radiator hose is hot.
5. With the engine idling, add coolant to the radiator until the level reaches the bottom of the filler neck.
6. Install the radiator cap.

DRAIN, FLUSH AND REFILL

The cooling system should be drained, flushed and refilled with fresh coolant every 2 years or 30,000 miles (48,000 km). This operation should be performed with the engine cold.

1. With the engine cold, remove the radiator cap. Turn the cap slowly to the left until it reaches a stop. Wait until pressure is relieved, then press down on cap and continue to rotate to the left.
2. With the radiator cap removed, run the engine until the upper radiator hose is hot (this shows that the thermostat is open and the coolant is flowing through the system).

✳✳ CAUTION:

Care should be taken as the antifreeze will be extremely hot.

3. Stop the engine and open the radiator drain plug to drain the coolant. Drain the coolant into a suitable container.

✳✳ CAUTION:

When draining the coolant, keep in mind that cats and dogs are attracted by the ethylene glycol antifreeze, and are quite likely to drink any that is left in an uncovered container or in puddles on the ground. This will prove fatal in sufficient quantity. Always drain the coolant into a sealable container. Coolant should be reused unless it is contaminated or several years old.

4. Close the drain plug. Add water until the system is filled and run the engine until the upper radiator hose is hot again.
5. Repeat Steps 3 and 4 until the drained liquid is nearly colorless.
6. Drain the system and close the radiator drain plug tightly.
7. Disconnect the hose from the water reservoir tank. Remove the tank and pour out any coolant. Clean the inside of the tank, then reinstall.
8. Add a 50/50 mixture of good quality ethylene glycol antifreeze and water to the radiator and reservoir tank. Fill the radiator to the base of the filler neck and the reservoir tank to the **FULL** mark.
9. Run the engine, with the radiator cap removed, until the upper radiator hose is hot.
10. With the engine idling, add coolant to the radiator until the level reaches the bottom of the filler neck. Install the radiator cap.

Master Cylinder

At least twice a year the brake master cylinder reservoir should be checked for the proper fluid level. A low fluid level can indicate worn disc brake pads. A large loss in fluid may indicate a problem or leak in the system. Have it serviced immediately.

FLUID RECOMMENDATIONS

When adding fluid to the brake master cylinder, use only heavy-duty Delco Supreme 11 or DOT 3 brake fluid.

LEVEL CHECK

See Figure 118

The brake master cylinder reservoir is made of translucent plastic so that the fluid level may be checked without removing the cap. If the fluid level in the master cylinder reservoir falls below the **MIN** line molded on the side of the reservoir, add brake fluid to bring the level up to the **MAX** line.

Clean the top of the reservoir off before removing the cap to prevent dirt from entering the master cylinder. Pour the fluid slowly to prevent air bubbles from forming. Reinstall the cap immediately.

Fig. 118 Brake master cylinder reservoir

CAUTION:

Brake fluid damages paint. It also absorbs moisture from the air; never leave a container or the master cylinder uncovered any longer than necessary. All parts in contact with the brake fluid (master cylinder, hoses, plunger assemblies and etc.) must be kept clean, since any contamination of the brake fluid will adversely affect braking performance.

Power Steering Pump

FLUID RECOMMENDATIONS

Dexron, III Automatic Transmission Fluid (GM P/N 12346143) or the equivalent

LEVEL CHECK

1. Drive vehicle onto a level surface.
2. Inspect reservoir for foaming or milky colored fluid.
3. If foaming or milky fluid is found bleed the power steering system. For additional information, please refer to Steering and Suspension, Steering.
4. If the fluid in the reservoir if found to be below the min. line after bleeding, then fill with DEXRON III Automatic Transmission Fluid.

Chassis Greasing

Under normal conditions regular chassis greasing should be performed at 7,500 mile (12,500 km) intervals or at least once a year. If a component is replaced, or a dust boot or seal is damaged or leaking, the component will have to be removed, repacked with grease, and a new boot or seal installed.

Points to be lubricated:

- Parking brake cable
- Underbody contact points
- Any and all linkage components

Body Lubrication

Body lubrication should be performed at regularly scheduled intervals. Apply multipurpose chassis grease to the hood hinges, lock and striker, the door hinges, latch and striker, and the trunk hinges and striker. Use grease sparingly on the door and trunk strikers, as they may come into contact with clothing.

The clutch, brake, and accelerator linkages should be lubricated at regular intervals, with multipurpose chassis grease. Working inside the car, apply a small amount of grease to the pedal pivots and linkage. Working under the hood, grease all pivoting and sliding parts of the accelerator and brake linkages.

Use powdered graphite to lubricate the door key lock cylinders and trunk key lock cylinders. Do not use oil or grease to lubricate the insides of lock cylinders.

Use silicone lubricant to preserve the rubber weather stripping around the doors and trunk. This will prevent the rubber stripping from sticking to the painted surfaces of the body and also prevent the rubber from dry rotting.

Rear Wheel Bearings

The wheel bearings are a sealed type bearing. They are not serviceable and should be replaced if found to be defective. Always replace wheel bearings as an axle set.

TOWING

Towing

Two styles of towing are recommended, either a car carrier or a wheel lift tow truck.

Note: A sling type tow truck should never be used to tow the vehicle as it will damage the front or rear bumper fascia or the fog lamps.

When towing the vehicle, have the ignition switch turned to the **LOCK** position. The steering wheel should be clamped in a straight ahead position using a device designed for towing services. Do not use the vehicle's steering column lock. The transaxle should be in the **N** position and the parking brake released.

For front towing hookup using a wheel lift tow truck, attach wheel straps to both front wheels. Attach safety chains to the front tie down brackets.

For rear towing hookup using a wheel lift tow truck, attach wheel straps to both rear wheels. Dollies are required under the front wheels when the vehicle is equipped with an automatic transaxle. Attach safety chains to the rear tie down brackets.

Note: On automatic transaxle equipped vehicles, never tow from the rear with the front wheels on the road. The front wheels must be supported on dollies before towing. Damage to the transaxle will result if dollies are not used.

JUMP STARTING A DEAD BATTERY

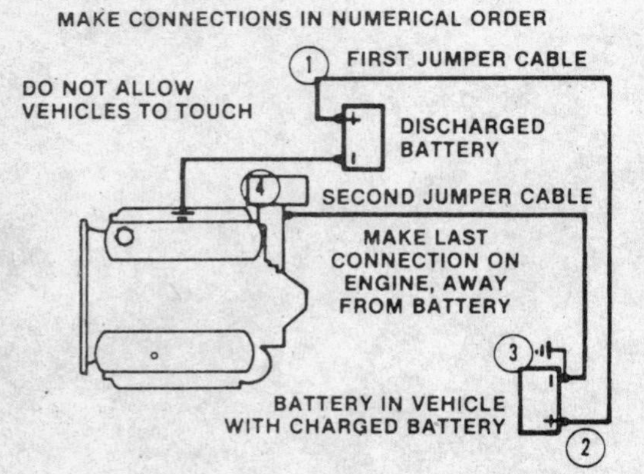

Fig. 119 Connect the jumper cables to the batteries and engine in the order shown

See Figure 119

Whenever a vehicle is jump started, precautions must be followed in order to prevent the possibility of personal injury. Remember that batteries contain a small amount of explosive hydrogen gas which is a by-product of battery charging. Sparks should always be avoided when working around batteries, especially when attaching jumper cables. To minimize the possibility of accidental sparks, follow the procedure carefully.

CAUTION:

NEVER hook the batteries up in a series circuit or the entire electrical system will go up in smoke, including the starter!

Vehicles equipped with a diesel engine may utilize two 12 volt batteries. If so, the batteries are connected in a parallel circuit (positive terminal to positive terminal, negative terminal to negative terminal). Hooking the batteries up in parallel circuit increases battery cranking power without increasing total battery voltage output. Output remains at 12 volts. On the other hand, hooking two 12 volt batteries up in a series circuit (positive terminal to negative terminal, positive terminal to negative terminal) increases total battery output to 24 volts (12 volts plus 12 volts).

Jump Starting Precautions

• Be sure that both batteries are of the same voltage. Vehicles covered by this manual and most vehicles on the road today utilize a 12 volt charging system.

• Be sure that both batteries are of the same polarity (have the same terminal, in most cases NEGATIVE grounded).

• Be sure that the vehicles are not touching or a short could occur.

• On serviceable batteries, be sure the vent cap holes are not obstructed.

• Do not smoke or allow sparks anywhere near the batteries.

• In cold weather, make sure the battery electrolyte is not frozen. This can occur more readily in a battery that has been in a state of discharge.

• Do not allow electrolyte to contact your skin or clothing.

Jump Starting Procedure

SINGLE BATTERY GASOLINE ENGINE MODELS

1. Make sure that the voltages of the 2 batteries are the same. Most batteries and charging systems are of the 12 volt variety.

2. Pull the jumping vehicle (with the good battery) into a position so the jumper cables can reach the dead battery and that vehicle's engine. Make sure that the vehicles do NOT touch.

3. Place the transmissions of both vehicles in **NEUTRAL** (MT) or **P** (AT), as applicable, then firmly set their parking brakes.

Note: If necessary for safety reasons, the hazard lights on both vehicles may be operated throughout the entire procedure without significantly increasing the difficulty of jumping the dead battery.

4. Turn all lights and accessories OFF on both vehicles. Make sure the ignition switches on both vehicles are turned to the **OFF** position.

5. Cover the battery cell caps with a rag, but do not cover the terminals.

6. Make sure the terminals on both batteries are clean and free of corrosion or proper electrical connection will be impeded. If necessary, clean the battery terminals before proceeding.

7. Identify the positive (+) and negative (–) terminals on both batteries.

8. Connect the first jumper cable to the positive (+) terminal of the dead battery, then connect the other end of that cable to the positive (+) terminal of the booster (good) battery.

9. Connect one end of the other jumper cable to the negative (–) terminal on the booster battery and the final cable clamp to an engine bolt head, alternator bracket or other solid, metallic point on the engine with the dead battery. Try to pick a ground on the engine that is positioned away from the battery in order to minimize the possibility of the 2 clamps touching should one loosen during the procedure. DO NOT connect this clamp to the negative (–) terminal of the bad battery.

❄ CAUTION:

Be very careful to keep the jumper cables away from moving parts (cooling fan, belts, etc.) on both engines.

10. Check to make sure that the cables are routed away from any moving parts, then start the donor vehicle's engine. Run the engine at moderate speed for several minutes to allow the dead battery a chance to receive some initial charge.

11. With the donor vehicle's engine still running slightly above idle, try to start the vehicle with the dead battery. Crank the engine for no more than 10 seconds at a time and let the starter cool for at least 20 seconds between tries. If the vehicle does not start in 3 tries, it is likely that something else is also wrong or that the battery needs additional time to charge.

12. Once the vehicle is started, allow it to run at idle for a few seconds to make sure that it is operating properly.

13. Turn ON the headlights, heater blower and, if equipped, the rear defroster of both vehicles in order to reduce the severity of voltage spikes and subsequent risk of damage to the vehicles' electrical systems when the cables are disconnected. This step is especially important to any vehicle equipped with computer control modules.

14. Carefully disconnect the cables in the reverse order of connection. Start with the negative cable that is attached to the engine ground, then the negative cable on the donor battery. Disconnect the positive cable from the donor battery and finally, disconnect the positive cable from the formerly dead battery. Be careful when disconnecting the cables from the positive terminals not to allow the alligator clips to touch any metal on either vehicle or a short and sparks will occur.

JACKING

See Figures 120, 121 and 122

For lifting a vehicle with equipment other than original equipment jack, various lift points have been established and are recommended.

Note: When jacking a vehicle at the frame side rails or other established lift points, be certain that lift pads do not contact the catalytic converter, brake pipes or cables or fuel pipes/hoses. Such contact may result in damage or unsatisfactory vehicle performance.

Fig. 120 Jacking point at the rear of the vehicle

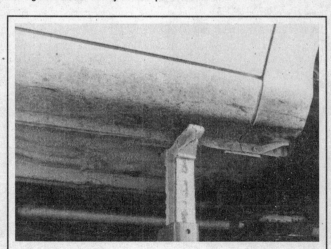

Fig. 121 Support point at the front of the vehicle

The center line of gravity on front wheel drive vehicles is further forward than on rear wheel drive vehicles. Therefore, whenever removing major components from the rear of a front wheel drive vehicle supported on a hoist, it is mandatory to support the vehicle in such a way that reduces the likelihood of the vehicle tipping forward.

❉❉ CAUTION:

To help avoid personal injury when a vehicle is on a jack, provide additional support for the vehicle at the end from which components are being removed. This will reduce the possibilities of the vehicle falling off of the jack.

When supporting a vehicle with jackstands, the supports should be placed under the body side rail pinch welds or a similar strong, stable structure.

Fig. 122 Support point at the rear of the vehicle

ITEM NO.	TO BE SERVICED	WHEN TO PERFORM Miles (kilometers) or Months, Whichever Occurs First	The services shown in this schedule up to 48,000 miles (80 000 km) are to be performed after 48,000 miles at the same intervals														
		MILES (000)	3	6	9	12	15	18	21	24	27	30	33	36	39	42	45	48
		KILOMETERS (000)	5	10	15	20	25	30	35	40	45	50	55	60	65	70	75	80
1	Engine Oil & Oil Filter Change*	Every 3,000 Miles (5 000 km) or 3 Months	•	•	•	•	•	•	•	•	•	•	•	•	•	•	•	•
2	Chassis Lubrication	Every Other Oil Change		•		•		•		•		•		•		•		•
3	Carburetor Choke Inspection*	At 6,000 Miles (10 000 km), then every 30,000 Miles (50 000 km)		•								•†						
4	Engine Idle Speed Inspection*	At 6,000 Miles (10 000 km), then every 15,000 Miles (25 000 km)		•			•					•					•	
5	Valve Lash Inspection*	Every 15,000 Miles (25 000 km)					•					•					•	
6	Water Pump Belt Inspection*	Every 30,000 Miles (50 000 km) or 24 Months										•†						
7	Cooling System Service*	See Explanation of Scheduled Maintenance Services																
8	Fuel Cut System Inspection*	Every 30,000 Miles (50 000 km) or 24 Months										•						
9	Transaxle Service	Every 30,000 Miles (50 000 km) or 24 Months										•						
10	Fuel Filter Replacement	Every 30,000 Miles (50 000 km)										•						
11	Spark Plug Replacement*	Every 30,000 Miles (50 000 km)										•†						
12	PCV System Inspection*	Every 30,000 Miles (50 000 km) or 24 Months										•						
13	Air Cleaner Element Replacement*	Every 30,000 Miles (50 000 km) or 24 Months										•						
14	Oxygen Sensor Inspection*	Every 30,000 Miles (50 000 km)										•						
15	Pulse Air Control System Inspection*	Every 30,000 Miles (50 000 km) or 24 Months										•						
16	Spark Plug Wires & Distributor Inspection*	Every 30,000 Miles (50 000 km) or 24 Months										•						
17	Fuel Tank, Cap & Lines — Inspection	Every 15,000 Miles (25 000 km) or 12 Months					•					•				•		
18	Thermostatically Controlled Air Cleaner*	Every 30,000 Miles (50 000 km) or 12 Months										•						

Maintenance interval chart, 1985-88 vehicles - Normal

ITEM NO.	TO BE SERVICED	WHEN TO PERFORM Miles (kilometers) or Months, Whichever Occurs First	The services shown in this schedule up to 45,000 miles (75 000 km) are to be performed after 45,000 miles at the same intervals					
		MILES (000)	7.5	15	22.5	30	37.5	45
		KILOMETERS (000)	12.5	25	37.5	50	62.5	75
1	Engine Oil & Oil Filter Change*	Every 7,500 Miles (12 500 km) or 12 Months	•	•	•	•	•	•
2	Chassis Lubrication	Every 7,500 Miles (12 500 km) or 12 Months	•	•	•	•	•	•
3	Carburetor Choke Inspection*	Every 30,000 Miles (50 000 km) or 24 Months				•†		
4	Engine Idle Speed Inspection*	At 7,500 Miles (12 500 km), then at 15,000 Mile (25 000 km) intervals	•	•		•		•
5	Valve Lash Inspection*	Every 15,000 Miles (25 000 km)		•		•		•
6	Water Pump Belt Inspection*	Every 30,000 Miles (50 000 km) or 24 Months				•†		
7	Cooling System Service*	See Explanation of Scheduled Maintenance Services						
8	Fuel Cut System Inspection*	Every 30,000 Miles (50 000 km) or 24 Months				•		
9	Transaxle Service	Every 30,000 Miles (50 000 km) or 24 Months				•		
10	Fuel Filter Replacement	Every 30,000 Miles (50 000 km)				•		
11	Spark Plug Replacement*	Every 30,000 Miles (50 000 km)				•†		
12	PCV System Inspection*	Every 30,000 Miles (50 000 km) or 24 Months				•		
13	Air Cleaner Element Replacement*	Every 30,000 Miles (50 000 km) or 24 Months				•		
14	Oxygen Sensor Inspection*	Every 30,000 Miles (50 000 km)				•		
15	Pulse Air Control System Inspection*	Every 30,000 Miles (50 000 km) or 24 Months				•		
16	Spark Plug Wires & Distributor Inspection*	Every 30,000 Miles (50 000 km) or 24 Months				•		
17	Fuel Tank, Cap & Lines — Inspection	Every 15,000 Miles (25 000 km) or 12 Months			•	•		•
18	Thermostatically Controlled Air Cleaner*	Every 30,000 Miles (50 000 km) or 12 Months				•		

FOOTNOTES:

* An Emission Control Service

† In California, these are the minimum Emission Control Maintenance Services an owner must perform according to the California Air Resources Board. General Motors, however, urges that all Emission Control Maintenance Services shown above be performed. To maintain your other new car warranties, all services shown in this section should be performed.

Maintenance interval chart, 1985-88 vehicles - Severe usage

TO BE SERVICED	WHEN TO PERFORM MILES (KILOMETERS) OR MONTHS WHICHEVER OCCURS FIRST	THE SERVICES SHOWN IN THIS SCHEDULE UP TO 60,000 MILES (100 000 km) ARE TO BE PERFORMED AFTER 60,000 MILES (100 000 km) AT THE SAME INTERVALS																		
	MILES (000)	3	6	9	12	15	18	21	24	27	30	33	36	39	42	45	48	51	54	57	60
	KILOMETERS (000)	5	10	15	20	25	30	35	40	45	50	55	60	65	70	75	80	85	90	95	100
ENGINE OIL & OIL FILTER CHANGE*	EVERY 3,000 mi. (5 000 km) OR 3 mos.	•	•	•	•	•	•	•	•	•	•	•	•	•	•	•	•	•	•	•	•
CHASSIS LUBRICATION	EVERY OTHER OIL CHANGE		•		•		•		•		•		•		•		•		•		•
THROTTLE BODY MOUNT BOLT TORQUE*	AT 6,000 mi. (10 000 km) ONLY		•																		
TIRE & WHEEL INSPECTION AND ROTATION	AT 6,000 mi. (10 000 km) AND THEN EVERY 15,000 mi. (25 000 km)		•					•					•					•			
ENGINE ACCESSORY DRIVE BELT(S) INSPECTION*	EVERY 30,000 mi. (50 000 km) OR 24 mos.										•										•
COOLING SYSTEM SERVICE*											•										•
TRANSAXLE SERVICE	SEE EXPLANATION FOR SERVICE INTERVAL																				
SPARK PLUG REPLACEMENT*	EVERY 30,000 mi. (50 000 km)										•										•
SPARK PLUG (SECONDARY) WIRE INSPECTION*	EVERY 60,000 mi. (100 000 km) OR 60 mos.																				•
EGR SYSTEM INSPECTION* ††	EVERY 30,000 mi. (50 000 km) OR 36 mos.										•										•
AIR CLEANER & PCV INLET FILTER REPLACEMENT*											•										•
ENGINE TIMING CHECK*	EVERY 30,000 mi. (50 000 km)										•										
FUEL TANK, CAP & PIPES/HOSES INSPECTION* ††	EVERY 15,000 mi. (25 000 km) OR 15 mos.					•					•					•					•
PCV SYSTEM INSPECTION	EVERY 60,000 mi. (100 000 km)																				•

FOOTNOTES:

* AN EMISSION CONTROL SERVICE

†† THE U.S. ENVIRONMENTAL AGENCY HAS DETERMINED THAT THE FAILURE TO PERFORM THIS MAINTENANCE ITEM WILL NOT NULLIFY THE EMISSION WARRANTY OR LIMIT RECALL LIABILITY PRIOR TO THE COMPLETION OF VEHICLE USEFUL LIFE. GENERAL MOTORS, HOWEVER, URGES THAT ALL RECOMMENDED MAINTENANCE SERVICES BE PERFORMED AT THE INDICATED INTERVALS AND THE MAINTENANCE BE RECORDED IN SECTION E OF THE OWNER'S MAINTENANCE SCHEDULE.

Maintenance interval chart, 1989-00 vehicles and all turbocharged vehicles - Normal usage

TO BE SERVICED	WHEN TO PERFORM MILES (KILOMETERS) OR MONTHS WHICHEVER OCCURS FIRST	THE SERVICES SHOWN IN THIS SCHEDULE UP TO 60,000 MILES (100 000 km) ARE TO BE PERFORMED AFTER 60,000 MILES (100 000 km) AT THE SAME INTERVALS							
	MILES (000)	7.5	15	22.5	30	37.5	45	52.5	60
	KILOMETERS (000)	12.54	25	37.5	50	62.5	75	87.5	100
ENGINE OIL CHANGE*	EVERY 7,500 mi. (12 500 km) OR 7.5 mos.	•	•	•	•	•	•	•	•
OIL FILTER CHANGE*	EVERY 7,500 mi. (12 500 km) OR 7.5 mos.	•	•	•	•	•	•	•	•
CHASSIS LUBRICATION	EVERY 7,500 mi. (12 500 km) OR 12 mos.	•	•	•	•	•	•	•	•
THROTTLE BODY MOUNT BOLT TORQUE*	AT 7,500 mi. (12 500 km) ONLY	•							
TIRE & WHEEL INSPECTION AND ROTATION	AT 7,500 mi. (12 500 km) AND THEN EVERY 15,000 mi. (25 000 km)	•		•		•		•	
ENGINE ACCESSORY DRIVE BELT(S) INSPECTION*	EVERY 30,000 mi. (50 000 km) OR 24 mos.				•				•
COOLING SYSTEM SERVICE*					•				•
TRANSAXLE SERVICE	SEE EXPLANATION FOR SERVICE INTERVAL								
SPARK PLUG REPLACEMENT*	EVERY 30,000 mi. (50 000 km)				•				•
SPARK PLUG (SECONDARY) WIRE INSPECTION*	EVERY 60,000 mi. (100 000 km) OR 60 mos.								•
EGR SYSTEM INSPECTION* ††	EVERY 30,000 mi. (50 000 km) OR 36 mos.				•				•
AIR CLEANER & PCV INLET FILTER REPLACEMENT*					•				•
ENGINE TIMING CHECK*	EVERY 30,000 mi. (50 000 km) OR 36 mos.				•				•
FUEL TANK, CAP & PIPES/HOSES INSPECTION* ††	EVERY 15,000 mi. (25 000 km) OR 15 mos.		•		•		•		•
PCV SYSTEM INSPECTION*	EVERY 60,000 mi. (100 000 km)								•

FOOTNOTES:

* AN EMISSION CONTROL SERVICE

†† THE U.S. ENVIRONMENTAL AGENCY HAS DETERMINED THAT THE FAILURE TO PERFORM THIS MAINTENANCE ITEM WILL NOT NULLIFY THE EMISSION WARRANTY OR LIMIT RECALL LIABILITY PRIOR TO THE COMPLETION OF VEHICLE USEFUL LIFE. GENERAL MOTORS, HOWEVER, URGES THAT ALL RECOMMENDED MAINTENANCE SERVICES BE PERFORMED AT THE INDICATED INTERVALS AND THE MAINTENANCE BE RECORDED IN SECTION E OF THE OWNER'S MAINTENANCE SCHEDULE.

Maintenance interval chart, 1989-00 vehicles and all turbocharged vehicles - Severe usage

CAPACITIES

Year	Model	Engine Displacement Liters (cc)	Engine ID/VIN	Engine Oil with Filter (qts.)	Transmission (qts.) Manual	Transmission (qts.) Auto.	Transfer Case (qts.)	Drive Axle Front (qts.)	Drive Axle Rear (qts.)	Fuel Tank (gal.)	Cooling System (qts.)
1985	Sprint	1.0 (1000)	M	3.5	2.5	—	—	—	—	8.3	4.5
1986	Sprint	1.0 (1000)	5	3.5	2.5	4.75 ①	—	—	—	8.3	4.5
1987	Sprint	1.0 (1000)	2	3.5	2.5	4.75 ①	—	—	—	8.3	4.5
	Sprint	1.0 (1000)	5	3.5	2.5	4.75 ①	—	—	—	8.3	4.5
1988	Sprint	1.0 (1000)	2	3.5	2.5	4.75 ①	—	—	—	8.3	4.5
	Sprint	1.0 (1000)	5	3.5	2.5	4.75 ①	—	—	—	8.3	4.5
1989	Metro	1.0 (1000)	5	3.7	2.5	4.75 ①	—	—	—	8.7	4.5
	Swift	1.3 (1300)	3								
	Swift	1.3 (1300)	3								
1990	Metro	1.0 (1000)	5	3.7	2.5	5.2 ①	—	—	—	10.0	4.2
	Swift	1.3 (1300)	3								
	Swift	1.3 (1300)	3								
1991	Metro	1.0 (1000)	6	3.7	2.5	5.2 ①	—	—	—	10.6	4.2
	Swift	1.3 (1300)	3								
	Swift	1.3 (1300)	3								
1992	Metro	1.0 (1000)	6	3.7	2.5	5.2 ①	—	—	—	10.6	4.2
	Swift	1.3 (1300)	3								
	Swift	1.3 (1300)	3								
1993	Metro	1.0 (1000)	6	3.7	2.5	5.2 ①	—	—	—	10.6	4.2
	Swift	1.3 (1300)	3								
	Swift	1.3 (1300)	3								
1994	Metro	1.0 (1000)	6	3.7	2.5	5.2 ①	—	—	—	10.6	4.2
	Swift	1.3 (1300)	3								
	Swift	1.3 (1300)	3								
1995	Metro	1.0 (1000)	6	3.7	2.5	5.0 ①	—	—	—	10.6	②
	Metro	1.3 (1300)	9	3.7	2.5	5.2 ①	—	—	—	10.6	4.9
	Swift	1.3 (1300)	3								
1996	Metro	1.0 (1000)	6	3.7	2.5	5.0 ①	—	—	—	10.6	②
	Metro	1.3 (1300)	9	3.7	2.5	5.0 ①	—	—	—	10.6	4.9
	Swift	1.3 (1300)	3								
1997	Metro	1.0 (1000)	6	3.7	2.5	5.0 ①	—	—	—	10.6	②
	Metro	1.3 (1300)	9	3.7	2.5	5.0 ①	—	—	—	10.6	4.9
	Swift	1.3 (1300)	3								
1998	Metro	1.0 (1000)	6	3.7	2.5	5.0 ①	—	—	—	10.6	②
	Metro	1.3 (1300)	9	3.7	2.5	5.0 ①	—	—	—	10.6	4.9
	Swift	1.3 (1300)	3								
1999	Metro	1.0 (1000)	6	3.7	2.5	5.0 ①	—	—	—	10.6	②
	Metro	1.3 (1300)	9	3.7	2.5	5.0 ①	—	—	—	10.6	4.9
	Swift	1.3 (1300)	3								
2000	Metro	1.0 (1000)	6	3.7	2.5	5.0 ①	—	—	—	10.6	②
	Metro	1.3 (1300)	9	3.7	2.5	5.0 ①	—	—	—	10.6	4.9
	Swift	1.3 (1300)	3								

NOTE: All capacities are approximate. Add fluid gradually and ensure a proper fluid level is obtained.

① Automatic transmission - Specification is after complete overhaul. Drain and fill will be less

② Manual transaxle: 4.1 qts.

Automatic transaxle: 4.2 qts.

SCHEDULED MAINTENANCE INTERVALS
SPRINT & METRO & SWIFT

TO BE SERVICED	TYPE OF SERVICE	VEHICLE MILEAGE INTERVAL (x1000)												
		7.5	15	22.5	30	37.5	45	52.5	60	67.5	75	82.5	90	97.5
Engine oil & filter	R	✓	✓	✓	✓	✓	✓	✓	✓	✓	✓	✓	✓	✓
Chassis lubrication	S/I	✓	✓	✓	✓	✓	✓	✓	✓	✓	✓	✓	✓	✓
Lubricate parking brake cable guides, underbody contact points & linkage	S/I	✓	✓	✓	✓	✓	✓	✓	✓	✓	✓	✓	✓	✓
Rotate tires	S/I	✓	✓	✓	✓	✓	✓	✓	✓	✓	✓	✓	✓	✓
Brake system	S/I	✓		✓		✓		✓		✓		✓		✓
Exhaust system	S/I	✓		✓		✓		✓		✓		✓		✓
Valve clearance	S/I		✓		✓		✓		✓		✓		✓	
Air cleaner element	R				✓				✓				✓	
Engine coolant	R				✓				✓				✓	
Spark plugs	R				✓				✓				✓	
Fuel filter	R				✓				✓				✓	
Ball joints & steering linkage seals	S/I				✓				✓				✓	
Drive belt(s)	S/I				✓				✓				✓	
Fuel tank, cap, & lines	S/I				✓				✓				✓	
Manual transaxle oil	R				✓				✓				✓	
Cooling system	S/I				✓				✓				✓	
EGR system	S/I				✓				✓				✓	
PCV system	S/I				✓				✓				✓	
PCV valve (1996-2000)①	R													
Ignition cables	R								✓					
Timing belt(s)	R								✓					
Automatic transaxle fluid & filter	R							✓						
Distributor cap & rotor	S/I								✓					
EVAP system (except canister)	S/I								✓					
Throttle body unit mount torque	S/I	✓												

① PCV valve (1996-2000)
replace at 50,000 miles

R - Replace   S/I - Service or Inspect

FREQUENT OPERATION MAINTENANCE (SEVERE SERVICE)

If a vehicle is operated under any of the following conditions it is considered severe service:

- Extremely dusty areas.
- 50% or more of the vehicle operation is in 32°C (90°F) or higher temperatures, or constant operation in temperatures below 0°C (32°F).
- Prolonged idling (vehicle operation in stop and go traffic).
- Frequent short running periods (engine does not warm to normal operating temperatures).
- Police, taxi, delivery usage or trailer towing usage.

Oil & oil filter change - change every 3000 miles.

Chassis lubrication - lubricate every 6000 miles.

Air filter element - service or inspect every 15,000 miles.

Automatic transaxle fluid & filter - replace every 50,000 miles.

Rotate tires - rotate at 6000 miles and then every 15,000 miles therafter.

Throttle body mount torque - torque at 6000 miles.

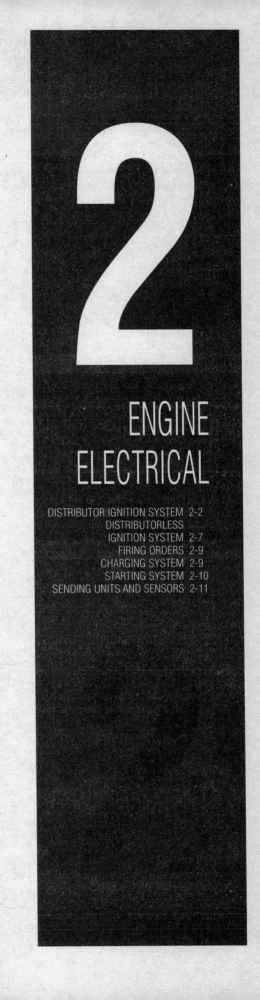

2

ENGINE ELECTRICAL

DISTRIBUTOR IGNITION SYSTEM

Note: For information on understanding electricity and troubleshooting electrical circuits, please refer to Chassis Electrical, Understanding and Trouble Shooting Electrical Systems.

General Information

DESCRIPTION AND OPERATION

Conventional Spark Control Ignition System

See Figure 1

A conventional electronic ignition system with vacuum/centrifugal spark control is used on carbureted 1985 - 88 Sprint and 1989 - 98 Metro models.

The basic components of this ignition system are the ignition coil, the distributor, the spark plugs, and spark plug wiring. The distributor consists of a signal generator (signal rotor and pick-up coil), igniter, rotor, ignition module, vacuum advancer, and centrifugal advancer.   When the distributor shaft rotates, a fluctuating magnetic field is generated due to changes in the air gap between the pick-up coil and signal rotor. Therefore, an alternating current (AC) voltage is induced in the pick-up coil. This induced AC voltage peaks when a ridge on the signal rotor is adjacent to the ridge on the pick-up coil. When the voltage peaks, the igniter breaks the circuit to ground from the negative side of the coil primary winding. With the circuit broken, the magnetic field in the ignition coil, which has been generated by the electrical current passing through it, collapses. The high voltage induced by the collapsing field is then forced to find a ground through the secondary coil wire, the distributor cap, the rotor, the spark plug wire and finally across the spark plug air gap to the engine block.

Spark timing is mechanically controlled by a vacuum advance system which uses engine manifold vacuum and a centrifugal advance mechanism.

Electronic Ignition System With Knock Controller

See Figure 2

An electronic ignition system with knock controller is used on turbocharged 1987 - 88 Chevrolet Sprint vehicles only.

This system functions in much the same manner as a conventional electronic ignition system except it utilizes an igniter with knock controller which electrically controls the ignition timing based on signal received from a knock sensor. The system ensures that optimum ignition timing is always obtained for best engine output and drive train protection. When there is no knocking, the ignition system operates in the same way as an ordinary ignition system. When knocking occurs, the system can retard the ignition timing up to 12-degrees, according to the degree of knocking.

The distributor uses a rotor, signal generator, vacuum advance unit and centrifugal advancer. The vacuum advance unit controls the ignition timing as follows. The throttle body bore and surge tank internal pressure is delivered into the vacuum advance unit through hoses. When the pressure is negative (vacuum), it moves the breaker clockwise (in reverse direction to rotor rotation) to advance the ignition timing. On the other hand, the positive pressure causes the breaker to move counterclockwise to retard the ignition timing.

The igniter with knock controller is located at the left side of the engine compartment. It has two main circuits, one serving as a fully transistorized igniter and the other as a knock controller. Based on the engine speed and signals from the Electronic Control Module (ECM) and knock sensor, the knock controller gives the igniter an instruction to retard the ignition timing so that engine knocking is suppressed.

The controller also has a fail safe circuit built-in. It gives an instruction to retard ignition timing by a certain amount if the knock sensor fails or a short or open circuit occurs in the output leads.

The knock sensor is located on the cylinder block at the intake manifold side. It detects engine vibration and converts it into an electrical signal, which is transmitted to the igniter.

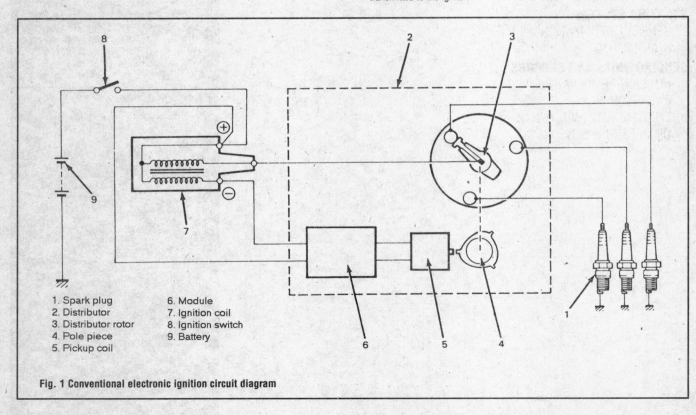

1. Spark plug
2. Distributor
3. Distributor rotor
4. Pole piece
5. Pickup coil
6. Module
7. Ignition coil
8. Ignition switch
9. Battery

Fig. 1 Conventional electronic ignition circuit diagram

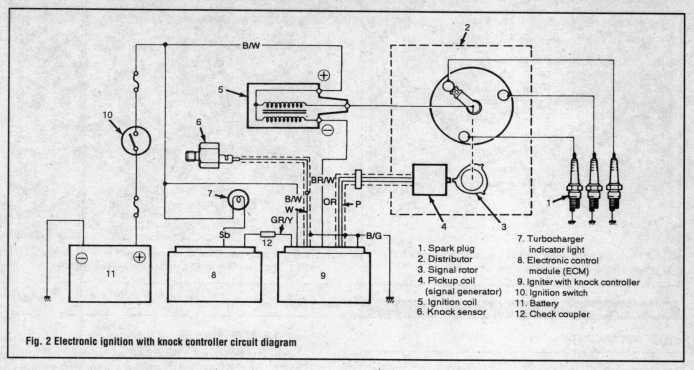

Fig. 2 Electronic ignition with knock controller circuit diagram

1. Spark plug
2. Distributor
3. Signal rotor
4. Pickup coil (signal generator)
5. Ignition coil
6. Knock sensor
7. Turbocharger indicator light
8. Electronic control module (ECM)
9. Igniter with knock controller
10. Ignition switch
11. Battery
12. Check coupler

Electronic Spark Control (ESC) Ignition System

See Figure 3

An electronic spark control ignition system is used on 1989 - 91 Metro Base and XFi models, and all 1992 - 00 Metro (3-cylinder) models.

The ignition circuit consists of the battery, distributor, ignition switch spark plugs, primary and secondary wiring. The ESC system is monitored and controlled by the engine control module (ECM). The distributor used in this system consists of a signal generator (signal rotor and pick-up coil), and rotor. The igniter is located in the ECM.

All spark timing changes in the distributor are performed electronically by the ECM. After receiving signals indicating engine speed, manifold vacuum, coolant temperature and other engine functions, the ECM selects the most appropriate timing setting from memory and signals the distributor to change the timing accordingly. No vacuum or mechanical advance mechanisms are used.

The ECM controls a driver to ground, which is connected to negative side from the coil's primary circuit. When this ground is interrupted, the field around the primary coil collapses and a high voltage is induced in the secondary coil. The high voltage induced in the secondary coil is then forced to find a ground through the coil wire, distributor cap, rotor, spark plug wire and across the spark plug air gap to the engine block.

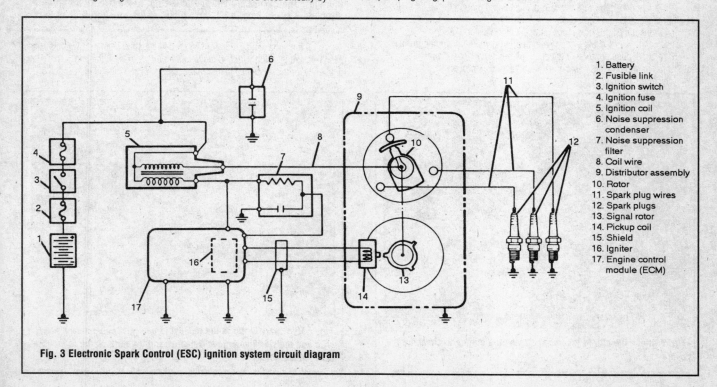

1. Battery
2. Fusible link
3. Ignition switch
4. Ignition fuse
5. Ignition coil
6. Noise suppression condenser
7. Noise suppression filter
8. Coil wire
9. Distributor assembly
10. Rotor
11. Spark plug wires
12. Spark plugs
13. Signal rotor
14. Pickup coil
15. Shield
16. Igniter
17. Engine control module (ECM)

Fig. 3 Electronic Spark Control (ESC) ignition system circuit diagram

Fig. 4 This spark tester looks just like a spark plug; attach the clip to ground and crank the engine to check for spark

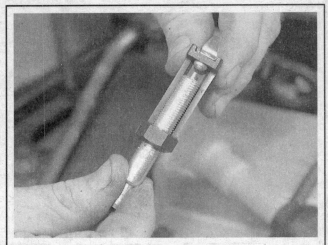

Fig. 5 This spark tester has an adjustable air-gap for measuring spark strength and testing different voltage ignition systems

Diagnosis and Testing

SECONDARY SPARK TEST

See Figures 4, 5, 6 and 7

The best way to perform this procedure is to use a spark tester (available at most automotive parts stores). Three types of spark testers are commonly available. The Neon Bulb type is connected to the spark plug wire and flashes with each ignition pulse. The Air Gap type must be adjusted to the individual spark plug gap specified for the engine. The last type of spark plug tester looks like a spark plug with a grounding clip on the side, but there is no side electrode for the spark to jump to. The last two types of testers allows the user to not only detect the presence of spark, but also the intensity (orange/yellow is weak, blue is strong).

1. Disconnect a spark plug wire at the spark plug end.
2. Connect the plug wire to the spark tester and ground the tester to an appropriate location on the engine.
3. Crank the engine and check for spark at the tester.
4. If spark exists at the tester, the ignition system is functioning properly.
5. If spark does not exist at the spark plug wire, perform diagnosis of the ignition system using individual component diagnosis procedures.

CYLINDER DROP TEST

See Figures 8, 9 and 10

The cylinder drop test is performed when an engine misfire is evident. This test helps determine which cylinder is not contributing the proper power. The easiest way to perform this test is to remove the plug wires one at a time from the cylinders with the engine running.

1. Place the transaxle in P or N, engage the emergency brake, and start the engine and let it idle.
2. Using a spark plug wire removing tool, preferably, the plier type, carefully remove the boot from one of the cylinders.

❊❊ WARNING:

Make sure your body is free from touching any part of the car which is metal. The secondary voltage in the ignition system is high and although it is unlikely to kill you, it will shock you and it does hurt.

3. The engine will sputter, run worse, and possibly nearly stall. If this happens reinstall the plug wire and move to the next cylinder. If the engine runs no differently, or the difference is minimal, shut the engine off and inspect the spark

Fig. 6 Attach the clip to ground and crank the engine to check for spark

Fig. 7 This spark tester is the easiest to use; just place it on a plug wire and the spark voltage is detected and the bulb on the top will flash with each pulse

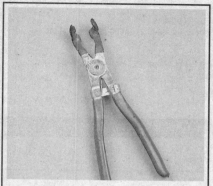

Fig. 8 These pliers are insulated and help protect the user from shock as well as the plug wires from being damaged

Fig. 9 To perform the cylinder drop test, remove one wire at a time and . . .

Fig. 10 . . . note the idle speed and idle characteristics of the engine. The cylinder(s) with the least drop is the non-contributing cylinder(s)

plug wire, spark plug, and if necessary, perform component diagnostics as covered in this section. Perform the test on all cylinders to verify which cylinders are suspect.

Adjustments

PICK-UP COIL AIR GAP ADJUSTMENT

1. Remove the distributor cap and rotor.
2. Using a nonmagnetic thickness gauge, measure the air gap between the pole piece tooth and pick-up coil.
3. The air gap should be 0.009-0.015 in. (0.2-0.4 mm). If the gap is out of specification, adjust it.
4. Remove the module and loosen the screws securing the pick-up coil. Using a screw driver, move the generator pick-up coil and adjust the gap to specification.
5. After adjustment, tighten the screws and recheck the air gap. Install the module, rotor, and distributor cap.

Ignition Coil

IGNITION COIL TESTING

See Figures 11 and 12

1. Check for spark at each spark plug with a spark plug tester. If no spark

is detected, proceed to Step 2. If spark is only detected on some spark plugs, check for a faulty distributor cap or rotor. Also check the spark plugs and wires. Replace as needed.
2. Check for voltage at the ignition coil positive terminal with a voltmeter. If battery voltage is detected, proceed to Step 3. If battery voltage is not detected, repair the open in the wiring between the battery and the ignition coil.
3. Disconnect the connector on the negative coil wire. Check ignition coil resistance. If resistance is within specification, proceed to Step 4. If resistance is not within specification, replace the coil.
    a. Measure the resistance between the positive and negative terminals. Resistance should be 1.08 - 1.32 ohms electronic ignition with knock control and 1.33 - 1.55 ohms for all others.
    b. Measure the resistance between the positive/negative terminals and the coil high tension wire terminal. Resistance should be 11.6 - 15.8 kilo-ohms for electronic ignition with knock control and 10.7 - 14.5 kilo-ohms up to 1993. 22.1 - 30 kilo-ohms for vehicles 1994 - 00.
4. On Conventional and ESC ignitions, check the resistance of the noise

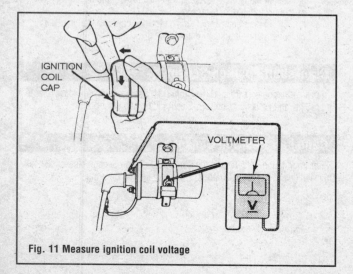

Fig. 11 Measure ignition coil voltage

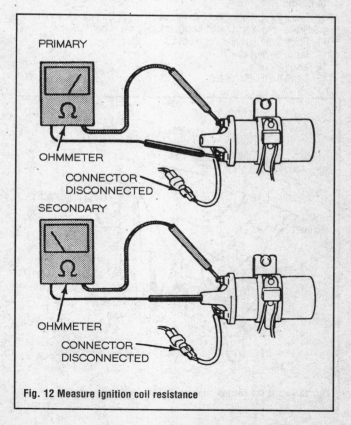

Fig. 12 Measure ignition coil resistance

filter and condenser with an ohmmeter. If the resistance is 2.0 - 2.5 ohms for both units, proceed to Step 5. If the resistance is not within specification, replace both units as a set.

5. On Conventional ignitions, check the continuity of the brown/white wire between the ignition coil negative terminal and the distributor. If continuity exists, replace the pick-up coil and igniter. If continuity does not exist, repair the open in the wire.

REMOVAL & INSTALLATION

1. Disconnect the negative battery terminal.
2. Twist and pull the secondary wire from the coil.
3. Remove the electrical connector from the coil.
4. Remove the relays from the coil mounting bracket.
5. Unbolt the coil and ignition control module from the firewall.
6. Unscrew the coil from the mounting bracket.

To install:

7. Reverse above procedure, torquing the mounting bracket to the firewall to 11 ft. lbs. (15 Nm).

Ignition Module

IGNITION MODULE REPLACEMENT

Conventional Spark Control Ignition

1. Disconnect the negative battery cable.
2. Remove the distributor and place it in a suitable holding device.
3. Remove the distributor cap if not already removed.
4. Remove the rotor by pulling upward with a twist.
5. Remove the pick-up coil and module dust covers.
6. Disconnect the wires from the ignition module.
7. Remove the module attaching screws from the outside of the distributor housing.
8. Remove the ignition module.

To install:

9. Install the ignition module. As necessary, adjust the pole piece air gap to specification and tighten the attaching screws to 44 inch lbs. (5 Nm).
10. Connect the ignition module wires.
11. Install the dust covers.
12. Install the rotor
13. Install the distributor cap.

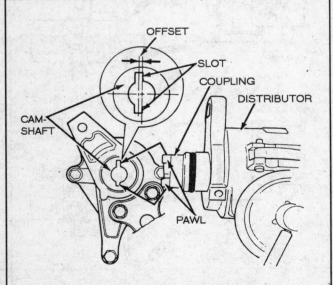

Fig. 13 This is the correct alignment of the distributor shaft

14. Install the distributor.
15. Connect the negative battery cable.
16. Start the engine and adjust the ignition timing to specification.

1992 - 00

The ignition module is an integral part of the ignition coil. If the module is found to be faulty, the coil must be replaced. Refer to Ignition Coil Pack, found in this section (Engine Electrical).

Distributor

DISTRIBUTOR REPLACEMENT

See Figure 13

1. Disconnect the negative battery cable.
2. Disconnect the wiring harness at the distributor and the vacuum line at the distributor vacuum advance unit.
3. Remove the distributor cap.

Note: Mark the distributor body in reference to where the rotor is pointing. Mark the distributor hold-down bracket and cylinder head for a reinstallation location point.

4. Remove the hold-down bolt and the distributor from the cylinder head. Do not rotate the engine after the distributor has been removed.

To install:

5. If the engine was not rotated proceed as follows:
   a. Align the reference marks on the distributor housing to the distributor hold-down bracket.
   b. Install the distributor into the offset slot in the camshaft, then the hold-down bolt.
   c. Connect vacuum hoses and electrical connectors to the distributor.
   d. Install the distributor cap, then connect the battery negative cable. Check and/or adjust the ignition timing.
6. If the engine was rotated while the distributor was removed, place the engine on TDC of the compression stroke to obtain the proper ignition timing.
7. Remove the No. 1 spark plug.
   a. Place thumb over the spark plug hole. Crank the engine slowly until compression is felt. It will be easier to have someone rotate the engine by hand, using a wrench on the crankshaft pulley.
   b. Align the timing mark on the crankshaft pulley with the 0 degrees mark on the timing scale attached to the front of the engine. This places the engine at TDC of the compression stroke.
   c. Turn the distributor shaft until the rotor points to the No. 1 spark plug tower on the cap.
   d. Install the distributor into the engine. Be sure to align the distributor-to-engine block mark made earlier.
   e. Install the No. 1 spark plug. Connect all vacuum hoses and electrical connectors to the distributor.
   f. Install distributor cap, then connect the battery negative cable.
   g. Check and/or adjust ignition timing.

Crankshaft Position Sensor

For information on servicing the Crankshaft Position Sensor, please refer to Driveability and Emission Controls, Electronic Engine Controls.

Camshaft Position Sensor

For information on servicing the Camshaft Position Sensor, please refer to Driveability and Emission Controls, Electronic Engine Controls.

Fig. 14 This spark tester looks just like a spark plug - attach the clip to ground and crank the engine to check for spark

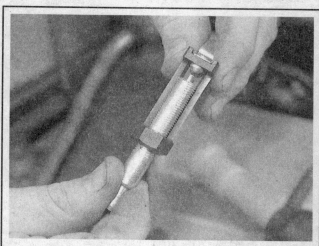

Fig. 15 This spark tester has an adjustable air-gap for measuring spark strength and testing different voltage ignition systems

Fig. 16 Attach the clip to ground and crank the engine to check for spark

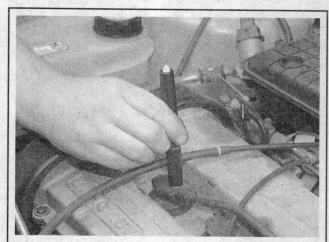

Fig. 17 This spark tester is the easiest to use; just place it on a plug wire and the spark voltage is detected and the bulb on the top will flash with each pulse

DISTRIBUTORLESS IGNITION SYSTEM

General Information

The 1998 - 00 1.3L Engine uses a distributorless ignition system (DIS). The system utilizes coil packs with built in ignition modules. Each coil pack fires two cylinders simultaneously. Being companion cylinders, one of the cylinders will be on compression while its companion will be on the exhaust segment of its stroke. Firing both cylinders in this manner reduces emissions by burning off any residual fuel left behind from the power stroke. The secondary voltage produced by this system is very high, in excess of 40,000 volts. The PCM controls all the adjustments for timing in this system.

Diagnosis and Testing

SECONDARY SPARK TEST

See Figures 14, 15, 16 and 17

The best way to perform this procedure is to use a spark tester (available at most automotive parts stores). Three types of spark testers are commonly avail-

able. The Neon Bulb type is connected to the spark plug wire and flashes with each ignition pulse. The Air Gap type must be adjusted to the individual spark plug gap specified for the engine. The last type of spark plug tester looks like a spark plug with a grounding clip on the side, but there is no side electrode for the spark to jump to. The last two types of testers allows the user to not only detect the presence of spark, but also the intensity (orange/yellow is weak, blue is strong).

1. Disconnect a spark plug wire at the spark plug end.
2. Connect the plug wire to the spark tester and ground the tester to an appropriate location on the engine.
3. Crank the engine and check for spark at the tester.
4. If spark exists at the tester, the ignition system is functioning properly.
5. If spark does not exist at the spark plug wire, perform diagnosis of the ignition system using individual component diagnosis procedures.

CYLINDER DROP TEST

See Figures 18, 19 and 20

The cylinder drop test is performed when an engine misfire is evident. This

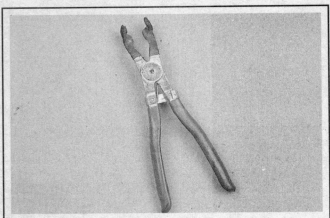

Fig. 18 These pliers are insulated and help protect the user from shock as well as the plug wires from being damaged

Fig. 20 . . . note the idle speed and idle characteristics of the engine. the cylinder(s) with the least drop is the non-contributing cylinder(s)

test helps determine which cylinder is not contributing the proper power. The easiest way to perform this test is to remove the plug wires one at a time from the cylinders with the engine running.

Place the transaxle in P or N, engage the emergency brake, and start the engine and let it idle.

1. Using a spark plug wire removing tool, preferably, the plier type, carefully remove the boot from one of the cylinders.

❊❊ WARNING

Make sure your body is free from touching any part of the car which is metal. The secondary voltage in the ignition system is extremely high and although it is unlikely to kill you, it will shock you and it does hurt.

2. The engine will sputter, run worse, and possibly nearly stall. If this happens reinstall the plug wire and move to the next cylinder. If the engine runs no differently, or the difference is minimal, shut the engine off and inspect the spark plug wire, spark plug, and if necessary, perform component diagnostics as covered in this section. Perform the test on all cylinders to verify which cylinders are suspect.

Adjustments

No adjustments are necessary, or possible for this system. The PCM (powertrain control module) controls all aspects of the ignition timing. If the timing

Fig. 19 To perform the cylinder drop test, remove one wire at a time and . . .

falls out of parameters, individual component testing is required.

Ignition Coil Pack

TESTING

1. Check for spark at each spark plug with a spark plug tester. If no spark is detected, proceed to Step 2. If spark is only detected on some spark plugs, check for a faulty distributor cap or rotor. Also check the spark plugs and wires.

2. Check for voltage at the ignition coil positive terminal with a voltmeter. If battery voltage is detected, proceed to Step 3. If battery voltage is not detected, repair the open in the wiring between the battery and the ignition coil.

3. Disconnect the connector on the negative coil wire. Check ignition coil resistance. If resistance is within specification, proceed to Step 4. If resistance is not within specification, replace the coil.

   a. Measure the resistance between the positive and negative terminals. Resistance should be 1.08 - 1.32 ohms electronic ignition with knock control and 1.33 - 1.55 ohms for all others.

   b. Measure the resistance between the positive/negative terminals and the coil high tension wire terminal. Resistance should be 11.6 - 15.8 kilo-ohms.

4. On ESC ignitions, check the resistance of the noise filter and condenser with an ohmmeter. If the resistance is 2.0 - 2.5 ohms for both units, proceed to Step 5. If the resistance is not within specification, replace both units as a set.

REMOVAL & INSTALLATION

See Figure 21

Fig. 21 The coils are located on the valve cover

1. Disconnect negative battery terminal.
2. Remove the appropriate secondary ignition wires from the coil.
3. Remove the electrical connector from the ignition coil.
4. Unbolt the coil from the cylinder head and remove the coil.

To install

5. Place the ignition coil in place on the cylinder head.
6. Torque the retaining bolt to 7.5 ft. lbs. (10 Nm).
8. Connect the electrical connector to the new coil.
9. Reconnect the secondary wires.
10 Connect the negative battery terminal.

Ignition Module

REMOVAL & INSTALLATION

The ignition module is an integral part of the ignition coil. If the module is found to be faulty, the coil must be replaced. Refer to Ignition Coil Pack, found in this section (Engine Electrical).

Crankshaft and Camshaft Position Sensors

For procedures on the position sensors, please refer to Driveability and Emission Controls, Electronic Engine Controls.

FIRING ORDERS

See Figures 22 and 23

Note: To avoid confusion, remove and tag the spark plug wires one at a time, for replacement.

If a distributor is not keyed for installation with only one orientation, it could have been removed previously and rewired. The resultant wiring would hold the correct firing order, but could change the relative placement of the plug towers in relation to the engine. For this reason it is imperative that you label all wires

before disconnecting any of them. Also, before removal, compare your wiring with the accompanying illustrations. If the wiring on your engine does not match, make notes in your book to reflect how your engine is wired.

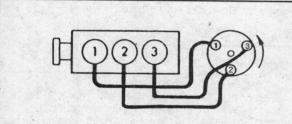

Fig. 22 1.0L Engine
Firing order: 1 - 3 - 2

Fig. 23 1.3L Engine (1997 and earlier with distributor shown, firing order same for later distributorless models)
Firing order: 1 - 3 - 4 - 2

CHARGING SYSTEM

General Information

All models utilize an integral regulator charging system. The integrated circuit (IC) regulator is a solid state unit that is mounted inside the alternator to the rear end frame. All regulator components are enclosed in a solid mold to protect them from the heat and corrosive elements.

The alternator rotor bearings contain enough grease to eliminate the need for periodic lubrication. Two brushes carry current through two slip rings to the field coil, mounted on the rotor. Under normal conditions, this arrangement is capable of providing long periods for attention-free service.

Stator windings are assembled inside a laminated core that forms part of the alternator drive end frame. A rectifier bridge, that contains six diodes, is connected to the stator windings. These diodes electrically change stator AC voltage into DC voltage. The DC voltage is then transmitted to the alternator output terminal.

Two neutral diodes are utilized to smooth out voltage fluctuations caused by varying alternator speeds. A capacitor (condenser), mounted in the regulator, protects the rectifier bridge and neutral diodes. This capacitor also suppresses radio interference noise.

Alternator Precautions

To prevent damage to the on-board computer, alternator and regulator, the following precautionary measures must be taken when working with the electrical system.

- Never reverse the battery connections. Always check the battery polarity visually. This is to be done before any connections are made to be sure that all of the connections correspond to the battery ground polarity.
- Booster batteries for starting must be connected properly. Make sure that the positive cable of the booster battery is connected to the positive terminal of the battery that is getting the boost. This applies to both negative and ground cables.
- Make sure the ignition switch is OFF when connecting or disconnecting any electrical component.
- Disconnect the battery cables before using a fast charger; the charger has a tendency to force current through the diodes in the opposite direction for which they were designed. This burns out the diodes.
- Never use a fast charger as a booster for starting the vehicle.
- Never disconnect the voltage regulator while the engine is running.
- Do not ground the alternator output terminal.
- Do not attempt to polarize an alternator.

Alternator

Note: Before beginning any electrical testing be sure that the battery is fully charged. False readings can result from not having a fully charged battery. This could lead to improper diagnosis of components, resulting in costly, non-refundable purchases.

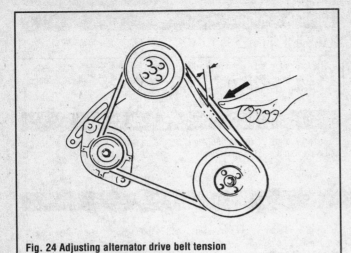

Fig. 24 Adjusting alternator drive belt tension

Fig. 25 The alternator is located next to the water pump at the front of the engine

TESTING

Note: Before any electrical testing can be accomplished, the battery must be fully charged. If the electrical system source voltage is not to 12.66 volts, all of the readings may be inaccurate.

Voltage Drop Testing

1. Start the engine and let it reach operating temperature.
2. Shut off the engine.
3. Set the parking brake.
4. Connect a tachometer.
5. Start the engine. Turn on all the accessories.
6. Rev the engine to 2000 RPM. Hold the engine speed there.
7. Test the ground circuits.
   a. Connect the negative lead of voltmeter to the positive Battery terminal.
   b. Connect the positive lead to the output terminal of the alternator. The reading should be no higher than 0.6 volts. If found to be higher than 0.6 volt, connect to the terminal mounting stud and the wiring connector. If the reading is now below 0.6 volts, look for loose, dirty, or poor connections. This test can be done at all ground connections in the circuit to find excessive resistance.
8. Test for the positive circuit.
   a. Connect the positive lead to the negative battery terminal.
   b. Connect the negative lead to the ground terminal of the alternator. The

voltage should not exceed 0.3 volts. If it is higher move to the terminal mounting stud and the wiring connector. If found to be lower look for loose, dirty, or poor connections. This test can be done at all positive connections in the circuit to find excessive resistance.

9. Perform this test between the alternator case and the engine block to find corrosion or loose alternator mounting points.

REMOVAL & INSTALLATION

See Figures 24 and 25

1. Disconnect the negative battery cable.
2. Remove other components as necessary to gain access to the alternator.
3. Label and disconnect the alternator's electrical connectors.
4. Remove the alternator brace bolt and the drive belt.
5. Support the alternator while removing the mounting bolts, then remove the alternator.

To install:

6. Install the alternator and loosely tighten the mounting bolts.
7. Install the drive belt and tension to obtain a deflection of 1/4-inch on the longest span of the belt.
8. Tighten the alternator drive belt adjuster bolt to 17 ft. lbs. (23 Nm).
9. Reconnect the electrical connector and tighten nut to 71 inch lbs.. (8 Nm).
10. Connect the negative battery cable.

STARTING SYSTEM

General Information

Four types of starter motor are utilized depending upon the vehicle transaxle and assembly plant location. Manual transaxle equipped vehicles utilize a conventional starter motor which consists of a yoke, an armature assembly, an overrunning clutch assembly, a solenoid, a commutator end cover, a brush holder and a pinion drive lever. Automatic transaxle equipped vehicles utilize a reduction type starter motor which has, in addition to the components found on conventional starter motors, a reduction gear and shock absorber assembly.

In the basic circuit, the solenoid windings are energized when the ignition switch is turn to the START position and the clutch start/neutral safety switch is closed. The resulting plunger and shift lever movement causes the pinion to engage the engine flywheel ring gear. This movement also causes the starter solenoid contacts to close.

With the contacts closed, the starter solenoid provides a closed circuit between the battery positive terminal and the starter motor. Because the starter

motor is permanently grounded to the engine block, the circuit is complete and cranking occurs as soon as the starter solenoid contacts are closed.

When the engine starts, the pinion is designed to overrun and protect the armature from excessive speed until the ignition switch is released from the START position. With the ignition switch released, a return spring in the solenoid assembly forces the starter solenoid contacts open, breaks the circuit between the battery and the starter motor, and disengages the pinion. To prevent prolonged overrun, the ignition switch should be immediately released upon engine.

Starter

Note: Before beginning any electrical testing be sure that the battery is fully charged. False readings can result from not having a fully charged battery. This could lead to improper diagnosis of components, resulting in costly, non-refundable purchases.

TESTING

1. Connect a voltmeter in conjunction with an inductive amp probe to the battery.
2. Disable the ignition system.
3. Set the vehicle in park or neutral and set the parking brake.
4. Turn the key to the START position and read the meters.
5. If the voltage reads 12 volts or greater and the amperage reads 0 - 10 amps, further testing to the solenoid and relays are applicable.
6. If the voltage reads 7.5 and above with the amperage readings above 150 amps, move onto the testing of feed circuit resistance to establish a properly functioning starter circuit.

Feed Circuit Resistance

1. Connect a voltmeter to the negative battery post and the negative battery cable clamp.
2. Turn the key to the START position and read the meter.
3. If any voltage is recorded, Clean the contact area of the two items.
4. Do the same test for the positive battery terminal post and clamp.
5. If any voltage is recorded, Clean the contact area of the two items.
6. Connect to the negative battery terminal and the engine block near the ground cable.
7. Turn the key and take reading.
8. If the reading is above 0.3 volts, clean up the contact area.
9. If this does not correct the high reading, replace the cable.
10. Connect to the positive battery terminal and the terminal on the starter solenoid.
11. Turn key and take reading.
12. If the reading is above 0.3 volts, clean up the contact area.
13. If this does not correct the high reading, replace the cable.
14. If necessary, move onto solenoid testing.

Starter Solenoid

1. Connect the voltmeter to the Solenoid terminal to ground.
2. Turn the key to START.
3. If battery voltage is not found, check the ignition switch circuit.
4. If battery voltage is found, proceed by connecting an ohmmeter to the battery and the ground terminal of the solenoid.
5. Turn the key and take reading.
6. The ohmmeter should read zero, if not repair ground connection.
7. If these tests are performed and the solenoid still does not energize, replace the solenoid.

REMOVAL & INSTALLATION

See Figure 26

1. Disconnect the negative battery cable.
2. Raise and support the vehicle safely.
3. Label and disconnect the starter solenoid electrical connector.

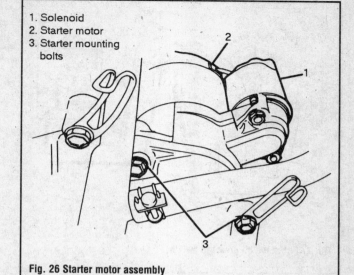

1. Solenoid
2. Starter motor
3. Starter mounting bolts

Fig. 26 Starter motor assembly

4. Remove the mounting bolts from the starter motor, then carefully lower the assembly from the vehicle.

To install:

5. Install the starter motor assembly complete with any shims that may be used between the engine block and the starter.
6. Install and tighten the starter mounting bolts to 17 ft. lbs.. (23 Nm).
7. Connect the starter solenoid electrical connector.
8. Lower the vehicle and connect the negative battery cable.

SOLENOID OR RELAY REPLACEMENT

See Figure 26

1. Disconnect the negative battery cable.
2. Raise and support the vehicle safely.
3. Label and disconnect the starter solenoid electrical connector.
4. Remove the mounting bolts from the starter motor, then carefully lower the assembly from the vehicle.

To install:

5. Install the starter motor assembly complete with any shims that may be used between the engine block and the starter.
6. Install and tighten the starter mounting bolts to 17 ft. lbs.. (23 Nm).
7. Connect the starter solenoid electrical connector.
8. Lower the vehicle and connect the negative battery cable.

SENDING UNITS AND SENSORS

Note: This section describes the operating principles of sending units, warning lights and gauges. Sensors which provide information to the Electronic Control Module (ECM) are covered in The Driveability and Emission Controls Section of this manual.

Instrument panels contain a number of indicating devices (gauges and warning lights). These devices are composed of two separate components. One is the sending unit, mounted on the engine or other remote part of the vehicle, and the other is the actual gauge or light in the instrument panel.

Several types of sending units exist, however most can be characterized as being either a pressure type or a resistance type. Pressure type sending units convert liquid pressure into an electrical signal which is sent to the gauge. Resistance type sending units are most often used to measure temperature and

use variable resistance to control the current flow back to the indicating device. Both types of sending units are connected in series by a wire to the battery (through the ignition switch). When the ignition is turned ON, current flows from the battery through the indicating device and on to the sending unit.

Coolant Temperature Sensor

TESTING

1. With the use of a scan tool, bring up the ECT reading.
2. Disconnect the sensor. It should read -40-degrees (-40-degrees C).

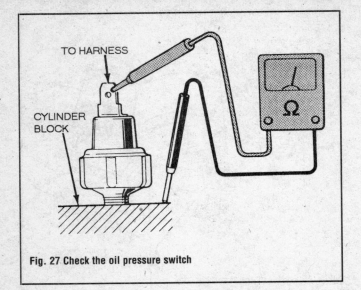

Fig. 27 Check the oil pressure switch

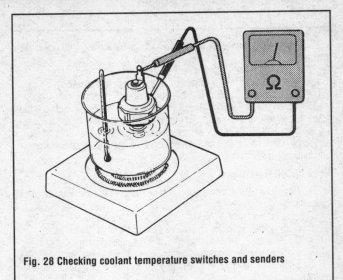

Fig. 28 Checking coolant temperature switches and senders

3. Place a paper clip into the electrical connector. It should 250-degrees F (120-degrees C). If the sensor wire is a one wire connection, ground the wire to the block. The gauge on the instrument panel will begin to read hot. Do not let the needle stay all the way pinned for any extended period of time. This will burn out the gauge.

4. If the gauge is good move on to testing the sending unit.

5. Connect an ohmmeter to the sending unit and its ground. Resistance is relative to temperature. The hotter the coolant gets, the less resistance will be found in the sending unit.

6. With the coolant temperature at 77-degrees F (25-degrees C), the resistance should be 2796 ohms.

7. With the engine at operating temperature, approximately 212-degrees F (100-degrees C), the resistance should be 177 ohms.

8. If the sending unit does not render the correct values at these temperatures, replace the sensor.

REMOVAL & INSTALLATION

Note: Be careful when handling the sensor. Damage to the sensor can and will affect the operation of the fuel delivery system.

1. Drain the cooling system.
2. Disconnect the electrical connector from the sensor.
3. Remove the engine coolant temperature sensor from the thermostat housing.

To install:

4. Thread the new sensor into the housing and torque to 7.5-14.0 ft. lbs. (10-20 Nm).
5. Connect the electrical connector to the sensor.
6. Fill the coolant system with a 50/50 mix of antifreeze and water.

Oil Pressure Sensor

TESTING

To test when the indicator lamp does not illuminate.

1. Turn ON the ignition switch.
2. If the lamp does not illuminate, check for an open in the oil pressure sensor circuit.
3. If the circuit checks out to be good, disconnect the wire from the sensor and using a jumper wire, ground the wire.
4. If the lamp illuminates, check the sensor for a good ground. If necessary, replace the sensor.
5. If the lamp does not illuminate, check for a burnt out bulb or disconnected socket in the instrument cluster.

To test when the indicator lamp does not go out.

1. Check the oil level and top off as needed.
2. If the engine was low on oil, test start the engine and check to see if the lamp goes out. If the lamp stays on, immediately stop the engine and go to the next step.
3. Disconnect the wire from the oil pressure sensor. If the lamp stays illuminated, check the harness for a short to ground. If the lamp goes out, go to the next step.
4. Replace the oil pressure sensor.
5. Start the engine and check the indicator lamp. If the lamp still has not gone out, immediately stop the engine to avoid severe damage.
6. Check for the possible causes:
-   Pinched or grounded sensor wire.
-   Defective oil pressure sending unit.
-   Restricted or severely leaking oil filter.
-   Excessive internal engine bearing clearance.
-   Insufficient or severely contaminated engine oil.
-   Blocked oil pump pickup screen or severely worn oil pump.

REMOVAL & INSTALLATION

See Figure 27

1. Disconnect the negative battery cable.
2. Drain the engine oil.
3. Disconnect the oil pressure switch electrical connector.
4. Remove the switch from the cylinder block.

To install:

5. Coat the sending unit threads with sealant and install in the cylinder block.
6. Connect the oil pressure switch electrical connector.
8. Fill the engine with oil.
9. Connect the negative battery cable.

Electric Fan Switch

Up until 1996, the coolant fan was controlled by a thermostat switch. At the manufacturer specified temperature the switch closes the path to ground and energizes the cooling fan relay. The relay in turn completes the path to the permanently grounded fan, thus energizing the fan.

In 1996, the switch was removed from the process. The PCM took over the job of the switch. When the PCM sees a manufacturer specified temperature from the ECT it energizes the relay and powers the fan. This simplifies the wiring and troubleshooting.

TESTING

1. Bring the engine to operating temperature.

2. The switch should ground the fan circuit at approximately 205-degrees F (96-degrees C).

3. If the fan does not run, disconnect the electrical harness.

4. Using a fused jumper wire, connect the two wires in the harness to each other.

5. If the fan runs, replace the switch.

6. If the fan does not run, check for the open in the circuit.

REMOVAL & INSTALLATION

1985 - 96

See Figure 28

1. Disconnect the negative battery cable.
2. Drain the cooling system below the level of the thermostat housing.

❊❊ CAUTION:

When draining the coolant, keep in mind that cats and dogs are attracted by the ethylene glycol antifreeze, and are quite likely to drink any that is left in an uncovered container or in puddles on the ground. This will prove fatal in sufficient quantity. Always drain the coolant into a sealable container. Coolant should be reused unless it is contaminated or several years old.

3. Disconnect the radiator fan thermostat switch electrical connector.

4. Remove the switch from the thermostat housing.

To install:

5. Coat the threads of the thermostat switch with sealant and install in the thermostat housing.

6. Connect the radiator fan thermostat switch electrical connector.

7. Fill the cooling system.

8. Connect the negative battery cable.

1996 - 00

The PCM controls the electric cooling fan operation for this system. If the switching device is faulty, the PCM must be replaced. Refer to Driveability and Emission Controls, Electronic Engine Controls.

Notes

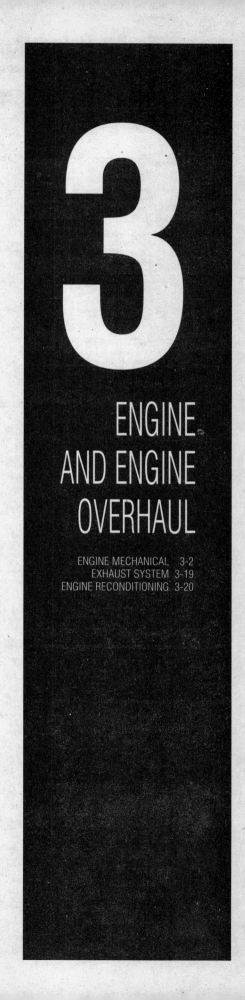

3

ENGINE
AND ENGINE
OVERHAUL

ENGINE MECHANICAL

1.0L ENGINE MECHANICAL SPECIFICATIONS

Description	English Specifications	Metric Specifications
General Information		
Engine type	3 Cylinder In-Line Overhead Camshaft	
Displacement	61.0 cubic in.	1.0L
Bore	2.91in.	73.914mm
Stroke	3.03in.	76.962mm
Compression ratio	9.5:1	
Firing order	1-3-2	
Cylinder Head		
Cylinder Head Bore	1.2205-1.2214 in.	31.000-31.025 mm
Cylinder Head Gasket Surface Surface Distortion (Maximum)	0.002 in.	0.05 mm
Cylinder Head to Manifold Seating Distortion Intake and Exhaust (Maximum)	0.004 in.	0.010 mm
Cylinder Bore Diameter Limit	2.9193 in.	74.15 mm
Taper and Out-of-Round Limit	0.004 in.	0.10 mm
Camshaft		
Camshaft height		
Standard	1.5911-1.5974 in.	40.415-40.575 mm
Limit	1.5872 in.	40.315 mm
Bearing oil clearance		
Standard	0.0024-0.0039 in.	0.06-0.10mm
Limit	0.0055 in.	0.14mm
Hydraulic Valve Lash Adjusters		
Outer Diameter	1.2188-1.2194 in.	30.959-30.975 mm
Adjuster -to- Cylinder Head Bore Clearance	0.0010-0.0025 in.	0.025-0.066 mm
Adjuster -to- Cylinder Head Bore Minimum	0.0059 in.	0.15 mm
Valves		
Valve Guide Inside Diameter	0.2165-0.2170 in.	5.500-5.512 mm
Valve Head Thickness		
Intake Standard	0.039 in.	1.0 mm
Intake Minimum	0.02 in.	0.6 mm
Exhaust Standard	0.047 in.	1.2 mm
Exhaust Minimum	0.027 in.	0.7 mm
Valve Seat Contact Width Intake and Exhaust	0.0512-0.0590 in.	1.30-1.50 mm
Valve Stem Outside Diameter		
Intake	0.2148-0.2157 in.	5.457-5.480 mm
Exhaust	0.2142-0.2148 in.	5.440-5.455 mm
Valve Stem Radial Runout (Minimum) Intake and Exhaust	0.003 in.	0.08 mm
Valve Stem -to- Valve Guide Clearance		
Intake Standard	0.0008-0.0022 in.	0.020-0.055 mm
Intake Maximum Limit	0.0027 in.	0.070 mm
Exhaust Standard	0.0018-0.0028 in.	0.045-0.072 mm
Exhaust Maximum Limit	0.0035 in.	0.090 mm
Valve Spring Free Length Standard	1.6649 in.	42.29 mm
Valve Spring Free Length Limit (Minimum)	1.6142 in.	41.00 mm
Valve Spring Preload Standard	46.1-51.8 lbs. at 1.28 in.	20.9-23.5 kg. at 32.6 mm
Valve Spring Preload Limit (Minimum)	41.2 lbs. at 1.28 in.	18.7 kg. at 32.6 mm
Valve Spring Squareness Deviation (Maximum)	0.079 in.	2.0 mm
Pistons		
Piston to Cylinder Bore Clearance	0.0008-0.0015 in.	0.02-0.04 mm
Piston Diameter		
Oringinal Piston	2.9122-2.9130 in.	73.970-73.990 mm
0.0098 in. (0.25 mm) Oversize Piston	2.9220-2.9224 in.	74.220-74.230 mm
0.0197 in. (0.50 mm) Oversize Piston	2.9319-2.9323 in.	74.470-74.480 mm
Piston Ring End Gap		
Top Ring (Standard)	0.0079-0.0118 in.	0.2-0.3 mm
Top Ring (Maximum Limit)	0.0276 in.	0.7 mm
Second Ring (Standard)	0.0079-0.018 in.	0.2-0.3 mm
Second Ring (Maximum Limit)	0.0276 in.	0.7 mm
Oil Ring (Standard)	0.0079-0.0275 in.	0.2-0.6 mm
Oil Ring (Maximum Limit)	0.0708 in.	1.8 mm
Piston Groove Clearance		
First Ring	0.0012-0.0027 in.	0.03-0.07 mm
Second Ring	0.0008-0.0023 in.	0.02-0.06 mm
Main Bearings		
Main Bearing Clearance Standard	0.00008-0.00015 in.	0.0020-0.0040 mm
Main Bearing Clearance Limit	0.0023 in.	0.060 mm
0.0098 in. (0.25 mm) Undersized Bearings Green and Red	0.0835-0.0836 in	2.121-2.125 mm
0.0098 in. (0.25 mm) Undersized Bearings Black and Red	0.0836-0.0838 in.	2.124-2.128 mm
Red	0.0837-0.0839 in.	2.127-2.131 mm
Yellow and Red	0.0839-0.0840 in.	2.130-2.134 mm
Blue and Red	0.0840-0.0841 in.	2.133-2.137 mm
Crankshaft Journal Diameter 1 Stamping	1.7714-1.7716 in.	44.994-45.000 mm
Crankshaft Journal Diameter 2 Stamping	1.7712-1.7714 in.	44.988-44.994 mm
Crankshaft Journal Diameter 3 Stamping	1.7710-1.7712 in.	44.982-44.988 mm
(Undersized)	1.7611-1.7618 in.	44.732-44.750 mm
Main Bearing Cap Bore Diameter (Without Bearing) A Stamping	1.9292-1.9294 in.	49.000-49.006 mm
Main Bearing Cap Bore Diameter (Without Bearing) B Stamping	1.9294-1.9296 in.	49.006-49.012 mm
Main Bearing Cap Bore Diameter (Without Bearing) C Stamping	1.9296-1.9298 in.	49.012-49.018 mm
Connecting Rods and Bearings		
Connecting Rod Bow Limit	0.0002 in.	0.005 mm
Connecting Rod Twist Limit	0.004 in.	0.10 mm
Crank Pin Diameter Standard	1.6529-1.6535 in.	41.982-42.000 mm
Crank Pin Diameter 0.0098 in. (0.25 mm) Undersize	1.6430-1.6437 in.	41.732-41.750 mm
Crank Pin Diameter Out-of-Round and Taper Limit	0.0004 in.	0.01 mm
Connecting Rod Bearing Clearance Standard	0.0008-0.0019 in.	0.020-0.050 mm
Connecting Rod Bearing Clearance Limit	0.0031 in.	0.080 mm
Oil Pump		
Oil Pump Rotor-to-Oil Pump Body Radial Clearance (Maximum)	0.0122 in.	0.310 mm
Oil Pump Housing -to- Oil Pump Gear Set (Side Clearance) (Maximum)	0.0059 in.	0.15 mm

1.3L ENGINE MECHANICAL SPECIFICATIONS

Description	English Specifications	Metric Specifications
General Information		
Engine type	4 Cylider In-Line Overhead Camshaft	
Displacement	79 cubic in.	1.3 L
Bore	2.91in.	73.914mm
Stroke	2.97 in.	75.5 mm
Compression ratio	9.5:1	
Firing order	1-3-4-2	
Cylinder Head		
Cylinder Head Gasket Surface Distortion (Maximum)	0.002 in.	0.05 mm
Cylinder Head to Manifold Seating Distortion Intake and Exhaust (Maximum)	0.004 in.	0.010 mm
Camshaft		
Camshaft height		
Standard	1.5014 in.	38.136 mm
Limit	1.4975 in.	38.036 mm
Bearing oil clearance		
Standard	0.0020-0.0036 in.	0.050-0.091 mm
Limit	0.0059 in.	0.15 mm
Camshaft Runout (Maximum)	0.0039 in.	0.10 mm
Rocker Arms		
Rocker Arm Clearance Standard	0.0005-0.0017 in.	0.012-0.045 mm
Rocker Arm Clearance Limit (Maximum)	0.035 in.	0.9 mm
Rocker Arm Inside Diameter	0.629-0.630 in.	16.00-16.018 mm
Rocker Arm Shaft Runout Limit	0.004 in.	0.12 mm
Rocker Arm Shaft Diameter	0.628-0.629 in.	15.973-15.988 mm
Valves		
Valve Guide Inside Diameter	0.2756-0.2761 in.	7.000-7.015 mm
Valve Head Thickness		
Intake Standard	0.039 in.	1.0 mm
Intake Minimum	0.023 in.	0.6 mm
Exhaust Standard	0.039 in.	1.0 mm
Exhaust Minimum	0.027 in.	0.7 mm
Valve Seat Contact Width Intake and Exhaust	0.0512-0.0590 in.	1.30-1.50 mm
Valve Stem Outside Diameter		
Intake	0.2742-0.2748 in.	6.965-6.980 mm
Exhaust	0.2737-0.2742 in.	6.950-6.965 mm
Valve Stem Radial Runout (Minimum) Intake and Exhaust	0.003 in.	0.08 mm
Valve Stem -to- Valve Guide Clearance		
Intake Standard	0.0008-0.0019 in.	0.020-0.055 mm
Intake Maximum Limit	0.0027 in.	0.070 mm
Exhaust Standard	0.0014-0.0025 in.	0.035-0.065mm
Exhaust Maximum Limit	0.0035 in.	0.090 mm
Valve Spring Free Length Standard	1.9409 in.	49.30 mm
Valve Spring Free Length Limit (Minimum)	1.8937 in.	48.10 mm
Valve Spring Preload Standard	54.7-64.3 lbs. at 1.63 in.	24.8-29.2 kg. at 41.5
Valve Spring Preload Limit (Minimum)	50.2 lbs. at 1.63 in.	22.8 kg. at 41.5 mm
Valve Spring Squareness Deviation (Maximum)	0.079 in.	2.0 mm
Cylinder Block		
Cylinder Bore Stamped 1	2.9138-2.9142 in.	74.01-74.02 mm
Cylinder Bore Stamped 2	2.9134-2.9138 in.	74.00-74.01 mm
Cylinder Bore Diameter Limit	2.9193 in.	74.15 mm
Taper and Out-of-Round Limits	.0.004 in.	0.10 mm
Pistons		
Piston to Cylinder Bore Clearance	0.0008-0.0015 in.	0.02-0.04 mm
Piston Diameter		
Stamped 1	2.9126-2.9130 in.	73.980-79.990 mm
Stamped 2	2.912-2.9126 in.	73.970-73.980 mm
0.0098 in. (0.25 mm) Oversize Piston	2.9220-2.9224 in.	74.220-74.230 mm
0.0197 in. (0.50 mm) Oversize Piston	2.9319-2.9323 in.	74.470-74.480 mm
Piston Ring End Gap		
Top Ring (Standard)	0.0079-0.0118 in.	0.2-0.3 mm
Top Ring (Maximum Limit)	0.0276 in.	0.7 mm
Second Ring (Standard)	0.0079-0.00118 in.	0.2-0.3 mm
Second Ring (Maximum Limit)	0.0276 in.	0.7 mm
Oil Ring (Standard)	0.0079-0.0275 in.	0.2-0.6 mm
Oil Ring (Maximum Limit)	0.0708 in.	1.8 mm
Piston Groove Clearance		
First Ring	0.0012-0.0027 in.	0.03-0.07 mm
Second Ring	0.0008-0.0023 in.	0.02-0.06 mm
Main Bearings		
Main Bearing Clearance Standard	0.00008-0.00015 in.	0.0020-0.0040 mm
Main Bearing Clearance Limit	0.0023 in.	0.060 mm
0.0098 in. (0.25 mm) Undersized Bearings Green and Red	0.0835-0.0836 in.	2.121-2.125 mm
0.0098 in. (0.25 mm) Undersized Bearings Black and Red	0.0836-0.0838 in.	2.124-2.128 mm
Red	0.0837-0.0839 in.	2.127-2.131 mm
Yellow and Red	0.0839-0.0840 in.	2.130-2.134 mm
Blue and Red	0.0840-0.0841 in.	2.133-2.137 mm
Crankshaft Journal Diameter 1 Stamping	1.7714-1.7716 in.	44.994-45.000 mm
Crankshaft Journal Diameter 2 Stamping	1.7712- 1.7714 in.	44.988-44.994 mm
Crankshaft Journal Diameter 3 Stamping	1.7710-1.7712 in.	44.982-44.988 mm
(Undersized)	1.7611-1.7618 in.	44.732-44.750 mm
Main Bearing Cap Bore Diameter (Without Bearing) A Stamping	1.9292-1.9294 in.	49.000-49.006 mm
Main Bearing Cap Bore Diameter (Without Bearing) B Stamping	1.9294-1.9296 in.	49.006-49.012 mm
Main Bearing Cap Bore Diameter (Without Bearing) C Stamping	1.9296-1.9298 in.	49.012-49.018 mm

1.3L ENGINE MECHANICAL SPECIFICATIONS (CONTINUED)

Description	English Specifications	Metric Specifications
Connecting Rods and Bearings		
Connecting Rod Side Clearance Standard	0.0039-0.0078 in.	0.10-0.20mm
Connecting Rod Side Clearance Maximum Limit	0.0137	0.35 mm
Connecting Rod Bow Limit	0.0002 in.	0.005 mm
Connecting Rod Twist Limit	0.004 in.	0.10 mm
Crank Pin Diameter Standard	1.6529-1.6535 in.	41.982-42.000 mm
Crank Pin Diameter 0.0098 in. (0.25 mm) Undersize	1.6430-1.6437 in.	41.732-41.750 mm
Crank Pin Diameter Out-of-Round and Taper Limit	0.0004 in.	0.01 mm
Connecting Rod Bearing Clearance Standard	0.0008-0.0019 in.	0.020-0.050 mm
Connecting Rod Bearing Clearance Limit	0.0031 in.	0.080 mm
Oil Pump		
Oil Pump Rotor-to-Oil Pump Body Radial Clearance (Maximum)	0.0122 in.	0.310 mm
Oil Pump Housing -to- Oil Pump Gear Set (Side Clearance) (Maximum)	0.0059 in.	0.15 mm

TORQUE SPECIFICATIONS
1.0L Engine

Components	English	Metric
Air Cleaner -to- Cylinder Head Bolt	89 inch lbs.	10 Nm
Connecting Rod Bearing Cap Nuts	26 ft. lbs.	35 Nm
Camshaft Housing Bolts	97 inch lbs.	11 Nm
Camshaft Timing Gear Bolt	44 ft. lbs.	60 Nm
Coolant Pump Pulley Bolts	18 ft. lbs.	24 Nm
Crankshaft Pulley Bolts	12 ft. lbs.	16 Nm
Crankshaft Timing Gear Bolt	96 ft. lbs.	130 Nm
Cylinder Head -to- Block Bolts	54 ft. lbs.	73 Nm
Cylinder Head Cover Bolts	44 inch lbs.	5 Nm
Engine Oil Drain Plug	26 ft. lbs.	35 Nm
Engine Oil Pan Bolts and Nuts	97 inch lbs.	11 Nm
Exhaust Manifold Bolts and Nuts	17 ft. lbs.	23 Nm
Exhaust Manifold-to-Cylinder Head Bolts and Nuts	17 ft. lbs.	23 Nm
Exhaust Manifold-to-Front Pipe/Three Way Catalytic Converter Assembly Bolts	33 ft. lbs.	45 Nm
Flywheel Retaining Bolts: Automatic Transaxle	45 ft. lbs.	61 Nm
Flywheel Retaining Bolts: Manual Transaxle	45 ft. lbs.	61 Nm
Alternator Mounting Bolts and Nuts	57 ft. lbs.	77 Nm
Guide Tube Bolts	97 inch lbs.	11 Nm
Heat Shield Bolts	4 ft. lbs.	6 Nm
Intake Manifold Mounting Bolts	17 ft. lbs.	23 Nm
Lower Alternator Cover Bolts	49 inch lbs.	5.5 Nm
Lower Rear Mounting Bracket Retaining Bolts and Nuts	41 ft.lbs.	55 Nm
Main Bearing Bolts	40 ft. lbs.	54 Nm
Mount Through Bolt	41 ft.lbs.	55 Nm
Mounting Bracket Bolts	41 ft.lbs.	55 Nm
Oil Pressure Switch	10 ft. lbs.	14 Nm
Oil Pump Mounting Bolts	97 inch lbs.	11 Nm
Oil Pump Strainer Bolt	97 inch lbs.	11 Nm
Oil Pump Strainer Bracket Bolt	97 inch lbs.	11 Nm
Rear Engine Mount Through Bolt and Nut	41 ft.lbs.	55 Nm
Rear Engine Mount -to- Bulkhead Bolts	41 ft.lbs.	55 Nm
Rear Main Seal Housing Bolts	106 inch lbs.	12 Nm
Muffler/Tail Pipe Assembly -to- Front Pipe	29 ft. lbs.	40 Nm
Right Engine Mount -to- Mounting Bracket Bolts	41 ft.lbs.	55 Nm
Timing Belt Cover Nuts and Bolts	97 inch lbs.	11 Nm
Timing Belt Tensioner Bolt	20 ft. lbs.	27 Nm
Timing Belt Tensioner Stud	97 inch lbs.	11 Nm
Torque Rod Bracket Bolts	41 ft.lbs.	55 Nm
Torque Rod -to- Frame Through Bolt	41 ft.lbs.	55 Nm
Torque Rod -to- Torque Rod Bracket Through Bolt and Nut	41 ft.lbs.	55 Nm
Upper Alternator Adjustment Bolt	17 ft. lbs.	23 Nm
Upper Rear Mounting Bracket Retaining Nuts	41 ft.lbs.	55 Nm

TORQUE SPECIFICATIONS
1.3L Engine

Components	English	Metric
Adjusting Screw Locknut	13 ft. lbs.	17 Nm
Air Cleaner -to- Cylinder Head Bolt	89 inch lbs.	10 Nm
Connecting Rod Bearing Cap Nuts	26 ft. lbs.	35 Nm
Camshaft Timing Gear Bolt	44 ft. lbs.	60 Nm
Coolant Pump Pulley Bolts	18 ft. lbs.	24 Nm
Crankshaft Pulley Bolts	12 ft. lbs.	16 Nm
Crankshaft Timing Gear Bolt	96 ft. lbs.	130 Nm
Cylinder Head -to- Block Bolts		
1998 and earlier models	54 ft. lbs.	73 Nm
1999 and later models	49 ft. lbs.	68 Nm
Cylinder Head Cover Bolts		
1998 and earlier models	44 inch lbs.	5 Nm
1999 and later models	97 inch lbs.	11 Nm
Engine Oil Drain Plug	26 ft. lbs.	35 Nm
Engine Oil Pan Bolts and Nuts	97 inch lbs.	11 Nm
Exhaust Manifold Bolts and Nuts	17 ft. lbs.	23 Nm
Exhaust Manifold-to-Cylinder Head Bolts and Nuts	17 ft. lbs.	23 Nm
Exhaust Manifold-to-Front Pipe/Three Way Catalytic Converter Assembly Bolts	33 ft. lbs.	45 Nm
Front Pipe/Catalytic Converter Assembly -to- Resonator/Center Pipe Nuts	26 ft. lbs.	35 Nm
Flywheel Retaining Bolts: Automatic Transaxle	45 ft. lbs.	61 Nm
Flywheel Retaining Bolts: Manual Transaxle	45 ft. lbs.	61 Nm
Alternator Mounting Bolts and Nuts	17 ft. lbs.	23 Nm
Guide Tube Bolts	97 inch lbs.	11 Nm
Heat Shield Bolts	11 ft. lbs.	15 Nm
Intake Maninfold Mounting Bolts	17 ft. lbs.	23 Nm
Lower Rear Mounting Bracket Retaining Bolts and Nuts	41 ft.lbs.	55 Nm
Main Bearing Bolts	40 ft. lbs.	54 Nm
Mounting Bracket Bolts	41 ft.lbs.	55 Nm
Oil Pressure Switch	10 ft. lbs.	14 Nm
Oil Pump Mounting Bolts	97 inch lbs.	11 Nm
Oil Pump Strainer Bolt	97 inch lbs.	11 Nm
Oil Pump Strainer Bracket Bolt	97 inch lbs.	11 Nm
Rear Engine Mount Through Bolt and Nut	41 ft.lbs.	55 Nm
Rear Engine Mount -to- Bulkhead Bolts	41 ft.lbs.	55 Nm
Rear Main Seal Housing Bolts	106 inch lbs.	12 Nm
Muffler/Tail Pipe Assembly -to- Front Pipe	26 ft. lbs.	35 Nm
Right Engine Mount -to- Mounting Bracket Bolts	41 ft.lbs.	55 Nm
Right Engine Mount Through Bolt	41 ft.lbs.	55 Nm
Timing Belt Cover Nuts and Bolts	97 inch lbs.	11 Nm
Timing Belt Tensioner Bolt	20 ft. lbs.	27 Nm
Timing Belt Tensioner Stud	97 inch lbs.	11 Nm
Torque Rod Bracket Bolts	41 ft.lbs.	55 Nm
Torque Rod -to- Frame Through Bolt	41 ft.lbs.	55 Nm
Torque Rod -to- Torque Rod Bracket Through Bolt and Nut	41 ft.lbs.	55 Nm
Upper Alternator Adjustment Bolt	17 ft. lbs.	23 Nm
Upper Rear Mounting Bracket Retaining Nuts	41 ft.lbs.	55 Nm

Engine 1.0L & 1.3L

REMOVAL & INSTALLATION

In the process of removing the engine, you will come across a number of steps which call for the removal of a separate component or system, such as "disconnect the exhaust system" or "remove the radiator." In most instances, a detailed removal procedure can be found elsewhere in this manual.

It is virtually impossible to list each individual wire and hose which must be disconnected. Careful observation and common sense are the best possible approaches to any repair procedure.

Removal and installation of the engine can be made easier if you follow these basic points:

- If you have to drain any of the fluids, use a suitable container.
- Always tag any wires or hoses and, if possible, the components they came from before disconnecting them.
- Because there are so many bolts and fasteners involved, store and label the retainers from components separately in muffin pans, jars or coffee cans. This will prevent confusion during installation.
- After unbolting the transmission or transaxle, always make sure it is properly supported.
- If it is necessary to disconnect the air conditioning system, have this service performed by a qualified technician using a recovery/recycling station. If the system does not have to be disconnected, unbolt the compressor and set it aside.
- When unbolting the engine mounts, always make sure the engine is properly supported. When removing the engine, make sure that any lifting devices are properly attached to the engine. It is recommended that if your engine is supplied with lifting hooks, your lifting apparatus be attached to them.
- Lift the engine from its compartment slowly, checking that no hoses, wires or other components are still connected.
- After the engine is clear of the compartment, place it on an engine stand or workbench.
- After the engine has been removed, you can perform a partial or full teardown of the engine using the procedures outlined in this manual.

1. Relieve the fuel system pressure on fuel injected vehicles.
2. Using a scratch awl, scribe the hood hinge-to-hood outline, then, using an assistant remove the hood.
3. Make a note of all radio pre-sets and the radio code.
4. Disconnect the negative battery cable. Drain the cooling system.

❄❊❄ CAUTION:

When draining the coolant, keep in mind that cats and dogs are attracted by the ethylene glycol antifreeze, and are quite likely to drink any that is left in an uncovered container or in puddles on the ground. This will prove fatal in sufficient quantity. Always drain the coolant into a sealable container. Coolant should be reused unless it is contaminated or several years old.

5. Remove the air cleaner assembly. Remove the radiator assembly along with the cooling fan.
6. Disconnect and tag all necessary electrical connections.
7. Disconnect and tag all necessary vacuum lines.
8. Disconnect, tag and plug all necessary fuel lines.
9. Disconnect the heater inlet and outlet hoses.
10. Disconnect the following cables:
    a. The accelerator cable from the throttle body or carburetor.
    b. The clutch cable from the transaxle (for manual transaxle models).
    c. The gear select cable and the oil pressure control cable from the transaxle (for automatic transaxle models).
    d. The speedometer cable from the transaxle.
11. Raise and safely support the vehicle safely.
12. Disconnect the exhaust pipe from the exhaust manifold.
13. Disconnect the gear shift control shaft and the extension to the transaxle for (manual transaxle models).
14. Drain the engine oil and transaxle oil.
15. Remove the drive axles from the differential side gears of the transaxle. For the engine/transaxle removal, it is not necessary to remove the drive axle

from the steering knuckle.
16. Remove the engine rear torque rod bracket from the transaxle (for automatic transaxle models).
17. Lower the vehicle.
18. Install a suitable chain hoist to the lifting device on the engine.
19. Remove the right side engine mounting from its bracket.
20. On vehicles equipped with a automatic transaxle, remove the transaxle rear mounting nut.
21. On vehicles equipped with a manual transaxle, remove the transaxle rear mounting from the body.
22. Remove the transaxle left side mounting bracket.
23. Lift the engine and transaxle assembly out from the vehicle. Separate the transaxle from the engine.

To install:

24. Install the transaxle to the engine, then a suitable hoist onto the engine lifting brackets.
25. Install engine and transaxle into vehicle and leave the hoist connected to the lifting device.
26. On vehicles equipped with a automatic transaxle, install the transaxle rear mounting nut.
27. On vehicles equipped with a manual transaxle, install the transaxle rear mounting from the body.
28. Install the transaxle left side mounting bracket.
29. Install the transaxle right side engine mounting to its bracket.
30. Tighten all the bolts and nuts.
31. Remove the lifting device.
32. To complete the installation procedure, reverse the removal procedure.
33. Adjust the clutch pedal free-play.
34. Adjust the gear select cable, and oil pressure control cable.
35. Adjust the accelerator cable play.
36. Refill the transaxle with the recommended fluid. Do the same for the engine oil and engine coolant.
37. Reconnect the negative battery cable. Start the engine and check for leakage of any kind. Make all necessary repairs and adjustments.
38. Torque the transaxle-to-engine bolts and nuts to 37 ft. lbs.. (50 Nm).
39. Torque the engine mounting nuts to 37 ft. lbs.. (50 Nm).
40. Torque the engine mounting left hand bracket bolts to 37 ft. lbs.. (50 Nm).
41. Torque the exhaust pipe to manifold bolts to 37 ft. lbs.. (50 Nm).
42. Torque the flywheel retaining bolts to 47 ft. lbs.. (64 Nm).

Rocker Arm (Valve) Cover

REMOVAL & INSTALLATION

See Figures 1, 2, 3, 4, 5 and 6

1. Disconnect the negative battery cable.
2. Remove the air cleaner assembly.
3. Remove the spark plug wire retaining clips. Lay the spark plug wires aside.
4. Disconnect the PCV valve hose.
5. Remove the nuts and seal washers located under the nuts.
6. Remove the valve cover from the cylinder head.

To install:

7. Apply a small amount of silicone sealant to the corners of the new valve cover gasket.

❄❊❄ CAUTION:

Be sure not to block the oil drain hole, located at the front of the cylinder head opening, with silicone sealant. This could cause excessive oil pressure with the cylinder head, resulting in a possible oil leak.

8. Install the new gasket.
9. Install the valve cover and secure with new seal washers and nuts.

Fig. 1 Overall view of the valve cover at the top of the engine.

Fig. 2 Removing the air cleaner-to-valve cover brace bolt

Fig. 3 Removing the PCV valve hose from the valve cover

Fig. 4 Removing the valve cover retaining nuts

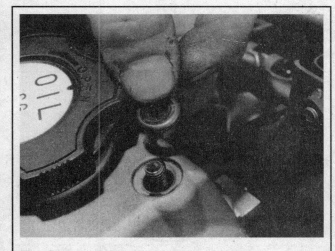

Fig. 5 Removing the valve cover seal washers. Always use new seal washers during installation

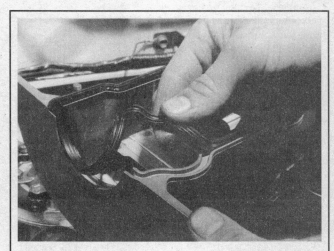

Fig. 6 When installing the valve cover gasket, place a small amount of silicone sealant at the corners of the valve cover

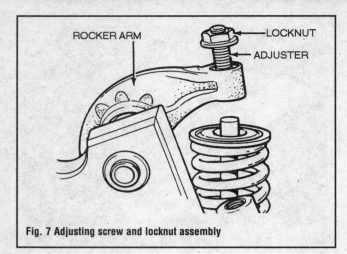

Fig. 7 Adjusting screw and locknut assembly

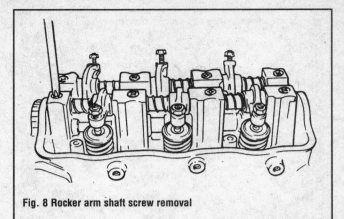

Fig. 8 Rocker arm shaft screw removal

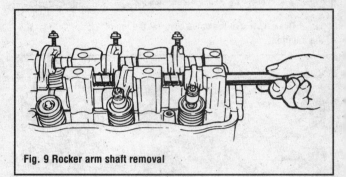

Fig. 9 Rocker arm shaft removal

Tighten nuts to 44 inch lbs. (5 Nm).

10. Install the spark plug wire retaining clips. Route the spark plug wires in their original position.

11. Install the air cleaner assembly.

12. Connect the negative battery cable.

Rocker Arm/Shafts

REMOVAL & INSTALLATION

1985 - 88 Sprint & 1.3L Engine
See Figures 7, 8 and 9

1. Disconnect the negative battery cable.
2. Disconnect positive battery cable and remove the battery.
3. Remove the A/C compressor and bracket if equipped.
4. Remove the air cleaner and cylinder head cover.
5. Remove the distributor cap, then mark the position of the rotor and the distributor housing with the cylinder head. Remove the distributor and the case from the cylinder head.
6. After loosening all valve adjusting screw lock nuts, turn the adjusting screws back all the way to allow all rocker arms to move freely (Sprint only).

Note: Rocker arm shafts are of different sizes. Mark the intake and exhaust rocker arm shafts for installation reference.

7. Remove the rocker shaft screws.
8. Remove the intake and exhaust rocker arm shafts, then the rocker arms and springs.

To install:

9. Apply engine oil to all rocker arms and rocker arm shafts.
10. Install rocker arms, springs and rocker arm shafts.

Note: Rocker arm shafts are of different sizes. Install the intake rocker arm shaft facing its stepped end to the camshaft pulley side. Install the exhaust rocker arm shaft facing its stepped end to the distributor side.

11. Tighten rocker arm shaft bolts to 7 - 9 ft. lbs.. (9 - 12 Nm).
12. Install distributor and distributor cap, aligning them with the match-marks make during removal.
13. Adjust the valve lash.
14. Install the cylinder head cover.
15. Install the air cleaner.
16. Install the A/C compressor and bracket if equipped.
17. Install the battery and connect positive battery cable.
18. Connect the negative battery cable.
19. Start the engine and allow it to reach operating temperature. Check for leaks.

1.0L Metro

The 1.0L Metro does not use rocker arms or rocker arm shafts. It is equipped with hydraulic valve lash adjusters, which are incorporated into the head.

Thermostat

REMOVAL & INSTALLATION

See Figure 10

1. Disconnect the battery negative cable.
2. Drain cooling system to a level below the thermostat.
3. Remove the air cleaner.
4. Disconnect the electrical connectors at the thermostat cap.
5. Remove the inlet hose, cap mounting bolts and the thermostat from the thermostat housing.
6. Clean the gasket mounting surfaces. Ensure that the thermostat air bleed hose is clear.

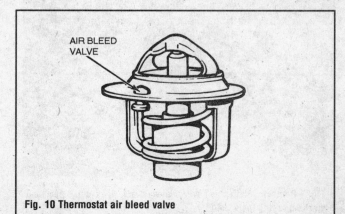

Fig. 10 Thermostat air bleed valve

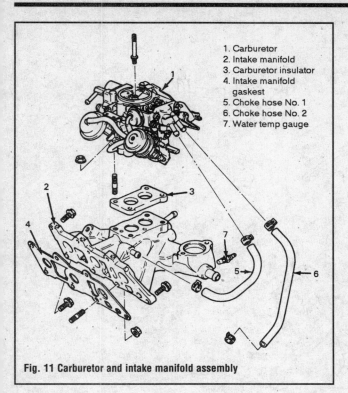

1. Carburetor
2. Intake manifold
3. Carburetor insulator
4. Intake manifold gaskest
5. Choke hose No. 1
6. Choke hose No. 2
7. Water temp gauge

Fig. 11 Carburetor and intake manifold assembly

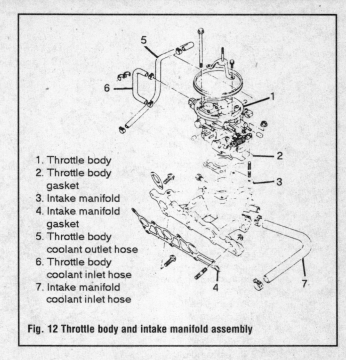

1. Throttle body
2. Throttle body gasket
3. Intake manifold
4. Intake manifold gasket
5. Throttle body coolant outlet hose
6. Throttle body coolant inlet hose
7. Intake manifold coolant inlet hose

Fig. 12 Throttle body and intake manifold assembly

To install:

7. Install thermostat into housing with the spring side down.
8. Install the thermostat housing using a new gasket. Tighten bolts to 15 ft. lbs.. (20 Nm).
9. Install the inlet hose and tighten clap securely.
10. Fill cooling system.
11. Connect the battery negative cable. Start engine and check for leaks.

Intake Manifold

REMOVAL & INSTALLATION

See Figures 11 and 12

1. On fuel injected models, relieve the fuel system pressure.
2. Disconnect the negative battery cable.
3. Drain the cooling system.

❊❊ CAUTION:

When draining the coolant, keep in mind that cats and dogs are attracted by the ethylene glycol antifreeze, and are quite likely to drink any that is left in an uncovered container or in puddles on the ground. This will prove fatal in sufficient quantity. Always drain the coolant into a sealable container. Coolant should be reused unless it is contaminated or several years old.

4. Remove the air cleaner assembly.
5. Label and disconnect all electrical connectors from the intake manifold.
6. Label and disconnect the fuel return and feed hoses from the throttle body or carburetor.
7. Disconnect the water hoses from the throttle body and the intake manifold.
8. Label and disconnect all vacuum hoses from the intake manifold.
9. Remove the air intake hose from intercooler to throttle body on turbocharged models.
10. Disconnect the PCV hose from the cylinder head cover.

11. Disconnect the accelerator cable from the throttle body or carburetor.
12. Disconnect any other lines and cables, as necessary.
13. Remove the intake manifold with the throttle body or carburetor from the cylinder head.

To install:

14. Install the intake manifold to the cylinder head, using a new gasket, install the clamps, and tighten the intake manifold retaining bolts to 17 ft. lbs.. (23 Nm).
15. Reinstall all vacuum and water hoses.
16. Install the fuel feed and return hoses.
17. Install all electrical lead wires.
18. Install the air intake hose from intercooler to throttle body on turbocharged models.
19. Install the accelerator cable to the throttle body or carburetor. Adjust to specification.
20. Install the air cleaner assembly.
21. Fill the cooling system and reconnect the negative battery cable.
22. Start the engine and check for vacuum leaks.

Exhaust Manifold

REMOVAL & INSTALLATION

1.0L Engine

1. Disconnect the negative battery cable.
2. Remove the turbocharger assembly, as required.
3. Disconnect the oxygen sensor coupler.
4. Remove the exhaust pipe from the exhaust manifold.
5. Remove the manifold retaining bolts and remove the exhaust manifold and gaskets.

To install:

6. Install a new manifold gasket and torque the bolts to 17 ft. lbs.. (23 Nm).
7. Install the turbocharger assembly, as required.
8. Install the exhaust pipe and tighten bolts to 30 - 43 ft. lbs.. (40 - 60 Nm).
9. Reconnect the oxygen sensor coupler.
10. Connect the negative battery cable. Start the engine and check for leaks.

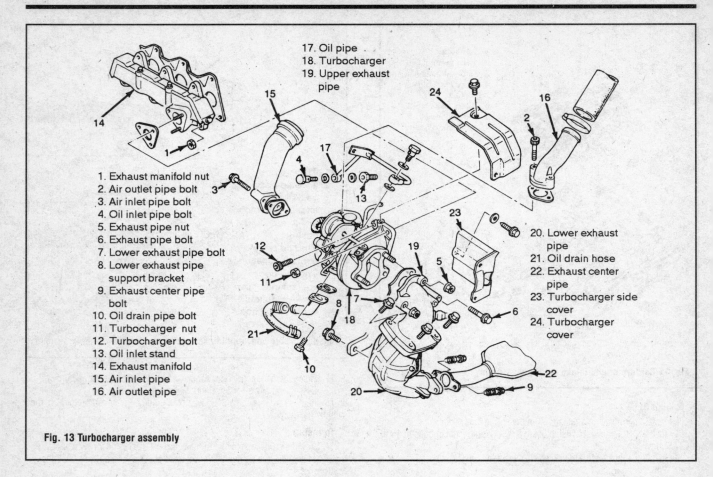

17. Oil pipe
18. Turbocharger
19. Upper exhaust pipe

1. Exhaust manifold nut
2. Air outlet pipe bolt
3. Air inlet pipe bolt
4. Oil inlet pipe bolt
5. Exhaust pipe nut
6. Exhaust pipe bolt
7. Lower exhaust pipe bolt
8. Lower exhaust pipe support bracket
9. Exhaust center pipe bolt
10. Oil drain pipe bolt
11. Turbocharger nut
12. Turbocharger bolt
13. Oil inlet stand
14. Exhaust manifold
15. Air inlet pipe
16. Air outlet pipe

20. Lower exhaust pipe
21. Oil drain hose
22. Exhaust center pipe
23. Turbocharger side cover
24. Turbocharger cover

Fig. 13 Turbocharger assembly

1.3L Engine

1. Disconnect the negative battery cable.
2. Raise and safely support the vehicle.
3. Separate the front pipe/catalytic converter assembly from the exhaust manifold.
4. Lower the vehicle.
5. Disconnect the oxygen sensor electrical connector.
6. Remove the heat shield from the manifold.
7. Remove the spark plug wires from the spark plugs.
8. Remove the exhaust manifold and gasket from the cylinder head.

To install

9. Be sure the mating surface is clean and free or debris.
10. Install a new manifold gasket and torque the bolts to 17 ft. lbs.. (23 Nm).
11. Install the heat shield..
12. Raise the vehicle.
13. Connect the front pipe/catalytic converter assembly to the exhaust manifold using a new seal. Torque to 37 ft. lbs. (50 Nm).
14. Lower the vehicle.
15. Connect the oxygen sensor electrical connector.
16. Connect the negative battery cable. Start the engine and check for leaks.

Turbocharger

REMOVAL & INSTALLATION

See Figure 13

1. Disconnect the negative battery cable.
2. Drain the cooling system.

☀ CAUTION:

When draining the coolant, keep in mind that cats and dogs are attracted by the ethylene glycol antifreeze, and are quite likely to drink any that is left in an uncovered container or in puddles on the ground. This will prove fatal in sufficient quantity. Always drain the coolant into a sealable container. Coolant should be reused unless it is contaminated or several years old.

3. As required, remove the hood and front grille to gain access to components.
4. Remove the intercooler.
5. Remove the radiator hoses and fan motor electrical connector.
6. Remove the front upper member.
7. Remove the radiator and air conditioning condenser.
8. Remove the front bumper.
9. Remove the exhaust pipe bolts.
10. Remove the air conditioning compressor and lay it aside.
11. Remove the turbocharger top and side covers.
12. Disconnect the oxygen sensor electrical connector.
13. Remove the upper and lower exhaust pipes as a unit after removing the bracket bolt.
14. Remove the air inlet and outlet pipes from the turbocharger.
15. Remove the turbocharger oil pipes from the cylinder block.
16. Remove the turbocharger water pipes.
17. Unbolt and remove the turbocharger.

To install:

18. Turn the turbocharger by hand and check the blades for damage. Check the inside of the housing for oil deposits. If found, replace the turbocharger assembly.
19. Check the oil pipe orifices for clogs. If found clear the obstruction.

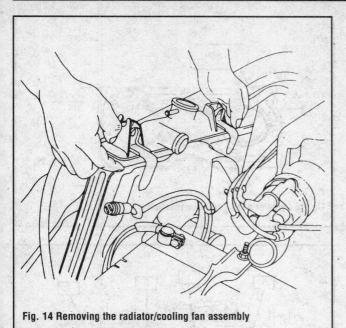

Fig. 14 Removing the radiator/cooling fan assembly

20. Install the air inlet pipe to the turbocharger using a new gasket. Tighten bolts to 6 - 8 ft. lbs. (8 - 12 Nm).

21. Install the oil pipe to the turbocharger and air inlet pipe using a new gasket.

22. Install the turbocharger on the exhaust manifold using a new gasket. Tighten bolts to 13 - 20 ft. lbs.. (18 - 28 Nm).

23. Install the water hoses to the turbocharger and cylinder head.

24. Install the oil drain hose. Tighten to 3 - 5 ft. lbs.. (4 - 7 Nm).

25. Install the oil inlet pipe on the cylinder head using a new gasket. Tighten to 8 - 10 ft. lbs.. (11 - 15 Nm).

26. Install the air inlet tube clamp bolt to the cylinder head.

27. Install the air outlet pipe using a new gasket. Tighten bolt to 6 - 8 ft. lbs.. (8 - 12 Nm).

28. Install the upper and lower exhaust pipes. Tighten bolts to 18 - 25 ft. lbs.. (25 - 35 Nm) and nuts to 13 - 20 ft. lbs.. (18 - 28 Nm).

29. Install the lower exhaust pipe bracket bolt and tighten to 29 - 43 ft. lbs.. (40 - 60 Nm).

30. Install the turbocharger covers.

31. Connect the oxygen sensor electrical connector.

32. Install the air conditioning compressor and belt.

33. Install the front bumper, radiator, and air conditioning condenser.

34. Connect the radiator fan motor electrical connector.

35. Install the radiator hoses, intercooler, front grille, and hood.

36. Fill the engine with coolant and connect the negative battery cable.

37. Start the engine and allow it to reach normal operating temperature. Check for leaks.

Intercooler

REMOVAL & INSTALLATION

1. Remove the intercooler cover.
2. Remove the intercooler inlet and outlet hoses
3. Remove the intercooler.
4. Remove the relief valve from the intercooler.

To install:

5. Check the intercooler for cracks or damage. Blow air into the relief valve and confirm that air does not come through. Also push relief valve and check spring for setting and damage, and valve for looseness. If defective replace valve.

6. Install relief valve using new gasket. Install screws using Loctite, or equivalent.

7. Install intercooler.

8. Install inlet and outlet hoses.

9. Install intercooler cover.

Radiator

REMOVAL & INSTALLATION

See Figure 14

1. Disconnect the battery negative cable.
2. Drain the cooling system.

✻✻ CAUTION:

When draining the coolant, keep in mind that cats and dogs are attracted by the ethylene glycol antifreeze, and are quite likely to drink any that is left in an uncovered container or in puddles on the ground. This will prove fatal in sufficient quantity. Always drain the coolant into a sealable container. Coolant should be reused unless it is contaminated or several years old.

3. Disconnect the cooling fan motor electrical connector and the air inlet hose.

4. Remove the upper, lower and reservoir tank hoses from the radiator.

5. If equipped with automatic transaxle, disconnect the oil cooler lines from the radiator and plug them to prevent oil spills.

6. Remove the mounting bolts and lift the radiator from the vehicle with the cooling fan attached.

7. Remove the cooling fan and shroud.

To install:

8. Install the cooling fan and shroud on the radiator. Tighten bolts to 89 inch lbs.. (10 Nm).

9. Place the radiator in the vehicle and install the mounting bolts. Tighten bolts to 89 inch lbs.. (10 Nm).

10. If equipped with automatic transaxle, connect the oil cooler lines to the radiator.

11. Install the upper, lower and reservoir tank hoses on the radiator.

12. Connect the cooling fan motor electrical connector and the air inlet hose.

13. Fill the cooling system and connect the negative battery cable.

14. Start the engine, allow it to reach operating temperature and check the cooling system for leaks. Refill the system as necessary.

Engine Fan

REMOVAL & INSTALLATION

1. Disconnect the negative battery cable.
2. Label and disconnect the electrical connector from the cooling fan motor.

3. Remove the fan shroud-to-radiator frame bolts and the fan/shroud assembly from the vehicle.

4. Remove the fan blade-to-motor nut, fan blade, and washer.

5. Remove the fan-to-shroud bolts and the fan motor from the shroud.

To install:

6. Install the fan motor in the shroud.
7. Install the fan blade on the motor.
8. Install the fan shroud on the radiator and tighten bolts to 89 inch lbs.. (10 Nm).

9. Connect the fan motor electrical connector.
10. Connect the negative battery cable.
11. Test fan motor for proper operation.

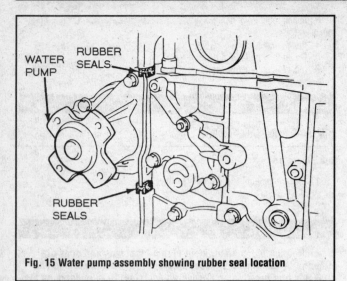

Fig. 15 Water pump assembly showing rubber seal location

Water Pump

REMOVAL & INSTALLATION

See Figure 15

1. Disconnect the negative battery cable.
2. Drain the cooling system.

✳ CAUTION:

When draining the coolant, keep in mind that cats and dogs are attracted by the ethylene glycol antifreeze, and are quite likely to drink any that is left in an uncovered container or in puddles on the ground. This will prove fatal in sufficient quantity. Always drain the coolant into a sealable container. Coolant should be reused unless it is contaminated or several years old.

3. Remove the air cleaner assembly.
4. Loosen but do not remove the four water pump pulley bolts.
5. Raise and support the vehicle safely.
6. Remove the lower splash shield.
7. Remove the air conditioner compressor drive belt.
8. Remove the lower alternator cover plate bolts, loosen the alternator adjusting bolt, and remove the drive belt.
9. Remove the crankshaft pulley.
10. Remove the water pump pulley.
11. Remove the timing belt.
12. Remove the oil level dipstick and guide tube.
13. Remove the alternator adjusting bracket from the water pump.
14. Remove the water pump rubber seals.
15. Remove the water pump mounting bolts and nuts. Remove the water pump from the vehicle.

To install:

16. Clean the gasket mating surfaces thoroughly.
17. Check the water pump by hand for smooth operation. If the pump does not operate smoothly or is noisy, replace it.
18. Install the pump using a new gasket. Tighten bolts to 115 inch lbs.. (13 Nm).
19. Install new rubber seals.
20. Install the upper alternator adjusting bracket and tighten bolt to 17 ft. lbs.. (23 Nm).
21. Install the oil level dipstick and guide tube.
22. Install the timing belt.

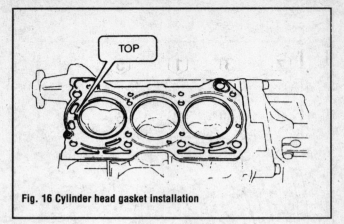

Fig. 16 Cylinder head gasket installation

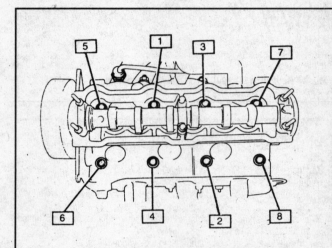

Fig. 17 Cylinder head tightening sequence - 3-cylinder Metro shown, 3-cylinder Sprint similar

23. Install the water pump pulley and leave the bolts hand tight.
24. Install the crankshaft pulley.
25. Install the water pump/alternator drive belt.
26. Install the lower alternator cover plate and tighten bolts to 89 inch lbs.. (10 Nm).
27. Install the air conditioner compressor drive belt by releasing the tensioner pulley and installing belt.
28. Install the lower splash shield and lower vehicle.
29. Tighten water pump pulley mounting bolts to 18 ft. lbs.. (24 Nm).
30. Adjust the water pump drive belt tension and tighten alternator adjustment bolt to 17 ft. lbs.. (23 Nm).
31. Install the air cleaner assembly.
32. Refill the cooling system.
33. Connect the negative battery cable.
34. Start the engine and allow it to reach operating temperature. Check for leaks and refill cooling system as necessary.

Cylinder Head

REMOVAL & INSTALLATION

See Figures 16, 17 and 18

1. On fuel injected vehicles, relieve the fuel system pressure.
2. Disconnect the negative battery cable.
3. Drain the cooling system.

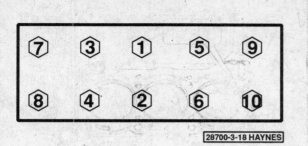

Fig. 18 Cylinder head tightening sequence - 1.3L four-cylinder engine

✳✳ CAUTION:

When draining the coolant, keep in mind that cats and dogs are attracted by the ethylene glycol antifreeze, and are quite likely to drink any that is left in an uncovered container or in puddles on the ground. This will prove fatal in sufficient quantity. Always drain the coolant into a sealable container. Coolant should be reused unless it is contaminated or several years old.

4. Label and disconnect all necessary electrical connectors.
5. Label and disconnect all necessary vacuum, fuel, and water hoses.
6. Remove the intake manifold with the carburetor or throttle body installed.
7. Remove the exhaust manifold.
8. Remove the timing belt and belt tensioner.
9. Remove the distributor cap, then mark the position of the rotor and the distributor housing with the cylinder head. Remove the distributor and the case from the cylinder head.
10. Remove the cylinder head cover.
11. Back off all valve lash adjusters until valves are closed if applicable.
12. Loosen and remove the cylinder head bolts in the reverse order of the tightening sequence.
13. Remove the cylinder head from the engine. Discard the cylinder head gasket.

To install:

Note: Before reassembly, the cylinder head should be cleaned and inspected. Refer to Engine Reconditioning for further information on the procedures that should be followed.

14. Install the cylinder head gasket with the TOP indicator facing upward and to the crankshaft pulley side.
15. Install the cylinder head and eight cylinder head bolts. Lubricate the head bolts with engine oil prior to installation.
16. Tighten cylinder head bolts in the proper sequence to 54 ft. lbs. (73 Nm) on 1998 and earlier models, or 49 ft. lbs. (68 Nm) on 1999 and later models.. Repeat tighten sequence several times before reaching specified torque figure.
17. Install rubber seals between the water pump and the cylinder head.
18. Install the cylinder head cover and secure with nuts and new seal washers. Tighten nuts to 44 inch lbs.. (5 Nm) on 1998 and earlier models, or 97 inch lis (11 Nm) on 1999 and later models.
19. Install timing belt and tensioner.
20. Install the distributor, aligning the matchmarks made during removal.
21. Install the intake manifold.
22. Install the exhaust manifold.
23. Connect all previously removed electrical connectors.
24. Connect all previously removed vacuum, fuel, and water hoses.
25. Adjust the accessory drive belt tension.
26. Adjust the accelerator cable play.
27. Refill the cooling system.
28. Connect the negative battery cable.
29. Start the engine and allow it to reach operating temperature.
30. Check for leaks.
31. Make any necessary adjustments.

Oil Pan

REMOVAL & INSTALLATION

See Figures 19 and 20

1. Remove the negative battery cable.
2. Raise and support the vehicle safely.
3. Drain the engine oil.
4. Remove the flywheel dust cover.
5. Remove the exhaust pipe at the exhaust manifold. The 1.3L Engine will require you to separate the pipe from the center pipe and then remove the hanger in order to gain access to the oil pan.
6. Remove the crankshaft position sensor.
7. Remove the oil pan bolts, the pan and the oil pump strainer.

To install:

8. Clean the oil pan and oil pump strainer screen. Clean the gasket mating surfaces.
9. Install the oil pump strainer with a new seal. Secure with bolt and tighten to 97 inch lbs.. (11 Nm).

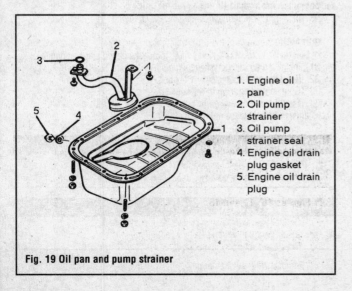

1. Engine oil pan
2. Oil pump strainer
3. Oil pump strainer seal
4. Engine oil drain plug gasket
5. Engine oil drain plug

Fig. 19 Oil pan and pump strainer

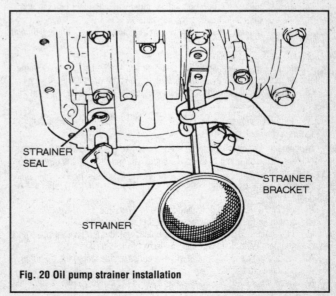

Fig. 20 Oil pump strainer installation

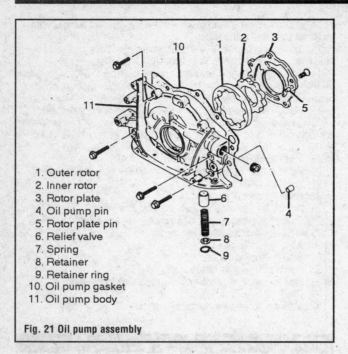

1. Outer rotor
2. Inner rotor
3. Rotor plate
4. Oil pump pin
5. Rotor plate pin
6. Relief valve
7. Spring
8. Retainer
9. Retainer ring
10. Oil pump gasket
11. Oil pump body

Fig. 21 Oil pump assembly

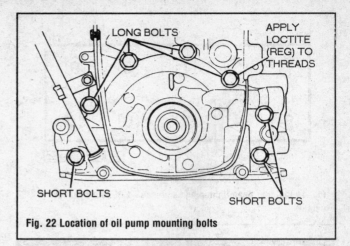

Fig. 22 Location of oil pump mounting bolts

10. Apply a continuous bead of RTV sealant to the engine oil pan and install. Tighten the oil pan bolts to 9 ft. lbs.. (11 Nm).

11. Install the oil pan drain plug with a new gasket and tighten to 26 ft. lbs. (35 Nm).

12. Install the exhaust system as necessary

13. Install the flywheel dust cover.

14. Lower the vehicle and fill the engine with oil.

15. Connect the negative battery cable, start the engine, and check for proper oil pressure and any signs of leaks.

Oil Pump

REMOVAL & INSTALLATION

See Figures 21 and 22

1. Remove the negative battery cable.
2. Raise and support the vehicle safely.
3. Drain the engine oil.
4. Remove the water pump belt, pulley, alternator, alternator bracket, and air conditioning mounting bracket, if equipped.
5. Remove the crankshaft pulley, timing belt outside cover, timing belt, and tensioner.
6. Disconnect the engine oil level gauge.
7. Remove the crankshaft timing belt gear and timing belt guide. With the crankshaft locked, remove the crankshaft timing belt pulley bolt.
8. Remove the oil pan bolts, oil pan, oil strainer fixing bolt and the oil strainer assembly.
9. Remove the oil pump bolts and the oil pump assembly.

To install:

10. Install a new oil seal into oil pump body using a seal driver.
11. Install the oil pump to the block being careful not to rip the new seal on the crankshaft.
12. Apply a thread locking compound to the four upper (short) bolts of the oil pump.
13. Install the mounting bolts and torque to 97 in. lbs. (11 Nm).
14. Install the rubber seal between the oil pump and water pump.
15. If the edge of the oil pump gasket bulges out, cut it off with a sharp knife to make it smooth and flush with the end faces of the case and block.
16. Install the timing belt guide with the concave side facing the oil pump.
17. Lock the crankshaft.
18. Install the A/C compressor and bracket to the cylinder block if equipped.

19. Install the oil strainer and oil pan.
20. Install the timing belt and the tensioner.
21. Lower the vehicle.
22. Install the guide tube with a new seal and torque to 97 inch lbs.
23. Install the dipstick.
24. Fill the engine with oil.
25. Connect negative battery cable. Start the engine and check for exhaust and oil leaks and then for oil pressure.

Crankshaft Timing Pulley

REMOVAL & INSTALLATION

1. Disconnect the negative battery cable.
2. Remove the air cleaner assembly.
3. Raise and safely support the vehicle.
4. Remove the right side splash shield.
5. Remove the A/C compressor drive belt by releasing the tensioner and removing the belt from the crankshaft pulley.
6. Lower the vehicle.
7. Remove the water pump/alternator belt by loosening the upper mounting bolt on the alternator.
8. Raise and safely support the vehicle.
9. Remove the flywheel inspection cover.
10. Lock the crankshaft.

Note: 1.3L: If the engine is still in the vehicle, the crankshaft timing sprocket bolt must be removed. If the engine is out, it is not necessary to loosen the crankshaft timing sprocket bolt.

11. Remove the crankshaft timing pulley from the engine.

To install

12. Install the crankshaft timing pulley. Torque the timing sprocket bolt to 96 ft. lbs. (130 Nm). Torque the crankshaft timing pulley bolts to 12 ft. lbs. (16 Nm).
13. Install the water pump/alternator belt.
14. Raise and safely support the vehicle.
15. Install the A/C compressor belt.
16. Install the right side splash shield.
17. Lower the vehicle.
18. Adjust the belts to proper tension.
19. torque the upper alternator mounting bolt to 17 ft. lbs. (23 Nm).
20. Install the air cleaner assembly.
21. Install the negative battery cable.

Timing Belt Cover

REMOVAL & INSTALLATION

1. Remove the crankshaft pulley.

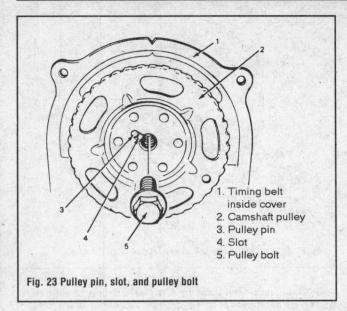

1. Timing belt inside cover
2. Camshaft pulley
3. Pulley pin
4. Slot
5. Pulley bolt

Fig. 23 Pulley pin, slot, and pulley bolt

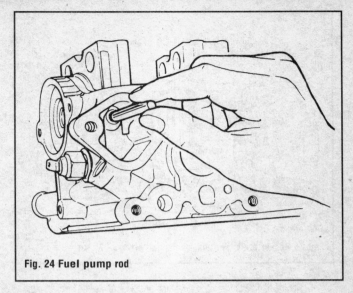

Fig. 24 Fuel pump rod

2. Disconnect the wiring harness and retaining clips from the timing belt cover.
3. Remove the air cleaner resonator.
4. Remove the water pump pulley.
5. Remove the eight bolts and one nut to remove the cover from the engine.

To install

6. Install the cover and torque the bolts and nut to 97 in. lbs. (11 Nm).
7. Install the water pump pulley.
8. Install the air cleaner resonator.
9. Connect the wiring harness to the timing belt cover.
10. Install the crankshaft pulley.

Timing Belt and Sprockets

For the service intervals please refer to General Information and Maintenance.

The timing belt is the component that allows the engine to breathe. With the tolerances of today's engines, maximum efficiency is achieved by timing the opening of valves against the rise of the piston. If the two come out of time, mechanical contact will occur and damage is a certainty. It is an absolute must that you follow the recommended service interval for the timing belt. Should the timing belt break or jump a few teeth, a very hefty repair bill will follow. As stated earlier in this book, maintenance is cheaper than repair.

REMOVAL & INSTALLATION

Timing Belt

1. Remove the timing belt cover.
2. Align the upper and lower timing marks.
3. Loosen the timing belt tensioner. Push the tensioner by hand.
4. Remove the belt.
5. Remove the tensioner, tensioner plate, tensioner spring, and the spring damper.
6. Inspect the components thoroughly. Refer to the inspection points below.

To install

7. Install the tensioner plate to the tensioner.
8. Install the tensioner assembly to the block but, do not torque down. Make sure that the arrow matches the plate movement.
9. Be sure that the timing marks are aligned.
10. Remove the cylinder head cover.
11. Loosen all the valve adjusting screws.
12. Install the timing belt with the tensioner spring and damper with the tim-

ing mark aligned and the tensioner pushed up.
13. With no slack, install the timing belt. Then put the tensioner stud in.
14. Turn the crankshaft two rotations clockwise after installing it. Make sure that there is no slack in the belt and torque the stud to 97 in. lbs. (11 Nm) and the tensioner bolt to 20 ft. lbs. (27 Nm).
15. Install the timing belt cover.

Camshaft Timing Sprocket

1. Lock the camshaft using a 0.39 in. (10 mm) rod inserted into the hole in the cam.

Note: Be sure to protect the machined surfaces of the cylinder head with a shop rag or other suitable object during the removal and installation of the sprocket.

2. Remove the retaining bolt from the cam.
3. Remove the sprocket.

To install

4. Place the sprocket on the cam.
5. Torque the bolt to 44 ft. lbs. (60 Nm).
6. Remove the locking rod from the cam.

INSPECTION

The belt and tensioner should be checked for:
- Hardening of the rubber.
- Cracking or peeling of the backing.
- Cracking ribs.
- Cracking on the side of the belt.
- Missing teeth or parts of teeth.
- Abnormal wear on the side of the belt.
- Rough operation of the tensioner.

If any of these are noticed, replace the belt. If the belt does not exhibit any of the above mentioned conditions, the belt is good. The belt MUST be replaced at the recommended service interval.

Camshaft, Bearings and Lifters

REMOVAL & INSTALLATION

Sprint & 1.3L Engine

See Figures 23, 24 and 25

1. Disconnect the negative battery cable.
2. Remove the air cleaner assembly.
3. Remove the cylinder head cover assembly.

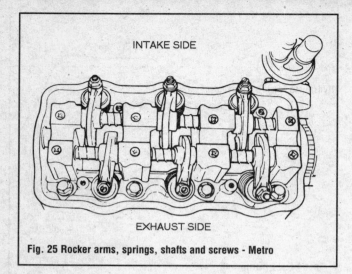

Fig. 25 Rocker arms, springs, shafts and screws - Metro

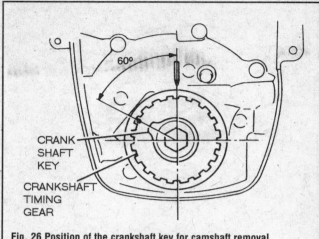

Fig. 26 Position of the crankshaft key for camshaft removal

4. Set the engine up on top dead center of the compression stroke on the No. 1 cylinder. Make an alignment mark on the distributor cap and engine block and remove the distributor assembly.

5. Remove the crankshaft pulley, timing belt outside cover, and the timing belt.

Note: After removing the timing belt, set the key on the crankshaft in position by turning the crankshaft. This is to prevent interference between the valves and the piston when reinstalling the camshaft.

6. Remove the camshaft timing belt gear. Lock the camshaft with a proper size rod inserted into the hole 0.39 in. (10mm) in it. Loosen the camshaft timing belt gear bolt.

Note: The mating surface of the cylinder head and cover must not be damaged in this work. So, put a clean shop cloth between the rod and mating surfaces and use care not to bump the rod against the mating surfaces hard when loosening.

7. Remove the fuel pump and fuel pump rod. Remove the camshaft from the cylinder head.

To install:

8. Apply engine oil to lobes and journals on camshaft and oil seal on cylinder head.

9. Install the camshaft into the cylinder head.

10. Install the timing belt inside cover and camshaft pulley. Fit pulley pin on camshaft into slot on camshaft pulley. Tighten the pulley bolt to 41 - 46 ft. lbs.. (55 - 64 Nm).

11. Install the fuel pump rod, gasket, and fuel pump to the cylinder head.

12. Apply engine oil to rocker arms and rocker arm shafts.

Note: The two rocker arm shafts are different. To distinguish between the two, the dimensions of their stepped ends differ. The intake rocker arm step measures 0.55 in. (14mm). The exhaust rocker arm step measures 0.59 in. (15 mm).

13. Install the intake rocker arm shaft facing its stepped end to camshaft pulley side, and the exhaust rocker arm shaft facing its stepped end to distributor side.

14. Install rocker arms, springs, and rocker arm shafts. Tighten the rocker arm shaft screws to 7 - 9 ft. lbs.. (9 - 12 Nm).

15. Install the distributor.

16. Install the belt tensioner, timing belt, outside cover, crankshaft pulley and water pump belt.

17. Adjust the intake and exhaust valves.

18. Install the cylinder head cover and air cleaner.

19. Connect the negative battery cable.

20. Adjust the ignition timing.

1.0L Engine
See Figures 26, 27, 28 and 29

1. Disconnect the negative battery cable.

2. Remove the air cleaner assembly.

3. Remove the cylinder head cover assembly.

4. Set the engine up on top dead center of the compression stroke on the No. 1 cylinder. Make an alignment mark on the distributor cap and engine block and remove the distributor assembly.

5. Remove the crankshaft pulley, timing belt outside cover, and the timing belt.

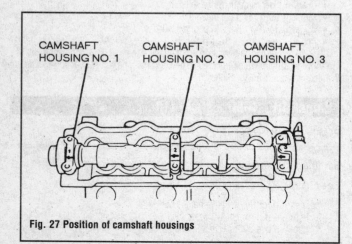

Fig. 27 Position of camshaft housings

Fig. 28 Removing the valve cover to expose the camshaft - Metro

Fig. 29 The camshaft on 3-cylinder engines is held in place by three bearing caps - Metro

Note: After removing the timing belt, set the key on the crankshaft in position by turning the crankshaft. This is to prevent interference between the valves and the piston when reinstalling the camshaft.

6. Remove the camshaft timing belt gear. Lock the camshaft with a proper size rod inserted into the hole 0.39 in. (10mm) in it. Loosen the camshaft timing belt gear bolt.

Note: The mating surface of the cylinder head and cover must not be damaged in this work. So, put a clean shop cloth between the rod and mating surfaces and use care not to bump the rod against the mating surfaces hard when loosening.

7. Remove the camshaft housings from the cylinder head.
8. Remove the camshaft from the cylinder head.
9. Remove the HVL adjusters and submerge in oil until reinstallation.

To install:

10. Fill the oil passage in the cylinder head with engine oil. Pour engine oil through camshaft journal oil holes and check that engine oil comes out from oil holes in HVL adjuster bores. Install HVL adjusters.
11. Install the camshaft to the cylinder head. After applying engine oil to the camshaft journal and all around the cam, position the camshaft into the cylinder head so that the camshaft timing belt gear pin hole in camshaft is at the lower position.
12. Install the camshaft housing to the camshaft and the cylinder head.
13. Apply the engine oil to the sliding surface of each housing against the camshaft journal.
14. Apply the sealant to the mating surface of the No. 1 and No. 3 housing which will mate with the cylinder head.
15. There are marks provided on each camshaft housing indicating position and direction for installation. Install the housing as indicated by these marks.
16. As the camshaft housing No. 1 retains the camshaft in the proper position as to the thrust direction, make sure to first fit the No. 1 housing to the No. 1 journal of the camshaft securely.
17. After applying the engine oil to the housing bolts, tighten them temporarily. Then tighten in the proper sequence. Tighten the bolts a little at a time and evenly among bolts, repeat the tightening sequence 3 to 4 times before they are tighten to the proper torque of 8 ft. lbs.. (11 Nm).
18. Install the camshaft oil seal. After applying engine oil to the oil seal lip, press-fit the camshaft oil seal until the oil seal surface becomes flush with the housing surfaces.
19. Install the camshaft timing belt gear to the camshaft after installing the dwell pin to the camshaft. While locking the camshaft, install the camshaft pulley and retaining bolt and torque the bolt to 44 ft. lbs.. (60 Nm).
20. Install the cylinder head cover to the cylinder head.
21. Install the timing belt, timing belt outside cover, crankshaft pulley, water pump pulley and water pump belt.
22. Install the distributor assembly into the engine.

23. Install the air cleaner assembly and reinstall the negative battery cable.
24. Adjust the ignition timing.

INSPECTION

Hydraulic Valve Lash Adjusters (HVL)

1. Check for pitting, scratches, or damage. If these condition occur, replace the adjuster.
2. Measure the cylinder head adjuster bore and the outside diameter to determine the clearance.
3. The standard clearance is 0.0010-0.0025 in. (0.025-0.066 mm). The limit is 0.0059 (0.15 mm).
4. If the clearance does not meet the specifications, replace the adjuster or the head.

Camshaft Runout

1. Set the camshaft on two V-blocks.
2. Using a dial indicator, measure the runout by spinning the cam.
3. If the runout exceeds 0.0039 in. (0.10 mm) replace the cam.

Journal Wear 1.0L Engine

1. Check the journals and the housing for pitting, wear, damage, or scratches.
2. Do not proceed if the above mentioned conditions are found. Replace the cam or the head if present.
3. Clean the housings and the cam.
4. Remove the HVLs and install the cam in the head.
5. Place Plastigage, across the journal parallel to the cam.
6. Install the housings, making sure not to rotate the cam, and tighten the housings to specification.
7. Start the torque sequence in the center working to the outside. Repeat the process four times.
8. Remove the housings.
9. Measure the Plastigage, at its widest point.
10. The clearance should be 0.0008-0.0024 in. (0.020-0.062 mm).
11. If the clearance exceeds 0.0047 in. (0.12 mm), proceed to the next step.
12. Using special tool J 26900-14 (Dial Bore Gauge) measure the camshaft housing bore.
13. Measure the camshaft journal diameter using special tool J 26900-2 (outside micrometer).
14. The standard diameter for the #1 journal bore is 1.0236-1.0244 in. (26.000-26.021 mm). For the #2 and the #3 journal bores, the standard is 1.1811-1.1819 in. (30.000-30.021 mm).
15. The standard for the #1 outside journal diameter is 1.0220-1.0228 in. (25.959-25.980 mm). The standard for the #2 and the #3 outside journal diameters is 1.1795-1.1803 in. (29.959-29.980 mm).
16. Replace the camshaft or the cylinder head, base the decision on the one with the furthest reading from specification.

Journal Wear 1.3L Engine

1. Measure the camshaft bore diameter using a dial bore gauge or another accurate measuring instrument.
2. Measure the journal diameters in two places using an outside micrometer.
3. Subtract the two measurements from each other to get the clearance.
4. Standard clearance is 0.0020-0.0036 in. (0.050-0.091 mm). The limit is 0.0059 in. (0.15 mm).

Rear Main Seal

REMOVAL & INSTALLATION

1. Remove the transaxle from the engine assembly. Refer to Drivetrain, Manual/Automatic Transaxle.
2. If manual transaxle, remove the pressure plate and clutch disc.
3. Make a mark on the flywheel and the crankshaft to keep them in balance upon reassembly.
4. Remove the flywheel/flexplate.

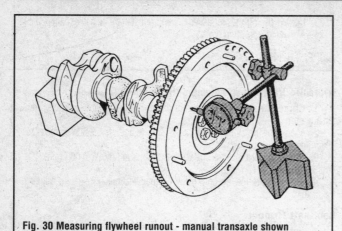

Fig. 30 Measuring flywheel runout - manual transaxle shown

5. Remove the rear main seal.
6. Clean the area that the seal came out of.

To install

7. Install the new rear main seal.
8. Apply a thread sealer to the flywheel/flexplate retaining bolts.
9. Install the flywheel/flexplate being sure to line up the marks made previously.
10. Torque the bolts to 45 ft. lbs. (61 Nm).
11. Install the clutch disc and the pressure plate if applicable.
12. Install the transaxle to the engine. Refer to Drivetrain, Manual/Automatic Transaxle.

Flywheel/Flexplate

REMOVAL & INSTALLATION

See Figure 30

The terms flywheel and flexplate are used interchangeably. They describe the gear toothed ring attached to the crankshaft that the starter uses to turn the engine over. The automatic transaxle flywheel is sometimes referred to as a flexplate.

On manual transaxle equipped vehicles, the flywheel is the mounting point and friction surface for the clutch disc and pressure plate. On automatic transaxle equipped vehicles, the flywheel is the attaching point for the torque converter.

The flywheel and ring gear are machined from one piece of metal and cannot be separated. If gear teeth are damaged, the flywheel must be replaced as an assembly.

1. Disconnect the negative battery cable. Raise and support the vehicle safely.
2. Remove the transaxle from the vehicle.

3. On manual transaxle equipped vehicles, inspect the flywheel/pressure plate assembly for match marks. If no mark exists, mark the flywheel and the pressure plate for installation reference.

Note: The flywheel is balanced and must be replaced in the same position to ensure trouble free operation of the engine.

4. On manual transaxle equipped vehicles, loosen the clutch-to-flywheel bolts, evenly (one turn at a time), until the spring tension is relieved, then remove the retaining bolts, the pressure plate and the clutch assembly.

✳ CAUTION:

The clutch driven disc contains asbestos, which has been determined to be a cancer causing agent. Never clean clutch surfaces with compressed air! Avoid inhaling any dust from any clutch surface! When cleaning clutch surfaces, use a commercially available brake cleaning fluid.

5. Check the flywheel face for runout using a dial indicator. If runout exceeds 0.0078 in. (0.2 mm), resurface the flywheel prior to installation.
6. Remove the flywheel-to-crankshaft bolts and the flywheel from the engine.

To install:

7. On manual transaxle equipped vehicles, clean the clutch disc (use a stiff brush), the pressure plate and the flywheel of all dirt, oil and grease.
8. Inspect the flywheel, the pressure plate and the clutch disc for scoring, cracks, heat checking and/or other defects.
9. If flywheel resurfacing is needed send the flywheel to an experienced machine shop.

Note: When the flywheel is removed, it is a good idea to replace the rear main oil seal and the pilot bushing.

10. Install the flywheel on the crankshaft and align the matchmarks.
11. Apply Loctite, sealant, or equivalent, to the flywheel retaining bolt threads.
12. Install the flywheel retaining bolts and tighten to 41 - 47 ft. lbs.. (56 - 64 Nm).
13. On manual transaxle equipped vehicles, position a clutch disc aligner tool in the pilot bushing (to support the clutch disc), then assemble the clutch disc (the damper springs facing the transaxle) and pressure plate. Align the matchmarks made during removal and install the retaining bolts into the flywheel.
15. Tighten the pressure plate-to-flywheel bolts to 17 ft. lbs.. (23 Nm) gradually and evenly (to prevent clutch plate distortion). Then remove the alignment tool.
16. On manual transaxle equipped vehicles, lubricate the pilot bushing and the clutch release lever.
17. Install the transaxle, lower the vehicle, and connect the negative battery cable.
18. On manual transaxle equipped vehicles, adjust the clutch linkage.

EXHAUST SYSTEM

Inspection

See Figures 31, 32, 33, 34, 35, 36 and 37

Note: Safety glasses should be worn at all times when working on or near the exhaust system. Older exhaust systems will usually be covered with loose rust particles that will shower you when disturbed. These particles are more than a nuisance and could injure your eye.

✳ CAUTION:

DO NOT perform exhaust repairs or inspection with the engine or exhaust hot. Allow the system to cool completely before attempting any work. Exhaust systems are noted for sharp edges, flaking metal and rusted bolts. Gloves and eye protection are required. A healthy supply of penetrating oil and rags is highly recommended.

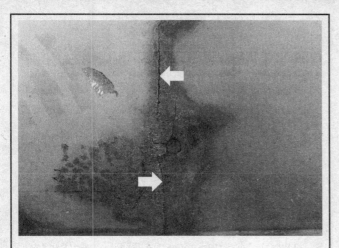

Fig. 31 Cracks in the muffler are a guaranteed leak

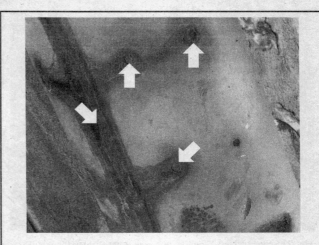

Fig. 32 Check the muffler for rotted spot welds and seams

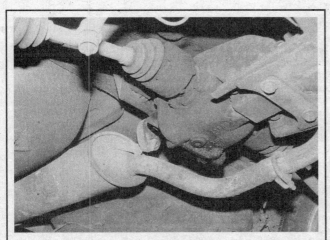

Fig. 33 Make sure the exhaust components are not contacting the body or suspension

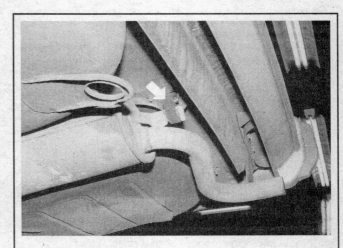

Fig. 34 Check for overstretched or torn exhaust hangers

Fig. 35 Example of a badly deteriorated exhaust pipe

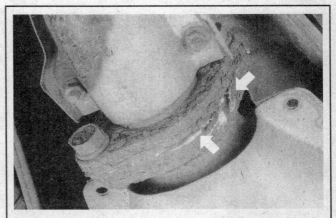

Fig. 36 Inspect flanges for gaskets that have deteriorated and need replacement

Your vehicle must be raised and supported safely to inspect the exhaust system properly. By placing 4 safety stands under the vehicle for support should provide enough room for you to slide under the vehicle and inspect the system completely. Start the inspection at the exhaust manifold or turbocharger pipe where the header pipe is attached and work your way to the back of the vehicle. On dual exhaust systems, remember to inspect both sides of the vehicle. Check the complete exhaust system for open seams, holes loose connections, or other deterioration which could permit exhaust fumes to seep into the passenger compartment. Inspect all mounting brackets and hangers for deterioration, some models may have rubber O-rings that can be overstretched and non-supportive.

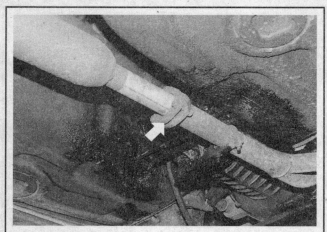

Fig. 37 Some systems, like this one, use large O-rings (doughnuts) in between the flanges

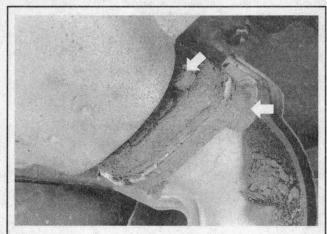

Fig. 38 Nuts and bolts will be extremely difficult to remove when deteriorated with rust

These components will need to be replaced if found. It has always been a practice to use a pointed tool to poke up into the exhaust system where the deterioration spots are to see whether or not they crumble. Some models may have heat shield covering certain parts of the exhaust system , it will be necessary to remove these shields to have the exhaust visible for inspection also.

REPLACEMENT

See Figure 38

There are basically two types of exhaust systems. One is the flange type where the component ends are attached with bolts and a gasket in-between. The other exhaust system is the slip joint type. These components slip into one another using clamps to retain them together.

✳✳ CAUTION:

Allow the exhaust system to cool sufficiently before spraying a solvent exhaust fasteners. Some solvents are highly flammable and could ignite when sprayed on hot exhaust components.

Before removing any component of the exhaust system, ALWAYS squirt a liquid rust dissolving agent onto the fasteners for ease of removal. A lot of knuckle skin will be saved by following this rule. It may even be wise to spray the fasteners and allow them to sit overnight.

Flange Type
See Figure 39

✳✳ CAUTION:

DO NOT perform exhaust repairs or inspection with the engine or exhaust hot. Allow the system to cool completely before attempting any work. Exhaust systems are noted for sharp edges, flaking metal and rusted bolts. Gloves and eye protection are required. A healthy supply of penetrating oil and rags is highly recommended. Never spray liquid rust dissolving agent onto a hot exhaust component.

Before removing any component on a flange type system, ALWAYS squirt a liquid rust dissolving agent onto the fasteners for ease of removal. Start by unbolting the exhaust piece at both ends (if required). When unbolting the headpipe from the manifold, make sure that the bolts are free before trying to remove them. if you snap a stud in the exhaust manifold, the stud will have to be removed with a bolt extractor, which often means removal of the manifold itself. Next, disconnect the component from the mounting; slight twisting and turning may be required to remove the component completely from the vehicle. You may need to tap on the component with a rubber mallet to loosen the component. If all else fails, use a hacksaw to separate the parts. An oxy-acetylene cutting torch may be faster but the sparks are DANGEROUS near the fuel tank, and at the very least, accidents could happen, resulting in damage to the under-car parts, not to mention yourself.

Fig. 39 Example of a flange type exhaust system joint

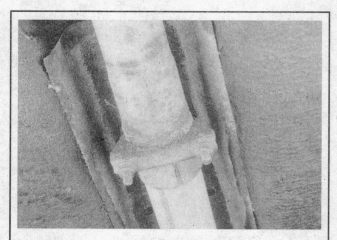

Fig. 40 Example of a common slip joint type system

Slip Joint Type
See Figure 40

Before removing any component on the slip joint type exhaust system, ALWAYS squirt a liquid rust dissolving agent onto the fasteners for ease of removal. Start by unbolting the exhaust piece at both ends (if required). When unbolting the headpipe from the manifold, make sure that the bolts are free

before trying to remove them. if you snap a stud in the exhaust manifold, the stud will have to be removed with a bolt extractor, which often means removal of the manifold itself. Next, remove the mounting U-bolts from around the exhaust pipe you are extracting from the vehicle. Do not be surprised if the U-bolts break while removing the nuts. Loosen the exhaust pipe from any mounting brackets retaining it to the floor pan and separate the components.

ENGINE RECONDITIONING

Determining Engine Condition

Anything that generates heat and/or friction will eventually burn or wear out (for example, a light bulb generates heat, therefore its life span is limited). With this in mind, a running engine generates tremendous amounts of both; friction is encountered by the moving and rotating parts inside the engine and heat is created by friction and combustion of the fuel. However, the engine has systems designed to help reduce the effects of heat and friction and provide added longevity. The oiling system reduces the amount of friction encountered by the moving parts inside the engine, while the cooling system reduces heat created by friction and combustion. If either system is not maintained, a break-down will be inevitable. Therefore, you can see how regular maintenance can affect the service life of your vehicle. If you do not drain, flush, and refill your cooling system at the proper intervals, deposits will begin to accumulate in the radiator, thereby reducing the amount of heat it can extract from the coolant. The same applies to your oil and filter; if it is not changed often enough it becomes laden with contaminates and is unable to properly lubricate the engine. This increases friction and wear.

There are a number of methods for evaluating the condition of your engine. A compression test can reveal the condition of your pistons, piston rings, cylinder bores, head gasket(s), valves, and valve seats. An oil pressure test can warn you of possible engine bearing, or oil pump failures. Excessive oil consumption, evidence of oil in the engine air intake area and/or bluish smoke from the tailpipe may indicate worn piston rings, worn valve guides, and/or valve seals. As a general rule, an engine that uses no more than one quart of oil every 1000 miles is in good condition. Engines that use one quart of oil or more in less than 1000 miles should first be checked for oil leaks. If any oil leaks are present, have them fixed before determining how much oil is consumed by the engine, especially if blue smoke is not visible at the tailpipe.

COMPRESSION TEST

See Figure 41

A noticeable lack of engine power, excessive oil consumption, and/or poor

fuel mileage measured over an extended period are all indicators of internal engine wear. Worn piston rings, scored or worn cylinder bores, blown head gaskets, sticking or burnt valves, and worn valve seats are all possible culprits. A check of each cylinder's compression will help locate the problem.

Note: A screw-in type compression gauge is more accurate than the type you simply hold against the spark plug hole. Although it takes slightly longer to use, it is worth the effort to obtain a more accurate reading.

1. Make sure that the proper amount and viscosity of engine oil is in the crankcase, then ensure the battery is fully charged.
2. Warm-up the engine to normal operating temperature, then shut the engine OFF .
3. Disable the ignition system.
4. Label and disconnect all of the spark plug wires from the plugs.
5. Thoroughly clean the cylinder head area around the spark plug ports, then remove the spark plugs.
6. Set the throttle plate to the fully open (wide-open throttle) position. You can block the accelerator linkage open for this, or you can have an assistant fully depress the accelerator pedal.
7. Install a screw-in type compression gauge into the No. 1 spark plug hole until the fitting is snug.

❋ WARNING:

Be careful not to crossthread the spark plug hole.

8. According to the tool manufacturer's instructions, connect a remote starting switch to the starting circuit.
9. With the ignition switch in the OFF position, use the remote starting switch to crank the engine through at least five compression strokes (approximately 5 seconds of cranking) and record the highest reading on the gauge.
10. Repeat the test on each cylinder, cranking the engine approximately the same number of compression strokes and/or time as the first.
11. Compare the highest readings from each cylinder to that of the others. The indicated compression pressures are considered within specifications if the lowest reading cylinder is within 75 percent of the pressure recorded for the highest reading cylinder. For example, if your highest reading cylinder pressure was 150 psi (1034 kPa), then 75 percent of that would be 113 psi (779 kPa). So the lowest reading cylinder should be no less than 113 psi (779 kPa).
12. If a cylinder exhibits an unusually low compression reading, pour a tablespoon of clean engine oil into the cylinder through the spark plug hole and repeat the compression test. If the compression rises after adding oil, it means that the cylinder's piston rings and/or cylinder bore are damaged or worn. If the pressure remains low, the valves may not be seating properly (a valve job is needed), or the head gasket may be blown near that cylinder. If compression in any two adjacent cylinders is low, and if the addition of oil does not help raise compression, there is leakage past the head gasket. Oil and coolant in the combustion chamber, combined with blue or constant white smoke from the tailpipe, are symptoms of this problem. However, do not be alarmed by the normal white smoke emitted from the tailpipe during engine warm-up or from cold weather driving. There may be evidence of water droplets on the engine dipstick and/or oil droplets in the cooling system if a head gasket is blown.

OIL PRESSURE TEST

Check for proper oil pressure at the sending unit passage with an externally mounted mechanical oil pressure gauge (as opposed to relying on a factory

Fig. 41 A screw-in type compression gauge is more accurate and easier to use without an assistant

installed dash-mounted gauge). A tachometer may also be needed, as some specifications may require running the engine at a specific rpm.

1. With the engine cold, locate and remove the oil pressure sending unit.

2. Following the manufacturer's instructions, connect a mechanical oil pressure gauge and, if necessary, a tachometer to the engine.

3. Start the engine and allow it to idle.

4. Check the oil pressure reading when cold and record the number. You may need to run the engine at a specified rpm, so check the specifications.

5. Run the engine until normal operating temperature is reached (upper radiator hose will feel warm).

6. Check the oil pressure reading again with the engine hot and record the number. Turn the engine OFF .

7. Compare your hot oil pressure reading to that given in the chart. If the reading is low, check the cold pressure reading against the chart. If the cold pressure is well above the specification, and the hot reading was lower than the specification, you may have the wrong viscosity oil in the engine. Change the oil, making sure to use the proper grade and quantity, then repeat the test.

8 Low oil pressure readings could be attributed to internal component wear, pump related problems, a low oil level, or oil viscosity that is too low. High oil pressure readings could be caused by an overfilled crankcase, too high of an oil viscosity or a faulty pressure relief valve.

Buy or Rebuild?

Now that you have determined that your engine is worn out, you must make some decisions. The question of whether or not an engine is worth rebuilding is largely a subjective matter and one of personal worth. Is the engine a popular one, or is it an obsolete model? Are parts available? Will it get acceptable gas mileage once it is rebuilt? Is the car it is being put into worth keeping? Would it be less expensive to buy a new engine, have your engine rebuilt by a pro, rebuild it yourself or buy a used engine from a salvage yard? Or would it be simpler and less expensive to buy another car? If you have considered all these matters and more, and have still decided to rebuild the engine, then it is time to decide how you will rebuild it.

Note: The editors at Chilton feel that most engine machining should be performed by a professional machine shop. Do not think of it as wasting money, rather, as an assurance that the job has been done right the first time. There are many expensive and specialized tools required to perform such tasks as boring and honing an engine block or having a valve job done on a cylinder head. Even inspecting the parts requires expensive micrometers and gauges to properly measure wear and clearances. Also, a machine shop can deliver to you clean, and ready to assemble parts, saving you time and aggravation. Your maximum savings will come from performing the removal, disassembly, assembly and installation of the engine and purchasing or renting only the tools required to perform the above tasks. Depending on the particular circumstances, you may save 40 to 60 percent of the cost doing these yourself.

A complete rebuild or overhaul of an engine involves replacing all of the moving parts (pistons, rods, crankshaft, camshaft, etc.) with new ones and machining the non-moving wearing surfaces of the block and heads. Unfortunately, this may not be cost effective. For instance, your crankshaft may have been damaged or worn, but it can be machined undersize for a minimal fee.

So, as you can see, you can replace everything inside the engine, but, it is wiser to replace only those parts which are really needed, and, if possible, repair the more expensive ones. Later in this section, we will break the engine down into its two main components: the cylinder head and the engine block. We will discuss each component, and the recommended parts to replace during a rebuild on each.

Engine Overhaul Tips

Most engine overhaul procedures are fairly standard. In addition to specific parts replacement procedures and specifications for your individual engine, this section is also a guide to acceptable rebuilding procedures. Examples of standard rebuilding practice are given and should be used along with specific details concerning your particular engine.

Competent and accurate machine shop services will ensure maximum performance, reliability and engine life. In most instances it is more profitable for the

do-it-yourself mechanic to remove, clean and inspect the component, buy the necessary parts and deliver these to a shop for actual machine work.

Much of the assembly work (crankshaft, bearings, piston rods, and other components) is well within the scope of the do-it-yourself mechanic's tools and abilities. You will have to decide for yourself the depth of involvement you desire in an engine repair or rebuild.

TOOLS

The tools required for an engine overhaul or parts replacement will depend on the depth of your involvement. With a few exceptions, they will be the tools found in a mechanic's tool kit (see Section 1 of this manual). More in-depth work will require some or all of the following:

• A dial indicator (reading in thousandths) mounted on a universal base
• Micrometers and telescope gauges
• Jaw and screw-type pullers
• Scraper
• Valve spring compressor
• Ring groove cleaner
• Piston ring expander and compressor
• Ridge reamer
• Cylinder hone or glaze breaker
• Plastigage,
• Engine stand

The use of most of these tools is illustrated in this section. Many can be rented for a one-time use from a local parts jobber or tool supply house specializing in automotive work.

Occasionally, the use of special tools is called for. See the information on Special Tools and the Safety Notice in the front of this book before substituting another tool.

OVERHAUL TIPS

Aluminum has become extremely popular for use in engines, due to its low weight. Observe the following precautions when handling aluminum parts:

• Never hot tank aluminum parts (the caustic hot tank solution will eat the aluminum.
• Remove all aluminum parts (identification tag, etc.) from engine parts prior to the tanking.
• Always coat threads lightly with engine oil or anti-seize compounds before installation, to prevent seizure.
• Never overtighten bolts or spark plugs especially in aluminum threads.

When assembling the engine, any parts that will be exposed to frictional contact must be prelubed to provide lubrication at initial start-up. Any product specifically formulated for this purpose can be used, but engine oil is not recommended as a prelube in most cases.

When semi-permanent (locked, but removable) installation of bolts or nuts is desired, threads should be cleaned and coated with Loctite® or another similar, commercial non-hardening sealant.

CLEANING

See Figures 42, 43, 44 and 45

Before the engine and its components are inspected, they must be thoroughly cleaned. You will need to remove any engine varnish, oil sludge and/or carbon deposits from all of the components to insure an accurate inspection. A crack in the engine block or cylinder head can easily become overlooked if hidden by a layer of sludge or carbon.

Most of the cleaning process can be carried out with common hand tools and readily available solvents or solutions. Carbon deposits can be chipped away using a hammer and a hard wooden chisel. Old gasket material and varnish or sludge can usually be removed using a scraper and/or cleaning solvent. Extremely stubborn deposits may require the use of a power drill with a wire brush. If using a wire brush, use extreme care around any critical machined surfaces (such as the gasket surfaces, bearing saddles, cylinder bores, etc.). Use of a wire brush is NOT RECOMMENDED on any aluminum components. Always follow any safety recommendations given by the manufacturer of the tool and/or solvent. You should always wear eye protection during any cleaning process involving scraping, chipping, or spraying of solvents.

Fig. 42 Use a gasket scraper to remove the old gasket material from the mating surfaces

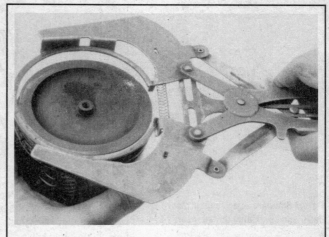
Fig. 43 Use a ring expander tool to remove the piston rings

Fig. 44 Clean the piston ring grooves using a ring groove cleaner tool, or . . .

Fig. 45 . . . use a piece of an old ring to clean the grooves. Be careful, the ring can be quite sharp

An alternative to the mess and hassle of cleaning the parts yourself is to drop them off at a local garage or machine shop. They will, more than likely, have the necessary equipment to properly clean all of the parts for a nominal fee.

✳✳ CAUTION:

Always wear eye protection during any cleaning process involving scraping, chipping, or spraying of solvents.

Remove any oil galley plugs, freeze plugs and/or pressed-in bearings and carefully wash and degrease all of the engine components including the fasteners and bolts. Small parts such as the valves, springs, etc., should be placed in a metal basket and allowed to soak. Use pipe cleaner type brushes, and clean all passageways in the components. Use a ring expander and remove the rings from the pistons. Clean the piston ring grooves with a special tool or a piece of broken ring. Scrape the carbon off of the top of the piston. You should never use a wire brush on the pistons. After preparing all of the piston assemblies in this manner, wash and degrease them again.

✳✳ WARNING:

Use extreme care when cleaning around the cylinder head valve seats. A mistake or slip may cost you a new seat.

When cleaning the cylinder head, remove carbon from the combustion chamber with the valves installed. This will avoid damaging the valve seats.

REPAIRING DAMAGED THREADS

See Figures 46, 47, 48, 49 and 50

Several methods of repairing damaged threads are available. Heli-Coil®

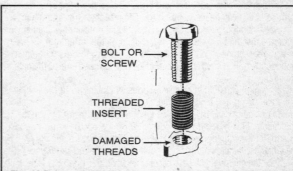
Fig. 46 Damaged bolt hole threads can be replaced with thread repair inserts

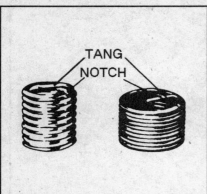

Fig. 47 Standard thread repair insert (left), and spark plug thread insert

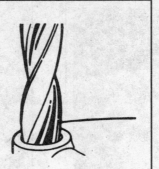

Fig. 48 Drill out the damaged threads with the specified size bit. Be sure to drill completely through the hole or to the bottom of a blind hole

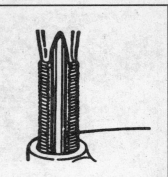

Fig. 49 Using the kit, tap the hole in order to receive the thread insert. Keep the tap well oiled and back it out frequently to avoid clogging the threads

(shown here), Keenserts®, and Microdot® are among the most widely used. All involve basically the same principle - drilling out stripped threads, tapping the hole and installing a prewound insert - making welding, plugging and over-size fasteners unnecessary.

Two types of thread repair inserts are usually supplied: a standard type for most inch coarse, inch fine, metric course and metric fine thread sizes and a spark lug type to fit most spark plug port sizes. Consult the individual tool manufacturer's catalog to determine exact applications. Typical thread repair kits will contain a selection of prewound threaded inserts, a tap (corresponding to the outside diameter threads of the insert) and an installation tool. Spark plug inserts usually differ because they require a tap equipped with pilot threads and a combined reamer/tap section. Most manufacturers also supply blister-packed thread repair inserts separately in addition to a master kit containing a variety of taps and inserts plus installation tools.

Before attempting to repair a threaded hole, remove any snapped, broken or damaged bolts or studs. Penetrating oil can be used to free frozen threads. The offending item can usually be removed with locking pliers or using a screw/stud extractor. After the hole is clear, the thread can be repaired, as shown in the series of accompanying illustrations and in the kit manufacturer's instructions.

Engine Preparation

To properly rebuild an engine, you must first remove it from the vehicle, then disassemble, and diagnose it. Ideally you should place your engine on an engine stand. This affords you the best access to the engine components. Follow the manufacturer's directions for using the stand with your particular engine. Remove the flywheel or flexplate before installing the engine to the stand.

Now that you have the engine on a stand, and assuming that you have drained the oil and coolant from the engine, it is time to strip it of all but the necessary components. Before you start disassembling the engine, you may want to take a moment to draw some pictures, or fabricate some labels or containers to mark the locations of various components and the bolts and/or studs which fasten them. Modern day engines use a lot of little brackets and clips which hold wiring harnesses and such, and these holders are often mounted on studs and/or bolts that can be easily mixed up. The manufacturer spent a lot of time and money designing your vehicle, and they would not have wasted any of it by haphazardly placing brackets, clips or fasteners on the vehicle. If it's present when you disassemble it, put it back when you assemble, you will regret not remembering that little bracket which holds a wire harness out of the path of a rotating part.

You should begin by unbolting any accessories still attached to the engine, such as the water pump, power steering pump, alternator, etc. Then, unfasten any manifolds (intake or exhaust) which were not removed during the engine removal procedure. Finally, remove any covers remaining on the engine such as the rocker arm, front, or timing cover and oil pan. Some front covers may require the vibration damper and/or crank pulley to be removed beforehand. The idea is to reduce the engine to the bare necessities (cylinder head(s), valve train, engine block, crankshaft, pistons and connecting rods), plus any other 'in block' components such as oil pumps, balance shafts and auxiliary shafts.

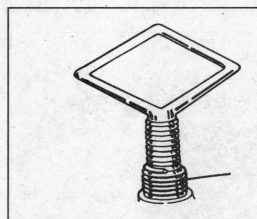

Fig. 50 Screw the insert onto the installer tool until the tang engages the slot. Thread the insert into the hole until it is 1/4 - 1/2 turn below the top surface, then remove the tool and break off the tang using a punch

Finally, remove the cylinder head(s) from the engine block and carefully place on a bench. Disassembly instructions for each component follow later in this section.

Cylinder Head

There are two basic types of cylinder heads used on today's automobiles: the Overhead Valve (OHV) and the Overhead Camshaft (OHC). The latter can also be broken down into two subgroups: the Single Overhead Camshaft (SOHC) and the Dual Overhead Camshaft (DOHC). Generally, if there is only a single camshaft on a head, it is just referred to as an OHC head. Also, an engine with an OHV cylinder head is also known as a pushrod engine.

Most cylinder heads these days are made of an aluminum alloy due to its light weight, durability, and heat transfer qualities. However, cast iron was the material of choice in the past, and is still used on many vehicles today. Whether made from aluminum or iron, all cylinder heads have valves and seats. Some use two valves per cylinder, while the more hi-tech engines will utilize a multi-valve configuration using 3, 4 and even 5 valves per cylinder. When the valve contacts the seat, it does so on precision machined surfaces, which seals the combustion chamber. All cylinder heads have a valve guide for each valve. The guide centers the valve to the seat and allows it to move up and down within it. The clearance between the valve and guide can be critical. Too much clearance and the engine may consume oil, lose vacuum, and/or damage the seat. Too little, and the valve can stick in the guide causing the engine to run poorly if at all, and possibly causing severe damage. The last component all cylinder heads

Fig. 51 Exploded view of a valve, seal, spring, retainer and locks from an OHC cylinder head

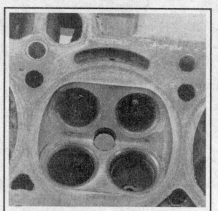

Fig. 52 Example of a multi-valve cylinder head. Note how it has 2 intake and 2 exhaust valve ports

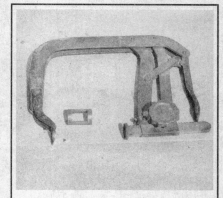

Fig. 53 C-clamp type spring compressor and an OHC spring removal tool (center) for cup type followers

Fig. 54 Most cup type follower cylinder heads retain the camshaft using bolt-on bearing caps

Fig. 55 Position the OHC spring tool in the follower bore, then compress the spring with a C-clamp type tool

have are valve springs. The spring holds the valve against its seat. It also returns the valve to this position when the valve has been opened by the valve train or camshaft. The spring is fastened to the valve by a retainer and valve locks (sometimes called keepers). Aluminum heads will also have a valve spring shim to keep the spring from wearing away the aluminum.

An ideal method of rebuilding the cylinder head would involve replacing all of the valves, guides, seats, springs, etc. with new ones. However, depending on how the engine was maintained, often this is not necessary. A major cause of valve, guide, and seat wear is an improperly tuned engine. An engine that is running too rich, will often wash the lubricating oil out of the guide with gasoline, causing it to wear rapidly. Conversely, an engine which is running too lean will place higher combustion temperatures on the valves and seats allowing them to wear or even burn. Springs fall victim to the driving habits of the individual. A driver who often runs the engine rpm to the redline will wear out or break the springs faster then one that stays well below it. Unfortunately, mileage takes it toll on all of the parts. Generally, the valves, guides, springs and seats in a cylinder head can be machined and re-used, saving you money. However, if a valve is burnt, it may be wise to replace all of the valves, since they were all operating in the same environment. The same goes for any other component on the cylinder head. Think of it as an insurance policy against future problems related to that component.

Unfortunately, the only way to find out which components need replacing, is to disassemble and carefully check each piece. After the cylinder head(s) are disassembled, thoroughly clean all of the components.

DISASSEMBLY

OHC Heads
See Figures 51 and 52

Whether it is a single or dual overhead camshaft cylinder head, the disassembly procedure is relatively unchanged. One aspect to pay attention to is careful labeling of the parts on the dual camshaft cylinder head. There will be an intake camshaft and followers as well as an exhaust camshaft and followers and they must be labeled as such. In some cases, the components are identical and could easily be installed incorrectly. DO NOT MIX THEM UP! Determining which is which is very simple; the intake camshaft and components are on the same side of the head as was the intake manifold. Conversely, the exhaust camshaft and components are on the same side of the head as was the exhaust manifold.

CUP TYPE CAMSHAFT FOLLOWERS
See Figures 53, 54 and 55

Most cylinder heads with cup type camshaft followers will have the valve spring, retainer and locks recessed within the follower's bore. You will need a C-clamp style valve spring compressor tool, an OHC spring removal tool (or equivalent) and a small magnet to disassemble the head.

1. If not already removed, remove the camshaft(s) and/or followers. Mark

Fig. 56 Example of the shaft mounted rocker arms on some OHC heads

Fig. 57 Another example of the rocker arm type OHC head. This model uses a follower under the camshaft

Fig. 58 Before the camshaft can be removed, all of the followers must first be removed . . .

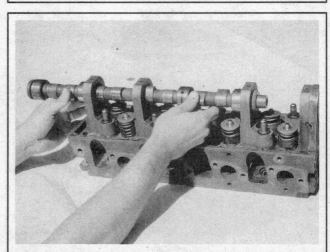

Fig. 59 . . . then the camshaft can be removed by sliding it out (shown), or unbolting a bearing cap (not shown)

their positions for assembly.

2. Position the cylinder head to allow use of a C-clamp style valve spring compressor tool.

Note: It is preferred to position the cylinder head gasket surface facing you with the valve springs facing the opposite direction and the head laying horizontal.

3. With the OHC spring removal adapter tool positioned inside of the follower bore, compress the valve spring using the C-clamp style valve spring compressor.

4. Remove the valve locks. A small magnetic tool or screwdriver will aid in removal.

5. Release the compressor tool and remove the spring assembly.

6. Withdraw the valve from the cylinder head.

7. If equipped, remove the valve seal.

Note: Special valve seal removal tools are available. Regular or needlenose type pliers, if used with care, will work just as well. If using ordinary pliers, be sure not to damage the follower bore. The follower and its bore are machined to close tolerances and any damage to the bore will effect this relationship.

8. If equipped, remove the valve spring shim. A small magnetic tool or screwdriver will aid in removal.

9. Repeat Steps 3 through 8 until all of the valves have been removed.

ROCKER ARM TYPE CAMSHAFT FOLLOWERS
See Figures 56, 57, 58, 59, 60, 61, 62, 63 and 64

Most cylinder heads with rocker arm-type camshaft followers are easily disassembled using a standard valve spring compressor. However, certain models may not have enough open space around the spring for the standard tool and may require you to use a C-clamp style compressor tool instead.

1. If not already removed, remove the rocker arms and/or shafts and the camshaft. If applicable, also remove the hydraulic lash adjusters. Mark their positions for assembly.

2. Position the cylinder head to allow access to the valve spring.

3. Use a valve spring compressor tool to relieve the spring tension from the retainer.

Note: Due to engine varnish, the retainer may stick to the valve locks. A gentle tap with a hammer may help to break it loose.

4. Remove the valve locks from the valve tip and/or retainer. A small magnet may help in removing the small locks.

5. Lift the valve spring, tool and all, off of the valve stem.

6. If equipped, remove the valve seal. If the seal is difficult to remove with the valve in place, try removing the valve first, then the seal. Follow the steps below for valve removal.

7. Position the head to allow access for withdrawing the valve.

Fig. 60 Compress the valve spring . . .

Fig. 61 . . . then remove the valve locks from the valve stem and spring retainer

Fig. 62 Remove the valve spring and retainer from the cylinder head

Fig. 63 Remove the valve seal from the guide. Some gentle prying or pliers may help to remove stubborn ones

Note: Cylinder heads that have seen a lot of miles and/or abuse may have mushroomed the valve lock grove and/or tip, causing difficulty in removal of the valve. If this has happened, use a metal file to carefully remove the high spots around the lock grooves and/or tip. Only file it enough to allow removal.

8. Remove the valve from the cylinder head.
9. If equipped, remove the valve spring shim. A small magnetic tool or screwdriver will aid in removal.
10. Repeat Steps 3 though 9 until all of the valves have been removed.

INSPECTION

Now that all of the cylinder head components are clean, it is time to inspect them for wear and/or damage. To accurately inspect them, you will need some specialized tools:
- A 0 - 1 in. micrometer for the valves
- A dial indicator or inside diameter gauge for the valve guides
- A spring pressure test gauge

If you do not have access to the proper tools, you may want to bring the components to a shop that does.

Fig. 64 All aluminum and some cast iron heads will have these valve spring shims. Remove all of them as well

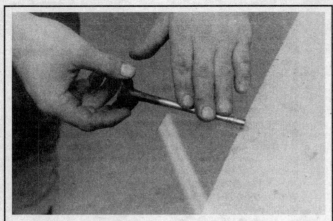

Fig. 65 Valve stems may be rolled on a flat surface to check for bends

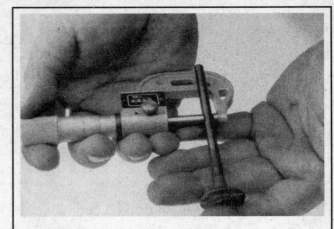

Fig. 66 Use a micrometer to check the valve stem diameter

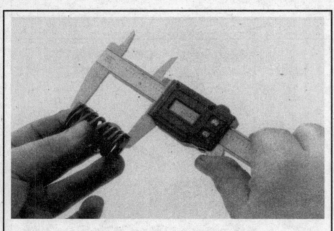

Fig. 67 Use a caliper to check the valve spring free-length

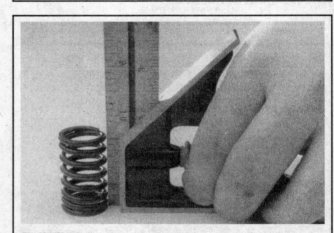

Fig. 68 Check the valve spring for squareness on a flat surface; a carpenter's square can be used

Valves

See Figures 65 and 66

The first thing to inspect are the valve heads. Look closely at the head, margin and face for any cracks, excessive wear or burning. The margin is the best place to look for burning. It should have a squared edge with an even width all around the diameter. When a valve burns, the margin will look melted and the edges rounded. Also inspect the valve head for any signs of tulipping. This will show as a lifting of the edges or dishing in the center of the head and will usually not occur to all of the valves. All of the heads should look the same, any that seem dished more than others are probably bad. Next, inspect the valve lock grooves and valve tips. Check for any burrs around the lock grooves, especially if you had to file them to remove the valve. Valve tips should appear flat, although slight rounding with high mileage engines is normal. Slightly worn valve tips will need to be machined flat. Last, measure the valve stem diameter with the micrometer. Measure the area that rides within the guide, especially towards the tip where most of the wear occurs. Take several measurements along its length and compare them to each other. Wear should be even along the length with little to no taper. If no minimum diameter is given in the specifications, then the stem should not read more than 0.001 in. (0.025 mm) below the unworn area of the valve stem. Any valves that fail these inspections should be replaced.

Springs, Retainers and Valve Locks

See Figures 67 and 68

The first thing to check is the most obvious, broken springs. Next check the free length and squareness of each spring. If applicable, insure to distinguish between intake and exhaust springs. Use a ruler and/or carpenter's square to measure the length. A carpenter's square should be used to check the springs for squareness. If a spring pressure test gauge is available, check each springs rating and compare to the specifications chart. Check the readings against the specifications given. Any springs that fail these inspections should be replaced.

The spring retainers rarely need replacing, however they should still be checked as a precaution. Inspect the spring mating surface and the valve lock retention area for any signs of excessive wear. Also check for any signs of cracking. Replace any retainers that are questionable.

Valve locks should be inspected for excessive wear on the outside contact area as well as on the inner notched surface. Any locks which appear worn or broken and its respective valve should be replaced.

Cylinder Head

There are several things to check on the cylinder head: valve guides, seats, cylinder head surface flatness, cracks and physical damage.

VALVE GUIDES

See Figure 69

Now that you know the valves are good, you can use them to check the guides, although a new valve, if available, is preferred. Before you measure anything, look at the guides carefully and inspect them for any cracks, chips or breakage. Also if the guide is a removable style (as in most aluminum heads), check them for any looseness or evidence of movement. All of the guides should appear to be at the same height from the spring seat. If any seem lower (or higher) from another, the guide has moved. Mount a dial indicator onto the spring side of the cylinder head. Lightly oil the valve stem and insert it into the

Fig. 69 A dial gauge may be used to check valve stem-to-guide clearance; read the gauge while moving the valve stem

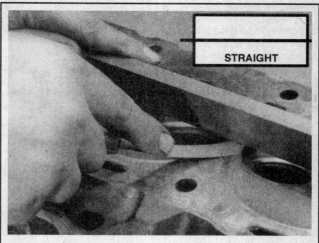

Fig. 70 Check the head for flatness across the center of the head surface using a straightedge and feeler gauge

cylinder head. Position the dial indicator against the valve stem near the tip and zero the gauge. Grasp the valve stem and wiggle towards and away from the dial indicator and observe the readings. Mount the dial indicator 90 degrees from the initial point and zero the gauge and again take a reading. Compare the two readings for a out of round condition. Check the readings against the specifications given. An Inside Diameter (I.D.) gauge designed for valve guides will give you an accurate valve guide bore measurement. If the I.D. gauge is used, compare the readings with the specifications given. Any guides that fail these inspections should be replaced or machined.

VALVE SEATS

A visual inspection of the valve seats should show a slightly worn and pitted surface where the valve face contacts the seat. Inspect the seat carefully for severe pitting or cracks. Also, a seat that is badly worn will be recessed into the cylinder head. A severely worn or recessed seat may need to be replaced. All cracked seats must be replaced. A seat concentricity gauge, if available, should be used to check the seat run-out. If run-out exceeds specifications the seat must be machined (if no specification is given use 0.002 in. or 0.051 mm).

CYLINDER HEAD SURFACE FLATNESS
See Figures 70 and 71

After you have cleaned the gasket surface of the cylinder head of any old gasket material, check the head for flatness.

Place a straightedge across the gasket surface. Using feeler gauges, determine the clearance at the center of the straightedge and across the cylinder head at several points. Check along the centerline and diagonally on the head surface. If the warpage exceeds 0.003 in. (0.076 mm) within a 6.0 in. (15.2 cm) span, or 0.006 in. (0.152 mm) over the total length of the head, the cylinder head must be resurfaced. After resurfacing the heads of a V-type engine, the intake manifold flange surface should be checked, and if necessary, milled proportionally to allow for the change in its mounting position.

CRACKS AND PHYSICAL DAMAGE

Generally, cracks are limited to the combustion chamber, however, it is not uncommon for the head to crack in a spark plug hole, port, outside of the head or in the valve spring/rocker arm area. The first area to inspect is always the hottest: the exhaust seat/port area.

A visual inspection should be performed, but just because you don't see a crack does not mean it is not there. Some more reliable methods for inspecting for cracks include Magnaflux, a magnetic process or Zyglo, a dye penetrant. Magnaflux, is used only on ferrous metal (cast iron) heads. Zyglo uses a spray on fluorescent mixture along with a black light to reveal the cracks. It is strongly recommended to have your cylinder head checked professionally for cracks, especially if the engine was known to have overheated and/or leaked or consumed coolant. Contact a local shop for availability and pricing of these services.

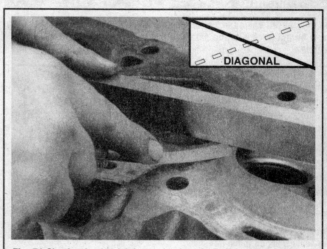

Fig. 71 Checks should also be made along both diagonals of the head surface

Physical damage is usually very evident. For example, a broken mounting ear from dropping the head or a bent or broken stud and/or bolt. All of these defects should be fixed or, if unrepairable, the head should be replaced.

Camshaft and Followers

Inspect the camshaft(s) and followers as described earlier in this section.

REFINISHING & REPAIRING

Many of the procedures given for refinishing and repairing the cylinder head components must be performed by a machine shop. Certain steps, if the inspected part is not worn, can be performed yourself inexpensively. However, you spent a lot of time and effort so far, why risk trying to save a couple bucks if you might have to do it all over again?

Valves

Any valves that were not replaced should be refaced and the tips ground flat. Unless you have access to a valve grinding machine, this should be done by a machine shop. If the valves are in extremely good condition, as well as the valve seats and guides, they may be lapped in without performing machine work.

It is a recommended practice to lap the valves even after machine work has been performed and/or new valves have been purchased. This insures a positive seal between the valve and seat.

LAPPING THE VALVES

Note 1: Before lapping the valves to the seats, read the rest of the cylinder head section to insure that any related parts are in acceptable enough condition to continue.

Note 2: Before any valve seat machining and/or lapping can be performed, the guides must be within factory recommended specifications.

1. Invert the cylinder head.
2. Lightly lubricate the valve stems and insert them into the cylinder head in their numbered order.
3. Raise the valve from the seat and apply a small amount of fine lapping compound to the seat.
4. Moisten the suction head of a hand-lapping tool and attach it to the head of the valve.
5. Rotate the tool between the palms of both hands, changing the position of the valve on the valve seat and lifting the tool often to prevent grooving.
6. Lap the valve until a smooth, polished circle is evident on the valve and seat.
7. Remove the tool and the valve. Wipe away all traces of the grinding compound and store the valve to maintain its lapped location.

✳✳ WARNING:

Do not get the valves out of order after they have been lapped. They must be put back with the same valve seat with which they were lapped.

Springs, Retainers and Valve Locks

There is no repair or refinishing possible with the springs, retainers and valve locks. If they are found to be worn or defective, they must be replaced with new (or known good) parts.

Cylinder Head

Most refinishing procedures dealing with the cylinder head must be performed by a machine shop. Read the sections below and review your inspection data to determine whether or not machining is necessary.

VALVE GUIDE

Note: If any machining or replacements are made to the valve guides, the seats must be machined.

Unless the valve guides need machining or replacing, the only service to perform is to thoroughly clean them of any dirt or oil residue.

There are only two types of valve guides used on automobile engines: the replaceable-type (all aluminum heads) and the cast-in integral-type (most cast iron heads). There are four recommended methods for repairing worn guides.
- Knurling
- Inserts
- Reaming oversize
- Replacing

Knurling is a process in which metal is displaced and raised, thereby reducing clearance, giving a true center, and providing oil control. It is the least expensive way of repairing the valve guides. However, it is not necessarily the best, and in some cases, a knurled valve guide will not stand up for more than a short time. It requires a special knurlizer and precision reaming tools to obtain proper clearances. It would not be cost effective to purchase these tools, unless you plan on rebuilding several of the same cylinder head.

Installing a guide insert involves machining the guide to accept a bronze insert. One style is the coil-type which is installed into a threaded guide. Another is the thin-walled insert where the guide is reamed oversize to accept a split-sleeve insert. After the insert is installed, a special tool is then run through the guide to expand the insert, locking it to the guide. The insert is then reamed to the standard size for proper valve clearance.

Reaming for oversize valves restores normal clearances and provides a true valve seat. Most cast-in type guides can be reamed to accept an valve with an oversize stem. The cost factor for this can become quite high as you will need to purchase the reamer and new, oversize stem valves for all guides which were

reamed. Oversizes are generally 0.003 to 0.030 in. (0.076 to 0.762 mm), with 0.015 in. (0.381 mm) being the most common.

To replace cast-in type valve guides, they must be drilled out, then reamed to accept replacement guides. This must be done on a fixture which will allow centering and leveling off of the original valve seat or guide, otherwise a serious guide-to-seat misalignment may occur making it impossible to properly machine the seat.

Replaceable-type guides are pressed into the cylinder head. A hammer and a stepped drift or punch may be used to install and remove the guides. Before removing the guides, measure the protrusion on the spring side of the head and record it for installation. Use the stepped drift to hammer out the old guide from the combustion chamber side of the head. When installing, determine whether or not the guide also seals a water jacket in the head, and if it does, use the recommended sealing agent. If there is no water jacket, grease the valve guide and its bore. Use the stepped drift, and hammer the new guide into the cylinder head from the spring side of the cylinder head. A stack of washers the same thickness as the measured protrusion may help the installation process.

VALVE SEATS

Note 1: Before any valve seat machining can be performed, the guides must be within factory recommended specifications.

Note 2: If any machining or replacements were made to the valve guides, the seats must be machined.

If the seats are in good condition, the valves can be lapped to the seats, and the cylinder head assembled. See the valves section for instructions on lapping.

If the valve seats are worn, cracked or damaged, they must be serviced by a machine shop. The valve seat must be perfectly centered to the valve guide, which requires very accurate machining.

CYLINDER HEAD SURFACE

If the cylinder head is warped, it must be machined flat. If the warpage is extremely severe, the head may need to be replaced. In some instances, it may be possible to straighten a warped head enough to allow machining. In either case, contact a professional machine shop for service.

Note: Any OHC cylinder head that shows excessive warpage should have the camshaft bearing journals align bored after the cylinder head has been resurfaced.

✳✳ WARNING:

Failure to align bore the camshaft bearing journals could result in severe engine damage including but not limited to: valve and piston damage, connecting rod damage, camshaft and/or crankshaft breakage.

CRACKS AND PHYSICAL DAMAGE

Certain cracks can be repaired in both cast iron and aluminum heads. For cast iron, a tapered threaded insert is installed along the length of the crack. Aluminum can also use the tapered inserts, however welding is the preferred method. Some physical damage can be repaired through brazing or welding. Contact a machine shop to get expert advice for your particular dilemma.

ASSEMBLY

The first step for any assembly job is to have a clean area in which to work. Next, thoroughly clean all of the parts and components that are to be assembled. Finally, place all of the components onto a suitable work space and, if necessary, arrange the parts to their respective positions.

OHC Engines
See Figure 72

CUP TYPE CAMSHAFT FOLLOWERS

To install the springs, retainers and valve locks on heads which have these components recessed into the camshaft follower's bore, you will need a small screwdriver-type tool, some clean white grease and a lot of patience. You will

Fig. 72 Once assembled, check the valve clearance and correct as needed

Fig. 73 Place rubber hose over the connecting rod studs to protect the crankshaft and cylinder bores from damage

also need the C-clamp style spring compressor and the OHC tool used to disassemble the head.

1. Lightly lubricate the valve stems and insert all of the valves into the cylinder head. If possible, maintain their original locations.
2. If equipped, install any valve spring shims which were removed.
3. If equipped, install the new valve seals, keeping the following in mind:
• If the valve seal presses over the guide, lightly lubricate the outer guide surfaces.
• If the seal is an O-ring type, it is installed just after compressing the spring but before the valve locks.
4. Place the valve spring and retainer over the stem.
5. Position the spring compressor and the OHC tool, then compress the spring.
6. Using a small screwdriver as a spatula, fill the valve stem side of the lock with white grease. Use the excess grease on the screwdriver to fasten the lock to the driver.
7. Carefully install the valve lock, which is stuck to the end of the screwdriver, to the valve stem then press on it with the screwdriver until the grease squeezes out. The valve lock should now be stuck to the stem.
8. Repeat Steps 6 and 7 for the remaining valve lock.
9. Relieve the spring pressure slowly and insure that neither valve lock becomes dislodged by the retainer.
10. Remove the spring compressor tool.
11. Repeat Steps 2 through 10 until all of the springs have been installed.
12. Install the followers, camshaft(s) and any other components that were removed for disassembly.

ROCKER ARM TYPE CAMSHAFT FOLLOWERS

1. Lightly lubricate the valve stems and insert all of the valves into the cylinder head. If possible, maintain their original locations.
2. If equipped, install any valve spring shims which were removed.
3. If equipped, install the new valve seals, keeping the following in mind:
• If the valve seal presses over the guide, lightly lubricate the outer guide surfaces.
• If the seal is an O-ring type, it is installed just after compressing the spring but before the valve locks.
4. Place the valve spring and retainer over the stem.
5. Position the spring compressor tool and compress the spring.
6. Assemble the valve locks to the stem.
7. Relieve the spring pressure slowly and insure that neither valve lock becomes dislodged by the retainer.
8. Remove the spring compressor tool.
9. Repeat Steps 2 through 8 until all of the springs have been installed.
10. Install the camshaft(s), rockers, shafts and any other components that were removed for disassembly.

Engine Block

A thorough overhaul or rebuild of an engine block would include replacing

the pistons, rings, bearings, timing belt/chain assembly and oil pump. For OHV engines also include a new camshaft and lifters. The block would then have the cylinders bored and honed oversize (or if using removable cylinder sleeves, new sleeves installed) and the crankshaft would be cut undersize to provide new wearing surfaces and perfect clearances. However, your particular engine may not have everything worn out. What if only the piston rings have worn out and the clearances on everything else are still within factory specifications? Well, you could just replace the rings and put it back together, but this would be a very rare example. Chances are, if one component in your engine is worn, other components are sure to follow, and soon. At the very least, you should always replace the rings, bearings and oil pump. This is what is commonly called a "freshen up".

Cylinder Ridge Removal

Because the top piston ring does not travel to the very top of the cylinder, a ridge is built up between the end of the travel and the top of the cylinder bore.

Pushing the piston and connecting rod assembly past the ridge can be difficult, and damage to the piston ring lands could occur. If the ridge is not removed before installing a new piston or not removed at all, piston ring breakage and piston damage may occur.

Note: It is always recommended that you remove any cylinder ridges before removing the piston and connecting rod assemblies. If you know that new pistons are going to be installed and the engine block will be bored oversize, you may be able to forego this step. However, some ridges may actually prevent the assemblies from being removed, necessitating its removal.

There are several different types of ridge reamers on the market, none of which are inexpensive. Unless a great deal of engine rebuilding is anticipated, borrow or rent a reamer.

1. Turn the crankshaft until the piston is at the bottom of its travel.
2. Cover the head of the piston with a rag.
3. Follow the tool manufacturers instructions and cut away the ridge, exercising extreme care to avoid cutting too deeply.
4. Remove the ridge reamer, the rag and as many of the cuttings as possible. Continue until all of the cylinder ridges have been removed.

DISASSEMBLY

See Figures 73 and 74

The engine disassembly instructions following assume that you have the engine mounted on an engine stand. If not, it is easiest to disassemble the engine on a bench or the floor with it resting on the bell housing or transmission mounting surface. You must be able to access the connecting rod fasteners and turn the crankshaft during disassembly. Also, all engine covers (timing, front, side, oil pan, whatever) should have already been removed. Engines which are seized or locked up may not be able to be completely disassembled, and a core (salvage yard) engine should be purchased.

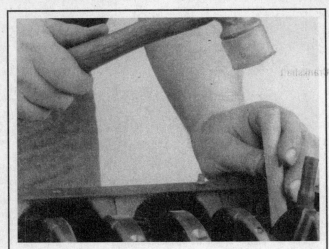

Fig. 74 Carefully tap the piston out of the bore using a wooden dowel

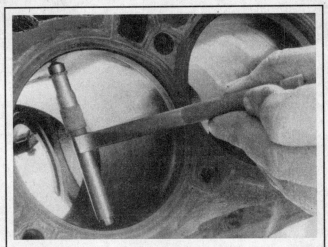

Fig. 75 Use a telescoping gauge to measure the cylinder bore diameter - take several readings within the same bore

OHC Engines

If not done during the cylinder head removal, remove the timing chain/belt and/or gear/sprocket assembly. Remove the oil pick-up and pump assembly and, if necessary, the pump drive. If equipped, remove any balance or auxiliary shafts. If necessary, remove the cylinder ridge from the top of the bore. See the cylinder ridge removal procedure earlier in this section.

All Engines

Rotate the engine over so that the crankshaft is exposed. Use a number punch or scribe and mark each connecting rod with its respective cylinder number. The cylinder closest to the front of the engine is always number 1. However, depending on the engine placement, the front of the engine could either be the flywheel or damper/pulley end. Generally the front of the engine faces the front of the vehicle. Use a number punch or scribe and also mark the main bearing caps from front to rear with the front most cap being number 1 (if there are five caps, mark them 1 through 5, front to rear).

> **✳✳ WARNING:**
>
> Take special care when pushing the connecting rod up from the crankshaft because the sharp threads of the rod bolts/studs will score the crankshaft journal. Insure that special plastic caps are installed over them, or cut two pieces of rubber hose to do the same.

Again, rotate the engine, this time to position the number one cylinder bore (head surface) up. Turn the crankshaft until the number one piston is at the bottom of its travel, this should allow the maximum access to its connecting rod. Remove the number one connecting rods fasteners and cap and place two lengths of rubber hose over the rod bolts/studs to protect the crankshaft from damage. Using a sturdy wooden dowel and a hammer, push the connecting rod up about 1 in. (25 mm) from the crankshaft and remove the upper bearing insert. Continue pushing or tapping the connecting rod up until the piston rings are out of the cylinder bore. Remove the piston and rod by hand, put the upper half of the bearing insert back into the rod, install the cap with its bearing insert installed, and hand-tighten the cap fasteners. If the parts are kept in order in this manner, they will not get lost and you will be able to tell which bearings came form what cylinder if any problems are discovered and diagnosis is necessary. Remove all the other piston assemblies in the same manner. On V-style engines, remove all of the pistons from one bank, then reposition the engine with the other cylinder bank head surface up, and remove that banks piston assemblies.

The only remaining component in the engine block should now be the crankshaft. Loosen the main bearing caps evenly until the fasteners can be turned by hand, then remove them and the caps. Remove the crankshaft from the engine block. Thoroughly clean all of the components.

INSPECTION

Now that the engine block and all of its components are clean, it's time to inspect them for wear and/or damage. To accurately inspect them, you will need some specialized tools:

- Two or three separate micrometers to measure the pistons and crankshaft journals
- A dial indicator
- Telescoping gauges for the cylinder bores
- A rod alignment fixture to check for bent connecting rods

If you do not have access to the proper tools, you may want to bring the components to a shop that does.

Generally, you shouldn't expect cracks in the engine block or its components unless it was known to leak, consume or mix engine fluids, it was severely overheated, or there was evidence of bad bearings and/or crankshaft damage. A visual inspection should be performed on all of the components, but just because you don't see a crack does not mean it is not there. Some more reliable methods for inspecting for cracks include Magnaflux,, a magnetic process or Zyglo,, a dye penetrant. Magnaflux, is used only on ferrous metal (cast iron). Zyglo, uses a spray on fluorescent mixture along with a black light to reveal the cracks. It is strongly recommended to have your engine block checked professionally for cracks, especially if the engine was known to have overheated and/or leaked or consumed coolant. Contact a local shop for availability and pricing of these services.

Engine Block

ENGINE BLOCK BEARING ALIGNMENT

Remove the main bearing caps and, if still installed, the main bearing inserts. Inspect all of the main bearing saddles and caps for damage, burrs or high spots. If damage is found, and it is caused from a spun main bearing, the block will need to be align-bored or, if severe enough, replacement. Any burrs or high spots should be carefully removed with a metal file.

Place a straightedge on the bearing saddles, in the engine block, along the centerline of the crankshaft. If any clearance exists between the straightedge and the saddles, the block must be align-bored.

Align-boring consists of machining the main bearing saddles and caps by means of a flycutter that runs through the bearing saddles.

DECK FLATNESS

The top of the engine block where the cylinder head mounts is called the deck. Insure that the deck surface is clean of dirt, carbon deposits and old gasket material. Place a straightedge across the surface of the deck along its centerline and, using feeler gauges, check the clearance along several points. Repeat the checking procedure with the straightedge placed along both diagonals of the deck surface. If the reading exceeds 0.003 in. (0.076 mm) within a 6.0 in. (15.2 cm) span, or 0.006 in. (0.152 mm) over the total length of the deck, it must be machined.

CYLINDER BORES
See Figure 75

The cylinder bores house the pistons and are slightly larger than the pistons themselves. A common piston-to-bore clearance is 0.0015 - 0.0025 in. (0.0381 mm - 0.0635 mm). Inspect and measure the cylinder bores. The bore should be checked for out-of-roundness, taper and size. The results of this inspection will determine whether the cylinder can be used in its existing size and condition, or a rebore to the next oversize is required (or in the case of removable sleeves, have replacements installed).

The amount of cylinder wall wear is always greater at the top of the cylinder than at the bottom. This wear is known as taper. Any cylinder that has a taper of 0.0012 in. (0.305 mm) or more, must be rebored. Measurements are taken at a number of positions in each cylinder: at the top, middle and bottom and at two points at each position; that is, at a point 90 degrees from the crankshaft centerline, as well as a point parallel to the crankshaft centerline. The measurements are made with either a special dial indicator or a telescopic gauge and micrometer. If the necessary precision tools to check the bore are not available, take the block to a machine shop and have them mike it. Also if you don't have the tools to check the cylinder bores, chances are you will not have the necessary devices to check the pistons, connecting rods and crankshaft. Take these components with you and save yourself an extra trip.

For our procedures, we will use a telescopic gauge and a micrometer. You will need one of each, with a measuring range which covers your cylinder bore size.

1. Position the telescopic gauge in the cylinder bore, loosen the gauges lock and allow it to expand.

Note: Your first two readings will be at the top of the cylinder bore, then proceed to the middle and finally the bottom, making a total of six measurements.

2. Hold the gauge square in the bore, 90 degrees from the crankshaft centerline, and gently tighten the lock. Tilt the gauge back to remove it from the bore.
3. Measure the gauge with the micrometer and record the reading.
4. Again, hold the gauge square in the bore, this time parallel to the crankshaft centerline, and gently tighten the lock. Again, you will tilt the gauge back to remove it from the bore.
5. Measure the gauge with the micrometer and record this reading. The difference between these two readings is the out-of-round measurement of the cylinder.
6. Repeat steps 1 through 5, each time going to the next lower position, until you reach the bottom of the cylinder. Then go to the next cylinder, and continue until all of the cylinders have been measured.

The difference between these measurements will tell you all about the wear in your cylinders. The measurements which were taken 90 degrees from the crankshaft centerline will always reflect the most wear. That is because at this position is where the engine power presses the piston against the cylinder bore the hardest. This is known as thrust wear. Take your top, 90 degree measurement and compare it to your bottom, 90 degree measurement. The difference between them is the taper. When you measure your pistons, you will compare these readings to your piston sizes and determine piston-to-wall clearance.

Crankshaft

Inspect the crankshaft for visible signs of wear or damage. All of the journals should be perfectly round and smooth. Slight scores are normal for a used crankshaft, but you should hardly feel them with your fingernail. When measuring the crankshaft with a micrometer, you will take readings at the front and rear of each journal, then turn the micrometer 90 degrees and take two more readings, front and rear. The difference between the front-to-rear readings is the journal taper and the first-to-90 degree reading is the out-of-round measurement. Generally, there should be no taper or out-of-roundness found, however, up to 0.0005 in. (0.0127 mm) for either can be overlooked. Also, the readings should fall within the factory specifications for journal diameters.

If the crankshaft journals fall within specifications, it is recommended that it be polished before being returned to service. Polishing the crankshaft insures that any minor burrs or high spots are smoothed, thereby reducing the chance of scoring the new bearings.

Pistons and Connecting Rods
PISTONS
See Figure 76

The piston should be visually inspected for any signs of cracking or burning (caused by hot spots or detonation), and scuffing or excessive wear on the skirts. The wrist pin attaches the piston to the connecting rod. The piston should move freely on the wrist pin, both sliding and pivoting. Grasp the connecting rod securely, or mount it in a vise, and try to rock the piston back and forth along the centerline of the wrist pin. There should not be any excessive play evident between the piston and the pin. If there are C-clips retaining the pin in the piston then you have wrist pin bushings in the rods. There should not be any excessive play between the wrist pin and the rod bushing. Normal clearance for the wrist pin is approx. 0.001 - 0.002 in. (0.025 mm - 0.051 mm).

Use a micrometer and measure the diameter of the piston, perpendicular to the wrist pin, on the skirt. Compare the reading to its original cylinder measurement obtained earlier. The difference between the two readings is the piston-to-wall clearance. If the clearance is within specifications, the piston may be used as is. If the piston is out of specification, but the bore is not, you will need a new piston. If both are out of specification, you will need the cylinder rebored and oversize pistons installed. Generally if two or more pistons/bores are out of specification, it is best to rebore the entire block and purchase a complete set of oversize pistons.

CONNECTING ROD

You should have the connecting rod checked for straightness at a machine shop. If the connecting rod is bent, it will unevenly wear the bearing and piston, as well as place greater stress on these components. Any bent or twisted connecting rods must be replaced. If the rods are straight and the wrist pin clearance is within specifications, then only the bearing end of the rod need be checked. Place the connecting rod into a vice, with the bearing inserts in place, install the cap to the rod and torque the fasteners to specifications. Use a telescoping gauge and carefully measure the inside diameter of the bearings. Compare this reading to the rods original crankshaft journal diameter measurement. The difference is the oil clearance. If the oil clearance is not within specifications, install new bearings in the rod and take another measurement. If the clearance is still out of specifications, and the crankshaft is not, the rod will need to be reconditioned by a machine shop.

Note: You can also use Plastigage, to check the bearing clearances. The assembling section has complete instructions on its use.

Camshaft

Inspect the camshaft and lifters/followers as described earlier in this section.

Bearings

All of the engine bearings should be visually inspected for wear and/or damage. The bearing should look evenly worn all around with no deep scores or pits. If the bearing is severely worn, scored, pitted or heat blued, then the bearing, and the components that use it, should be brought to a machine shop for

Fig. 76 Measure the piston's outer diameter, perpendicular to the wrist pin, with a micrometer

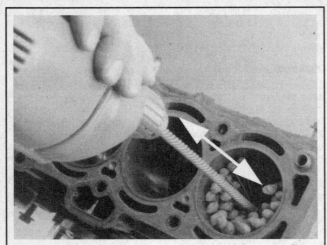

Fig. 77 Use a ball type cylinder hone to remove any glaze and provide a new surface for seating the piston rings

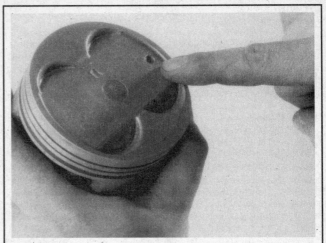

Fig. 78 Most pistons are marked to indicate positioning in the engine (usually a mark means the side facing the front)

inspection. Full-circle bearings (used on most camshafts, auxiliary shafts, balance shafts, etc.) require specialized tools for removal and installation, and should be brought to a machine shop for service.

Oil Pump

Note: The oil pump is responsible for providing constant lubrication to the whole engine and so it is recommended that a new oil pump be installed when rebuilding the engine.

Completely disassemble the oil pump and thoroughly clean all of the components. Inspect the oil pump gears and housing for wear and/or damage. Insure that the pressure relief valve operates properly and there is no binding or sticking due to varnish or debris. If all of the parts are in proper working condition, lubricate the gears and relief valve, and assemble the pump.

REFINISHING

See Figure 77

Almost all engine block refinishing must be performed by a machine shop. If the cylinders are not to be rebored, then the cylinder glaze can be removed with a ball hone. When removing cylinder glaze with a ball hone, use a light or penetrating type oil to lubricate the hone. Do not allow the hone to run dry as this may cause excessive scoring of the cylinder bores and wear on the hone. If new

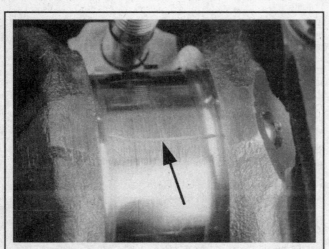

Fig. 79 Apply a strip of gauging material to the bearing journal, then install and torque the cap

pistons are required, they will need to be installed to the connecting rods. This should be performed by a machine shop as the pistons must be installed in the correct relationship to the rod or engine damage can occur.

Pistons and Connecting Rods
See Figure 78

Only pistons with the wrist pin retained by C-clips are serviceable by the home-mechanic. Press fit pistons require special presses and/or heaters to remove/install the connecting rod and should only be performed by a machine shop.

All pistons will have a mark indicating the direction to the front of the engine and the must be installed into the engine in that manner. Usually it is a notch or arrow on the top of the piston, or it may be the letter F cast or stamped into the piston.

ASSEMBLY

Before you begin assembling the engine, first give yourself a clean, dirt free work area. Next, clean every engine component again. The key to a good assembly is cleanliness.

Mount the engine block into the engine stand and wash it one last time using water and detergent (dishwashing detergent works well). While washing it, scrub the cylinder bores with a soft bristle brush and thoroughly clean all of the oil passages. Completely dry the engine and spray the entire assembly down with an anti-rust solution such as WD-40, or similar product. Take a clean lint-free rag and wipe up any excess anti-rust solution from the bores, bearing saddles, etc. Repeat the final cleaning process on the crankshaft. Replace any freeze or oil galley plugs which were removed during disassembly.

Crankshaft
See Figures 79, 80, 81 and 82

1. Remove the main bearing inserts from the block and bearing caps.
2. If the crankshaft main bearing journals have been refinished to a definite undersize, install the correct undersize bearing. Be sure that the bearing inserts and bearing bores are clean. Foreign material under inserts will distort bearing and cause failure.
3. Place the upper main bearing inserts in bores with tang in slot.

Note: The oil holes in the bearing inserts must be aligned with the oil holes in the cylinder block.

4. Install the lower main bearing inserts in bearing caps.
5. Clean the mating surfaces of block and rear main bearing cap.
6. Carefully lower the crankshaft into place. Be careful not to damage bearing surfaces.
7. Check the clearance of each main bearing by using the following procedure:

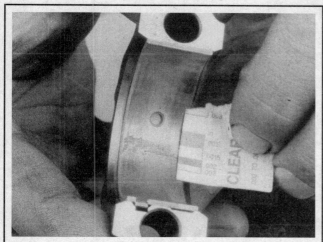

Fig. 80 After the cap is removed again, use the scale supplied with the gauging material to check the clearance

Fig. 81 A dial gauge may be used to check crankshaft end-play

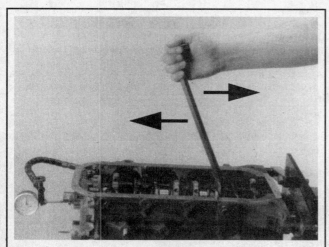

Fig. 82 Carefully pry the crankshaft back and forth while reading the dial gauge for end-play

Fig. 83 Checking the piston ring-to-ring groove side clearance using the ring and a feeler gauge

a.   Place a piece of Plastigage, or its equivalent, on bearing surface across full width of bearing cap and about 1/4 in. off center.

b.   Install cap and tighten bolts to specifications. Do not turn crankshaft while Plastigage, is in place.

c.   Remove the cap. Using the supplied Plastigage, scale, check width of Plastigage, at widest point to get maximum clearance. Difference between readings is taper of journal.

d.   If clearance exceeds specified limits, try a 0.001 in. or 0.002 in. undersize bearing in combination with the standard bearing. Bearing clearance must be within specified limits. If standard and 0.002 in. undersize bearing does not bring clearance within desired limits, refinish crankshaft journal, then install undersize bearings.

8. Install the rear main seal.

9. After the bearings have been fitted, apply a light coat of engine oil to the journals and bearings. Install the rear main bearing cap. Install all bearing caps except the thrust bearing cap. Be sure that main bearing caps are installed in original locations. Tighten the bearing cap bolts to specifications.

10. Install the thrust bearing cap with bolts finger-tight.

11. Pry the crankshaft forward against the thrust surface of upper half of bearing.

12. Hold the crankshaft forward and pry the thrust bearing cap to the rear. This aligns the thrust surfaces of both halves of the bearing.

13. Retain the forward pressure on the crankshaft. Tighten the cap bolts to

specifications.

14. Measure the crankshaft end-play as follows:

a.   Mount a dial gauge to the engine block and position the tip of the gauge to read from the crankshaft end.

b.   Carefully pry the crankshaft toward the rear of the engine and hold it there while you zero the gauge.

c.   Carefully pry the crankshaft toward the front of the engine and read the gauge.

d.   Confirm that the reading is within specifications. If not, install a new thrust bearing and repeat the procedure. If the reading is still out of specifications with a new bearing, have a machine shop inspect the thrust surfaces of the crankshaft, and if possible, repair it.

15. Rotate the crankshaft so as to position the first rod journal to the bottom of its stroke.

Pistons and Connecting Rods
See Figures 83, 84, 85 and 86

1. Before installing the piston/connecting rod assembly, oil the pistons, piston rings and the cylinder walls with light engine oil. Install connecting rod bolt protectors or rubber hose onto the connecting rod bolts/studs. Also perform the following:

a.   Select the proper ring set for the size cylinder bore.

b.   Position the ring in the bore in which it is going to be used.

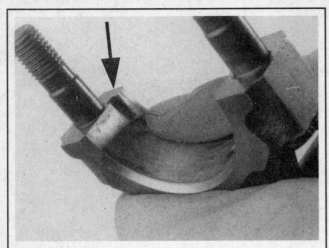

Fig. 84 The notch on the side of the bearing cap matches the tang on the bearing insert

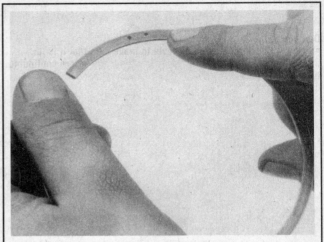

Fig. 85 Most rings are marked to show which side of the ring should face up when installed to the piston

c. Push the ring down into the bore area where normal ring wear is not encountered.

d. Use the head of the piston to position the ring in the bore so that the ring is square with the cylinder wall. Use caution to avoid damage to the ring or cylinder bore.

e. Measure the gap between the ends of the ring with a feeler gauge. Ring gap in a worn cylinder is normally greater than specification. If the ring gap is greater than the specified limits, try an oversize ring set.

f. Check the ring side clearance of the compression rings with a feeler gauge inserted between the ring and its lower land according to specification. The gauge should slide freely around the entire ring circumference without binding. Any wear that occurs will form a step at the inner portion of the lower land. If the lower lands have high steps, the piston should be replaced.

2. Unless new pistons are installed, be sure to install the pistons in the cylinders from which they were removed. The numbers on the connecting rod and bearing cap must be on the same side when installed in the cylinder bore. If a connecting rod is ever transposed from one engine or cylinder to another, new bearings should be fitted and the connecting rod should be numbered to correspond with the new cylinder number. The notch on the piston head goes toward the front of the engine.

3. Install all of the rod bearing inserts into the rods and caps.

4. Install the rings to the pistons. Install the oil control ring first, then the

second compression ring and finally the top compression ring. Use a piston ring expander tool to aid in installation and to help reduce the chance of breakage.

5. Make sure the ring gaps are properly spaced around the circumference of the piston. Fit a piston ring compressor around the piston and slide the piston and connecting rod assembly down into the cylinder bore, pushing it in with the wooden hammer handle. Push the piston down until it is only slightly below the top of the cylinder bore. Guide the connecting rod onto the crankshaft bearing journal carefully, to avoid damaging the crankshaft.

6. Check the bearing clearance of all the rod bearings, fitting them to the crankshaft bearing journals. Follow the procedure in the crankshaft installation above.

7. After the bearings have been fitted, apply a light coating of assembly oil to the journals and bearings.

8. Turn the crankshaft until the appropriate bearing journal is at the bottom of its stroke, then push the piston assembly all the way down until the connecting rod bearing seats on the crankshaft journal. Be careful not to allow the bearing cap screws to strike the crankshaft bearing journals and damage them.

9. After the piston and connecting rod assemblies have been installed, check the connecting rod side clearance on each crankshaft journal.

10. Prime and install the oil pump and the oil pump intake tube.

OHC Engines
CYLINDER HEAD(S)

1. Install the cylinder head(s) using new gaskets.
2. Install the timing sprockets/gears and the belt/chain assemblies.

Engine Covers and Components

Install the timing cover(s) and oil pan. Refer to your notes and drawings made prior to disassembly and install all of the components that were removed. Install the engine into the vehicle.

Engine Start-up and Break-in

STARTING THE ENGINE

Now that the engine is installed and every wire and hose is properly connected, go back and double check that all coolant and vacuum hoses are connected. Check that your oil drain plug is installed and properly tightened. If not already done, install a new oil filter onto the engine. Fill the crankcase with the proper amount and grade of engine oil. Fill the cooling system with a 50/50 mixture of coolant/water.

1. Connect the vehicle battery.
2. Start the engine. Keep your eye on your oil pressure indicator; if it does not indicate oil pressure within 10 seconds of starting, turn the vehicle off.

Fig. 86 Install the piston and rod assembly into the block using a ring compressor and the handle of a hammer

✳✳ WARNING:

Damage to the engine can result if it is allowed to run with no oil pressure. Check the engine oil level to make sure that it is full. Check for any leaks and if found, repair the leaks before continuing. If there is still no indication of oil pressure, you may need to prime the system.

3. Confirm that there are no fluid leaks (oil or other).

4. Allow the engine to reach normal operating temperature (the upper radiator hose will be hot to the touch).

5. At this point you can perform any necessary checks or adjustments, such as checking the ignition timing.

6. Install any remaining components or body panels which were removed.

BREAKING IT IN

Make the first miles on the new engine, easy ones. Vary the speed but do not accelerate hard. Most importantly, do not lug the engine, and avoid sustained high speeds until at least 100 miles. Check the engine oil and coolant levels frequently. Expect the engine to use a little oil until the rings seat. Change the oil and filter at 500 miles, 1500 miles, then every 3000 miles past that.

KEEP IT MAINTAINED

Now that you have just gone through all of that hard work, keep yourself from doing it all over again by thoroughly maintaining it. Not that you may not have maintained it before, heck you could have had one to two hundred thousand miles on it before doing this. However, you may have bought the vehicle used, and the previous owner did not keep up on maintenance. Which is why you just went through all of that hard work. See?

Notes

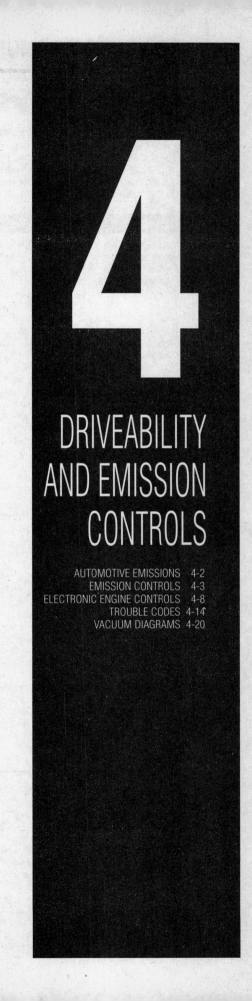

4

DRIVEABILITY AND EMISSION CONTROLS

AUTOMOTIVE EMISSIONS

Before emission controls were mandated on internal combustion engines, other sources of engine pollutants were discovered along with the exhaust emissions. It was determined that engine combustion exhaust produced approximately 60 percent of the total emission pollutants, fuel evaporation from the fuel tank and carburetor vents produced 20 percent, with the final 20 percent being produced through the crankcase as a by-product of the combustion process.

Exhaust Gases

The exhaust gases emitted into the atmosphere are a combination of burned and unburned fuel. To understand the exhaust emission and its composition, we must review some basic chemistry.

When the air/fuel mixture is introduced into the engine, we are mixing air, composed of nitrogen (78 percent), oxygen (21 percent) and other gases (1 percent) with the fuel, which is 100 percent hydrocarbons (HC), in a semi-controlled ratio. As the combustion process is accomplished, power is produced to move the vehicle while the heat of combustion is transferred to the cooling system. The exhaust gases are then composed of nitrogen, a diatomic gas (N2), the same as was introduced in the engine, carbon dioxide (CO2), the same gas that is used in beverage carbonation, and water vapor (H2O). The nitrogen (N2), for the most part, passes through the engine unchanged, while the oxygen (O2) reacts (burns) with the hydrocarbons (HC) and produces the carbon dioxide (CO2) and the water vapors (H2O). If this chemical process would be the only process to take place, the exhaust emissions would be harmless. However, during the combustion process, other compounds are formed which are considered dangerous. These pollutants are hydrocarbons (HC), carbon monoxide (CO), oxides of nitrogen (NOx), oxides of sulfur (SOx), and engine particulates.

HYDROCARBONS

Hydrocarbons (HC) are essentially fuel which was not burned during the combustion process or which has escaped into the atmosphere through fuel evaporation. The main sources of incomplete combustion are rich air/fuel mixtures, low engine temperatures and improper spark timing. The main sources of hydrocarbon emission through fuel evaporation on most vehicles used to be the vehicle's fuel tank and carburetor float bowl.

To reduce combustion hydrocarbon emission, engine modifications were made to minimize dead space and surface area in the combustion chamber. In addition, the air/fuel mixture was made more lean through the improved control which feedback carburetion and fuel injection offers and by the addition of external controls to aid in further combustion of the hydrocarbons outside the engine. Two such methods were the addition of air injection systems, to inject fresh air into the exhaust manifolds and the installation of catalytic converters, units that are able to burn traces of hydrocarbons without affecting the internal combustion process or fuel economy.

To control hydrocarbon emissions through fuel evaporation, modifications were made to the fuel tank to allow storage of the fuel vapors during periods of engine shut-down. Modifications were also made to the air intake system so that at specific times during engine operation, these vapors may be purged and burned by blending them with the air/fuel mixture.

CARBON MONOXIDE

Carbon monoxide is formed when not enough oxygen is present during the combustion process to convert carbon (C) to carbon dioxide (CO2). An increase in the carbon monoxide (CO) emission is normally accompanied by an increase in the hydrocarbon (HC) emission because of the lack of oxygen to completely burn all of the fuel mixture.

Carbon monoxide (CO) also increases the rate at which the photo chemical smog is formed by speeding up the conversion of nitric oxide (NO) to nitrogen dioxide (NO2). To accomplish this, carbon monoxide (CO) combines with oxygen (O2) and nitric oxide (NO) to produce carbon dioxide (CO2) and nitrogen dioxide (NO2). (CO + O2 + NO = CO2 + NO2).

The dangers of carbon monoxide, which is an odorless and colorless toxic gas are many. When carbon monoxide is inhaled into the lungs and passed into the blood stream, oxygen is replaced by the carbon monoxide in the red blood cells, causing a reduction in the amount of oxygen supplied to the many parts of the body. This lack of oxygen causes headaches, lack of coordination, reduced mental alertness and, should the carbon monoxide concentration be high enough, death could result.

NITROGEN

Normally, nitrogen is an inert gas. When heated to approximately 2500-degrees F (1371-degrees C) through the combustion process, this gas becomes active and causes an increase in the nitric oxide (NO) emission.

Oxides of nitrogen (NOx) are composed of approximately 97 - 98 percent nitric oxide (NO). Nitric oxide is a colorless gas but when it is passed into the atmosphere, it combines with oxygen and forms nitrogen dioxide (NO2). The nitrogen dioxide then combines with chemically active hydrocarbons (HC) and when in the presence of sunlight, causes the formation of photo-chemical smog.

Ozone

To further complicate matters, some of the nitrogen dioxide (NO2) is broken apart by the sunlight to form nitric oxide and oxygen. (NO2) + sunlight = NO + O). This single atom of oxygen then combines with diatomic (meaning 2 atoms) oxygen (O2) to form ozone (O3). Ozone is one of the smells associated with smog. It has a pungent and offensive odor, irritates the eyes and lung tissues, affects the growth of plant life and causes rapid deterioration of rubber products. Ozone can be formed by sunlight as well as electrical discharge into the air.

The most common discharge area on the automobile engine is the secondary ignition electrical system, especially when inferior quality spark plug cables are used. As the surge of high voltage is routed through the secondary cable, the circuit builds up an electrical field around the wire, which acts upon the oxygen in the surrounding air to form the ozone. The faint glow along the cable with the engine running that may be visible on a dark night, is called the "corona discharge." It is the result of the electrical field passing from a high along the cable, to a low in the surrounding air, which forms the ozone gas. The combination of corona and ozone has been a major cause of cable deterioration. Recently, different and better quality insulating materials have lengthened the life of the electrical cables.

Although ozone at ground level can be harmful, ozone is beneficial to the earth's inhabitants. By having a concentrated ozone layer called the "ozonosphere," between 10 and 20 miles (16 - 32 km) up in the atmosphere, much of the ultra violet radiation from the sun's rays are absorbed and screened. If this ozone layer were not present, much of the earth's surface would be burned, dried and unfit for human life.

OXIDES OF SULFUR

Oxides of sulfur (SOx) were initially ignored in the exhaust system emissions, since the sulfur content of gasoline as a fuel is less than 1/10 of 1 percent. Because of this small amount, it was felt that it contributed very little to the overall pollution problem. However, because of the difficulty in solving the sulfur emissions in industrial pollution and the introduction of catalytic converters to automobile exhaust systems, a change was mandated. The automobile exhaust system, when equipped with a catalytic converter, changes the sulfur dioxide (SO2) into sulfur trioxide (SO3).

When this combines with water vapors (H2O), a sulfuric acid mist (H2SO4) is formed and is a very difficult pollutant to handle since it is extremely corrosive. This sulfuric acid mist that is formed, is the same mist that rises from the vents of an automobile battery when an active chemical reaction takes place within the battery cells.

When a large concentration of vehicles equipped with catalytic converters are operating in an area, this acid mist may rise and be distributed over a large ground area causing land, plant, crop, paint and building damage.

PARTICULATE MATTER

A certain amount of particulate matter is present in the burning of any fuel, with carbon constituting the largest percentage of the particulates. In gasoline, the remaining particulates are the burned remains of the various other compounds used in its manufacture. When a gasoline engine is in good internal condition, the particulate emissions are low but as the engine wears internally, the particulate emissions increase. By visually inspecting the tail pipe emissions, a determination can be made as to where an engine defect may exist. An engine with light gray or blue smoke emitting from the tail pipe normally indicates an increase in the oil consumption through burning due to internal engine wear. Black smoke would indicate a defective fuel delivery system, causing the engine to operate in a rich mode. Regardless of the color of the smoke, the internal part of the engine or the fuel delivery system should be repaired to prevent excess particulate emissions.

Diesel and turbine engines emit a darkened plume of smoke from the exhaust system because of the type of fuel used. Emission control regulations are mandated for this type of emission and more stringent measures are being used to prevent excess emission of the particulate matter. Electronic components are being introduced to control the injection of the fuel at precisely the proper time of piston travel, to achieve the optimum in fuel ignition and fuel usage. Other particulate after-burning components are being tested to achieve a cleaner emission.

Good grades of engine lubricating oils should be used, which meet the manufacturer's specification. Cut-rate oils can contribute to the particulate emission problem because of their low flash or ignition temperature point. Such oils burn prematurely during the combustion process causing emission of particulate matter.

The cooling system is an important factor in the reduction of particulate matter. The optimum combustion will occur with the cooling system operating at a temperature specified by the manufacturer. The cooling system must be maintained in the same manner as the engine oiling system, as each system is required to perform properly in order for the engine to operate efficiently for a long time.

Crankcase Emissions

Crankcase emissions are made up of water, acids, unburned fuel, oil fumes and particulates. These emissions are classified as hydrocarbons (HC) and are formed by the small amount of unburned, compressed air/fuel mixture entering the crankcase from the combustion area (between the cylinder walls and piston rings) during the compression and power strokes. The heat of the compression and combustion help to form the remaining crankcase emissions.

Since the first engines, crankcase emissions were allowed into the atmosphere through a road draft tube, mounted on the lower side of the engine block. Fresh air came in through an open oil filler cap or breather. The air passed through the crankcase mixing with blow-by gases. The motion of the vehicle and the air blowing past the open end of the road draft tube caused a low pressure area (vacuum) at the end of the tube. Crankcase emissions were simply drawn out of the road draft tube into the air.

To control the crankcase emission, the road draft tube was deleted. A hose and/or tubing was routed from the crankcase to the intake manifold so the blow-by emission could be burned with the air/fuel mixture. However, it was found

that intake manifold vacuum, used to draw the crankcase emissions into the manifold, would vary in strength at the wrong time and not allow the proper emission flow. A regulating valve was needed to control the flow of air through the crankcase.

Testing, showed the removal of the blow-by gases from the crankcase as quickly as possible, was most important to the longevity of the engine. Should large accumulations of blow-by gases remain and condense, dilution of the engine oil would occur to form water, soots, resins, acids and lead salts, resulting in the formation of sludge and varnishes. This condensation of the blow-by gases occurs more frequently on vehicles used in numerous starting and stopping conditions, excessive idling and when the engine is not allowed to attain normal operating temperature through short runs.

Evaporative Emissions

Gasoline fuel is a major source of pollution, before and after it is burned in the automobile engine. From the time the fuel is refined, stored, pumped and transported, again stored until it is pumped into the fuel tank of the vehicle, the gasoline gives off unburned hydrocarbons (HC) into the atmosphere. Through the redesign of storage areas and venting systems, the pollution factor was diminished, but not eliminated, from the refinery standpoint. However, the automobile still remained the primary source of vaporized, unburned hydrocarbon (HC) emissions.

Fuel pumped from an underground storage tank is cool but when exposed to a warmer ambient temperature, will expand. Before controls were mandated, an owner might fill the fuel tank with fuel from an underground storage tank and park the vehicle for some time in warm area, such as a parking lot. As the fuel would warm, it would expand and should no provisions or area be provided for the expansion, the fuel would spill out of the filler neck and onto the ground, causing hydrocarbon (HC) pollution and creating a severe fire hazard. To correct this condition, the vehicle manufacturers added overflow plumbing and/or gasoline tanks with built in expansion areas or domes.

However, this did not control the fuel vapor emission from the fuel tank. It was determined that most of the fuel evaporation occurred when the vehicle was stationary and the engine not operating. Most vehicles carry 5 - 25 gallons (19 - 95 liters) of gasoline. Should a large concentration of vehicles be parked in one area, such as a large parking lot, excessive fuel vapor emissions would take place, increasing as the temperature increases.

To prevent the vapor emission from escaping into the atmosphere, the fuel systems were designed to trap the vapors while the vehicle is stationary, by sealing the system from the atmosphere. A storage system is used to collect and hold the fuel vapors from the carburetor (if equipped) and the fuel tank when the engine is not operating. When the engine is started, the storage system is then purged of the fuel vapors, which are drawn into the engine and burned with the air/fuel mixture.

EMISSION CONTROLS

See Figure 1

Crankcase Ventilation System

OPERATION

See Figure 2

The PCV valve system is designed to force blow-by gases generated in the engine crankcase back into the carburetor or throttle body, then deliver them together with the fuel mixture into the combustion chambers. This system is a closed type and consists of a PCV valve in the cylinder head cover for separating oil particles from blow-by gases and a hose to the carburetor or throttle body. The air cleaner allows fresh air into the system.

Under normal operating conditions, blow-by gases passing between the piston rings and fuel vapor from the fuel tank are mixed with the ambient temperature supplies from the air cleaner. This mixture is then drawn through the PCV valve into the intake manifold for burning. When the engine is operating with the throttle wide open, part of the blow-by generated is drawn directly into the air cleaner via a hose in the cylinder head cover.

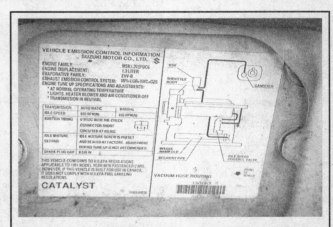

Fig. 1 The emission label under the hood will give you system specifications for a quick reference

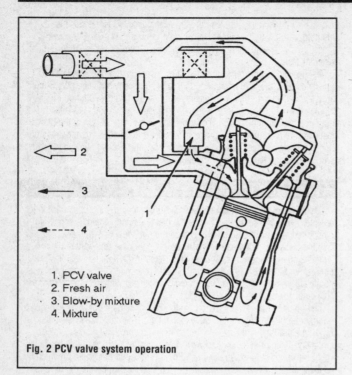

1. PCV valve
2. Fresh air
3. Blow-by mixture
4. Mixture

Fig. 2 PCV valve system operation

TESTING

The PCV system should be inspected every 60,000 miles (100,000 km). Check the PCV valve for blockage or deterioration. Clean the valve and hoses with carburetor cleaner and dry with compressed air. Check the mounting grommet and hoses for deterioration and leakage; replace as necessary.

1. Run the engine at idle.
2. Place a finger over the end of the PCV valve to check for vacuum. If there is no vacuum, check for clogged valve.
3. If the engine is idling rough, this may be caused by a clogged valve or plugged hoses. Never adjust idle speed without checking the PCV valve first.
4. Turn the engine OFF and remove the valve. Shake the valve and listen for a rattle of the needle inside the valve. If the valve does not rattle, replace the valve.

REMOVAL & INSTALLATION

For this procedure please refer to General Information and Maintenance, Routine Maintenance and Tune-Up.

Evaporative Emission Controls

OPERATION

See Figures 3, 4, 5, 6, 7 and 8

The basic evaporative emission control system used on all fuel injected vehi-

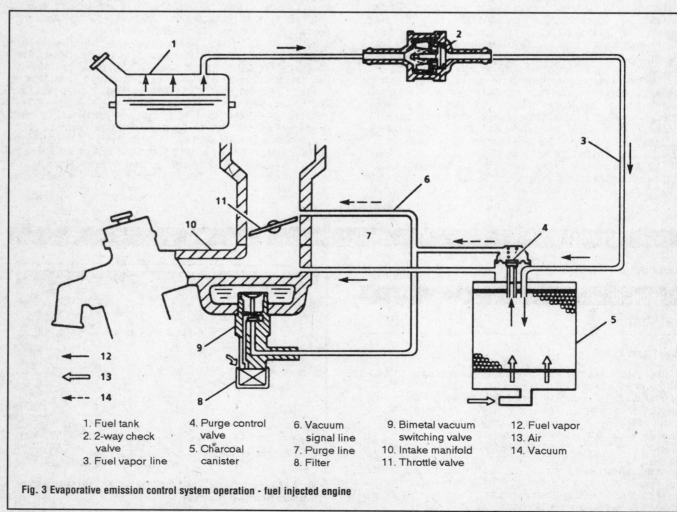

1. Fuel tank
2. 2-way check valve
3. Fuel vapor line
4. Purge control valve
5. Charcoal canister
6. Vacuum signal line
7. Purge line
8. Filter
9. Bimetal vacuum switching valve
10. Intake manifold
11. Throttle valve
12. Fuel vapor
13. Air
14. Vacuum

Fig. 3 Evaporative emission control system operation - fuel injected engine

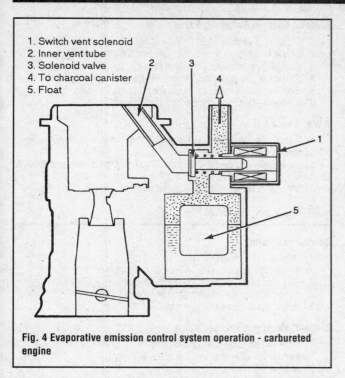

1. Switch vent solenoid
2. Inner vent tube
3. Solenoid valve
4. To charcoal canister
5. Float

Fig. 4 Evaporative emission control system operation - carbureted engine

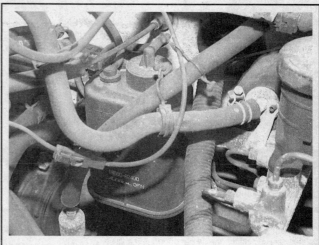

Fig. 5 Charcoal canister and valve

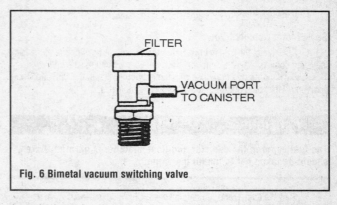

FILTER

VACUUM PORT TO CANISTER

Fig. 6 Bimetal vacuum switching valve

cles is the charcoal canister storage method. This method transfers fuel vapor from the fuel tank and, if equipped, the carburetor bowl, to an activated charcoal storage device. This canister stores the vapors in activated charcoal when the vehicle is not running. When the engine is started, the fuel vapor is purged from the carbon element by intake air flow and consumed in the normal combustion process.

Carbureted Engines

Carbureted vehicles use a switch vent solenoid operated by the ignition switch and the Electronic Control Module (ECM). The switch vent prevents the fuel vapor in the float chamber of the carburetor from flowing out into the atmosphere.

When the ignition switch is in the OFF position, or when cranking the engine, the vent tube is closed by the solenoid valve and allows the fuel vapor to flow from the float chamber into the vapor storage canister. When the engine is operating, the solenoid receives an electrical signal from the ECM to keep the inner vent tube open. As a result, the vapor passes through the tube into the carburetor and is drawn into the engine.

Fuel Injected Engines

Fuel injected vehicles use a vacuum operated canister purge control valve. The canister purge control valve prevents the vapor in the fuel tank from flowing out into the atmosphere.

Certain conditions must be satisfied for the canister purge to occur. When

the engine is running, the coolant temperature is operational and the throttle valve is at any position other than idle, the canister purge control valve will receive ported vacuum. As a result, fuel vapor in the canister is sucked into the intake manifold through the purge control valve and purge line.

When coolant temperature is below normal (cold start), the vacuum signal is interrupted by a bimetal vacuum switching valve and ported vacuum is not applied to the purge control valve. In this condition, the canister is not purged.

A 2-way check valve is also used to keep pressure in the fuel tank constant. When the pressure in the fuel tank becomes positive and reaches its specified value, it opens the valve to let the vapor flow to the charcoal canister. If a vacuum develops in the fuel tank, it opens the valve to let air flow into the tank.

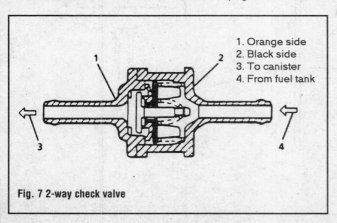

1. Orange side
2. Black side
3. To canister
4. From fuel tank

Fig. 7 2-way check valve

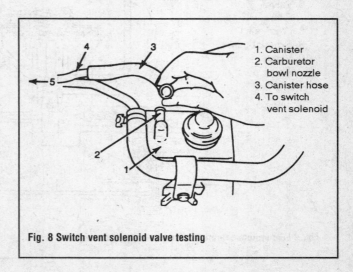

1. Canister
2. Carburetor bowl nozzle
3. Canister hose
4. To switch vent solenoid

Fig. 8 Switch vent solenoid valve testing

SERVICE

The evaporative emissions system should be inspected at least once a year. Inspect the canister for internal damage or clogging. Clean with compressed air, as necessary. Inspect the fuel tank, cap and evaporative emission hoses for damage or leaks. Replace hoses as necessary.

Canister Purge Control Valve

1. Using a small length of vacuum hose connected to the tank tube, blow into the canister. Air should escape the air tube at the bottom of the canister.

> ※※ **CAUTION:**
>
> **The fuel vapor in the canister is harmful. Care should be taken not to inhale the vapor.**

2. Using a small length of vacuum hose connected to the purge tube, blow into the canister. No air should pass through the valve.
3. Apply 20 in. Hg of vacuum to the vacuum signal line tube of the valve, while blowing air into purge tube. Air should come out of the throttle body (TB) tube.
4. If the valve fails to function as specified, replace the canister.

Switch Vent Solenoid Valve

1. Disconnect the canister hose from the carburetor bowl nozzle of the canister, and connect a new hose to the pipe connecting with the solenoid.
2. Blow air into the new hose with the ignition switch in the OFF and ON positions. Air should not pass through the solenoid valve.

> ※※ **CAUTION:**
>
> **The fuel vapor in the canister and float chamber is harmful. Care should be taken not to inhale the vapor.**

3. Start the engine and run at idle speed. Check the solenoid valve as before. Air should not pass through the solenoid.
4. If the valve fails to function as specified, replace the canister.

Bi-Metal Vacuum Switching Valve

1. Remove the vacuum hoses from the VSV.
2. Connect a length of hose to the valve with the engine cold.
3. Blow into the valve, air should not pass through the valve.
4. Start the engine and allow to reach 140-degrees F (60-degrees C).
5. Blow air into the valve, air should pass through the valve.
6. If the valve fails to function as specified, replace it.

2-Way Check Valve

1. Remove the valve and blow hard into the BLACK side of the valve. Air should pass through the valve.
2. Blow lightly into the ORANGE side of the valve, air should pass through the valve.
3. If the valve fails to function as specified, replace it.

REMOVAL & INSTALLATION

Charcoal Canister

1. Label and disconnect all vacuum lines from the canister.
2. As required, disconnect the electrical connector from the canister.
3. Loosen the canister mounting bracket and remove the canister.
4. Inspect and replace vacuum lines as necessary.
5. Installation is the reverse of removal.

Bi-Metal Vacuum Switching Valve

1. Label and disconnect all vacuum lines from the valve.
2. Remove the valve attaching screw, as required.
3. Remove the valve.
4. Inspect and replace vacuum lines as necessary.
5. Installation is the reverse of removal.

2-Way Check Valve

The valve may be located either in the engine compartment or near the fuel tank at the rear of the vehicle.
1. Raise and support the vehicle safely, as required.
2. Locate the check valve.

Note: The valve must be replaced in the same position. Take note which way the valve is removed.

3. Label and disconnect the hoses from the valve.

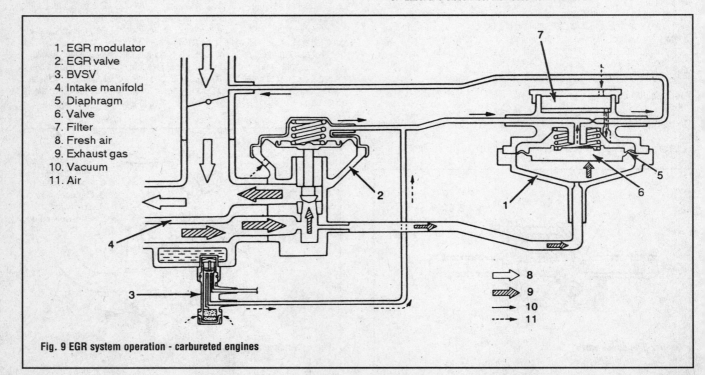

1. EGR modulator
2. EGR valve
3. BVSV
4. Intake manifold
5. Diaphragm
6. Valve
7. Filter
8. Fresh air
9. Exhaust gas
10. Vacuum
11. Air

Fig. 9 EGR system operation - carbureted engines

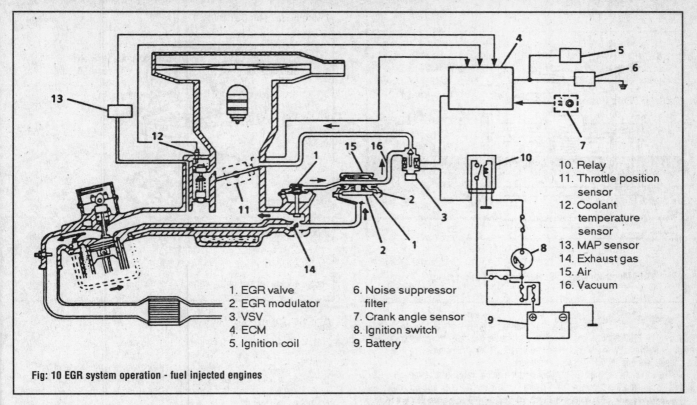

10. Relay
11. Throttle position sensor
12. Coolant temperature sensor
13. MAP sensor
14. Exhaust gas
15. Air
16. Vacuum

1. EGR valve
2. EGR modulator
3. VSV
4. ECM
5. Ignition coil
6. Noise suppressor filter
7. Crank angle sensor
8. Ignition switch
9. Battery

Fig: 10 EGR system operation - fuel injected engines

4. Remove the valve.
5. Installation is the reverse of removal.

Exhaust Gas Recirculation System

OPERATION

See Figures 9, 10, 11, 12, 13 and 14

The EGR system lowers combustion temperatures in the combustion chamber to reduce NOx (Oxides of Nitrogen) emissions. The exhaust gases are drawn from the cylinder head exhaust port into the intake manifold riser portion through the passages in the cylinder head, the intake manifold, and the EGR valve.

The diaphragm mounted in the EGR modulator is operated by the back pressure of the exhaust gas on carbureted engines, or by the Engine Control Module (ECM) on fuel injected engines, to open and close the valve. By this opening and closing action, the EGR modulator controls the vacuum transmitted to the EGR valve.

Under low load condition such as low speed driving, the exhaust pressure is low. In this state, the diaphragm in the EGR modulator is pushed down by the spring force and the modulator valve opens to allow the air into the vacuum passage from the outside.

As a result, the vacuum transmitted to the EGR valve becomes less and so does the opening of the EGR valve. Thus, less exhaust gas is recirculated to the intake manifold.

Under a high load condition such as high speed driving, the exhaust pressure is high. By the high exhaust pressure, the diaphragm in the modulator is pushed up and closes its valve. As the air does not enter the vacuum passage in this state, the vacuum transmitted to the EGR valve becomes larger and so does the opening of the EGR valve. Thus, a larger amount of exhaust gas is recirculated to the intake manifold

When coolant temperature is low, the vacuum passage of the EGR valve is opened to the air through the bi-metal vacuum switching valve (BVSV) on carbureted vehicles, or the vacuum switching valve (VSV) on fuel injected vehicles. In this state, because vacuum is not transmitted to the EGR valve, it remains closed.

On the other hand, when the coolant temperature is normal, the BVSV or VSV is closed. So the EGR valve opens and closes in accordance with the EGR modulator operation.

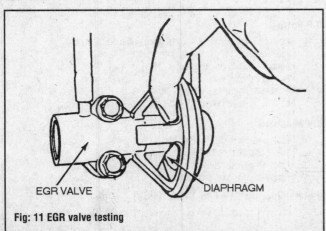

Fig: 11 EGR valve testing

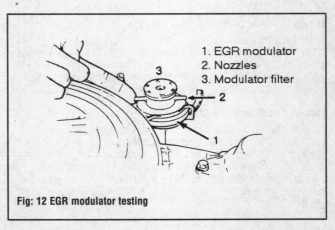

1. EGR modulator
2. Nozzles
3. Modulator filter

Fig: 12 EGR modulator testing

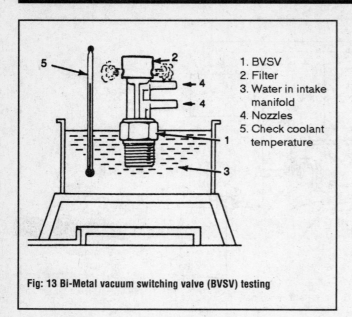

1. BVSV
2. Filter
3. Water in intake manifold
4. Nozzles
5. Check coolant temperature

Fig: 13 Bi-Metal vacuum switching valve (BVSV) testing

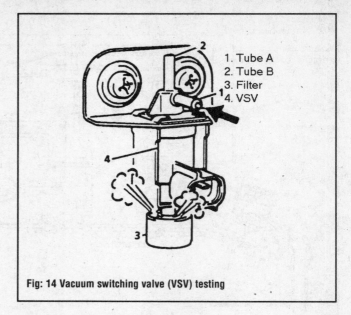

1. Tube A
2. Tube B
3. Filter
4. VSV

Fig: 14 Vacuum switching valve (VSV) testing

On later models, the operation is similar to previous years with a few exceptions. The PCM controls the operation of the solenoid vacuum valve, which regulates the vacuum to the back pressure transducer. The back pressure transducer controls the EGR valve operation.

The PCM checks the EGR passage and the actual valve for blockage. It does this by utilizing the bypass valve. The PCM turns the valve on and off while watching the MAP sensor for variations against the preset values that the PCM expects to see. The only function of the bypass valve is for diagnostic purposes.

TESTING

EGR Valve

1. Run the engine until normal operating temperature.
2. Place a finger on the EGR valve diaphragm and accelerate the engine, the diaphragm should move.
3. Disconnect the vacuum hose from the EGR valve.
4. Apply 10 in. Hg of vacuum to the valve and place a finger on the diaphragm. The valve should move and the engine should stall.

EGR Modulator

1. Check the filter for contamination and damage. Clean using compressed air.
2. Remove the modulator and plug the nozzle with a finger. Blow air into another nozzle and check that air passes through to the air filter side freely.
3. Install a vacuum pump to nozzle **P** and plug nozzle **Q** with a finger. Blow air into nozzle **A** and operate the vacuum pump. Should not be able to obtain vacuum on the pump.

Bi-metal Vacuum Switching Valve (BVSV)

1. Disconnect the hoses from the valve.
2. With the BVSV cool (engine temperature below 113-degrees F, blow into both nozzles individually. Air should come out of the filter.
3. With the BVSV warm (engine temperature above 140-degrees F, blow into both nozzles individually. Air should not come out of the filter.

Vacuum Switching Valve (VSV)

1. Disconnect the hoses and electrical connectors from the solenoid.
2. Use a DVOM to check the resistance between the 2 terminals; should be 33 - 39 ohms resistance. If not, replace the solenoid.
3. Blow into tube **A**, air should exhaust through the filter, not tube **B**.
4. Reconnect the electrical connector. With the ignition switch **ON** and ALDL connector grounded, blow air into tube **A**. The air should exhaust from tube **B**.

Solenoid Vacuum Valve

1. Remove the electrical connector from the valve.
2. Label and remove the two vacuum hoses from the valve.
3. Using an Ohmmeter, check the resistance between the two terminals. The reading should be 33 ohms to 39 ohms at 68-degrees F (20-degrees C).
4. Blow into the tube that is parallel to the electrical terminals. Air should pass out of the other tube.
5. Supply the terminals with power and ground (12v).
6. Blow into the tube that is parallel to the electrical terminals. Air should pass out of the filter but not the other tube.
7. Replace the valve if it does not pass any one of these tests.

Bypass Valve

1. Remove the electrical connector from the valve.
2. Label and remove the three vacuum lines from the valve.
3. Using an Ohmmeter, check the resistance between the two terminals. The reading should be 33 ohms to 39 ohms at 68-degrees F (20-degrees C).
4. Check the resistance between the terminal and the body. The reading should be at least 1M ohm.
5. Blow into the tube that is parallel to the terminal and closer to the terminal. Air should only pass out of the tube that stands by itself.
6. Supply power and ground to the terminals (12v).
7. Blow into the same tube. Air should pass out of the other tube only.
8. Replace the valve if it does not pass any one of these tests.

REMOVAL & INSTALLATION

EGR Valve

1. Allow the engine to cool prior to removing the EGR valve
2. Disconnect the EGR valve vacuum hose.
3. Remove the EGR valve retaining bolts.
4. Remove the EGR valve.
5. When installing the valve use a new gasket.
6. Installation is the reverse of removal.

EGR Modulator

1. Remove the air cleaner assembly.
2. Label and disconnect the modulator vacuum hoses.
3. Remove the modulator.
4. Installation is the reverse of removal.

Bi-Metal Vacuum Switching Valve (BVSV)

1. Drain engine coolant below the level of the valve.

✳✳ CAUTION:

When draining the coolant, keep in mind that cats and dogs are attracted by the ethylene glycol antifreeze, and are quite likely to drink any that is left in an uncovered container or in puddles on the ground. This will prove fatal in sufficient quantity. Always drain the coolant into a sealable container. Coolant should be reused unless it is contaminated or several years old.

2. Label and disconnect the vacuum hoses from the valve.
3. Remove the valve from the intake manifold.
4. Installation is the reverse of removal.

Vacuum Switching Valve (VSV)

1. Disconnect the valve electrical connector.
2. Label and disconnect the vacuum hoses.
3. Remove the fasteners the hold the valve to the firewall.
4. Remove the vacuum switching valve.
5. Installation is the reverse of removal.

Solenoid Vacuum Valve & Bypass Valve

The Solenoid Vacuum Valve and the Bypass Valve are replaced as a unit.
1. Label and remove all of the vacuum lines.
2. Disconnect the electrical connectors from the valves.
3. Unscrew the mounting bracket from the vehicle.
4. Installation is the reverse of the removal.

ELECTRONIC ENGINE CONTROLS

There are two forms of electronic powertrain control systems. Prior to 1996, the system that is used is called On Board Diagnostic first version (OBD-I). As of January 1, 1996, any vehicle built or sold in the United States is required to comply with On Board Diagnostics second version (OBD-II). Unlike its older brother, OBD-II systems have the ability to test itself. This enables the system to find the beginning of problems and not just the failures. The codes in the OBD-II system have a sort of ranking system. Any fault that is set due to an emission failure above federally mandated specification will turn on the MIL and store freeze-frame data and also store a DTC in the first trip. This is referred to as a One Trip Monitor. A Two Trip Monitor is anything that causes the PCM to store a temporary DTC. If the PCM does not see the failure on the next trip, it will erase the DTC. If the PCM sees the failure on the next trip it will store the DTC and freeze-frame data and illuminate the MIL. When the PCM sees an engine misfire that is bad enough to cause damage to the catalytic converter, it will flash the MIL. This condition is falls under the Two Trip Monitor.

The OBD-I system is only able to inform the driver that there is a failure. The system monitors voltage on each circuit and when it sees the wrong voltage, it sets a code.

Engine Control Module (ECM)

OPERATION

The PCM/ECM works by receiving inputs from various sensors, comparing the information received, and making the necessary corrections. The output side of the computer actually supplies ground to the majority of the components. By controlling how long the component is grounded the computer is able to make all the necessary corrections. For example the pulse width of the injector(s).

REMOVAL & INSTALLATION

See Figure 15

1. Disconnect the negative battery cable.
2. Locate the ECM/PCM.
   a. On models through 1994, the ECM is located on the drivers side of the vehicle behind and below the instrument panel.
   b. On 1995 and newer models the ECM/PCM is located behind the glove box.
1. Remove the attaching hardware from the module.
2. Disconnect the electrical connectors.

To install:

3. Connect the electrical connectors.
4. Mount the module and screw into place.
5. Connect the negative battery cable.

Oxygen Sensor

See Figure 16

OPERATION

An oxygen sensor does exactly what its name implies. It monitors the amount of oxygen in the exhaust. By comparing the ambient air, which has approximately 20% oxygen to the air stream in the exhaust, the sensor is able to send a signal to the PCM. This input is created by a chemical reaction that

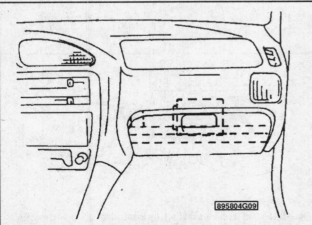

Fig: 15 The PCM in 1995 and newer models is located behind the glove box

Fig: 16 View of Oxygen Sensor from under the vehicle

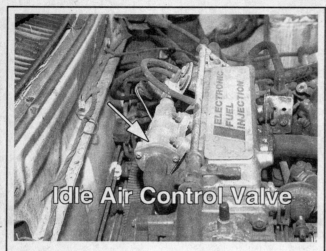

Fig: 17 The IAC is located on the intake manifold

happens when the sensor reaches 600-degrees F (315-degrees C) at this point the sensor begins to create its own voltage. When there is a high Oxygen content in the exhaust, the voltage will be low. The voltage is high when the Oxygen content is low. This allows the PCM to constantly fine tune the fuel delivery in order to maintain the perfect air to fuel ratio.

TESTING

The preferred method for testing this sensor is with the use of an automotive oscilloscope, but any digital multimeter with an internal impedance of 10 megaohms will work just fine. The use of a scan tool that has the ability to monitor the Oxygen sensor's voltage is also helpful. Before the testing can begin, there are a few things that the do it yourselfer should know. Digital Multimeters (DMM) average the readings that they receive. That simply means that the meter takes the average and displays it. There is usually a bar graph at the bottom of the display screen, this is where the most accurate signal is. This is what all of your findings should be based on. The average is an important reading but means nothing if other factors do not fall into place. Amplitude of the signal needs to be at least 650 millivolts, there should be a switching time from high to low of no more than 100 milliseconds or low to high of no more than 125 milliseconds, and the number of crosscounts, or the number of times the signal crosses the 450 millivolt mark per second.

1. Bring the vehicle to normal operating temperature.
2. Rev the engine to 2000rpms and hold the engine speed there.
3. Using a pin, backprobe into the Oxygen sensor's signal wire.
4. Attach the device that is to be used for the testing to the pin and a known good ground.
5. Be sure to write down all findings for future reference.
6. Be sure to check for a post catalytic Oxygen sensor. These are found on OBD-II compliant vehicles.

Note: The post catalytic Oxygen sensor should not be switching at the same rate as the pre cat sensor. This sensor is used by the vehicle to monitor the effectiveness of the catalytic converter. If this sensor reaches within 75% of the pre cat sensor, the catalytic converter is bad.

7. Be sure to remove all pins from the sensors. If sensor checks out to be good but problem still present, continue on to next step.
8. In order to perform this next test a scan tool should be used.
9. Disconnect the sensor from the harness.
10. Grab the harness side connector with your fingers.
11. Now with your other hand touch the positive terminal of the battery and look at the scanner. The reading on the scanner should go to the high side of the scale.
12. Now touch the negative terminal of the battery. The reading should go to the low side of the scale.
13 If the readings switch, the PCM side of the circuit is good.

REMOVAL & INSTALLATION

14. Disconnect negative battery cable.
15. Disconnect the electrical connector of the Oxygen sensor.
16. Using suitable tool unscrew the oxygen sensor from the manifold or pipe.
17. Take care not to damage the tip of the sensor. It is not to come in contact with dirt or fluid and do not attempt to clean the sensor.
18. Installation is the reverse of the removal.

Idle Air Control Valve

See Figure 17

OPERATION

The Idle Air Control Valve is used on ported fuel injection systems. The Idle Air Control Valve (IAC) controls the flow of air allowed past the throttle blade during idle. This is controlled by the PCM. This component is necessary in order to compensate for additional loads that are placed on the engine at idle.

TESTING

Before testing this component, check all electrical connections along with all air supply lines that are involved in this application. Vacuum leaks can lead you down the wrong track.
1. Locate and visually inspect the idle control valve.
2. With the aid of a scan tool, check the idle air counts. When the IAC is fully closed the count is zero and when it is fully open the count is around 140.
3. With the aid of an assistant, check for valve operation.
4. Place hand on the valve while an assistant turn the ignition switch to the on position. Do this several times continuously in order to feel for operation.
5. Replace as needed.

REMOVAL & INSTALLATION

1. Remove the throttle body from the manifold.
2. Remove the IAC from the throttle body assembly.

To install:
3. Using a new O-ring, install the IAC to the throttle body.
4. Torque the IAC to the throttle body to 2.5 ft. lbs. (3.3 Nm).
5. Reinstall the throttle body assembly to the manifold.

Idle Speed Control Motor

See Figure 18

OPERATION

The ISC (Idle Speed Control Motor) is used on carbureted and throttle body injected vehicles. The PCM uses the ISC to control the idle speed of the vehicle.

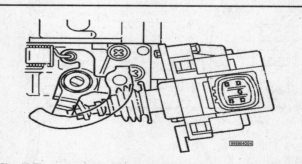

Fig. 18 The two terminals that are by themselves are the terminals for the ISC

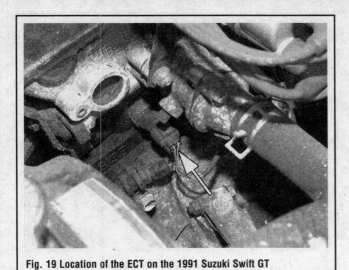

Fig. 19 Location of the ECT on the 1991 Suzuki Swift GT

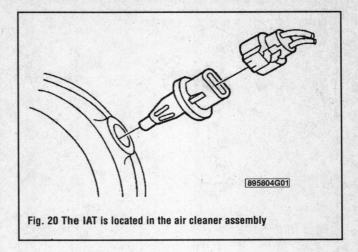

Fig. 20 The IAT is located in the air cleaner assembly

If the PCM push the plunger on the ISC forward, it will increase the engine idle speed. The PCM decreases the idle speed by moving the ISC plunger to the rear. The plunger simply pushes on the throttle valve in order to control the amount of air that is allowed to pass into the engine.

TESTING

1. Make sure that the ISC plunger is in contact with the throttle valve lever.
2. Disconnect the electrical connector from the ISC.
3. Connect 6v to the GRY/YEL wire and ground to the GRY/RED wire.
4. If the plunger does not extend outward, replace the ISC.
5. If the plunger does extend and the code is present, check the rest of the circuit for continuity.

REMOVAL & INSTALLATION

1. Remove the air cleaner assembly.
2. Disconnect the electrical connector from the motor.
3. Remove the ISC from the throttle body by removing the three screws.

To install:
4. Place the new ISC on the throttle body and secure with the three screws.
5. Torque the screws to 24 - 36 inch lbs. (2.8 - 4 Nm).
6. Connect the electrical connector.
7. Install the air cleaner assembly.

Coolant Temperature Sensor

OPERATION

This sensor is located in the thermostat housing and is used to measure the temperature of the coolant in the engine. The sensor uses resistance to turn temperature into a voltage that the PCM can use. As the temperature goes up the resistance goes down. The PCM has a fixed resistor located internally. It uses this resistor to reference the sensor. This sensor signal is used through all the phases of engine operation from cold start to closed loop operation to tune fuel delivery.

TESTING

1. Disconnect the electrical connector from the sensor.
2. Using a DMM set to read Ohms, connect to the sensor.
3. Start the vehicle and take a reading every few minutes as the engine warms up.
4. If the resistance does not decrease, the sensor is bad and must be replaced.
5. If the sensor checks out okay, check the circuit from the sensor back to the PCM and to ground for any voltage drops.

REMOVAL & INSTALLATION

See Figure 19

1. Drain enough coolant so that the level is below the sensor.
2. Disconnect the electrical connector.
3. Remove the sensor from the thermostat housing.

To install:
4. Clean the mating surface of the housing and the sensor.
5. Replace the o-ring as necessary.
6. Torque the sensor to 11 ft. lbs. (15 Nm).
7. Connect the electrical connector to the sensor.

Intake Air Temperature Sensor

See Figure 20

OPERATION

This sensor is located in the air cleaner assembly and is used to measure the temperature of the intake air about to be used by the engine. The sensor uses resistance to turn temperature into a voltage that the PCM can use. As the temperature goes up the resistance goes down. The PCM has a fixed resistor located internally. It uses this resistor to reference the sensor. This sensor signal is used through all the phases of engine operation from cold start to closed loop operation to tune fuel delivery.

TESTING

1. Remove the sensor.
2. Place the tip of the sensor in water.
3. Begin to heat the water while taking readings of the resistance.
4. If the resistance does not decrease as the temperature goes up, replace the sensor.
5. If the sensor checks out okay, check the circuit from the sensor back to the PCM and to ground for any voltage drops.

REMOVAL & INSTALLATION

1. Disconnect the negative battery cable.
2. Remove the electrical connector from the sensor.
3. Remove the sensor from the air cleaner housing.

To install:
4. Clean the mating surfaces.
5. Install and torque the sensor to 9.5 - 12.0 ft. lbs. (13 - 17 Nm).
6. Connect the electrical connector to the sensor.
7. Reconnect the negative battery cable.

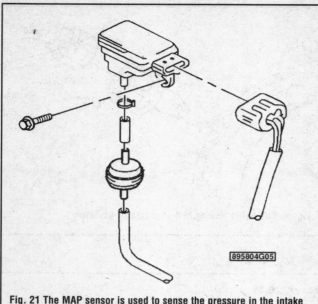

Fig. 21 The MAP sensor is used to sense the pressure in the intake manifold.

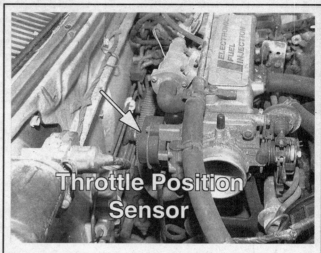

Fig. 22 The TPS is located on the end of the throttle blade shaft

Manifold Absolute Pressure Sensor

See Figure 21

OPERATION

This sensor measures engine vacuum or pressure. The PCM supplies a reference voltage to the sensor. The sensor converts the change in vacuum to an electrical signal that is then sent to the PCM. A low voltage signal at the PCM means that there is low manifold pressure or high engine manifold vacuum. For example: At idle 18" hg. Map sensor voltage is 1.1v-1.3v; as the vacuum decreases or the pressure goes up, the voltage goes up.

TESTING

1. Turn the key to the ON position but do not start the vehicle.
2. Backprobe the signal wire of the sensor.
3. Connect a DMM to the sensor and a known good ground.
4. The voltage should be 4v to 5v.
5. Start the vehicle, the reading should be 1.1v to 1.3v.
6. Replace the sensor as needed.

REMOVAL & INSTALLATION

1. Remove the electrical connector from the sensor.
2. Remove the vacuum lines from the sensor.
3. Unbolt the sensor bracket for the firewall.
4. Remove the sensor from the mounting bracket.
To install:
5. Place new sensor into mounting bracket.
6. Bolt the mounting bracket to the firewall and torque to 89 inch lbs. (10 Nm).
7. Connect the vacuum lines and electrical connector to the sensor.

Barometric Pressure Sensor

This vehicle is equipped with a BARO Sensor that enables the PCM to make correction for changes in altitude while the vehicle is operating. The sensor is an integral part of the PCM and can not be replaced separately. If it is necessary to replace the Baro Sensor, the new PCM must be programmed by the dealer.

Throttle Position Sensor

See Figure 22

OPERATION

The TPS (throttle position sensor) measures the percentage of throttle valve opening. The sensor is connected to the throttle valve shaft. The PCM supplies a reference voltage to the sensor. The PCM uses this signal in order to control the fuel delivery, the IAC, the EGR solenoid vacuum valve, and in the automatic transmission models, the shift points.

TESTING

1. Backprobe the signal wire and connect a DMM to the signal and a known good ground.
2. Turn the key to ON but do not start the vehicle.
3. With the throttle closed, the reading should be less than 1 volt. 900mv to 1.02v is normal.
4. Slowly open the throttle by hand while watching the voltage reading change. Look for dead spots where the voltage drops off.
5. When the throttle is wide open, the reading should be close to 5v. 4.85v to 4.95v is normal.
6. Replace the sensor if the readings are bad.

REMOVAL & INSTALLATION

1. Disconnect the negative battery cable.
2. Remove the air cleaner assembly if necessary.
3. Remove the electrical connector from the sensor.
4. Remove the sensor.
To install:
5. Place the new sensor on the throttle valve shaft in such a way that screw holes are a little out of alignment.
6. Turn the sensor clockwise until the holes line up.
7. Hand tighten the screws.
8. Connect the negative battery cable.
9. Connect the electrical connector to the sensor..
10. Models equipped with ISC motors, place a 0.14 inch (3.5 mm) feeler blade between the stop screw and the throttle lever.
11. Turn the sensor until the voltage reading is 0.98v to 1.02v.
12. Torque the screws to 1.2 to 1.7 ft. lbs. (1.6 to 2.4 Nm).
13. Replace the air cleaner assembly if removed.

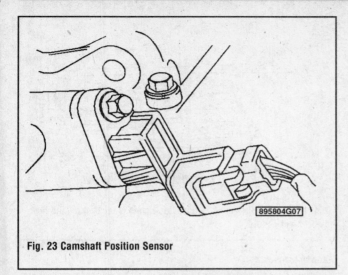

Fig. 23 Camshaft Position Sensor

Camshaft Position Sensor

See Figure 23

OPERATION

See Figure 24

The CMP (camshaft position sensor) has an air gap between the sensor and the rotor. This produces a digital signal, which is sent to the PCM. The PCM uses the signal to watch for misfires and to determine which cylinder the engine is about to fire.

TESTING

1. Disconnect the sensor and check for voltage on the pins. The left terminal or B+ should be 10v to 14v. The center or Vout should be 4v to 5v. The right terminal should be ground.
2. Reconnect the harness to the sensor.
3. Crank the engine while probing pin C22-2 at the PCM.
4. Look for varying voltage of 0v to 1v low and 4v to 5v high.
5. Remove the sensor and visually inspect the rotor using a mirror.
6. Replace sensor if the rotor checks out to be good.

REMOVAL & INSTALLATION

1. Disconnect the electrical connector from the sensor.
2. Remove the sensor from the sensor case.

To install:
3. Check the O-ring for damage and replace as necessary.
4. Install the sensor into casing and torque to 6.5 ft. lbs. (9 Nm).
5. Connect the electrical connector.

Crankshaft Position Sensor

See Figure 25

OPERATION

This sensor produces an AC wave by producing a magnetic field. As the rotor passes through the magnetic field, it breaks the flow of current in turn producing a signal. The pulse that is produced is used by the PCM to control ignition and fuel delivery, it is also used to monitor engine speed and misfires.

TESTING

1. Check the sensor for resistance. Between the two terminals should be

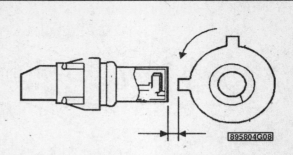

Fig. 24 The CMP uses the air gap to produce a usable signal for the PCM

360 ohms to 460 ohms.
2. Check the resistance between each terminal and ground. The readings should be At least 1M ohms
3. Visually inspect the sensor and the sensor pulley for damage, metal particles in the teeth, or incorrect set up.
4. Replace or correct any component found that is out of parameters.

REMOVAL & INSTALLATION

1. Raise and support the vehicle safely.
2. Remove the inner fender extension on the right side.
3. Remove the electrical connector from the sensor.
4. Remove the sensor from the oil pan.

To install:
5. Install the sensor to the oil pan.
6. Reconnect the electrical connector to the sensor.
7. Install the inner fender apron.
8. Lower the vehicle.

Vehicle Speed Sensor

OPERATION

On manual transmission models, the sensor is part of the speedometer and is located in the dash. There is a magnet which turns with the speedometer cable, this turns a reed switch off and on, producing a digital signal that is sent to the PCM. On automatic transmission models, the sensor is slightly different. The sensor is located in the transaxle assembly near the countershaft. Using a magnetic core with a magnet and coil, the sensor produces the signal when the magnetic field is broken and completed by the rotating countershaft. The countershaft speed determines the signal pulses, which are sent to the PCM.

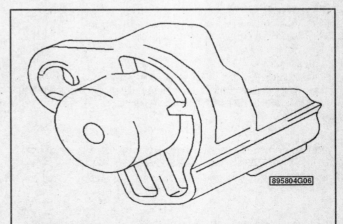

Fig. 25 Crankshaft Position Sensor from a 2000 Chevrolet Metro

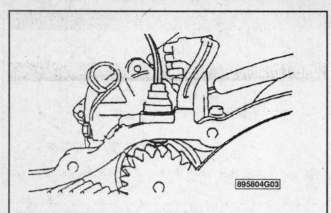

Fig. 26 The VSS for the automatic transaxle is located in the transaxle casing

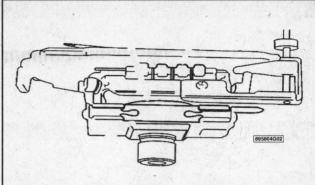

Fig. 27 The VSS for manual transaxle models is located behind the instrument panel

TESTING

Automatic Transaxle

See Figure 26

1. Disconnect the electrical connector from the sensor.
2. Using an Ohmmeter, check the resistance of the sensor.
3. The resistance between the terminals should be 100 ohms to 300 ohms.
4. The resistance between the terminal and the transaxle case should be 1M ohm or more.
5. Replace the sensor if the test do not produce the correct results.
6. Remove the sensor and check for damage, correct installation, and foreign material on the sensor or on the countershaft.

Manual Transaxle

See Figure 27

1. Backprobe the sensor.
2. Raise and safely support the vehicle.
3. Connect a DMM or an oscilloscope to the sensor.
4. Start the vehicle and put the transaxle into gear allowing the front wheels to spin freely.
5. Make sure that the sensor is receiving a reference voltage from the PCM.
6. If no signal is present, check the wiring back to the PCM.
7. Make needed repairs.

REMOVAL & INSTALLATION

Automatic Transaxle

1. Disconnect the electrical connector from the sensor.
2. Unbolt the sensor from the transaxle case.
3. Remove the sensor.

To install:

4. Install the new sensor into the transaxle case.
5. Bolt the sensor to the transaxle case and torque to 72 inch lbs. (8 Nm).
6. Connect the electrical connector to the sensor.

Manual Transaxle

Please refer to Chassis Electrical, Instruments, and Switches for removal procedures.

Fuel Tank Pressure Sensor

OPERATION

The Fuel Tank Pressure Sensor is used to monitor the pressure or vacuum in the fuel tank much like the way the MAP sensor monitors the intake manifold. The PCM supplies the sensor with a reference voltage. When the gas cap is removed, the signal voltage back to the PCM is 2.0v to 2.6v. This system is designed to monitor the EVAP system for failures.

TESTING

1. Be sure that the sensor is receiving the reference voltage from the PCM.
2. Make sure that the fuel tank pressure sensor air hole is clear of obstruction.
3. Backprobe the signal wire and connect a DMM.
4. Remove the gas cap and turn the ignition to ON .
5. Check the voltage reading, it should be 2.0v to 2.6v.
6. Check the continuity of the harness back to the PCM.
7. Repair as needed.
8. If the harness is good, replace the sensor.

REMOVAL & INSTALLATION

1. Remove or lower the fuel tank.
2. Remove the sensor and disconnect the electrical harness from the sensor.

To install:

3. Replace O-ring as needed.
4. Install the sensor pointing the terminals toward the fuel level sensor.
5. Torque the sensor to 1 ft. lbs. (2 Nm).
6. Connect the electrical connector to the sensor.
7. Reinstall the fuel tank.

TROUBLE CODES

Diagnostic Trouble Codes

Trouble codes are faults that the PCM recognizes. These faults are then translated into a number form and stored in the PCM.

General Information

The Chevrolet Sprint, Geo/Chevrolet Metro, and the Suzuki Swift all use an Engine Control Module/Powertrain Control Module (ECM/PCM) to control different components on the vehicle. The module is designed to sense, compare, and correct as the inputs are fed to the system. It is very important to test the components before condemning and replacing anything. If the input is not the proper signal, then the output is not going to perform properly. When a code is gathered and read, it is important to look at the entire circuit. There will be times that components share grounds or even power supplies. A good understanding of electricity is an essential key to diagnostic troubleshooting on today's vehicles. As the control module becomes more advanced, it will monitor more parameters and perform more tests. When the data from the module is available, use as much as possible to find clues to why the codes were set.

Diagnostic Connector

The diagnostic connector or the DLC (Data Link Connector) is where connection can be made in order to retrieve information from the control module. All OBD-II models have the connector in the same place. It is under the instrument panel in between the steering column and the center console. Do not attempt to ground out the pins in order to get flash codes. The system may become damaged and rendered inoperative. OBD-II systems do not give flash codes.

On the earlier models, there are two data link connectors. One is located under the left hand side of the dash next to the junction block. The other is located in the engine compartment near the left side strut tower.

Reading Codes

There are a few ways to read codes on pre 1996 vehicles. The best way is to use a Diagnostic Scan Tool (DST). The Data Link Connector is located on the drivers side of the engine compartment near the strut tower. Once connected to the vehicle with the scanner, follow the instructions for that specific scanner. If the use of a DST is not available, the diagnostic request terminal can be grounded. This sends a signal to the PCM, which then flashes the MIL. The number of flashes will equal the trouble code that the PCM is sending.

The junction block can also be used to retrieve codes from the PCM. Under the left side of the instrument panel, the junction block has a built in DLC or data link connector. This is very useful when data must be monitored while driving.

Clearing Codes

There are a couple of ways to clear codes on today's vehicles. The least recommended way is to disconnect the negative battery cable for 60 seconds. The problem with this is that the control module learns to adapt to the way you drive and when it loses power, it loses that part of the memory. This can lead you to believe that your repair is bad. On the OBD-II vehicles the module will lose all the freeze frame data it recorded, the readiness monitors that it is trying to run, and the adaptive memory.

The second way of clearing codes is to use a scan tool. This is the best way to clear codes on OBD-I vehicles. It will allow the codes to be cleared without erasing the adaptive memory. Unfortunately, for those with an OBD-II vehicle, the readiness monitors are reset and the vehicle has to go through another drive cycle in order to give a status report.

OBD-I Diagnostic Trouble Codes

The following is a list of OBD I Diagnostic Trouble Codes, for 1989 - 95 vehicles:

12	No Failures
13	Oxygen Sensor
14	Coolant Temperature Sensor
15	Coolant Temperature Sensor
21	Throttle Switch (Manual Transaxle)
21	Throttle Position Sensor (Automatic Transaxle)
22	Throttle Position Sensor (Automatic Transaxle)
23	Manifold Air Temperature Sensor
25	Manifold Air Temperature Sensor
24	Speed Sensor
31	Manifold Absolute Pressure Sensor
32	Manifold Absolute Pressure Sensor
41	Ignition Signal
42	Crank Angle Sensor
51	EGR System
ON	ECM Failure

OBD-II Diagnostic Trouble Codes

Following is a list of OBD II Diagnostic Trouble Codes, for 1996 - 00 vehicles:

P0000	No Failures
P0100	Mass or Volume Air Flow Circuit Malfunction
P0101	Mass or Volume Air Flow Circuit Range/Performance Problem
P0102	Mass or Volume Air Flow Circuit Low Input
P0103	Mass or Volume Air Flow Circuit High Input
P0104	Mass or Volume Air Flow Circuit Intermittent
P0105	Manifold Absolute Pressure/Barometric Pressure Circuit Malfunction
P0106	Manifold Absolute Pressure/Barometric Pressure Circuit Range/Performance Problem
P0107	Manifold Absolute Pressure/Barometric Pressure Circuit Low Input
P0108	Manifold Absolute Pressure/Barometric Pressure Circuit High Input
P0109	Manifold Absolute Pressure/Barometric Pressure Circuit Intermittent

OBD-II Diagnostic Trouble Codes (continued)

P0110...... Intake Air Temperature Circuit Malfunction

P0111...... Intake Air Temperature Circuit Range/Performance Problem

P0112...... Intake Air Temperature Circuit Low Input

P0113...... Intake Air Temperature Circuit High Input

P0114...... Intake Air Temperature Circuit Intermittent

P0115...... Engine Coolant Temperature Circuit Malfunction

P0116...... Engine Coolant Temperature Circuit Range/Performance Problem

P0117...... Engine Coolant Temperature Circuit Low Input

P0118...... Engine Coolant Temperature Circuit High Input

P0119...... Engine Coolant Temperature Circuit Intermittent

P0120...... Throttle/Pedal Position Sensor/Switch "A" Circuit Malfunction

P0121...... Throttle/Pedal Position Sensor/Switch "A" Circuit Range/Performance Problem

P0122...... Throttle/Pedal Position Sensor/Switch "A" Circuit Low Input

P0123...... Throttle/Pedal Position Sensor/Switch "A" Circuit High Input

P0124...... Throttle/Pedal Position Sensor/Switch "A" Circuit Intermittent

P0125...... Insufficient Coolant Temperature For Closed Loop Fuel Control

P0126...... Insufficient Coolant Temperature For Stable Operation

P0130...... O2 Circuit Malfunction (Bank no. 1 Sensor no. 1)

P0131...... O2 Sensor Circuit Low Voltage (Bank no. 1 Sensor no. 1)

P0132...... O2 Sensor Circuit High Voltage (Bank no. 1 Sensor no. 1)

P0133...... O2 Sensor Circuit Slow Response (Bank no. 1 Sensor no. 1)

P0134...... O2 Sensor Circuit No Activity Detected (Bank no. 1 Sensor no. 1)

P0135...... O2 Sensor Heater Circuit Malfunction (Bank no. 1 Sensor no. 1)

P0136...... O2 Sensor Circuit Malfunction (Bank no. 1 Sensor no. 2)

P0137...... O2 Sensor Circuit Low Voltage (Bank no. 1 Sensor no. 2)

P0138...... O2 Sensor Circuit High Voltage (Bank no. 1 Sensor no. 2)

P0139...... O2 Sensor Circuit Slow Response (Bank no. 1 Sensor no. 2)

P0140...... O2 Sensor Circuit No Activity Detected (Bank no. 1 Sensor no. 2)

P0141...... O2 Sensor Heater Circuit Malfunction (Bank no. 1 Sensor no. 2)

P0142...... O2 Sensor Circuit Malfunction (Bank no. 1 Sensor no. 3)

P0143...... O2 Sensor Circuit Low Voltage (Bank no. 1 Sensor no. 3)

P0144...... O2 Sensor Circuit High Voltage (Bank no. 1 Sensor no. 3)

P0145...... O2 Sensor Circuit Slow Response (Bank no. 1 Sensor no. 3)

P0146...... O2 Sensor Circuit No Activity Detected (Bank no. 1 Sensor no. 3)

P0147...... O2 Sensor Heater Circuit Malfunction (Bank no. 1 Sensor no. 3)

P0150...... O2 Sensor Circuit Malfunction (Bank no. 2 Sensor no. 1)

P0151...... O2 Sensor Circuit Low Voltage (Bank no. 2 Sensor no. 1)

P0152...... O2 Sensor Circuit High Voltage (Bank no. 2 Sensor no. 1)

P0153...... O2 Sensor Circuit Slow Response (Bank no. 2 Sensor no. 1)

P0154...... O2 Sensor Circuit No Activity Detected (Bank no. 2 Sensor no. 1)

P0155...... O2 Sensor Heater Circuit Malfunction (Bank no. 2 Sensor no. 1)

P0156...... O2 Sensor Circuit Malfunction (Bank no. 2 Sensor no. 2)

P0157...... O2 Sensor Circuit Low Voltage (Bank no. 2 Sensor no. 2)

P0158...... O2 Sensor Circuit High Voltage (Bank no. 2 Sensor no. 2)

P0159...... O2 Sensor Circuit Slow Response (Bank no. 2 Sensor no. 2)

P0160...... O2 Sensor Circuit No Activity Detected (Bank no. 2 Sensor no. 2)

P0161...... O2 Sensor Heater Circuit Malfunction (Bank no. 2 Sensor no. 2)

P0162...... O2 Sensor Circuit Malfunction (Bank no. 2 Sensor no. 3)

P0163...... O2 Sensor Circuit Low Voltage (Bank no. 2 Sensor no. 3)

P0164...... O2 Sensor Circuit High Voltage (Bank no. 2 Sensor no. 3)

P0165...... O2 Sensor Circuit Slow Response (Bank no. 2 Sensor no. 3)

P0166...... O2 Sensor Circuit No Activity Detected (Bank no. 2 Sensor no. 3)

P0167...... O2 Sensor Heater Circuit Malfunction (Bank no. 2 Sensor no. 3)

P0170...... Fuel Trim Malfunction (Bank no. 1)

P0171...... System Too Lean (Bank no. 1)

P0172...... System Too Rich (Bank no. 1)

P0173...... Fuel Trim Malfunction (Bank no. 2)

P0174...... System Too Lean (Bank no. 2)

P0175...... System Too Rich (Bank no. 2)

P0176...... Fuel Composition Sensor Circuit Malfunction

P0177...... Fuel Composition Sensor Circuit Range/Performance

P0178...... Fuel Composition Sensor Circuit Low Input

P0179...... Fuel Composition Sensor Circuit High Input

P0180...... Fuel Temperature Sensor "A" Circuit Malfunction

P0181...... Fuel Temperature Sensor "A" Circuit Range/Performance

P0182...... Fuel Temperature Sensor "A" Circuit Low Input

P0183...... Fuel Temperature Sensor "A" Circuit High Input

P0184...... Fuel Temperature Sensor "A" Circuit Intermittent

P0185...... Fuel Temperature Sensor "B" Circuit Malfunction

P0186...... Fuel Temperature Sensor "B" Circuit Range/Performance

P0187...... Fuel Temperature Sensor "B" Circuit Low Input

P0188...... Fuel Temperature Sensor "B" Circuit High Input

P0189...... Fuel Temperature Sensor "B" Circuit Intermittent

P0190...... Fuel Rail Pressure Sensor Circuit Malfunction

P0191...... Fuel Rail Pressure Sensor Circuit Range/Performance

P0192...... Fuel Rail Pressure Sensor Circuit Low Input

P0193...... Fuel Rail Pressure Sensor Circuit High Input

P0194...... Fuel Rail Pressure Sensor Circuit Intermittent

P0195...... Engine Oil Temperature Sensor Malfunction

P0196...... Engine Oil Temperature Sensor Range/Performance

P0197...... Engine Oil Temperature Sensor Low

P0198...... Engine Oil Temperature Sensor High

P0199...... Engine Oil Temperature Sensor Intermittent

P0200...... Injector Circuit Malfunction

P0201...... Injector Circuit Malfunction - Cylinder no. 1

P0202...... Injector Circuit Malfunction - Cylinder no. 2

P0203...... Injector Circuit Malfunction - Cylinder no. 3

P0204...... Injector Circuit Malfunction - Cylinder no. 4

P0205...... Injector Circuit Malfunction - Cylinder no. 5

P0206...... Injector Circuit Malfunction - Cylinder no. 6

P0207...... Injector Circuit Malfunction - Cylinder no. 7

P0208...... Injector Circuit Malfunction - Cylinder no. 8

P0209...... Injector Circuit Malfunction - Cylinder no. 9

P0210...... Injector Circuit Malfunction - Cylinder no. 10

P0211...... Injector Circuit Malfunction - Cylinder no. 11

P0212...... Injector Circuit Malfunction - Cylinder no. 1

P0213...... Cold Start Injector no. 1 Malfunction

P0214...... Cold Start Injector no. 2 Malfunction

P0215...... Engine Shutoff Solenoid Malfunction

P0216...... Injection Timing Control Circuit Malfunction

P0217...... Engine Over Temperature Condition

P0218...... Transmission Over Temperature Condition

P0219...... Engine Over Speed Condition

P0220...... Throttle/Pedal Position Sensor/Switch "B" Circuit Malfunction

P0221...... Throttle/Pedal Position Sensor/Switch "B" Circuit Range/Performance Problem

P0222...... Throttle/Pedal Position Sensor/Switch "B" Circuit Low Input

P0223...... Throttle/Pedal Position Sensor/Switch "B" Circuit High Input

P0224...... Throttle/Pedal Position Sensor/Switch "B" Circuit Intermittent

P0225...... Throttle/Pedal Position Sensor/Switch "C" Circuit Malfunction

P0226...... Throttle/Pedal Position Sensor/Switch "C" Circuit Range/Performance Problem

P0227...... Throttle/Pedal Position Sensor/Switch "C" Circuit Low Input

P0228...... Throttle/Pedal Position Sensor/Switch "C" Circuit High Input

P0229...... Throttle/Pedal Position Sensor/Switch "C" Circuit Intermittent

P0230...... Fuel Pump Primary Circuit Malfunction

P0231...... Fuel Pump Secondary Circuit Low

P0232 ..... Fuel Pump Secondary Circuit High

P0233...... Fuel Pump Secondary Circuit Intermittent

P0234...... Engine Over Boost Condition

P0261...... Cylinder no. 1 Injector Circuit Low

P0262...... Cylinder no. 1 Injector Circuit High

P0263...... Cylinder no. 1 Contribution/Balance Fault

P0264...... Cylinder no. 2 Injector Circuit Low

P0265...... Cylinder no. 2 Injector Circuit High

P0266...... Cylinder no. 2 Contribution/Balance Fault

P0267...... Cylinder no. 3 Injector Circuit Low

P0268...... Cylinder no. 3 Injector Circuit High

P0269...... Cylinder no. 3 Contribution/Balance Fault

P0270...... Cylinder no. 4 Injector Circuit Low

P0271...... Cylinder no. 4 Injector Circuit High

P0272...... Cylinder no. 4 Contribution/Balance Fault

P0273...... Cylinder no. 5 Injector Circuit Low

P0274...... Cylinder no. 5 Injector Circuit High

P0275...... Cylinder no. 5 Contribution/Balance Fault

P0276...... Cylinder no. 6 Injector Circuit Low

P0277...... Cylinder no. 6 Injector Circuit High

P0278...... Cylinder no. 6 Contribution/Balance Fault

P0279...... Cylinder no. 7 Injector Circuit Low

P0280...... Cylinder no. 7 Injector Circuit High

P0281...... Cylinder no. 7 Contribution/Balance Fault

P0282...... Cylinder no. 8 Injector Circuit Low

P0283...... Cylinder no. 8 Injector Circuit High

P0284...... Cylinder no. 8 Contribution/Balance Fault

P0285...... Cylinder no. 9 Injector Circuit Low

P0286...... Cylinder no. 9 Injector Circuit High

P0287...... Cylinder no. 9 Contribution/Balance Fault

P0288...... Cylinder no. 10 Injector Circuit Low

P0289...... Cylinder no. 10 Injector Circuit High

P0290...... Cylinder no. 10 Contribution/Balance Fault

P0291...... Cylinder no. 11 Injector Circuit Low

P0292...... Cylinder no. 11 Injector Circuit High

P0293...... Cylinder no. 11 Contribution/Balance Fault

P0294...... Cylinder no. 12 Injector Circuit Low

P0295...... Cylinder no. 12 Injector Circuit High

P0296...... Cylinder no. 12 Contribution/Balance Fault

P0300...... Random/Multiple Cylinder Misfire Detected

P0301...... Cylinder no. 1 - Misfire Detected

P0302...... Cylinder no. 2 - Misfire Detected

P0303...... Cylinder no. 3 - Misfire Detected

P0304...... Cylinder no. 4 - Misfire Detected

P0305...... Cylinder no. 5 - Misfire Detected

P0306...... Cylinder no. 6 - Misfire Detected

OBD-II Diagnostic Trouble Codes (continued)

P0307...... Cylinder no. 7 - Misfire Detected

P0308...... Cylinder no. 8 - Misfire Detected

P0309...... Cylinder no. 9 - Misfire Detected

P0310...... Cylinder no. 10 - Misfire Detected

P0311...... Cylinder no. 11 - Misfire Detected

P0312...... Cylinder no. 12 - Misfire Detected

P0320...... Ignition/Distributor Engine Speed Input Circuit Malfunction

P0321...... Ignition/Distributor Engine Speed Input Circuit Range/Performance

P0322...... Ignition/Distributor Engine Speed Input Circuit No Signal

P0323...... Ignition/Distributor Engine Speed Input Circuit Intermittent

P0325...... Knock Sensor no. 1 - Circuit Malfunction (Bank no. 1 or Single Sensor)

P0326...... Knock Sensor no. 1 - Circuit Range/Performance (Bank no. 1 or Single Sensor)

P0327...... Knock Sensor no. 1 - Circuit Low Input (Bank no. 1 or Single Sensor)

P0328...... Knock Sensor no. 1 - Circuit High Input (Bank no. 1 or Single Sensor)

P0329...... Knock Sensor no. 1 - Circuit Input Intermittent (Bank No. 1 or Single Sensor)

P0330...... Knock Sensor no. 2 - Circuit Malfunction (Bank no. 2)

P0331...... Knock Sensor no. 2 - Circuit Range/Performance (Bank no. 2)

P0332...... Knock Sensor no. 2 - Circuit Low Input (Bank no. 2)

P0333...... Knock Sensor no. 2 - Circuit High Input (Bank no. 2)

P0334...... Knock Sensor no. 2 - Circuit Input Intermittent (Bank no. 2)

P0335...... Crankshaft Position Sensor "A" Circuit Malfunction

P0336...... Crankshaft Position Sensor "A" Circuit Range/Performance

P0337...... Crankshaft Position Sensor "A" Circuit Low Input

P0338...... Crankshaft Position Sensor "A" Circuit High Input

P0339...... Crankshaft Position Sensor "A" Circuit Intermittent

P0340...... Camshaft Position Sensor Circuit Malfunction

P0341...... Camshaft Position Sensor Circuit Range/Performance

P0342...... Camshaft Position Sensor Circuit Low Input

P0343...... Camshaft Position Sensor Circuit High Input

P0344...... Camshaft Position Sensor Circuit Intermittent

P0350...... Ignition Coil Primary/Secondary Circuit Malfunction

P0351...... Ignition Coil "A" Primary/Secondary Circuit Malfunction

P0352...... Ignition Coil "B" Primary/Secondary Circuit Malfunction

P0353...... Ignition Coil "C" Primary/Secondary Circuit Malfunction

P0354...... Ignition Coil "D" Primary/Secondary Circuit Malfunction

P0355...... Ignition Coil "E" Primary/Secondary Circuit Malfunction

P0356...... Ignition Coil "F" Primary/Secondary Circuit Malfunction

P0357...... Ignition Coil "G" Primary/Secondary Circuit Malfunction

P0358...... Ignition Coil "H" Primary/Secondary Circuit Malfunction

P0359...... Ignition Coil "I" Primary/Secondary Circuit Malfunction

P0360...... Ignition Coil "J" Primary/Secondary Circuit Malfunction

P0361...... Ignition Coil "K" Primary/Secondary Circuit Malfunction

P0362...... Ignition Coil "L" Primary/Secondary Circuit Malfunction

P0370...... Timing Reference High Resolution Signal "A" Malfunction

P0371...... Timing Reference High Resolution Signal "A" Too Many Pulses

P0372...... Timing Reference High Resolution Signal "A" Too Few Pulses

P0373...... Timing Reference High Resolution Signal "A" Intermittent/Erratic Pulses

P0374...... Timing Reference High Resolution Signal "A" No Pulses

P0375...... Timing Reference High Resolution Signal "B" Malfunction

P0376...... Timing Reference High Resolution Signal "B" Too Many Pulses

P0377...... Timing Reference High Resolution Signal "B" Too Few Pulses

P0378...... Timing Reference High Resolution Signal "B" Intermittent/Erratic Pulses

P0379...... Timing Reference High Resolution Signal "B" No Pulses

P0380...... Glow Plug/Heater Circuit "A" Malfunction

P0381...... Glow Plug/Heater Indicator Circuit Malfunction

P0382...... Glow Plug/Heater Circuit "B" Malfunction

P0385...... Crankshaft Position Sensor "B" Circuit Malfunction

P0386...... Crankshaft Position Sensor "B" Circuit Range/Performance

P0387...... Crankshaft Position Sensor "B" Circuit Low Input

P0388...... Crankshaft Position Sensor "B" Circuit High Input

P0389...... Crankshaft Position Sensor "B" Circuit Intermittent

P0400...... Exhaust Gas Recirculation Flow Malfunction

P0401...... Exhaust Gas Recirculation Flow Insufficient Detected

P0402...... Exhaust Gas Recirculation Flow Excessive Detected

P0403...... Exhaust Gas Recirculation Circuit Malfunction

P0404...... Exhaust Gas Recirculation Circuit Range/Performance

P0405...... Exhaust Gas Recirculation Sensor "A" Circuit Low

P0406...... Exhaust Gas Recirculation Sensor "A" Circuit High

P0407...... Exhaust Gas Recirculation Sensor "B" Circuit Low

P0408...... Exhaust Gas Recirculation Sensor "B" Circuit High

P0410...... Secondary Air Injection System Malfunction

P0411...... Secondary Air Injection System Incorrect Flow Detected

P0412...... Secondary Air Injection System Switching Valve "A" Circuit Malfunction

P0413...... Secondary Air Injection System Switching Valve "A" Circuit Open

P0414...... Secondary Air Injection System Switching Valve "A" Circuit Shorted

P0415...... Secondary Air Injection System Switching Valve "B" Circuit Malfunction

P0416...... Secondary Air Injection System Switching Valve "B" Circuit Open

P0417...... Secondary Air Injection System Switching Valve "B" Circuit Shorted

P0418...... Secondary Air Injection System Relay "A" Circuit Malfunction

P0419...... Secondary Air Injection System Relay "B" Circuit Malfunction

P0420...... Catalyst System Efficiency Below Threshold (Bank no. 1)

P0421...... Warm Up Catalyst Efficiency Below Threshold (Bank no. 1)

P0422...... Main Catalyst Efficiency Below Threshold (Bank no. 1)

P0423...... Heated Catalyst Efficiency Below Threshold (Bank no. 1)

P0424...... Heated Catalyst Temperature Below Threshold (Bank no. 1)

P0430...... Catalyst System Efficiency Below Threshold (Bank no. 2)

P0431...... Warm Up Catalyst Efficiency Below Threshold (Bank no. 2)

P0432...... Main Catalyst Efficiency Below Threshold (Bank no. 2)

P0433...... Heated Catalyst Efficiency Below Threshold (Bank no. 2)

P0434...... Heated Catalyst Temperature Below Threshold (Bank no. 2)

P0440...... Evaporative Emission Control System Malfunction

P0441...... Evaporative Emission Control System Incorrect Purge Flow

P0442...... Evaporative Emission Control System Leak Detected (Small Leak)

P0443...... Evaporative Emission Control System Purge Control Valve Circuit Malfunction

P0444...... Evaporative Emission Control System Purge Control Valve Circuit Open

P0445...... Evaporative Emission Control System Purge Control Valve Circuit Shorted

P0446...... Evaporative Emission Control System Vent Control Circuit Malfunction

P0447...... Evaporative Emission Control System Vent Control Circuit Open

P0448...... Evaporative Emission Control System Vent Control Circuit Shorted

P0449...... Evaporative Emission Control System Vent Valve/Solenoid Circuit Malfunction

P0450...... Evaporative Emission Control System Pressure Sensor Malfunction

P0451...... Evaporative Emission Control System Fuel Tank Pressure Sensor Range/Performance

P0452...... Evaporative Emission Control System Fuel Tank Pressure Sensor Lowput

P0453...... Evaporative Emission Control System Fuel Tank Pressure Sensor High Input

P0454...... Evaporative Emission Control System Pressure Sensor Intermittent

P0455...... Evaporative Emission Control System Leak Detected (Gross Leak)

P0460...... Fuel Level Sensor Circuit Malfunction

P0461...... Fuel Level Sensor Circuit Range/Performance

P0462...... Fuel Level Sensor Circuit Low Input

P0463...... Fuel Level Sensor Circuit High Input

P0464...... Fuel Level Sensor.Circuit Intermittent

P0465...... Purge Flow Sensor Circuit Malfunction

P0466...... Purge Flow Sensor Circuit Range/Performance

P0467...... Purge Flow Sensor Circuit Low Input

P0468...... Purge Flow Sensor Circuit High Input

P0469...... Purge Flow Sensor Circuit Intermittent

P0470...... Exhaust Pressure Sensor Malfunction

P0471...... Exhaust Pressure Sensor Range/Performance

P0472...... Exhaust Pressure Sensor Low

P0473...... Exhaust Pressure Sensor High

P0474...... Exhaust Pressure Sensor Intermittent

P0475...... Exhaust Pressure Control Valve Malfunction

P0476...... Exhaust Pressure Control Valve Range/Performance

P0477...... Exhaust Pressure Control Valve Low

P0478...... Exhaust Pressure Control Valve High

P0479...... Exhaust Pressure Control Valve Intermittent

P0480...... Cooling Fan no. 1 Control Circuit Malfunction

P0481...... Cooling Fan no. 2 Control Circuit Malfunction

P0482...... Cooling Fan no. 3 Control Circuit Malfunction

P0483...... Cooling Fan Rationality Check Malfunction

P0484...... Cooling Fan Circuit Over Current

P0485...... Cooling Fan Power/Ground Circuit Malfunction

P0500...... Vehicle Speed Sensor Malfunction

P0501...... Vehicle Speed Sensor Range/Performance

P0502...... Vehicle Speed Sensor Circuit Low Input

P0503...... Vehicle Speed Sensor Intermittent/Erratic/High

P0505...... Idle Control System Malfunction

P0506...... Idle Control System RPM Lower Than Expected

P0507...... Idle Control System RPM Higher Than Expected

P0510...... Closed Throttle Position Switch Malfunction

P0520...... Engine Oil Pressure Sensor/Switch Circuit Malfunction

P0521...... Engine Oil Pressure Sensor/Switch Range/Performance

P0522...... Engine Oil Pressure Sensor/Switch Low Voltage

P0523...... Engine Oil Pressure Sensor/Switch High Voltage

P0530...... A/C Refrigerant Pressure Sensor Circuit Malfunction

P0531...... A/C Refrigerant Pressure Sensor Circuit Range/Performance

P0532...... A/C Refrigerant Pressure Sensor Circuit Low Input

P0533...... A/C Refrigerant Pressure Sensor Circuit High Input

OBD-II Diagnostic Trouble Codes (continued)

P0534...... A/C Refrigerant Charge Loss

P0550...... Power Steering Pressure Sensor Circuit Malfunction

P0551...... Power Steering Pressure Sensor Circuit Range/Performance

P0552...... Power Steering Pressure Sensor Circuit Low Input

P0553...... Power Steering Pressure Sensor Circuit High Input

P0554...... Power Steering Pressure Sensor Circuit Intermittent

P0560...... System Voltage Malfunction

P0561...... System Voltage Unstable

P0562...... System Voltage Low

P0563...... System Voltage High

P0565...... Cruise Control On Signal Malfunction

P0566...... Cruise Control Off Signal Malfunction

P0567...... Cruise Control Resume Signal Malfunction

P0568...... Cruise Control Set Signal Malfunction

P0569...... Cruise Control Coast Signal Malfunction

P0570...... Cruise Control Accel Signal Malfunction

P0571...... Cruise Control/Brake Switch "A" Circuit Malfunction

P0572...... Cruise Control/Brake Switch "A" Circuit Low

P0573...... Cruise Control/Brake Switch "A" Circuit High

P0574...... Through P0580 Reserved for Cruise Codes

P0600...... Serial Communication Link Malfunction

P0601...... Internal Control Module Memory Check Sum Error

P0602...... Control Module Programming Error

P0603...... Internal Control Module Keep Alive Memory (KAM) Error

P1410...... Fuel Tank Pressure Control Solenoid Control Circuit

P1451...... Barometric Pressure (BARO) Sensor Performance

P1500...... Start Switch Circuit

P1510...... Control Module Long Term Memory Resets

P1530...... Ignition Timing Adjustment Switch Circuit

VACUUM DIAGRAMS

See Figures 28 through 38

Following are vacuum diagrams for most of the engine and emissions package combinations covered by this manual. Because vacuum circuits will vary based on various engine and vehicle options, always refer first to the vehicle emission control information label, if present. Should the label be missing, or should vehicle be equipped with a different engine from the vehicle's original equipment, refer to the diagrams below for the same or similar configuration.

If you wish to obtain a replacement emissions label, most manufacturers make the labels available for purchase. The labels can usually be ordered from a local dealer.

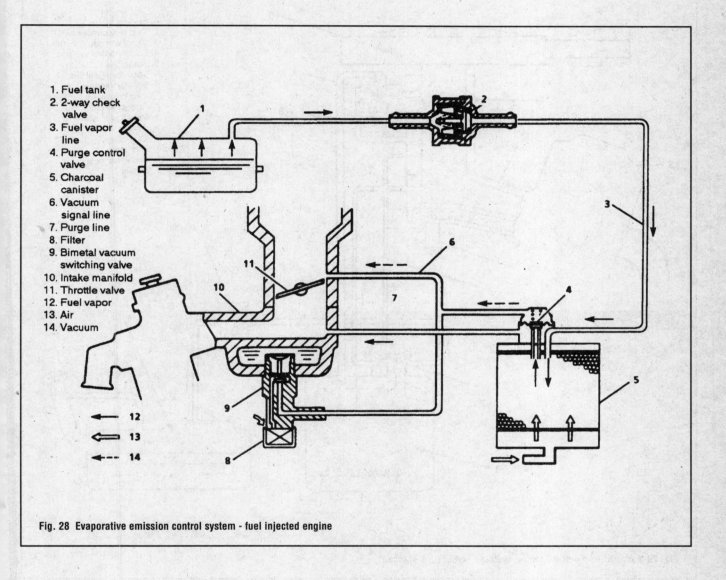

1. Fuel tank
2. 2-way check valve
3. Fuel vapor line
4. Purge control valve
5. Charcoal canister
6. Vacuum signal line
7. Purge line
8. Filter
9. Bimetal vacuum switching valve
10. Intake manifold
11. Throttle valve
12. Fuel vapor
13. Air
14. Vacuum

Fig. 28 Evaporative emission control system - fuel injected engine

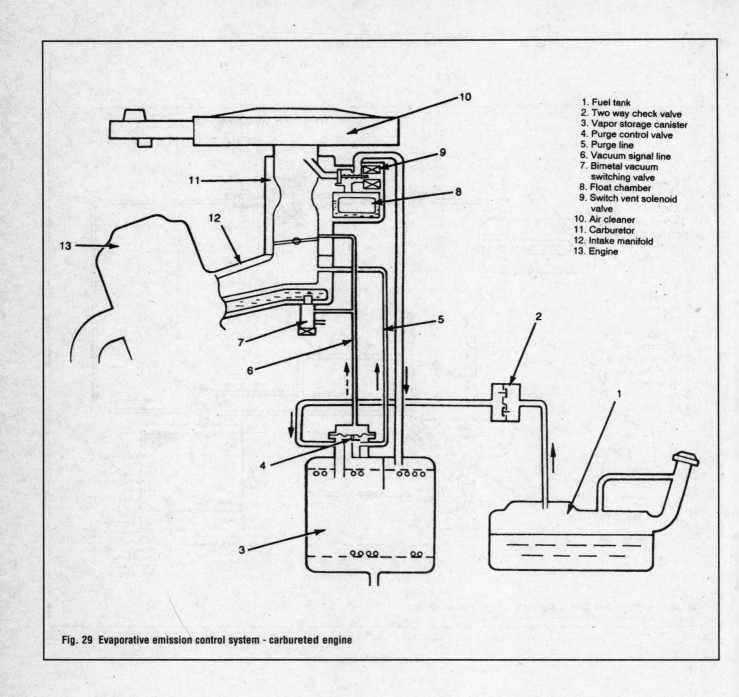

1. Fuel tank
2. Two way check valve
3. Vapor storage canister
4. Purge control valve
5. Purge line
6. Vacuum signal line
7. Bimetal vacuum switching valve
8. Float chamber
9. Switch vent solenoid valve
10. Air cleaner
11. Carburetor
12. Intake manifold
13. Engine

Fig. 29 Evaporative emission control system - carbureted engine

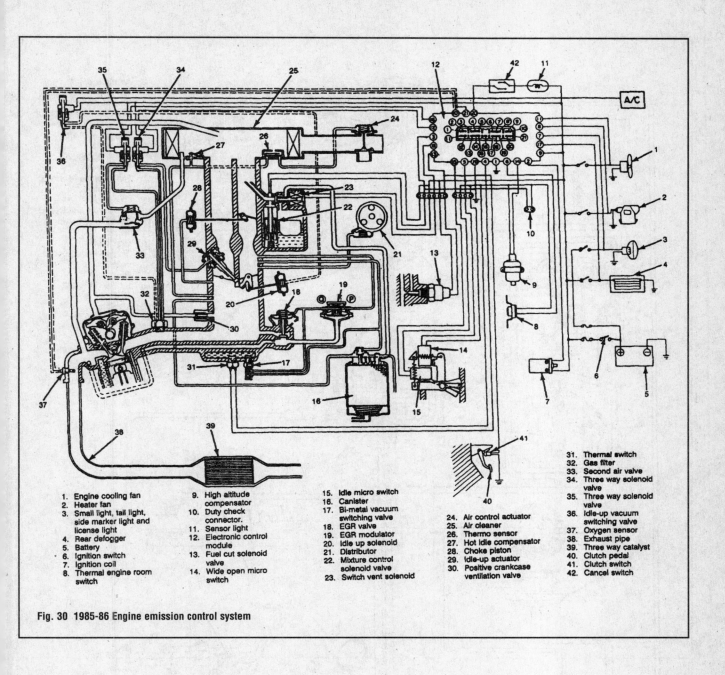

1. Engine cooling fan
2. Heater fan
3. Small light, tail light, side marker light and license light
4. Rear defogger
5. Battery
6. Ignition switch
7. Ignition coil
8. Thermal engine room switch
9. High altitude compensator
10. Duty check connector.
11. Sensor light
12. Electronic control module
13. Fuel cut solenoid valve
14. Wide open micro switch
15. Idle micro switch
16. Canister
17. Bi-metal vacuum switching valve
18. EGR valve
19. EGR modulator
20. Idle up solenoid
21. Distributor
22. Mixture control solenoid valve
23. Switch vent solenoid
24. Air control actuator
25. Air cleaner
26. Thermo sensor
27. Hot idle compensator
28. Choke piston
29. Idle-up actuator
30. Positive crankcase ventilation valve
31. Thermal switch
32. Gas filter
33. Second air valve
34. Three way solenoid valve
35. Three way solenoid valve
36. Idle-up vacuum switching valve
37. Oxygen sensor
38. Exhaust pipe
39. Three way catalyst
40. Clutch pedal
41. Clutch switch
42. Cancel switch

Fig. 30 1985-86 Engine emission control system

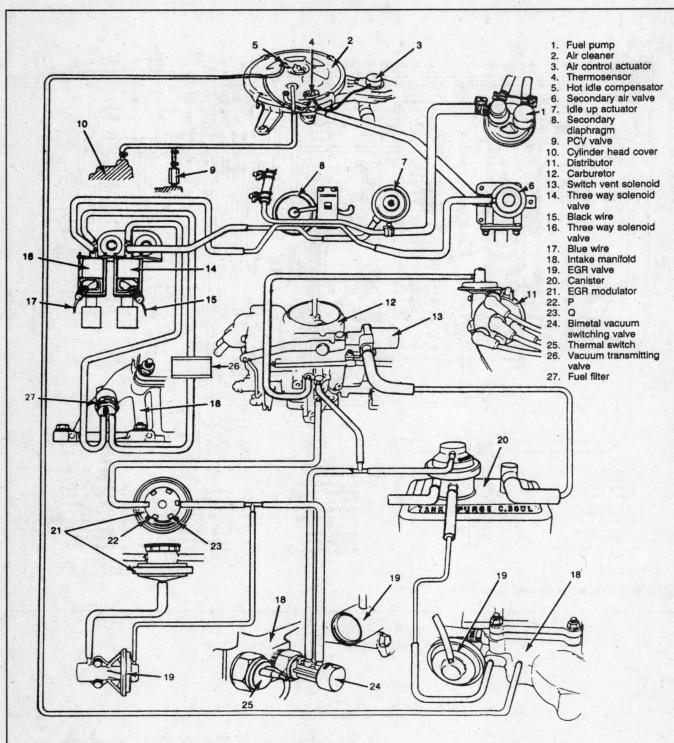

1. Fuel pump
2. Air cleaner
3. Air control actuator
4. Thermosensor
5. Hot idle compensator
6. Secondary air valve
7. Idle up actuator
8. Secondary diaphragm
9. PCV valve
10. Cylinder head cover
11. Distributor
12. Carburetor
13. Switch vent solenoid
14. Three way solenoid valve
15. Black wire
16. Three way solenoid valve
17. Blue wire
18. Intake manifold
19. EGR valve
20. Canister
21. EGR modulator
22. P
23. Q
24. Bimetal vacuum switching valve
25. Thermal switch
26. Vacuum transmitting valve
27. Fuel filter

Fig. 31 1985-86 Engine emission control system vacuum hose schematic

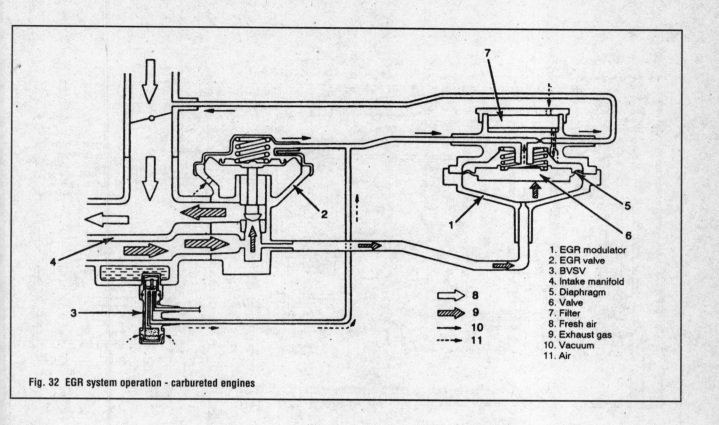

1. EGR modulator
2. EGR valve
3. BVSV
4. Intake manifold
5. Diaphragm
6. Valve
7. Filter
8. Fresh air
9. Exhaust gas
10. Vacuum
11. Air

Fig. 32 EGR system operation - carbureted engines

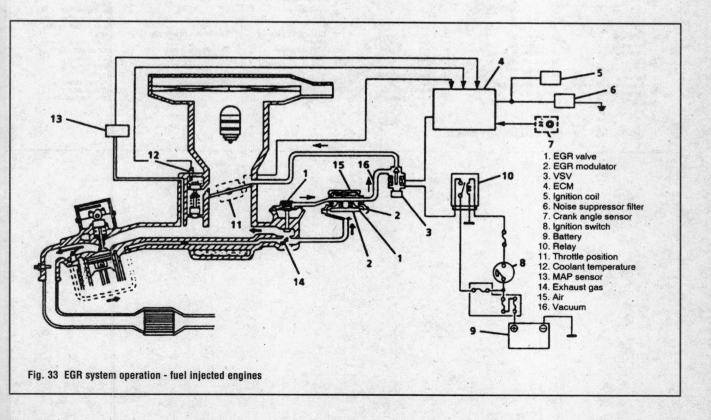

1. EGR valve
2. EGR modulator
3. VSV
4. ECM
5. Ignition coil
6. Noise suppressor filter
7. Crank angle sensor
8. Ignition switch
9. Battery
10. Relay
11. Throttle position
12. Coolant temperature
13. MAP sensor
14. Exhaust gas
15. Air
16. Vacuum

Fig. 33 EGR system operation - fuel injected engines

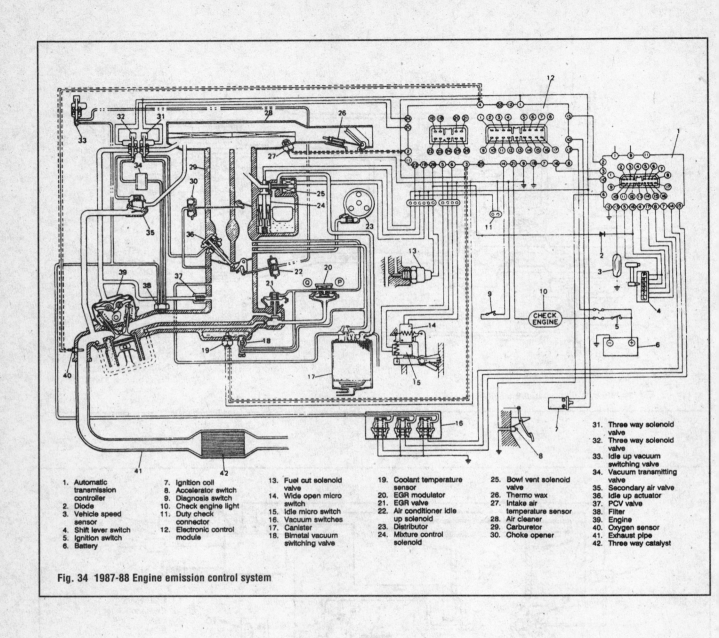

Fig. 34 1987-88 Engine emission control system

1. Automatic transmission controller	7. Ignition coil	13. Fuel cut solenoid valve	19. Coolant temperature sensor	25. Bowl vent solenoid valve	31. Three way solenoid valve
2. Diode	8. Accelerator switch	14. Wide open micro switch	20. EGR modulator	26. Thermo wax	32. Three way solenoid valve
3. Vehicle speed sensor	9. Diagnosis switch	15. Idle micro switch	21. EGR valve	27. Intake air temperature sensor	33. Idle up vacuum switching valve
4. Shift lever switch	10. Check engine light	16. Vacuum switches	22. Air conditioner idle up solenoid	28. Air cleaner	34. Vacuum transmitting valve
5. Ignition switch	11. Duty check connector	17. Canister	23. Distributor	29. Carburetor	35. Secondary air valve
6. Battery	12. Electronic control module	18. Bimetal vacuum switching valve	24. Mixture control solenoid	30. Choke opener	36. Idle up actuator
					37. PCV valve
					38. Filter
					39. Engine
					40. Oxygen sensor
					41. Exhaust pipe
					42. Three way catalyst

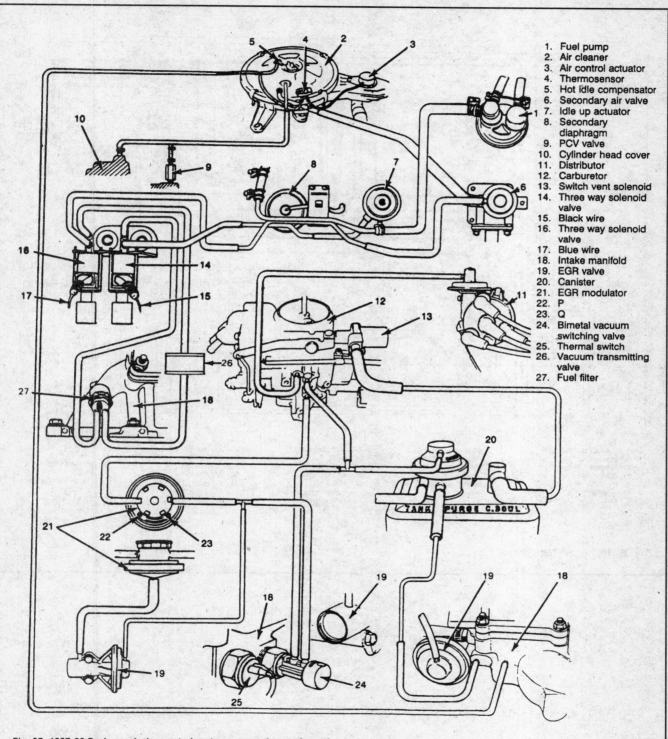

1. Fuel pump
2. Air cleaner
3. Air control actuator
4. Thermosensor
5. Hot idle compensator
6. Secondary air valve
7. Idle up actuator
8. Secondary diaphragm
9. PCV valve
10. Cylinder head cover
11. Distributor
12. Carburetor
13. Switch vent solenoid
14. Three way solenoid valve
15. Black wire
16. Three way solenoid valve
17. Blue wire
18. Intake manifold
19. EGR valve
20. Canister
21. EGR modulator
22. P
23. Q
24. Bimetal vacuum switching valve
25. Thermal switch
26. Vacuum transmitting valve
27. Fuel filter

Fig. 35 1987-88 Engine emission control system vacuum hose schematic

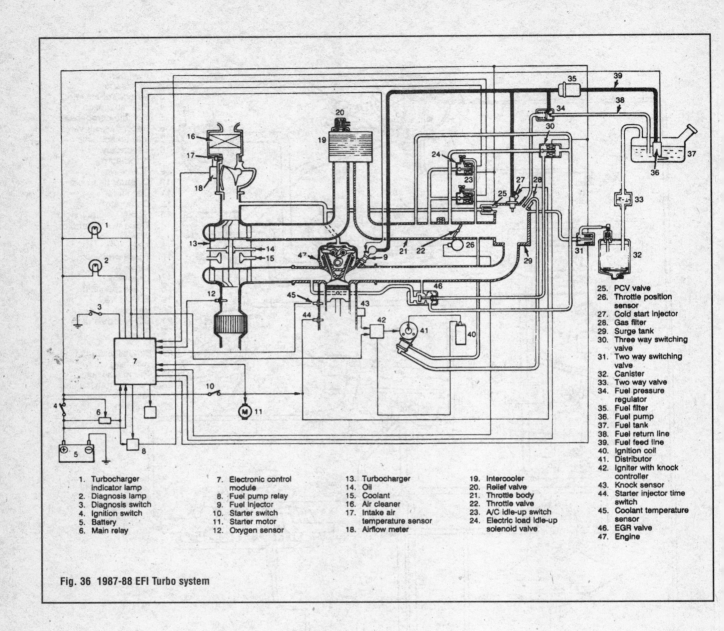

25. PCV valve
26. Throttle position sensor
27. Cold start injector
28. Gas filter
29. Surge tank
30. Three way switching valve
31. Two way switching valve
32. Canister
33. Two way valve
34. Fuel pressure regulator
35. Fuel filter
36. Fuel pump
37. Fuel tank
38. Fuel return line
39. Fuel feed line
40. Ignition coil
41. Distributor
42. Igniter with knock controller
43. Knock sensor
44. Starter injector time switch
45. Coolant temperature sensor
46. EGR valve
47. Engine

1. Turbocharger indicator lamp
2. Diagnosis lamp
3. Diagnosis switch
4. Ignition switch
5. Battery
6. Main relay

7. Electronic control module
8. Fuel pump relay
9. Fuel injector
10. Starter switch
11. Starter motor
12. Oxygen sensor

13. Turbocharger
14. Oil
15. Coolant
16. Air cleaner
17. Intake air temperature sensor
18. Airflow meter

19. Intercooler
20. Relief valve
21. Throttle body
22. Throttle valve
23. A/C idle-up switch
24. Electric load idle-up solenoid valve

Fig. 36 1987-88 EFI Turbo system

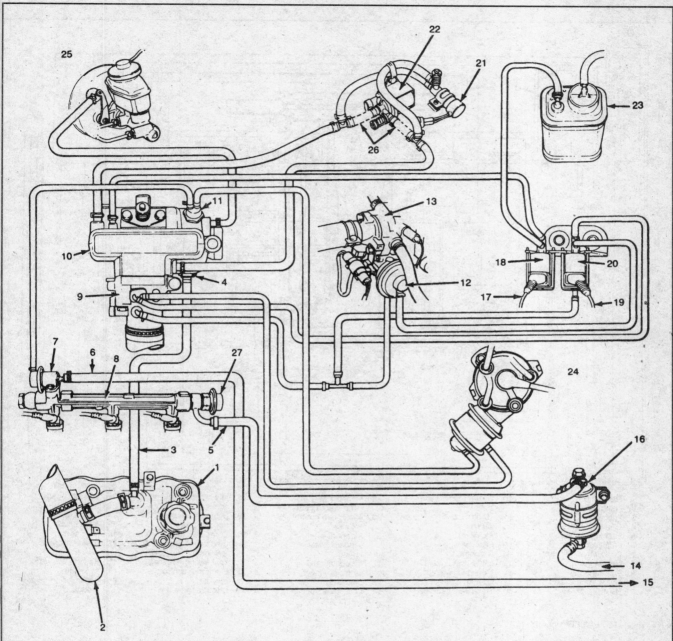

1. Cylinder head	9. Throttle body	18. Canister vacuum switching valve	22. Air conditioner idle up vacuum switching valve
2. Turbocharger intake pipe	10. Surge tank	19. White/Blue and Red/green wires	23. Canister
3. PCV hose	11. Gas filter	20. EGR vacuum switching valve	24. Distributor
4. PCV valve	12. EGR valve	21. Electric load idle up vacuum switching valve	25. Brake booster
5. Fuel feed hose	13. Intake manifold		26. Only for air conditioning equipped vehicle
6. Fuel return hose	14. From fuel pump		27. Fuel pulsation damper
7. Fuel pressure regulator	15. To fuel tank		
8. Fuel delivery pipe	16. Fuel filter		
	17. White/Blue and Red/Yellow wires		

Fig. 37 1987-88 EFI Turbo system vacuum hose schematic

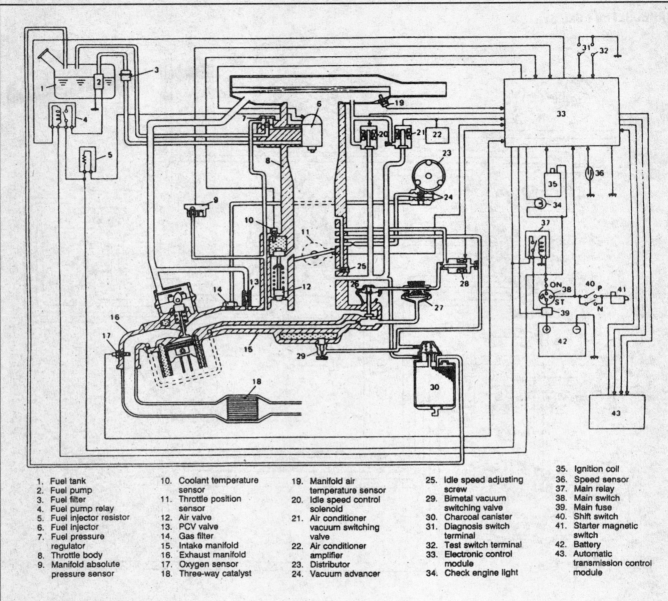

1. Fuel tank
2. Fuel pump
3. Fuel filter
4. Fuel pump relay
5. Fuel injector resistor
6. Fuel injector
7. Fuel pressure regulator
8. Throttle body
9. Manifold absolute pressure sensor
10. Coolant temperature sensor
11. Throttle position sensor
12. Air valve
13. PCV valve
14. Gas filter
15. Intake manifold
16. Exhaust manifold
17. Oxygen sensor
18. Three-way catalyst
19. Manifold air temperature sensor
20. Idle speed control solenoid
21. Air conditioner vacuum switching valve
22. Air conditioner amplifier
23. Distributor
24. Vacuum advancer
25. Idle speed adjusting screw
29. Bimetal vacuum switching valve
30. Charcoal canister
31. Diagnosis switch terminal
32. Test switch terminal
33. Electronic control module
34. Check engine light
35. Ignition coil
36. Speed sensor
37. Main relay
38. Main switch
39. Main fuse
40. Shift switch
41. Starter magnetic switch
42. Battery
43. Automatic transmission control module

Fig. 38 1989-93 EFI system

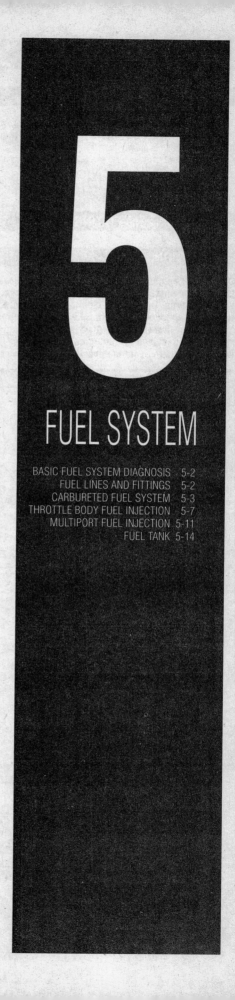

5
FUEL SYSTEM

BASIC FUEL SYSTEM DIAGNOSIS

When there is a problem starting or driving a vehicle, two of the most important checks involve the ignition and the fuel systems. The questions most mechanics attempt to answer first, "is there spark?" and "is there fuel?" will often lead to solving most basic problems. For ignition system diagnosis and testing, please refer to the information on engine electrical components and ignition systems found earlier in this manual. If the ignition system checks out (there is spark), then you must determine if the fuel system is operating properly (is there fuel?).

FUEL LINES AND FITTINGS

✳✳ CAUTION:

Observe all applicable safety precautions when working around fuel. Whenever servicing the fuel system, always work in a well ventilated area. Do not allow fuel spray or vapors to come in contact with a spark or open flame. Keep a dry chemical fire extinguisher near the work area. Always keep fuel in a container specifically designed for fuel storage; also, always properly seal fuel containers to avoid the possibility of fire or explosion.

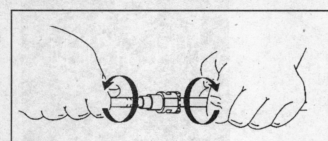

Fig. 1 Be sure to twist the connector...

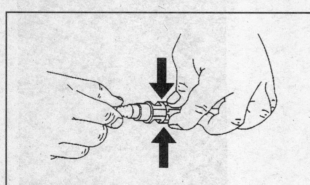

Fig. 2 ...before the connector is squeezed...

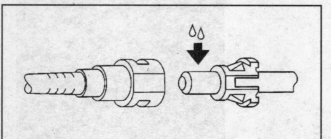

Fig. 4 Place the oil on the male end of the connector as shown here

Type of Fuel Fittings

Most of the models use simple hose clamps to secure the fuel lines, but there are a few out there that use quick connect fittings. The fitting is designed to make a good leak-free connection while at the same time being easy to service. Once mastered, the quick connect fitting is a great innovation. No tools are required, but first attempts can be quite nerve racking.

REMOVAL & INSTALLATION

See Figures 1, 2, 3, 4 and 5

1. Relieve the fuel system pressure.
2. Twist the connector 1/4 turn to loosen the dirt.
3. Blow out the dirt with compressed air.
4. Squeeze the release tabs on the retainer together.
5. Separate the two lines. Be sure to be ready to catch the residual fuel that is going to come out of the lines.
6. Clean the male end of the fitting. If there are any burrs on the end be sure to remove them before reconnecting the lines.

To install:
7. Place a few drops of engine oil to the male end of the fitting.
8. Insert the male end into the female end.
9. Push the two together until the connector makes an audible click.
10. Pull on the connector a few times to make sure that the connection is solid.

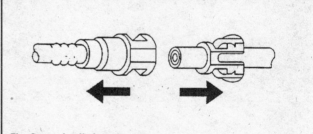

Fig. 3 ...and pulled apart

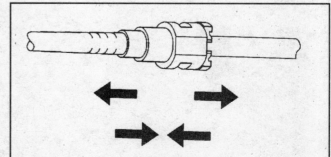

Fig. 5 Be sure that the connector is truly connected

CARBURETED FUEL SYSTEM

Mechanical Fuel Pump

A mechanical fuel pump is mounted on the cylinder head. The diaphragm in fuel pump is actuated from the cam on the engine camshaft, through a fuel pump rod and rocker arm of the fuel pump.

REMOVAL & INSTALLATION

See Figure 6

1. Disconnect the negative battery cable.
2. Remove the fuel filler cap to release the fuel vapor pressure in the fuel tank. Reinstall the cap.
3. Remove the air cleaner
4. Remove the fuel inlet, outlet and return hoses from the fuel pump.
5. Remove the fuel pump from the cylinder head.
6. Remove the fuel pump rod from the cylinder head.

To install:

7. Lubricate and install the fuel pump rod.
8. Install the fuel pump using a new gasket.
9. Install the inlet, outlet and return hoses to the fuel pump.
10. Install the air cleaner
11. Connect the negative battery cable. Start the engine and check for leaks.

TESTING

1. Disconnect the fuel outlet hose from the fuel pump.
2. Connect a pressure gauge to the outlet hose using a T-fitting.
3. Start the engine and read the fuel pressure on the gauge.
4. Fuel pressure should be at least 3.5 psi. If not, check for clogs or leaks in the fuel system.
5. If the fuel system hoses and pipes are clear, replace the fuel pump.

Carburetor

This 2-barrel, downdraft type carburetor has primary and secondary systems. The primary system operates under normal driving conditions and the secondary system operates under high speed, high load driving conditions. The choke valve is provided in the primary system.

The main components and their functions are as follows:

• The primary system has a mixture control solenoid valve which is operated by the electrical signals from the Electronic Control Module (ECM). The solenoid maintains the optimum air/fuel ratio of the primary slow and the primary main fuel systems at all times.

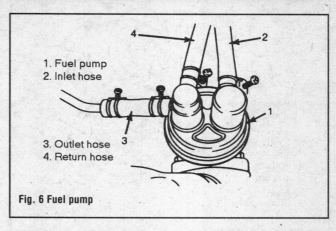

1. Fuel pump
2. Inlet hose
3. Outlet hose
4. Return hose

Fig. 6 Fuel pump

• A fuel cut solenoid valve stops fuel flow under deceleration and prevents dieseling when the engine is stopped.
• An accelerator pump system provides additional fuel for acceleration.
• The secondary system has a secondary vacuum break unit which is operated by the vacuum from the primary side and actuates the secondary throttle valve.
• The choke system is a full automatic type using a thermo-wax element.
• The switch vent solenoid valve provided on top of the float chamber is to reduce evaporative emissions.

ADJUSTMENTS

See Figures 7, 8, 9, 10, 11, 12, 13, 14, 15 and 16

Accelerator Cable

1. Check accelerator cable for play. Move the accelerator cable up and down to determine free-play.
2. Accelerator cable free-play should not exceed 0.40 - 0.59 in. (10 - 15mm) when engine and carburetor are cold or 0.12 - 0.19 in. (3 - 5mm) when engine and carburetor are warm.
3. If out of specification loosen locknut and adjust by turning adjusting nut.

Float

1. The fuel level in float chamber should be within round mark at the center

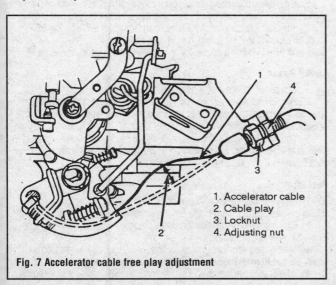

1. Accelerator cable
2. Cable play
3. Locknut
4. Adjusting nut

Fig. 7 Accelerator cable free play adjustment

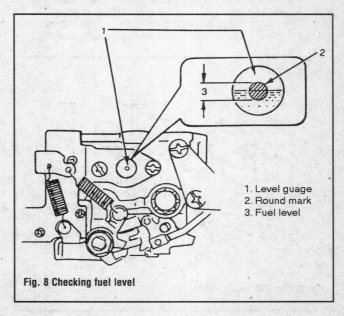

1. Level guage
2. Round mark
3. Fuel level

Fig. 8 Checking fuel level

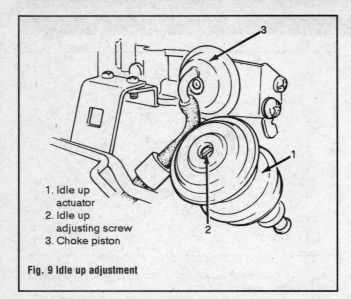

1. Idle up actuator
2. Idle up adjusting screw
3. Choke piston

Fig. 9 Idle up adjustment

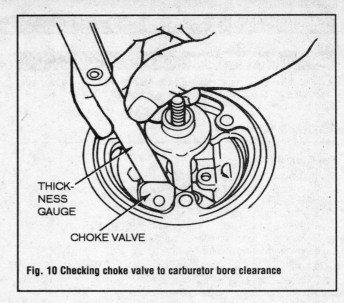

THICK-NESS GAUGE

CHOKE VALVE

Fig. 10 Checking choke valve to carburetor bore clearance

of the level gauge.

2. If the fuel level is not found within the round mark check the float level and adjust.

3. Remove the air horn and invert it.

4. Measure the distance between the float and the surface of the choke chamber. the measured distance is the float level. Measurement should be 0.21 - 0.24 in. (5.3 - 6.3 mm).

5. If the float level is out of specification, adjust it by bending the tongue up and down. This measurement should be made without a gasket on the air horn.

Idle Up Actuator

The idle-up actuator operates even when cooling fan is running. Therefore, idle-up adjustment must be performed when cooling fan is not running.

Manual Transaxle

1. Warm engine to normal operating temperature.

2. While running engine at idle speed, check to ensure that idle up adjusting screw moves down when lights are turned **ON**.

3. With lights turned **ON** check engine rpm. Be sure that heater fan, rear defogger, engine cooling fan and air conditioner are **OFF**.

4. Engine rpm should be at specified idle speed or 50 rpm higher. If not, adjust using idle up adjusting screw located at top of idle up solenoid.

5. Check idle up system as described above with the heater fan, rear defogger, engine cooling fan and air conditioner are all operated separately.

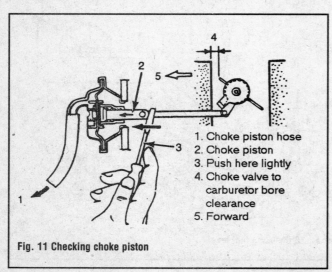

1. Choke piston hose
2. Choke piston
3. Push here lightly
4. Choke valve to carburetor bore clearance
5. Forward

Fig. 11 Checking choke piston

Automatic Transaxle

1. Warm engine to normal operating temperature.

2. While running engine at idle speed, check to ensure that idle up adjusting screw moves down when brake pedal is depressed and shift selector lever is moved to D range. All accessories should be OFF.

3. Check engine rpm. Engine rpm should be at specified idle speed or 50 rpm higher. If not, adjust using idle up adjusting screw located at top of idle up solenoid.

Choke Valve

Perform the following adjustment with the air cleaner top removed and the engine cold.

1. Check choke valve for smooth movement by pushing it with a finger.

2. Make sure that choke valve is closed almost completely when ambient temperature is below 77-degrees F (25-degrees C) and engine is cold.

3. Check to ensure that choke valve to carburetor bore clearance is 0.004 - 0.019 in. (0.1 - 0.5mm) when air temperature is 77-degrees F (25-degrees C) and 0.03 - 0.06 in. (0.7 - 1.7mm) when air temperature is 95-degrees F (35-degrees C).

4. If clearance is not within specification, remove the air cleaner case, and check strangler spring, choke piston and each link in choke system for smooth operation. Lubricate choke valve shaft and each link with lubricant if necessary. Do not remove riveted choke lever guide.

5. If the clearance is still out of specification, even after lubrication, remove carburetor from intake manifold and remove idle up actuator from carburetor.

6. Turn fast idle cam counterclockwise and insert an available pin into holes on cam and bracket to lock cam. In this state, bend the choke lever up or down with pliers. Bending up causes choke valve to close and vice-versa.

Choke Piston

1. Disconnect choke piston hose at throttle chamber.

2. With choke valve pushed down to its closing side lightly by finger pressure, apply vacuum to choke piston hose and check to ensure that choke valve to carburetor bore clearance is within 0.09 - 0.10 in. (2.3 - 2.6mm).

3. With vacuum applied, move choke piston rod toward diaphragm with small screwdriver and check to ensure that choke valve to carburetor bore clearance is within 0.16 - 0.18 in. (4.0 - 4.7mm).

Fast Idle

1. Allow the engine to cool completely, then remove the radiator cap to relieve any residual pressure in the cooling system..

2. Clamp off and disconnect the choke hoses from the carburetor thermo element holder and plug them.

3. Start engine and check hoses for leakage. After making sure that both hoses are free from leakage, warm engine to normal operating temperature.

4. With engine running at idle speed, force fast idle cam to rotate counter-

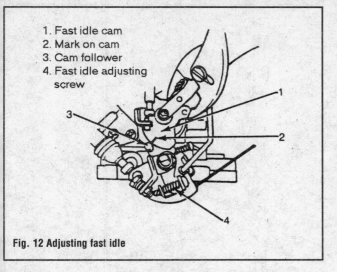

1. Fast idle cam
2. Mark on cam
3. Cam follower
4. Fast idle adjusting screw

Fig. 12 Adjusting fast idle

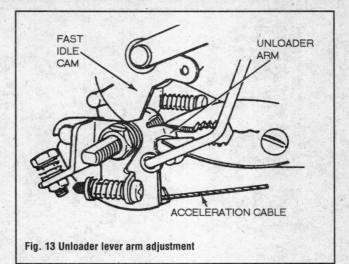

FAST IDLE CAM

UNLOADER ARM

ACCELERATION CABLE

Fig. 13 Unloader lever arm adjustment

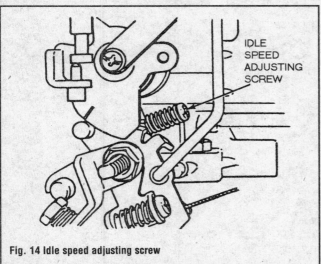

IDLE SPEED ADJUSTING SCREW

Fig. 14 Idle speed adjusting screw

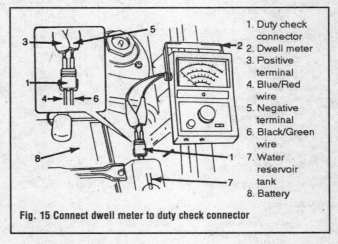

1. Duty check connector
2. Dwell meter
3. Positive terminal
4. Blue/Red wire
5. Negative terminal
6. Black/Green wire
7. Water reservoir tank
8. Battery

Fig. 15 Connect dwell meter to duty check connector

clockwise with pliers until mark on cam aligns with center of cam follower.

5. Check to ensure that engine speed is within 2100-2700 rpm.

6. If engine speed is not within specification, adjust by turning fast idle adjusting screw.

7. After adjusting fast idle speed, allow the engine to cool completely, then reconnect the hoses.

8 Check the coolant level.

Unloader

1. Perform this adjustment when engine is cold.
2. Remove air cleaner cover.
3. Make sure that choke valve is closed.
4. Fully open throttle valve and check choke valve to carburetor bore clearance to ensure is within 0.10 - 0.12 in. (2.5 - 3.3mm).
5. If clearance is out of specification, adjust by bending the unloader arm.

Idle Speed

1. Check emission control system wires, accelerator cable, ignition timing and valve lash prior to setting idle speed.
2. Connect a tachometer to the engine.
3. Place transaxle in **N** and set parking brake.
4. Warm engine to normal operating temperature.
5. With lights, heater fan, rear defogger, cooling fan and air conditioner all **OFF**, check idle speed.
6. If idle speed is not within specification adjust by turning throttle screw.
7. After idle speed adjustment, check idle up system.

8. Stop engine and check accelerator cable to ensure that free-play is within specification.

Idle Mixture

The carburetor has been calibrated at the factory and should not normally need adjustment. For this reason, the mixture adjustment should never be changed from the original factory setting. However, if during diagnosis, the check indicates the carburetor to be the cause of a driver performance complaint or emission failure, or the carburetor is overhauled or replaced, the idle mixture can be adjusted using the following procedure.

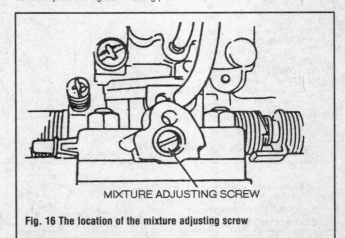

MIXTURE ADJUSTING SCREW

Fig. 16 The location of the mixture adjusting screw

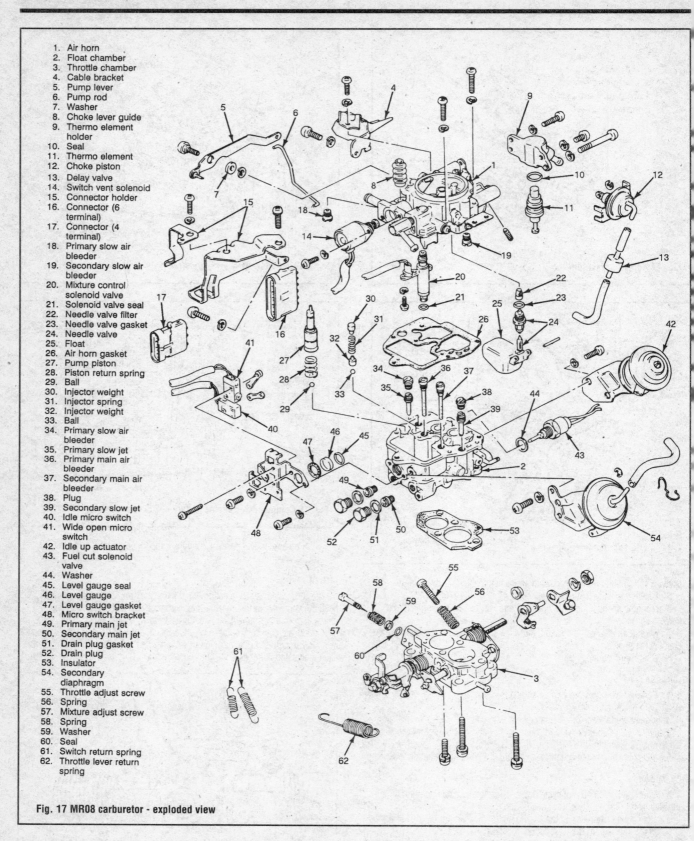

1. Air horn
2. Float chamber
3. Throttle chamber
4. Cable bracket
5. Pump lever
6. Pump rod
7. Washer
8. Choke lever guide
9. Thermo element holder
10. Seal
11. Thermo element
12. Choke piston
13. Delay valve
14. Switch vent solenoid
15. Connector holder
16. Connector (6 terminal)
17. Connector (4 terminal)
18. Primary slow air bleeder
19. Secondary slow air bleeder
20. Mixture control solenoid valve
21. Solenoid valve seal
22. Needle valve filter
23. Needle valve gasket
24. Needle valve
25. Float
26. Air horn gasket
27. Pump piston
28. Piston return spring
29. Ball
30. Injector weight
31. Injector spring
32. Injector weight
33. Ball
34. Primary slow air bleeder
35. Primary slow jet
36. Primary main air bleeder
37. Secondary main air bleeder
38. Plug
39. Secondary slow jet
40. Idle micro switch
41. Wide open micro switch
42. Idle up actuator
43. Fuel cut solenoid valve
44. Washer
45. Level gauge seal
46. Level gauge
47. Level gauge gasket
48. Micro switch bracket
49. Primary main jet
50. Secondary main jet
51. Drain plug gasket
52. Drain plug
53. Insulator
54. Secondary diaphragm
55. Throttle adjust screw
56. Spring
57. Mixture adjust screw
58. Spring
59. Washer
60. Seal
61. Switch return spring
62. Throttle lever return spring

Fig. 17 MR08 carburetor - exploded view

1. Check the ignition timing and valve lash. Ensure the idle up actuator does not operate and the cooling fan does not run.
2. Remove the carburetor from the intake manifold following normal service procedure to again access to the mixture adjust screw pin covering the

mixture adjust screw.
3. Using a 4 - 4.5mm drill, drill a hole in pin. After drilling, remove pin by punch or equivalent.
4. Reinstall the carburetor and air cleaner following normal service proce-

dures. Connect emission control system hoses and lead wires. Make specified play on accelerator cable and refill cooling system.

5. Place transaxle gear shift lever in N and set parking brake.

6. Start engine and allow it to reach operating temperature.

7. Remove coupler on duty check connector in engine compartment and connect a dwell meter to the connector. Connect the positive terminal of dwell meter to Blue/Red wire and the negative terminal to Black/Green wire.

8. Set dwell meter to 6-cylinder position.

9. Check idle speed and adjust if not within specification.

10. Run engine at idle speed and adjust mixture screw slowly. Adjust until the desired 21 - 27 degrees is obtained. Allow time for dwell to stabilize after turning screw.

11. Check idle speed after setting mixture and adjust as required.

12. If adjustment cannot be made because the dwell meter does not deflect, check the feedback system.

REMOVAL & INSTALLATION

1. Disconnect the negative battery cable.

2. Allow the engine to cool completely, then remove the radiator cap to relieve any residual pressure in the cooling system. Clamp off and disconnect the choke hoses from the carburetor thermo element holder and plug them.

3. Remove the air cleaner element.

4. Disconnect warm air hose, cool air hose, second air hose, vacuum hose and EGR modulator from air cleaner case.

5. Remove air cleaner, accelerator cable, electric lead wires, emission control hoses, choke hoses and fuel hose.

6. Remove carburetor from intake manifold.

To install:

7. Using a new gasket, install carburetor on intake manifold.

8. Install air cleaner, accelerator cable, electric lead wires, emission control hoses, choke hoses and fuel hose.

9. Connect warm air hose, cool air hose, second air hose, vacuum hose and EGR modulator on air cleaner case.

10. Install the air cleaner element.

11. Check the coolant level.

12. Connect the negative battery cable.

OVERHAUL

See Figure 17

Disassembly

1. Remove air horn from float chamber after disconnecting hoses and pump lever and removing screws from air horn.

2. Remove float and needle valve from air horn and then needle valve seat and filter.

3. Remove micro switch bracket after removing springs and set screws. Do not remove micro switches from bracket.

3. Remove lockplate and drain plugs and then primary and secondary main jets in float chamber through plug holes using a screwdriver.

4. Remove throttle chamber from float chamber after removing screws.

Cleaning

5. Wash all removable air jets and fuel jets, needle valve, valve seat, filter and float in carburetor cleaner and then dry with compressed air.

6. Blow compressed air into all passages to clean.

7. Clean bottom of float chamber.

8. Do not clean the following parts: micro switches, switch vent solenoid, fuel cut solenoid, mixture control solenoid valve, accelerator pump piston, secondary diaphragm, choke piston, idle up actuator, rubber parts and gaskets or thermo-wax element.

9. Do not put drills or wires into fuel passages and metering jets for cleaning. It may cause damage in passages and jets.

10. Do not remove the mixture adjust screw pin located in front of mixture adjust screw.

Inspection

11. Check choke valve and throttle valve for smooth operation.

12. Check rubber cup of pump piston and seal of mixture control solenoid valve for deterioration and damage.

13. Check needle valve and valve seat for wear.

Assembly

14. Install the gasket on the float chamber.

15. After attaching both ends of throttle lever return spring, install throttle chamber to float chamber. Hook throttle valve side end of return spring over the boss on float chamber.

16. Two of the four washers for the throttle chamber securing screws are toothed washers and the other two are spring washers. Install each washer to the throttle chamber and tighten to 3 - 5 ft. lbs. (4 - 7 Nm).

17. Install the primary and secondary main jets.

18. Install the gaskets and drain plugs, and then lock plate after installing main jets.

19. Install level gauge seal and level gauge. When installing level gauge, direct its face with small round mark in its center toward float chamber.

20. Install micro switch bracket with micro switches and springs. Do not remove the micro switches from the bracket.

Note: When bracket with micro switches has been removed from float chamber for any service and reinstalled after service work, make sure to check switches for operation and adjust if necessary.

21. Install jets, air bleeders and plug to float chamber.

22. Install balls, injector spring and weights to accelerator pump. Direct "U" bend end side of piston return spring downward.

23. Install needle valve filter, valve seat, gasket, needle valve and float to air horn. After installing float, check for float level and adjust.

24. Install primary and secondary slow air bleeders to air horn.

25. Be sure to apply silicone grease to mixture control solenoid valve seal before installing air horn to float chamber.

26. Install air horn gasket to float chamber. Use new gasket.

27. Install air horn to float chamber. After installing accelerator pump lever to air horn, check the lever for smooth operation.

28. Connect hoses to carburetor.

THROTTLE BODY FUEL INJECTION

General Information

See Figures 18, 19, 20, 21, 22 and 23

Electronic throttle body fuel injection (TBI) is a fuel metering system which provides a means of fuel distribution for controlling exhaust emissions. By precisely controlling the air/fuel mixture under all operating conditions, the system provides as near as possible complete combustion.

The amount of fuel delivered by the throttle body injector is determined by a signal supplied by the Electronic Control Module (ECM). The ECM monitors various engine and vehicle conditions to calculate the fuel delivery time (pulse width) of the injector(s). The fuel pulse may be modified by the ECM to account for special operating conditions, such as cranking, cold starting, altitude, accel-

eration, and deceleration.

An oxygen sensor in the main exhaust stream functions to provide feedback information to the ECM as to the oxygen content, lean or rich, in the exhaust. The ECM uses this information from the oxygen sensor, and other sensors, to modify fuel delivery to achieve, as near as possible, an ideal air/fuel ratio of 14.7:1. This air/fuel ratio allows the 3-way catalytic converter to be more efficient in the conversion process of reducing exhaust emissions while at the same time providing acceptable levels of driveability and fuel economy.

A single fuel injector is mounted on top of a throttle body, which replaces the carburetor on the intake manifold. The injector is a solenoid-operated device controlled by the ECM. The incoming fuel is directed to the lower end of the injector assembly which has a fine screen filter surrounding the injector inlet. The ECM turns on the solenoid, which lifts a normally closed ball valve off a

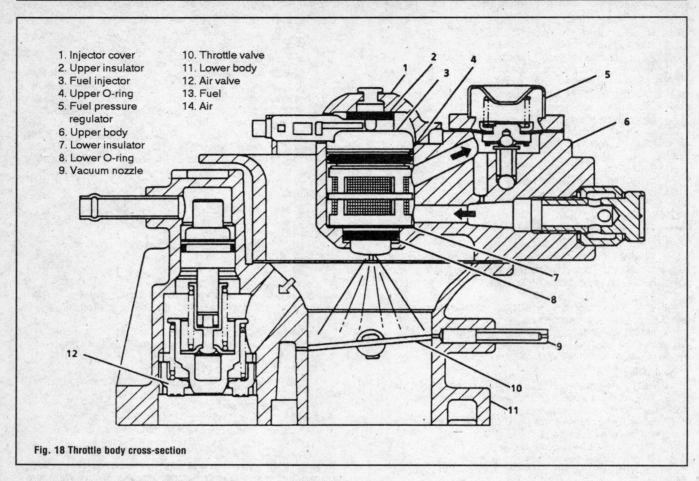

1. Injector cover
2. Upper insulator
3. Fuel injector
4. Upper O-ring
5. Fuel pressure regulator
6. Upper body
7. Lower insulator
8. Lower O-ring
9. Vacuum nozzle
10. Throttle valve
11. Lower body
12. Air valve
13. Fuel
14. Air

Fig. 18 Throttle body cross-section

seat. The fuel, under pressure, is injected in a conical spray pattern at the walls of the throttle body bore above the throttle valve. The excess fuel passes through a pressure regulator before being returned to the vehicle fuel tank.

The pressure regulator is a diaphragm-operated relief valve with the injector pressure on one side, and the air cleaner pressure on the other. The function of the regulator is to maintain constant pressure (approximately 11 psi) to the injector throughout the operating loads and speed ranges of the engine. If the regulator pressure is too low, below 9 psi, it can cause poor performance. Too high a pressure could cause detonation and a strong fuel odor.

The fuel pump is mounted in the fuel tank. This electrically operated pump supplies sufficient pressure (10 - 13 psi) to provide proper fuel atomization at the injector. The fuel pump also uses a check valve to hold fuel pressure within

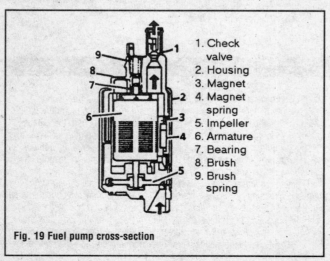

1. Check valve
2. Housing
3. Magnet
4. Magnet spring
5. Impeller
6. Armature
7. Bearing
8. Brush
9. Brush spring

Fig. 19 Fuel pump cross-section

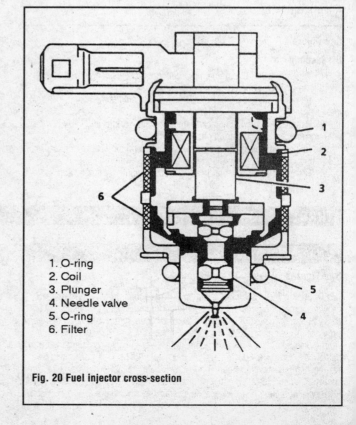

1. O-ring
2. Coil
3. Plunger
4. Needle valve
5. O-ring
6. Filter

Fig. 20 Fuel injector cross-section

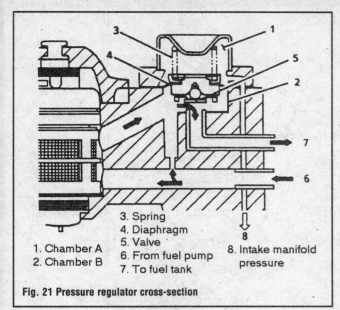

Fig. 21 Pressure regulator cross-section

1. Chamber A
2. Chamber B
3. Spring
4. Diaphragm
5. Valve
6. From fuel pump
7. To fuel tank
8. Intake manifold pressure

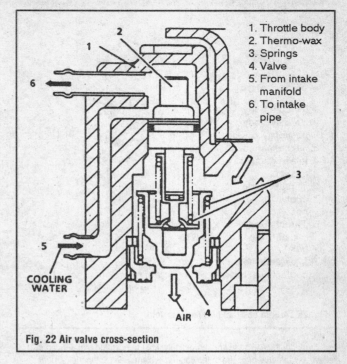

Fig. 22 Air valve cross-section

1. Throttle body
2. Thermo-wax
3. Springs
4. Valve
5. From intake manifold
6. To intake pipe

COOLING WATER

AIR

the fuel feed line when the vehicle is not running.

A relay is used to control voltage to the fuel pump. When the ignition key is turned **ON**, the ECM will initialize (start program running) and energize the fuel pump relay. The fuel pump pressurizes the system to approximately 10 psi. If the ECM does not receive a distributor reference pulse (telling the ECM the engine is turning) within 2 seconds, the ECM will then de-energize the fuel pump relay, turning off the fuel pump. If a distributor reference pulse is later received, the ECM will turn the fuel pump back on.

An air valve is used to control intake air during cold start conditions. The air valve consist of thermo-wax, springs and a valve. When the engine is cold, the thermo-wax contracts. In this state, the valve opens by the spring force, allowing the air to be drawn into the intake manifold. Thus the amount of intake air increases even when throttle valve is at idle position and engine speed rises to the fast idle state.

Relieving Fuel System Pressure

See Figure 24

If the fuel pressure is not released prior to system service, fuel may be forced out through the fuel hoses during servicing.
1. Remove the gas tank cap.
2. Place the gearshift selector in **NEUTRAL** on manual transaxle equipped vehicles or in **PARK** on automatic transaxle equipped vehicles.
3. Remove the fuel pump relay from the main fuse box in the engine compartment.

4. Start the engine and allow it to stall.
5. Crank the engine 2 - 3 times for approximately 3 seconds each time to ensure fuel pressure dissipation with fuel lines.
6. Disconnect the negative battery cable.
7. The fuel system components are now ready to be serviced.
8. Once the system has been serviced, reinstall the relay and reconnect the battery.
9. Turn the key to the **ON** position without starting the vehicle. Do this three or four times.
10. Start the vehicle.

Throttle Body

REMOVAL & INSTALLATION

See Figure 25

Note: Do not remove the fuel pressure regulator or air valve from the throttle body. They are calibrated at the factory and are not serviceable.

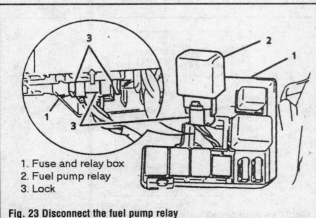

1. Fuse and relay box
2. Fuel pump relay
3. Lock

Fig. 23 Disconnect the fuel pump relay

Fig. 24 Fuel pump relay is located at the lower left side of the relay box - fuel injected engine.

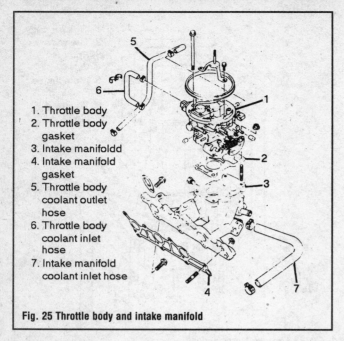

1. Throttle body
2. Throttle body gasket
3. Intake manifoldd
4. Intake manifold gasket
5. Throttle body coolant outlet hose
6. Throttle body coolant inlet hose
7. Intake manifold coolant inlet hose

Fig. 25 Throttle body and intake manifold

1. Allow the engine to cool completely, then remove the radiator cap to relieve any residual pressure in the cooling system. Relieve the fuel system pressure and disconnect the negative battery cable.
2. Remove the air cleaner assembly.
3. Clamp off the coolant hoses connected to the throttle body.
4. Label and disconnect the throttle position sensor, fuel injector and coolant temperature sensor electrical connectors.
5. Label and disconnect the fuel feed and return hoses, coolant hoses and all vacuum hoses.
6. Remove the accelerator cable.
7. Remove the throttle body attaching bolts.
8. Lift the throttle body from the intake manifold.

To install:
9. Install the throttle body on the intake manifold using a new gasket.
10. Tighten throttle body bolts evenly to 17 ft. lbs. (23 Nm).
11. Remove the accelerator cable.
12. Connect the fuel feed and return hoses, coolant hoses and all vacuum hoses.
13. Connect the throttle position sensor, fuel injector and coolant temperature electrical connectors.
14. Check the coolant level.
15. Install the air cleaner assembly.
16. Connect the negative battery cable. Start the engine and check for leaks.

INJECTOR REPLACEMENT

See Figure 26

Note: Do not remove the fuel pressure regulator or air valve from the throttle body. They are calibrated at the factory and are not serviceable.

1. Depressurize the fuel system, then disconnect the negative battery cable.
2. Remove the intake air hose and air cleaner.
3. Remove the injector cover and upper insulator.
4. Gently pull the injector out of the throttle body.

To install:
5. Replace both injector O-rings with new.
6. Apply a thin coat of automatic transmission fluid to the O-rings and then install the injector into the throttle body. Make sure the injector is facing the proper direction.

Note: Do not twist the injector while installing as damage or misalignment of the O-rings may occur.

7. Install the upper insulator, cover, electrical connector and connect the

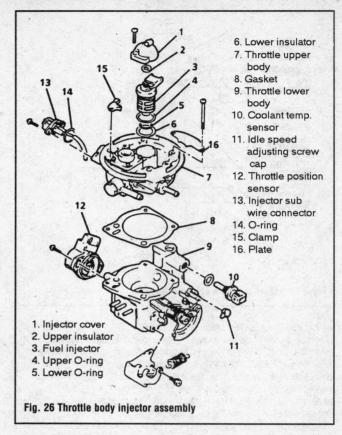

6. Lower insulator
7. Throttle upper body
8. Gasket
9. Throttle lower body
10. Coolant temp. sensor
11. Idle speed adjusting screw cap
12. Throttle position sensor
13. Injector sub wire connector
14. O-ring
15. Clamp
16. Plate

1. Injector cover
2. Upper insulator
3. Fuel injector
4. Upper O-ring
5. Lower O-ring

Fig. 26 Throttle body injector assembly

negative battery cable.
8. With the ignition switch **ON** and the engine **OFF**, check for fuel leaks.
9. Install the air cleaner and inlet hose.

Fuel Pressure Regulator

The fuel pressure regulator is calibrated at the factory and is not serviceable. No attempt should be made to remove the regulator from the throttle body. If the regulator is defective, the throttle body must be replaced as an assembly.

Air Valve

REMOVAL & INSTALLATION

The air valve is calibrated at the factory and is not serviceable. No attempt should be made to remove it from the throttle body. If the air valve is defective, the throttle body must be replaced as an assembly.

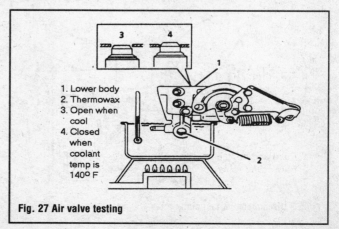

1. Lower body
2. Thermowax
3. Open when cool
4. Closed when coolant temp is 140° F

Fig. 27 Air valve testing

TESTING

See Figure 27

Note: Use care not to submerge throttle body in water to prevent possible damage due to corrosion. Only the air valve should be submersed in water.

1. Remove the throttle body assembly.
2. Separate the throttle body halves.

3. Remove the coolant temperature sensor.
4. Immerse air valve in water.
5. Check that air valve closes as the water temperature rises. The valve should fully close at 140-degrees F (60-degrees C). If it does not, replace the valve.
6. Install the coolant temperature sensor.
7. Join the upper and lower halves of the throttle body using a new gasket.
8. Tighten attaching screws to 3 - 5 ft. lbs. (4 - 7 Nm).
9. Install throttle body on intake manifold using a new gasket. Tighten bolts to 17 ft. lbs. (23 Nm).

MULTIPORT FUEL INJECTION

Description

See Figure 28

Electronic fuel injection (EFI) is a fuel metering system which provides a means of fuel distribution for controlling exhaust emissions. By precisely controlling the air/fuel mixture under all operating conditions, the system provides as near as possible complete combustion.

The amount of fuel delivered by the injectors is determined by adding several compensations to the basic injection time (pulse width) which is calculated on the basis of the intake air volume and engine speed. The information of the intake air volume and that of the engine speed are sent to the ECM from the airflow meter and the ignition coil respectively.

An oxygen sensor in the main exhaust stream functions to provide feedback information to the ECM as to the oxygen content, lean or rich, in the exhaust. The ECM uses this information from the oxygen sensor, and other sensors, to modify fuel delivery to achieve, as near as possible, an ideal air/fuel ratio of 14.7:1. This air/fuel ratio allows the 3-way catalytic converter to be more efficient in the conversion process of reducing exhaust emissions while at the same time providing acceptable levels of driveability and fuel economy.

Three or four (depending on engine) individual fuel injectors are mounted on the intake manifold. The injector is a solenoid-operated device controlled by the ECM. The incoming fuel is directed to the lower end of the injector assembly which has a fine screen filter surrounding the injector inlet. The ECM turns on the solenoid, which lifts a normally closed ball valve off a seat. The fuel is then atomized directly behind the intake valve. The excess fuel passes through a pressure regulator before being returned to the vehicle fuel tank.

The pressure regulator is a diaphragm-operated relief valve with the injector pressure on one side, and intake manifold vacuum on the other. The function of the regulator is to maintain constant pressure (approximately 30 psi) to the injector throughout the operating loads and speed ranges of the engine. If the regulator pressure is too low, below 25 psi, it can cause poor performance. Too high a pressure will cause an overly rich mixture.

The fuel pump is mounted in the fuel tank. This electrically operated pump supplies sufficient pressure (25 - 33 psi) to provide proper fuel atomization at the injector. The fuel pump also uses a check valve to hold fuel pressure within the fuel feed line when the vehicle is not running.

A relay is used to control voltage to the fuel pump. When the ignition key is turned **ON**, the ECM will initialize (start program running) and energize the fuel pump relay. If the ECM does not receive a distributor reference pulse (telling the ECM the engine is turning) within 2 seconds, the ECM will then de-energize the fuel pump relay, turning off the fuel pump. If a distributor reference pulse is later received, the ECM will turn the fuel pump back on.

An air valve is used to control intake air during cold start conditions. The air valve consist of thermo-wax, springs and a valve. When the engine is cold, the thermo-wax contracts. In this state, the valve opens by the spring force, allowing the air to be drawn into the intake manifold. Thus the amount of intake air increases even when throttle valve is at idle position and engine speed rises to the fast idle state.

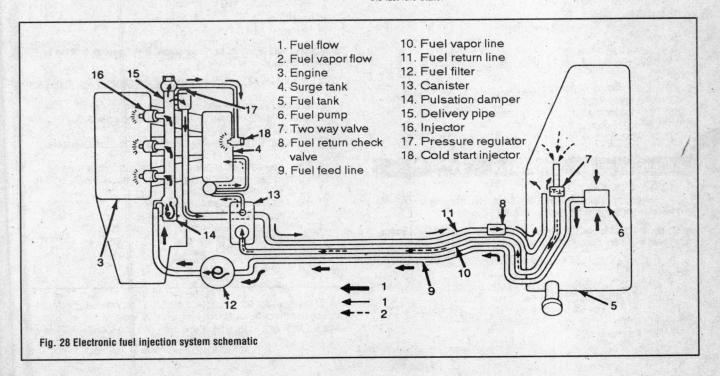

1. Fuel flow
2. Fuel vapor flow
3. Engine
4. Surge tank
5. Fuel tank
6. Fuel pump
7. Two way valve
8. Fuel return check valve
9. Fuel feed line
10. Fuel vapor line
11. Fuel return line
12. Fuel filter
13. Canister
14. Pulsation damper
15. Delivery pipe
16. Injector
17. Pressure regulator
18. Cold start injector

Fig. 28 Electronic fuel injection system schematic

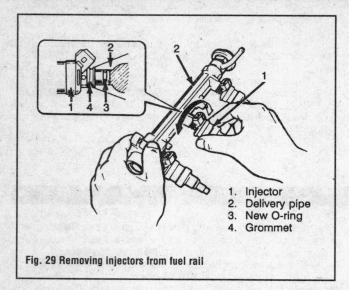

1. Injector
2. Delivery pipe
3. New O-ring
4. Grommet

Fig. 29 Removing injectors from fuel rail

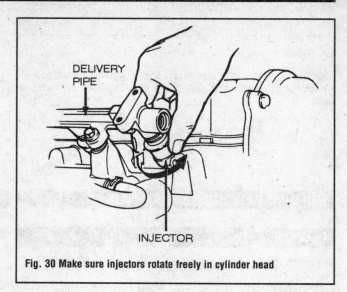

DELIVERY PIPE

INJECTOR

Fig. 30 Make sure injectors rotate freely in cylinder head

Throttle Body

REMOVAL & INSTALLATION

❉ CAUTION:

Wait until the engine is cool before starting this procedure.

1. Disconnect the negative battery cable.
2. Allow the engine to cool completely, then remove the radiator cap to relieve any residual pressure in the cooling system..
3. Remove inlet air hose.
4. Remove throttle position sensor coupler.
5. Remove accelerator cable.
6. Clamp off and detach the water hoses from throttle body.
7. Label and remove vacuum hoses.
8. Remove throttle body.

To install:
9. Install throttle body using a new gasket.
10. Connect vacuum hoses.
11. Connect water hoses.
12. Connect accelerator cable and adjust free-play to 0.32 - 0.35 in. (8 - 9mm).
13. Install throttle position sensor coupler.
14. Install inlet air hose.
15. Check the coolant level.
16. Connect the negative battery cable.
17. Start engine and check for leaks.

Relieving Fuel System Pressure

1. Remove the gas tank cap.
2. With engine running, remove connector of fuel pump relay (see Fig. 36) and wait until the engine stops, due to a lack of fuel.

Note: The main relay and fuel pump relay are identical. The fuel pump relay lead wires are Pink, Pink/White, White/Blue, and White/Blue.

3. Engage the starter for a few seconds to assure relief of remaining fuel pressure.
4. Disconnect the negative battery cable before working on the fuel system.
5. Once the system has been serviced, reinstall the relay.
6. Turn the key to the **ON** position without starting the vehicle. Do this three or four times.
7. Start the vehicle.

Fuel Injector(s)

REMOVAL & INSTALLATION

See Figures 29 and 30

1. Relieve fuel system pressure and disconnect the negative battery cable.
2. Remove intake air hose between throttle body and intercooler.
3. Remove accelerator cable.
4. Unclamp PCV and fuel return hoses from delivery pipe.
5. Unclamp injector wiring harness.
6. Disconnect injector coupler.
7. Remove cold start injector pipe from delivery pipe.
8. Remove vacuum hose from pressure regulator.
9. Remove fuel feed hose from delivery pipe.
10. Remove pressure regulator from delivery pipe.
11. Remove delivery pipe with injectors.
12. Remove injectors from delivery pipe.

To install:
13. Replace injector O-rings and lubricate with fuel.

Note: Make sure injectors rotate smoothly. If not, probable cause is incorrect installation of O-ring.

14. Check if insulator is cracked or otherwise damaged. If it is, replace with new one.
15. Connect delivery pipe with injectors.
16. Install pressure regulator to delivery pipe using a new O-ring.
17. Install fuel feed hose to delivery pipe.
18. Install vacuum and fuel return hoses to pressure regulator and clamp securely.
19. Install cold start injector pipe to delivery pipe using new gaskets.
20. Install injector coupler. Clamp injector wiring harness.
21. Install PCV hose to cylinder head.
22. Install throttle position sensor coupler.
23. Install accelerator cable and adjust free-play.
24. Install intake air hose to throttle body and intercooler.
25. Connect the negative battery cable.
26. Start engine and check for leaks.

TESTING

The easiest way to test the operation of the fuel injectors is to listen for a clicking sound coming from the injectors while the engine is running. This is accomplished using a mechanic's stethoscope, or a long screwdriver. Place the

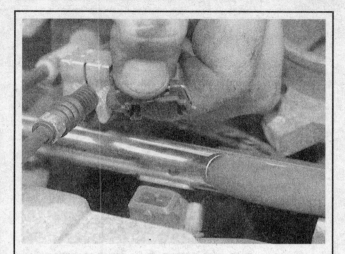

Fig. 31 Unplug the fuel injector connector

Fig. 32 Probe the two terminals of a fuel injector to check its resistance

end of the stethoscope or the screwdriver (tip end, not handle) onto the body of the injector. Place the ear pieces of the stethoscope in your ears, or if using a screwdriver, place your ear on top of the handle. An audible clicking noise should be heard; this is the solenoid operating. If the injector makes this noise, the injector driver circuit and computer are operating as designed. Continue testing all the injectors this way.

CAUTION:

Be extremely careful while working on an operating engine, make sure you have no dangling jewelry, extremely loose clothes, long hair, power tool cords or other items that might get caught in a moving part of the engine.

All Injectors Clicking

If all the injectors are clicking, but you have determined that the fuel system is the cause of your driveability problem, continue diagnostics. Make sure that you have checked fuel pump pressure as outlined. An easy way to determine a weak or unproductive cylinder is a cylinder drop test. This is accomplished by removing one spark plug wire at a time, and seeing which cylinder causes the least difference in the idle. The one that causes the least change is the weak cylinder.

If the injectors were all clicking and the ignition system is functioning prop-

erly, remove the injector of the suspect cylinder and bench test it. This is accomplished by checking for a spray pattern from the injector itself. Install a fuel supply line to the injector (or rail if the injector is left attached to the rail) and momentarily apply 12 volts DC and a ground to the injector itself; a visible fuel spray should appear. If no spray is achieved, replace the injector and check the running condition of the engine.

One or More Injectors Are Not Clicking
See Figures 31, 32, 33 and 34

If one or more injectors are found to be not operating, testing the injector driver circuit and computer can be accomplished using a "noid" light. First, with the engine not running and the ignition key in the **OFF** position, remove the connector from the injector you plan to test, then plug the "noid" light tool into the injector connector. Start the engine and the "noid" light should flash, signaling that the injector driver circuit is working. If the "noid" light flashes, but the injector does not click when plugged in, test the injector's resistance. Resistance should be between 12.0 to 13.0 ohms.

If the "noid" light does not flash, the injector driver circuit is faulty. Disconnect the negative battery cable. Unplug the "noid" light from the injector connector and also unplug the PCM. Check the harness between the appropriate pins on the harness side of the PCM connector and the injector connector. Resistance should be less than 5.0 ohms; if not, repair the circuit. If resistance is within specifications, the injector driver inside the PCM is faulty and replacement of the PCM will be necessary.

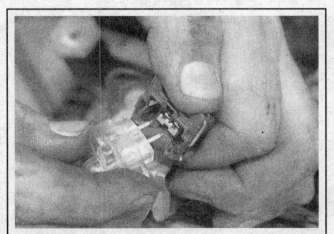

Fig. 33 Plug the correct "noid" light directly into the injector harness connector

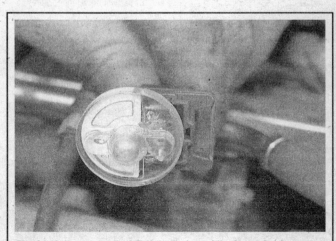

Fig. 34 If the correct "noid" light flashes while the engine is running, the injector driver circuit inside the PCM is working

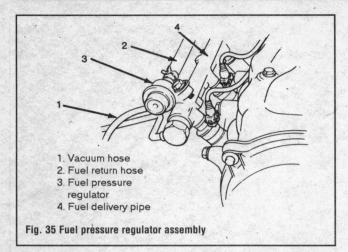

1. Vacuum hose
2. Fuel return hose
3. Fuel pressure regulator
4. Fuel delivery pipe

Fig. 35 Fuel pressure regulator assembly

Fuel Pressure Regulator

REMOVAL & INSTALLATION

See Figure 35

1. Relieve fuel system pressure and disconnect the negative battery cable.
2. Put ample rags under fuel pressure regulator.
3. Disconnect vacuum hose and fuel return hose from regulator.
4. Remove fuel pressure regulator from fuel delivery pipe.

To install:

5. Install the pressure regulator using a new O-ring. Tighten bolt to 6 - 8 ft. lbs. (8 - 12 Nm).
6. Connect vacuum hose and fuel return hose to regulator.
7. Start engine and check for leaks.

Fuel Pump Relay

Fig. 36 The fuel pump relay is located in the engine compartment on the driver's side

Fuel Pump Relay

REMOVAL & INSTALLATION

See Figure 36

1. The fuel pump relay is located near the right front strut in the engine compartment.
2. The main relay and fuel pump relay are identical. The fuel pump relay lead wires are Pink, Pink/White, White/Blue, and White/Blue.
3. Simply unplug the relay from the connector.
4. Installation is the reverse of removal procedure.

FUEL TANK

Tank Assembly

REMOVAL & INSTALLATION

1. Relieve the fuel system pressure and disconnect the negative battery cable.
2. Remove the fuel filler cap from the fuel tank.
3. Have a Class B fire extinguisher near the work area. Use a hand operated pump device to drain as much fuel through the fuel filler neck as possible.
4. Use a siphon to remove the remainder of the fuel in the tank by connecting the siphon to the fuel pump outlet fitting.

❄ CAUTION:

Never drain or store fuel in an open container because there is the possibility of a fire or an explosion.

5. Reinstall the fuel filler cap.
6. Remove the rear seat cushion from vehicle (if so equipped).
7. Disconnect the fuel pump motor connector and sending unit electrical connectors.
8. Disconnect the wire harness grommet and harness through the vehicle floor pan.
9. Raise and safely support the vehicle.

10. Remove the fuel filler hose clamp from the filler neck assembly.
11. Remove the fuel breather hose clamp from the filler neck assembly.
12. Remove the fuel filter inlet hose clamp and hose from the filter.

Note: A small amount of fuel may be released after the fuel hose is disconnected. In order to reduce the chance of personal injury, cover the fitting to be disconnected with a shop towel.

13. Remove the fuel vapor clamp and hose, and fuel return hose clamps and hose from the respective fuel lines.
14. Using a suitable transaxle jack, support the fuel tank.
15. Remove the fuel tank retaining bolts and lower the tank.

To install:

16. Reconnect all fuel hoses, lines and the fuel breather hose to the fuel tank.
17. Place the fuel tank in its proper space using the transaxle jack, Install the fuel tank retaining bolts.
18. Remove the transaxle jack.
19. Reconnect all fuel hoses, lines and the fuel breather hose to the fuel tank.
20. Install the fuel breather hose and hose clamp to the filler neck assembly.
21. Install the fuel vapor hose and hose clamps. Install the fuel return hose and hose clamp to the respective fuel lines.
22. Install the fuel filter inlet hose and hose clamp to the filter.
23. Lower the vehicle. Install the wire harness and grommet through the vehicle floor pan.
24. Connect the fuel pump motor and the sending unit connectors.
25. Install the rear seat cushion. Reconnect the negative battery cable.

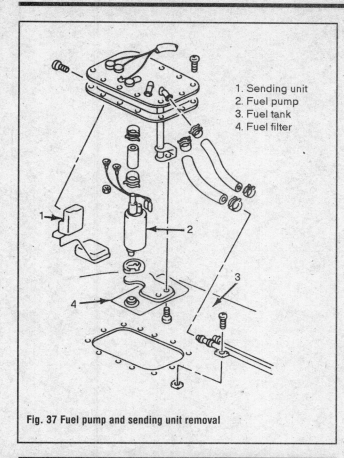

1. Sending unit
2. Fuel pump
3. Fuel tank
4. Fuel filter

Fig. 37 Fuel pump and sending unit removal

Electric Fuel Pump

REMOVAL & INSTALLATION

See Figures 37 and 38

1. Relieve the fuel system pressure.
2. Disconnect the negative battery cable.
3. Raise and support the vehicle safely.
4. Drain the fuel tank by pumping or siphoning the fuel out through the fuel feed line (tank to fuel filter line).
5. Remove the tank from the vehicle.
6. Remove the fuel feed and return clamps and hoses from the fuel pump assembly.
7. Remove the 12 attaching screws from the fuel pump assembly and remove the assembly with the gasket from the fuel tank.
8. Remove the 1 mounting screw from the fuel pump motor assembly.

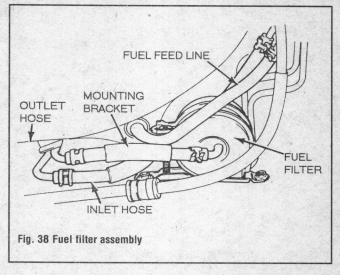

Fig. 38 Fuel filter assembly

Remove the 2 fuel pump motor connectors and remove the fuel pump motor from the fuel pump assembly.

To install:

9. Install the 2 fuel pump motor connectors. Install the fuel pump motor on the fuel pump assembly and tighten the mounting screw.
10. Install the assembly with the gasket on the fuel tank. Install the 12 attaching screws and tighten securely.
11. Install the fuel feed and return clamps and hoses on the fuel pump assembly.
12. Install the fuel tank in the vehicle.
13. Lower the vehicle and connect the negative battery cable.
14. Fill the fuel tank. Turn the ignition key **ON** and allow the fuel system to prime.
15. Start the engine and check for leaks.

TESTING

1. Relieve fuel system pressure.
2. Disconnect the fuel inlet line at the fuel filter and install a suitable pressure gauge on the line.
3. Connect a jumper wire between the terminals of the fuel pump relay connector and check the system pressure on the gauge.
4. Fuel pressure should be 25 - 33 lbs.
5. As the pressure reaches 33 lbs., the relief valve in the pump should pulsate the pressure so it is always within specification.
6. If the pressure is above specification, check for restrictions in the fuel lines. If no restrictions are found, replace the fuel pump. If the pressure is below specifications, check for battery voltage to the fuel pump and correct as required. If battery voltage is found, replace the fuel pump or fuel pump relay.
7. Before removing the pressure gauge, relieve the fuel pressure again.
8. Reconnect the fuel line. Start the engine and check for leaks.

TORQUE SPECIFICATIONS

Component	Standard	Metric
Fuel Pressure Regulator	6-8 ft. lbs.	8-12 Nm
Throttle Body	17 ft. lbs.	23 Nm
Throttle Chamber	3-5 ft. lbs.	4-7 Nm
Throttle Position Sensor	18 inch lbs.	2 Nm

Notes

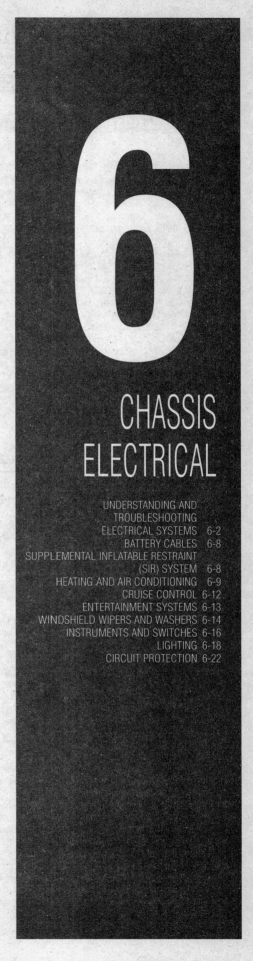

6

CHASSIS ELECTRICAL

UNDERSTANDING AND TROUBLESHOOTING ELECTRICAL SYSTEMS

Basic Electrical Theory

See Figure 1

For any 12-volt negative ground electrical system to operate, the electricity must travel in a complete circuit. This simply means that current (power) from the positive (+) terminal of the battery must eventually return to the negative (−) terminal of the battery. Along the way, this current will travel through wires, fuses, switches, and components. If, for any reason, the flow of current through the circuit is interrupted, the component fed by that circuit will cease to function properly.

Perhaps the easiest way to visualize a circuit is to think of connecting a light bulb (with two wires attached to it) to the battery - one wire attached to the negative (−) terminal of the battery and the other wire to the positive (+) terminal. With the two wires touching the battery terminals, the circuit would be complete and the light bulb would illuminate. Electricity would follow a path from the battery to the bulb and back to the battery. It's easy to see that with longer wires on our light bulb, it could be mounted anywhere. Further, one wire could be fitted with a switch so that the light could be turned on and off.

The normal automotive circuit differs from this simple example in two ways. First, instead of having a return wire from the bulb to the battery, the current travels through the frame of the vehicle. Since the negative (−) battery cable is attached to the frame (made of electrically conductive metal), the frame of the vehicle can serve as a ground wire to complete the circuit. Secondly, most automotive circuits contain multiple components which receive power from a single circuit. This lessens the amount of wire needed to power components on the vehicle.

HOW DOES ELECTRICITY WORK: THE WATER ANALOGY

Electricity is the flow of electrons - the subatomic particles that constitute the outer shell of an atom. Electrons spin in an orbit around the center core of an atom. The center core is comprised of protons (positive charge) and neutrons (neutral charge). Electrons have a negative charge and balance out the positive charge of the protons. When an outside force causes the number of electrons to unbalance the charge of the protons, the electrons will split off the atom and look for another atom to balance out. If this imbalance is kept up, electrons will continue to move and an electrical flow will exist.

Many people have been taught electrical theory using an analogy with water. In a comparison with water flowing through a pipe, the electrons would be the water and the wire is the pipe.

The flow of electricity can be measured much like the flow of water through a pipe. The unit of measurement used is amperes, frequently abbreviated as amps (a). You can compare amperage to the volume of water flowing through a pipe. When connected to a circuit, an ammeter will measure the actual amount of current flowing through the circuit. When relatively few electrons flow through a circuit, the amperage is low. When many electrons flow, the amperage is high.

Water pressure is measured in units such as pounds per square inch (psi); The electrical pressure is measured in units called volts (v). When a voltmeter is connected to a circuit, it is measuring the electrical pressure.

The actual flow of electricity depends not only on voltage and amperage, but also on the resistance of the circuit. The higher the resistance, the higher the force necessary to push the current through the circuit. The standard unit for measuring resistance is an ohm. Resistance in a circuit varies depending on the amount and type of components used in the circuit. The main factors which determine resistance are:

• **Material** - some materials have more resistance than others. Those with high resistance are said to be insulators. Rubber materials (or rubber-like plastics) are some of the most common insulators used in vehicles as they have a very high resistance to electricity. Very low resistance materials are said to be conductors. Copper wire is among the best conductors. Silver is actually a superior conductor to copper and is used in some relay contacts, but its high cost prohibits its use as common wiring. Most automotive wiring is made of copper.

• **Size** - the larger the wire size being used, the less resistance the wire will have. This is why components which use large amounts of electricity usually have large wires supplying current to them.

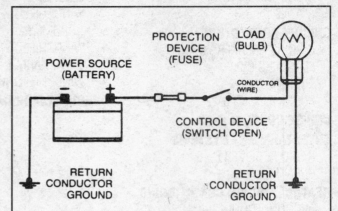

Fig. 1 This example illustrates a simple circuit. When the switch is closed, power from the positive (+) battery terminal flows through the fuse and the switch, and then to the light bulb. The light illuminates and the circuit is completed through the ground wire back to the negative (−) battery terminal. In reality, the two ground points shown in the illustration are attached to the metal frame of the vehicle, which completes the circuit back to the battery

• **Length** - for a given thickness of wire, the longer the wire, the greater the resistance. The shorter the wire, the less the resistance. When determining the proper wire for a circuit, both size and length must be considered to design a circuit that can handle the current needs of the component.

• **Temperature** - with many materials, the higher the temperature, the greater the resistance (positive temperature coefficient). Some materials exhibit the opposite trait of lower resistance with higher temperatures (negative temperature coefficient). These principles are used in many of the sensors on the engine.

OHM'S LAW

There is a direct relationship between current, voltage, and resistance. The relationship between current, voltage, and resistance can be summed up by a statement known as Ohm's law.

• Voltage (E) is equal to amperage (I) times resistance (R): $E = I \times R$
• Other forms of the formula are $R = E/I$ and $I = E/R$

In each of these formulas, E is the voltage in volts, I is the current in amps and R is the resistance in ohms. The basic point to remember is that as the resistance of a circuit goes up, the amount of current that flows in the circuit will go down, if voltage remains the same.

The amount of work that the electricity can perform is expressed as power. The unit of power is the watt (w). The relationship between power, voltage and current is expressed as:

• Power (w) is equal to amperage (I) times voltage (E): $W = I \times E$

This is only true for direct current (DC) circuits; The alternating current formula is a tad different, but since the electrical circuits in most vehicles are DC type, we need not get into AC circuit theory.

Electrical Components

POWER SOURCE

Power is supplied to the vehicle by two devices: The battery and the alternator. The battery supplies electrical power during starting or during periods when the current demand of the vehicle's electrical system exceeds the output capacity of the alternator. The alternator supplies electrical current when the engine is running. Just not does the alternator supply the current needs of the vehicle, but it recharges the battery.

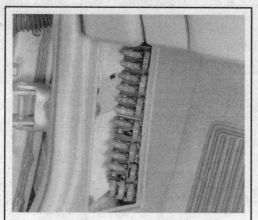

Fig. 2 Most vehicles use one or more fuse panels. This one is located on the driver's side kick panel

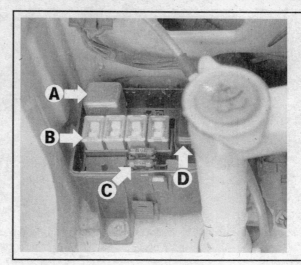

Fig. 3 The underhood fuse and relay panel usually contains fuses, relays, flashers and fusible links

A. Relay
B. Fusible link
C. Fuse
D. Flasher

The Battery

In most modern vehicles, the battery is a lead/acid electrochemical device consisting of six 2 volt subsections (cells) connected in series, so that the unit is capable of producing approximately 12 volts of electrical pressure. Each subsection consists of a series of positive and negative plates held a short distance apart in a solution of sulfuric acid and water.

The two types of plates are of dissimilar metals. This sets up a chemical reaction, and it is this reaction which produces current flow from the battery when its positive and negative terminals are connected to an electrical load. The power removed from the battery is replaced by the alternator, restoring the battery to its original chemical state.

The Alternator

On some vehicles there isn't an alternator, but a generator. The difference is that an alternator supplies alternating current which is then changed to direct current for use on the vehicle, while a generator produces direct current. Alternators tend to be more efficient and that is why they are used.

Alternators and generators are devices that consist of coils of wires wound together making big electromagnets. One group of coils spins within another set and the interaction of the magnetic fields causes a current to flow. This current is then drawn off the coils and fed into the vehicles electrical system.

GROUND

Two types of grounds are used in automotive electric circuits. Direct ground components are grounded to the frame through their mounting points. All other components use some sort of ground wire which is attached to the frame or chassis of the vehicle. The electrical current runs through the chassis of the vehicle and returns to the battery through the ground (−) cable; if you look, you'll see that the battery ground cable connects between the battery and the frame or chassis of the vehicle.

Note: It should be noted that a good percentage of electrical problems can be traced to bad grounds.

PROTECTIVE DEVICES

See Figure 2

It is possible for large surges of current to pass through the electrical system of your vehicle. If this surge of current were to reach the load in the circuit, the surge could burn it out or severely damage it. It can also overload the wiring, causing the harness to get hot and melt the insulation. To prevent this, fuses, circuit breakers and/or fusible links are connected into the supply wires of the electrical system. These items are nothing more than a built-in weak spot in the system. When an abnormal amount of current flows through the system, these protective devices work as follows to protect the circuit:

• Fuse - when an excessive electrical current passes through a fuse, the

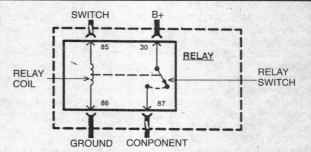

Fig. 4 Relays are composed of a coil and a switch. These two components are linked together so that when one operates, the other operates at the same time. The large wires in the circuit are connected from the battery to one side of the relay switch (B+) and from the opposite side of the relay switch to the load (component). Smaller wires are connected from the relay coil to the control switch for the circuit and from the opposite side of the relay coil to ground

fuse "blows" (the conductor melts) and opens the circuit, preventing the passage of current.

• Circuit Breaker - a circuit breaker is basically a self-repairing fuse. It will open the circuit in the same fashion as a fuse, but when the surge subsides, the circuit breaker can be reset and does not need replacement.

• Fusible Link - a fusible link (fuse link or main link) is a short length of special, high temperature insulated wire that acts as a fuse. When an excessive electrical current passes through a fusible link, the thin gauge wire inside the link melts, creating an intentional open to protect the circuit. To repair the circuit, the link must be replaced. Some newer type fusible links are housed in plug-in modules, which are simply replaced like a fuse, while older type fusible links must be cut and spliced if they melt. Since this link is very early in the electrical path, it's the first place to look if nothing on the vehicle works, yet the battery seems to be charged and is properly connected.

❈❈ CAUTION:

Always replace fuses, circuit breakers and fusible links with identically rated components. Under no circumstances should a component of higher or lower amperage rating be substituted.

SWITCHES & RELAYS

See Figures 3 and 4

Switches are used in electrical circuits to control the passage of current. The

Fig. 5 Hard shell (left) and weatherproof (right) connectors have replaceable terminals

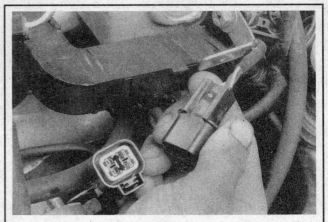

Fig. 6 Weatherproof connectors are most commonly used in the engine compartment or where the connector is exposed to the elements

most common use is to open and close circuits between the battery and the various electric devices in the system. Switches are rated according to the amount of amperage they can handle. If a sufficient amperage rated switch is not used in a circuit, the switch could overload and cause damage.

Some electrical components which require a large amount of current to operate use a special switch called a relay. Since these circuits carry a large amount of current, the thickness of the wire in the circuit is also greater. If this large wire were connected from the load to the control switch, the switch would have to carry the high amperage load and the fairing or dash would be twice as large to accommodate the increased size of the wiring harness. To prevent these problems, a relay is used.

Relays are composed of a coil and a set of contacts. When the coil has a current passed though it, a magnetic field is formed and this field causes the contacts to move together, completing the circuit. Most relays are normally open, preventing current from passing through the circuit, but they can take any electrical form depending on the job they are intended to do. Relays can be considered "remote control switches." They allow a smaller current to operate devices that require higher amperages. When a small current operates the coil, a larger current is allowed to pass by the contacts. Some common circuits which may use relays are the horn, headlights, starter, electric fuel pump and other high draw circuits.

LOAD

Every electrical circuit must include a "load" (something to use the electricity coming from the source). Without this load, the battery would attempt to deliver its entire power supply from one pole to another. This is called a "short circuit." All this electricity would take a short cut to ground and cause a great amount of damage to other components in the circuit by developing a tremendous amount of heat. This condition could develop sufficient heat to melt the insulation on all the surrounding wires and reduce a multiple wire cable to a lump of plastic and copper.

WIRING & HARNESSES

The average vehicle contains meters and meters of wiring, with hundreds of individual connections. To protect the many wires from damage and to keep them from becoming a confusing tangle, they are organized into bundles, enclosed in plastic or taped together and called wiring harnesses. Different harnesses serve different parts of the vehicle. Individual wires are color coded to help trace them through a harness where sections are hidden from view.

Automotive wiring or circuit conductors can be either single strand wire, multi-strand wire or printed circuitry. Single strand wire has a solid metal core and is usually used inside such components as alternators, motors, relays and other devices. Multi-strand wire has a core made of many small strands of wire twisted together into a single conductor. Most of the wiring in an automotive electrical system is made up of multi-strand wire, either as a single conductor or grouped together in a harness. All wiring is color coded on the insulator, either as a solid color or as a colored wire with an identification stripe. A printed

circuit is a thin film of copper or other conductor that is printed on an insulator backing. Occasionally, a printed circuit is sandwiched between two sheets of plastic for more protection and flexibility. A complete printed circuit, consisting of conductors, insulating material and connectors for lamps or other components is called a printed circuit board. Printed circuitry is used in place of individual wires or harnesses in places where space is limited, such as behind instrument panels.

Since automotive electrical systems are very sensitive to changes in resistance, the selection of properly sized wires is critical when systems are repaired. A loose or corroded connection or a replacement wire that is too small for the circuit will add extra resistance and an additional voltage drop to the circuit.

The wire gauge number is an expression of the cross-section area of the conductor. Vehicles from countries that use the metric system will typically describe the wire size as its cross-sectional area in square millimeters. In this method, the larger the wire, the greater the number. Another common system for expressing wire size is the American Wire Gauge (AWG) system. As gauge number increases, area decreases and the wire becomes smaller. An 18 gauge wire is smaller than a 4 gauge wire. A wire with a higher gauge number will carry less current than a wire with a lower gauge number. Gauge wire size refers to the size of the strands of the conductor, not the size of the complete wire with insulator. It is possible, therefore, to have two wires of the same gauge with different diameters because one may have thicker insulation than the other.

It is essential to understand how a circuit works before trying to figure out why it doesn't. An electrical schematic shows the electrical current paths when a circuit is operating properly. Schematics break the entire electrical system down into individual circuits. In a schematic, usually no attempt is made to represent wiring and components as they physically appear on the vehicle; switches and other components are shown as simply as possible. Face views of harness connectors show the cavity or terminal locations in all multi-pin connectors to help locate test points.

CONNECTORS

See Figures 5 and 6

Three types of connectors are commonly used in automotive applications - weatherproof, molded and hard shell.

• Weatherproof - these connectors are most commonly used where the connector is exposed to the elements. Terminals are protected against moisture and dirt by sealing rings which provide a weathertight seal. All repairs require the use of a special terminal and the tool required to service it. Unlike standard blade type terminals, these weatherproof terminals cannot be straightened once they are bent. Make certain that the connectors are properly seated and all of the sealing rings are in place when connecting leads.

• Molded - these connectors require complete replacement of the connector if found to be defective. This means splicing a new connector assembly into the harness. All splices should be soldered to insure proper contact. Use care when probing the connections or replacing terminals in them, as it is possible to cre-

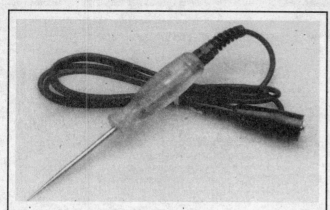

Fig. 7 A 12 volt test light is used to detect the presence of voltage in a circuit

ate a short circuit between opposite terminals. If this happens to the wrong terminal pair, it is possible to damage certain components. Always use jumper wires between connectors for circuit checking and NEVER probe through weatherproof seals.

• Hard Shell - unlike molded connectors, the terminal contacts in hard-shell connectors can be replaced. Replacement usually involves the use of a special terminal removal tool that depresses the locking tangs (barbs) on the connector terminal and allows the connector to be removed from the rear of the shell. The connector shell should be replaced if it shows any evidence of burning, melting, cracks, or breaks. Replace individual terminals that are burnt, corroded, distorted or loose.

Test Equipment

Pinpointing the exact cause of trouble in an electrical circuit is most times accomplished by the use of special test equipment. The following describes different types of commonly used test equipment and briefly explains how to use them in diagnosis. In addition to the information covered below, the tool manufacturer's instructions booklet (provided with the tester) should be read and clearly understood before attempting any test procedures.

JUMPER WIRES

❄ CAUTION:

Never use jumper wires made from a thinner gauge wire than the circuit being tested. If the jumper wire is of too small a gauge, it may overheat and possibly melt. Never use jumpers to bypass high resistance loads in a circuit. Bypassing resistances, in effect, creates a short circuit. This may, in turn, cause damage and fire. Jumper wires should only be used to bypass lengths of wire or to simulate switches.

Jumper wires are simple, yet extremely valuable, pieces of test equipment. They are basically test wires which are used to bypass sections of a circuit. Although jumper wires can be purchased, they are usually fabricated from lengths of standard automotive wire and whatever type of connector (alligator clip, spade connector or pin connector) that is required for the particular application being tested. In cramped, hard-to-reach areas, it is advisable to have insulated boots over the jumper wire terminals in order to prevent accidental grounding. It is also advisable to include a standard automotive fuse in any jumper wire. This is commonly referred to as a "fused jumper." By inserting an in-line fuse holder between a set of test leads, a fused jumper wire can be used for bypassing open circuits. Use a 5 amp fuse to provide protection against voltage spikes.

Jumper wires are used primarily to locate open electrical circuits, on either the ground (–) side of the circuit or on the power (+) side. If an electrical component fails to operate, connect the jumper wire between the component and a good ground. If the component operates only with the jumper installed, the

ground circuit is open. If the ground circuit is good, but the component does not operate, the circuit between the power feed and component may be open. By moving the jumper wire successively back from the component toward the power source, you can isolate the area of the circuit where the open is located. When the component stops functioning, or the power is cut off, the open is in the segment of wire between the jumper and the point previously tested.

You can sometimes connect the jumper wire directly from the battery to the "hot" terminal of the component, but first make sure the component uses 12 volts in operation. Some electrical components, such as fuel injectors or sensors, are designed to operate on about 4 to 5 volts, and running 12 volts directly to these components will cause damage.

TEST LIGHTS

See Figure 7

The test light is used to check circuits and components while electrical current is flowing through them. It is used for voltage and ground tests. To use a 12 volt test light, connect the ground clip to a good ground and probe wherever necessary with the pick. The test light will illuminate when voltage is detected. This does not necessarily mean that 12 volts (or any particular amount of voltage) is present; it only means that some voltage is present. It is advisable before using the test light to touch its ground clip and probe across the battery posts or terminals to make sure the light is operating properly.

❄ WARNING:

Do not use a test light to probe electronic ignition, spark plug or coil wires. Never use a pick-type test light to probe wiring on computer controlled systems unless specifically instructed to do so. Any wire insulation that is pierced by the test light probe should be taped and sealed with silicone after testing.

Like the jumper wire, the 12 volt test light is used to isolate opens in circuits. But, whereas the jumper wire is used to bypass the open to operate the load, the 12 volt test light is used to locate the presence of voltage in a circuit. If the test light illuminates, there is power up to that point in the circuit; if the test light does not illuminate, there is an open circuit (no power). Move the test light in successive steps back toward the power source until the light in the handle illuminates. The open is between the probe and a point which was previously probed.

The self-powered test light is similar in design to the 12 volt test light, but contains a 1.5 volt penlight battery in the handle. It is most often used in place of a multimeter to check for open or short circuits when power is isolated from the circuit (continuity test).

The battery in a self-powered test light does not provide much current. A weak battery may not provide enough power to illuminate the test light even when a complete circuit is made (especially if there is high resistance in the circuit). Always make sure that the test battery is strong. To check the battery, briefly touch the ground clip to the probe; if the light glows brightly, the battery is strong enough for testing.

Note: A self-powered test light should not be used on any computer controlled system or component. The small amount of electricity transmitted by the test light is enough to damage many electronic automotive components.

MULTIMETERS

Multimeters are an extremely useful tool for troubleshooting electrical problems. They can be purchased in either analog or digital form and have a price range to suit any budget. A multimeter is a voltmeter, ammeter and ohmmeter (along with other features) combined into one instrument. It is often used when testing solid state circuits because of its high input impedance (usually 10 megaohms or more). A brief description of the multimeter main test functions follows:

• **Voltmeter** - the voltmeter is used to measure voltage at any point in a circuit, or to measure the voltage drop across any part of a circuit. Voltmeters usually have various scales and a selector switch to allow the reading of different voltage ranges. The voltmeter has a positive and a negative lead. To avoid damage to the meter, always connect the negative lead to the negative (–) side of the circuit (to ground or nearest the ground side of the circuit) and connect the positive lead to the positive (+) side of the circuit (to the power source or the nearest power source). Note that the negative voltmeter lead will always be black and that the positive voltmeter will always be some color other than black (usually red).

• **Ohmmeter** - the ohmmeter is designed to read resistance (measured in ohms) in a circuit or component. Most ohmmeters will have a selector switch which permits the measurement of different ranges of resistance (usually the selector switch allows the multiplication of the meter reading by 10, 100, 1,000 and 10,000). Some ohmmeters are "auto-ranging" which means the meter itself will determine which scale to use. Since the meters are powered by an internal battery, the ohmmeter can be used like a self-powered test light. When the ohmmeter is connected, current from the ohmmeter flows through the circuit or component being tested. Since the ohmmeter's internal resistance and voltage are known values, the amount of current flow through the meter depends on the resistance of the circuit or component being tested. The ohmmeter can also be used to perform a continuity test for suspected open circuits. In using the meter for making continuity checks, do not be concerned with the actual resistance readings. Zero resistance, or any ohm reading, indicates continuity in the circuit. Infinite resistance indicates an opening in the circuit. A high resistance reading where there should be none indicates a problem in the circuit. Checks for short circuits are made in the same manner as checks for open circuits, except that the circuit must be isolated from both power and normal ground. Infinite resistance indicates no continuity, while zero resistance indicates a dead short.

• **Ammeter** - an ammeter measures the amount of current flowing through a circuit in units called amperes or amps. At normal operating voltage, most circuits have a characteristic amount of amperes, called "current draw" which can be measured using an ammeter. By referring to a specified current draw rating, then measuring the amperes and comparing the two values, one can determine what is happening within the circuit to aid in diagnosis. An open circuit, for example, will not allow any current to flow, so the ammeter reading will be zero. A damaged component or circuit will have an increased current draw, so the reading will be high. The ammeter is always connected in series with the circuit being tested. All of the current that normally flows through the circuit must also flow through the ammeter; if there is any other path for the current to follow, the ammeter reading will not be accurate. The ammeter itself has very little resistance to current flow and, therefore, will not affect the circuit, but it will measure current draw only when the circuit is closed and electricity is flowing. Excessive current draw can blow fuses and drain the battery, while a reduced current draw can cause motors to run slowly, lights to dim and other components to not operate properly.

Troubleshooting Electrical Systems

When diagnosing a specific problem, organized troubleshooting is a must. The complexity of a modern automotive vehicle demands that you approach any problem in a logical, organized manner. There are certain troubleshooting techniques, however, which are standard:

• Establish when the problem occurs. Does the problem appear only under certain conditions? Were there any noises, odors or other unusual symptoms? Isolate the problem area. To do this, make some simple tests and observations, then eliminate the systems that are working properly. Check for obvious problems, such as broken wires and loose or dirty connections. Always check the obvious before assuming something complicated is the cause.

• Test for problems systematically to determine the cause once the problem area is isolated. Are all the components functioning properly? Is there power going to electrical switches and motors. Performing careful, systematic checks will often turn up most causes on the first inspection, without wasting time checking components that have little or no relationship to the problem.

• Test all repairs after the work is done to make sure that the problem is fixed. Some causes can be traced to more than one component, so a careful

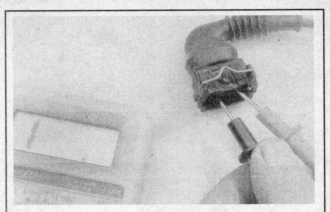

Fig. 8 The infinite reading on this multimeter indicates that the circuit is open

verification of repair work is important in order to pick up additional malfunctions that may cause a problem to reappear or a different problem to arise. A blown fuse, for example, is a simple problem that may require more than another fuse to repair. If you don't look for a problem that caused a fuse to blow, a shorted wire (for example) may go undetected.

Experience has shown that most problems tend to be the result of a fairly simple and obvious cause, such as loose or corroded connectors, bad grounds or damaged wire insulation which causes a short. This makes careful visual inspection of components during testing essential to quick and accurate troubleshooting.

Testing

OPEN CIRCUITS

See Figure 8

This test already assumes the existence of an open in the circuit and it is used to help locate the open portion.

1. Isolate the circuit from power and ground.
2. Connect the self-powered test light or ohmmeter ground clip to the ground side of the circuit and probe sections of the circuit sequentially.
3. If the light is out or there is infinite resistance, the open is between the probe and the circuit ground.
4. If the light is on or the meter shows continuity, the open is between the probe and the end of the circuit toward the power source.

SHORT CIRCUITS

Note: Never use a self-powered test light to perform checks for opens or shorts when power is applied to the circuit under test. The test light can be damaged by outside power.

1. Isolate the circuit from power and ground.
2. Connect the self-powered test light or ohmmeter ground clip to a good ground and probe any easy-to-reach point in the circuit.
3. If the light comes on or there is continuity, there is a short somewhere in the circuit.
4. To isolate the short, probe a test point at either end of the isolated circuit (the light should be on or the meter should indicate continuity).
5. Leave the test light probe engaged and sequentially open connectors or switches, remove parts, etc. until the light goes out or continuity is broken.
6. When the light goes out, the short is between the last two circuit components which were opened.

VOLTAGE

This test determines voltage available from the battery and should be the first step in any electrical troubleshooting procedure after visual inspection. Many electrical problems, especially on computer controlled systems, can be caused

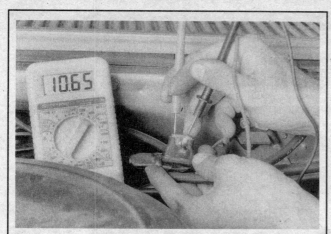

Fig. 9 This voltage drop test revealed high resistance (low voltage) in the circuit

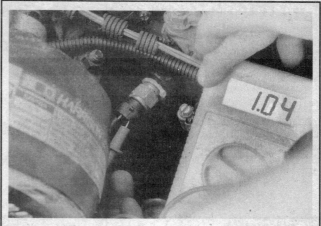

Fig. 10 Checking the resistance of a coolant temperature sensor with an ohmmeter. Reading is 1.04 k-ohms

by a low state of charge in the battery. Excessive corrosion at the battery cable terminals can cause poor contact that will prevent proper charging and full battery current flow.

1. Set the voltmeter selector switch to the 20V position.
2. Connect the multimeter negative lead to the battery's negative (−) post or terminal and the positive lead to the battery's positive (+) post or terminal.
3. Turn the ignition switch **ON** to provide a load.
4. A well charged battery should register over 12 volts. If the meter reads below 11.5 volts, the battery power may be insufficient to operate the electrical system properly.

VOLTAGE DROP

See Figure 9

When current flows through a load, the voltage beyond the load drops. This voltage drop is due to the resistance created by the load and also by small resistances created by corrosion at the connectors and damaged insulation on the wires. The maximum allowable voltage drop under load is critical, especially if there is more than one load in the circuit, since all voltage drops are cumulative.

1. Set the voltmeter selector switch to the 20 volt position.
2. Connect the multimeter negative lead to a good ground.
3. Operate the circuit and check the voltage prior to the first component (load).

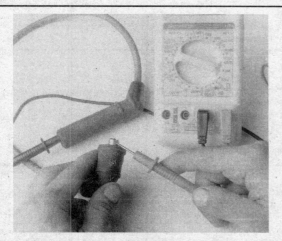

Fig. 11 Spark plug wires can be checked for excessive resistance using an ohmmeter

4. There should be little or no voltage drop in the circuit prior to the first component. If a voltage drop exists, the wire or connectors in the circuit are suspect.
5. While operating the first component in the circuit, probe the ground side of the component with the positive meter lead and observe the voltage readings. A small voltage drop should be noticed. This voltage drop is caused by the resistance of the component.
6. Repeat the test for each component (load) down the circuit.
7. If a large voltage drop is noticed, the preceding component, wire or connector is suspect.

RESISTANCE

See Figures 10 and 11

✴✴ WARNING:

Never use an ohmmeter with power applied to the circuit. The ohmmeter is designed to operate on its own power supply. The normal 12 volt electrical system voltage could damage the meter!

1. Isolate the circuit from the vehicle's power source.
2. Ensure that the ignition key is **OFF** when disconnecting any components or the battery.
3. Where necessary, also isolate at least one side of the circuit to be checked, in order to avoid reading parallel resistances. Parallel circuit resistances will always give a lower reading than the actual resistance of either of the branches.
4. Connect the meter leads to both sides of the circuit (wire or component) and read the actual measured ohms on the meter scale. Make sure the selector switch is set to the proper ohm scale for the circuit being tested, to avoid misreading the ohmmeter test value.

Wire and Connector Repair

Almost anyone can replace damaged wires, as long as the proper tools and parts are available. Wire and terminals are available to fit almost any need. Even the specialized weatherproof, molded and hard shell connectors are now available from aftermarket suppliers.

Be sure the ends of all the wires are fitted with the proper terminal hardware and connectors. Wrapping a wire around a stud is never a permanent solution and will only cause trouble later. Replace wires one at a time to avoid confusion. Always route wires exactly the same as the factory.

Note: If connector repair is necessary, only attempt it if you have the proper tools. Weatherproof and hard shell connectors require special tools to release the pins inside the connector. Attempting to repair these connectors with conventional hand tools will damage them.

BATTERY CABLES

Disconnecting the Cables

When working on any electrical component on the vehicle, it is always a good idea to disconnect the negative (−) battery cable. This will prevent potential damage to many sensitive electrical components such as the Engine Control Module (ECM), radio, alternator, etc.

Note: Any time you disengage the battery cables, it is recommended that you disconnect the negative (−) battery cable first. This will prevent your accidentally grounding the positive (+) terminal to the body of the vehicle when disconnecting it, thereby preventing damage to the above mentioned components.

Before you disconnect the cable(s), first turn the ignition to the **OFF** position. This will prevent a draw on the battery which could cause arcing (electricity trying to ground itself to the body of a vehicle, just like a spark plug jumping the gap) and, of course, damaging some components such as the alternator diodes.

When the battery cable(s) are reconnected (negative cable last), be sure to check that your lights, windshield wipers and other electrically operated safety components are all working correctly. If your vehicle contains an Electronically Tuned Radio (ETR), don't forget to also reset your radio stations. Ditto for the clock.

SUPPLEMENTAL INFLATABLE RESTRAINT (SIR) SYSTEM

General Information

The air bag system used on CHEVROLET/GEO and SUZUKI vehicles is referred to as Supplemental Inflatable Restraint (SIR) system. The SIR system provides additional protection for the driver, if a forward collision of sufficient force is encountered. The SIR assists the normal sea belt restraining system by deploying an air bag, via the steering column. A knee pad, located beneath the driver's side instrument panel, also aid in absorbing collision impact. The steering column, as in previous design, still continues to be collapsible.

The SIR system contains a deployment loop and a Diagnostic Energy Reserve Module (DERM). The function of the deployment loop is to supply current through the inflator module in the steering wheel, which will cause air bag deployment during a severe accident. The DERM supplies the necessary power, even if the battery has been damaged.

The deployment loop is made up of the arming sensors, coil assembly, inflator module and the discriminating sensors. The inflator module is only supplied sufficient current to deploy the air bag, when the arming sensors and at least 1 of the discriminating sensors close simultaneously. The function of the DERM is to supply the deployment loop a 36 Volt Loop Reserve (36VLR) to assure air bag deployment for seconds after ignition voltage is lost during an accident.

The DERM, in conjunction with the resistors make it possible to detect circuit and component faults within the deployment loop. If the voltages monitored by the DERM fall outside expected limits, the DERM will indicate a fault code through the storage of a malfunction code and turning **ON** the INFLATABLE RESTRAINT lamp.

SERVICE PRECAUTIONS

✳✳ CAUTION:

To avoid deployment when servicing the SIR system or components in the immediate area, do not use electrical test equipment such as battery or AC powered voltmeter, ohmmeter, etc. or any type of tester other than specified. Do not use a non-powered probe tester. To avoid personal injury, all precautions must be strictly adhered to.

• Never disconnect any electrical connection with the ignition switch **ON** unless instructed to do so in a test.
• Before disconnecting the negative battery cable, make a record of the contents memorized by each memory system like the clock, audio, etc. When service or repairs are completed make certain to reset these memory system.
• Always wear a grounded wrist static strap when servicing any control module or component labeled with a Electrostatic Discharge (ESD) sensitive device symbol.
• Avoid touching module connector pins.
• Leave new components and modules in the shipping package until ready to install them.
• Always touch a vehicle ground after sliding across a vehicle seat or walk-

ing across vinyl or carpeted floors to avoid static charge damage.
• The DERM can maintain sufficient voltage to cause a deployment for up to 10 minutes, even if the battery is disconnected.
• All sensors are specifically calibrated to each series vehicle's series. The sensors, mounting brackets and wiring harness must never be modified from original design.
• Never strike or jar a sensor, or deployment could happen.
• Never power up the SIR system when any sensor is not rigidly attached to the vehicle.
• Always carry an inflator module with the trim cover facing away.
• Always place an inflator module on the workbench with the trim cover up, away from loose objects.
• The inflator module is to be stored and shipped under DOT E - 8236 flammable solid regulations.
• The inflator module must be deployed before it is scrapped.
• After deployment the air bag surface may contain sodium hydroxide dust. Always wear gloves and safety glasses when handling the assembly. Wash hands with mild soap and water afterwards.
• Any visible damage to sensors requires component replacement.
• Wire and connector repair must be performed using kit J - 38125 - A, or equivalent. Use special crimping tools, heat torch and seals.
• Absolutely no wire connector, or terminal repair is to be attempted on the arming sensor, passenger compartment discriminating sensor, forward discriminating sensor, inflator module or SIR coil assembly
• Never bake dry paint on vehicle or allow to exceed temperatures over 300-degrees F, without disabling the SIR system and removing the inflator module.
• Do not interchange sensors between models or years.
• Do not install used SIR system parts from another vehicle.
• Never allow welding cables to lay on, near or across any vehicle electrical wiring.

DISARMING THE SYSTEM

1. Turn the ignition switch **OFF**.
2. Remove the SIR IG fuse from the SIR fuse block.
3. Remove the access cover at the back of the steering wheel to gain access to the 2-way SIR connector.
4. Remove the Connector Position Assurance (CPA) lock and disconnect the yellow 2-way connector inside the inflator module housing.

ARMING THE SYSTEM

1. Turn the ignition switch **OFF**.
2. Reconnect the yellow 2-way connector at the back of the steering wheel and install the CPA lock.
3. Install the SIR IG fuse.
4. Refit the rear plastic access cover to the inflator module housing.
5. Turn the ignition switch **ON** and observe the inflatable restraint indicator lamp. If the lamp does not flash 7 to 9 times and then remain **OFF**, perform the SIR diagnostic system check.

HEATING AND AIR CONDITIONING

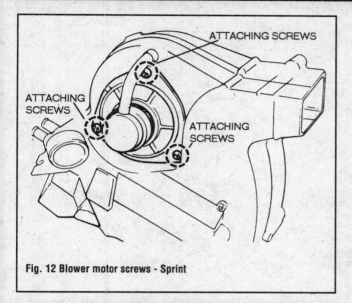

Fig. 12 Blower motor screws - Sprint

Blower Motor

REMOVAL & INSTALLATION

See Figures 12 and 13

Sprint

1. Disconnect the negative battery cable.
2. Disconnect the defroster hose on the steering column side.
3. Disconnect the blower motor lead wire.
4. Remove the attaching screws and blower motor.
5. Installation is the reverse of removal.

Metro/Swift

1. Disconnect the negative battery cable.
2. On Metro, remove the glove compartment to access the blower motor electrical connectors.
3. Disconnect the blower motor and resistor wiring connectors.
4. Disconnect the air control cable from the blower case assembly.
5. Remove the blower case mounting bolts and case from the vehicle.
6. Remove the three motor retaining screws and blower motor. Disconnect the air hose, if equipped.

To install:

7. Install the blower motor case and secure with screws.
8. Connect the air hose to the blower motor case.
9. Install the blower motor case in the vehicle and tighten bolts to 89 inch lbs. (10 Nm).
10. Connect the air control cable. Connect the electrical connectors.
11. Install the glove compartment.
12. Connect the negative battery cable.

Heater Core

REMOVAL & INSTALLATION

See Figures 14 and 15

Sprint

1. Drain the cooling system.
2. Remove the glove compartment.
3. Remove the defroster hoses from the heater case.
4. Disconnect the wiring connectors from the blower motor and resistor.
5. Disconnect the control cables from the heater case.
6. Pull out center vent louver.
7. Disconnect side vent ducts from center vent duct.
8. Remove center vent duct, ashtray upper plate and instrument panel member stay.
9. Remove the heater assembly attaching nuts.
10. Loosen the heater case top side mounting bolt through box wrench from

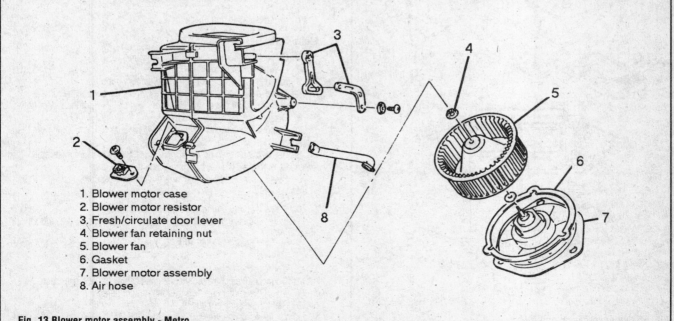

1. Blower motor case
2. Blower motor resistor
3. Fresh/circulate door lever
4. Blower fan retaining nut
5. Blower fan
6. Gasket
7. Blower motor assembly
8. Air hose

Fig. 13 Blower motor assembly - Metro

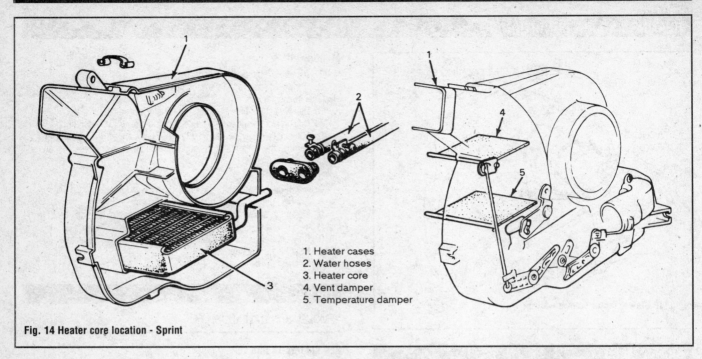

1. Heater cases
2. Water hoses
3. Heater core
4. Vent damper
5. Temperature damper

Fig. 14 Heater core location - Sprint

glove compartment side.
11. Remove the heater control assembly by raising the dash panel.
12. Remove clips to separate the heater case into right and left sections.
13. Pull out the heater core from the heater case.

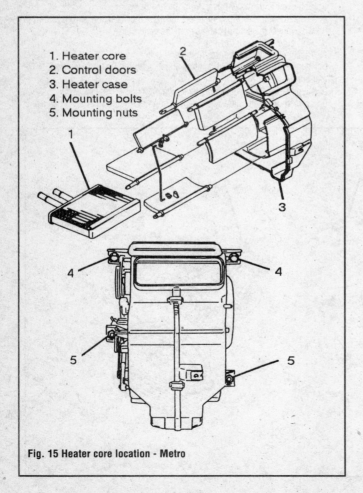

1. Heater core
2. Control doors
3. Heater case
4. Mounting bolts
5. Mounting nuts

Fig. 15 Heater core location - Metro

To install:
14. Install the heater core in the heater case.
15. Install clips to join the heater case sections.
16. Install the heater control assembly by raising the dash panel.
17. Tighten the heater case top side mounting bolt through box wrench from glove compartment side.
18. Install the heater assembly attaching nuts.
19. Install center vent duct, ashtray upper plate and instrument panel member stay.
20. Connect side vent ducts from center vent duct.
21. Install center vent louver.
22. Connect the control cables to the heater case.
23. Connect the wiring connectors to the blower motor and resistor.
24. Install the defroster hoses to the heater case.
25. Install the glove compartment.
26. Fill the cooling system.
27. Run the engine and check for leaks.

Metro/Swift
1. Disconnect the negative battery cable.
2. Drain the engine coolant.
3. Remove the instrument panel and center supports.
4. Remove the heater control assembly from the support member.
5. Disconnect all electrical connectors and cables from the heater case.
6. Disconnect the heater core hoses.
7. Remove the defrost duct and speedometer retaining bracket from the heater case.
8. Remove the fastening bolts, grommets and floor duct, if equipped, from the case and remove the case from the vehicle.
9. Separate the heater case and remove the heater core.

To install:
10. Install the core and assemble the heater case.
11. Install the fastening bolts, grommets and floor duct to the case after installation.
12. Install the defrost duct and speedometer retaining bracket to the heater case.
13. Connect the heater core hoses.
14. Connect all electrical connectors and cables to the heater case.
15. Install the center supports and instrument panel.
16. Refill the engine coolant.
17. Connect the negative battery cable.
18. Run engine and check for coolant leaks.

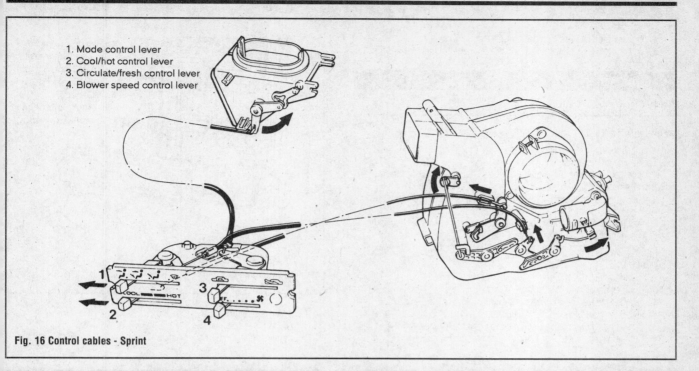

1. Mode control lever
2. Cool/hot control lever
3. Circulate/fresh control lever
4. Blower speed control lever

Fig. 16 Control cables - Sprint

Air Conditioning Components

REMOVAL & INSTALLATION

Repair or service of air conditioning components is not covered by this manual, because of the risk of personal injury or death, and because of the legal ramifications of servicing these components without the proper EPA certification and experience. Cost, personal injury or death, environmental damage, and legal considerations (such as the fact that it is a federal crime to vent refrigerant into the atmosphere), dictate that the A/C components on your vehicle should be serviced only by a Motor Vehicle Air Conditioning (MVAC) trained, and EPA certified automotive technician.

Note: If your vehicle's A/C system uses R-12 refrigerant and is in need of recharging, the A/C system can be converted over to R-134a refrigerant (less environmentally harmful and expensive). Refer to Air Conditioning System for additional information on R-12 to R-134a conversions, and for additional considerations dealing with your vehicle's A/C system.

Control Cable

ADJUSTMENT

1. Set the temperature control lever to HOT.
2. Set the mode control lever to the DEFROST position.
3. Set the fresh/recirculate control lever to the FRESH position.
4. Connect and clamp each respective control cable to the heater and blower case with the heater control assembly set.

REMOVAL & INSTALLATION

See Figures 16 and 17

1. Remove the heater control unit from the instrument panel.
2. Remove the mode and temperature control cables at the heater case. Remove the cables from the vehicle.
3. Remove the fresh/recirculate control cable at blower case and remove

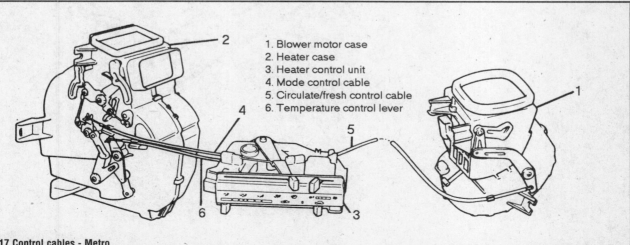

1. Blower motor case
2. Heater case
3. Heater control unit
4. Mode control cable
5. Circulate/fresh control cable
6. Temperature control lever

Fig. 17 Control cables - Metro

from vehicle.
    4. Installation is the reverse of removal.
    5. Adjust the cables prior to attaching at heater control unit.

Control Panel

REMOVAL & INSTALLATION

See Figure 18

    1. Disconnect the negative battery cable.
    2. Pull the control knobs from the levers.
    3. Release the latches at the rear of the bezel. Remove the control assembly lens and disconnect the bulb.
    4. Disconnect the control cables at the blower and heater assembly.
    5. Remove the control assembly fasteners.
    6. Pull the control assembly out and disconnect the electrical connections.
    7. Disconnect the control cables from the levers.
    8. Remove the blower, air conditioning and heater switch.

To install:

    9. Install the blower, air conditioning and heater switch.
  10. Connect the control cables to the levers.
  11. Connect the electrical connections and install the control assembly.
  12. Install the control assembly fasteners.
  13. Connect the control cables at the blower and heater assembly.
  14. Connect the bulb and install the control assembly lens.

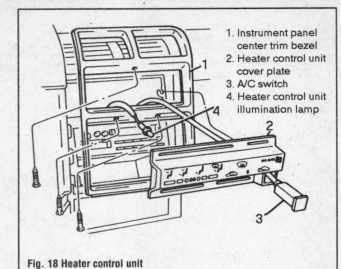

1. Instrument panel center trim bezel
2. Heater control unit cover plate
3. A/C switch
4. Heater control unit illumination lamp

Fig. 18 Heater control unit

  15. Install the control knobs.
  16. Adjust the control cables.
  17. Connect the negative battery cable.

CRUISE CONTROL

See Figure 19

    The cruise control system consists of a mode control switch, electronics module, servo unit, speed sensor and wiring harness. Throttle actuation is accomplished by an electrically operated servo motor attached by cable to the vehicles throttle linkage. Maximum and minimum cruise speeds are 85 and 25 miles per hour.

    The vehicle speed is provided to the electronics module by the use of a speed sensor. The sensor utilizes a magnetic reed switch which opens and closes 4 times per revolution of the speedometer cable. The sensor is located in the speedometer head.

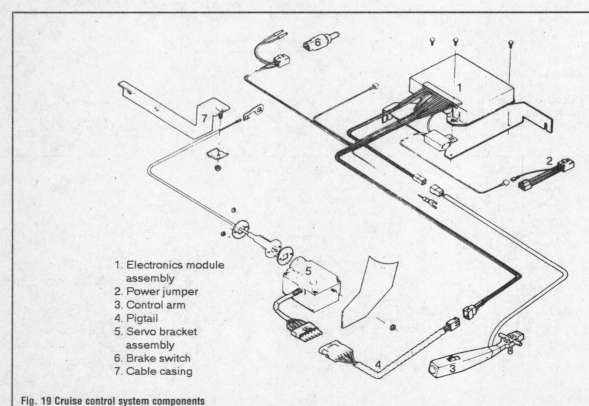

1. Electronics module assembly
2. Power jumper
3. Control arm
4. Pigtail
5. Servo bracket assembly
6. Brake switch
7. Cable casing

Fig. 19 Cruise control system components

The electronics module is the brain of the system. The module interprets the position of the servo unit, the position of the mode control switches and the output of the speed sensor. In response to these inputs, the module electrically signals the servo motor drive in or out. The electronic module is located under the dash on the driver side.

The disengagement switches, brake and clutch, are operated by the use of the brake and clutch pedals. The brake switch operates the stoplights and cancels the signal to the cruise control module when the lights are illuminated. The clutch switch disengages the cruise control if the pedal is depressed for up shifting or down shifting.

The servo consists of an electric motor with reduction gearing, electromag-

netic clutch, actuating rack and a variable voltage position sensor. The servo operates the throttle in response to signal from the electronics module.

✳✳ CAUTION:

If vehicle is equipped with an supplemental inflatable restraint system (SIR), the system must be fully disarmed before performing cruise control repairs. Failure to disarm the system could result in personal injury and/or property damage.

ENTERTAINMENT SYSTEMS

Radio Receiver

REMOVAL & INSTALLATION

1985 - 94 Models
See Figure 20

1. Disconnect the negative battery cable.
2. Open the glove box. Remove the glove box open panel.
3. Remove the air conditioning switch connector and heater control unit lever knobs. Pull heater control unit cover plate from instrument panel.
4. Remove the gearshift control lever upper boot and center console.
5. Remove the ashtray.
6. Remove the instrument panel center trim bezel and radio face plate.
7. Remove the screw from the back of the radio receiver and the screws from the front face of the radio.
8. Remove the radio.

To install:
9. Install the radio. Tighten screws securely.
10. Install the instrument panel center trim bezel and radio face plate.
11. Install the ashtray.
12. Install the gearshift control lever upper boot and center console.
13. Pull heater control unit cover plate from instrument panel. Install the air conditioning switch connector and heater control unit lever knobs.
14. Install the glove box open panel.
15. Connect the negative battery cable.

1995 - 00 Models
1. Disconnect the antenna and the radio electrical connector by accessing through the instrument panel compartment.
2. Remove the ashtray from the track.
3. Remove the center trim by removing the four screws.
4. Remove the screw under the radio.
5. Unscrew the four screws from the front of the radio.
6. Pull the radio out with the mounting bracket out of the vehicle. Remove the brackets if necessary.

To install:
7. Install the mounting bracket if they were removed.
8. Place the radio back into the instrument panel.
9. Install the four screws into the face of the radio.
10. Reinstall the screw in the underside of the radio.
11. Install the center trim and secure with the screws removed in the removal procedure.
12. Reconnect all the connectors that were removed.

Speakers

REMOVAL & INSTALLATION

See Figures 21, 22, 23 and 24

Front Speakers
1. Disconnect the negative battery cable.
2. Remove the speaker grills.
3. Remove the speaker retaining screws.

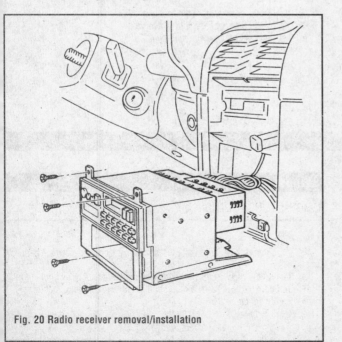

Fig. 20 Radio receiver removal/installation

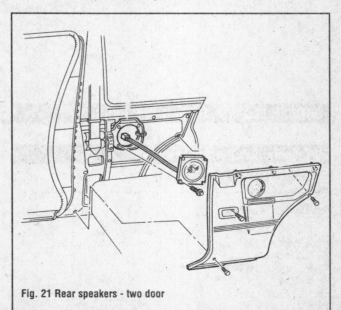

Fig. 21 Rear speakers - two door

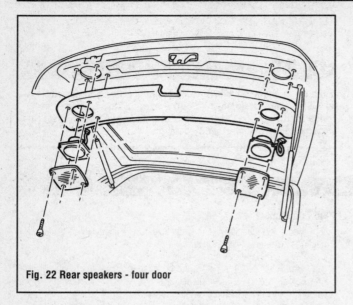

Fig. 22 Rear speakers - four door

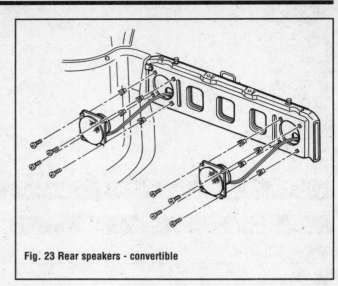

Fig. 23 Rear speakers - convertible

4. Remove the speaker from the instrument panel.
5. Disconnect the speaker electrical connector.
6. Installation is the reverse of removal.

Rear Speakers

2-DOOR MODELS

1. Disconnect the negative battery cable.
2. Remove the rear quarter trim panel.
3. Remove the speaker retaining screws.
4. Remove the speaker from the rear quarter panel.
5. Disconnect the speaker electrical connector.
6. Installation is the reverse of removal.

4-DOOR MODELS

1. Disconnect the negative battery cable.
2. Remove the speaker grilles and from the hatchback door.
3. Remove the speaker from the hatchback door.
4. Disconnect the speaker electrical connector.
5. Installation is the reverse of removal.

CONVERTIBLE MODELS

1. Disconnect the negative battery cable.
2. Remove the speaker trim panels.

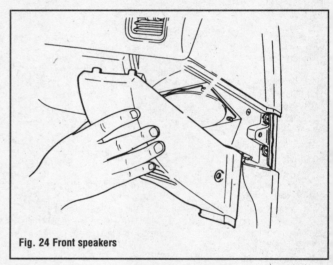

Fig. 24 Front speakers

3. Remove the speaker from the seat belt tower.
4. Disconnect the speaker electrical connector.
5. Installation is the reverse of removal.

WINDSHIELD WIPERS AND WASHERS

Windshield Wiper Blade and Arm

REMOVAL & INSTALLATION

See Figures 25 and 26

1. Note the location of the wiper arm prior to removal.
2. Remove the nut cover and retaining nut securing the wiper arm.
3. Remove the wiper from the linkage
4. Installation is the reverse of removal.
5. Tighten wiper retaining nut to 15 ft. lbs. (20 Nm).

Windshield Wiper Motor

REMOVAL & INSTALLATION

Front

1. Disconnect the negative battery cable and wiper motor electrical connectors.
2. Remove the wiper motor retaining bolts and pull motor away from firewall.
3. On Sprint, remove crank arm nut and crank arm. On Metro, gently pry wiper linkage from crank arm.
4. Remove the wiper motor from the vehicle.

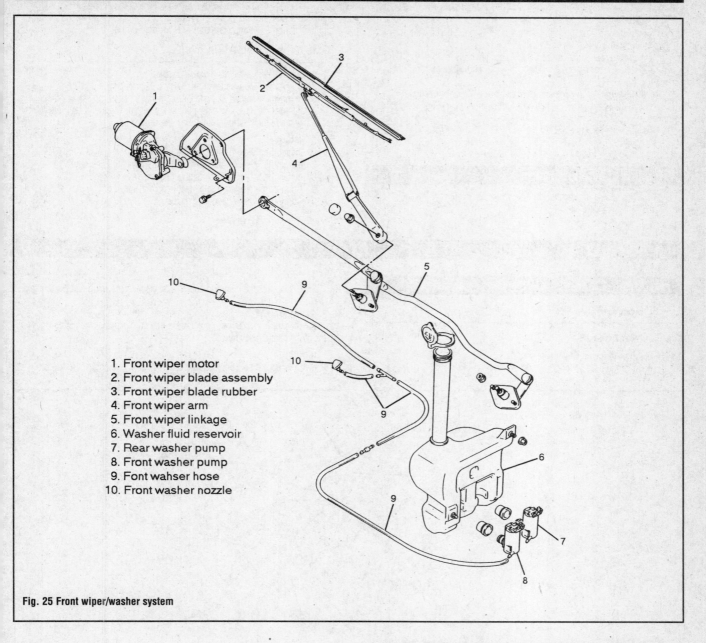

1. Front wiper motor
2. Front wiper blade assembly
3. Front wiper blade rubber
4. Front wiper arm
5. Front wiper linkage
6. Washer fluid reservoir
7. Rear washer pump
8. Front washer pump
9. Font wahser hose
10. Front washer nozzle

Fig. 25 Front wiper/washer system

To install:

5. Connect wiper linkage to wiper motor. On Sprint, tighten wiper crank arm nut to 96 inch lbs. (10 Nm).

6. Install the wiper motor to the vehicle. Tighten bolts to 15 ft. lbs. (20 Nm).

7. Connect wiper motor electrical connectors, then negative battery cable.

Rear

1. Disconnect the negative battery cable.

2. Remove the speakers from the hatchback door inner trim panel, if so equipped.

3. Remove the retaining clips and hatchback door inner trim panel from the vehicle.

4. Remove the wiper motor electrical connector and wiper motor ground screw.

5. Remove the wiper motor mounting screws and lower the wiper m

6. On Sprint, remove the wiper cranking arm retaining nut from the wiper motor shaft. On Metro, pry the wiper linkage from the cranking arm.

7. Remove the rear wiper motor.

Fig. 26 Windshield wiper motor

To install:

8. Connect wiper linkage to wiper motor. On Sprint, tighten wiper crank arm nut to 96 inch lbs. (10 Nm).

9. Install the wiper motor to the vehicle. Tighten bolts to 15 ft. lbs. (20 Nm).

10. Install the wiper motor electrical connector and wiper motor ground screw.

11. Install the retaining clips and hatchback door inner trim panel.

12. Install the speakers in the hatchback door inner trim panel, if so equipped.

13. Connect the negative battery cable.

Windshield Washer Pump

Dual washer pumps are located on the washer reservoir. One feeds the front

windshield washer system, the other feeds the rear windshield washer. Removal and installation procedures are the same for both pumps.

REMOVAL & INSTALLATION

1. Disconnect the negative battery cable.
2. Disconnect the washer pump electrical connectors.
3. Remove the screws and clips attaching the reservoir to the wheel housing.
4. Remove the attaching nuts and the washer fluid reservoir from the vehicle.
5. Remove the washer pumps from the reservoir.

To install:

6. Install the washer pumps on the reservoir.
7. Install the washer fluid reservoir on the vehicle.
8. Install the screws and clips attaching the reservoir to the wheel housing.
9. Connect the washer pump electrical connectors.
10. Connect the negative battery cable.

INSTRUMENTS AND SWITCHES

Instrument Cluster

REMOVAL & INSTALLATION

See Figures 27 and 28

1. Disconnect the negative battery cable.
2. Remove the instrument panel trim bezel.

3. Disconnect the retaining clip and the speedometer cable at the transaxle to ease cluster removal.

4. Remove the cluster assembly from the instrument panel.

5. Disconnect the speedometer cable and all electrical connectors from the back of the cluster assembly.

To install:

6. Connect the speedometer cable and all electrical connectors to the

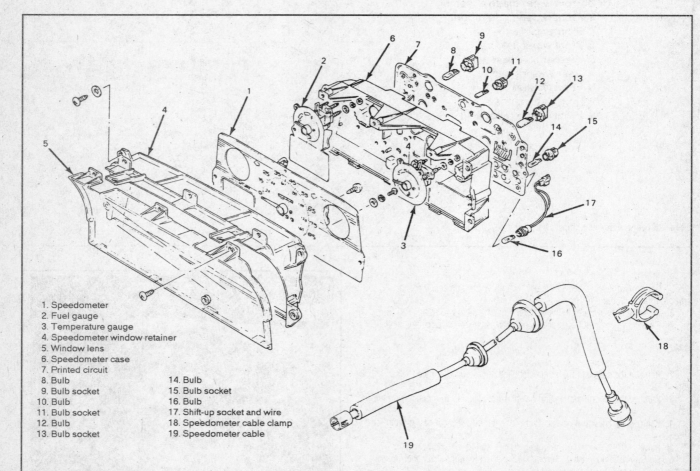

1. Speedometer
2. Fuel gauge
3. Temperature gauge
4. Speedometer window retainer
5. Window lens
6. Speedometer case
7. Printed circuit
8. Bulb
9. Bulb socket
10. Bulb
11. Bulb socket
12. Bulb
13. Bulb socket
14. Bulb
15. Bulb socket
16. Bulb
17. Shift-up socket and wire
18. Speedometer cable clamp
19. Speedometer cable

Fig. 27 Instrument panel cluster - Sprint

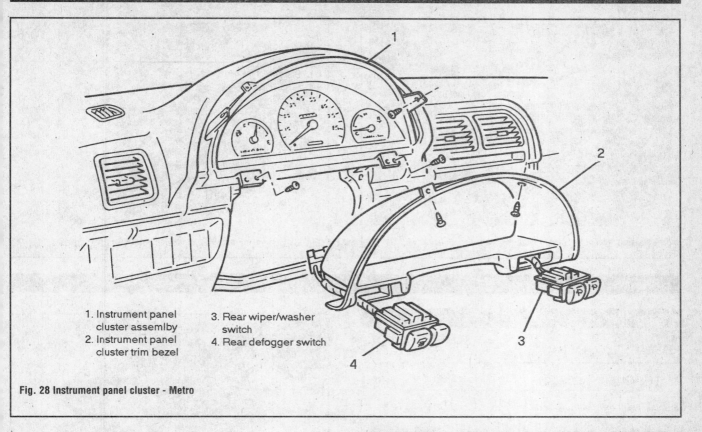

1. Instrument panel cluster assemlby
2. Instrument panel cluster trim bezel
3. Rear wiper/washer switch
4. Rear defogger switch

Fig. 28 Instrument panel cluster - Metro

back of the cluster assembly.

7. Install the cluster assembly in the instrument panel.

8. Connect the retaining clip and the speedometer cable at the transaxle.

9. Install the instrument panel trim bezel.

10. Connect the negative battery cable.

Speedometer

REMOVAL & INSTALLATION

See Figure 29

1. Remove the instrument cluster from the vehicle.
2. Remove the cluster lens and bezel.
3. Remove the screws attaching the speedometer to the cluster from the back of the cluster.
4. Remove the speedometer.
5. Installation is the reverse of removal.

Tachometer and Gauges

REMOVAL & INSTALLATION

1. Remove the instrument cluster from the vehicle.
2. Remove the cluster lens and bezel.
3. Remove the speedometer.
4. Remove the screws attaching the gauges to the cluster from the back of the cluster.
5. Remove the gauges.
6. Installation is the reverse of removal.

Rear Windshield Wiper Switch

The rear windshield wiper/washer switch is located in the instrument panel cluster bezel.

REMOVAL & INSTALLATION

1. Disconnect the negative battery cable.
2. Remove the instrument panel cluster bezel.
3. Disconnect the electrical connector.
4. Remove the switch from the bezel.
5. Installation is the reverse of removal.

1. Tachometer mounting screws
2. Speedometer mounting screws
3. Fuel gauge mounting screws
4. Temperature gauge mounting screws

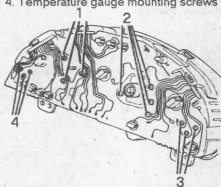

Fig. 29 Gauge mounting screws

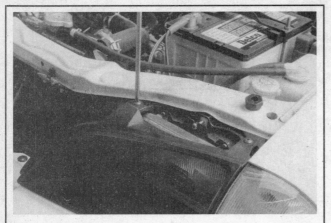

Fig. 30 Remove the headlamp bezel screws...

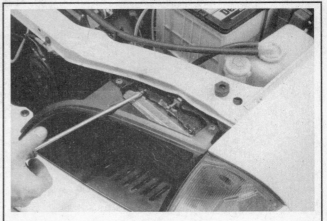

Fig. 31 ...then, remove the headlamp retaining ring screws...

LIGHTING

Headlights

REMOVAL & INSTALLATION

See Figures 30, 31, 32 and 33

Sealed Beam Headlamp Assembly

1. Remove the trim bezel.
2. Remove the retaining ring.
3. Disconnect the headlamp bulb electrical connector.
4. Remove the headlamp from the vehicle.
5. Installation is the reverse of removal.

Composite Headlamp Assembly

See Figure 34

1. Remove the composite headlamp bulb from the headlamp lens assembly.
2. Remove the parking lamp housing.
3. Remove the plastic retaining clips and screw from the wheel housing. Pull the wheel housing back to gain access to the mounting nuts.
4. Remove the rubber retaining strap and air cleaner resonator, as required.
5. Remove the retaining nuts and then remove the composite headlamp assembly.

Fig. 32 ...carefully, remove the headlamp...

To install:

6. Install the composite headlamp assembly and tighten retaining nuts to 89 inch lbs. (10 Nm).
7. Install the rubber retaining strap and air cleaner resonator, as required.

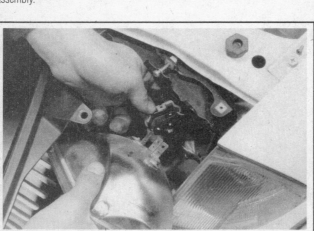

Fig. 33 ...and disconnect the headlamp connector

Fig. 34 Remove the bulb from the headlamp assembly

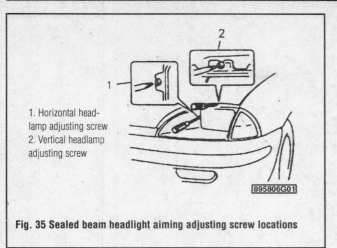

1. Horizontal headlamp adjusting screw
2. Vertical headlamp adjusting screw

895806G01

Fig. 35 Sealed beam headlight aiming adjusting screw locations

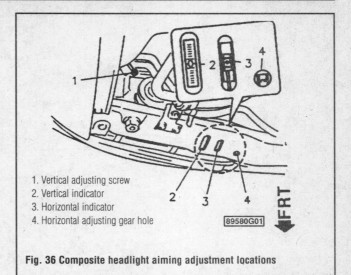

1. Vertical adjusting screw
2. Vertical indicator
3. Horizontal indicator
4. Horizontal adjusting gear hole

89580G01

Fig. 36 Composite headlight aiming adjustment locations

8. Install the plastic retaining clips and screw in the wheel housing.
9. Install the parking lamp housing.
10. the composite headlamp bulb from the headlamp lens assembly.

AIMING THE HEADLIGHTS

See Figures 35, 36, 37 and 38

The headlights must be properly aimed to provide the best, safest road illumination. The lights should be checked for proper aim and adjusted as necessary. Certain state and local authorities have requirements for headlight aiming; these should be checked before adjustment is made.

✳✳ CAUTION:

About once a year, when the headlights are replaced or any time front end work is performed on your vehicle, the headlight should be accurately aimed by a reputable repair shop using the proper equipment. Headlights not properly aimed can make it virtually impossible to see and may blind other drivers on the road, possibly causing an accident. Note that the following procedure is a temporary fix, until you can take your vehicle to a repair shop for a proper adjustment.

Headlight adjustment may be temporarily made using a wall, as described below, or on the rear of another vehicle. When adjusted, the lights should not glare in oncoming car or truck windshields, nor should they illuminate the passenger compartment of vehicles driving in front of you. These adjustments are rough and should always be fine-tuned by a repair shop, which is equipped with headlight aiming tools. Improper adjustments may be both dangerous and illegal.

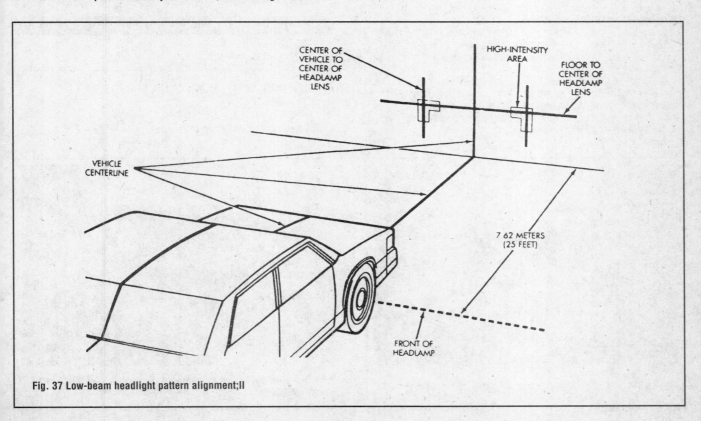

Fig. 37 Low-beam headlight pattern alignment;ll

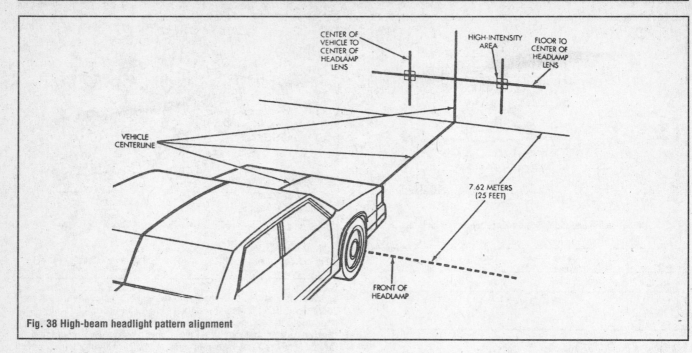

Fig. 38 High-beam headlight pattern alignment

For most of the vehicles covered by this manual, horizontal and vertical aiming of each sealed beam unit is provided by two adjusting screws which move the retaining ring and adjusting plate against the tension of a coil spring. There is no adjustment for focus; this is done during headlight manufacturing.

Before removing the headlight bulb or disturbing the headlamp in any way, note the current settings in order to ease headlight adjustment upon reassembly. If the high or low beam setting of the old lamp still works, this can be done using the wall of a garage or a building:

1. Park the vehicle on a level surface, with the fuel tank about 1/2 full and with the vehicle empty of all extra cargo (unless normally carried). The vehicle should be facing a wall, which is no less than 6 feet (1.8m) high and 12 feet (3.7m) wide. The front of the vehicle should be about 25 feet from the wall.

2. If aiming is to be performed outdoors, it is advisable to wait until dusk in order to properly see the headlight beams on the wall. If done in a garage, darken the area around the wall as much as possible by closing shades or hanging cloth over the windows.

3. Turn the headlights **ON** and mark the wall at the center of each light's low beam, then switch on the brights and mark the center of each light's high beam. A short length of masking tape, which is visible from the front of the vehicle, may be used. Although marking all four positions is advisable, marking one position from each light should be sufficient.

4. If neither beam on one side is working, and if another like-sized vehicle is available, park the second one in the exact spot where the vehicle was and mark the beams using the same-side light. Then switch the vehicles so the one to be aimed is back in the original spot. It must be parked no closer to or farther away from the wall than the second vehicle.

5. Perform any necessary repairs, but make sure the vehicle is not moved, or is returned to the exact spot from which the lights were marked. Turn the headlights **ON** and adjust the beams to match the marks on the wall.

6. Have the headlight adjustment checked as soon as possible by a reputable repair shop.

Signal and Marker Lights

REMOVAL & INSTALLATION

See Figures 39, 40, 41, 42, 43, 44 and 45

Fog Lamps

1. Turn the weather seal cap counterclockwise and pull back.

Fig. 39 Remove the retaining screws from the turn signal assembly

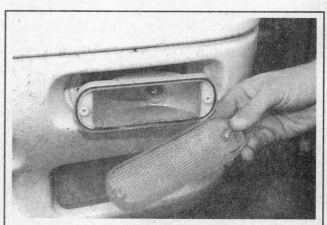

Fig. 40 Once the screws are removed, the lens can be pulled away from the housing

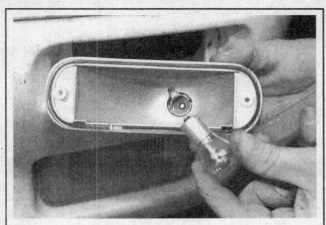

Fig. 41 Turn the bulb counterclockwise 1/4 of a turn to remove the bulb

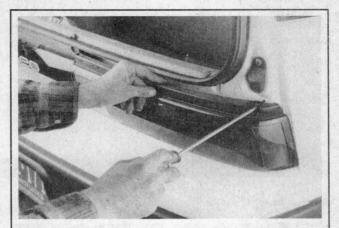

Fig. 42 Removing the rear combination lamp attaching screws

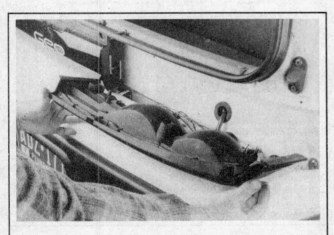

Fig. 43 Pull the combination lamp assembly away from the vehicle.

Fig. 44 Remove the bulb socket from the lamp assembly by turning counterclockwise

2. Push on the retaining clip and push it upward.
3. Remove the bulb from the lamp assembly.
4. Pull the connector away from the bulb so there is no strain placed on the wiring harness.
5. Installation is the reverse of removal.

Turn Signal and Parking Lights

1. Remove the screws from the parking lamp assembly.
2. Remove the parking lamp assembly.
3. Remove the socket from the lamp assembly.
4. Remove the bulb from the socket.
5. Installation is the reverse of removal.

Front Turn Signal Lamps

1. Remove the screws from the turn signal lamp assembly.
2. Remove the turn signal lamp assembly.
3. Remove the socket from the lamp assembly.
4. Remove the bulb from the socket.
5. Installation is the reverse of removal.

License Plate Lamps

1. Remove the screws from the license plate lamp assembly.
2. Remove the license plate lamp assembly.
3. Remove the socket from the lamp assembly.
4. Remove the bulb from the socket.
5. Installation is the reverse of removal.

Rear Combination Lamp

The rear combination lamp assembly contains the backup lights, rear parking lights and brake lights.
1. Remove the rear garnish from vehicle.
2. Remove the rear combination lamp assembly attaching screws and pull the lamp assembly away from the end panel.
3. Remove the four bulb sockets from the lamp assembly.

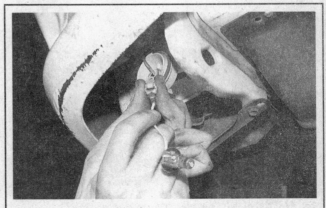

Fig. 45 Pull the connector away from the bulb

4. Remove the lamp assembly, then remove the bulbs from the sockets.
5. Installation is the reverse of removal.

Dome Lamp

1. Gently pry dome lamp lens from lamp assembly.
2. Remove dome lamp bulb.
3. Installation is the reverse of removal.

Instrument Panel Cluster Lamps

1. Remove the instrument cluster from the vehicle.
2. Remove the bulb sockets from the back of the cluster assembly.
3. Remove the bulbs from the sockets.
4. Installation is the reverse of removal.

CIRCUIT PROTECTION

See Figures 46, 47 and 48

Fuses

All electrical circuits are protected against excessive loads, which might occur because of shorts or overloads in the wiring system. Such protection is provided by fuses. The fuse box is located under the left side of the dash. Additional fuses are located in the fuse and relay box in the engine compartment

REPLACEMENT

To replace a blown fuse, simply remove the fuse box cover and locate the blown fuse. Remove the fuse from the box by gently pulling and replace with a fuse of the same amperage rating.

Note: Prior to replacing the fuse, inspect the circuit covered by the fuse to find the problem that caused the fuse to blow.

Fusible Links

In addition to fuses, some circuits use fusible links to protect the wiring. Like fuses, fusible links are one time protection devices that will melt and create an open circuit.

Note: Not all fusible link open circuits can be detected by observation. Always inspect that there is battery voltage past the fusible link to verify continuity.

Fusible links are used instead of a fuse in wiring circuits that are not normally fused, such as the ignition circuit. Each fusible link is four wire gage sizes smaller than the cable it is designed to protect. Links are marked on the insulation with wire gage size because the heavy insulation makes the link appear to

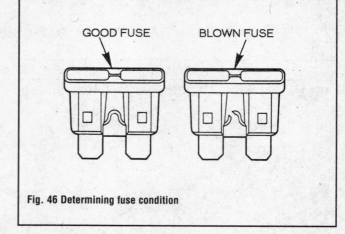

Fig. 46 Determining fuse condition

be a heavier gage than it actually is. The same wire size fusible link must be used when replacing an open fusible link.

REPLACEMENT

See Figure 49

To replace a damaged fusible link, disconnect the negative battery cable, cut the link off beyond the splice, and replace with a repair link. When connecting the repair link, strip the wire and use staking type pliers to crimp the splice securely in two places.

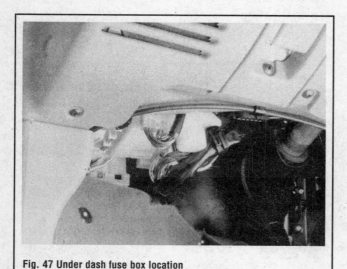

Fig. 47 Under dash fuse box location

Fig. 48 Engine compartment fuse/relay box location

Circuit Breakers

RESETTING AND/OR REPLACEMENT

A Positive Temperature Coefficient (PTC) Circuit Breaker greatly increases resistance when current exceeds its limit. Eventually the circuit breaker will not allow any current to flow through it. The PTC circuit breaker will not reset itself until voltage is removed from it. After the voltage is removed the circuit breaker resets in about two seconds.

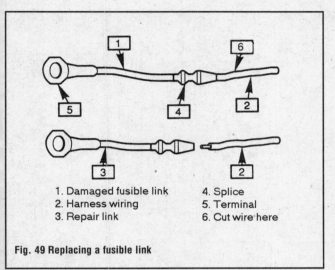

1. Damaged fusible link
2. Harness wiring
3. Repair link
4. Splice
5. Terminal
6. Cut wire here

Fig. 49 Replacing a fusible link

Flashers

REPLACEMENT

See Figure 50

The hazard/turn signal relay (flasher) is located on top of the under dash fuse box. To replace the flasher, remove the fuse box retaining bolts and locate the flasher at the right rear corner. Pull gently to remove the flasher. Replace the one of like kind.

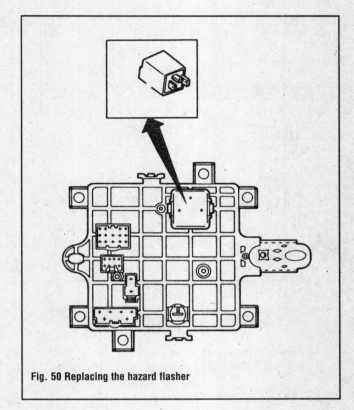

Fig. 50 Replacing the hazard flasher

WIRING DIAGRAMS

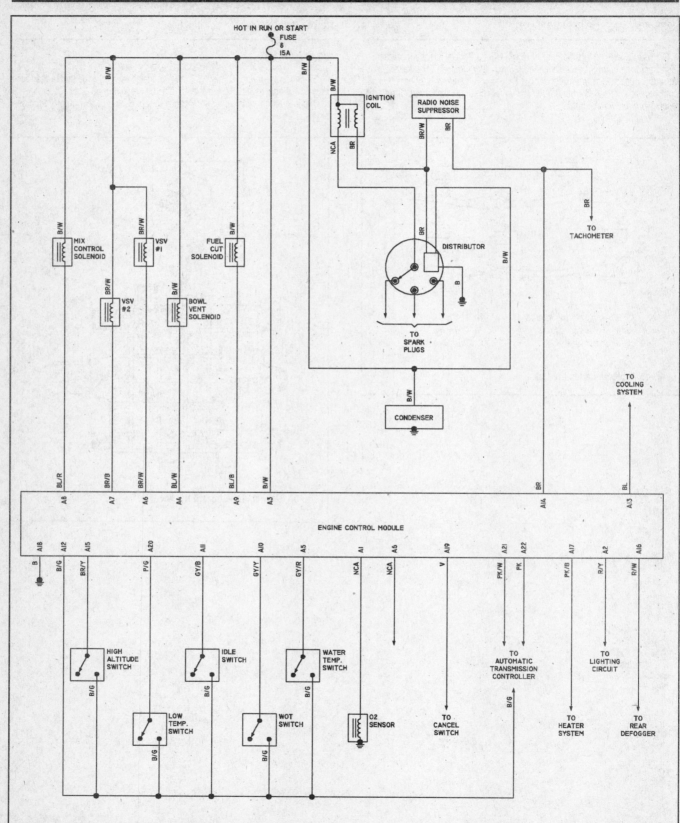

Fig. 51 1985 Chevrolet Sprint 1.0L engine wiring diagram

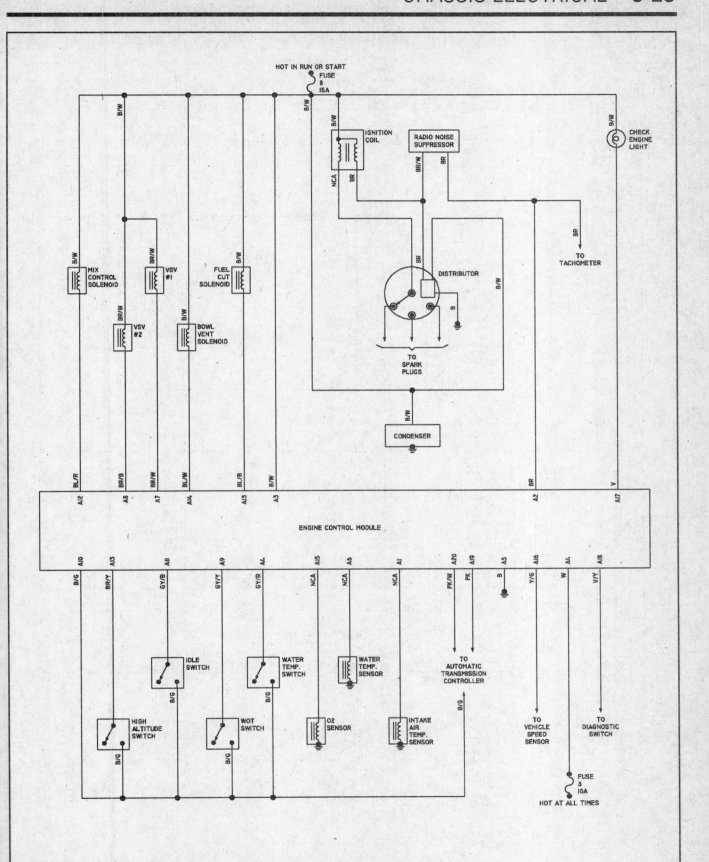

Fig. 52 1986 - 1988 Chevrolet Sprint 1.0L engine wiring diagram - carbureted models

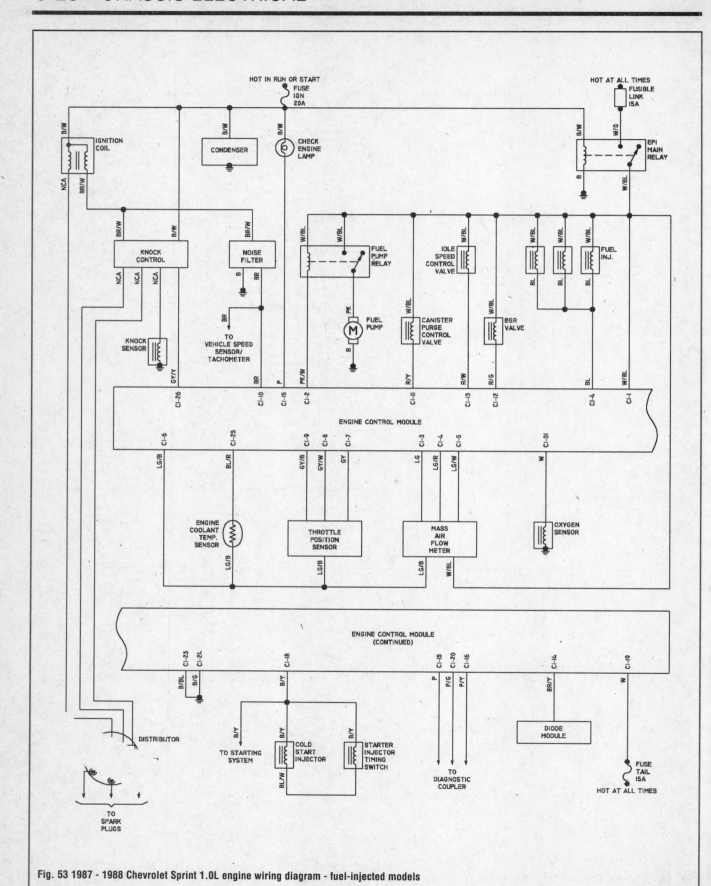

Fig. 53 1987 - 1988 Chevrolet Sprint 1.0L engine wiring diagram - fuel-injected models

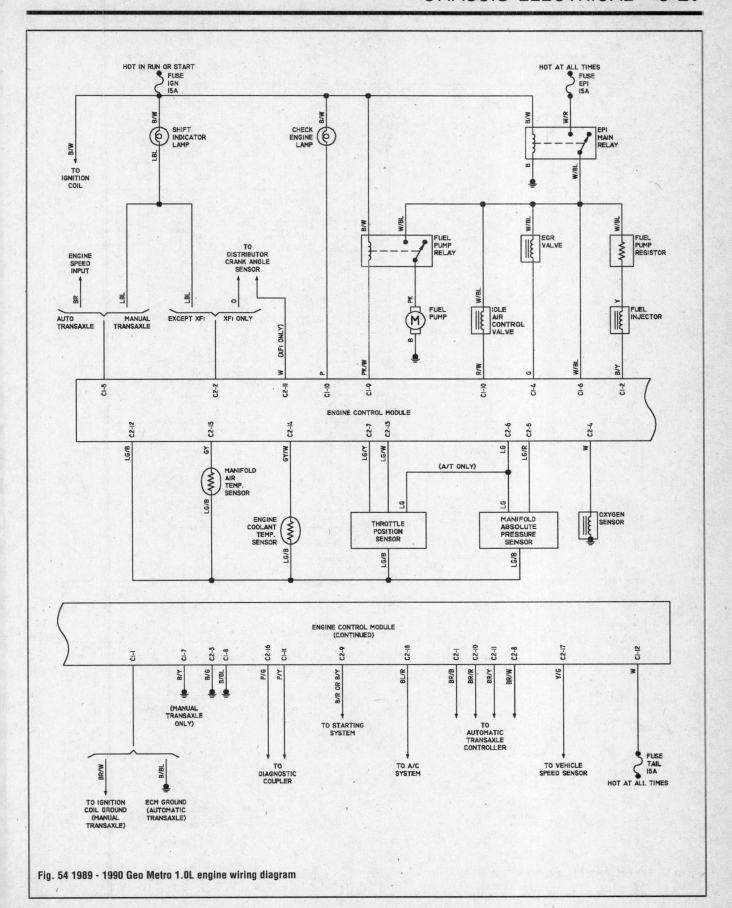

Fig. 54 1989 - 1990 Geo Metro 1.0L engine wiring diagram

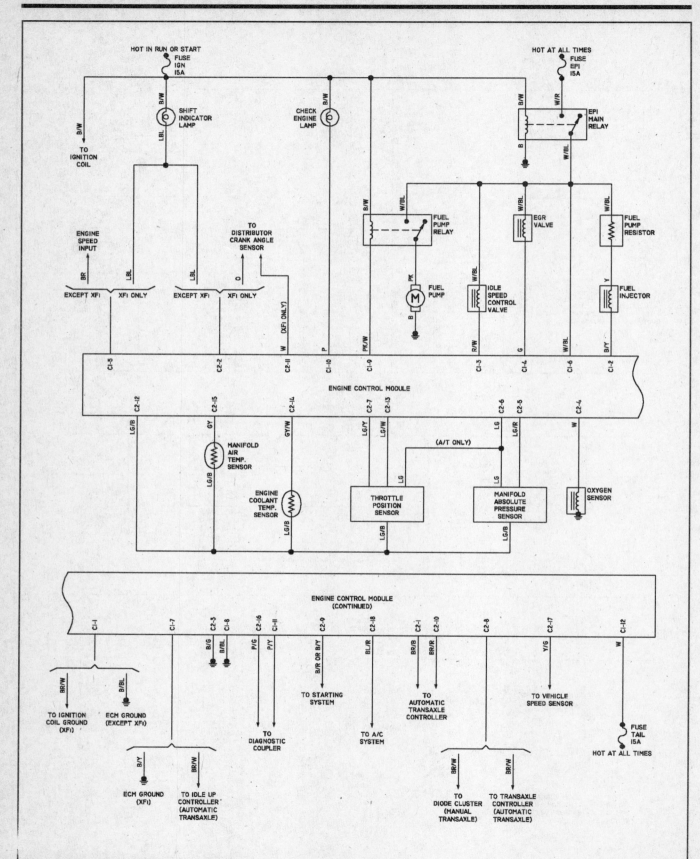

Fig. 55 1991 Geo Metro 1.0L engine wiring diagram

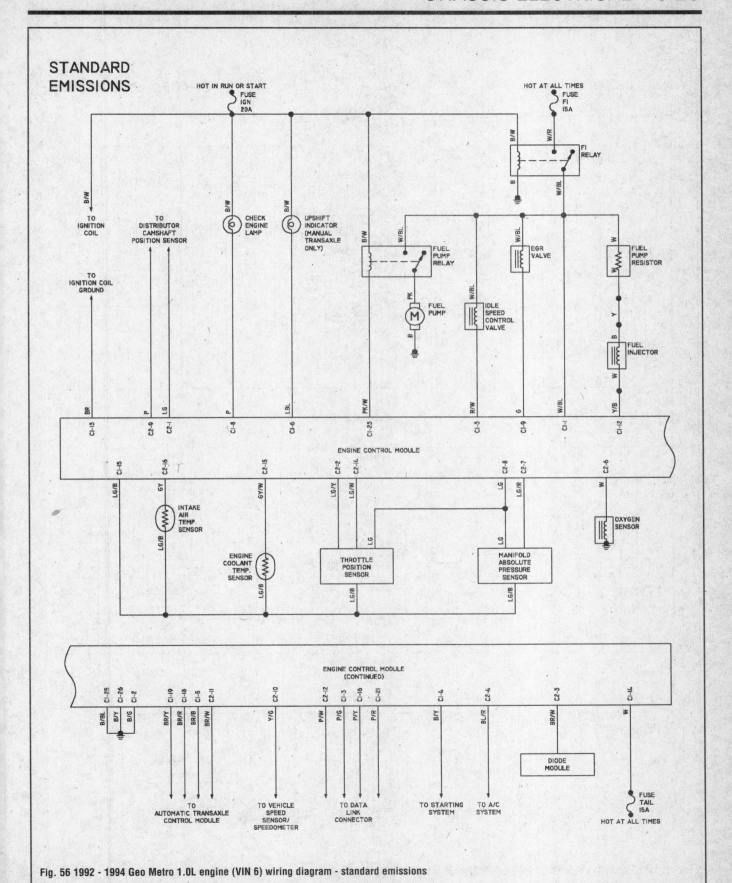

Fig. 56 1992 - 1994 Geo Metro 1.0L engine (VIN 6) wiring diagram - standard emissions

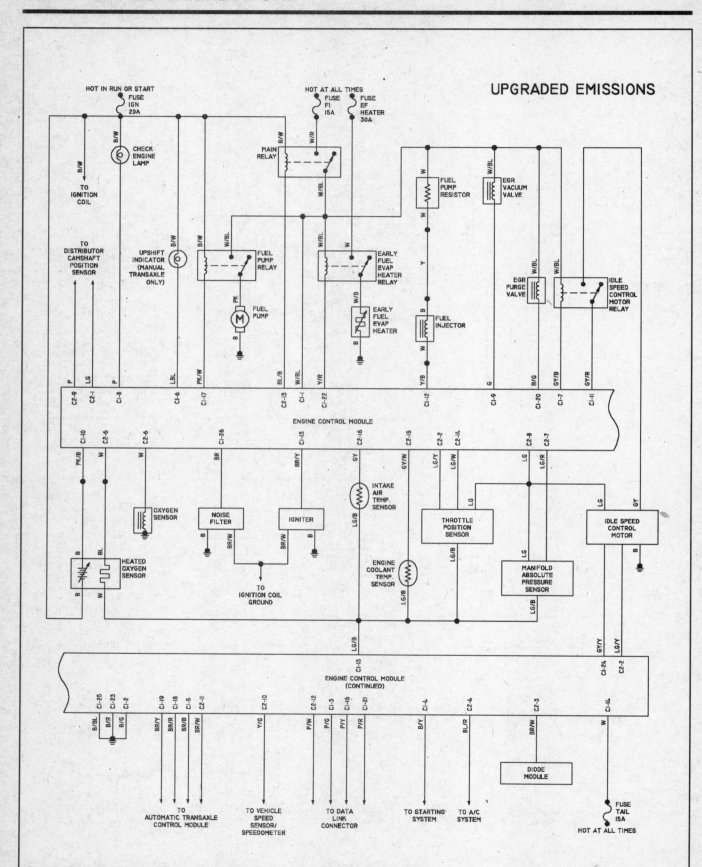

Fig. 57 1992 - 1994 Geo Metro 1.0L engine (VIN 6) wiring diagram - upgraded emissions

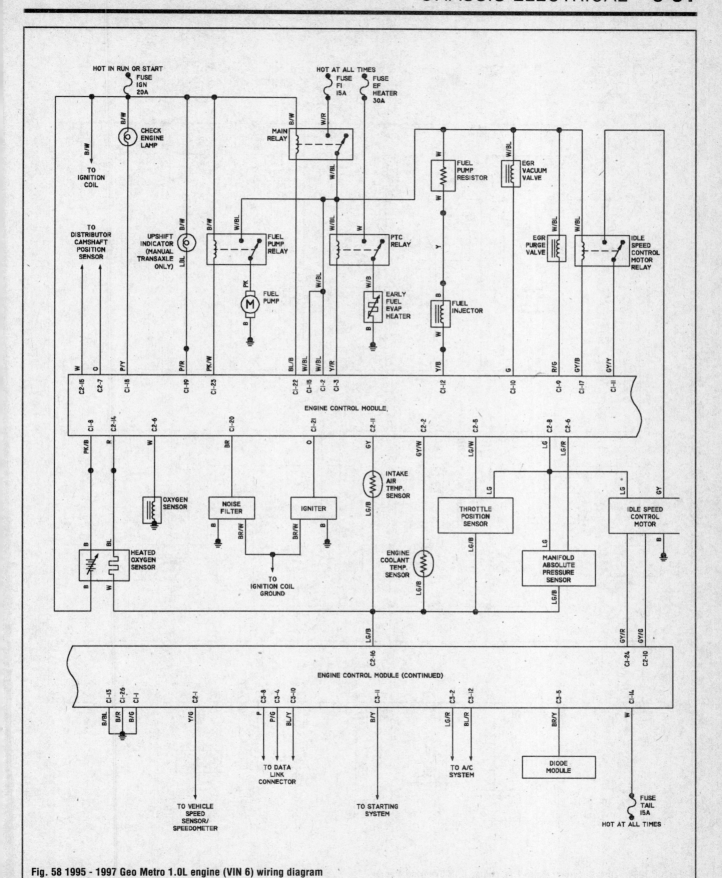

Fig. 58 1995 - 1997 Geo Metro 1.0L engine (VIN 6) wiring diagram

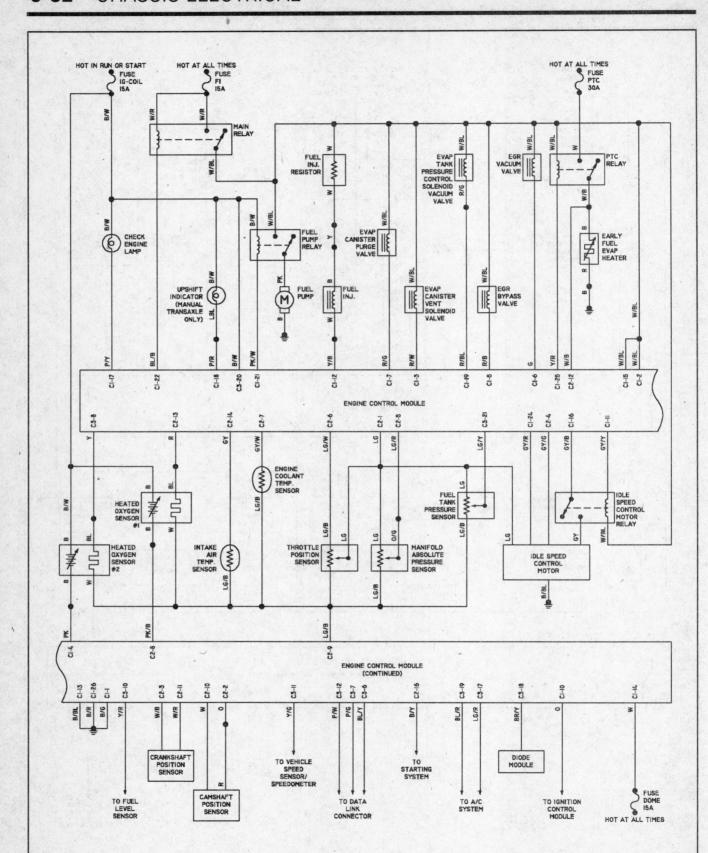

Fig. 59 1998 - 2000 Chevrolet Metro 1.0L engine (VIN 6) wiring diagram

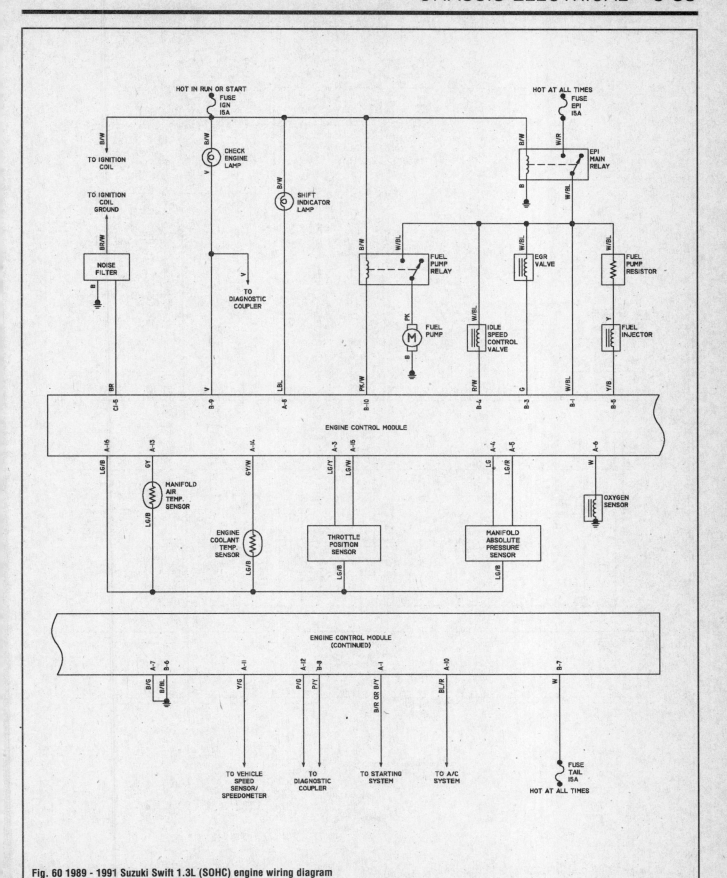

Fig. 60 1989 - 1991 Suzuki Swift 1.3L (SOHC) engine wiring diagram

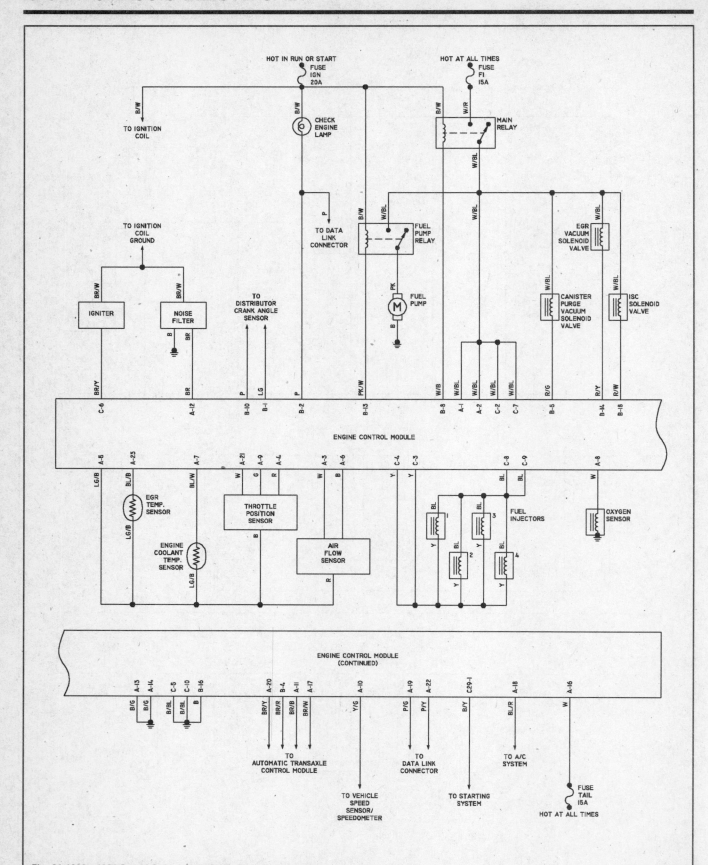

Fig. 61 1989 - 1991 Suzuki Swift 1.3L (DOHC) engine wiring diagram

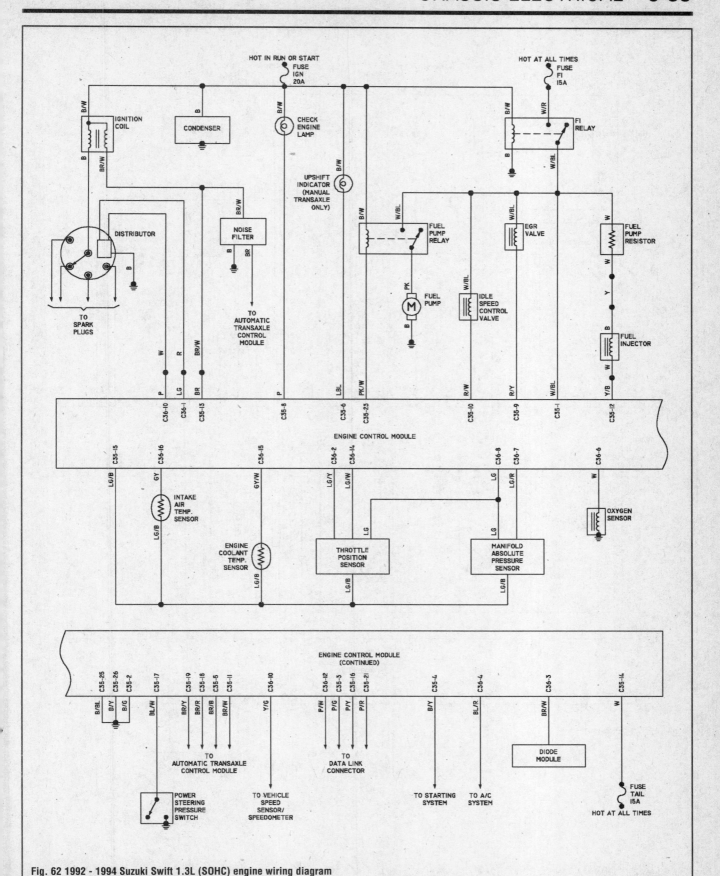

Fig. 62 1992 - 1994 Suzuki Swift 1.3L (SOHC) engine wiring diagram

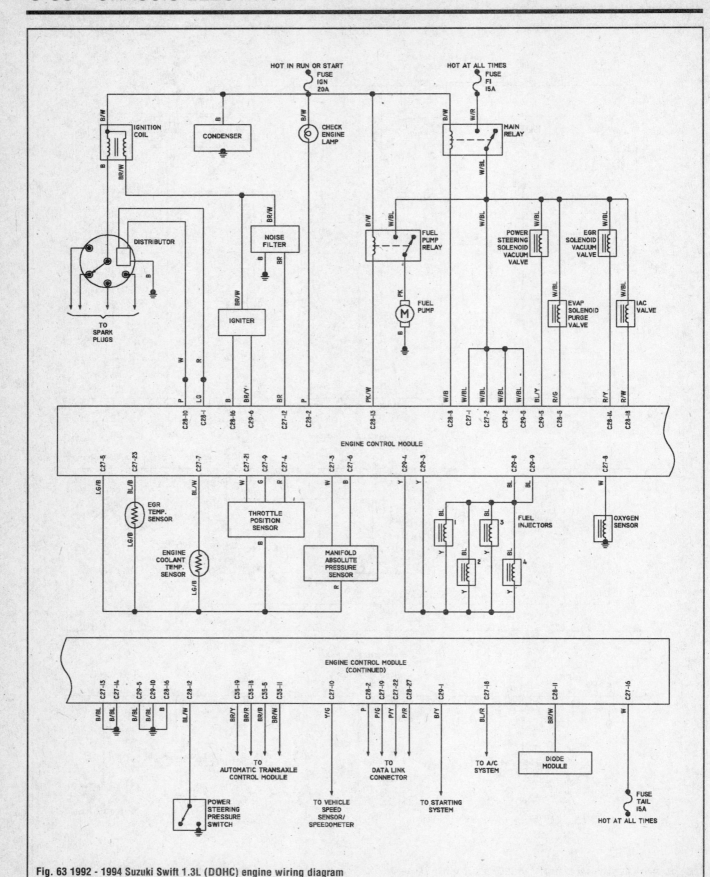

Fig. 63 1992 - 1994 Suzuki Swift 1.3L (DOHC) engine wiring diagram

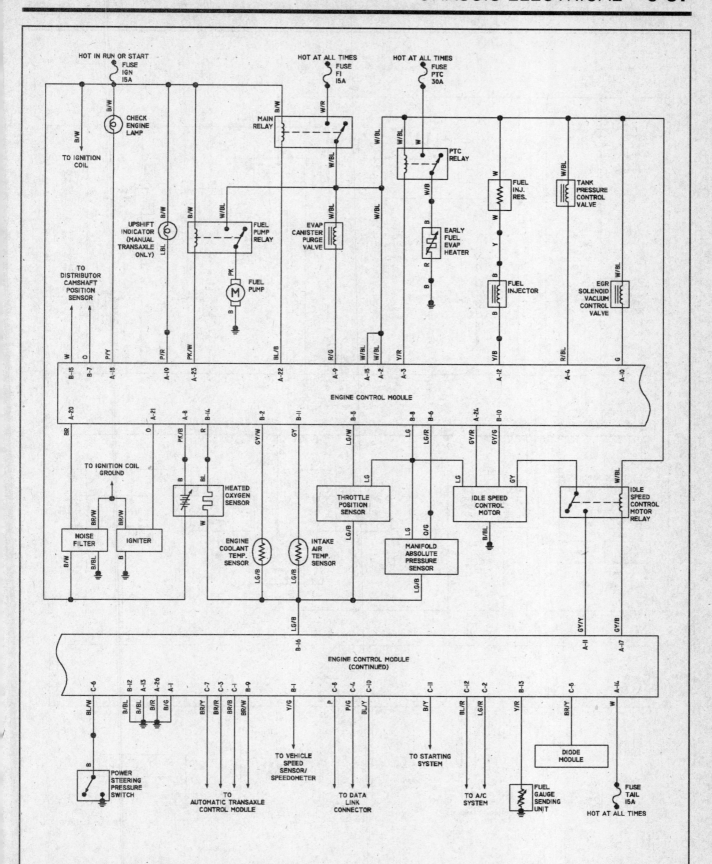

Fig. 64 1995 Geo Metro/Suzuki Swift 1.3L engine wiring diagram

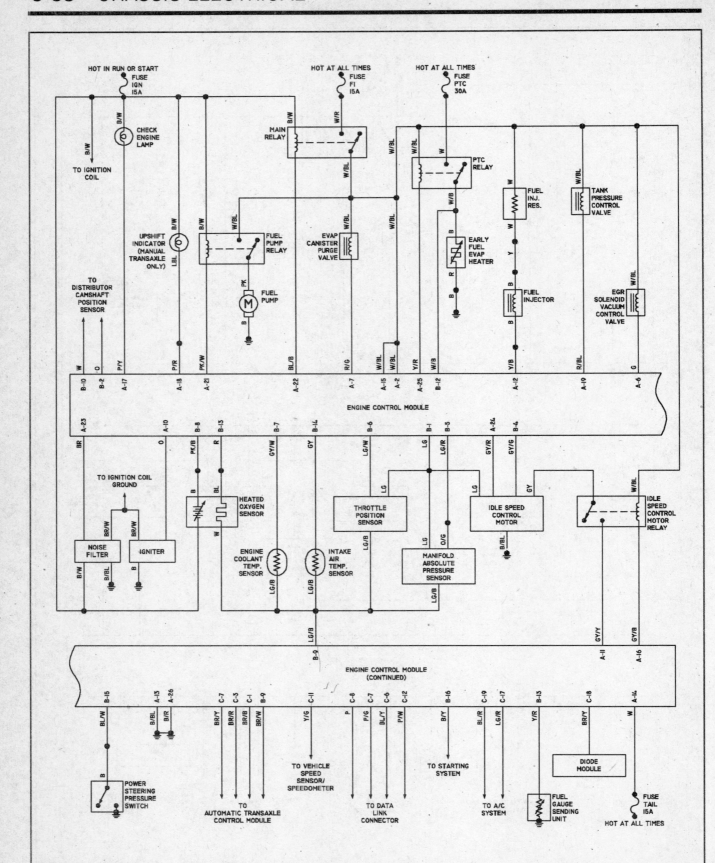

Fig. 65 1996 - 1997 Geo Metro/Suzuki Swift 1.3L engine wiring diagram

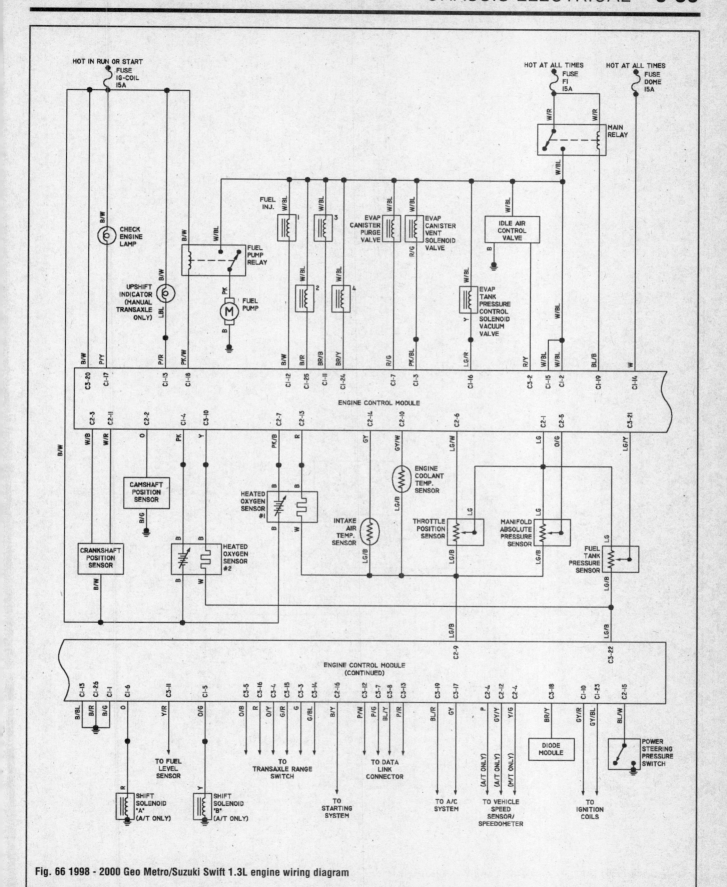

Fig. 66 1998 - 2000 Geo Metro/Suzuki Swift 1.3L engine wiring diagram

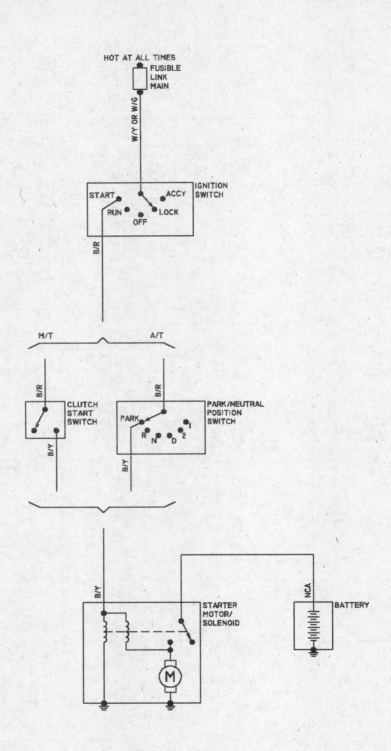

Fig. 67 1985 - 1988 Chevrolet Sprint starting system wiring diagram

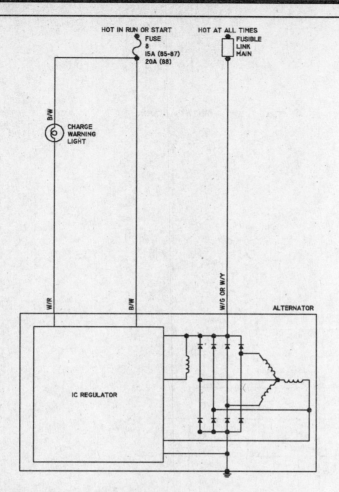

Fig. 68 1985 - 1988 Chevrolet Sprint charging system wiring diagram

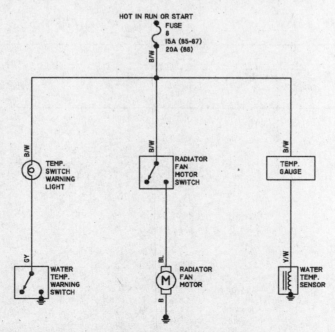

Fig. 69 1985 - 1988 Chevrolet Sprint engine cooling fan/temperature indicator wiring diagram

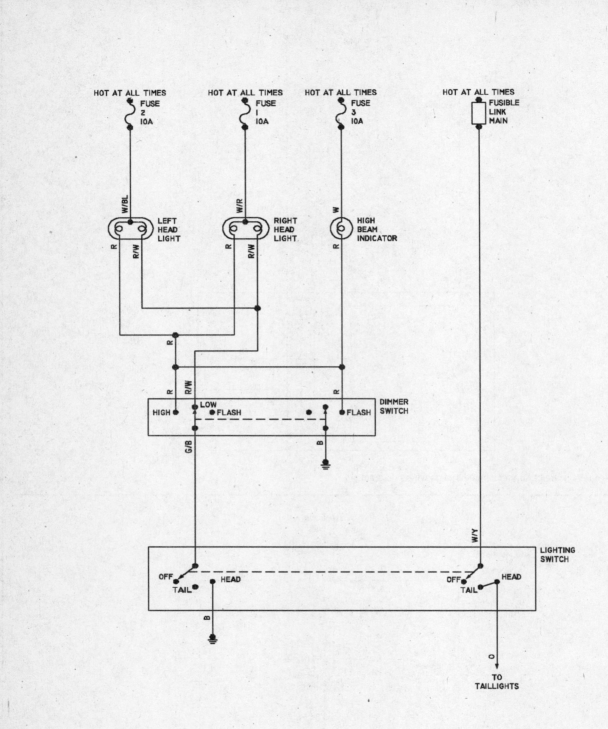

Fig. 70 1985 - 1988 Chevrolet Sprint headlight system wiring diagram

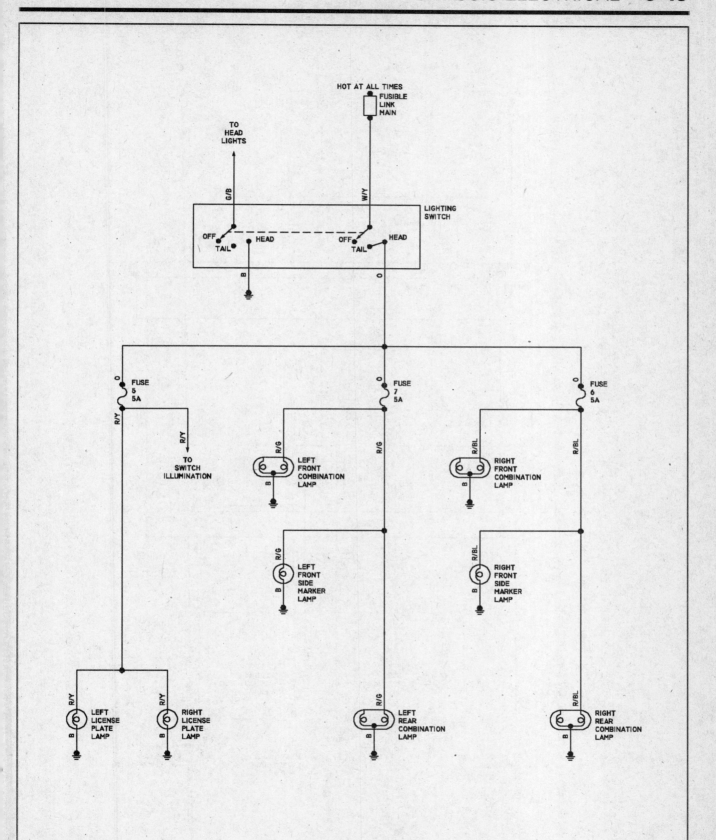

Fig. 71 1985 - 1988 Chevrolet Sprint exterior lighting system wiring diagram

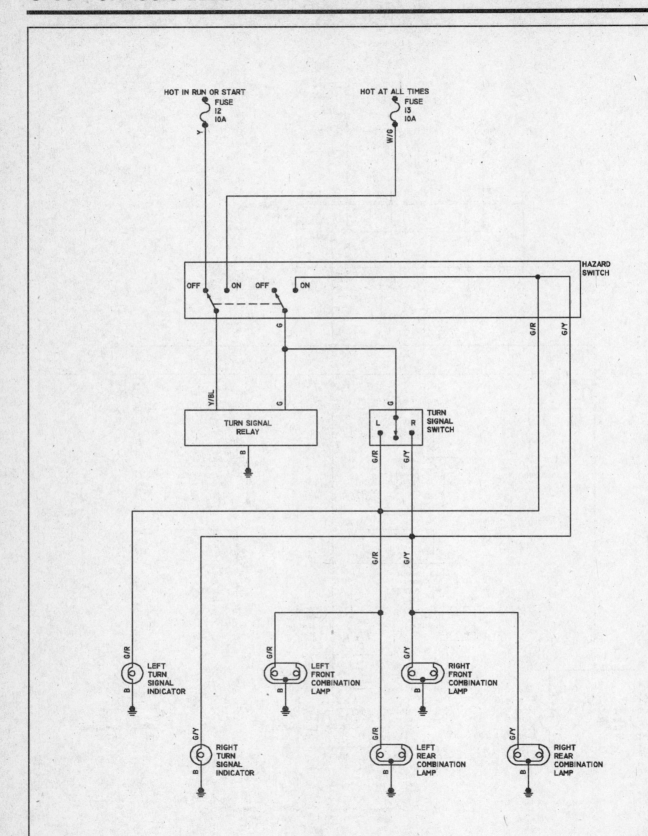

Fig. 72 1985 - 1988 Chevrolet Sprint turn signal/hazard flasher wiring diagram

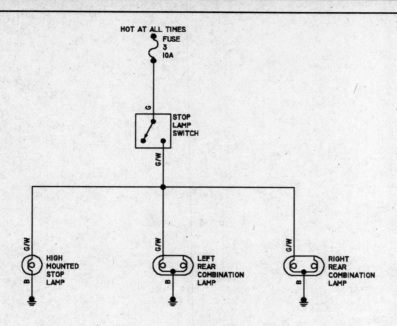

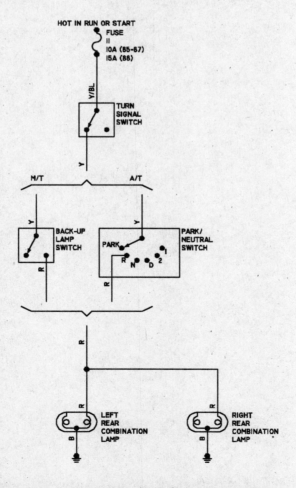

Fig. 73 1985 - 1988 Chevrolet Sprint brake light system (top) and back-up light system (bottom) wiring diagrams

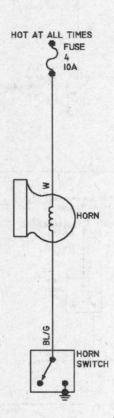

Fig. 74 1985 - 1988 Chevrolet Sprint horn wiring diagram

FRONT

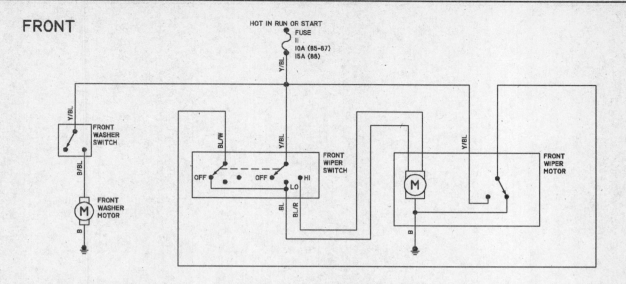

FRONT W/ INT.

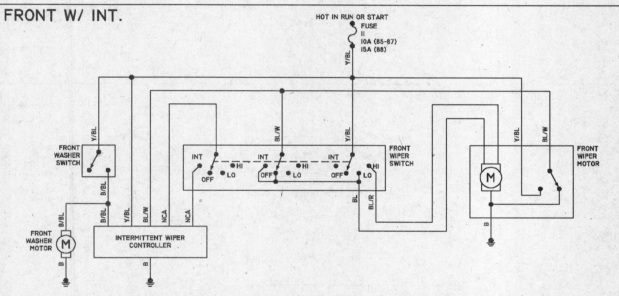

REAR

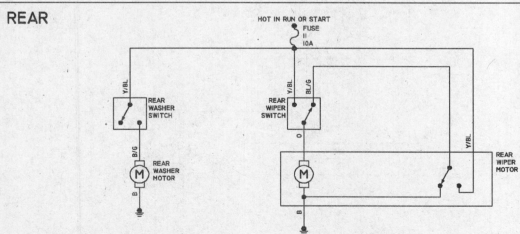

Fig. 75 1985 - 1988 Chevrolet Sprint wiper/washer wiring diagram

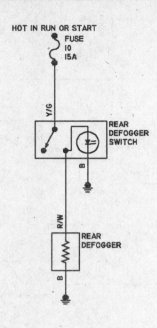

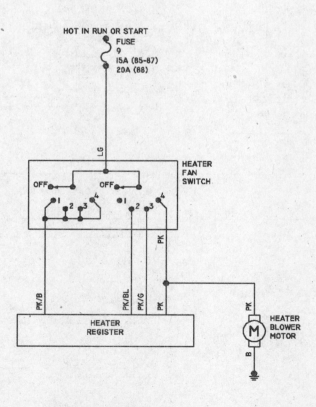

Fig. 76 1985 - 1988 Chevrolet Sprint rear window defogger (top) and heater (bottom) wiring diagrams

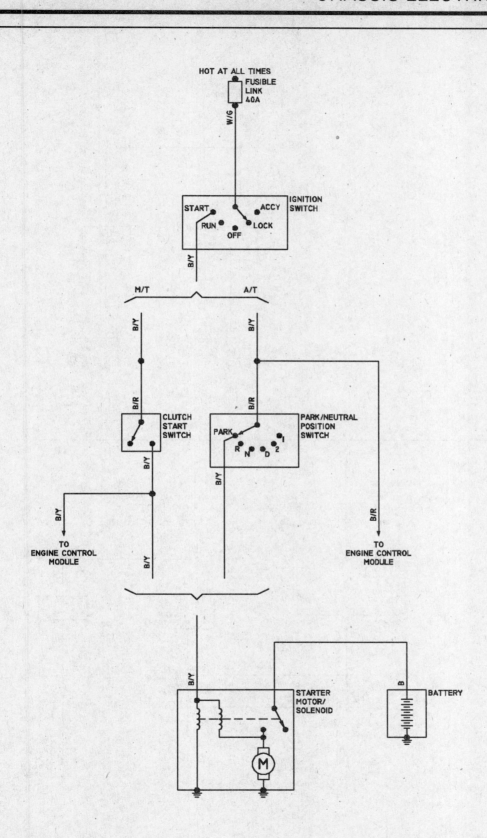

Fig. 77 1989 - 1994 Geo Metro/Suzuki Swift starting system wiring diagram

1989-90

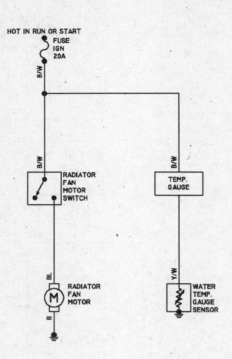

1991-94

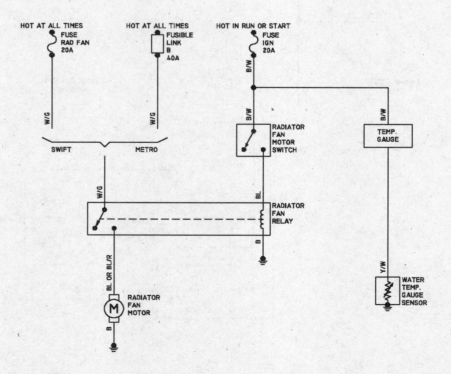

Fig. 78 1989 - 1994 Geo Metro/Suzuki Swift engine cooling fan/temperature indicator wiring diagram

1989-1991

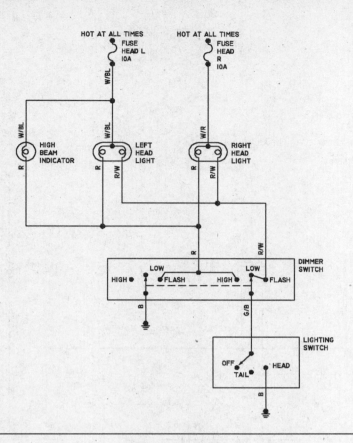

1992-94

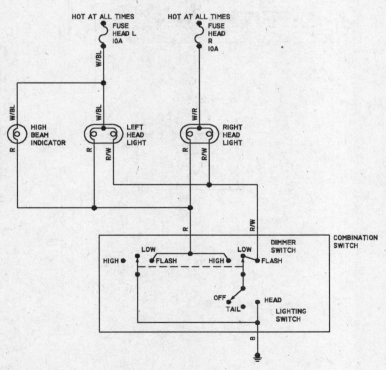

Fig. 79 1989 - 1994 Geo Metro/Suzuki Swift headlight system (without Daytime Running Lamps) wiring diagram

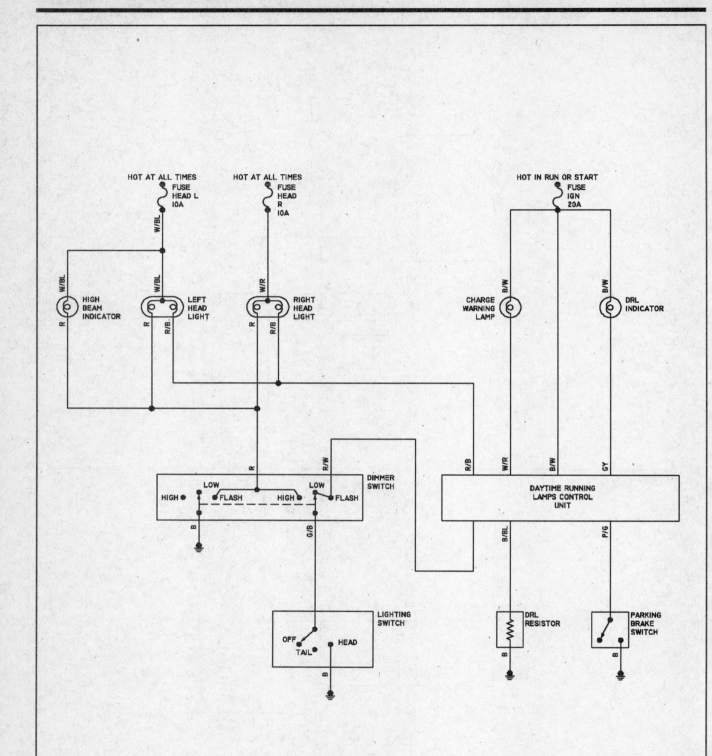

Fig. 80 1991 - 1994 Geo Metro/Suzuki Swift headlight system (with Daytime Running Lamps) wiring diagram

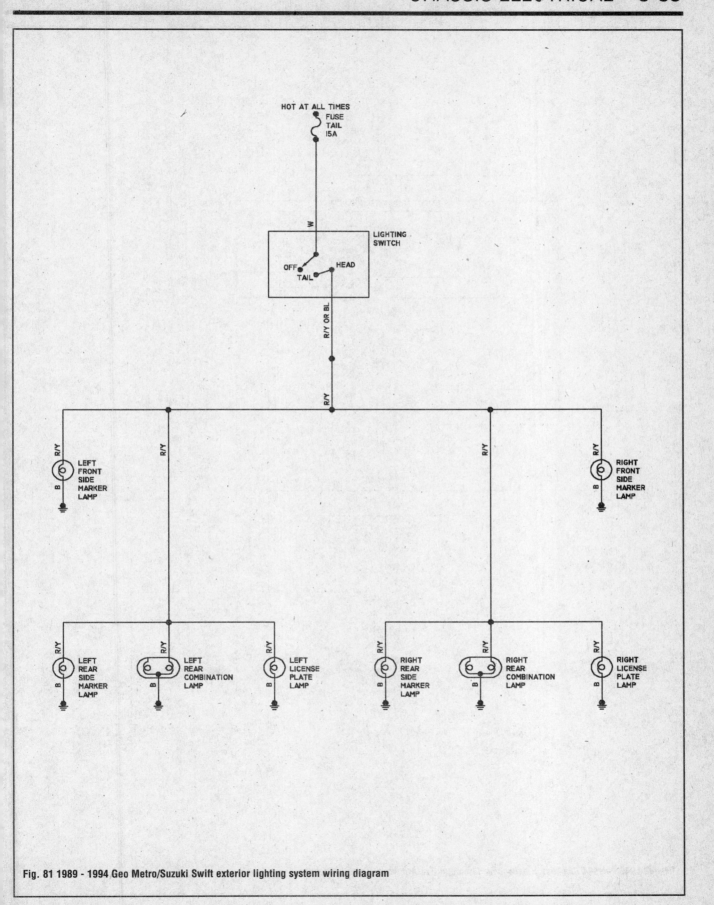

Fig. 81 1989 - 1994 Geo Metro/Suzuki Swift exterior lighting system wiring diagram

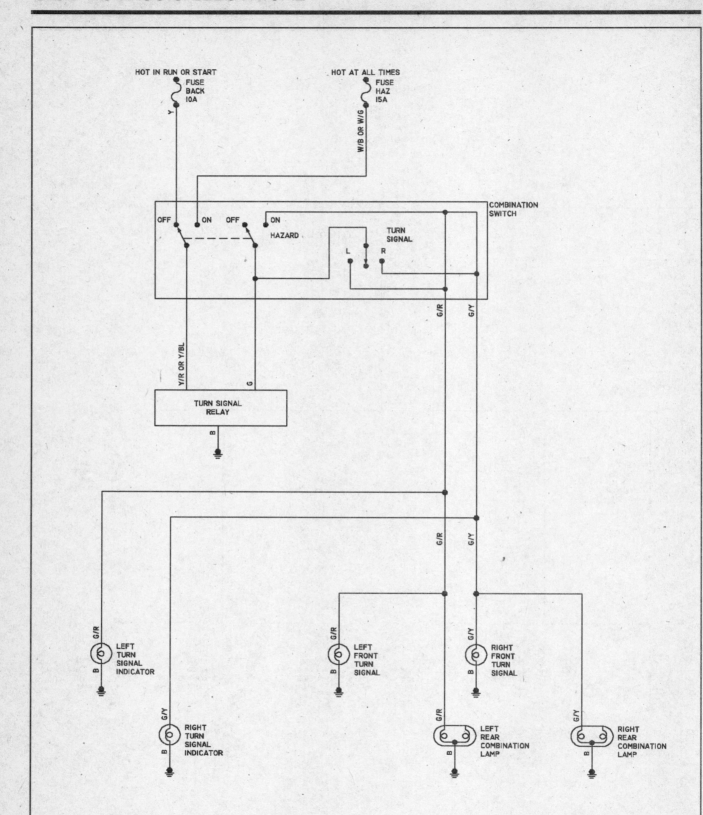

Fig. 82 1989 - 1994 Geo Metro/Suzuki Swift turn signal/hazard flasher wiring diagram

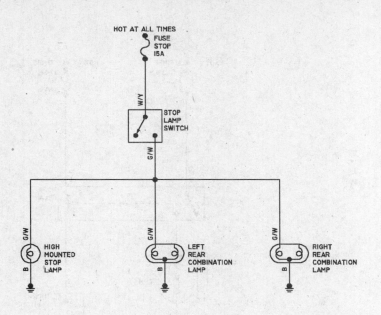

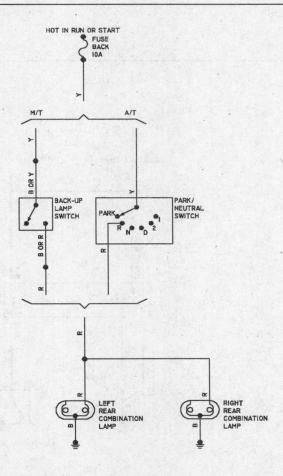

Fig. 83 1989 - 1994 Geo Metro/Suzuki Swift brake light system (top) and back-up light system (bottom) wiring diagrams

1989-91

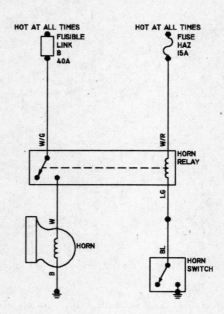

1992-94

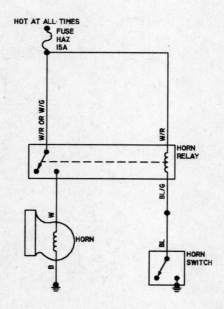

Fig. 84 1989 - 1994 Geo Metro/Suzuki Swift horn wiring diagram

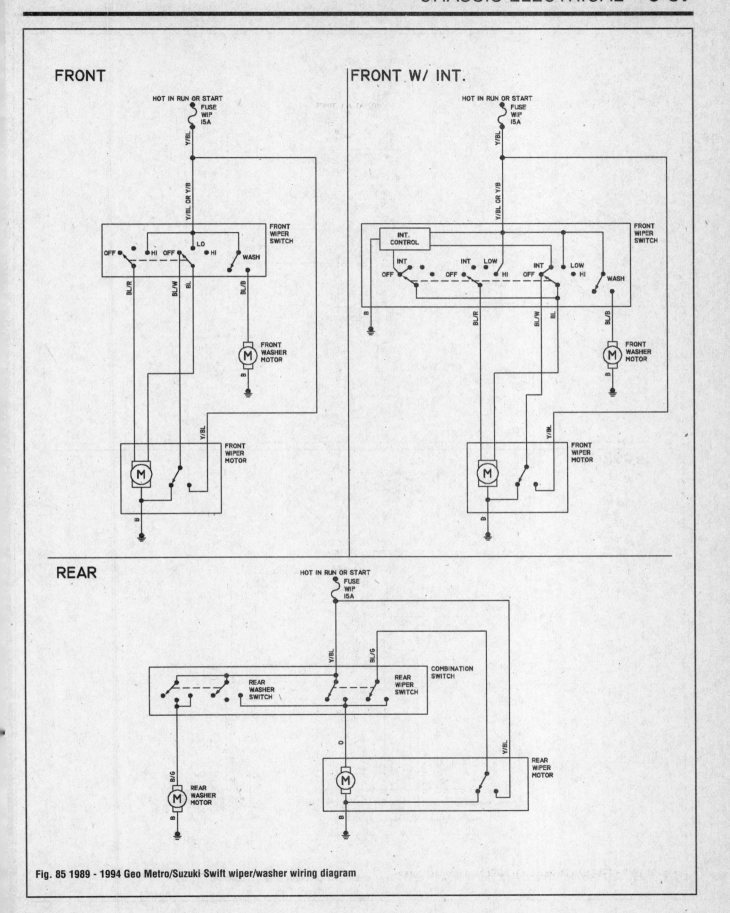

Fig. 85 1989 - 1994 Geo Metro/Suzuki Swift wiper/washer wiring diagram

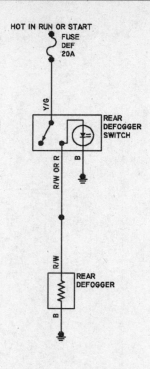

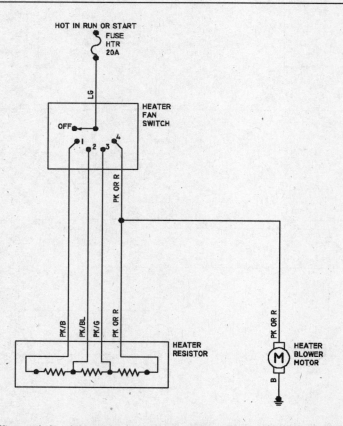

Fig. 86 1989 - 1994 Geo Metro/Suzuki Swift rear window defogger (top) and heater (bottom) wiring diagrams

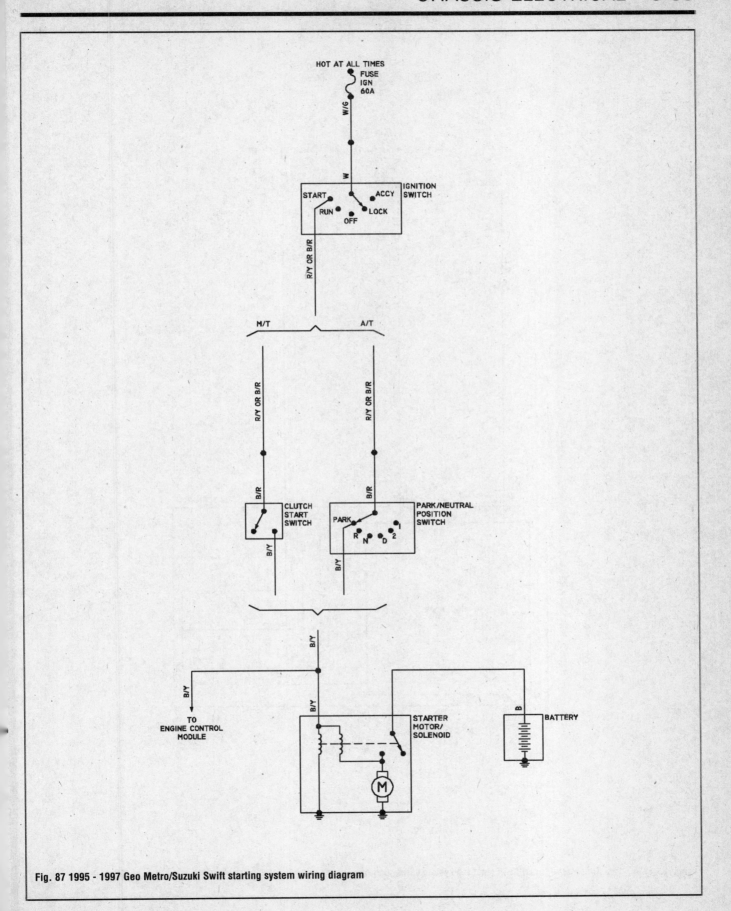

Fig. 87 1995 - 1997 Geo Metro/Suzuki Swift starting system wiring diagram

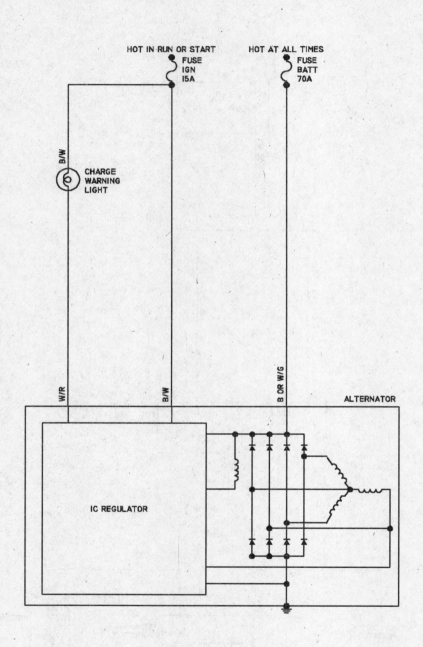

Fig. 88 1995 - 1997 Geo Metro/Suzuki Swift charging system wiring diagram

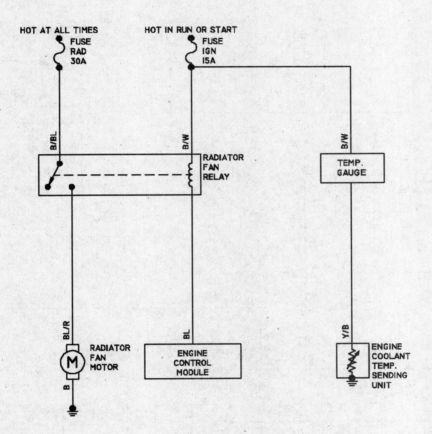

Fig. 89 1995 - 1997 Geo Metro/Suzuki Swift engine cooling fan/temperature indicator wiring diagram

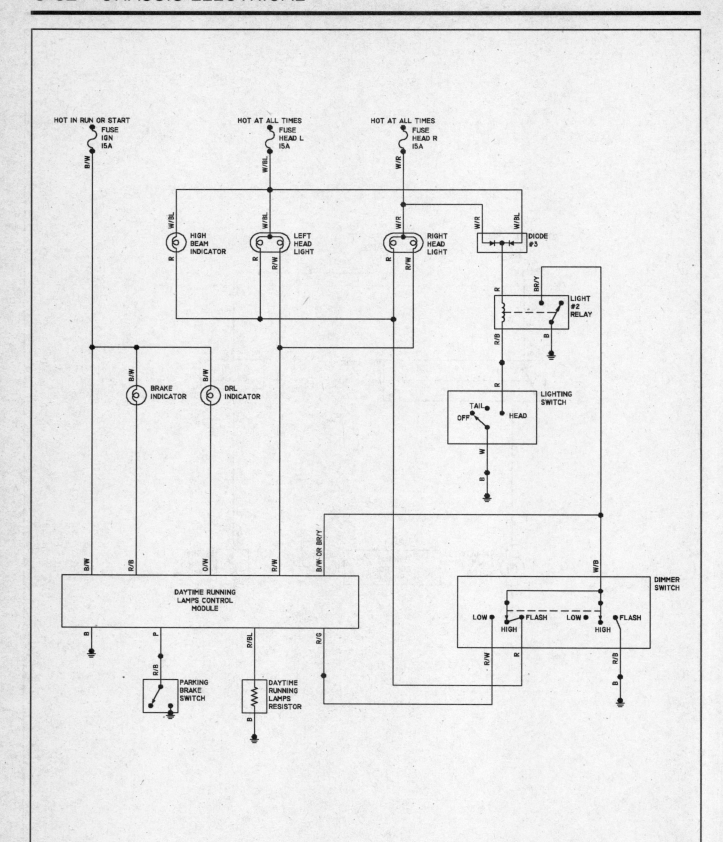

Fig. 90 1995 - 1997 Geo Metro/Suzuki Swift headlight system wiring diagram

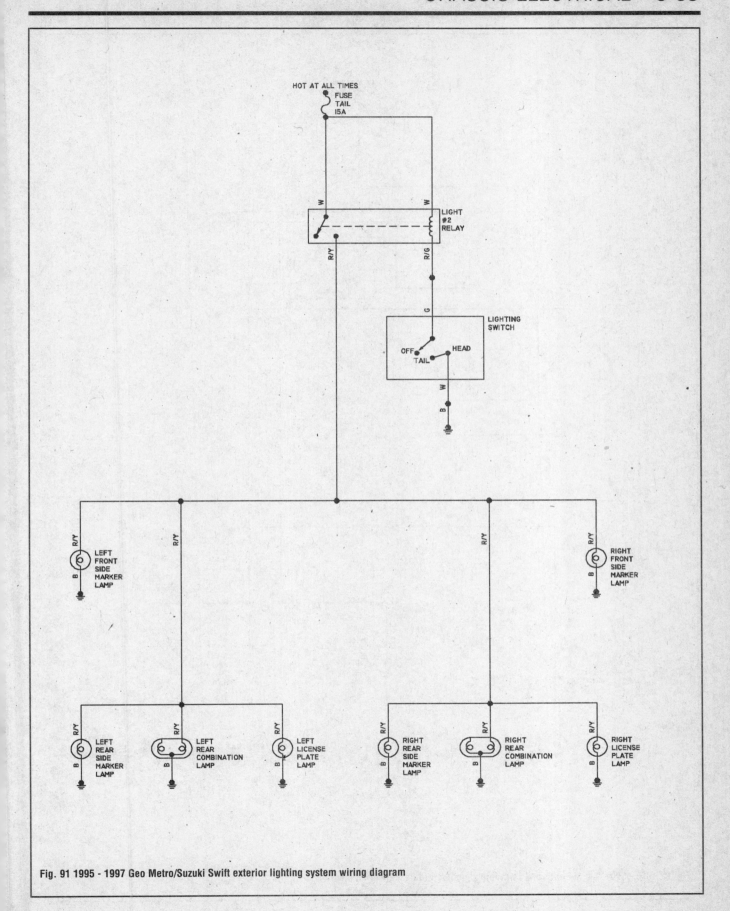

Fig. 91 1995 - 1997 Geo Metro/Suzuki Swift exterior lighting system wiring diagram

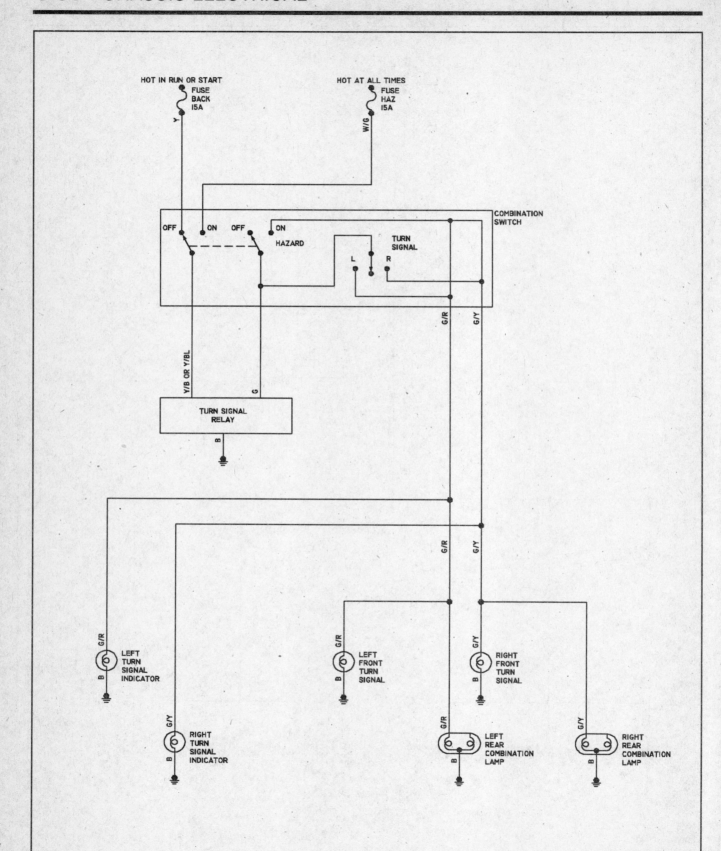

Fig. 92 1995 - 1997 Geo Metro/Suzuki Swift turn signal/hazard flasher wiring diagram

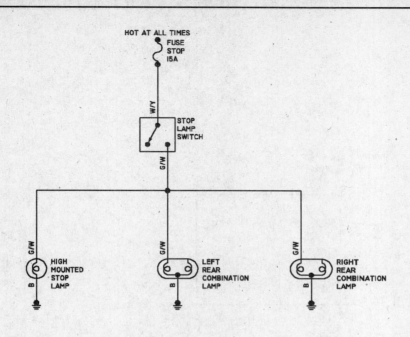

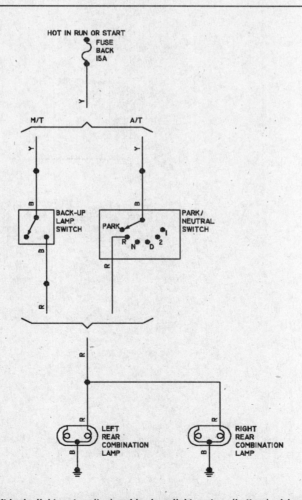

Fig. 93 1995 - 1997 Geo Metro/Suzuki Swift brake light system (top) and back-up light system (bottom) wiring diagrams

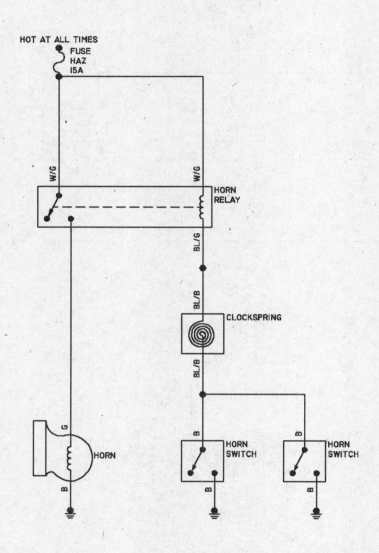

Fig. 94 1995 - 1997 Geo Metro/Suzuki Swift horn wiring diagram

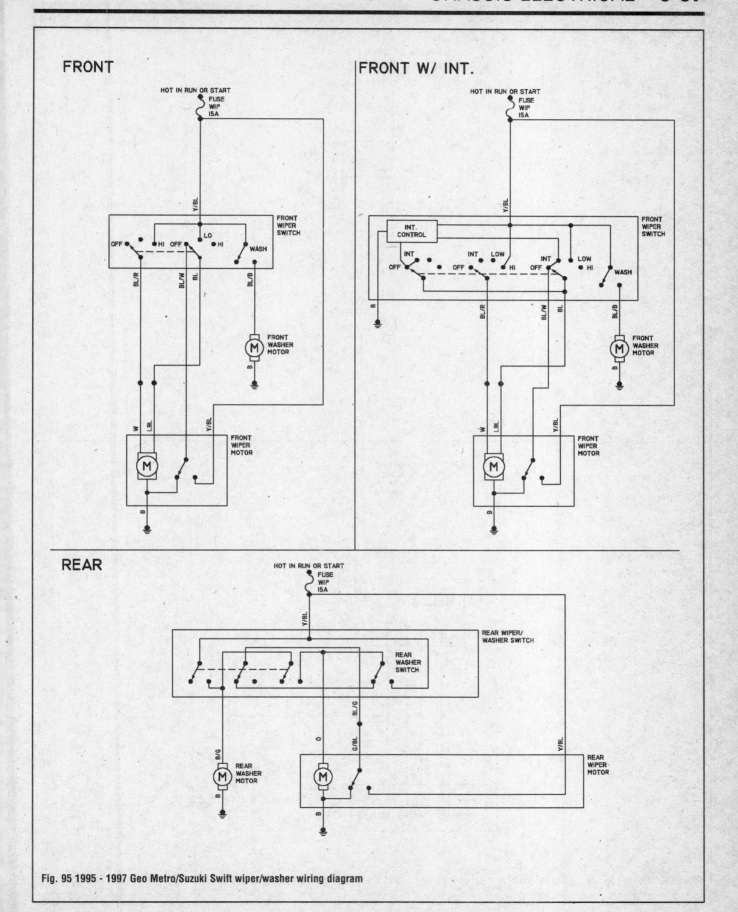

Fig. 95 1995 - 1997 Geo Metro/Suzuki Swift wiper/washer wiring diagram

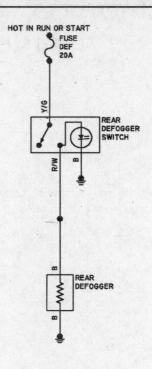

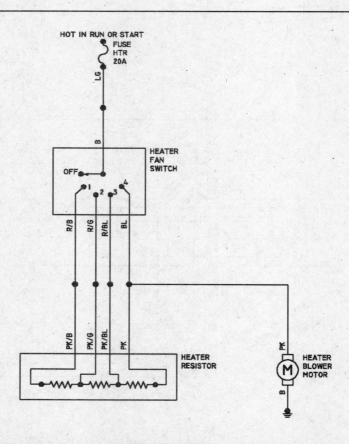

Fig. 96 1995 - 1997 Geo Metro/Suzuki Swift rear window defogger (top) and heater (bottom) wiring diagrams

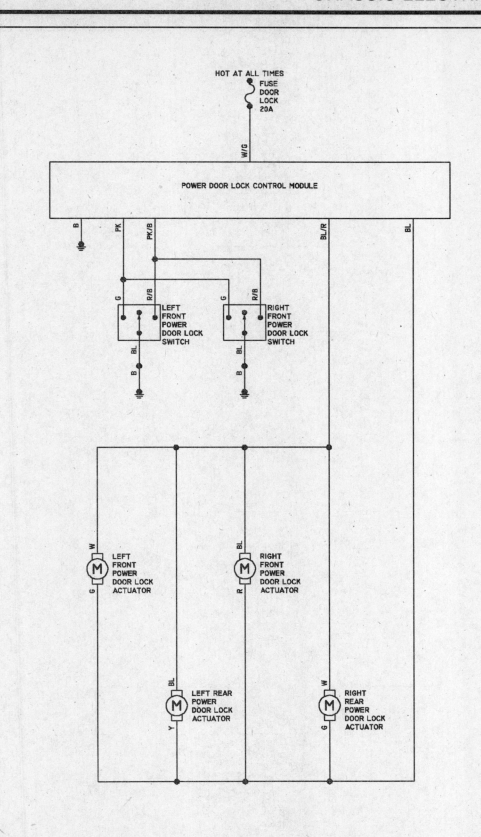

Fig. 97 1995 - 1997 Geo Metro/Suzuki Swift power door lock system wiring diagram

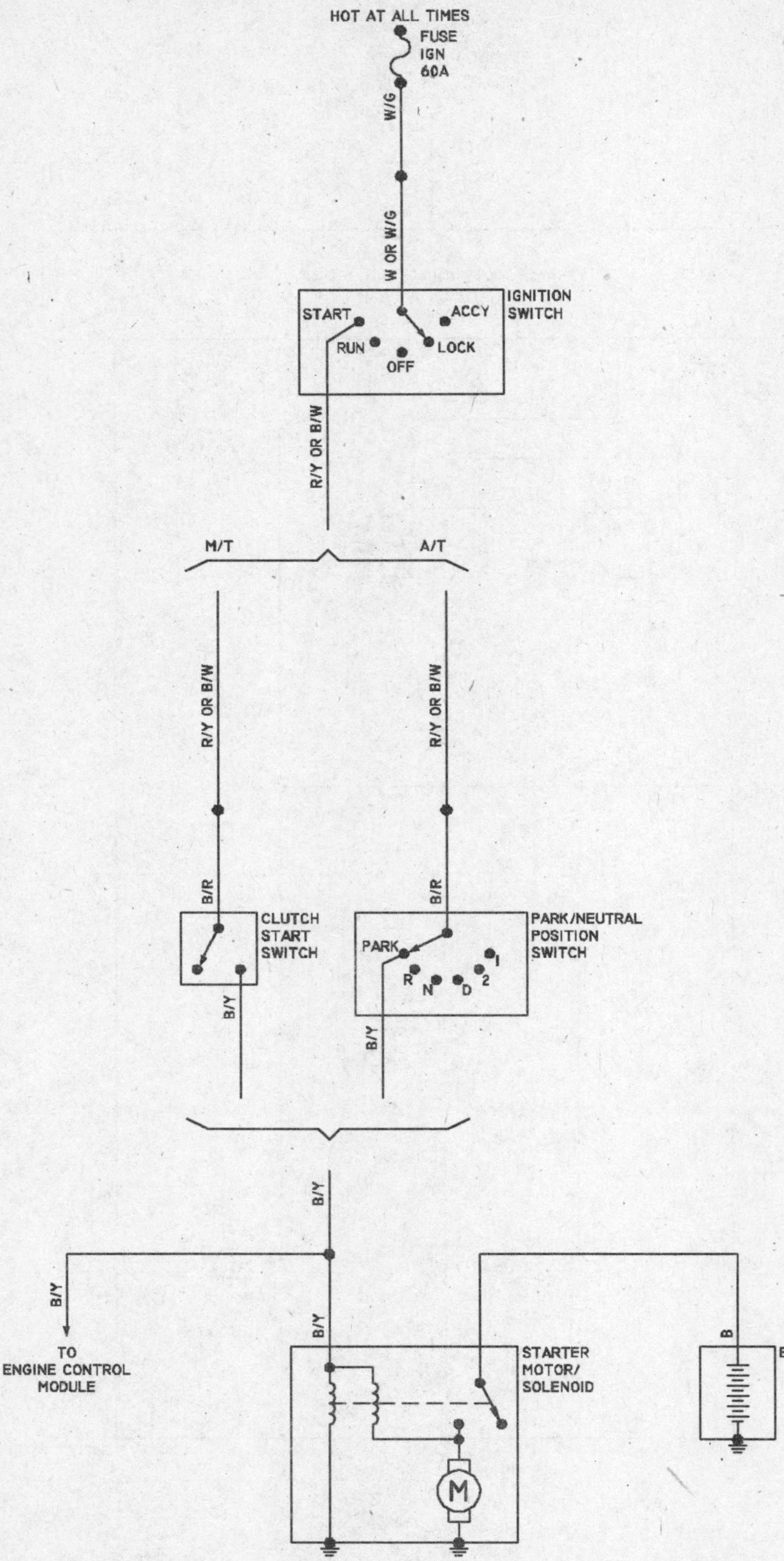

HOT AT ALL TIMES

FUSE
IGN
60A

W/G

W OR W/G

IGNITION
SWITCH

START

RUN   ACCY

OFF   LOCK

R/Y OR B/W

M/T   A/T

R/Y OR B/W   R/Y OR B/W

B/R   B/R

CLUTCH
START
SWITCH

PARK

PARK/NEUTRAL
POSITION
SWITCH

R   N   D   2   1

B/Y   B/Y

B/Y

B/Y

B/Y

TO
ENGINE CONTROL
MODULE

STARTER
MOTOR/
SOLENOID

B   BATTERY

M

Fig. 98 1998 - 2000 Chevrolet Metro/Suzuki Swift starting system wiring diagram

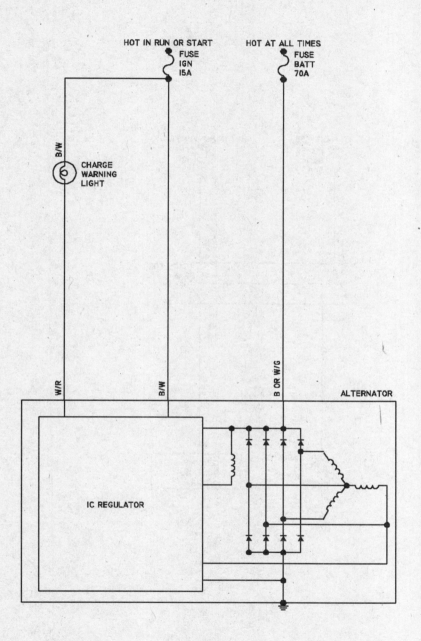

Fig. 99 1998 - 2000 Chevrolet Metro/Suzuki Swift charging system wiring diagram

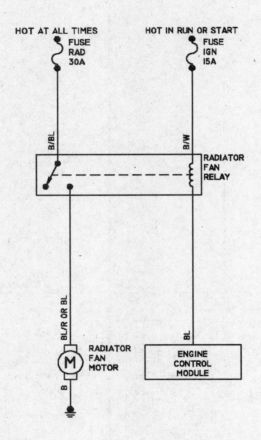

Fig. 100 1998 - 2000 Chevrolet Metro/Suzuki Swift engine cooling fan wiring diagram

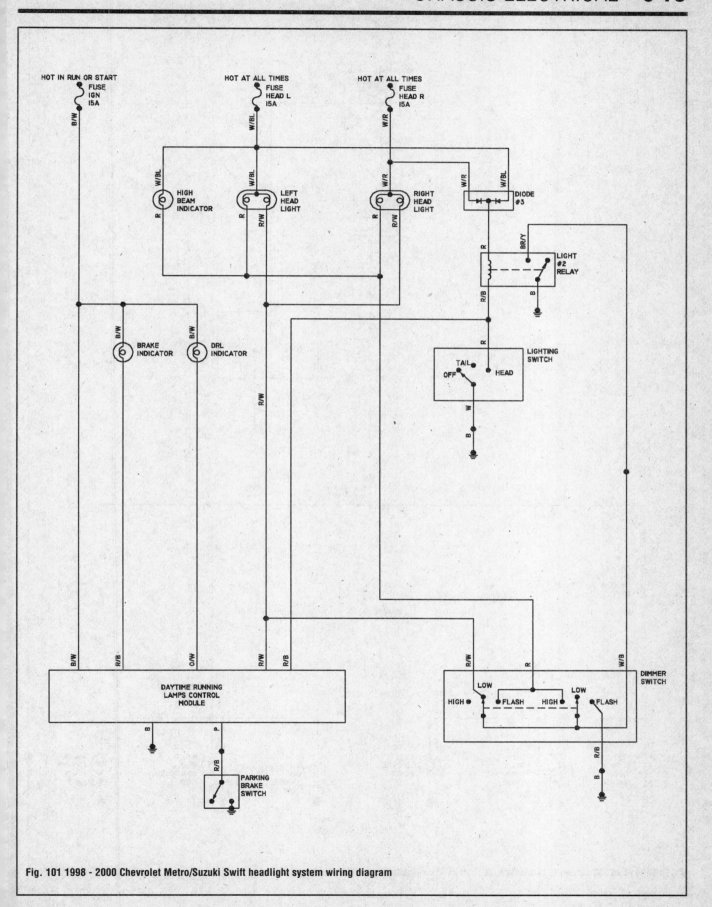

Fig. 101 1998 - 2000 Chevrolet Metro/Suzuki Swift headlight system wiring diagram

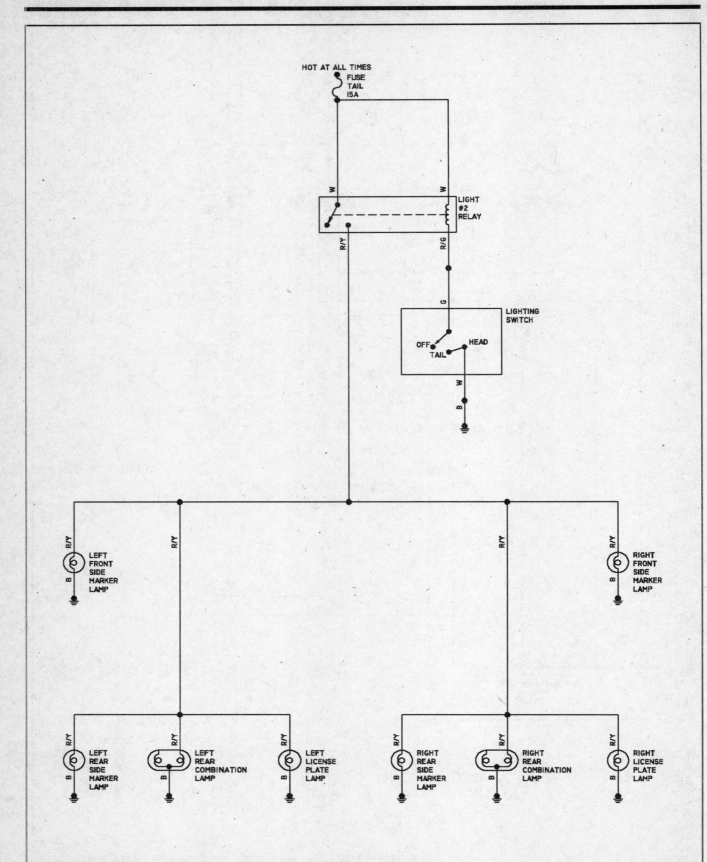

Fig. 102 1998 - 2000 Chevrolet Metro/Suzuki Swift exterior lighting system wiring diagram

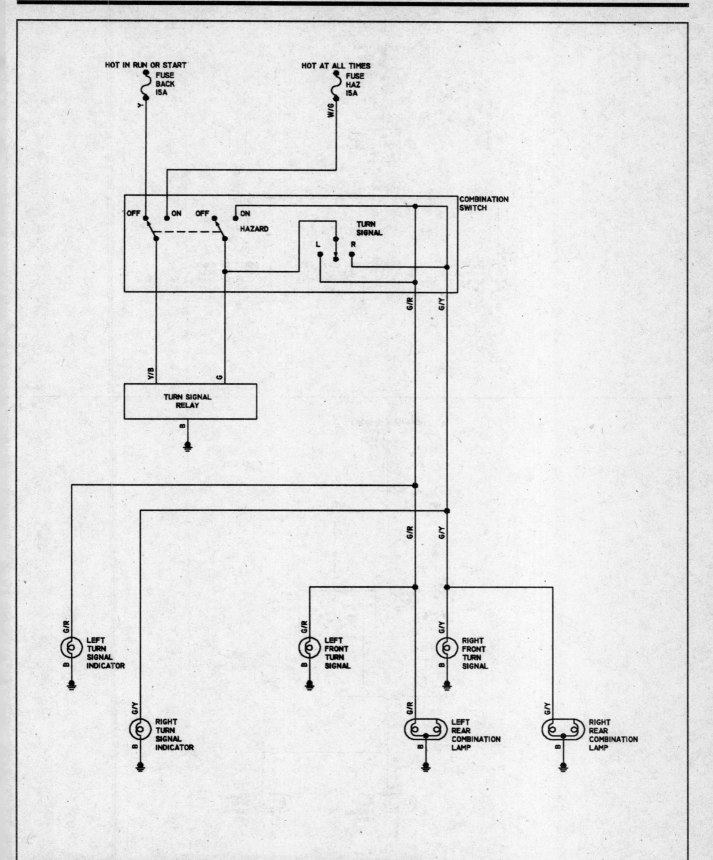

Fig. 103 1998 - 2000 Chevrolet Metro/Suzuki Swift turn signal/hazard flasher wiring diagram

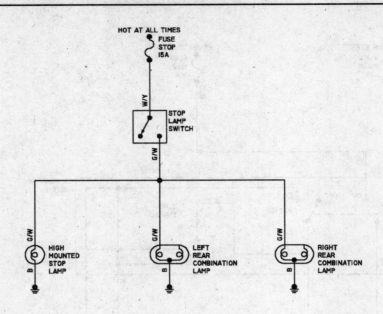

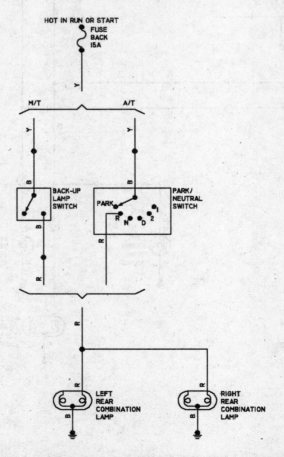

Fig. 104 1998 - 2000 Chevrolet Metro/Suzuki Swift brake light system (top) and back-up light system (bottom) wiring diagrams

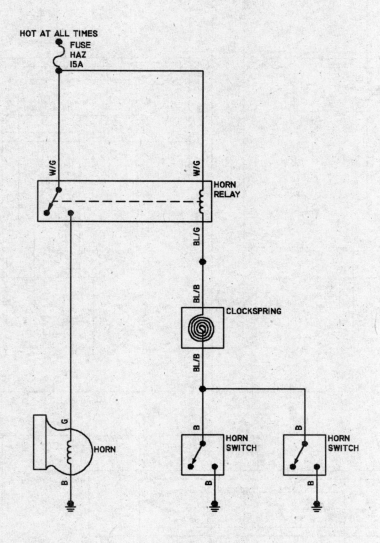

Fig. 105 1998 - 2000 Chevrolet Metro/Suzuki Swift horn wiring diagram

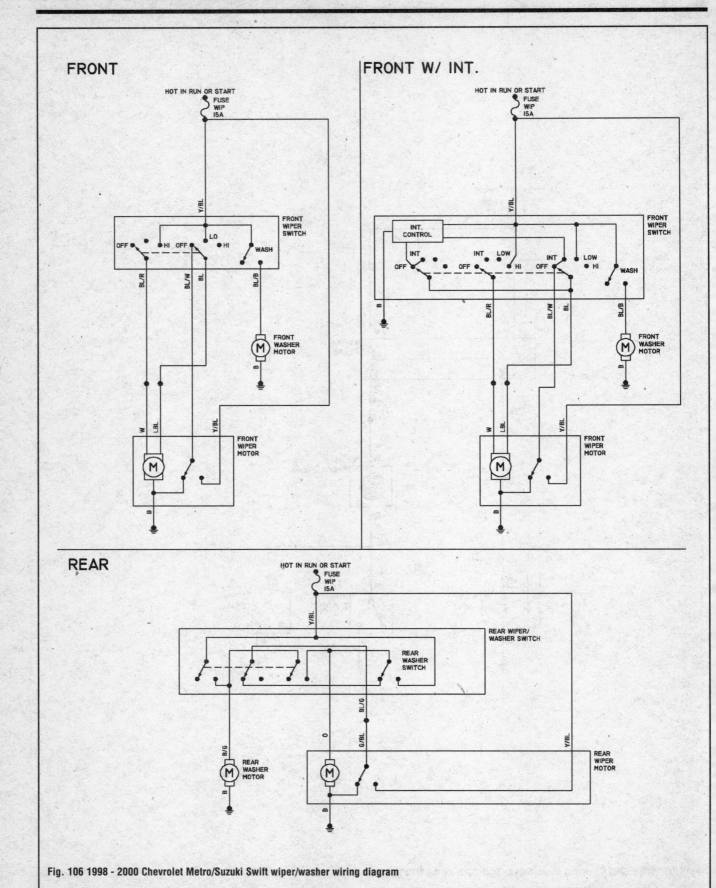

Fig. 106 1998 - 2000 Chevrolet Metro/Suzuki Swift wiper/washer wiring diagram

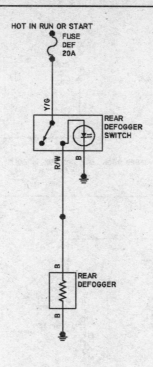

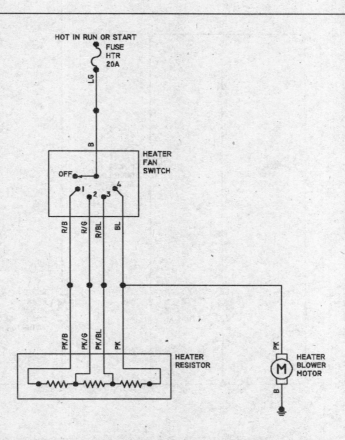

Fig. 107 1998 - 2000 Chevrolet Metro/Suzuki Swift rear window defogger (top) and heater (bottom) wiring diagrams

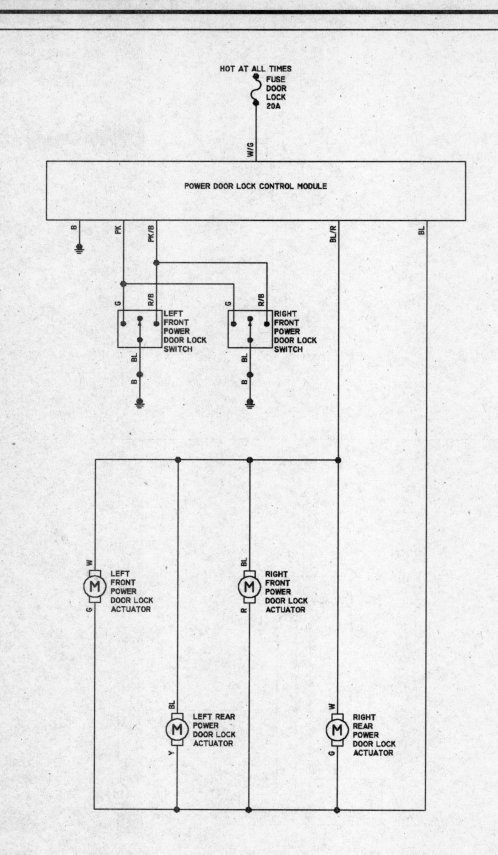

Fig. 108 1998 - 2000 Chevrolet Metro/Suzuki Swift power door lock system wiring diagram

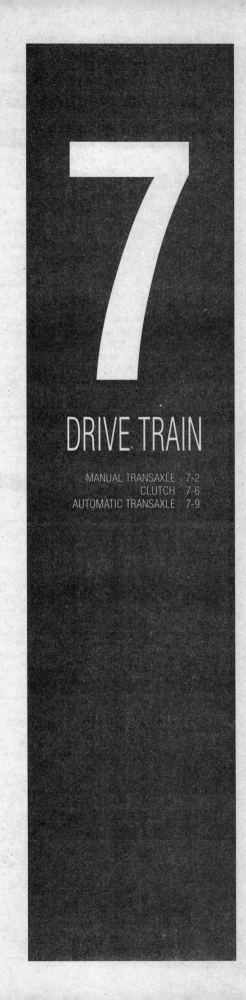

7

DRIVE TRAIN

MANUAL TRANSAXLE

Understanding the Manual Transaxle

Because of the way an internal combustion engine breathes, it can produce torque, or twisting force, only within a narrow speed range. Most modern, overhead valve pushrod engines must turn at about 2500 rpm to produce their peak torque. By 4500 rpm they are producing so little torque that continued increases in engine speed produce no power increases. The torque peak on overhead camshaft engines is generally much higher, but much narrower.

The manual transaxle and clutch are employed to vary the relationship between engine speed and the speed of the wheels so that adequate engine power can be produced under all circumstances. The clutch allows engine torque to be applied to the transaxle input shaft gradually, due to mechanical slippage. Consequently, the vehicle may be started smoothly from a full stop. The transaxle changes the ratio between the rotating speeds of the engine and the wheels by the use of gears. The gear ratios allow full engine power to be applied to the wheels during acceleration at low speeds and at highway/passing speeds.

In a front wheel drive transaxle, power is usually transmitted from the input shaft to a mainshaft or output shaft located slightly beneath and to the side of the input shaft. The gears of the mainshaft mesh with gears on the input shaft, allowing power to be carried from one to the other. All forward gears are in constant mesh and are free from rotating with the shaft unless the synchronizer and clutch are engaged. Shifting from one gear to the next causes one of the gears to be freed from rotating with the shaft and locks another to it. Gears are locked and unlocked by internal dog clutches which slide between the center of the gear and the shaft. The forward gears employ synchronizers; friction members which smoothly bring gear and shaft to the same speed before the toothed dog clutches are engaged.

Back-up Light Switch

REMOVAL & INSTALLATION

See Figure 1

1. Disconnect the negative battery cable.
2. Remove the back-up lamp switch electrical connector.
3. Remove the back-up lamp switch wire from retaining clamp.
4. Remove back-up lamp switch from case.

To install:

5. Using a new O-ring, install the back-up lamp switch. Tighten to 17 ft. lbs. (23 Nm).
6. Install the back-up lamp switch wire retaining clamp.
7. Install the back-up lamp switch electrical connector.
8. Connect the negative battery cable.

Manual Transaxle Assembly

REMOVAL & INSTALLATION

See Figure 2

1. Disconnect the negative battery cable and the ground strap at the transaxle.
2. Remove the clutch cable adjusting nuts, retaining clip from the cable and cable from the bracket.
3. Disconnect and tag all the wiring harness clamps and connectors involved with the transaxle removal.
4. Remove the speedometer cable boot, speedometer case clip and speedometer cable from the case.
5. Remove the transaxle retaining bolts.
6. Remove the starter assembly and starter motor plate.
7. Remove the vacuum hose from the pressure sensor.
8. Install the engine support to prevent the engine from lowering excessively.
9. Raise and support the vehicle safely. Drain the transaxle oil.
10. Remove the gear shift control shaft bolt and nut and detach the control shaft from the gear shift shaft.
11. Extension rod nut and remove the rod with washers.
12. Remove the exhaust pipe front and rear flange bolts.
13. Remove the clutch housing lower plate.
14. Remove the left front wheel.
15. Remove the left tie rod end.
16. Remove the left ball joint by removing the joint stud bolt.
17. Remove both halfshafts at the transaxle.
18. Support the transaxle with a suitable jack and remove the transaxle retaining bolts and nuts.
19. Remove the 2 rear engine mounting bolts.
20. Remove the 3 bolts and 2 nuts from the transaxle mounting left hand bracket, remove the left hand bracket.
21. Lower the transaxle with the engine attached in order to detach it from the stud bolt at the engine rear mounting portion. Pull the transaxle straight out toward the left side to disconnect the input shaft from the clutch cover, lower and remove the transaxle assembly.

To install:

22. While the transaxle is being raised into its correct position, install the right hand halfshaft into the differential.
23. Install the transaxle and the transaxle-to-engine nuts and bolts. Install the left hand bracket with its 3 bolts and 2 nuts. Torque them to 37 ft. lbs. (50 Nm).

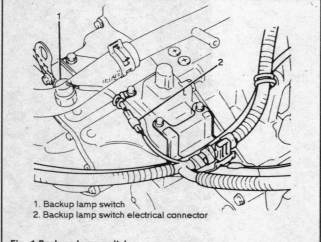

1. Backup lamp switch
2. Backup lamp switch electrical connector

Fig. 1 Back-up lamp switch

Fig. 2 Take care when raising or lowering the transaxle in and out of the vehicle

24. Install the 2 rear engine mounting nuts and torque them to 37 ft. lbs. (50 Nm).

25. Lower the transaxle supporting jack. Torque the transaxle to engine bolt and nut to 37 ft. lbs. (50 Nm).

26. Install the left hand halfshaft to the transaxle. Be sure to push each driveaxle in fully to engage the snaprings with the differential gear.

27. Install the left ball joint and ball joint stud bolt. Torque the ball joint bolt and nut to 44 ft. lbs. (60 Nm).

28. Install the left tie rod end, castle nut and cotter pin. Torque the castle nut to 32 ft. lbs. (43 Nm).

29. Install the left front wheel.

30. Install the clutch housing lower plate.

31. Install the exhaust pipe front and rear flange nuts.

32. Install the extension rod nut and washers. Torque the rod nut to 24 ft. lbs. (33 Nm).

33. Install the control shaft to gear shift and install the gear shift control shaft bolt and nut. Torque the gear shift control shaft bolt and nut to 13 ft. lbs. (18 Nm).

34. Refill the transaxle with the recommended lubricant.

35. Lower the vehicle.

36. Remove the engine support fixture.

37. Install the vacuum hose to the pressure sensor.

38. Install the starter, starter motor plate, and 2 bolts.

39. Install the transaxle retaining bolts. Torque the retaining bolts to 37 ft. lbs. (50 Nm).

40. Install the speedometer cable to case, speedometer case clip and speedometer cable boot.

41. Install the clutch cable bracket, retaining clip to cable and clutch cable adjusting nut. Adjust the clutch free-play as necessary.

42. Install the negative battery cable and the ground strap to the transaxle.

Halfshafts

REMOVAL & INSTALLATION

See Figure 3

1. Remove the grease cap, the cotter pin, and the halfshaft nut from both

front wheels.

2. Loosen the wheel nuts.

3. Raise and support the vehicle safely.

4. Remove the front wheels.

5. Drain the transaxle fluid.

6. Using a prybar, pry on the inboard joints of the right and left hand halfshafts to detach the halfshafts from the snaprings of the differential side gears.

7. Remove the stabilizer bar mounting bolts and the ball joint stud bolt. Pull down on the stabilizer bar and remove the ball joint stud from the steering knuckle.

8. Pull the halfshafts out of the transaxle's side gear, first, and then from the steering knuckles.

Note: To prevent the halfshaft boots from becoming damaged, be careful not to bring them into contact with any parts. If any malfunction is found in the either of the joints, replace the joints as an assembly.

To install:

9. To install, snap the halfshaft into the transaxle, first, and then into the steering knuckle.

10. Install ball joint and tighten nut to 44 ft. lbs. (60 Nm). Install the cotter pin.

11. Install the stabilizer bar and tighten mount bolts to 32 ft. lbs. (43 Nm).

12. Install the halfshaft nut and tighten to 129 ft. lbs. (175 Nm).

13. Fill the transaxle with fluid.

14. Install the front wheels.

15. Lower the vehicle.

CV-JOINTS OVERHAUL

See Figures 4, 5, 6, 7, 8, 9, 10, 11, 12, 13, 14, 15, 16 and 17

These vehicles use three different types of joints. Engine size, transaxle type, whether the joint is an inboard or outboard joint, even which side of the vehicle is being serviced could make a difference in joint type. Be sure to properly identify the joint before attempting joint or boot replacement. Look for identification numbers at the large end of the boots and/or on the end of the metal retainer bands.

The distance between the large and small boot bands is important and should be checked prior to and after boot service. This is so the boot will not be installed either too loose or too tight, which could cause early wear and cracking, allowing the grease to get out and water and dirt in, leading to early joint failure.

Note: The driveshaft joints use special grease; do not add any grease other than that supplied with the kit.

Double Offset Joint

The Double Offset Joint (D.O.J.) is bigger than other joints and, in these applications, is normally used as an inboard joint.

1. Remove the halfshaft from the vehicle.

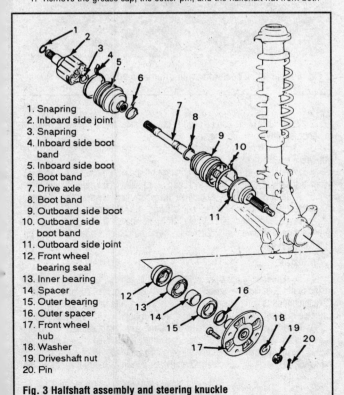

1. Snapring
2. Inboard side joint
3. Snapring
4. Inboard side boot band
5. Inboard side boot
6. Boot band
7. Drive axle
8. Boot band
9. Outboard side boot
10. Outboard side boot band
11. Outboard side joint
12. Front wheel bearing seal
13. Inner bearing
14. Spacer
15. Outer bearing
16. Outer spacer
17. Front wheel hub
18. Washer
19. Driveshaft nut
20. Pin

Fig. 3 Halfshaft assembly and steering knuckle

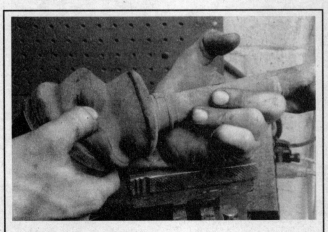

Fig. 4 Check the CV-boot for wear

Fig. 5 Removing the outer band from the CV-boot

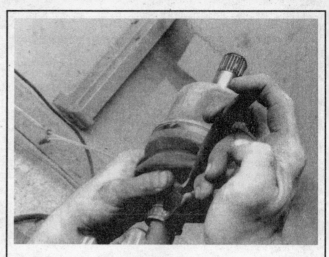

Fig. 6 Removing the inner band from the CV-boot

Fig. 7 Removing the CV-boot from the joint housing

Fig. 8 Clean the CV-joint housing prior to removing boot

Fig. 9 Removing the CV-joint housing assembly

2. Side cutter pliers can be used to cut the metal retaining bands. Remove the boot from the joint outer race.

3. Locate and remove the large circlip at the base of the joint. Remove the outer race (the body of the joint).

4. Remove the small snapring and take off the inner race, cage, and balls as an assembly. Clean the inner race, cage, and balls without disassembling.

5. If the boot is to be reused, wipe the grease from the splines and wrap the splines in vinyl tape before sliding the boot from the shaft.

6. Remove the inner (D.O.J.) boot from the shaft. If the outer (B.J.) boot is to be replaced, remove the boot retainer rings and slide the boot down and off of the shaft at this time.

To install:

7. Be sure to tape the shaft splines before installing the boots. Fill the inside of the boot with the specified grease. Often the grease supplied in the replacement parts kit is meant to be divided in half, with half being used to lubricate the joint and half being used inside the boot.

8. Install the cage onto the halfshaft so the small diameter side of the cage is installed first. With a brass drift pin, tap lightly and evenly around the inner race to install the race until it comes into contact with the rib of the shaft. Apply the specified grease to the inner race and cage and fit them together. Insert the balls into the cage.

9. Install the outer race (the body of the joint) after filling with the specified

Fig. 10 Removing the CV-joint

Fig. 11 Inspecting the CV-joint housing

Fig. 12 Removing the CV-joint outer snapring

Fig. 13 Checking the CV-joint snapring for wear

grease. The outer race should be filled with this grease.

10. Tighten the boot bands securely. Make sure the distance between the boot bands is correct.

11. Install the halfshaft to the vehicle.

Except Double Offset Joint

1. Disconnect the negative battery cable. Remove the halfshaft.

2. Use side cutter pliers to remove the metal retaining bands from the boot(s) that will be removed. Slide the boot from the T.J. case.

3. Remove the snapring and the tripod joint spider assembly from the halfshaft. Do not disassemble the spider and use care in handling.

4. If the boot is be reused, wrap vinyl tape around the spline part of the shaft so the boot(s) will not be damaged when removed. Remove the dynamic damper, if used, and the boots from the shaft.

Fig. 14 CV-joint snapring (typical)

Fig. 15 Removing the CV-joint assembly

Fig. 16 Removing the CV-joint inner snapring

Fig. 17 Installing the CV-joint assembly (typical)

To install:

5. Double check that the correct replacement parts are being installed. Wrap vinyl tape around the splines to protect the boot and install the boots and damper, if used, in the correct order.

6. Install the joint spider assembly to the shaft and install the snapring.

7. Fill the inside of the boot with the specified grease. Often the grease supplied in the replacement parts kit is meant to be divided in half, with half being used to lubricate the joint and half being used inside the boot. Keep grease off the rubber part of the dynamic damper (if used).

8. Secure the boot bands with the halfshaft in a horizontal position. Make sure distance between boot bands is correct.

9. Install the halfshaft to the vehicle and reconnect the negative battery cable.

CLUTCH

Understanding the Clutch

> **CAUTION:**
>
> The clutch driven disc may contain asbestos, which has been determined to be a cancer causing agent. **Never clean clutch surfaces with compressed air! Avoid inhaling any dust from any clutch surface! When cleaning clutch surfaces, use a commercially available brake cleaning fluid.**

The purpose of the clutch is to disconnect and connect engine power at the transaxle. A vehicle at rest requires a lot of engine torque to get all that weight moving. An internal combustion engine does not develop a high starting torque (unlike steam engines) so it must be allowed to operate without any load until it builds up enough torque to move the vehicle. Torque increases with engine rpm. The clutch allows the engine to build up torque by physically disconnecting the engine from the transaxle, relieving the engine of any load or resistance.

The transfer of engine power to the transaxle (the load) must be smooth and gradual; if it weren't, drive line components would wear out or break quickly. This gradual power transfer is made possible by gradually releasing the clutch pedal. The clutch disc and pressure plate are the connecting link between the engine and transaxle. When the clutch pedal is released, the disc and plate contact each other (the clutch is engaged) physically joining the engine and transaxle. When the pedal is pushed inward, the disc and plate separate (the clutch is disengaged) disconnecting the engine from the transaxle.

Most clutches utilize a single plate, dry friction disc with a diaphragm-style spring pressure plate. The clutch disc has a splined hub which attaches the disc to the input shaft. The disc has friction material where it contacts the flywheel and pressure plate. Torsion springs on the disc help absorb engine torque pulses. The pressure plate applies pressure to the clutch disc, holding it tight against the surface of the flywheel. The clutch operating mechanism consists of a release bearing, fork and cylinder assembly.

The release fork and actuating linkage transfer pedal motion to the release bearing. In the engaged position (pedal released) the diaphragm spring holds the pressure plate against the clutch disc, so engine torque is transmitted to the input shaft. When the clutch pedal is depressed, the release bearing pushes the diaphragm spring center toward the flywheel. The diaphragm spring pivots the fulcrum, relieving the load on the pressure plate. Steel spring straps riveted to the clutch cover lift the pressure plate from the clutch disc, disengaging the engine drive from the transaxle and enabling the gears to be changed.

The clutch is operating properly if:

1. It will stall the engine when released with the vehicle held stationary.

2. The shift lever can be moved freely between 1st and reverse gears when the vehicle is stationary and the clutch disengaged.

Driven Disc and Pressure Plate

REMOVAL & INSTALLATION

See Figures 18, 19, 20, 21, 22, 23, 24 and 25

1. Remove the transaxle.

2. Matchmark the clutch cover and flywheel for installation reference.

3. Loosen the clutch cover-to-flywheel bolts, one turn at a time (evenly) until the spring pressure is released.

4. Remove the clutch disc and clutch cover.

To install:

5. Clean the flywheel mating surfaces of all oil, grease, and metal deposits. Inspect flywheel for cracks, heat checking or other defects and replace or resurface as necessary.

6. Check the wear on the facings of the clutch disc by measuring the depth of each rivet head depression. Replace clutch disc when rivet heads are 0.02 in. below surface of clutch surface.

7. Check diaphragm spring and pressure plate for wear or damage. If the spring or plate is excessively worn, replace the clutch cover assembly.

8. Check the pilot bearing for smooth operation. If the bearing does not spin freely, replace it.

9. Position the clutch disc and clutch cover with the matchmarks aligned and support with pilot tool.

10. Install the clutch cover bolts and tighten evenly to 18 ft. lbs. (23 Nm). Remove the pilot tool.

11. Lightly lubricate the splines, pilot bearing surface of the input shaft and

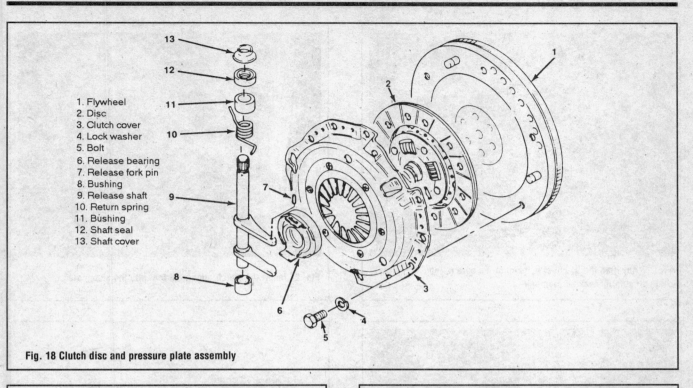

1. Flywheel
2. Disc
3. Clutch cover
4. Lock washer
5. Bolt
6. Release bearing
7. Release fork pin
8. Bushing
9. Release shaft
10. Return spring
11. Bushing
12. Shaft seal
13. Shaft cover

Fig. 18 Clutch disc and pressure plate assembly

Fig. 19 Remove the bolts that hold the pressure plate to the flywheel...

Fig. 20 ...and carefully remove the clutch disc and pressure plate from the flywheel...

Fig. 21 ...inspect the clutch disc for depth at the rivet heads...

Fig. 22 ...check the flywheel for cracks, grooves, or hard spots

Fig. 23 Any time the flywheel is taken off be sure to inspect the rear main oil seal for leaks or damage

Fig. 24 Insert the clutch alignment tool into the clutch disc...

Fig. 25 ...and carefully insert the tool into the pilot bearing of the crankshaft; the pressure plate can now be put on with greater ease

release bearing with grease.
12. Install the transaxle.
13. Adjust the clutch cable.

ADJUSTMENTS

Linkage
See Figure 26

1. At the console, loosen the gear shift control housing nuts and the guide plate bolts.
2. Adjust the guide plate by displacing it toward the front and rear so that the gear shift control lever is brought in the middle of the guide plate at the right angle.
3. Once the guide plate is positioned properly, tighten the guide plate bolts to 7 ft. lbs. (9 Nm) and then the housing nuts to 4 ft. lbs. (5 Nm).

Clutch Switch
See Figure 27

1. Disconnect the clutch switch electrical connector.
2. Depress the clutch pedal to the floor and return to within 0.6 - 0.12 in.

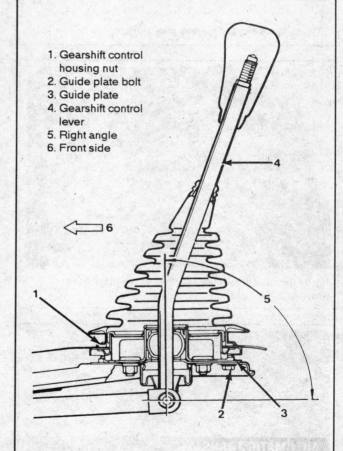

1. Gearshift control housing nut
2. Guide plate bolt
3. Guide plate
4. Gearshift control lever
5. Right angle
6. Front side

Fig. 26 Gearshift control lever adjustment

of its travel from the floor.
3. Attach an ohmmeter to the clutch switch connector.
4. Adjust the clutch switch until continuity is obtained.
5. Tighten the clutch switch to 115 inch lbs. (13 Nm).
6. Connect the electrical connector.

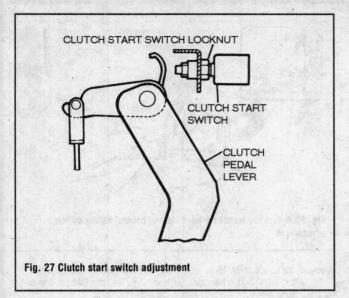

Fig. 27 Clutch start switch adjustment

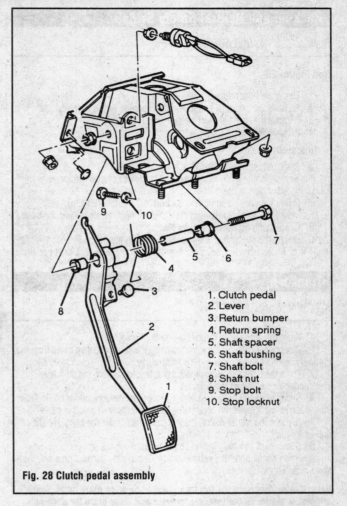

1. Clutch pedal
2. Lever
3. Return bumper
4. Return spring
5. Shaft spacer
6. Shaft bushing
7. Shaft bolt
8. Shaft nut
9. Stop bolt
10. Stop locknut

Fig. 28 Clutch pedal assembly

Release Arm Play

See Figure 28

1. At the transaxle, move the clutch release arm to check the free-play, it should be 0.08 - 0.16 in. on Sprint and 0.06-0.08 in. on Metro.
2. If necessary, turn the clutch cable joint nut to adjust the cable length.

Pedal Height

The clutch pedal height should be adjusted so the clutch pedal is the exact same height as the brake pedal. The pedal is adjusted at the stop bolt on the upper end of the pedal pivot.

Clutch Start Switch

1. Apply the parking brake firmly and place the gear shift lever in **N** position.
2. Disconnect the lead wire at the switch.
3. Loosen the locknut and screw the switch out.
4. Depress clutch pedal all the way to the floor and then return it back 0.4 - 1.1 in. along its travel from the floor.
5. Connect an ohmmeter to the switch and slowly screw the switch in until the switch is ON. Hold the switch at this position and tighten the locknut to 8 - 11 ft. lbs. (10 - 15 Nm).
6. Connect the lead wire.

Clutch Cable

REMOVAL & INSTALLATION

1. Disconnect the negative battery cable.

2. Remove the clutch cable joint nut and disconnect the cable from the release arm.
3. Remove the clutch cable bracket mounting nuts and remove the bracket from the cable.
4. Remove the cable retaining bolts at the clutch pedal.
5. Remove the cable from the vehicle.

To install:

6. Before installation, apply grease to the hook and pin end of the cable.
7. Connect the cable to the clutch pedal and install the retaining bolts.
8. Install the clutch cable bracket on the cable.
9. Position the bracket on the transaxle and install the mounting bolts.
10. Connect the cable to the release lever and install the joint nut on the cable.
11. Adjust the pedal free-play as previously outlined and connect the negative battery cable.

AUTOMATIC TRANSAXLE

Understanding the Automatic Transaxle

The automatic transaxle allows engine torque and power to be transmitted to the front wheels within a narrow range of engine operating speeds. It will allow the engine to turn fast enough to produce plenty of power and torque at very low speeds, while keeping it at a sensible rpm at high vehicle speeds (and it does this job without driver assistance). The transaxle uses a light fluid as the medium for the transmission of power. This fluid also works in the operation of various hydraulic control circuits and as a lubricant. Because the transaxle fluid performs all of these functions, trouble within the unit can easily travel from one part to another. For this reason, and because of the complexity and unusual operating principles of the transaxle, a very sound understanding of the basic principles of operation will simplify troubleshooting.

Back-up and Neutral Safety Switch

REMOVAL & INSTALLATION

See Figure 29

1. Disconnect the negative battery cable.
2. Remove the electrical connector at the engine wiring harness.
3. Remove the harness from the retaining clamps.
4. Remove the switch from the transaxle.

To install:

5. Place the transaxle in the **N** position.
6. Turn the shift switch assembly joint clockwise or counterclockwise until a distinct click noise is heard.
7. Install the switch and tighten the bolt to 17 ft. lbs. (23 Nm).
8. Install the harness retaining clips and connect the electrical connector.
9. Connect the negative battery cable.
10. Ensure the starter motor operates only when the transaxle shift lever is in the **P** or **N** positions and does not operate when in the **D**, **2**, **L** or **R** positions.

Transaxle

REMOVAL & INSTALLATION

1. From the air cleaner, remove the air suction guide.
2. Disconnect both cables from the battery and the negative cable from the transaxle. Remove the battery and the battery tray.
3. From the transaxle, disconnect the solenoid coupler, the shift lever switch coupler and the wiring harness.
4. Separate the oil pressure control cable from the accelerator cable. From the transaxle, disconnect the accelerator cable and the shift selector cable.
5. Remove the starter motor. Place a catch pan under the transaxle and drain the fluid.
6. Disconnect and plug the oil cooler tubes at the transaxle.
7. Raise and support the vehicle safely. Remove the exhaust pipe and the lower clutch housing plate.

Note: Before removing the torque converter-to-drive plate bolts, make alignment marks on the torque converter and drive plate for assembly purposes.

8. Using a prybar, insert it through the notch (underside of transaxle) to lock the drive plate gear. Remove the torque converter-to-drive plate bolts.
9. To remove the left halfshaft, perform the following procedures:
    a. From the wheel hub, remove the center cap, the split pin, and the driveshaft nut.
    b. Remove the lug nuts and the front wheels.
    c. Using a prybar, position it between the differential case and the halfshaft's inboard joint, pry the joint until the snap-ring disconnects from the side gear.
    d. Remove both stabilizer bar-to-chassis brackets and the ball stud-to-steering knuckle bolt. Pull the stabilizer bar downward to disconnect the ball joint from the steering knuckle.
    e. Carefully remove the halfshaft from the differential case and the steering knuckle to prevent tearing the boots.
10. Using a prybar, disconnect the right halfshaft from the differential case.
11. Remove the transaxle mounting member bolts and the member. Using a floor jack and a piece of wood, support the transaxle.
12. Remove the left transaxle mount.
13. Remove the transaxle-to-engine bolts. Slide the transaxle from the engine (to prevent damaging the crankshaft, drive plate, or torque converter) and lower it from the vehicle.

To install:

14. Using grease, lubricate the cup around the center of the torque converter.
15. Measure the distance between the torque converter and the transaxle housing; it should be at least 0.85 in. (21.4mm). If the distance is less than

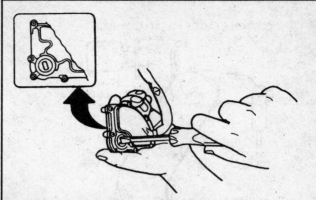

Fig. 29 Automatic transaxle back-up and neutral safety switch adjustment

specified, the torque converter is improperly installed; remove and reinstall it.
16. When installing the transaxle, guide the right halfshaft into the differential case; make sure the snapring seats in the differential gear.
17. To install the left halfshaft, perform the following procedures:
    a. Clean and lubricate the halfshaft splines with grease.
    b. Carefully install the halfshaft into the steering knuckle and the differential case to prevent tearing the boots; make sure the snapring seats in the differential gear.
    c. Install the ball joint stud into the steering knuckle and torque the bolt to 36 - 50 ft. lbs. (50 - 70 Nm).
    d. Install the stabilizer bar-to-chassis brackets and torque the bolts to 22 - 39 ft. lbs. (30 - 55 Nm).
    e. Torque the halfshaft hub nut to 108 - 195 ft. lbs. (150 - 270 Nm) and install the split pin (to the shaft) and the center cap.
    f. Torque the lug nuts to 29 - 50 ft. lbs. (40 - 70 Nm).
18. Torque the transaxle housing-to-engine bolts to 12 - 16.5 ft. lbs. (16 - 23 Nm), the mounting member-to-chassis bolts to 40 ft. lbs. (55 Nm), the mounting member-to-transaxle nuts to 33 ft. lbs. (45 Nm) and the transaxle-to-mount bolts to 40 ft. lbs. (55 Nm).
19. Using a prybar, insert it through the notch (underside of transaxle) to lock the drive plate gear and torque the torque converter-to-drive plate bolts to 13 - 14 ft. lbs. (18 - 19 Nm).
20. Install the oil cooler lines and the starter.
21. After connecting the oil pressure control cable to the accelerator cable, check and/or adjust the cable play.
22. Connect the wiring harness, the shift lever switch coupler and the solenoid coupler to the transaxle.
23. Install and adjust the select cable and shift switch.
24. Install the battery tray and the battery. Connect the battery cables to the battery and the negative battery cable to the transaxle.
25. Install the air suction guide to the air cleaner.
26. Refill and check the fluid level.

ADJUSTMENTS

Shift Linkage
See Figure 30

1. Place the shift lever in the N position.
2. Turn the adjusting nut in until it contacts the manual select cable joint.
3. Tighten the locknut.
4. To adjust the interlock cable (back drive cable), use the following procedure:
    a. Shift the selector to the P position.
    b. Loosen the adjusting and locknut on the interlock cable.
    c. Pull the outer wire (interlock cable) forward so there is no deflection on the inner wire, tighten the adjusting nut hand tight only, and then tighten the locknut.

Note: After tightening the nuts, make sure that with the shifter lever shifted to the PARK position, the ignition key can be turned from the ACC to the LOCK position and the key can be removed from the ignition switch. With the selector lever shifted to any range other than the PARK position, the ignition key can not be turned from the ACC to LOCK position.

5. On the Metro, adjust the shift lock solenoid so that it will operate as follows:

    a. When the ignition switch is turned **OFF**, the solenoid is not operated.

    b. When the ignition switch is turned **ON**, and the brake pedal is depressed, the solenoid is operated and the lock plate is positioned properly.

    c. There is no clearance between the lock plate and the guide plate.

    d. If the manual release knob is pulled when the ignition switch is turned **OFF**, the selector lever can be shifted from the P range to any other range.

Note: After tightening the solenoid retaining nuts, make sure that with the shifter lever shifted to the PARK position, the ignition key can be turned from the ACC to the LOCK position and the key can be removed from the ignition switch.

Oil Pressure Control Cable

6. Inspect and/or adjust the accelerator cable play by performing the following procedures:

    a. At the carburetor, check the amount of play in the accelerator cable; it should be 0.40 - 0.59 in. (10 - 15mm) cold or 0.12 - 0.19 in. (3 - 5mm) warm.

    b. If necessary to adjust, loosen the locknut and turn the adjustment nut until the correct specifications are met.

    c. After adjustment, tighten the locknut.

7. Operate the engine until normal operating temperatures are reached and allow the engine to idle; make sure the carburetor is not on the fast idle step.

8. From near transaxle's dipstick tube, remove the oil pressure control cable cover. Using a feeler gauge, check that the boot-to-inner cable stopper clearance is 0 - 0.02 in. (0 - 0.5mm).

9. If the clearance is not within specifications, perform the following procedures:

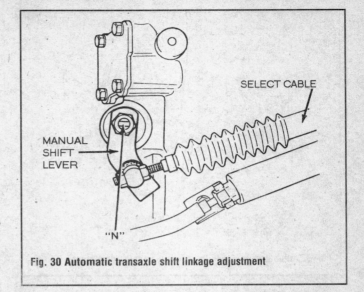

Fig. 30 Automatic transaxle shift linkage adjustment

    a. Loosen the adjusting nuts (engine side of bracket) and turn them to adjust the clearance.

    b. If the adjustment (engine side) fails to establish the clearance, tighten the nuts and move the other side (dipstick side) of the bracket.

    c. Loosen the adjusting nuts (dipstick side of bracket) and turn them to adjust the clearance.

    d. After adjustment is complete, tighten the adjusting nuts, recheck adjustment, and install the cover.

Interlock (back drive) Cable
See Figure 31

1. Place the shift selector into the P position.
2. Loosen both back drive cable nuts.
3. Pull the outer wire forward so there is no deflection on the inner wire and tighten both nuts (hand tight); tighten the nut farthest from the clevis end

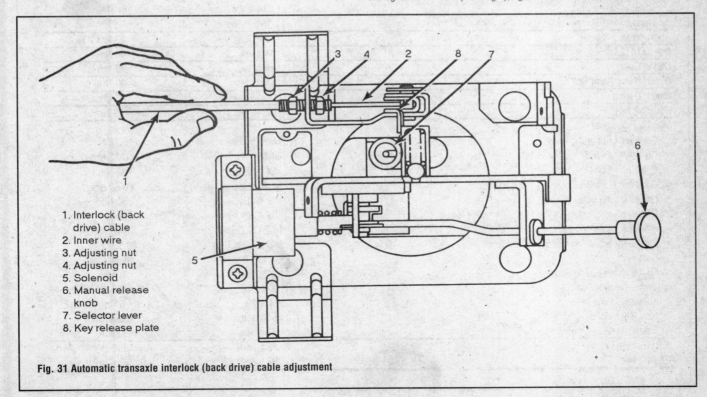

1. Interlock (back drive) cable
2. Inner wire
3. Adjusting nut
4. Adjusting nut
5. Solenoid
6. Manual release knob
7. Selector lever
8. Key release plate

Fig. 31 Automatic transaxle interlock (back drive) cable adjustment

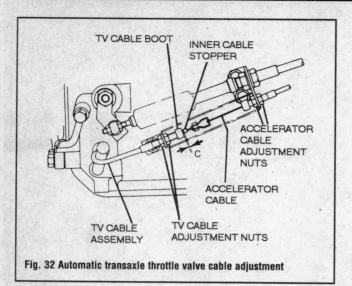

TV CABLE BOOT

INNER CABLE STOPPER

ACCELERATOR CABLE ADJUSTMENT NUTS

C

ACCELERATOR CABLE

TV CABLE ASSEMBLY

TV CABLE ADJUSTMENT NUTS

Fig. 32 Automatic transaxle throttle valve cable adjustment

turned from ACC to LOCK position and removed from the ignition switch.

b. With the shift selector in any position, other than P, the ignition key cannot be turned from ACC to LOCK position.

Throttle Valve (TV) Cable

See Figure 32

1. Inspect the accelerator cable for play and adjust if necessary.
2. Star the engine and allow it to reach normal operating temperature.
3. Remove the TV cable adjustment cover.
4. Measure the TV cable boot to inner cable stopper clearance with a feeler gauge. If clearance is more than 0.02 in. adjust the cable.
5. Adjust the clearance by turning the TV cable adjustment nuts until proper clearance is reached.
6. The accelerator cable nuts may also be used to adjust the TV cable if no further adjustment on the TV cable is available.

Halfshaft

REMOVAL & INSTALLATION

Halfshaft servicing procedures for the automatic transaxle are the same as for the manual transaxle. Refer to Halfshafts in the Manual Transaxle portion of this Section.

first and then tighten the other nut.
4. After tightening the nuts, check the following situations:
    a. With the shift selector in the P position, the ignition key can be

TORQUE SPECIFICATIONS

Components	English	Metric
Automatic transaxle		
Backup/Neutral safety switch	17 ft. lbs.	23 Nm
Crossmember-to-Chassis	40 ft. lbs.	55 Nm
Crossmember-to-Transaxle	33 ft. lbs.	45 Nm
Filter Screen	53 inch lbs.	6 Nm
Mount-to-Transaxle	40 ft. lbs.	55 Nm
Oil Pan	3-4 ft. lbs.	4-6 Nm
Torque Converter	13-14 ft. lbs.	18-19 Nm
Transaxle-to-Engine	12-16.5 ft. lbs.	16-23 Nm
Backup Lamp Switch	17 ft. lbs.	23 Nm
Ball Joint Nut	44 ft. lbs.	60 Nm
Clutch Cover	18 ft. lbs.	23 Nm
Clutch Pedal Shaft Bolt	15 ft. lbs.	20 Nm
Clutch Switch	115 inch lbs.	13 Nm
Halfshaft Nut	129 ft. lbs.	175 Nm
Manual Transaxle:		
Case Half Retaining Bolts	14-20 ft. lbs.	18-28 Nm
Countershaft Nut	44-58 ft.lbs.	60-80 Nm
Extension Rod Nuts	24 ft. lbs.	33 Nm
Gearshift Locating Bolts	30-43 ft.lbs.	40-60 Nm
Left Mounting Bracket	37 ft. lbs.	50 Nm
Rear Mounting Nuts	37 ft. lbs.	50 Nm
Reverse Gear Shift Lever	14-20 ft. lbs.	18-28 Nm
Ring Gear Retaining Bolts	58-72 ft. lbs.	80-100 Nm
Shift Fork	8-11 ft. lbs.	10-16 Nm
Shift Linkage Guide Plate	7 ft. lbs.	9 Nm
Shifter Control Shaft	13 ft. lbs.	18 Nm
Shifter Housing Nuts	4 ft. lbs.	5 Nm
Side Case Bolts	14-20 ft. lbs.	18-28 Nm
Transaxle-to-Engine	37 ft. lbs.	50 Nm
Stabilizer Bar	32 ft. lbs.	43 Nm
Tie Rod Nut	32 ft. lbs.	43 Nm

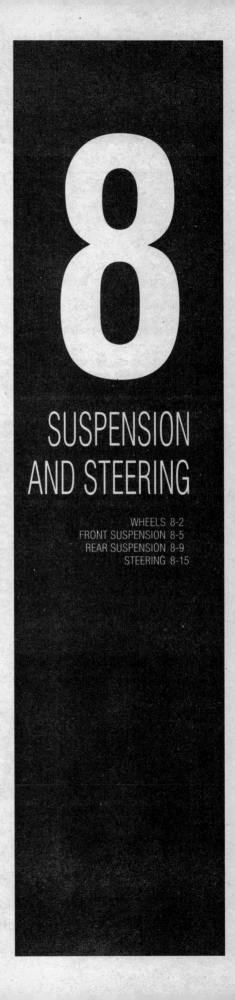

8

SUSPENSION AND STEERING

WHEELS

Wheels

REMOVAL & INSTALLATION

See Figures 1, 2, 3, 4, 5, 6 and 7

1. Park the vehicle on a level surface.
2. Remove the jack, tire iron and, if necessary, the spare tire from their storage compartments.
3. Check the owner's manual or refer to Jacking. Then, place the jack in the proper position.
4. If equipped with lug nut trim caps, remove them by either unscrewing or pulling them off the lug nuts, as appropriate. Consult the owner's manual, if necessary.
5. If equipped with a wheel cover or hub cap, insert the tapered end of the tire iron in the groove and pry off the cover.
6. Apply the parking brake and block the diagonally opposite wheel with a wheel chock or two.

Note: Wheel chocks may be purchased at your local auto parts store, or a block of wood cut into wedges may be used. If possible, keep one or two of the chocks in your tire storage compartment, in case any of the tires has to be removed on the side of the road.

Fig. 1 Place the jack at the proper lifting point on your vehicle

Fig. 2 Before jacking the vehicle, block the diagonally opposite wheel with one or, preferably, two chocks

Fig. 3 With the vehicle still on the ground, break the lug nuts loose using the wrench end of the tire iron

Fig. 4 After the lug nuts have been loosened, raise the vehicle using the jack until the tire is clear of the ground

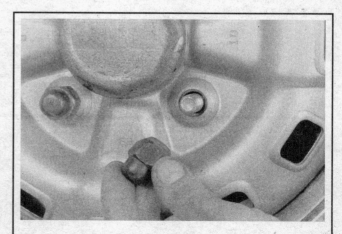

Fig. 5 Remove the lug nuts from the studs

Fig. 6 Remove the wheel from the vehicle

7. If equipped with an automatic transmission/transaxle, place the selector lever in P or Park; with a manual transmission/transaxle, place the shifter in Reverse.

8. With the tires still on the ground, use the tire iron/wrench to break the lug nuts loose.

Note: If a nut is stuck, never use heat to loosen it or damage to the wheel and bearings may occur. If the nuts are seized, one or two heavy hammer blows directly on the end of the bolt usually loosens the rust. Be careful, as continued pounding will likely damage the brake drum or rotor.

9. Using the jack, raise the vehicle until the tire is clear of the ground. Support the vehicle safely using jackstands.

10. Remove the lug nuts, then remove the wheel.

To install:

11. Make sure the wheel and hub mating surfaces, as well as the wheel lug studs, are clean and free of all foreign material. Always remove rust from the wheel mounting surface and the brake rotor or drum. Failure to do so may cause the lug nuts to loosen in service.

12. Install the wheel and hand-tighten the lug nuts.

13. Using the tire wrench, tighten all the lug nuts, in a crisscross pattern, until they are snug.

14. Raise the vehicle and withdraw the jackstand, then lower the vehicle.

15. Using a torque wrench, tighten the lug nuts in a crisscross pattern to 44 ft. lbs. (60 Nm). Check your owner's manual or refer to Wheels for the proper tightening sequence.

❊❊ WARNING:

Do not overtighten the lug nuts, as this may cause the wheel studs to stretch or the brake disc (rotor) to warp.

16. If so equipped, install the wheel cover or hub cap. Make sure the valve stem protrudes through the proper opening before tapping the wheel cover into position.

17. If equipped, install the lug nut trim caps by pushing them or screwing them on, as applicable.

18. Remove the jack from under the vehicle, and place the jack and tire iron/wrench in their storage compartments. Remove the wheel chock(s).

19. If you have removed a flat or damaged tire, place it in the storage compartment of the vehicle and take it to your local repair station to have it fixed or replaced as soon as possible.

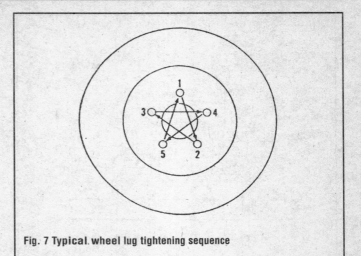

Fig. 7 Typical wheel lug tightening sequence

INSPECTION

Inspect the tires for lacerations, puncture marks, nails and other sharp objects. Repair or replace as necessary. Also check the tires for treadwear and air pressure.

Check the wheel assemblies for dents, cracks, rust and metal fatigue. Repair or replace as necessary.

Wheel Lug Studs

REMOVAL & INSTALLATION

With Disc Brakes
See Figures 8, 9 and 10

1. Raise and support the appropriate end of the vehicle safely using jackstands, then remove the wheel.

2. Remove the brake pads and caliper. Support the caliper aside using wire or a coat hanger.

3. Remove the outer wheel bearing and lift off the rotor.

4. Properly support the rotor using press bars, then drive the stud out using an arbor press.

Note: If a press is not available, CAREFULLY drive the old stud out using a blunt drift. MAKE SURE the rotor is properly and evenly supported or it may be damaged.

To install:

5. Clean the stud hole with a wire brush and start the new stud with a hammer and drift pin. Do not use any lubricant or thread sealer.

6. Finish installing the stud with the press.

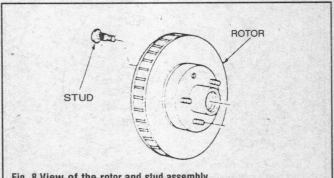

Fig. 8 View of the rotor and stud assembly

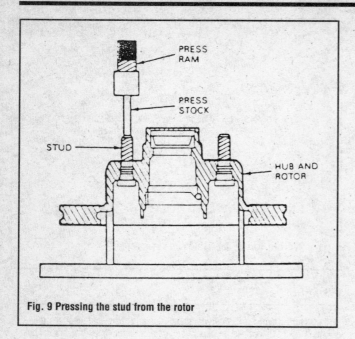

Fig. 9 Pressing the stud from the rotor

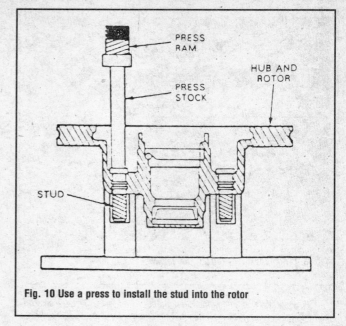

Fig. 10 Use a press to install the stud into the rotor

Note: If a press is not available, start the lug stud through the bore in the hub, then position about 4 flat washers over the stud and thread the lug nut. Hold the hub/rotor while tightening the lug nut, and the stud should be drawn into position. MAKE SURE THE STUD IS FULLY SEATED, then remove the lug nut and washers.

7. Install the rotor and adjust the wheel bearings.
8. Install the brake caliper and pads.

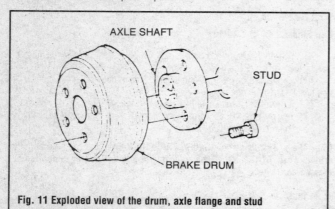

Fig. 11 Exploded view of the drum, axle flange and stud

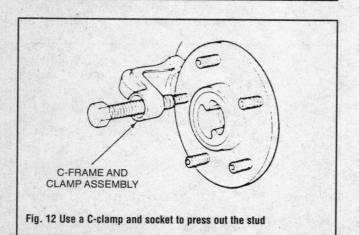

Fig. 12 Use a C-clamp and socket to press out the stud

9. Install the wheel, then remove the jackstands and carefully lower the vehicle.
10. Tighten the lug nuts to the proper torque.

With Drum Brakes
See Figures 11, 12 and 13

1. Raise the vehicle and safely support it with jackstands, then remove the wheel.
2. Remove the brake drum.
3. If necessary to provide clearance, remove the brake shoes.
4. Using a large C-clamp and socket, press the stud from the axle flange.
5. Coat the serrated part of the stud with liquid soap and place it into the hole.

To install:

6. Position about 4 flat washers over the stud and thread the lug nut. Hold the flange while tightening the lug nut, and the stud should be drawn into position. MAKE SURE THE STUD IS FULLY SEATED, then remove the lug nut and washers.
7. If applicable, install the brake shoes.
8. Install the brake drum.
9. Install the wheel, then remove the jackstands and carefully lower the vehicle.
10. Tighten the lug nuts to the proper torque.

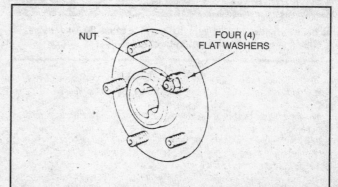

Fig. 13 Force the stud onto the axle flange using washers and a lug nut

FRONT SUSPENSION

See Figure 14

Coil Springs

REMOVAL & INSTALLATION

1. Remove the strut assembly from the vehicle.
2. Mount the strut into a suitable spring compressor.
3. Following the compressor manufacturer's instructions, compress the spring and remove the strut nut.
4. Remove the lockwasher, the strut stopper, and the spacer.
5. Release the tension on the spring.
6. Remove the spring from the strut.
7. Installation is the reverse of the removal.

MacPherson Strut

REMOVAL & INSTALLATION

1. Raise and support the vehicle safely.
2. Remove the wheel.
3. Remove the brake hose clip, then the hose from the strut.
4. Remove the upper strut support nuts from the engine compartment.
5. Remove the strut-to-steering knuckle bolts, then the strut assembly from the vehicle.

To install:

6. Install the strut assembly onto the vehicle. Install the upper support nuts loosely. Then install the strut-to-steering knuckle bolts and tighten to 59 ft. lbs. (80 Nm).
7. Tighten the upper strut support nuts to 20 ft. lbs. (27 Nm).
8. Install the brake hose clip.
9. Install the wheel.
10. Lower the vehicle.
11. Check front end alignment.

OVERHAUL

See Figure 15

1. Remove the strut from the vehicle.
2. Mount the strut in a suitable spring compressor.
3. Compress the strut spring slowly and evenly to approximately half is height after initial contact with top cap. Never bottom spring.
4. Remove the retainer nut from the strut shaft.
5. Remove the strut from the assembly.
6. Disassemble the strut components and inspect for damage or wear. Replace worn or damaged components as required.

Fig. 14 Front suspension components

1 Strut assembly	4 Control arm rear bracket	9 Stabilizer bar mounting bracket
2 Lower ball joint	6 Stabilizer bar	10 Steering knuckle
3 Stabilizer link	7 Rack and pinion steering gear	11 Tie rod end
4 Control arm front bracket	8 Control arm	

To assemble:

7. Mount strut on spring compressor.

8. Position spring on strut and ensure spring is properly seated on spring plate.

9. Install all shields, bumpers and insulators on shaft. Install spring seat on top of spring.

10. Lower the compressor to capture spring seat and pull up strut rod to full extension.

11. Compress spring and guide the strut rod through bearing cap.

Note: During compression of the spring be sure to guide the shaft through the exact center of the bearing. If the threads of the strut rod catch on the bearing cap and prevent the shaft from passing cleanly through the bearing, stop compressing immediately. Decompress the spring and begin again.

12. Compress spring until approximately 1 inch of the damper rod protrudes through the bearing cap. Do not compress the spring any further. Install and tighten nut to 29 ft. lbs. (40 Nm).

13. Apply grease to strut nut and threads.

14. Back off spring compressor and remove strut assembly.

15. Install the strut into the vehicle and tighten the fasteners to specifications.

16. Inspect the front alignment.

Lower Ball Joints

INSPECTION

Ball joints must be replace if any looseness is detected in the joint or if the ball joint seal is cut.

To inspect ball joints, raise and support the vehicle safely. Grasp the top and bottom of the tire and move the top of the tire with an in-and-out motion. Observe for any horizontal movement of the steering knuckle relative to the control arm.

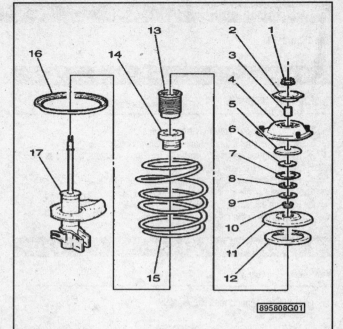

895808G01

Fig. 15 Exploded view of the strut assembly

1 Nut
2 Strut stopper
3 Inner spacer
4 Support
5 Bearing seat
6 Bearing upper washer
7 Bearing seal
8 Bearing
9 Bearing lower washer
10 Bearing spacer
11 Upper spring seat
12 Insulator
13 Cover
14 Bump stop
15 Coil spring
16 Lower spring seat
17 Strut

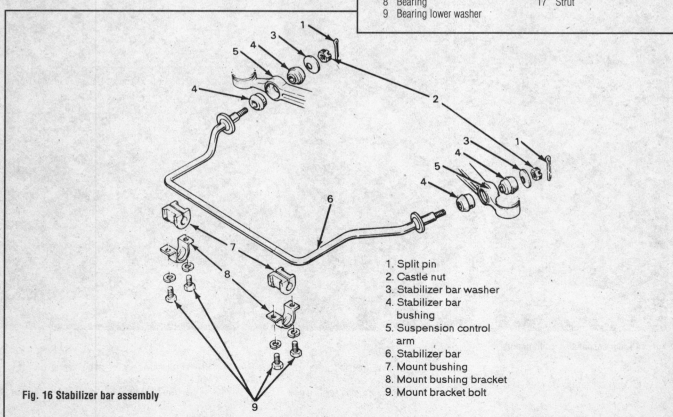

1. Split pin
2. Castle nut
3. Stabilizer bar washer
4. Stabilizer bar bushing
5. Suspension control arm
6. Stabilizer bar
7. Mount bushing
8. Mount bushing bracket
9. Mount bracket bolt

Fig. 16 Stabilizer bar assembly

Fig. 17a Front control arm front bushing

Fig. 17b Front control arm rear bushing

If the ball joint is disconnected from the knuckle and any looseness is detected, or if the ball joint can be twisted in its socket using finger pressure, replace the ball joint.

Ball joint tightness in the knuckle boss should also be checked when inspecting the ball joint. This may be done by shaking the wheel and feeling for movement of the stud end or castle nut at the knuckle boss. Checking the fastener torque at the castle nut is an alternative method of inspecting for wear. A loose nut can indicate a bend stud in the knuckle boss. Worn or damaged ball joints and knuckles must be replaced.

REMOVAL & INSTALLATION

The lower ball joint is an integral part of the lower control arm. Therefore, if ball joint replacement is necessary, the lower control arm must be replaced as an assembly.

Stabilizer Bar

REMOVAL & INSTALLATION

See Figure 16

1. Raise and support the vehicle safely.
2. Remove the wheels.
3. Remove the stabilizer bar mount bushing brackets.
4. Remove the castle nut, washer and bushing from the stabilizer at the lower control arm.
5. Remove the stabilizer bar from the vehicle.

To install:

6. Install the stabilizer bar and loosely install the castle nut, washer and bushing at the lower control arm.
7. Install the stabilizer bar mount bushing brackets.
8. Position stabilizer bar so that paint marks on the bar are centered between the mount bushings.
9. Tighten mount bolts to 29 - 65 ft. lbs. (40 - 90 Nm) and stabilizer bar castle nut to 22 - 39 ft. lbs. (30 - 55 Nm).
10. Install wheels. Lower the vehicle.

Lower Control Arm

REMOVAL & INSTALLATION

See Figures 17a and 17b

1. Raise and support the vehicle safely.

2. Remove the wheel.
3. Remove the ball joint nut and bolt. Separate the ball joint from the knuckle.
4. Remove the control arm front mounting bracket bolts.
5. Remove 2 bolts and the control arm rear mounting bracket.
6. Remove the control arm and the front mounting bracket from the vehicle.

To install:

7. Install the control arm to the vehicle and secure with 4 bolts. Do not fully tighten the bolts.
8. Install the ball joint to the knuckle and secure with nut and bolt.
9. Tighten control arm rear mounting bracket bolts to 32 ft. lbs. (43 Nm); front mounting bracket bolts to 66 ft. lbs. (90 Nm) and ball joint nut and bolt to 44 ft. lbs. (60 Nm).
10. Install wheel.
11. Lower the vehicle.
12. Check front wheel alignment.

Knuckle and Spindle

REMOVAL & INSTALLATION

See Figure 18

1. Raise and support the vehicle safely.
2. Remove the wheel.
3. Remove the hub from the steering knuckle, as outlined in this Section.
4. Remove the tie rod end cotter pin and nut.
5. Remove the ball joint bolt from the steering knuckle.
6. Using the ball joint removal tool J-21687-02 or equivalent, remove the ball joint from the steering knuckle.
7. Remove the strut-to-steering knuckle bolts.
8. Remove the steering knuckle from the vehicle. Support the axle shaft with a jackstand to prevent damage to the CV-joint.
9. Using a brass drift, drive the inner and outer wheel bearings from the steering knuckle.
10. Remove the spacer and clean the steering knuckle cavity.

To install:

11. Lubricate the new bearings and the steering knuckle cavity.
12. Using the installation tool J-34856, drive the new bearings, with the internal seals facing outward, into the steering knuckle.
13. Using the seal installation tool J-34881, drive the new seal into the steering knuckle, grease the seal lip.
14. Install the steering knuckle on the vehicle.
15. Install the strut-to-steering knuckle bolts. Tighten the strut-to-steering knuckle bolts to 59 ft. lbs. (80 Nm).

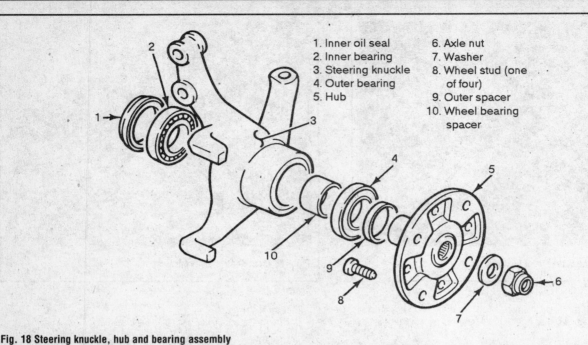

1. Inner oil seal
2. Inner bearing
3. Steering knuckle
4. Outer bearing
5. Hub
6. Axle nut
7. Washer
8. Wheel stud (one of four)
9. Outer spacer
10. Wheel bearing spacer

Fig. 18 Steering knuckle, hub and bearing assembly

16. Install the ball joint bolt through the steering knuckle.
17. Install the ball joint nut and tighten to 44 ft. lbs. (60 Nm).
18. Install the tie rod end cotter pin and nut. Tighten nut to 32 ft. lbs. (43 Nm).
19. Install the hub on the steering knuckle. Tighten axle shaft castle nut to 129 ft. lbs. (175 Nm).
20. Install the wheel.

Front Hub

REMOVAL & INSTALLATION

1. Raise and support the vehicle safely.
2. Remove the wheel.
3. Remove the brake caliper.
4. Unstake and remove the drive axle nut and washer.
5. Remove the hub retaining nuts.

6. Using a slide hammer, remove the hub from the vehicle.
7. Remove the brake rotor.

To install:

8. Install the brake rotor.
9. Apply a light coat of grease to the outside of the hub shaft.
10. Install the hub and outer spacer to the knuckle.
11. Install the hub retaining bolts and tighten to 37 ft. lbs. (50 Nm).
12. Install the drive axle nut and tighten to 129 ft. lbs. (137 Nm).
13. Install the caliper.
14. Install the wheel.
15. Lower the vehicle.

Front End Alignment

If the tires are worn unevenly, if the vehicle is not stable on the highway or if the handling seems uneven in spirited driving, the wheel alignment should be checked. If an alignment problem is suspected, first check for improper tire

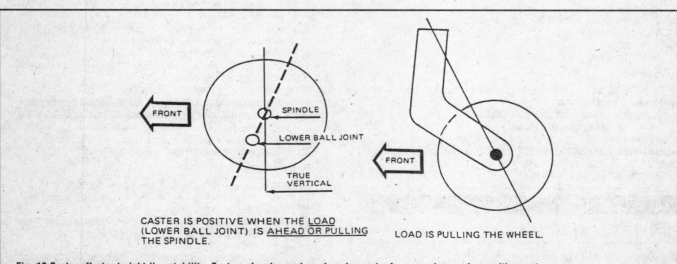

CASTER IS POSITIVE WHEN THE LOAD (LOWER BALL JOINT) IS AHEAD OR PULLING THE SPINDLE.

LOAD IS PULLING THE WHEEL.

Fig. 19 Caster affects straight-line stability. Caster wheels used on shopping carts, for example, employ positive caster

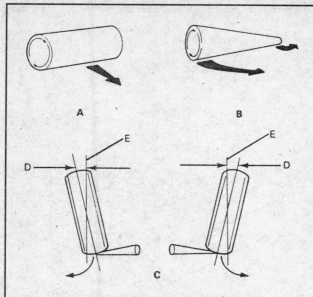

A A CYLINDER WILL ROLL STRAIGHT AHEAD
B A CONE WILL ROLL IN A CIRCLE TOWARD THE SMALL END
C TIRE CONTACTS THE ROAD SURFACE
D POSITIVE CAMBER ANGLE
E VERTICAL

Fig. 20 Camber influences tire contact with the road

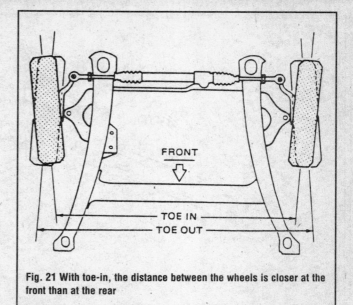

Fig. 21 With toe-in, the distance between the wheels is closer at the front than at the rear

inflation and other possible causes. These can be worn suspension or steering components, accident damage or even unmatched tires. If any worn or damaged components are found, they must be replaced before the wheels can be properly aligned. Wheel alignment requires very expensive equipment and involves minute adjustments, which must be accurate; it should only be performed by a trained technician. Take your vehicle to a properly equipped shop.

Following is a description of the alignment angles, which are adjustable on most vehicles and how they affect vehicle handling. Although these angles can apply to both the front and rear wheels, usually only the front suspension is adjustable.

CASTER

See Figure 19

Looking at a vehicle from the side, caster angle describes the steering axis rather than a wheel angle. The steering knuckle is attached to a control arm or strut at the top and a control arm at the bottom. The wheel pivots around the line between these points to steer the vehicle. When the upper point is tilted

back, this is described as positive caster. Having a positive caster tends to make the wheels self-centering, increasing directional stability. Excessive positive caster makes the wheels hard to steer, while an uneven caster will cause a pull to one side. Overloading the vehicle or sagging rear springs will affect caster, as will raising the rear of the vehicle. If the rear of the vehicle is lower than normal, the caster becomes more positive.

CAMBER

See Figure 20

Looking from the front of the vehicle, camber is the inward or outward tilt of the top of wheels. When the tops of the wheels are tilted in, this is negative camber; if they are tilted out, it is positive. In a turn, a slight amount of negative camber helps maximize contact of the tire with the road. However, too much negative camber compromises straight-line stability, increases bump steer and torque steer.

TOE

See Figure 21

Looking down at the wheels from above the vehicle, toe angle is the distance between the front of the wheels, relative to the distance between the back of the wheels. If the wheels are closer at the front, they are said to be toed-in or to have negative toe. A small amount of negative toe enhances directional stability and provides a smoother ride on the highway.

REAR SUSPENSION

Coil Springs

REMOVAL & INSTALLATION

1987 - 88 Sprint

See Figure 22

1. Raise and support the vehicle safely.
2. Place a jack under the rear axle and raise it slightly.

3. As required, disconnect the brake pipes and parking brake cable.
4. Remove the rear shock absorbers.
5. Disconnect the lateral rod.
6. Lower the rear axle until all tension is remove from the springs.
7. Remove the springs from the vehicle.

To install:

8. Install the springs in the vehicle with the flat side upward. Ensure the bottom of the spring is properly seated in the spring pocket on the rear axle.
9. Raise the rear axle to tension the springs.
10. Install the lateral rod and tighten bolt to 32 - 50 ft. lbs. (45 - 70 Nm).

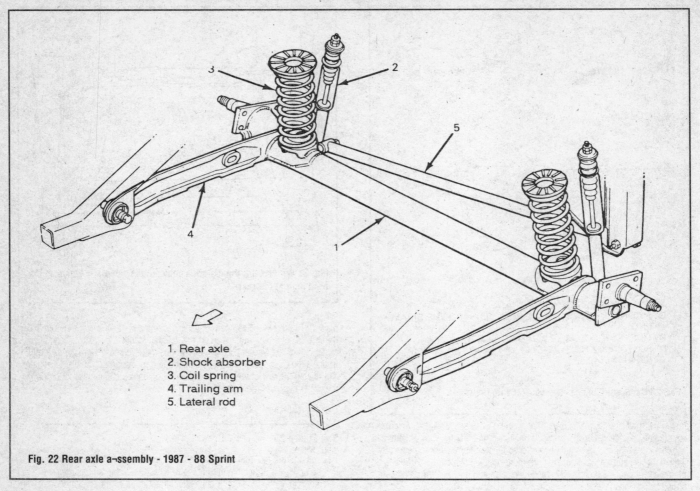

1. Rear axle
2. Shock absorber
3. Coil spring
4. Trailing arm
5. Lateral rod

Fig. 22 Rear axle a¬ssembly - 1987 - 88 Sprint

11. Install the shock absorbers. Tighten lower bolt to 32 - 50 ft. lbs. (45 - 70 Nm). Tighten upper nut to 13 - 20 ft. lbs. (18 - 28 Nm).
12. Connect the brake pipes and parking brake cable, as required.
13. Remove the jack under the rear axle and lower the vehicle.

1989 - 93 Metro
See Figure 23

1. Raise and support the vehicle safely.

Note: To facilitate the toe-in adjustment after reinstallation, confirm which one of the lines stamped on the washer is in the closest alignment with the stamped line on the control rod. If not marked, add the alignment marks.

2. Remove the control rod inside bolt (body center side).
3. Remove the outside (wheel side) of the control rod from the rear knuckle stud bolt.
4. Loosen the rear mount nut on the suspension arm, but do not remove the bolt.
5. Loosen the front nut of the suspension arm.
6. Loosen the lower mount nut on the knuckle. Place a jack under the suspension arm to prevent it from lowering and remove the lower mount nut on the knuckle.
7. Raise the jack placed under the suspension arm enough to allow the removal of the lower mount bolt of the knuckle.
8. Move the brake drum/backing plate toward the outside of the vehicle body so as to separate the lower mount of the knuckle from the suspension arm. Then lower the jack gradually and remove the coil spring.
9. Remove the suspension arm.

To install:

10. Install the 4 mounting bracket bolts. Torque the mounting bracket bolts to 33 ft. lbs. (45 Nm).
11. Install the rear and front mounting nuts, but do not torque them at this time.

Note: Make sure that the front mounting washer is installed in the proper direction.

12. Place the jack under the suspension arm.
13. Install the coil spring on the spring seat of the suspension arm then raise the suspension arm. When seating the coil spring, mate the spring end with the stepped part of the suspension arm spring.
14. Install the lower knuckle mount bolt. Torque the bolt to 37 ft. lbs. (50 Nm).
15. Remove the jack from under the suspension arm.
16. Install the inside and outside control rod bolts, but do not tighten them at this time.
17. Install the wheel assemblies and lower the vehicle.
18. Install the control rod inside and outside nut and torque them to 59 ft. lbs. (80 Nm).

Note: When tightening the nuts, it is most desirable to have the vehicle off the hoist, sitting at normal ride height. Also when tightening the inside nut, align the line stamped on the body with the line on the washer as confirmed before removal or align the matchmarks if marked.

19. Install the suspension arm front and rear nuts. Torque the front nuts to 44 ft. lbs. (60 Nm) and the rear nuts to 37 ft. lbs. (50 Nm). After tightening the suspension arm outer nut, make sure that the washer is not tilted.
20. Check the rear wheel alignment.

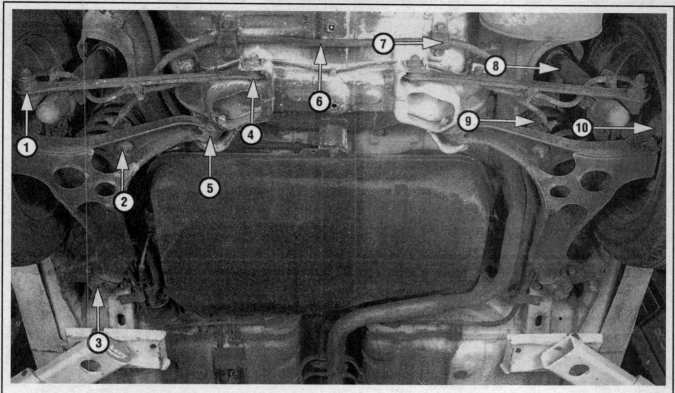

Fig. 23 Rear suspension components - 1989 and later Metro/Swift

1 Control rod bushing	5 Control arm rear bracket	8 Shock absorber
2 Control arm	6 Stabilizer bar	9 Coil spring
3 Control arm front bracket	7 Stabilizer bar mounting bracket	10 Knuckle
4 Control rod bushing		

Leaf Springs

REMOVAL & INSTALLATION

1985 - 86 Sprint
See Figure 24

1. Raise and support the vehicle safely. Raise rear axle assembly and place jackstands under suspension.
2. Disconnect lower portion of rear shock, as required. Remove the rear axle U-bolt nuts.
3. Remove shackle nuts and leaf spring front nut.
4. Pull out leaf spring front bolt and remove leaf spring from shackle pin.

To install:

5. Install front bolt and shackle pins with the threads facing outward. Tighten shackle pin nuts to 22 - 39 ft. lbs. (30 - 55 Nm). Tighten front bolt to 33 - 50 ft. lbs. (45 - 70 Nm).
6. Position axle on spring by aligning leaf spring pin with hole in under-side of axle.
7. Install bump stopper.
8. Align leaf spring underside pin with hole in spring seat. Install U-bolts from bump stopper side towards spring seat side and tighten to 22 - 32 ft. lbs. (30 - 45 Nm).
9. Install lower portion of shock, if removed.
10. Inspect all components for tightness and proper alignment. Lower the vehicle.

Shock Absorbers

REMOVAL & INSTALLATION

1985 - 88 Sprint
See Figure 25

1. Raise and safely support the vehicle. Remove the wheels.

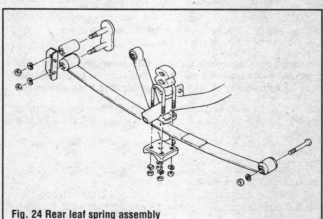

Fig. 24 Rear leaf spring assembly

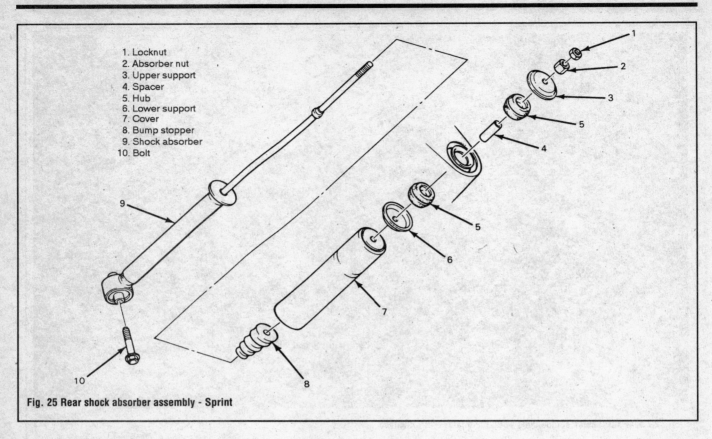

1. Locknut
2. Absorber nut
3. Upper support
4. Spacer
5. Hub
6. Lower support
7. Cover
8. Bump stopper
9. Shock absorber
10. Bolt

Fig. 25 Rear shock absorber assembly - Sprint

2. Support the rear axle assembly using jackstands.
3. Remove the upper shock absorber locknut and absorber nut.
4. Remove the lower shock mount bolt.
5. Remove the shock absorber from the vehicle.

To install:

6. Install the shock absorber.
7. Install the lower shock mount bolt and tighten to 32 - 50 ft. lbs. (45 - 70 Nm).
8. Install the upper shock locknut and absorber nut. Tighten to 13 - 20 ft. lbs. (18 - 28 Nm).
9. Remove the jackstand and lower the vehicle.

1989 and later Metro/Sprint
See Figure 26

1. Raise and safely support the vehicle. Remove the wheel.
2. Place a jackstand under the suspension arm for support when it lowers.
3. Remove the shock support nuts and push the shock down.
4. Remove the lower shock-to-knuckle bolt.

Note: Do not open the knuckle slit wider than necessary. Do not lower the jack more than necessary during the strut removal to prevent the coil spring from coming off, or a brake flexible hose from stretching.

5. Remove the shock from the knuckle. Compress the shock as short as possible for removal. If the shock is hard to remove, open the slit of the knuckle by inserting a wedge.

To install:

6. Install the shock absorber in the vehicle. Position the bottom of the alignment projection inside the knuckle opening.
7. Install the upper support nuts and tighten to 24 ft. lbs. (30 Nm).
8. Install shock absorber-to-knuckle bolt and tighten to 44 ft. lbs. (60 Nm).
9. Install the wheel.
10. Remove the jackstand and lower the vehicle.

TESTING

See Figure 27

The purpose of the shock absorber is simply to limit the motion of the spring during compression and rebound cycles. If the vehicle is not equipped with these motion dampers, the up and down motion would multiply until the vehicle was alternately trying to leap off the ground and to pound itself into the pavement.

Contrary to popular rumor, the shocks do not affect the ride height of the vehicle. This is controlled by other suspension components such as springs and tires. Worn shock absorbers can affect handling; if the front of the vehicle is rising or falling excessively, the "footprint" of the tires changes on the pavement and steering is affected.

The simplest test of the shock absorber is simply push down on one corner of the unladen vehicle and release it. Observe the motion of the body as it is released. In most cases, it will come up beyond it original rest position, dip back below it and settle quickly to rest. This shows that the damper is controlling the spring action. Any tendency to excessive pitch (up-and-down) motion or failure to return to rest within 2-3 cycles is a sign of poor function within the shock absorber. Oil-filled shocks may have a light film of oil around the seal, resulting from normal breathing and air exchange. This should NOT be taken as a sign of failure, but any sign of thick or running oil definitely indicates failure. Gas filled shocks may also show some film at the shaft; if the gas has leaked out, the shock will have almost no resistance to motion.

While each shock absorber can be replaced individually, it is recommended that they be changed as a pair to maintain equal response on both sides of the vehicle. Chances are quite good that if one has failed, its mate is weak also.

Rear Control Arms

REMOVAL & INSTALLATION

1989 and later Metro/Sprint
See Figures 28 and 29

1. Raise and support the vehicle safely.

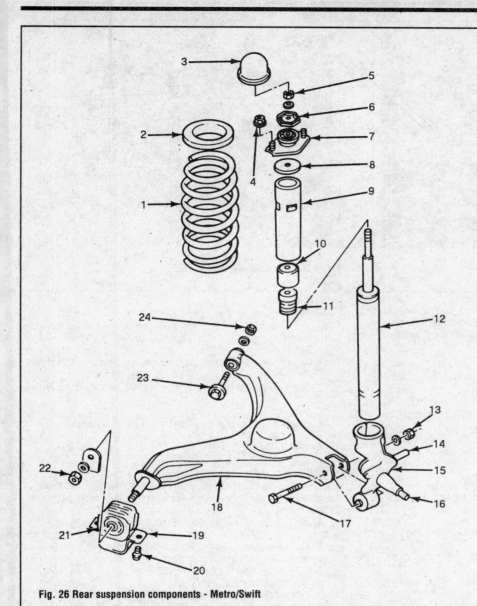

1. Coil spring
2. Coil spring upper seat
3. Strut upper cap
4. Strut upper support nut
5. Strut top nut
6. Strut upper seat
7. Strut upper support
8. Strut lower seat
9. Strut dust cover
10. Bumper stopper cap
11. Bumper stopper
12. Strut (shock absorber)
13. Suspension arm-to-knuckle nut
14. Suspension knuckle control rod stud
15. Suspension knuckle
16. Wheel spindle
17. Suspension arm-to-knuckle bolt
18. Suspension arm
19. Suspension arm front bracket
20. Bracket bolt
21. Suspension arm front bushing
22. Front bushing nut
23. Suspension arm rear mounting bolt
24. Suspension arm rear mounting nut

Fig. 26 Rear suspension components - Metro/Swift

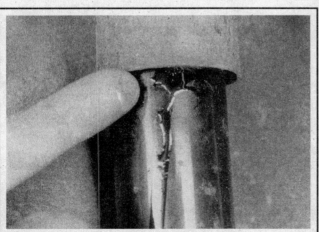

Fig. 27 When fluid is seeping out of the shock absorber, it's time to replace it

Fig. 28 Rear control arm front bushing

Fig. 29 Rear control arm rear bushing

Fig. 30 Lateral rod attaching point

Note: To facilitate the toe-in adjustment after reinstallation, confirm which one of the lines stamped on the washer is in the closest alignment with the stamped line on the control rod. If not marked, add the alignment marks.

2. Remove the brake hose from the control rod by pulling off the E-ring.

3. Remove the outside (wheel side) of the control rod from the rear knuckle stud bolt.

4. Remove the rear spring.

5. Remove the outermost control arm mounting bolts. Remove the washer and bushing as required.

6. Remove the inner control arm mounting bolt and nut. Hold the inside bolt with another wrench to prevent it from turning as the nut is turned.

7. Remove the control arm from the vehicle.

To install:

8. Install the control arm onto the vehicle. Install the bushing assembly and mounting bolts to the outer portion of the arm.

9. Install the inner mounting bolt and nut. Hold the inside bolt with another wrench to prevent it from turning as the nut is turned. Tighten mounting bolt to 59 ft. lbs. (80 Nm).

10. Install the lower knuckle to arm mounting bolt and nut, tightening to specifications.

11. Install the outside (wheel side) of the control rod to the rear knuckle stud bolt. Tighten bolt to 59 ft. lbs. (80 Nm).

12. Install the brake hose and secure with the E-ring.

13. Lower the vehicle. Check and adjust the rear alignment.

Rear Axle Assembly

REMOVAL & INSTALLATION

1985 - 86 Sprint

1. Raise and support the vehicle safely.

2. Remove the rear wheels and brake drums.

3. Remove the brake line at the flex hose. Remove the flex hose and brake line retainers.

4. Remove the brake hose pipe from bracket on the axle assembly.

5. Plug the brake flex hose to prevent loss of brake fluid and system contamination due to moisture.

6. Remove brake backing plate nuts, then remove backing plate.

7. If necessary, disconnect the parking brake cables and reposition out of the way.

8. Remove U-bolt nuts, U-bolts and jounce stop.

9. Remove the rear axle assembly from the vehicle.

To install:

10. Place axle on leaf spring by aligning pin on the top of the leaf spring with hole in underside of axle. Then fit pin on underside of leaf spring in hole of spring seat and tighten U-bolt nut to 22 - 32 ft. lbs. (30 - 45 Nm).

11. Apply watertight sealant to joint seam of axle and brake backing plate and tighten brake backing plate nuts to 13 - 20 ft. lbs. (18 - 28 Nm).

12. Install flex hose in bracket and secure with retainer. Install brake line at flex hose.

13. Install the brake drum and wheel.

14. Bleed the brake system and adjust the rear brakes as necessary.

1987 - 88 Sprint

1. Raise and support the vehicle safely.

2. Remove the wheel and brake drum.

3. Remove the brake hose attaching clip at the trailing arm bracket. Disconnect the brake pipe from the wheel cylinder and remove the brake hose/pipe from the trailing arm.

4. Remove the rear brakes and disconnect the parking brake from the brake shoe.

5. Remove the parking brake cable from the backing plate.

6. Remove the backing plate from the rear axle.

7. Support the center of the rear axle with a floor jack.

8. Remove the lateral rod body side bolt.

9. Remove the shock absorber lower mounting nut.

10. Lower the rear axle gradually until tension of suspension spring is relieved, then remove spring.

11. Remove trailing arm front bolts and remove rear axle from vehicle.

To install:

12. Raise the rear axle into the vehicle and loosely install the trailing arm front bolts.

13. Install coil spring on rear axle spring seat with flat face upward. Seat lower spring end with stepped part of rear axle seat.

14. Raise floor jack slightly and install shock absorber lower mounting bolt. Tighten to 32 - 50 ft. lbs. (45 - 70 Nm).

15. Install lateral rod and tighten nut to 32 - 50 ft. lbs. (45 - 70 Nm).

16. Tighten trailing arm nut to 50 - 65 ft. lbs. (70 - 90 Nm).

17. Apply watertight sealant to joint seam of axle and brake backing plate. Install backing plate and tighten bolts to 13 - 20 ft. lbs. (18 - 28 Nm).

18. Put brake hose/pipe through hole in bracket on trailing arm and install pipe flare nut to wheel cylinder. Tighten to 10 - 13 ft. lbs. (14 - 18 Nm).

19. Secure brake pipe/hose to bracket with E-clip.

20. Apply water tight sealant to parking brake cable and install on backing plate. Attach cable end to brake shoe.

21. Install rear brake shoes and brake drum. Install the wheel assembly.

22. Bleed brake system and adjust rear brakes.

23. Lower the vehicle.

Lateral Rod

REMOVAL & INSTALLATION

See Figure 30

1. Raise and support the vehicle safely. Support the rear axle with a floor jack.
2. Remove the lateral rod attaching bolts, then remove the lateral rod.
3. Installation is the reverse of removal. Tighten lateral rod bolts to 32 - 50 ft. lbs. (45 - 70 Nm)

Rear Spindle/Knuckle Assembly

REMOVAL & INSTALLATION

1985 - 88 Sprint

The 1985 - 88 Sprint uses a solid rear axle assembly. The rear spindle assembly is an integral part of the rear axle assembly. If the spindle is damaged, the rear axle assembly must be replace. The rear bearing and seal are located inside of the hub of the brake drum, which is then mounted to the spindle. Refer to Rear Axle removal and installation procedure in this Section for more information.

1989 and later Metro/Swift

The Metro uses an independent rear suspension. The rear wheels are mounted on knuckles much like the front wheels.

1. Raise and safely support the vehicle.
2. Remove the tire and wheel assemblies, then the brake line, retaining clip and flexible hose from the center of the rear axle.
3. Remove the tension spring from the rear axle, disconnect the parking brake cable from the turn buckle and the cable joint.
4. Remove the brake backing plate from the knuckle after removing the 4 plate retaining bolts.
5. Using a suitable jack, support under the lower suspension arm to prevent it from lowering.

Note: As a preparatory step for this removal, check the stamped line on the washer to use for a guide in the reinstallation.

6. Remove the lower strut mounting bolt.
7. Remove the lower knuckle mounting bolt.
8. Remove the knuckle (spindle) from the suspension arm and from the strut.

Note: If it is hard to remove the knuckle from the strut, open the slit in the knuckle by inserting a wedge. Do not open the slit wider than necessary.

To install:

9. Install the knuckle assembly onto the lower end of the strut. Align the projection on the strut against the slit of the knuckle and push the strut into the knuckle until it is properly positioned.
10. Install the lower strut retaining bolt and tighten to a torque of 44 ft. lbs. (60 Nm).
11. Install the lower mount end of the knuckle to suspension arm. Torque the nut to 44 ft. lbs. (60 Nm).
12. Remove the jack from under the suspension arm.
13. Torque the knuckle lower mount nut to 37 ft. lbs. (50 Nm).
14. Install the backing plate and secure with the retaining bolts. Torque the retaining bolts to 17 ft. lbs. (23 Nm).
15. Install the brake hose bracket to the knuckle. Install the brake line to the wheel cylinder and tighten the line to 12 ft. lbs. (16 Nm).
16. Install the breather plug cap to the breather plug. Install the brake drum assembly.
17. Install the control rod and control rod nuts. Torque the nuts to 59 ft. lbs. (80 Nm).
18. Confirm that all removed components are installed and securely in place.
19. Adjust the rear brakes and bleed the system.

Rear Wheel Bearings

REMOVAL & INSTALLATION

1. Raise and support the vehicle safely.
2. Remove the wheel assembly.
3. Remove the dust cap, the cotter pin, the castle nut and the washer.
4. Loosen the adjusting nuts of the parking brake cable.
5. Remove the plug from the rear of the backing plate. Insert a suitable tool through the hole, making contact with the shoe hold-down spring, then push the spring to release the parking brake shoe lever.
6. Using a slide hammer tool and a brake drum remover tool, pull the brake drum from the halfshaft.
7. Using a brass drift and a hammer, drive the rear wheel bearings from the brake drum.

Note: When installing the wheel bearings, face the sealed sides (numbered sides) outward. Fill the wheel bearing cavity with bearing grease.

8. Drive the new bearings into the brake drum with the bearing installation tool.
9. To install, use a new seal and reverse the removal procedures. Torque the hub castle nut to 41 ft. lbs. (55 Nm). Bleed the brake system. Operate the brakes 3 - 5 times to obtain the proper drum-to-shoe clearance. Adjust the parking brake cable.

STEERING

Steering Wheel

✳ CAUTION:

On vehicles equipped with an air bag, the air bag system must be disarmed before working around the steering wheel or instrument panel. Failure to do so may result in deployment of the air bag and possible personal injury. Refer to the Air Bag Disarming procedures later in this Section.

REMOVAL & INSTALLATION

See Figures 31 and 32

1. If equipped, with an air bag system, disable the air bag system as follows:
   a. Turn the ignition switch to the **OFF** position.
   b. Remove the **SIR IG** fuse in the supplemental inflatable restraint fuse block.
   c. Remove the rear plastic access cover to the air bag module.

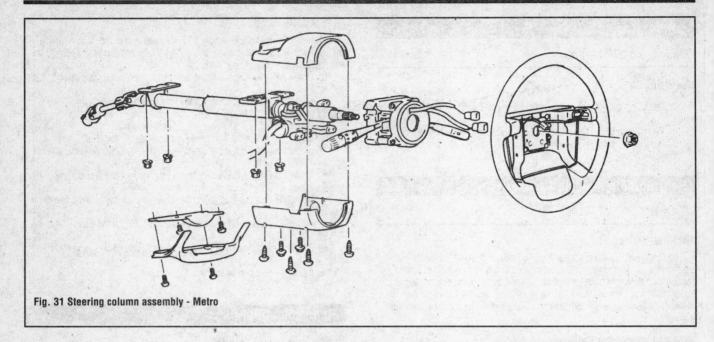

Fig. 31 Steering column assembly - Metro

d. Disconnect the yellow 2-way connector and connector position assurance (CPA) inside the inflator module housing.

2. Disconnect the negative battery cable.

3. Remove the air bag module attaching screws, then the air bag assembly from the vehicle.

⁂ CAUTION:

When carrying a live air bag module, make sure that the bag and trim cover are pointed away from you. Never carry the air bag module by the wires or the connector on the underside of the air bag module. In case of an accidental deployment, the bag will then deploy with minimal chance of injury. When placing a live air bag module on a bench or other surface, always face the bag and trim cover in the up position, away from the surface. Never rest a steering column assembly on the steering wheel with the air bag module face down and the column vertical. This is necessary so that a free space is provided to allow the air bag to expand in the unlikely event of accidental deployment. Otherwise, personal injury could result.

Note: The air bag system coil assembly is easily damaged if the correct steering wheel puller tools are not used.

4. Remove the steering wheel attaching nut, then using a suitable puller, remove the steering wheel.

5. Disconnect the electrical connectors from the steering wheel, then the rear steering wheel cover.

To install:

6. Reverse procedure to install. Torque steering nut to 25 ft. lbs. (34 Nm) and the air bag module attaching screws to 44 inch lbs. (5 Nm).

7. Reactivate the air bag system as follows:

a. Turn the ignition switch to the OFF position.

b. Connect the yellow 2-way connector and connector position assurance (CPA) inside the inflator module housing.

c. Install the SIR IG fuse in the supplemental inflatable restraint fuse block.

d. Install the rear plastic access cover to the air bag module.

e. Turn the ignition switch to the RUN position. Observe the INFLATABLE RESTRAINT indicator lamp. If the lamp does not flash 7 to 9 times and then remain off, there is a problem in the air bag system and further diagnostic testing of the system is needed.

Combination Switch

REMOVAL & INSTALLATION

See Figures 31 and 32

1. On vehicles equipped with an air bag, the air bag system must be disarmed before working around the steering wheel or instrument panel.

2. Remove the steering wheel.

3. Remove the lower steering column trim cover.

4. Loosen the steering column mounting nuts and lower column slightly.

5. Remove upper and lower steering column covers.

6. Disconnect combination switch electrical connector.

7. Remove switch from column.

To install:

8. Install switch to column.

9. Connect combination switch electrical connector.

10. Install upper and lower steering column covers.

11. Tighten the steering column mounting nuts to 10 ft. lbs. (14 Nm).

12. Install the lower steering column trim cover.

13. Install the steering wheel.

Ignition Switch

REMOVAL & INSTALLATION

1. Remove the steering column from the vehicle and mount in a table vise.

2. Remove ignition switch mounting bolts. Using a hammer and chisel, create slots on the top of the mounting bolts, then remove the bolts with a screwdriver.

3. Turn key in ignition switch to **ON** and remove switch from steering column.

To install:

4. Position the oblong hole in the steering shaft so that it is visible thorough, and in the center of the hole in the steering column.

5. Install ignition switch to column with the ignition key still in the **ON** position.

6. Turn the key to the **LOCK** position and remove the key from the ignition switch.

7. Align the ignition switch hub with the oblong hole in the steering shaft.

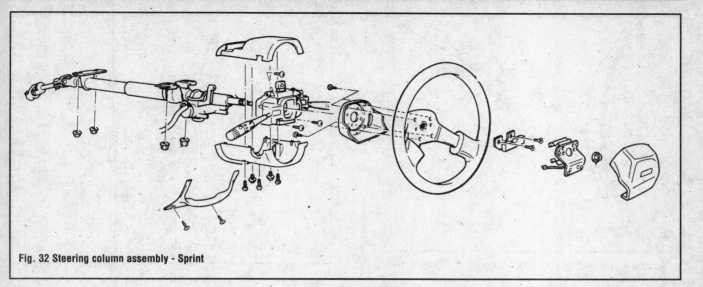

Fig. 32 Steering column assembly - Sprint

Rotate the shaft to ensure that the steering shaft is locked.

8. Install new break-away head bolts to ignition switch and tighten until break-away heads break off.

9. Turn ignition key to **ON** position and check that the shaft rotates smoothly. Remove the column from vise.

10. Install steering column in vehicle.

Steering Column

REMOVAL & INSTALLATION

See Figures 31 and 32

Note: The steering column is very susceptible to damage once it has been removed from the vehicle. The vehicle's wheels must be in a straight ahead position and the key must be in the LOCK position when removing or installing the steering column. Failure to do so may cause the air bag coil assembly to become off centered and may result in unneeded air bag system damage. In the event air bag deployment has occurred, replace the coil assembly. The steering column should never be supported by only the lower support bracket, damage to the column lower bearing adapter could result.

1. If equipped with an air bag system, disable the air bag system as follows:

a. Turn the ignition switch to the **OFF p**osition.

b. Remove the SIR IG fuse in the supplemental inflatable restraint fuse block.

c. Remove the rear plastic access cover to the air bag module.

d. Disconnect the yellow 2-way connector and connector position assurance (CPA) inside the inflator module housing.

2. Disconnect the negative battery cable.

3. Remove the air bag module attaching screws, then the air bag assembly from the vehicle.

❊❊ CAUTION:

When carrying a live air bag module, make sure that the bag and trim cover are pointed away from you. Never carry the air bag module by the wires or the connector on the underside of the air bag module. In case of an accidental deployment, the bag will then deploy with minimal chance of injury. When placing a live air bag module on a bench or other surface, always face the bag and trim cover in the up position, away from the surface. Never rest a steering column assembly on the steering wheel with the air bag module face down and the column vertical. This is necessary so that a free

space is provided to allow the air bag to expand in the unlikely event of accidental deployment. Otherwise, personal injury could result.

Note: The air bag system coil assembly is easily damaged if the correct steering wheel puller tools are not used.

4. Remove the steering wheel attaching nut, then using a suitable puller, remove the steering wheel.

5. Disconnect the electrical connectors from the steering wheel, then the rear steering wheel cover.

6. Remove the steering shaft trim panel. Remove the lower steering column trim panel and the steering column reinforcement plate.

7. Disconnect the steering column electrical connectors. Remove the brake transaxle shift interlock cable from the ignition switch.

8. Remove the steering column to steering shaft joint pinch bolt. Remove the upper and lower steering column mounting nuts and remove the steering column from the vehicle.

To install:

9. Installation is the reverse order of the removal procedure. Torque the steering column upper and lower mounting nuts to 10 ft. lbs. (14 Nm). Torque the steering column to steering shaft joint pinch bolt to 18 ft. lbs. (25 Nm).

10. Reactivate the air bag system as follows:

a. Turn the ignition switch to the **OFF** position.

b. Connect the yellow 2-way connector and connector position assurance (CPA) inside the inflator module housing.

c. Install the SIR IG fuse in the supplemental inflatable restraint fuse block.

d. Install the rear plastic access cover to the air bag module.

e. Turn the ignition switch to the **RUN** position. Observe the INFLATABLE RESTRAINT indicator lamp. If the lamp does not flash 7 to 8 times and then remain off, there is a problem in the air bag system and further diagnostic testing of the system is needed.

Steering Linkage

REMOVAL & INSTALLATION

Tie Rod End

See Figure 33

1. Raise and support the vehicle safely.

2. Remove the front wheel.

3. Remove the cotter pin and castle nut from the ball joint.

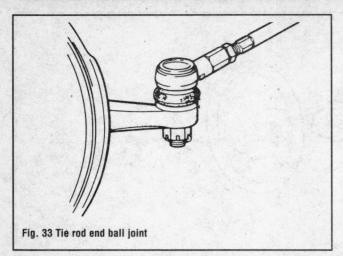

Fig. 33 Tie rod end ball joint

4. Remove the tie rod end from the knuckle using a ball joint separator.
5. Loosen the locknut on the threaded end of the tie rod.
6. Unscrew the tie rod end from the tie rod. Note the number of turns necessary for removal.

To install:

7. Screw the new tie rod end onto the tie rod the exact number of turns necessary to remove the old tie rod end. This will allow the alignment to be close enough to drive the vehicle to the alignment shop.
8. Tighten the locknut to 32 ft. lbs. (43 Nm).
9. Install the castle nut and tighten to 32 ft. lbs. (43 Nm). Install the cotter pin.
10. Install the front wheel.
11. Lower the vehicle.
12. Check and adjust the front wheel alignment.

Manual Rack and Pinion

REMOVAL & INSTALLATION

See Figures 34 and 35

1. Slide the driver's seat back as far as possible.
2. Pull off the front part of the floor mat on the driver's side and remove the steering shaft joint cover.
3. Loosen the steering shaft upper joint bolt, but do not remove.
4. Remove the steering shaft lower joint bolt and disconnect the lower joint from the pinion.
5. Raise and support the vehicle safely.
6. Remove the tie rod ends from the steering knuckles. Mark the left and right tie rods accordingly.
7. From under the dash, remove the steering joint cover.
8. Remove the lower steering shaft-to-steering gear clinch bolt and separate the steering shaft from the steering gear.
9. Remove the steering gear mounting bolts, the brackets and the steering gear case from the vehicle.

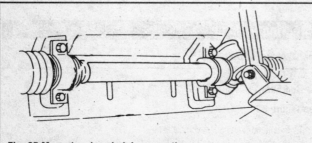

Fig. 35 Manual rack and pinion mounting

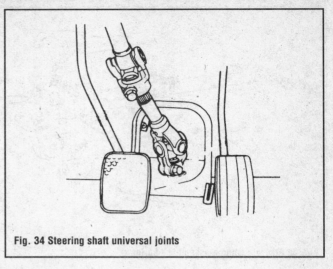

Fig. 34 Steering shaft universal joints

To install:

10. Install the steering gear, brackets and mounting bolts. Tighten bolts to 18 ft. lbs. (25 Nm).
11. Connect the steering shaft to the steering gear. Install the lower steering shaft-to-steering gear clinch bolt and tighten to 18 ft. lbs. (25 Nm).
12. Install the steering joint cover.
13. Install the tie rod ends to the steering knuckles. Tighten tie rod end-to-steering knuckle nut to 32 ft. lbs. (43 Nm).
14. Lower the vehicle.
15. Connect the lower joint to the pinion. Install the steering shaft lower joint bolt and tighten to 18 ft. lbs. (25 Nm).
16. Tighten the steering shaft upper joint bolt to 18 ft. lbs. (25 Nm).
17. Install the steering shaft joint cover.
18. Have the alignment checked by a professional shop.

Power Rack and Pinion

REMOVAL & INSTALLATION

1. Slide the driver's seat back as far as possible.
2. Pull off the front part of the floor mat on the driver's side and remove the steering shaft joint cover.
3. Loosen the steering shaft upper joint bolt, but do not remove.
4. Remove the steering shaft lower joint bolt and disconnect the lower joint from the pinion.
5. Raise and support the vehicle safely.
6. Remove the tie rod ends from the steering knuckles. Mark the left and right tie rods accordingly.
7. From under the dash, remove the steering joint cover.
8. Remove the lower steering shaft-to-steering gear clinch bolt and separate the steering shaft from the steering gear.
9. Disconnect the front exhaust pipe.
10. If equipped with manual transaxle, remove the shift linkage and the extension rod from the trans.
11. If equipped with automatic transaxle, remove the rear torque rod with bracket from the trans.
12. Disconnect the power steering lines from the rack. Be sure to plug the lines to prevent contamination.
13. Remove the steering gear mounting bolts.
14. Remove the rack from the vehicle.
    a. Move the rack to the driver's side and rotate the rack counterclockwise so that the pinion is positioned between the transaxle case and the frame rail.
    b. Now move the rack to the passenger's side until the outer tie rod is clear of the frame opening.
    c. Begin to lower the steering gear on a 45 degree angle and remove the rack from the vehicle.

To install:

15. Install the rack into the vehicle.

 a.   Position the rack so that the pinion shaft is facing downward and the rack assembly is at a 45 degree angle to the vehicle.

 b.   Slide the rack through the tie rod frame end opening on the passenger side of the vehicle.

 c.   Push the rack upward so that it is parallel to the vehicle and move the rack so the driver's side tie rod end goes through it's opening.

 d.   Begin to rotate the rack clockwise until it hit the transaxle case and then move the rack slightly to the driver's side until it can be rotated into position.

 e.   Align the pinion shaft through the floor opening.

16. Secure the rack to the vehicle. Torque the bolts to 18 ft. lbs. (25 Nm).

17. Connect the power steering lines to the rack. Be sure that all the plugs are removed first.

18. If equipped with a manual transaxle, install the shift linkage and the extension rod.

19. If equipped with an automatic transaxle, install the rear torque rod.

20. Install the front exhaust pipe.

21. Install the left and right tie rods to the steering knuckles. Torque the castlenuts to 32 ft. lbs. (43 Nm) and install the cotter pins.

22. Install the wheels and lower the vehicle.

23. Reconnect the pinion shaft to the joint and install the lower bolt and torque to 18 ft.lbs. (25 Nm).

24. Clip the cover back together by hand.

25. Place the driver's side carpet back into position.

26. Check the power steering fluid reservoir and fill as needed.

27 Bleed the system. Please refer to Suspension and Steering, Power Steering Pump, for more information.

28. Have the alignment checked by a professional shop.

Power Steering Pump

REMOVAL & INSTALLATION

1.   Remove the retaining bolt from the high pressure line and remove the line from the pump.

2.   Remove the high pressure hose from the high pressure line.

3.   Disconnect the return hose from the reservoir.

4.   Disconnect the power steering pressure switch electrical connector.

5.   Raise and support the vehicle.

6.   Remove the drive belt.

7.   Remove the A/C compressor and hang it off to the side if equipped.

8.   Remove the power steering pump A/C mounting bracket from the engine.

9.   Remove the power steering hose and bracket with the pump from the vehicle.

10. Remove the pump from the mounting bracket.

11. Remove the high pressure line from the pump.

12. Remove the return hose from the pump.

To install:

13. Install the return hose and the high pressure line to the pump.

14. Bolt the pump to the mounting bracket.

15. Install the assembly to the engine and torque to 64 ft. lbs. to 69 ft. lbs. (47 Nm to 51 Nm).

16. Install the A/C compressor to the mounting bracket and torque to 17 ft. lbs. to 20 ft. lbs. (23 Nm to 27 Nm).

17. Install the drive belt.

18. Lower the vehicle.

19. Reconnect the electrical connector to the power steering pressure switch.

20. Reconnect the return hose to the reservoir.

21. Reconnect the high pressure line. Torque components to : high pressure hose retaining bracket bolt to 89 inch lbs. (10 Nm). High pressure hose to high pressure pipe flare nut to 30 ft. lbs. (40 Nm).

22. Fill the power steering reservoir with new power steering fluid.

23. Bleed the system.

BLEEDING

1. Raise and support the vehicle.

2. Turn the wheels to the full left position and shut off the engine.

3. Fill the reservoir to the "MIN" mark.

4. Start the engine and allow to idle for 15 seconds.

5. Turn off the engine and recheck fluid level and if necessary bring back up to "MIN" mark.

6. Start the engine and turn the wheel lock to lock 3 or 4 times to bleed the system.

7. Turn engine off and check fluid. If there is a tan color present, there is still air in the system. Also look for the presence of visible bubbles. If either of these conditions are present the system must be bled further so that the power steering will operate properly. Repeat as necessary.

8. Lower the vehicle.

TORQUE SPECIFICATIONS

Components	Standard	Metric
Air Bag Module	44 inch lbs.	5 Nm
Axle Shaft Castle Nut (Front)	129 ft.lbs.	175 Nm
Control Arm:		
Rear Mount	32 ft. lbs.	43 Nm
Front Mount	66 ft. lbs.	90 Nm
Ball Joint	44 ft. lbs.	60 Nm
Control Rod	59 ft. lbs.	80 Nm
Damper Rod Locknut	29 ft. lbs	40 Nm
Hub Retaining Nut	37 ft. lbs.	50 Nm
Lateral Rod	32-50 ft. lbs.	45-70 Nm
Lower Knuckle	37 ft. lbs.	50 Nm
Lower Shock Mount	32-50 ft. lbs.	45-70 Nm
Lug Nuts	44 ft. lbs.	60 Nm
Shock Upper Support	24 ft. lbs.	30 Nm
Shock-to-Knuckle	44 ft. lbs.	60 Nm
Stabilizer Castle Nut	22-39 ft. lbs.	30-55 Nm
Stabilizer Mount	29-65 ft. lbs.	40-90 Nm
Steering Column	10 ft. lbs.	14 Nm
Steering Gear	18 ft. lbs.	25 Nm
Steering Pinch Bolts	18 ft. lbs.	25 Nm
Steering Wheel Nut	25 ft. lbs.	34 Nm
Strut to Knuckle	59 ft. lbs.	80 Nm
Suspension Arm		
Front	44 ft. lbs.	60 Nm
Rear	37 ft.lbs.	50 Nm
Tie Rod End	32 ft. lbs.	43 Nm
Upper Shock Mount	13-20 ft. lbs.	18-28 Nm
Upper Strut Support	20 ft. lbs.	27 Nm
Wheel Cylinder	12 ft. lbs.	16 Nm

895808G02

Notes

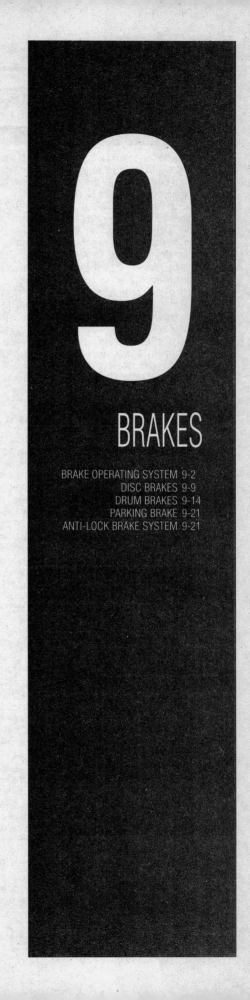

9

BRAKES

BRAKE OPERATING SYSTEM

Basic Operating Principles

Hydraulic systems are used to actuate the brakes of all modern automobiles. The system transports the power required to force the frictional surfaces of the braking system together from the pedal to the individual brake units at each wheel. A hydraulic system is used for two reasons.

First, fluid under pressure can be carried to all parts of an automobile by small pipes and flexible hoses without taking up a significant amount of room or posing routing problems.

Second, a great mechanical advantage can be given to the brake pedal end of the system, and the foot pressure required to actuate the brakes can be reduced by making the surface area of the master cylinder pistons smaller than that of any of the pistons in the wheel cylinders or calipers.

The master cylinder consists of a fluid reservoir along with a double cylinder and piston assembly. Double type master cylinders are designed to separate the front and rear braking systems hydraulically in case of a leak. The master cylinder converts mechanical motion from the pedal into hydraulic pressure within the lines. This pressure is translated back into mechanical motion at the wheels by either the wheel cylinder (drum brakes) or the caliper (disc brakes).

Steel lines carry the brake fluid to a point on the vehicle's frame near each of the vehicle's wheels. The fluid is then carried to the calipers and wheel cylinders by flexible tubes in order to allow for suspension and steering movements.

In drum brake systems, each wheel cylinder contains two pistons, one at either end, which push outward in opposite directions and force the brake shoe into contact with the drum.

In disc brake systems, the cylinders are part of the calipers. At least one cylinder in each caliper is used to force the brake pads against the disc.

All pistons employ some type of seal, usually made of rubber, to minimize fluid leakage. A rubber dust boot seals the outer end of the cylinder against dust and dirt. The boot fits around the outer end of the piston on disc brake calipers, and around the brake actuating rod on wheel cylinders.

The hydraulic system operates as follows: When at rest, the entire system, from the piston(s) in the master cylinder to those in the wheel cylinders or calipers, is full of brake fluid. Upon application of the brake pedal, fluid trapped in front of the master cylinder piston(s) is forced through the lines to the wheel cylinders. Here, it forces the pistons outward, in the case of drum brakes, and inward toward the disc, in the case of disc brakes. The motion of the pistons is opposed by return springs mounted outside the cylinders in drum brakes, and by spring seals, in disc brakes.

Upon release of the brake pedal, a spring located inside the master cylinder immediately returns the master cylinder pistons to the normal position. The pistons contain check valves and the master cylinder has compensating ports drilled in it. These are uncovered as the pistons reach their normal position. The piston check valves allow fluid to flow toward the wheel cylinders or calipers as the pistons withdraw. Then, as the brake pads or shoes return to the released position, the excess fluid flows into the reservoir through the compensating ports. It is during the time the pedal is in the released position that any fluid that has leaked out of the system will be replaced through the compensating ports.

Dual circuit master cylinders employ two pistons, located one behind the other, in the same cylinder. The primary piston is actuated directly by mechanical linkage from the brake pedal through the power booster. The secondary piston is actuated by fluid trapped between the two pistons. If a leak develops in front of the secondary piston, it moves forward until it bottoms against the front of the master cylinder, and the fluid trapped between the pistons will operate the rear brakes. If the rear brakes develop a leak, the primary piston will move forward until direct contact with the secondary piston takes place, and it will force the secondary piston to actuate the front brakes. In either case, the brake pedal moves farther when the brakes are applied, and less braking power is available.

All dual circuit systems use a switch to warn the driver when only half of the brake system is operational. This switch is usually located in a valve body which is mounted on the firewall or the frame below the master cylinder. A hydraulic piston receives pressure from both circuits, each circuit's pressure being applied to one end of the piston. When the pressures are in balance, the piston remains stationary. When one circuit has a leak, however, the greater pressure in that circuit during application of the brakes will push the piston to one side, closing the switch and activating the brake warning light.

In disc brake systems, this valve body also contains a metering valve and, in some cases, a proportioning valve. The metering valve keeps pressure from traveling to the disc brakes on the front wheels until the brake shoes on the rear wheels have contacted the drums, ensuring that the front brakes will never be used alone. The proportioning valve controls the pressure to the rear brakes to lessen the chance of rear wheel lock-up during very hard braking.

Warning lights may be tested by depressing the brake pedal and holding it while opening one of the wheel cylinder bleeder screws. If this does not cause the light to go on, substitute a new lamp, make continuity checks, and, finally, replace the switch as necessary.

The hydraulic system may be checked for leaks by applying pressure to the pedal gradually and steadily. If the pedal sinks very slowly to the floor, the system has a leak. This is not to be confused with a springy or spongy feel due to the compression of air within the lines. If the system leaks, there will be a gradual change in the position of the pedal with a constant pressure.

Check for leaks along all lines and at wheel cylinders. If no external leaks are apparent, the problem is inside the master cylinder.

DISC BRAKES

Instead of the traditional expanding brakes that press outward against a circular drum, disc brake systems utilize a disc (rotor) with brake pads positioned on either side of it. An easily-seen analogy is the hand brake arrangement on a bicycle. The pads squeeze onto the rim of the bike wheel, slowing its motion. Automobile disc brakes use the identical principle but apply the braking effort to a separate disc instead of the wheel.

The disc (rotor) is a casting, usually equipped with cooling fins between the two braking surfaces. This enables air to circulate between the braking surfaces making them less sensitive to heat buildup and more resistant to fade. Dirt and water do not drastically affect braking action since contaminants are thrown off by the centrifugal action of the rotor or scraped off the by the pads. Also, the equal clamping action of the two brake pads tends to ensure uniform, straight line stops. Disc brakes are inherently self-adjusting. There are three general types of disc brake:

- A fixed caliper.
- A floating caliper.
- A sliding caliper.

The fixed caliper design uses two pistons mounted on either side of the rotor (in each side of the caliper). The caliper is mounted rigidly and does not move. The sliding and floating designs are quite similar. In fact, these two types are often lumped together. In both designs, the pad on the inside of the rotor is moved into contact with the rotor by hydraulic force. The caliper, which is not held in a fixed position, moves slightly, bringing the outside pad into contact with the rotor. There are various methods of attaching floating calipers. Some pivot at the bottom or top, and some slide on mounting bolts. In any event, the end result is the same.

DRUM BRAKES

Drum brakes employ two brake shoes mounted on a stationary backing plate. These shoes are positioned inside a circular drum which rotates with the wheel assembly. The shoes are held in place by springs. This allows them to slide toward the drums (when they are applied) while keeping the linings and drums in alignment. The shoes are actuated by a wheel cylinder which is mounted at the top of the backing plate. When the brakes are applied, hydraulic pressure forces the wheel cylinder's actuating links outward. Since these links bear directly against the top of the brake shoes, the tops of the shoes are then forced against the inner side of the drum. This action forces the bottoms of the two shoes to contact the brake drum by rotating the entire assembly slightly (known as servo action). When pressure within the wheel cylinder is relaxed, return springs pull the shoes back away from the drum.

Most modern drum brakes are designed to self-adjust themselves during application when the vehicle is moving in reverse. This motion causes both shoes to rotate very slightly with the drum, rocking an adjusting lever, thereby causing rotation of the adjusting screw. Some drum brake systems are designed to self-adjust during application whenever the brakes are applied. This on-board adjustment system reduces the need for maintenance adjustments and keeps both the brake function and pedal feel satisfactory.

Troubleshooting the Brake System

Problem	Cause	Solution
Low brake pedal (excessive pedal travel required for braking action.)	• Excessive clearance between rear linings and drums caused by inoperative automatic adjusters	• Make 10 to 15 alternate forward and reverse brake stops to adjust brakes. If brake pedal does not come up, repair or replace adjuster parts as necessary.
	• Worn rear brakelining	• Inspect and replace lining if worn beyond minimum thickness specification
	• Bent, distorted brakeshoes, front or rear	• Replace brakeshoes in axle sets
	• Air in hydraulic system	• Remove air from system. Refer to Brake Bleeding.
Low brake pedal (pedal may go to floor with steady pressure applied.)	• Fluid leak in hydraulic system	• Fill master cylinder to fill line; have helper apply brakes and check calipers, wheel cylinders, differential valve tubes, hoses and fittings for leaks. Repair or replace as necessary.
	• Air in hydraulic system	• Remove air from system. Refer to Brake Bleeding.
	• Incorrect or non-recommended brake fluid (fluid evaporates at below normal temp).	• Flush hydraulic system with clean brake fluid. Refill with correct-type fluid.
	• Master cylinder piston seals worn, or master cylinder bore is scored, worn or corroded	• Repair or replace master cylinder
Low brake pedal (pedal goes to floor on first application—o.k. on subsequent applications.)	• Disc brake pads sticking on abutment surfaces of anchor plate. Caused by a build-up of dirt, rust, or corrosion on abutment surfaces	• Clean abutment surfaces
Fading brake pedal (pedal height decreases with steady pressure applied.)	• Fluid leak in hydraulic system	• Fill master cylinder reservoirs to fill mark, have helper apply brakes, check calipers, wheel cylinders, differential valve, tubes, hoses, and fittings for fluid leaks. Repair or replace parts as necessary.
	• Master cylinder piston seals worn, or master cylinder bore is scored, worn or corroded	• Repair or replace master cylinder
Decreasing brake pedal travel (pedal travel required for braking action decreases and may be accompanied by a hard pedal.)	• Caliper or wheel cylinder pistons sticking or seized	• Repair or replace the calipers, or wheel cylinders
	• Master cylinder compensator ports blocked (preventing fluid return to reservoirs) or pistons sticking or seized in master cylinder bore	• Repair or replace the master cylinder
	• Power brake unit binding internally	• Test unit according to the following procedure: (a) Shift transmission into neutral and start engine (b) Increase engine speed to 1500 rpm, close throttle and fully depress brake pedal (c) Slow release brake pedal and stop engine (d) Have helper remove vacuum check valve and hose from power unit. Observe for backward movement of brake pedal. (e) If the pedal moves backward, the power unit has an internal bind—replace power unit

Troubleshooting the Brake System (cont.)

Problem	Cause	Solution
Spongy brake pedal (pedal has abnormally soft, springy, spongy feel when depressed.)	• Air in hydraulic system • Brakeshoes bent or distorted • Brakelining not yet seated with drums and rotors • Rear drum brakes not properly adjusted	• Remove air from system. Refer to Brake Bleeding. • Replace brakeshoes • Burnish brakes • Adjust brakes
Hard brake pedal (excessive pedal pressure required to stop vehicle. May be accompanied by brake fade.)	• Loose or leaking power brake unit vacuum hose • Incorrect or poor quality brakelining • Bent, broken, distorted brakeshoes • Calipers binding or dragging on mounting pins. Rear brakeshoes dragging on support plate. • Caliper, wheel cylinder, or master cylinder pistons sticking or seized • Power brake unit vacuum check valve malfunction • Power brake unit has internal bind • Master cylinder compensator ports (at bottom of reservoirs) blocked by dirt, scale, rust, or have small burrs (blocked ports prevent fluid return to reservoirs). • Brake hoses, tubes, fittings clogged or restricted • Brake fluid contaminated with improper fluids (motor oil, transmission fluid, causing rubber components to swell and stick in bores • Low engine vacuum	• Tighten connections or replace leaking hose • Replace with lining in axle sets • Replace brakeshoes • Replace mounting pins and bushings. Clean rust or burrs from rear brake support plate ledges and lubricate ledges with molydisulfide grease. **NOTE:** If ledges are deeply grooved or scored, do not attempt to sand or grind them smooth—replace support plate. • Repair or replace parts as necessary • Test valve according to the following procedure: (a) Start engine, increase engine speed to 1500 rpm, close throttle and immediately stop engine (b) Wait at least 90 seconds then depress brake pedal (c) If brakes are not vacuum assisted for 2 or more applications, check valve is faulty • Test unit according to the following procedure: (a) With engine stopped, apply brakes several times to exhaust all vacuum in system (b) Shift transmission into neutral, depress brake pedal and start engine (c) If pedal height decreases with foot pressure and less pressure is required to hold pedal in applied position, power unit vacuum system is operating normally. Test power unit. If power unit exhibits a bind condition, replace the power unit. • Repair or replace master cylinder **CAUTION:** Do not attempt to clean blocked ports with wire, pencils, or similar implements. Use compressed air only. • Use compressed air to check or unclog parts. Replace any damaged parts. • Replace all rubber components, combination valve and hoses. Flush entire brake system with DOT 3 brake fluid or equivalent. • Adjust or repair engine

Troubleshooting the Brake System (cont.)

Problem	Cause	Solution
Grabbing brakes (severe reaction to brake pedal pressure.)	• Brakelining(s) contaminated by grease or brake fluid	• Determine and correct cause of contamination and replace brakeshoes in axle sets
	• Parking brake cables incorrectly adjusted or seized	• Adjust cables. Replace seized cables.
	• Incorrect brakelining or lining loose on brakeshoes	• Replace brakeshoes in axle sets
	• Caliper anchor plate bolts loose	• Tighten bolts
	• Rear brakeshoes binding on support plate ledges	• Clean and lubricate ledges. Replace support plate(s) if ledges are deeply grooved. Do not attempt to smooth ledges by grinding.
	• Incorrect or missing power brake reaction disc	• Install correct disc
	• Rear brake support plates loose	• Tighten mounting bolts
Dragging brakes (slow or incomplete release of brakes)	• Brake pedal binding at pivot	• Loosen and lubricate
	• Power brake unit has internal bind	• Inspect for internal bind. Replace unit if internal bind exists.
	• Parking brake cables incorrectly adjusted or seized	• Adjust cables. Replace seized cables.
	• Rear brakeshoe return springs weak or broken	• Replace return springs. Replace brakeshoe if necessary in axle sets.
	• Automatic adjusters malfunctioning	• Repair or replace adjuster parts as required
	• Caliper, wheel cylinder or master cylinder pistons sticking or seized	• Repair or replace parts as necessary
	• Master cylinder compensating ports blocked (fluid does not return to reservoirs).	• Use compressed air to clear ports. Do not use wire, pencils, or similar objects to open blocked ports.
Vehicle moves to one side when brakes are applied	• Incorrect front tire pressure	• Inflate to recommended cold (reduced load) inflation pressure
	• Worn or damaged wheel bearings	• Replace worn or damaged bearings
	• Brakelining on one side contaminated	• Determine and correct cause of contamination and replace brakelining in axle sets
	• Brakeshoes on one side bent, distorted, or lining loose on shoe	• Replace brakeshoes in axle sets
	• Support plate bent or loose on one side	• Tighten or replace support plate
	• Brakelining not yet seated with drums or rotors	• Burnish brakelining
	• Caliper anchor plate loose on one side	• Tighten anchor plate bolts
	• Caliper piston sticking or seized	• Repair or replace caliper
	• Brakelinings water soaked	• Drive vehicle with brakes lightly applied to dry linings
	• Loose suspension component attaching or mounting bolts	• Tighten suspension bolts. Replace worn suspension components.
	• Brake combination valve failure	• Replace combination valve
Chatter or shudder when brakes are applied (pedal pulsation and roughness may also occur.)	• Brakeshoes distorted, bent, contaminated, or worn	• Replace brakeshoes in axle sets
	• Caliper anchor plate or support plate loose	• Tighten mounting bolts
	• Excessive thickness variation of rotor(s)	• Refinish or replace rotors in axle sets

POWER BOOSTERS

Virtually all modern vehicles use a vacuum assisted power brake system to multiply the braking force and reduce pedal effort. Since vacuum is always available when the engine is operating, the system is simple and efficient. A vacuum diaphragm is located on the front of the master cylinder and assists the driver in applying the brakes, reducing both the effort and travel he must put into moving the brake pedal.

The vacuum diaphragm housing is normally connected to the intake manifold by a vacuum hose. A check valve is placed at the point where the hose enters the diaphragm housing, so that during periods of low manifold vacuum brakes assist will not be lost.

Depressing the brake pedal closes off the vacuum source and allows atmospheric pressure to enter on one side of the diaphragm. This causes the master cylinder pistons to move and apply the brakes. When the brake pedal is released, vacuum is applied to both sides of the diaphragm and springs return the diaphragm and master cylinder pistons to the released position.

If the vacuum supply fails, the brake pedal rod will contact the end of the master cylinder actuator rod and the system will apply the brakes without any power assistance. The driver will notice that much higher pedal effort is needed to stop the car and that the pedal feels harder than usual.

Vacuum Leak Test

1. Operate the engine at idle without touching the brake pedal for at least one minute.
2. Turn off the engine and wait one minute.
3. Test for the presence of assist vacuum by depressing the brake pedal and releasing it several times. If vacuum is present in the system, light application will produce less and less pedal travel. If there is no vacuum, air is leaking into the system.

System Operation Test

1. With the engine OFF, pump the brake pedal until the supply vacuum is entirely gone.
2. Put light, steady pressure on the brake pedal.
3. Start the engine and let it idle. If the system is operating correctly, the brake pedal should fall toward the floor if the constant pressure is maintained.

Power brake systems may be tested for hydraulic leaks just as ordinary systems are tested.

※※ WARNING:

Clean, high quality brake fluid is essential to the safe and proper operation of the brake system. You should always buy the highest quality brake fluid that is available. If the brake fluid becomes contaminated, drain and flush the system, then refill the master cylinder with new fluid. Never reuse any brake fluid. Any brake fluid that is removed from the system should be discarded.

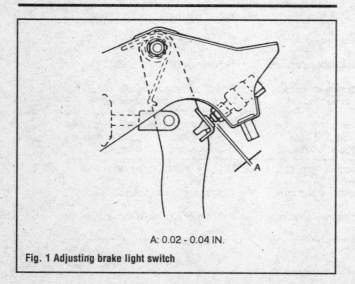

A: 0.02 - 0.04 IN.

Fig. 1 Adjusting brake light switch

Brake Light Switch

REMOVAL & INSTALLATION

See Figure 1

1. Disconnect the negative battery cable.
2. Remove the plastic cover from steering column, as required.
3. Disconnect the brake light switch electrical connector.
4. Depress the brake pedal and remove the locknut from the threaded portion of the brake light switch.
5. Remove the brake light switch.

To install:

6. Install brake light switch.
7. Adjust the switch so that the clearance between the end thread of the brake light switch and the brake pedal contact plate is 0.02 - 0.04 in. (0.5 - 1.0mm) with the brake pedal fully upward.
8. Depress brake pedal, install locknut and tighten to 115 inch lbs. (13 Nm).
9. Connect brake light switch electrical connector.
10. Install the plastic cover on steering column, as required.
11. Connect the negative battery cable.

Master Cylinder

REMOVAL & INSTALLATION

See Figure 2

Note: Be careful not to spill brake fluid on the painted surfaces of the vehicle; it will damage the finish.

1. Disconnect the negative battery cable. Clean around the reservoir cap and take some of the fluid out with a syringe.
2. Disconnect and plug the brake tubes from the master cylinder.
3. Remove the mounting nuts and washers.
4. Remove the master cylinder.

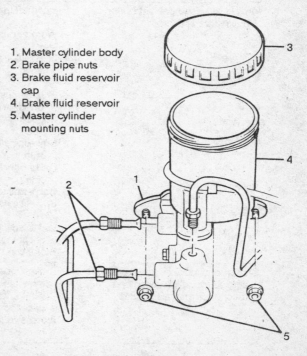

1. Master cylinder body
2. Brake pipe nuts
3. Brake fluid reservoir cap
4. Brake fluid reservoir
5. Master cylinder mounting nuts

Fig. 2 Removing the master cylinder

To install:

5. If a new master cylinder is to be installed, bleed as follows:
a. Install the master cylinder in a holding fixture, taking precautions to protect the cylinder body from damage.
b. Fill the fluid reservoir with clean brake fluid meeting DOT 3 recommendations.
c. Position a container under the outlet fittings. Depress the cylinder piston slowly through it's full travel. Cover both outlets and let the piston return to normal resting position.
d. Wait 5 seconds and then repeat the operation until the fluid exiting the master cylinder fittings is free of air bubbles.

6. Install the master cylinder. Tighten mounting bolts to 8 - 12 ft. lbs. (11 - 16 Nm).

7. Connect the brake tubes to the master cylinder. Tighten to 10 - 13 ft. lbs. (14 - 18 Nm).

8. Fill the master cylinder with clean brake fluid and bleed the brake system.

9. Connect the negative battery cable.

BENCH BLEEDING

✳✳ WARNING:

All new master cylinders should be bench bled prior to installation. Bleeding a new master cylinder on the vehicle is not a good idea. With air trapped inside, the master cylinder piston may bottom in the bore and possibly cause internal damage.

1. Secure the master cylinder in a bench vise using soft jaws.
2. Remove the master cylinder reservoir cap.
3. Manufacture or purchase bleeding tubes and install them on the master cylinder as illustrated.
4. Fill the master cylinder reservoir with clean, fresh brake fluid until the level is within 0.25 in. of the reservoir top.

Note: Ensure the bleeding tubes are below the level of the brake fluid, otherwise air may get into the system making your bleeding efforts ineffective.

5. Use a blunt tipped rod (a long socket extension works well) to slowly depress the master cylinder piston. Make sure the piston travels its full stroke.
6. As the piston is depressed, bubbles will come out of the bleeding tubes. Continue depressing and releasing the piston until all bubbles cease.
7. Refill the master cylinder with fluid.
8. Remove the bleeding tubes.
9. Install the master cylinder reservoir cap.
10. Install the master cylinder on the vehicle.

Power Brake Booster

REMOVAL & INSTALLATION

1. Disconnect the negative battery cable.
2. Remove the master cylinder.
3. Disconnect the pushrod clevis pin from the brake pedal arm.
4. Disconnect the vacuum hose from the brake booster.
5. Remove the mounting nuts from under the dash, then remove the booster.

To install:

6. Install the booster and tighten mounting nuts to 14 - 20 ft. lbs. (19 - 27 Nm).
7. Connect the vacuum hose from the brake booster.
8. Connect the pushrod clevis pin from the brake pedal arm.
9. Adjust the brake booster piston-to-master cylinder primary piston clearance.
10. Install the master cylinder.
11. Connect the negative battery cable.

Proportioning Valve

The proportioning valve is located along the right side of the engine compartment bulkhead.

REMOVAL & INSTALLATION

1. Clean dirt and foreign material from pipes and fittings.
2. Disconnect the proportioner valve electrical connector.
3. Disconnect the brake hoses.
4. Remove the proportioner valve mounting bolts.
5. Remove the valve from the engine compartment.

To install:

6. Install the valve on the engine compartment bulkhead.
7. Connect the brake hoses and tighten to 12 ft. lbs. (16 Nm).
8. Connect electrical connector.
9. Flush and bleed brake system.

Brake Hoses and Lines

Metal lines and rubber brake hoses should be checked frequently for leaks and external damage. Metal lines are particularly prone to crushing and kinking under the vehicle. Any such deformation can restrict the proper flow of fluid and therefore impair braking at the wheels. Rubber hoses should be checked for cracking or scraping; such damage can create a weak spot in the hose and it could fail under pressure.

Any time the lines are removed or disconnected, extreme cleanliness must be observed. Clean all joints and connections before disassembly (use a stiff bristle brush and clean brake fluid); be sure to plug the lines and ports as soon as they are opened. New lines and hoses should be flushed clean with brake fluid before installation to remove any contamination.

REMOVAL & INSTALLATION

See Figures 3, 4, 5 and 6

1. Disconnect the negative battery cable.
2. Raise and safely support the vehicle on jackstands.
3. Remove any wheel and tire assemblies necessary for access to the particular line you are removing.
4. Thoroughly clean the surrounding area at the joints to be disconnected.
5. Place a suitable catch pan under the joint to be disconnected.
6. Using two wrenches (one to hold the joint and one to turn the fitting), disconnect the hose or line to be replaced.
7. Disconnect the other end of the line or hose, moving the drain pan if necessary. Always use a back-up wrench to avoid damaging the fitting.
8. Disconnect any retaining clips or brackets holding the line and remove the line from the vehicle.

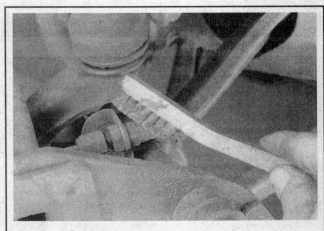

Fig. 3 Use a brush to clean the fittings of any debris

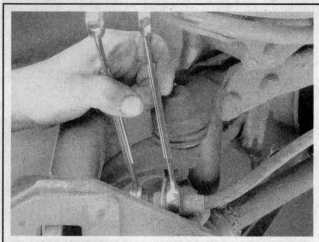

Fig. 4 Use two wrenches to loosen the fitting. If available, use flare nut type wrenches

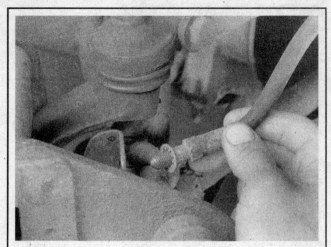

Fig. 5 Any gaskets/washers should be replaced with new ones during installation

Note: If the brake system is to remain open for more time than it takes to swap lines, tape or plug each remaining clip and port to keep contaminants out and fluid in.

To install:

9. Install the new line or hose, starting with the end farthest from the master cylinder. Connect the other end, then confirm that both fittings are correctly threaded and turn smoothly using finger pressure. Make sure the new line will not rub against any other part. Brake lines must be at least 1/2 in. (13mm) from the steering column and other moving parts. Any protective shielding or insulators must be reinstalled in the original location.

✲ WARNING:

Make sure the hose is NOT kinked or touching any part of the frame or suspension after installation. These conditions may cause the hose to fail prematurely.

10. Using two wrenches as before, tighten each fitting.
11. Install any retaining clips or brackets on the lines.
12. If removed, install the wheel and tire assemblies, then carefully lower the vehicle to the ground.
13. Refill the brake master cylinder reservoir with clean, fresh brake fluid, meeting DOT 3 specifications. Properly bleed the brake system.
14. Connect the negative battery cable.

Bleeding The Brake System

When any part of the hydraulic system has been disconnected for repair or replacement, air may get into the lines and cause spongy pedal action (because air can be compressed and brake fluid cannot). To correct this condition, it is necessary to bleed the hydraulic system so to be sure all air is purged.

When bleeding the brake system, bleed one brake cylinder at a time, beginning at the cylinder with the longest hydraulic line (farthest from the master cylinder) first. ALWAYS Keep the master cylinder reservoir filled with brake fluid during the bleeding operation. Never use brake fluid that has been drained from the hydraulic system, no matter how clean it is.

The primary and secondary hydraulic brake systems are separate and are bled independently. During the bleeding operation, do not allow the reservoir to run dry. Keep the master cylinder reservoir filled with brake fluid.

1. Clean all dirt from around the master cylinder fill cap, remove the cap and fill the master cylinder with brake fluid until the level is within 1/4 in.

(6mm) of the top edge of the reservoir.

2. Clean the bleeder screws at all 4 wheels. The bleeder screws are located on the back of the brake backing plate (drum brakes) and on the top of the brake calipers (disc brakes).

3. Attach a length of rubber hose over the bleeder screw and place the other end of the hose in a glass jar, submerged in brake fluid.

4. Open the bleeder screw 1/2 - 3/4 turn. Have an assistant slowly depress the brake pedal.

5. Close the bleeder screw and tell your assistant to allow the brake pedal to return slowly. Continue this process to purge all air from the system.

6. When bubbles cease to appear at the end of the bleeder hose, close the bleeder screw and remove the hose. Tighten the bleeder screw to the proper torque:

- 89 in. lbs. (10 Nm)

7. Check the master cylinder fluid level and add fluid accordingly. Do this after bleeding each wheel.

8. Repeat the bleeding operation at the remaining 3 wheels, ending with the one closest to the master cylinder.

9. Fill the master cylinder reservoir to the proper level.

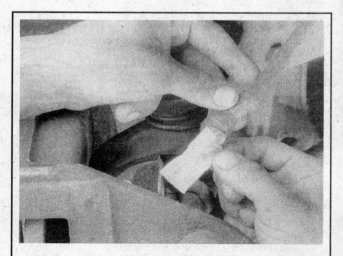

Fig. 6 Tape or plug the line to prevent contamination

DISC BRAKES

Brake Pads

REMOVAL & INSTALLATION

See Figures 7, 8, 9, 10, 11, 12, 13, 14, 15 and 16

✳ CAUTION

Brake pads or shoes may contain asbestos, which has been determined to be cancer causing agent. Never clean the brake surfaces with compressed air! Avoid inhaling any dust from any brake surface! When cleaning brake surfaces, use a commercially available brake cleaning fluid.

1. Raise and safely support the front of the vehicle. Set the parking brake and block the rear wheels.
2. Siphon a sufficient quantity of brake fluid from the master cylinder reservoir to prevent the brake fluid from overflowing from the master cylinder when removing or installing the brake pads. This is necessary as the piston must be forced into the cylinder bore to provide sufficient clearance to install the pads.
3. Remove the wheel, then reinstall 2 lug nuts finger tight to hold the disc in place.

Note: Disassemble brakes one wheel at a time. This will prevent parts confusion and also prevent the opposite caliper piston from popping out during pad installation.

4. Remove the 2 caliper mounting bolts and then remove the caliper from the mounting bracket. Position the caliper out of the way and support it with wire so it doesn't hang by the brake line.

Note: It may be necessary to rock the caliper back and forth a bit in order to reposition the piston so it will clear the brake pads.

5. Remove the brake pads, the wear indicators, the anti-squeal shims, the support plates and the anti squeal springs (if so equipped). Disassemble slowly and take note of how the parts fit together. This will save much time during reassembly.
6. Inspect the brake disc (both sides) for scoring or gouging. Measure the disc for both thickness and run-out. Complete inspection procedures are given later in this section.
7. Inspect the pads for remaining thickness and condition. Any sign of uneven wear, cracking, heat checking or spotting is cause for replacement. Compare the wear of the inner pad to the outer pad. While they will not wear at

Fig. 7 Front disc brake assembly

Fig. 8 Removing caliper mounting bolts

Fig. 9 Removing the caliper from the rotor

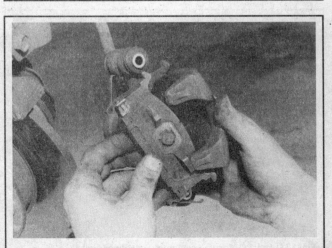

Fig. 10 Removing the outside brake pad

Fig. 11 Removing the inside brake pad

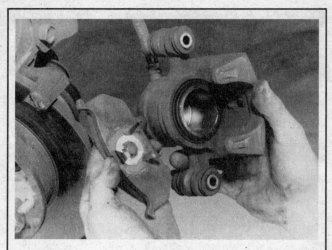

Fig. 12 The inside brake pad is attached to the caliper piston with a spring clip

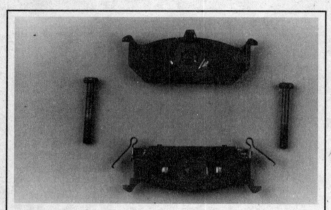

Fig. 13 Disc brake system hardware. Inside pad is at top and outside pad is on bottom. Note wear indicator springs protruding from sides of outside pad

Fig. 14 Removing the anti-squeal springs from the caliper wear indicators

exactly the same rate, the remaining thickness should be about the same on both pads. If one is heavily worn and the other is not, suspect either a binding caliper piston or dirty slides in the caliper mount.

8. Examine the 2 caliper retaining bolts and the slide bushings in which they run. Everything should be clean and dry. If cleaning is needed, use spray solvents and a clean cloth. Do not wire brush or sand the bolts - this will cause

Fig. 15 Using a C-clamp to compress the caliper piston

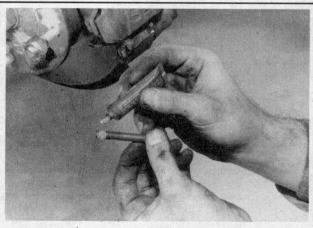

Fig. 16 Coat the caliper mounting bolts with anti-seize during installation

grooves in the metal which will trap more dirt. Check the condition of the rubber dust boots and replace them if damaged.

To install:

9. Install the pad support plates onto the mounting bracket.
10. Install new pad wear indicators onto each pad, making sure the arrow on the tab points in the direction of disc rotation.
11. Install new anti-squeal pads to the back of the pads.
12. Install the pads into the mounting bracket and install the anti-squeal springs.
13. Use a caliper compressor, or a C-clamp to slowly press the caliper piston back into the caliper. If the piston is frozen, or if the caliper is leaking hydraulic fluid, the caliper must be overhauled or replaced.
14. Install the caliper assembly to the mounting plate. Before installing the retaining bolts, apply a thin, even coating of anti-seize compound to the threads and slide surfaces. Don't use grease or spray lubricants; they will not hold up under the extreme temperatures generated by the brakes. Tighten the bolts to specification.
15. Remove the 2 lugs holding the disc in place and install the wheel.
16. Lower the vehicle to the ground. Check the level of the brake fluid in the master cylinder reservoir; it should be at least to the middle of the reservoir.
17. Depress the brake pedal several times and make sure that the movement feels normal. The first brake pedal application may result in a very "long" pedal due to the pistons being retracted. Always make several brake applications before starting the vehicle. Bleeding is not usually necessary after pad replacement.
18. Recheck the fluid level and add to the "MAX" line if necessary.

Note: Braking should be moderate for the first 5 miles or so until the new pads seat correctly. The new pads will bed best if put through several moderate heating and cooling cycles. Avoid hard braking until the brakes have experienced several long, slow stops with time to cool in between. Taking the time to properly bed the brakes will yield quieter operation, more efficient stopping and contribute to extended brake life.

INSPECTION

The brake linings should be checked anytime the car has any type of maintenance performed on it. Inspect for uneven wear, cracking, chipping, and thickness. Make sure that the lining is more than 0.030 in. (0.76 mm). If it is not replace the linings per axle.

Brake Caliper

REMOVAL & INSTALLATION

See Figures 7, 8, 9, 10, 11, 12, 13, 14, 15 and 16

1. Raise and safely support the front of the vehicle. Set the parking brake

and block the rear wheels.
2. Siphon a sufficient quantity of brake fluid from the master cylinder reservoir to prevent the brake fluid from overflowing the master cylinder when removing or installing the calipers. This is necessary as the piston must be forced into the cylinder bore to provide sufficient clearance to install the caliper.
3. Remove the wheel, then reinstall 2 lug nuts finger tight to hold the disc in place.

Note: Disassemble brakes one wheel at a time. This will prevent parts confusion and also prevent the opposite caliper piston from popping out during installation. Mark the relationship between the wheel and the axle hub before removing the tire and wheel assembly.

4. Disconnect the hose union at the caliper. Use a pan to catch any spilled fluid and immediately plug the disconnected hose.
5. Remove the 2 caliper mounting bolts and then remove the caliper from the mounting bracket.

To install:

6. Use a caliper compressor, a C-clamp or large pair of pliers to slowly press the caliper piston back into the caliper.
7. Install the caliper assembly to the mounting plate. Before installing the retaining bolts, apply a thin, even coating of anti-seize compound to the threads and slide surfaces. Don't use grease or spray lubricants; they will not hold up under the extreme temperatures generated by the brakes. Tighten the bolts.
8. Install the brake hose to the caliper. Always use a new gasket and tighten the union.
9. Bleed the brake system.
10. Remove the 2 lugs holding the disc in place and install the wheel.
11. Lower the vehicle to the ground. Check the level of the brake fluid in the master cylinder reservoir; it should be at least to the middle of the reservoir.

OVERHAUL

See Figures 17, 18, 19, 20, 21, 22, 23 and 24

Note: Some vehicles may be equipped dual piston calipers. The procedure to overhaul the caliper is essentially the same with the exception of multiple pistons, O-rings and dust boots.

1. Remove the caliper from the vehicle and place on a clean workbench.

❋❋ CAUTION:

NEVER place your fingers in front of the pistons in an attempt to catch or protect the pistons when applying compressed air. This could result in personal injury!

Fig. 17 For some types of calipers, use compressed air to drive the piston out of the caliper, but make sure to keep your fingers clear

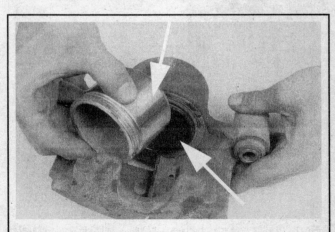
Fig. 18 Withdraw the piston from the caliper bore

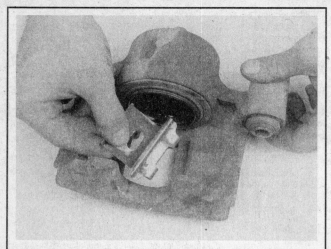

Fig. 19 On some vehicles, you must remove the anti-rattle clip

Fig. 20 Use a pry tool to carefully pry around the edge of the boot...

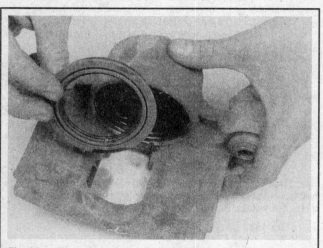

Fig. 21 ... then remove the boot from the caliper housing, taking care not to score or damage the bore

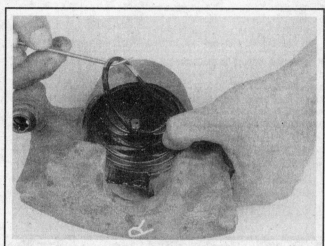

Fig. 22 Use extreme caution when removing the piston seal; DO NOT scratch the caliper bore

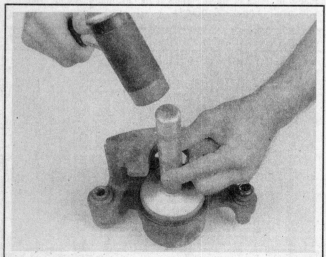

Fig. 23 Use the proper size driving tool and a mallet to properly seal the boot in the caliper housing

Note: Depending upon the vehicle, there are two different ways to remove the piston from the caliper. Refer to the brake pad replacement procedure to make sure you have the correct procedure for your vehicle.

2. The first method is as follows:
   a. Stuff a shop towel or a block of wood into the caliper to catch the piston.
   b. Remove the caliper piston using compressed air applied into the caliper inlet hole. Inspect the piston for scoring, nicks, corrosion and/or worn or damaged chrome plating. The piston must be replaced if any of these conditions are found.

3. For the second method, you must rotate the piston to retract it from the caliper.

4. If equipped, remove the anti-rattle clip.

5. Use a pry tool to remove the caliper boot, being careful not to scratch the housing bore.

6. Remove the piston seals from the groove in the caliper bore.

7. Carefully loosen the brake bleeder valve cap and valve from the caliper housing.

8. Inspect the caliper bores, pistons and mounting threads for scoring or excessive wear.

9. Use crocus cloth to polish out light corrosion from the piston and bore.

10. Clean all parts with denatured alcohol and dry with compressed air.

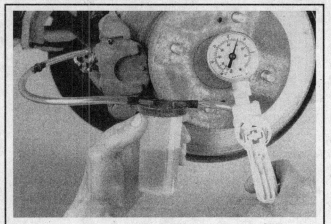

Fig. 24 There are tools, such as this Mighty-Vac, available to assist in proper brake system bleeding

To assemble:

11. Lubricate and install the bleeder valve and cap.
12. Install the new seals into the caliper bore grooves, making sure they are not twisted.
13. Lubricate the piston bore.
14. Install the pistons and boots into the bores of the calipers and push to the bottom of the bores.
15. Use a suitable driving tool to seat the boots in the housing.
16. Install the caliper in the vehicle.
17. Install the wheel and tire assembly, then carefully lower the vehicle.
18. Properly bleed the brake system.

Brake Disc (Rotor)

REMOVAL & INSTALLATION

See Figures 25, 26, 27 and 28

1. Elevate and safely support the vehicle. If only the front end is supported, set the parking brake and block the rear wheels.
2. Remove the wheel.
3. Remove the brake caliper from its mount and suspend it out of the way. Don't disconnect the hose and don't let the caliper hang by the hose. Remove the brake pads with all the clips, shims, etc.
4. If you're working on a 1995 or later model, install all the lug nuts to hold the rotor in place. If the nuts are open at both ends, it is helpful to install them backwards (tapered end out) to secure the disc. Tighten the nuts a bit tighter than finger tight, but make sure all are at approximately the same tightness.
5. Check the run-out and thickness measurements of the rotor. Also check the condition of the friction surfaces. Light scratches and shallow grooves are

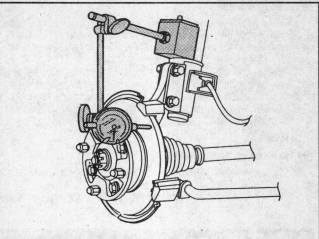

Fig. 25 Checking rotor runout with a dial indicator

normal after use and won't affect brake operation. Deep grooves require disc removal and refinishing by an automotive machine shop. Be sure to check both sides of the disc. If the runout exceeds the maximum allowed, the disc should be refinished by an automotive machine shop.

Note: The disc must not be machined to a thickness less than the specified minimum thickness, which is cast into the disc.

1994 and earlier models

6. Remove the driveaxle/hub nut and the four bolts securing the rotor to the hub.
7. Pull the hub and rotor off with a slide hammer and puller attachment.
8. Separate the rotor from the hub.

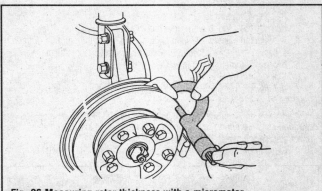

Fig. 26 Measuring rotor thickness with a micrometer

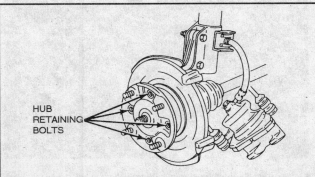

Fig. 27 Rotor hub retaining bolt locations (1994 and earlier models)

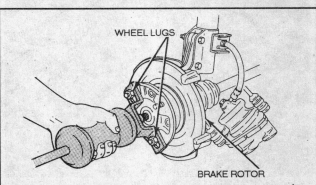

Fig. 28 Removing the rotor hub with a slide hammer (1994 and earlier models)

1995 and later models

9. When reinstalling, make certain the rotor is clean and free of any particles of rust or metal from resurfacing. Remove the 2 bolts holding the caliper mounting bracket to the steering knuckle. These bolts will be tight. Remove the bracket from the knuckle.

10. Before removing the rotor, make a mark on the rotor indexing one wheel stud to one hole in the rotor. This assures the rotor will be re-installed in its original position, serving to eliminate minor vibrations in the brake system.

11. Remove the two screws securing the rotor to the hub. Remove the 4 lug nuts holding the rotor and detach the rotor from the hub.

To install:

1994 and earlier models

12. Be sure the spacer on the hub is installed with the concave side to the hub.

13. Using a hammer and the proper driver, install the rotor and hub assem-

bly. Install the rotor retaining bolts and tighten them to 29 - 43 ft. lbs. (40 to 58 Nm).

14. Install the driveaxle/hub nut and tighten it to 129 ft. lbs. (175 Nm). Install a new cotter pin (castle nut types) or stake the nut into the groove (staked nut type).

1995 and later models

12. When reinstalling, make certain the rotor is clean and free of any particles of rust or metal from resurfacing. Observe the index mark made earlier and fit the rotor over the wheel lugs. Install 2 lug nuts to hold it in place.

13. Install the caliper mounting bracket in position and tighten the bolts.

All models

14. Install the brake pads and the hardware.

15. Install the caliper. Tighten the mounting bolts to the proper torque.

16. Install the wheel and lower the vehicle to the ground.

DRUM BRAKES

✳✳ CAUTION:

Older brake pads or shoes may contain asbestos, which has been determined to be cancer causing agent. Never clean the brake surfaces with compressed air! Avoid inhaling any; dust from any brake surface! When cleaning brake surfaces, use a commercially available brake cleaning fluid.

Brake Drums

REMOVAL & INSTALLATION

See Figures 29, 30, 31, 32, 33 and 34

1. Raise and support the vehicle safely.
2. Remove the tire and wheel assembly.
3. Remove the spindle cap without damaging the sealing portion of the cap.
4. Unfasten the staked portion of the nut using a suitable chisel.
5. Remove the castle nut and washer.
6. Slacken the parking brake cable by loosening its adjusting nuts.
7. Remove the backing plate plug, located on the back side of the backing plate.
8. Insert a suitable tool into the plug until its tip contacts the shoe hold-down and push the spring in the direction of the leading shoe. This allows a greater clearance between the shoes and the drum.
9. Remove the drum from the spindle.

Fig. 29 Rear drum brake assembly

To install:

10. Install the drum on the spindle.
11. Install the castle nut and washer.
12. Tighten nut to the proper torque:
- Castle nut = 58-86 ft.lbs, (80-120 Nm), install new cotter pin
- Staked-type nut = 125 ft.lbs (170 Nm), then stake in place. **Note:** *Always use a new nut.*

Fig. 30 Removing the spindle cap

Fig. 31 Unstake the nut using a suitable chisel

Fig. 32 Removing the drum from the spindle

Fig. 33 Tighten the nut to the specified torque using a torque wrench

13. Install the spindle cap.
14. Install the wheel, then lower the vehicle.

INSPECTION

15. Remove loose rust and other foreign matter from the outside surfaces of the drum with a wire brush.
16. Check the casting itself for cracks or other obvious damage. Bluing indicates overheating. If this can't be removed by an automotive machine shop, the drum should be replaced.
17. Clean the inside of the drum. Check for scoring or grooves. Any imperfections must be removed.

❊ CAUTION:

Never exceed the maximum allowable diameter when machining the braking surface.

18. Check the inside diameter of the drum. Maximum allowable inside diameter is stamped on the drum. If machining is needed to clean up the contact surface, the measurement must be taken afterwards. Replace the drum if it exceeds the specification.
19. Clean up the brake lining contact area with medium sandpaper. Be sure that you don't leave a directional pattern on the contact surface.
20. Perform a final cleaning of the contact area with a purpose-made commercial brake cleaning solvent to remove fingerprints and oily residue.

Fig. 34 Staking the nut in place

Brake Shoes

INSPECTION

Inspect the brake shoes for wear using a ruler or Vernier caliper. Compare measurements to the brake specifications chart. If the lining is thinner than specification or there is evidence of the lining being contaminated by brake fluid or oil, repair the leak and replace all brake shoe assemblies (a complete axle set).

In addition to the shoes, inspect all springs and brake shoe hardware for wear and replace as necessary (it is a good idea to replace the springs regardless off their apparent condition, since the heating and cooling cycles they are subjected to can weaken them, allowing the shoes to drag on the drum and wear at a more rapid rate than normal).

REMOVAL & INSTALLATION

See Figures 35, 36, 37, 38, 39, 40, 41, 42, 43, 44, 45 and 46

❊ CAUTION:

Brake shoes may contain asbestos, which has been determined to be a cancer causing agent. Never clean the brake surfaces with compressed air! Avoid inhaling any dust from any brake surface! When cleaning brake surfaces, us a commercially available brake cleaning fluid!

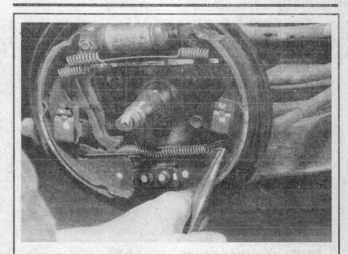

Fig. 35 Removing the lower brake shoe return spring

Fig. 36 Removing the anti-rattle spring

Fig. 37 Removing the brake shoe hold down springs

Fig. 38 Removing the parking brake lever from the cable

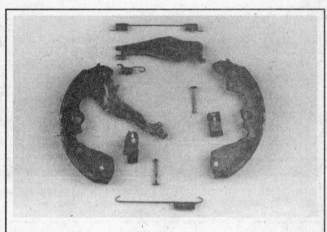

Fig. 39 Rear brake shoe assembly

1. Disconnect the battery negative cable.
2. Raise and support the vehicle safely.
3. Remove the brake drum.
4. Remove the upper and lower springs from the brake shoes.
5. Remove the anti rattle spring and brake shoe adjustment strut.

6. Remove the primary and secondary brake shoe hold down springs by turning hold down pins and removing shoes from vehicle.
7. Remove clip securing parking brake shoe lever to secondary shoe.
8. Remove parking brake cable from lever.
9. Remove hold down pins from brake backing plate.

Fig. 40 Lubricating the contact points with grease

Fig. 41 Installing the brake shoe hold down springs

Fig. 42 Installing the brake adjustment strut

Fig. 43 Installing the anti-rattle spring

Fig. 44 Installing the upper return spring

Fig. 45 Installing the lower return spring

To install:

10. Inspect all components for damage from heat and stress. Replace components as necessary. Lubricate all contact points on the backing plate with grease.
11. Install the hold down pins on the backing plate.
12. Install the parking brake cable to parking brake shoe lever.
13. Install clip securing parking brake shoe lever to secondary shoe.
14. Install primary and secondary brake shoes to vehicle and secure with hold down springs. Position hold down spring on hold down pins and turn pins downward.
15. Install brake adjustment strut and anti-rattle spring.
16. Install upper and lower return springs to primary and secondary brake shoes.
17. Install brake drum and tighten spindle nut to the proper torque:
- Castle nut = 58-86 ft.lbs. (80-120 Nm), install new cotter pin
- Staked-type nut = 125 ft.lbs (170 Nm), then stake in place. **Note:** *Always use a new nut.*
18. Install wheel and tire.
19. Lower vehicle.
20. Press brake pedal 3 - 5 times to adjust the brake shoe clearance.
21. Check to ensure the brake drum is free from dragging and proper braking is obtained.

ADJUSTMENTS

The rear brakes have a self-adjusting mechanism that does not require adjustment for proper drum to shoe clearance when brake shoe has been replaced or brake drum has been removed for some other service.

Adjustment is automatically accomplished by depressing brake pedal 3 - 5 times after all parts are installed. Then check brake drum for dragging and brake system for proper performance.

Wheel Cylinders

REMOVAL & INSTALLATION

See Figure 46

1. Disconnect the battery negative cable.
2. Raise and support the vehicle safely, then remove the tire and wheel assembly.
3. Remove the brake drum and shoes.
4. Remove the bleeder screw from the wheel cylinder.
5. Loosen the brake pipe flare nut and disconnect the brake pipe from the wheel cylinder.
6. Remove the wheel cylinder attaching bolts and the wheel cylinder from the backing plate.

To install:

7. Install the wheel cylinder and tighten mounting bolts to 115 inch lbs. (13 Nm).

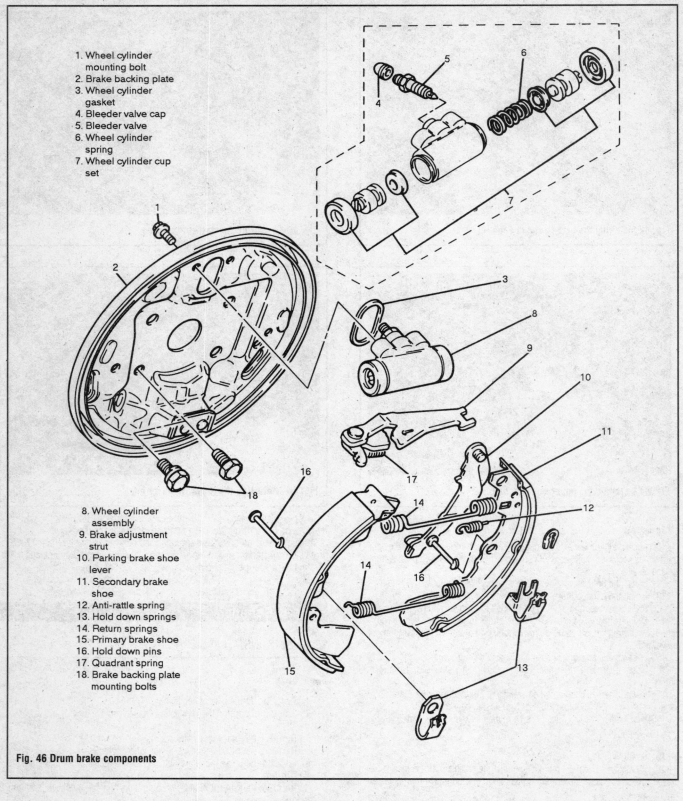

1. Wheel cylinder mounting bolt
2. Brake backing plate
3. Wheel cylinder gasket
4. Bleeder valve cap
5. Bleeder valve
6. Wheel cylinder spring
7. Wheel cylinder cup set

8. Wheel cylinder assembly
9. Brake adjustment strut
10. Parking brake shoe lever
11. Secondary brake shoe
12. Anti-rattle spring
13. Hold down springs
14. Return springs
15. Primary brake shoe
16. Hold down pins
17. Quadrant spring
18. Brake backing plate mounting bolts

Fig. 46 Drum brake components

8. Connect brake pipe to wheel cylinder and tighten to 12 ft. lbs. (16 Nm).
9. Install bleeder valve.
10. Install the brake drum and shoes.
11. Flush and bleed the brake system.
12. Install the wheel and tire. Lower the vehicle.

OVERHAUL

See Figures 47, 48, 49, 50, 51, 52, 53, 54, 55 and 56

Wheel cylinder overhaul kits may be available, but often at little or no sav-

Fig. 47 Remove the outer boots from the wheel cylinder

Fig. 48 Compressed air can be used to remove the pistons and seals

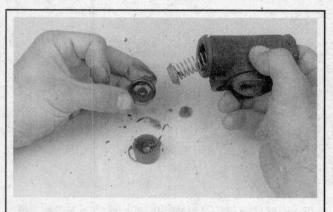

Fig. 49 Remove the pistons, cup seals and spring from the cylinder

Fig. 50 Use brake fluid and a soft brush to clean the pistons ...

ings over a reconditioned wheel cylinder. It often makes sense with these components to substitute a new or reconditioned part instead of attempting an overhaul.

If no replacement is available, or you would prefer to overhaul your wheel cylinders, the following procedure may be used. When rebuilding and installing wheel cylinders, avoid getting any contaminants into the system. Always use clean, new, high quality brake fluid. If dirty or improper fluid has been used, it will be necessary to drain the entire system, flush the system with proper brake fluid, replace all rubber components, then refill and bleed the system.

1. Remove the wheel cylinder from the vehicle and place on a clean workbench.

2. First remove and discard the old rubber boots, then withdraw the pistons. Wheel cylinders are equipped with seals and a spring assembly, all located behind the pistons in the cylinder bore.

3. Remove the remaining inner components, seals and spring assembly. Compressed air may be useful in removing these components. If no compressed air is available, be VERY careful not to score the wheel cylinder bore when removing parts from it. Discard all components for which replacements were supplied in the rebuild kit.

4. Wash the cylinder and metal parts with brake system cleaner. Clean brake fluid will also work.

Fig. 51 ... and the bore of the wheel cylinder

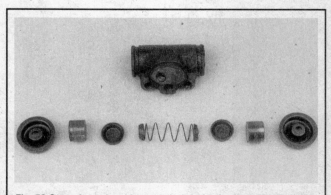

Fig. 52 Once cleaned and inspected, the wheel cylinder is ready for assembly

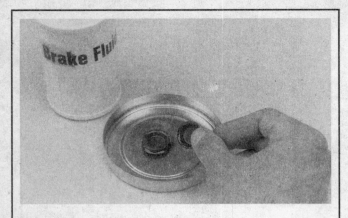

Fig. 53 Lubricate the cup seals with brake fluid

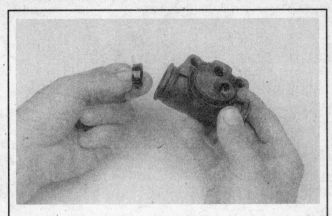

Fig. 54 Install the spring, then the cup seals in the bore

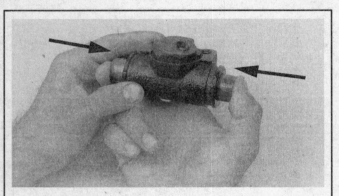

Fig. 55 Lightly lubricate the pistons, then install them

Fig. 56 The boots can now be installed over the wheel cylinder ends

✳✳ WARNING:

Never use a mineral-based solvent such as gasoline, kerosene or paint thinner for cleaning purposes. These solvents will swell rubber components and quickly deteriorate them.

5. Allow the parts to air dry or use compressed air. Do not use rags for cleaning, since lint will remain in the cylinder bore.

6. Inspect the piston and replace it if it shows scratches.
7. Lubricate the cylinder bore and seals using clean brake fluid.
8. Position the spring assembly.
9. Install the inner seals, then the pistons.
10. Insert the new boots into the counterbores by hand. Do not lubricate the boots.
11. Install the wheel cylinder.

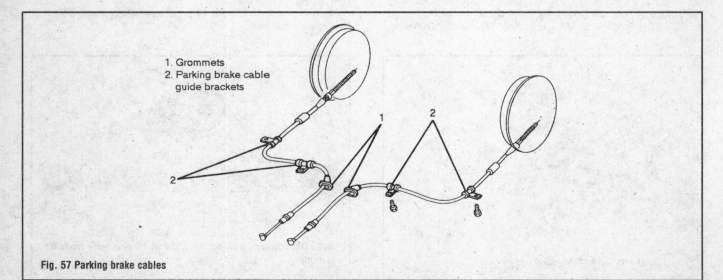

1. Grommets
2. Parking brake cable guide brackets

Fig. 57 Parking brake cables

PARKING BRAKE

Cable

REMOVAL & INSTALLATION

See Figure 57

1. Disconnect the negative battery cable.
2. Remove the parking brake lever assembly trim cover.
3. Disconnect the electrical connector from the parking brake switch.
4. Loosen the adjuster nut on the lever assembly.
5. Remove the parking brake cables from the equalizer plate.
6. Raise and support the vehicle safely.
7. Remove the wheel and tire assembly.
8. Remove the brake drum.
9. Remove the rear brakes and components.
10. Disconnect the parking brake cable from the brake shoe lever and the backing plate.
11. Remove the cable(s) from the chassis mounts, then the cable from the vehicle.

To install:

12. Install the cable(s) to the chassis mounts and tighten mount attaching bolts to 11 ft. lbs. (15 Nm).

13. Feed the cable(s) through the backing plate and connect to the brake shoe lever.
14. Install the rear brakes and components.
15. Install the brake drum.
16. Install the wheel and tire assembly.
17. Lower the vehicle.
18. Install the parking brake cables on the equalizer plate.
19. Adjust the parking brake lever assembly.
20. Connect the electrical connector to the parking brake switch.
21. Install the parking brake lever assembly trim cover.
22. Connect the negative battery cable.

ADJUSTMENT

1. Remove both door seal plates and the seat belt buckle bolts at the floor.
2. Disconnect the shoulder harness bolts at the floor and the interior, bottom trim panels.
3. Raise the rear seat cushion.
4. Pull up the carpet to gain access to the parking brake lever.
5. Loosen the parking brake cable adjusting nuts.
6. Adjust the parking brake cables, so they work evenly.
7. Adjust the cable, so when the parking brake handle is pulled, its travel is between 5 - 8 notches, with 44 lbs. of force.

ANTI-LOCK BRAKE SYSTEM

General Information

An ABS braking system will operate as a conventional braking system under normal conditions. They are similar in design and share many components. The major differences are seen and felt under heavy braking. A pulsation will be felt under foot and the car will be much easier to control compared to its conventional braking counterpart. The system uses various sensors to monitor speed and it has the ability to sense if one or more of the wheels is losing traction. Once the system senses that one of the wheels is losing traction, the system starts to change the braking pressures several times a second. This allows the vehicle to remain in control.

Diagnostics and Testing

The Electronic Control Brake Module (EBCM) is capable of storing DTCs just like the PCM. The DTCs can be accessed through the 16 pin DLC with the use of a scan tool. Due to the severe importance of correct system operation, it is recommended that a professional technician handle any ABS related problems.

ABS DIAGNOSTIC TROUBLE CODES:

C1214 ..... Brake Control Relay Contact Circuit Open
C1215 ..... Brake Control Relay Contact Circuit Active
C1216 ..... Brake Control Relay Coil Circuit Open
C1217 ..... Brake Control Relay Coil Circuit Short to Ground
C1218 ..... Brake Control Relay Coil Circuit Short to Voltage
C1221 ..... LF Wheel Speed Sensor Input Signal is 0
C1222 ..... RF Wheel Speed Sensor Input Signal is 0
C1223 ..... LR Wheel Speed Sensor Input Signal is 0
C1224 ..... RR Wheel Speed Sensor Input Signal is 0
C1225 ..... LF Excessive Wheel Speed Variation
C1226 ..... RF Excessive Wheel Speed Variation
C1227 ..... LR Excessive Wheel Speed Variation
C1228 ..... RR Excessive Wheel Speed Variation
C1232 ..... LF Wheel Speed Circuit Open or Shorted
C1233 ..... RF Wheel Speed Circuit Open or Shorted
C1234 ..... LR Wheel Speed Circuit Open or Shorted
C1235 ..... RR Wheel Speed Circuit Open or Shorted
C1236 ..... Low System Supply Voltage
C1237 ..... High System Supply Voltage
C1238 ..... Left Front ESB Does Not Hold Motor
C1241 ..... Right Front ESB Does Not Hold Motor
C1242 ..... Rear ESB Does Not Hold Motor
C1244 ..... Left Front ABS Channel Does Not Move
C1245 ..... Right Front ABS Channel Does Not Move
C1246 ..... Rear ABS Channel Does Not Move
C1247 ..... Left Front ABS Motor Free Spins
C1248 ..... Right Front ABS Motor Free Spins
C1251 ..... Rear ABS Motor Free Spins
C1255 ..... EBCM Internal Malfunction
C1256 ..... Left Front ABS Motor Circuit Open
C1257 ..... LF ABS Motor Circuit Shorted to Ground
C1258 ..... LF ABS Motor Circuit Shorted to Voltage
C1261 ..... Right Front ABS Motor Circuit Open
C1262 ..... RF ABS Motor Circuit Shorted to Ground
C1263 ..... RF ABS Motor Circuit Shorted to Voltage
C1264 ..... Rear ABS Motor Circuit Open
C1265 ..... Rear ABS Motor Circuit Shorted to Ground
C1266 ..... Rear ABS Motor Circuit Shorted to Voltage
C1276 ..... LF Solenoid Circuit Open or Short to Ground
C1277 ..... LF Solenoid Circuit Shorted to Voltage
C1278 ..... RF Solenoid Circuit Open or Short to Ground
C1281 ..... RF Solenoid Circuit Shorted to Voltage
C1282 ..... Calibration Malfunction

ABS DIAGNOSTIC TROUBLE CODES (continued):

C1286 ..... EBCM Turned On Brake Warning Indicator
C1287 ..... Brake Warning Indicator Circuit Open or Shorted to Voltage
C1291 ..... Open Brake Lamp Switch Contacts During Deceleration
C1292 ..... Open Brake Lamp Switch When ABS Was Required
C1293 ..... DTC C1291/C1292 Set in Current or Previous Ignition Cycle
C1294 ..... Brake Lamp Switch Circuit Always Active
C1295 ..... Brake Lamp Switch Circuit Open

Speed Sensors

REMOVAL & INSTALLATION

1. Raise and support the vehicle.

2. Remove the wheel.
3. Disconnect the electrical connector from the harness.
4. Unbolt the retaining bolt.
5. Remove the speed sensor.
6. Installation is the reverse of the removal.

Tone (Exciter) Ring

Front

Inspect the ring for debris or missing teeth. Clean or replace as necessary. The ring is part of the outer CV joint, so if it must be replaced so does the joint.

Rear

The rear ABS speed sensor tone ring is an integral part of the rear hub and wheel bearing assembly. If a problem develops with the tone ring, the hub and bearing assembly must be replaced as a unit.

BRAKE SPECIFICATIONS
All measurements in inches unless noted

Year	Model	Brake Disc Original Thickness	Brake Disc Minimum Thickness	Brake Disc Maximum Runout	Brake Drum Diameter Original Inside Diameter	Brake Drum Diameter Max. Wear Limit	Brake Drum Diameter Maximum Machine Diameter	Minimum Lining Thickness Front	Minimum Lining Thickness Rear	Brake Caliper Bracket Bolts (ft. lbs.)	Brake Caliper Mounting Bolts (ft. lbs.)
1985	Sprint	0.394	0.315	0.0028	7.09	7.16	—	0.315	0.110	—	22
1986	Sprint	0.394	0.315	0.0028	7.09	7.16	—	0.315	0.110	—	22
1987	Sprint	0.394	0.315	0.0028	7.09	7.16	—	0.315	0.110	—	22
1988	Sprint	0.394	0.315	0.0028	7.09	7.16	—	0.315	0.110	—	22
1989	Metro/Swift	0.394	0.315	0.0040	7.09	7.16	—	0.315	0.110	51–72	22
1990	Metro/Swift	0.394	0.315	0.0040	7.09	7.16	—	0.315	0.110	51–72	22
1991	Metro/Swift	0.394	0.315	0.0040	7.09	7.16	—	0.315	0.110	51–72	22
1992	Metro/Swift	0.394	0.315	0.0040	7.09	7.16	—	0.315	0.110	51–72	22
1993	Metro/Swift	0.394	0.315	0.0040	7.09	7.16	—	0.315	0.110	51–72	22
1994	Metro/Swift	0.394	0.315	0.0040	7.09	7.16	—	0.315	0.110	51–72	22
1995	Metro/Swift	0.670	0.590	0.0040	①	①	①	0.236	0.111	29–43	22
1996	Metro/Swift	0.670	0.590	0.0040	①	①	①	0.236	0.111	29–43	22
1997	Metro/Swift	0.670	0.590	0.0040	①	①	①	0.236	0.111	29–43	22
1998	Metro/Swift	0.670	0.590	0.0040	①	①	①	0.236	0.111	29–43	22
1999	Metro/Swift	0.670	0.590	0.0040	①	①	①	0.236	0.111	62	22
2000	Metro/Swift	0.670	0.590	0.0040	①	①	①	0.236	0.111	62	22

① 2 Door: 7.09
  4 Door: 7.87

895809G01

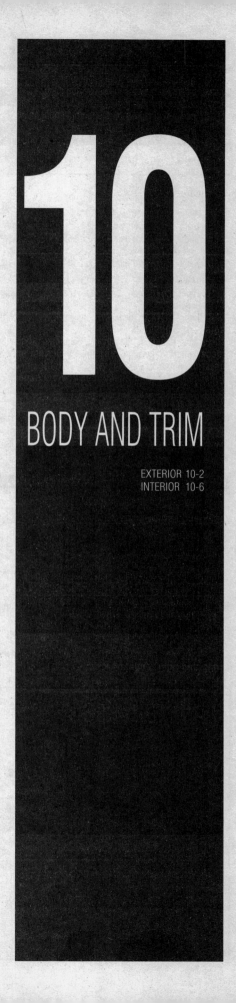

10
BODY AND TRIM

EXTERIOR

Doors

REMOVAL & INSTALLATION

See Figure 1

1. Remove the door stopper pin.
2. Matchmark the hinges to the body for installation reference.
3. Support the door using a floor jack with a piece of wood placed between the jack and panel.
4. Remove the door hinge bolts and then remove the door.

To install:

5. Using the jack, position the door and install hinge bolts. Align the door to the reference marks.
6. Loosely tighten the hinge bolts and close the door lightly to check alignment.
7. Align door and tighten hinge bolts to 25 ft. lbs. (34 Nm).
8. As necessary, align door striker by loosening the screws and adjusting.
9. Install the door stopper pin.

ADJUSTMENT

Door adjustment is made by loosening the mounting bolts and/or striker and adjusting position as required. Position the door so that a clearance of 0.20 - 0.26 in. exists between the door and the rocker panel, fender or other door. The door should be flush within 0.04 in.

Hood

REMOVAL & INSTALLATION

See Figure 2

1. Raise hood and suitably support.
2. Install protective covers over fenders to prevent paint damage.
3. Mark the position of the hinges to the hood for installation reference.

Note: A helper is necessary to hold the hood during removal.

4. Remove the hinge bolts and lift the hood from the vehicle.

To install:

5. Align the hood with the marks made during removal.
6. Install the hinge bolts but do not tighten fully.

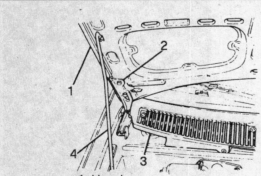

1. Hood
2. Hood hinge
3. Right side cowl vent grill
4. Hood prop rod

Fig. 2 Hood hinge assembly

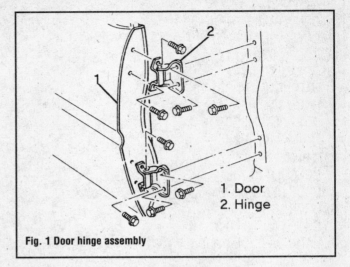

1. Door
2. Hinge

Fig. 1 Door hinge assembly

7. Adjust the hood to obtain the proper clearances.
8. Tighten hood hinge bolts to 20 ft. lbs. (27 Nm).

ADJUSTMENT

Hood adjustment is made by loosening the mounting bolts slightly and repositioning the hood. Always use an assistant during this procedure. The hood, when loosened, may come in contact with other painted surfaces and cause damage to their finish. Position the hood so that a clearance of 0.60 in. exists between the hood and cowl vent grille, a clearance of 0.20 in. exists between the hood and head lamps, and a clearance of 0.15 in. exists between the hood and fenders. The hood should be flush within 0.04 in.

Trunk Lid

REMOVAL & INSTALLATION

See Figure 3

Convertible Models

1. Raise and support the deck lid.
2. Remove the screws securing center high mounted stop lamp to the deck lid.
3. Pull stop lamp from deck lid and disconnect the electrical connector.
4. Remove stop light wiring from deck lid by removing grommets and feeding wiring through deck lid.
5. Remove the screw securing each deck lid side reveal molding to the deck lid.
6. Remove the screws securing each deck lid support to the deck lid.

Note: A helper is necessary to hold the hood during removal.

7. Remove the bolts securing the deck lid to each hinge and remove the deck lid from the vehicle.

To install:

8. Install the deck lid and secure with bolts.
9. Align deck lid and tighten bolts to 33 ft. lbs. (45 Nm).
10. Install the deck lid supports and secure with screws.
11. Install the screws to the deck lid reveal molding.
12. Feed wiring through deck lid and install grommets.
13. Connect the center high mounted stop light electrical connector.
14. Install the center high mounted stop lamp to the deck lid and secure with screw.
15. Lower deck lid and check adjustment.

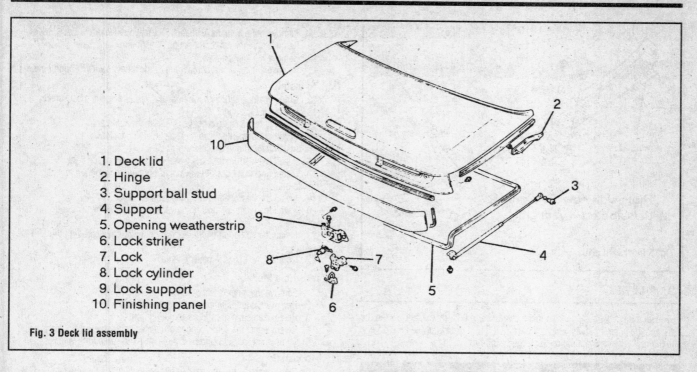

1. Deck lid
2. Hinge
3. Support ball stud
4. Support
5. Opening weatherstrip
6. Lock striker
7. Lock
8. Lock cylinder
9. Lock support
10. Finishing panel

Fig. 3 Deck lid assembly

ADJUSTMENT

Position the deck lid so that a clearance of 0.26 in. exists between the deck lid and the quarter panel. The deck lid should be flush within 0.04 in.

Hatchback Door

REMOVAL & INSTALLATION

See Figure 4

Hardtop Models

1. Raise and support the hatchback door.
2. Remove the screw securing each speaker grille and speaker to hatchback door.
3. Lower speakers and disconnect electrical connectors.
4. Remove plastic retaining clips and hatchback door interior trim panel.
5. Remove rear wiper motor, rear defogger, and center high mounted stop light electrical connectors.
6. Remove grommet from the upper right side of the hatchback door and feed wires through the opening.
7. Remove washer hose from the upper left side of the hatchback door.
8. Remove the screws from the hatchback door support and lower supports.
9. Mark position of hinges on door for installation reference.

Note: A helper is necessary to hold the door during removal.

10. Remove bolts from door hinge and lift hatchback door from vehicle.

To install:

11. Align the door hinges to the marks and install the hatchback door. Tighten hinge bolts to 33 ft. lbs. (45 Nm).
12. Install the door supports and washer hose.
13. Feed door wires through opening in hatchback door and install grommet.
14. Install rear wiper motor, rear window defogger and center high mounted stop light electrical connectors.
15. Install hatchback door interior trim panel.
16. Connect speaker electrical connectors and install speakers in place.
17. Lower hatchback door gently to check for proper alignment. Adjust as necessary.

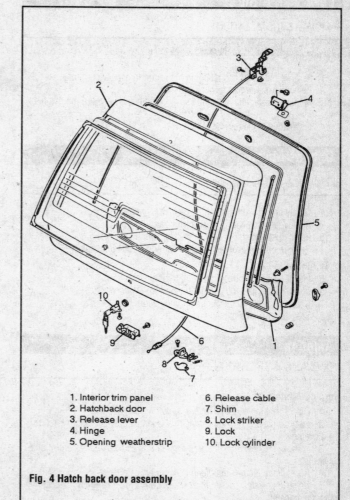

1. Interior trim panel	6. Release cable
2. Hatchback door	7. Shim
3. Release lever	8. Lock striker
4. Hinge	9. Lock
5. Opening weatherstrip	10. Lock cylinder

Fig. 4 Hatch back door assembly

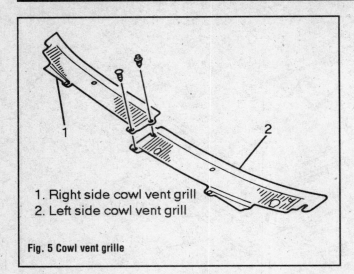

1. Right side cowl vent grill
2. Left side cowl vent grill

Fig. 5 Cowl vent grille

ADJUSTMENT

Position the hatchback door so that a clearance of 0.22 in. exists between the door and the quarter panel and a clearance of 0.34 in. exists between the door and the roof. The door should be flush within 0.04 in.

Cowl Vent Grille

REMOVAL & INSTALLATION

See Figure 5

1. Remove nut cover and retaining nut securing each wiper arm.
2. Remove wiper arms from linkage.
3. Remove plastic retaining clips securing the cowl vent and remove the vent.
4. Installation is the reverse of removal.

Outside Mirrors

REMOVAL & INSTALLATION

1. Gently pry off the inner mirror garnish.
2. Remove the screw and inner mirror garnish.
3. Remove screws and mirror assembly from door.
4. Remove outer mirror bezel from door and gasket from mirror.

To install:

5. Install gasket to mirror and bezel to door.
6. Install mirror assembly to door and secure with screws.
7. Install inner mirror bezel to door and secure with screw.
8. Snap inner mirror garnish into place.

Antenna

REMOVAL & INSTALLATION

Hardtop Models

1. Disconnect the negative battery cable.
2. Remove the air conditioner electrical connector by accessing through the glove box.
3. Remove the heater control unit lever knobs and the heater control unit cover plate.
4. Remove the illumination lamp from cover plate.
5. Remove gearshift control lever upper boot and console on manual transaxle models.
6. Remove the instrument panel bezel and front radio face panel.

7. Remove the radio from the instrument panel.
8. Remove radio antenna lead and electrical connectors.
9. Remove antenna cable from clips under instrument panel.
10. Remove left kick panel.
11. Remove antenna mast screws and guide antenna wire through hole.

To install:

12. Guide antenna wire through hole and install antenna mast screws.
13. Install left kick panel.
14. Install antenna cable on clips under instrument panel.
15. Install radio antenna lead and electrical connectors.
16. Install the radio in the instrument panel.
17. Install the instrument panel bezel and front radio face panel.
18. Install gearshift control lever upper boot and console on manual transaxle models.
19. Install the illumination lamp on cover plate.
20. Install the heater control unit lever knobs and the heater control unit cover plate.
21. Install the air conditioner electrical connector by accessing through the glove box.
22. Connect the negative battery cable.

Convertible Models

1. Remove the inner wheel housing.
2. Remove the antenna mast from ground base.
3. Remove antenna ground base mounting nut.
4. Remove antenna cable connector located behind wheel housing.
5. Remove antenna ground base assembly and cable from vehicle.

To install:

6. Install antenna ground base assembly and cable in vehicle.
7. Install antenna cable connector located behind wheel housing.
8. Install antenna ground base mounting nut and tighten to 11 ft. lbs. (15 Nm).
9. Install the antenna mast from ground base.
10. Install the inner wheel housing.

Fenders

REMOVAL & INSTALLATION

See Figure 6

1. Disconnect the negative battery cable.
2. Remove the parking lamp and slide away from fender. Disconnect bulb socket.
3. Raise and support the vehicle safely.
4. Remove tire and wheel.
5. Remove wheel housing.
6. Remove antenna from right fender, as required.
7. Remove fender bolts at door pillar.
8. Remove inner fender bolt.
9. Remove upper fender bolts.
10. Remove support nut securing fender to bumper fascia.
11. Remove retaining bolt from fender brace.
12. Slide fender off bumper side slider and remove.

To install:

13. Slide fender on bumper side slider and install.
14. Install retaining bolt on fender brace. Tighten to 15 ft. lbs. (20 Nm).
15. Install support nut securing fender to bumper fascia. Tighten to 15 ft. lbs. (20 Nm).
16. Install upper fender bolts. Tighten to 15 ft. lbs. (20 Nm).
17. Install inner fender bolt. Tighten to 15 ft. lbs. (20 Nm).
18. Install fender bolts at door pillar. Tighten to 15 ft. lbs. (20 Nm).
19. Install antenna on right fender, as required.
20. Install wheel housing.
21. Install tire and wheel.
22. Lower vehicle.
23. Connect bulb socket and install the parking lamp.
24. Connect the negative battery cable.

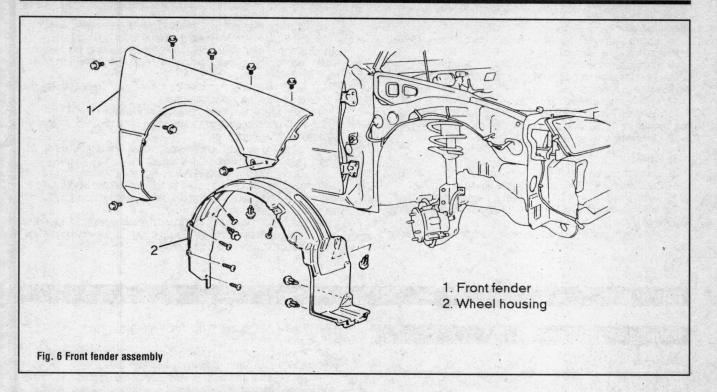

1. Front fender
2. Wheel housing

Fig. 6 Front fender assembly

Convertible Top

REMOVAL & INSTALLATION

See Figure 7

1. Unlatch the folding top at the windshield header. Raise top halfway and support.

2. Remove screws and header seal retainer from header.
3. Detach folded top edge of top material from header.
4. Remove screws from header extension.
5. Remove screws securing side rail, main arm seal retainer, top material, and cable guide to main arm. Separate top material from main arm seal retainer and cable guide. Bend metal tab of molding holder down with a hooked tip tool. The metal tab is located under the quarter molding.
6. Remove screws securing molding holder and side retainer.
7. Remove screws securing rear retainer and top material to vehicle and lift

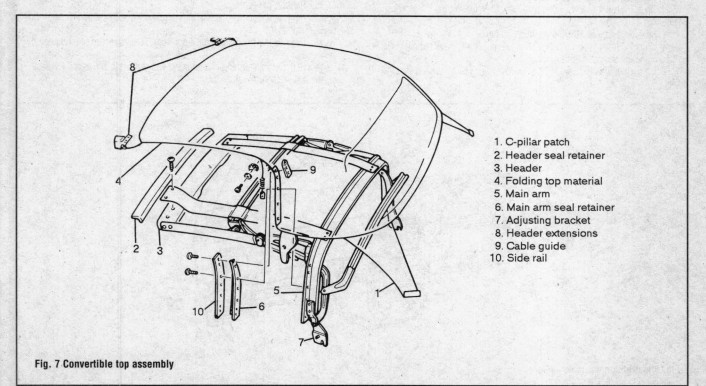

1. C-pillar patch
2. Header seal retainer
3. Header
4. Folding top material
5. Main arm
6. Main arm seal retainer
7. Adjusting bracket
8. Header extensions
9. Cable guide
10. Side rail

Fig. 7 Convertible top assembly

retainer from vehicle.

8. Remove plastic clips securing interior side trim panel to vehicle and position trim panel outside of vehicle.

9. Remove plastic retaining clip securing folding top material tongue to vehicle. Pull top material to gain access to the top pulleys and hold down cable brackets located on the main arm.

10. Remove screw and hold down cable bracket from main arm.

11. Remove screw and folding top pulley from main arm. Unfasten tension belt. Unfasten the C-pillar inner patches from rear bow.

12. Remove top from link assembly.

To install:

13. Install folding top material to link assembly.

14. Install top pulley to main arm and secure with screw.

15. Install hold down cable bracket to main arm and secure with screw.

16. Install top material tongue to side of vehicle and secure with plastic retaining clip.

17. Install interior side trim panel into position and secure with retaining clips.

18. Install rear retainer to vehicle and secure with screws. Lower deck lid.

19. Install side retainer and molding holder to vehicle and secure with screws. Straighten metal tab of molding holder and slide quarter molding into holder. Insert folding top material between the cable guide and the main arm seal retainer.

20. Install cable guide, folding rear top material, main arm seal retainer, and side rail to the main arm. Secure with screws.

21. Install weather strip to side rail and press into place.

22. Install header extensions to header and secure with screws. Attach double sided tape to folding top header.

23. Pull folding top material over header, fold top edge of material onto the header, and attach with a weatherstrip adhesive.

24. Install header seal retainer to header, align holes of folding top material, header and retainer. Secure with screws starting from center of header. Apply weatherstrip adhesive between header and material at both ends of header and press material securely into place.

25. Install latch to folding top to windshield header engaging the folding top latch handle lock. Fasten tension belt. Fasten C-pillar inner patches to rear bow to remove wrinkles in the folding top material.

INTERIOR

Instrument Panel and Pad

REMOVAL & INSTALLATION

See Figures 8 and 9

✳✳ CAUTION:

The Supplemental Inflatable Restraint (SIR) system must be disabled prior to performing this service. Refer to Section 6 for SIR disabling procedure.

1. Disconnect the negative battery cable.

2. On convertible models, remove the inflator module from the steering wheel.

3. Remove the lower steering column trim panel.

4. On convertible models, remove the steering wheel. Also remove the SIR coil/combination switch assembly.

5. On hardtop models, remove the combination switch from the steering wheel.

6. Remove the right and left kick panels by removing a plastic retaining nut and clip from each panel.

7. Remove the right and left speaker grilles from instrument panel by removing screws and plastic retaining clip from each grille.

8. On convertible models, remove the retaining clip securing instrument panel to each door jamb.

9. Remove the right and left front speakers from instrument panel by removing screws and one electrical connector from each speaker.

10. Remove the glove box inner panel.

11. Remove the A/C switch electrical connector through the glove box.

12. Remove the heater control unit lever knobs and pull the heater control unit from the instrument panel.

13. Disconnect the heater control unit illumination lamp from cover plate.

14. On manual transmission vehicles, remove the gearshift control lever upper boot from console, then remove the console.

15. Remove the ashtray.

16. Remove the center console trim bezel and instrument panel center trim bezel. Remove the radio.

17. Remove the electrical connectors from the cluster trim bezel mounted switches.

18. Remove the retaining clip and speedometer cable at transaxle to ease cluster assembly removal.

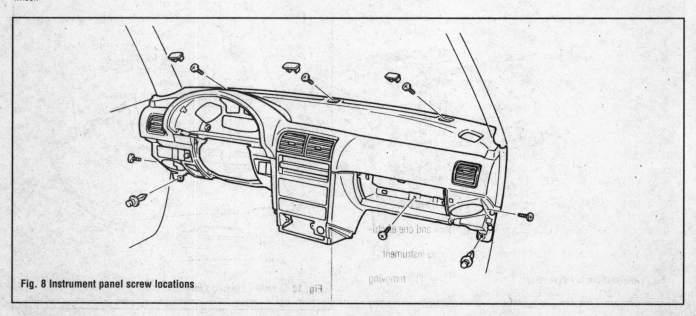

Fig. 8 Instrument panel screw locations

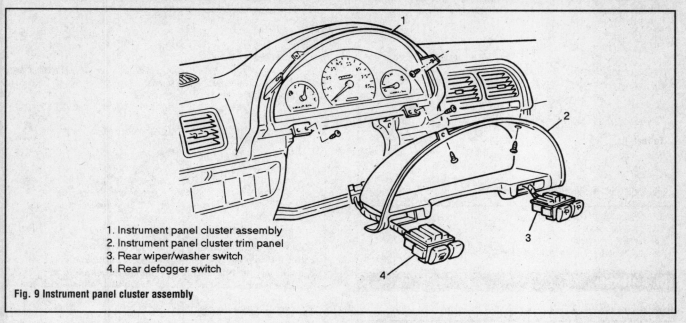

1. Instrument panel cluster assembly
2. Instrument panel cluster trim panel
3. Rear wiper/washer switch
4. Rear defogger switch

Fig. 9 Instrument panel cluster assembly

19. Remove cluster assembly from instrument panel.
20. Remove the speedometer cable and all electrical connectors from back of cluster assembly, then remove cluster assembly from vehicle.
21. Remove ashtray illumination lamp electrical connector.
22. Remove electrical connector from rear of cigar lighter, then remove retaining ring from rear of cigar lighter.
23. Remove the lower instrument panel retaining screws.
24. Remove the upper instrument panel retaining screws.
25. Remove screw retaining instrument panel bracket to floor pan.
26. Remove the illumination controller electrical connector.
27. Remove the hood latch release lever.
28. Remove instrument panel from vehicle.

To install:
29. Install instrument panel to vehicle.
30. Install the hood latch release lever.
31. Install the illumination controller electrical connector.
32. Install screw retaining instrument panel bracket to floor pan.
33. Install the upper instrument panel retaining screws.
34. Install the lower instrument panel retaining screws.
35. Install electrical connector to rear of cigar lighter then install retaining ring to rear of cigar lighter.
36. Install ashtray illumination lamp electrical connector.
37. Install the speedometer cable and all electrical connectors to back of cluster assembly, then install cluster assembly to vehicle.
38. Install cluster assembly to instrument panel.
39. Install the retaining clip and speedometer cable at transaxle.
40. Install the electrical connectors to the cluster trim bezel mounted switches.
41. Install the center console trim bezel and instrument panel center trim bezel. Install the radio.
42. Install the ashtray.
43. On manual transmission vehicles, install the console, then install the gearshift control lever upper boot to console.
44. Connect the heater control unit illumination lamp to cover plate.
45. Install the heater control unit lever knobs and push the heater control unit to the instrument panel.
46. Install the A/C switch electrical connector through the glove box.
47. Install the glove box inner panel.
48. Install the right and left to speakers to instrument panel and one electrical connector to each speaker.
49. On convertible models, install the retaining clip securing instrument panel to each door jamb.
50. Install the right and left speaker grilles to instrument panel by removing screws and plastic retaining clip to each grille.
51. Install the right and left kick panels by removing a plastic retaining nut

and clip to each panel.
52. On hardtop models, install the combination switch to the steering wheel.
53. On convertible models, install the SIR coil/combination switch assembly.
54. On convertible models, install the steering wheel.
55. Install the lower steering column trim panel.
56. On convertible models, install the inflator module to the steering wheel.
57. Connect the negative battery cable.

Console

REMOVAL & INSTALLATION

See Figure 10

1. Remove the gearshift control lever upper boot from console.

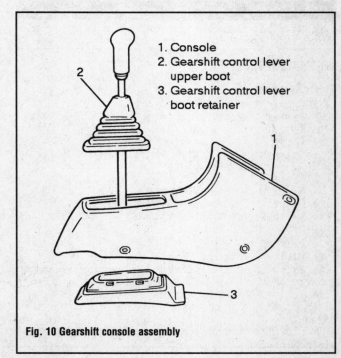

1. Console
2. Gearshift control lever upper boot
3. Gearshift control lever boot retainer

Fig. 10 Gearshift console assembly

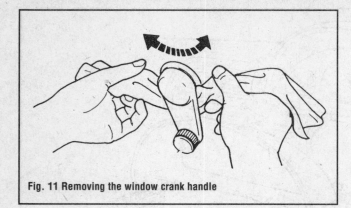

Fig. 11 Removing the window crank handle

2. Remove screws securing console to vehicle.
3. Remove console from vehicle.
4. Installation is the reverse of removal.

Door Panels

REMOVAL & INSTALLATION

See Figure 11

1. Remove the inside door handle bezel and gently pull from door trim.
2. Remove screws from armrest handle garnish.
3. Remove plastic screw covers from door armrest.
4. Remove screws and armrest from door.
5. Remove regulator handle using a cloth to remove snapring.
6. Gently pry door panel away from door, disengaging retaining clips.

To install:

7. Install door panel to door and press retaining clips into place.
8. Install snapring to window regulator handle and install handle.
9. Install armrest to door.
10. Install screws and plastic screw covers.
11. Install screw and armrest handle garnish.
12. Install inside door handle bezel.

Door Locks

REMOVAL & INSTALLATION

See Figures 12 and 13

Striker Assembly

1. Disconnect the negative battery cable.
2. Remove the door panel and unclip the outer sealing strip from door.
3. Remove the door trim bracket.
4. Disconnect the seat belt retractor electrical connector.
5. Remove the seat belt retractor and seat belt assembly from the door.
6. Remove the water deflector.
7. Remove the door glass.
8. Remove the rear window guide channel as required.
9. Remove the lock assembly switch electrical connector.
10. Remove the handle rod and lock rod from the door lock.
11. Remove the door lock assembly from the door.
12. Remove the lock striker from the door panel.

To install:

13. Install the lock striker and secure with screws. Adjust the lock striker to door distance to 0.51 - 0.59 in. (13 - 15 mm) by installing or removing shims.
14. Install the door lock assembly and secure with screws. Adjust the striker up and down measurement so that the striker shaft aligns with the center of the door lock.
15. Install the outside handle rod and outside handle lock rod. Adjust the lock rod distance to 0 - 0.08 in. (0 - 2 mm).

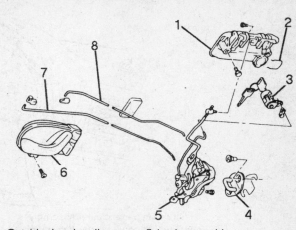

1. Outside door handle
2. Front side rib
3. Lock cylinder snapring
4. Lock striker
5. Lock assembly
6. Inside door handle
7. Inside door handle rod
8. Inside door handle lock rod

Fig. 12 Door lock assembly

16. Connect the lock assembly switch electrical connector.
17. Install the rear window guide channel as required.
18. Install the door glass.
19. Install the water deflector.
20. Install the seat belt retractor and seat belt assembly to the door. Tighten seat belt retractor assembly nut, bolts, and seat belt anchor to 33 ft. lbs. (45 Nm).
21. Connect the seat belt retractor electrical connector.
22. Install the door trim bracket.
23. Install the door panel and attach the outer sealing strip to door.
24. Connect the negative battery cable.

Lock Cylinder

1. Disconnect the negative battery cable.
2. Remove the door panel and pull water deflector far enough away from door to gain access to lock cylinder.
3. Remove lock rod from lock cylinder.
4. Remove retaining clip and lock cylinder from door.

To install:

5. Install lock cylinder and retaining clip.

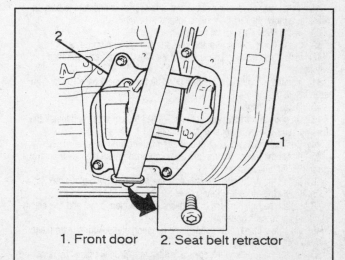

1. Front door
2. Seat belt retractor

Fig. 13 Seat belt retractor assembly

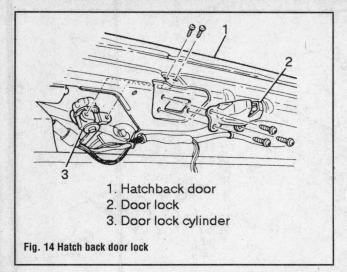

1. Hatchback door
2. Door lock
3. Door lock cylinder

Fig. 14 Hatch back door lock

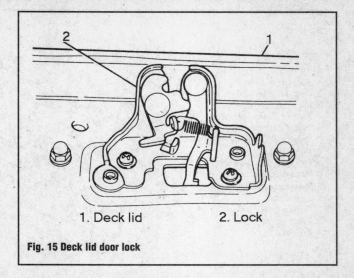

1. Deck lid   2. Lock

Fig. 15 Deck lid door lock

6. Install lock rod to lock cylinder.
7. Install water deflector and door panel.
8. Connect the negative battery cable.

Hatchback/Deck Lid Lock

REMOVAL & INSTALLATION

See Figures 14 and 15

Striker Assembly

1. Remove the rear end interior trim panel.
2. Remove the lock striker from the vehicle.
3. Installation is the reverse of removal.
4. Adjust the striker by loosening the screws and move the striker into position for proper alignment.

Lock Cylinder

1. On hatchback doors, remove the speaker grills and speakers. Lower

speakers and disconnect electrical connectors.
2. On hatchback doors, remove the door interior trim panel.
3. Remove the door lock from the door.
4. Installation is the reverse of removal.

Door Glass

REMOVAL & INSTALLATION

See Figures 16 and 17

Hardtop Models

1. Disconnect the negative battery cable.
2. Remove the front door trim and inner mirror garnish.
3. Remove the inner mirror garnish.
4. Unclip the outer sealing strip from the door. Pull the water deflector far enough away from the door to gain access to the bottom channel-to-regulator screws.
5. Remove the window bottom channel-to-regulator retaining screws.

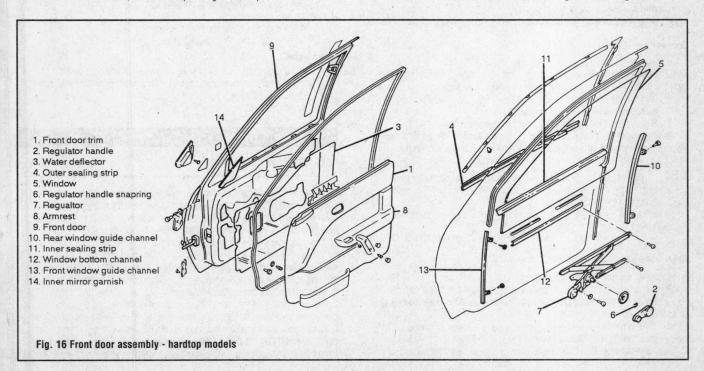

1. Front door trim
2. Regulator handle
3. Water deflector
4. Outer sealing strip
5. Window
6. Regulator handle snapring
7. Regualtor
8. Armrest
9. Front door
10. Rear window guide channel
11. Inner sealing strip
12. Window bottom channel
13. Front window guide channel
14. Inner mirror garnish

Fig. 16 Front door assembly - hardtop models

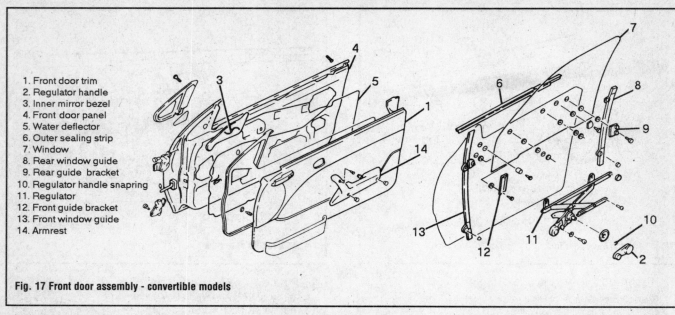

1. Front door trim
2. Regulator handle
3. Inner mirror bezel
4. Front door panel
5. Water deflector
6. Outer sealing strip
7. Window
8. Rear window guide
9. Rear guide bracket
10. Regulator handle snapring
11. Regulator
12. Front guide bracket
13. Front window guide
14. Armrest

Fig. 17 Front door assembly - convertible models

6. Remove the window assembly from the door.
7. Remove the window from the bottom channel.

To install:

8. Install the window to the bottom channel. Coat the bottom channel with soapy water to ease installation.
9. Install the window assembly to the door. Align the window bottom channel so that the distance from the bottom channel rear screw to the rear edge of the window is 11.95 in. on 2-door models or 9.96 in. on 4-door models.
10. Install the window bottom channel-to-regulator retaining screws. Tighten screws to 44 inch lbs. (5 Nm).

Note: Overtightening screws may break window.

11. Adjust regulator screws so that measurements between the front door window and the front door window frame are equal at the front and rear of the top edge.
12. Inspect window for correct front/rear and left/right position.
13. Place water deflector in its normal position.
14. Clip outer sealing strip onto door.
15. Install inner mirror garnish to door and install door panel.

Convertible Models

1. Remove the front door trim and inner mirror garnish.
2. Remove the inner mirror bezel. Pull the water deflector far enough away from the door to gain access to the bottom channel-to-regulator screws.
3. Remove the door trim support.
4. Remove the window regulator mounting nuts.
5. Remove the window assembly from the door.
6. Remove the regulator bottom bolts from the window, the window male stopper, the window male stabilizer and the front and rear guide brackets.

To install:

7. Loosen upper and lower front and rear window guide mounting nuts.
8. Install front and rear guide bracket to window and secure with bolts. Tighten bolts to 44 inch lbs. (5 Nm).
9. Install male stabilizer and stopper to window and secure with bolts. Tighten bolts to 44 inch lbs. (5 Nm).
10. Install regulator bottom bolts and tighten to 44 inch lbs. (5 Nm).

Note: Overtightening screws may break window.

11. Install window assembly to door.
12. Install regulator-to-window bolts and tighten to 44 inch lbs. (5 Nm).
13. Install door trim supports and secure with screw. Clip outer sealing strip to door.
14. Tighten front and rear window guide upper and lower mounting nuts at the center of the oblong holes in the door panel to 115 inch lbs. (13 Nm).
15. Raise window to its fully closed position. Inspect window for correct

front/rear and left/right position. If window is not properly positioned, correct by loosening the front and rear window guide mounting nuts and adjusting the front and rear window guides.

16. Adjust regulator equalizer screws so that measurements between the top stack link and the front door window are equal at the front and rear of the window top.

17. Install the water deflector, inner mirror bezel and door panel.

Window Regulator

REMOVAL & INSTALLATION

See Figures 16 and 17

1 Disconnect the negative battery cable.
2. Remove the window.
3. Pull water deflector far enough away from door to gain access to the regulator retaining screws.
4. Remove retaining screws from the regulator.
5. Remove the regulator through the large opening in the door.

To install:

6. Apply multipurpose grease to all lubrication and sliding points.
7. Install regulator to door and secure with screws. Position water deflector back to its normal position.
8. Install the window.

Windshield Glass

REMOVAL & INSTALLATION

If your windshield, or other fixed window, is cracked or chipped, you may decide to replace it with a new one yourself. However, there are two main reasons why replacement windshields and other window glass should be installed only by a professional automotive glass technician: safety and cost.

The most important reason a professional should install automotive glass is for safety. The glass in the vehicle, especially the windshield, is designed with safety in mind in case of a collision. The windshield is specially manufactured from two panes of specially-tempered glass with a thin layer of transparent plastic between them. This construction allows the glass to "give" in the event that a part of your body hits the windshield during the collision, and prevents the glass from shattering, which could cause lacerations, blinding and other harm to passengers of the vehicle. The other fixed windows are designed to be tempered so that if they break during a collision, they shatter in such a way that there are no large pointed glass pieces. The professional automotive glass tech-

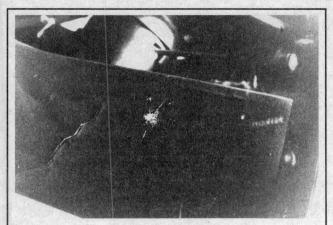

Fig. 18 Small chips on your windshield can be fixed with an aftermarket repair kit, such as the one from Loctite,

Fig. 19 To repair a chip, clean the windshield with glass cleaner and dry it completely

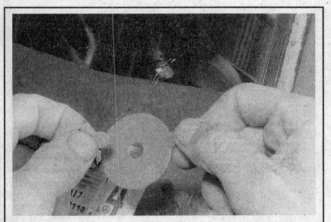

Fig. 20 Remove the center from the adhesive disc and peel off the backing from one side of the disc . . .

Fig. 21 . . . then press it on the windshield so that the chip is centered in the hole

nician knows how to install the glass in a vehicle so that it will function optimally during a collision. Without the proper experience, knowledge, and tools, installing a piece of automotive glass yourself could lead to additional harm if an accident should ever occur.

Cost is also a factor when deciding to install automotive glass yourself. Performing this could cost you much more than a professional may charge for the same job. Since the windshield is designed to break under stress, an often life saving characteristic, windshields tend to break VERY easily when an inexperienced person attempts to install one. Do-it-yourselfers buying two, three or even four windshields from a salvage yard because they have broken them during installation are common stories. Also, since the automotive glass is designed to prevent the outside elements from entering your vehicle, improper installation can lead to water and air leaks. Annoying whining noises at highway speeds from air leaks or inside body panel rusting from water leaks can add to your stress level and subtract from your wallet. After buying two or three windshields, installing them and ending up with a leak that produces a noise while driving and water damage during rainstorms, the cost of having a professional do it correctly the first time may be much more alluring. We here at Chilton, therefore, advise that you have a professional automotive glass technician service any broken glass on your vehicle.

WINDSHIELD CHIP REPAIR

See Figures 18, 19, 20, 21, 22, 23, 24, 25, 26, 27, 28, 29, 30, 31 and 32

Note: Check with your state and local authorities on the laws for state

safety inspection. Some states or municipalities may not allow chip repair as a viable option for correcting stone damage to your windshield.

Although severely cracked or damaged windshields must be replaced, there is something that you can do to prolong or even prevent the need for replacement of a chipped windshield. There are many companies which offer wind-

Fig. 22 Be sure that the tab points upward on the windshield

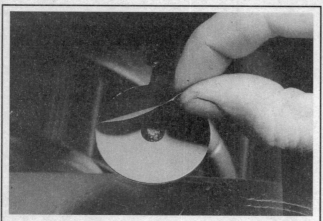

Fig. 23 Peel the backing off the exposed side of the adhesive disc . . .

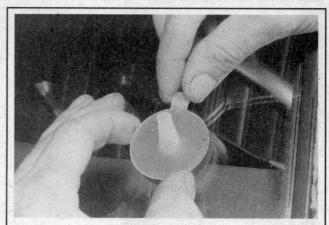

Fig. 24 . . . then position the plastic pedestal on the adhesive disc, ensuring that the tabs are aligned

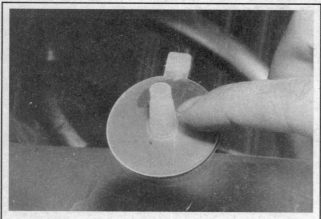

Fig. 25 Press the pedestal firmly on the adhesive disc to create an adequate seal . . .

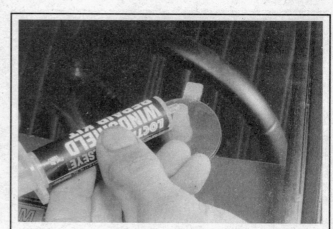

Fig. 26 . . . then install the applicator syringe nipple in the pedestal's hole

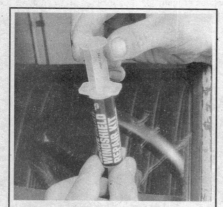

Fig. 27 Hold the syringe with one hand while pulling the plunger back with the other hand

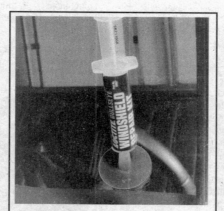

Fig. 28 After applying the solution, allow the entire assembly to sit until it has set completely

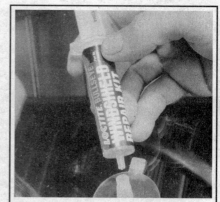

Fig. 29 After the solution has set, remove the syringe from the pedestal . . .

shield chip repair products, such as Loctite's, Bullseye' windshield repair kit. These kits usually consist of a syringe, pedestal, and a sealing adhesive. The syringe is mounted on the pedestal and is used to create a vacuum which pulls the plastic layer against the glass. This helps make the chip transparent. The adhesive is then injected which seals the chip and helps to prevent further stress cracks from developing. Refer to the sequence of photos to get a general idea of what windshield chip repair involves.

Note: Always follow the specific manufacturer's instructions.

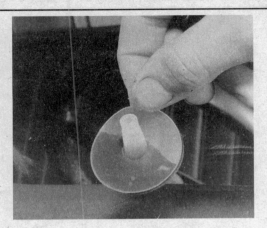

Fig. 30 . . . then peel the pedestal off of the adhesive disc . . .

Fig. 31 . . . and peel the adhesive disc off of the windshield

Inside Rear View Mirror

REMOVAL & INSTALLATION

1. Remove the dome lamp bezel.
2. Remove the rear view mirror mounting screws.
3. Remove the rear view mirror from the vehicle.
4. Installation is the reverse of removal.

Seats

REMOVAL & INSTALLATION

See Figures 33 and 34

Front

1. Disconnect the negative battery cable.
2. Remove the seat adjuster mounting bolts from seat assembly.
3. Disconnect seat belt switch electrical connector.
4. Remove seat from vehicle.

To install:

5. Install seat in vehicle.
6. Connect seat belt switch electrical connector.
7. Install the seat adjuster mounting bolts and tighten to 13 ft. lbs. (18 Nm).
8. Connect the negative battery cable.

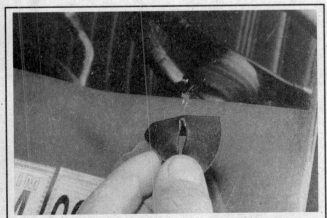

Fig. 32 The chip will still be slightly visible, but it should be filled with the hardened solution

Rear

1. Remove luggage compartment security shelf strings from hooks and lift the shelf out of the vehicle.
2. Disengage plastic snaps securing luggage compartment carpet to floor at rear of luggage compartment.
3. Remove plastic retaining clips along forward edge of luggage compartment floor.
4. Place rear seat back in folded position.
5. Lift carpet over the rear seat back to gain access to rear retaining clips

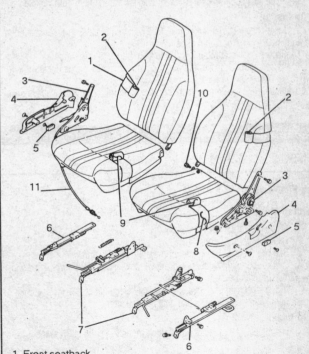

1. Front seatback
2. Front seatback cover
3. Recliner mechanism
4. Seat cushion side panel
5. Recliner handle
6. Outboard seat adjuster
7. Inboard seat adjusters
8. Front seat cushion
9. Front seat cushion cover
10. Inboard seatback hinge arm screw
11. Easy entry cable

Fig. 33 Front seat assembly

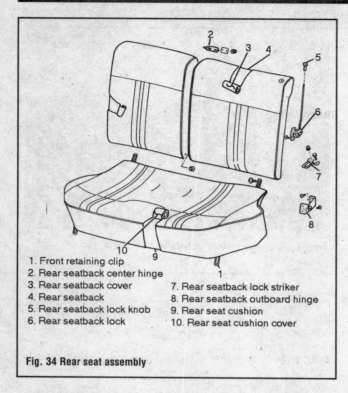

1. Front retaining clip
2. Rear seatback center hinge
3. Rear seatback cover
4. Rear seatback
5. Rear seatback lock knob
6. Rear seatback lock
7. Rear seatback lock striker
8. Rear seatback outboard hinge
9. Rear seat cushion
10. Rear seat cushion cover

Fig. 34 Rear seat assembly

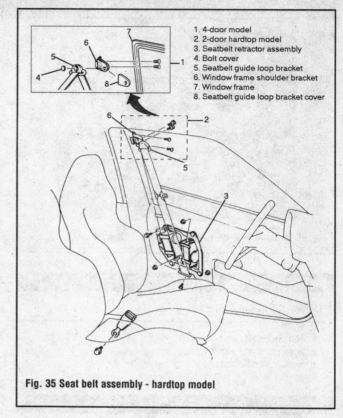

1. 4-door model
2. 2-door hardtop model
3. Seatbelt retractor assembly
4. Bolt cover
5. Seatbelt guide loop bracket
6. Window frame shoulder bracket
7. Window frame
8. Seatbelt guide loop bracket cover

Fig. 35 Seat belt assembly - hardtop model

which secure the rear seat cushion to the floor pan. Remove the screws and raise seat cushion at front edge disengaging front retaining slips.

6. Slide seat cushion over seat belt buckles and remove from vehicle.

To install:

7. Install seat cushion to vehicle, feed seat belt buckles through seat cushion and engage front retaining clips.

8. Secure each rear retaining clip to floor pan with one screw.

9. Place seat back in upright position and reinstall luggage compartment carpet.

10. Install luggage compartment security shelf into vehicle and attach security shelf strings to security shelf string hooks.

Seat Belts

REMOVAL & INSTALLATION

See Figure 35

Hardtop Model

1. Disconnect the negative battery cable.
2. Remove the front door panel.
3. Remove the seat belt guide loop bracket from window.
4. Pull rubber window channel from window and remove screws and window frame shoulder bracket.
5. Disconnect seat belt retractor assembly electrical connector.
6. Remove mounting bolts and seat belt retractor.

To install:

7. Install seat belt retractor and tighten mounting bolts to 33 ft. lbs. (45 Nm).

8. Connect seat belt retractor assembly electrical connector.
9. Install window frame shoulder bracket.
10. Install the seat belt guide loop bracket to window and tighten bolt to 33 ft. lbs. (45 Nm).
11. Install front door panel and connect negative battery cable.

Convertible Model

1. Disconnect the negative battery cable.
2. Remove the anchor bolt securing the seat belt to the floor.
3. Remove the plastic retaining clips and rear speaker panel.
4. Remove the plastic retaining clips and the passenger compartment quarter trim panel.
5. Remove the plastic cover and anchor bolt securing seat belt guide loop to vehicle.
6. Remove the anchor bolt and seat belt retractor assembly from the vehicle.
7. Remove the anchor bolt and remove the seat belt buckle from the vehicle.

To install:

8. Install the seat belt buckle and tighten bolt to 33 ft. lbs. (45 Nm).
9. Install the seat belt retractor and tighten bolt to 33 ft. lbs. (45 Nm).
10. Install the seat belt guide loop and tighten bolt to 33 ft. lbs. (45 Nm).
11. Install the plastic retaining clips and the passenger compartment quarter trim panel.
12. Install the plastic retaining clips and rear speaker panel.
13. Install the anchor bolt securing the seat belt to the floor. Tighten bolt to 33 ft. lbs. (45 Nm).
14. Connect the negative battery cable.

GLOSSARY

AIR/FUEL RATIO: The ratio of air-to-gasoline by weight in the fuel mixture drawn into the engine.

AIR INJECTION: One method of reducing harmful exhaust emissions by injecting air into each of the exhaust ports of an engine. The fresh air entering the hot exhaust manifold causes any remaining fuel to be burned before it can exit the tailpipe.

ALTERNATOR: A device used for converting mechanical energy into electrical energy.

AMMETER: An instrument, calibrated in amperes, used to measure the flow of an electrical current in a circuit. Ammeters are always connected in series with the circuit being tested.

AMPERE: The rate of flow of electrical current present when one volt of electrical pressure is applied against one ohm of electrical resistance.

ANALOG COMPUTER: Any microprocessor that uses similar (analogous) electrical signals to make its calculations.

ARMATURE: A laminated, soft iron core wrapped by a wire that converts electrical energy to mechanical energy as in a motor or relay. When rotated in a magnetic field, it changes mechanical energy into electrical energy as in a generator.

ATMOSPHERIC PRESSURE: The pressure on the Earth's surface caused by the weight of the air in the atmosphere. At sea level, this pressure is 14.7 psi at 32°F (101 kPa at 0°C).

ATOMIZATION: The breaking down of a liquid into a fine mist that can be suspended in air.

AXIAL PLAY: Movement parallel to a shaft or bearing bore.

BACKFIRE: The sudden combustion of gases in the intake or exhaust system that results in a loud explosion.

BACKLASH: The clearance or play between two parts, such as meshed gears.

BACKPRESSURE: Restrictions in the exhaust system that slow the exit of exhaust gases from the combustion chamber.

BAKELITE: A heat resistant, plastic insulator material commonly used in printed circuit boards and transistorized components.

BALL BEARING: A bearing made up of hardened inner and outer races between which hardened steel balls roll.

BALLAST RESISTOR: A resistor in the primary ignition circuit that lowers voltage after the engine is started to reduce wear on ignition components.

BEARING: A friction reducing, supportive device usually located between a stationary part and a moving part.

BIMETAL TEMPERATURE SENSOR: Any sensor or switch made of two dissimilar types of metal that bend when heated or cooled due to the different expansion rates of the alloys. These types of sensors usually function as an on/off switch.

BLOWBY: Combustion gases, composed of water vapor and unburned fuel, that leak past the piston rings into the crankcase during normal engine operation. These gases are removed by the PCV system to prevent the buildup of harmful acids in the crankcase.

BRAKE PAD: A brake shoe and lining assembly used with disc brakes.

BRAKE SHOE: The backing for the brake lining. The term is, however, usually applied to the assembly of the brake backing and lining.

BUSHING: A liner, usually removable, for a bearing; an anti-friction liner used in place of a bearing.

CALIPER: A hydraulically activated device in a disc brake system, which is mounted straddling the brake rotor (disc). The caliper contains at least one piston and two brake pads. Hydraulic pressure on the piston(s) forces the pads against the rotor.

CAMSHAFT: A shaft in the engine on which are the lobes (cams) which operate the valves. The camshaft is driven by the crankshaft, via a belt, chain or gears, at one half the crankshaft speed.

CAPACITOR: A device which stores an electrical charge.

CARBON MONOXIDE (CO): A colorless, odorless gas given off as a normal byproduct of combustion. It is poisonous and extremely dangerous in confined areas, building up slowly to toxic levels without warning if adequate ventilation is not available.

CARBURETOR: A device, usually mounted on the intake manifold of an engine, which mixes the air and fuel in the proper proportion to allow even combustion.

CATALYTIC CONVERTER: A device installed in the exhaust system, like a muffler, that converts harmful byproducts of combustion into carbon dioxide and water vapor by means of a heat-producing chemical reaction.

CENTRIFUGAL ADVANCE: A mechanical method of advancing the spark timing by using flyweights in the distributor that react to centrifugal force generated by the distributor shaft rotation.

CHECK VALVE: Any one-way valve installed to permit the flow of air, fuel or vacuum in one direction only.

CHOKE: A device, usually a moveable valve, placed in the intake path of a carburetor to restrict the flow of air.

CIRCUIT: Any unbroken path through which an electrical current can flow. Also used to describe fuel flow in some instances.

CIRCUIT BREAKER: A switch which protects an electrical circuit from overload by opening the circuit when the current flow exceeds a predetermined level. Some circuit breakers must be reset manually, while most reset automatically.

COIL (IGNITION): A transformer in the ignition circuit which steps up the voltage provided to the spark plugs.

COMBINATION MANIFOLD: An assembly which includes both the intake and exhaust manifolds in one casting.

COMBINATION VALVE: A device used in some fuel systems that routes fuel vapors to a charcoal storage canister instead of venting them into the atmosphere. The valve relieves fuel tank pressure and allows fresh air into the tank as the fuel level drops to prevent a vapor lock situation.

COMPRESSION RATIO: The comparison of the total volume of the cylinder and combustion chamber with the piston at BDC and the piston at TDC.

CONDENSER: 1. An electrical device which acts to store an electrical charge, preventing voltage surges. 2. A radiator-like device in the air conditioning system in which refrigerant gas condenses into a liquid, giving off heat.

CONDUCTOR: Any material through which an electrical current can be transmitted easily.

CONTINUITY: Continuous or complete circuit. Can be checked with an ohmmeter.

COUNTERSHAFT: An intermediate shaft which is rotated by a mainshaft and transmits, in turn, that rotation to a working part.

CRANKCASE: The lower part of an engine in which the crankshaft and related parts operate.

CRANKSHAFT: The main driving shaft of an engine which receives reciprocating motion from the pistons and converts it to rotary motion.

CYLINDER: In an engine, the round hole in the engine block in which the piston(s) ride.

CYLINDER BLOCK: The main structural member of an engine in which is found the cylinders, crankshaft and other principal parts.

CYLINDER HEAD: The detachable portion of the engine, usually fastened to the top of the cylinder block and containing all or most of the combustion chambers. On overhead valve engines, it contains the valves and their operating parts. On overhead cam engines, it contains the camshaft as well.

DEAD CENTER: The extreme top or bottom of the piston stroke.

DETONATION: An unwanted explosion of the air/fuel mixture in the combustion chamber caused by excess heat and compression, advanced timing, or an overly lean mixture. Also referred to as "ping".

DIAPHRAGM: A thin, flexible wall separating two cavities, such as in a vacuum advance unit.

DIESELING: A condition in which hot spots in the combustion chamber cause the engine to run on after the key is turned off.

DIFFERENTIAL: A geared assembly which allows the transmission of motion between drive axles, giving one axle the ability to turn faster than the other.

DIODE: An electrical device that will allow current to flow in one direction only.

DISC BRAKE: A hydraulic braking assembly consisting of a brake disc, or rotor, mounted on an axle, and a caliper assembly containing, usually two brake pads which are activated by hydraulic pressure. The pads are forced against the sides of the disc, creating friction which slows the vehicle.

DISTRIBUTOR: A mechanically driven device on an engine which is responsible for electrically firing the spark plug at a predetermined point of the piston stroke.

DOWEL PIN: A pin, inserted in mating holes in two different parts allowing those parts to maintain a fixed relationship.

DRUM BRAKE: A braking system which consists of two brake shoes and one or two wheel cylinders, mounted on a fixed backing plate, and a brake drum, mounted on an axle, which revolves around the assembly.

DWELL: The rate, measured in degrees of shaft rotation, at which an electrical circuit cycles on and off.

ELECTRONIC CONTROL UNIT (ECU): Ignition module, module, amplifier or igniter. See Module for definition.

ELECTRONIC IGNITION: A system in which the timing and firing of the spark plugs is controlled by an electronic control unit, usually called a module. These systems have no points or condenser.

END-PLAY: The measured amount of axial movement in a shaft.

ENGINE: A device that converts heat into mechanical energy.

EXHAUST MANIFOLD: A set of cast passages or pipes which conduct exhaust gases from the engine.

FEELER GAUGE: A blade, usually metal, or precisely predetermined thickness, used to measure the clearance between two parts.

FIRING ORDER: The order in which combustion occurs in the cylinders of an engine. Also the order in which spark is distributed to the plugs by the distributor.

FLOODING: The presence of too much fuel in the intake manifold and combustion chamber which prevents the air/fuel mixture from firing, thereby causing a no-start situation.

FLYWHEEL: A disc shaped part bolted to the rear end of the crankshaft. Around the outer perimeter is affixed the ring gear. The starter drive engages the ring gear, turning the flywheel, which rotates the crankshaft, imparting the initial starting motion to the engine.

FOOT POUND (ft. lbs. or sometimes, ft.lb.): The amount of energy or work needed to raise an item weighing one pound, a distance of one foot.

FUSE: A protective device in a circuit which prevents circuit overload by breaking the circuit when a specific amperage is present. The device is constructed around a strip or wire of a lower amperage rating than the circuit it is designed to protect. When an amperage higher than that stamped on the fuse is present in the circuit, the strip or wire melts, opening the circuit.

GEAR RATIO: The ratio between the number of teeth on meshing gears.

GENERATOR: A device which converts mechanical energy into electrical energy.

HEAT RANGE: The measure of a spark plug's ability to dissipate heat from its firing end. The higher the heat range, the hotter the plug fires.

HUB: The center part of a wheel or gear.

HYDROCARBON (HC): Any chemical compound made up of hydrogen and carbon. A major pollutant formed by the engine as a byproduct of combustion.

HYDROMETER: An instrument used to measure the specific gravity of a solution.

INCH POUND (inch lbs.; sometimes in.lb. or in. lbs.): One twelfth of a foot pound.

INDUCTION: A means of transferring electrical energy in the form of a magnetic field. Principle used in the ignition coil to increase voltage.

INJECTOR: A device which receives metered fuel under relatively low pressure and is activated to inject the fuel into the engine under relatively high pressure at a predetermined time.

INPUT SHAFT: The shaft to which torque is applied, usually carrying the driving gear or gears.

INTAKE MANIFOLD: A casting of passages or pipes used to conduct air or a fuel/air mixture to the cylinders.

JOURNAL: The bearing surface within which a shaft operates.

KEY: A small block usually fitted in a notch between a shaft and a hub to prevent slippage of the two parts.

MANIFOLD: A casting of passages or set of pipes which connect the cylinders to an inlet or outlet source.

MANIFOLD VACUUM: Low pressure in an engine intake manifold formed just below the throttle plates. Manifold vacuum is highest at idle and drops under acceleration.

MASTER CYLINDER: The primary fluid pressurizing device in a hydraulic system. In automotive use, it is found in brake and hydraulic clutch systems and is pedal activated, either directly or, in a power brake system, through the power booster.

MODULE: Electronic control unit, amplifier or igniter of solid state or integrated design which controls the current flow in the ignition primary circuit based on input from the pick-up coil. When the module opens the primary circuit, high secondary voltage is induced in the coil.

NEEDLE BEARING: A bearing which consists of a number (usually a large number) of long, thin rollers.

OHM: (Ω) The unit used to measure the resistance of conductor-to-electrical flow. One ohm is the amount of resistance that limits current flow to one ampere in a circuit with one volt of pressure.

OHMMETER: An instrument used for measuring the resistance, in ohms, in an electrical circuit.

OUTPUT SHAFT: The shaft which transmits torque from a device, such as a transmission.

OVERDRIVE: A gear assembly which produces more shaft revolutions than that transmitted to it.

OVERHEAD CAMSHAFT (OHC): An engine configuration in which the camshaft is mounted on top of the cylinder head and operates the valve either directly or by means of rocker arms.

OVERHEAD VALVE (OHV): An engine configuration in which all of the valves are located in the cylinder head and the camshaft is located in the cylinder block. The camshaft operates the valves via lifters and pushrods.

OXIDES OF NITROGEN (NOx): Chemical compounds of nitrogen produced as a byproduct of combustion. They combine with hydrocarbons to produce smog.

OXYGEN SENSOR: Use with the feedback system to sense the presence of oxygen in the exhaust gas and signal the computer which can reference the voltage signal to an air/fuel ratio.

PINION: The smaller of two meshing gears.

PISTON RING: An open-ended ring with fits into a groove on the outer diameter of the piston. Its chief function is to form a seal between the piston and cylinder wall. Most automotive pistons have three rings: two for compression sealing; one for oil sealing.

PRELOAD: A predetermined load placed on a bearing during assembly or by adjustment.

PRIMARY CIRCUIT: the low voltage side of the ignition system which consists of the ignition switch, ballast resistor or resistance wire, bypass, coil, electronic control unit and pick-up coil as well as the connecting wires and harnesses.

PRESS FIT: The mating of two parts under pressure, due to the inner diameter of one being smaller than the outer diameter of the other, or vice versa; an interference fit.

RACE: The surface on the inner or outer ring of a bearing on which the balls, needles or rollers move.

REGULATOR: A device which maintains the amperage and/or voltage levels of a circuit at predetermined values.

RELAY: A switch which automatically opens and/or closes a circuit.

RESISTANCE: The opposition to the flow of current through a circuit or electrical device, and is measured in ohms. Resistance is equal to the voltage divided by the amperage.

RESISTOR: A device, usually made of wire, which offers a preset amount of resistance in an electrical circuit.

RING GEAR: The name given to a ring-shaped gear attached to a differential case, or affixed to a flywheel or as part of a planetary gear set.

ROLLER BEARING: A bearing made up of hardened inner and outer races between which hardened steel rollers move.

ROTOR: 1. The disc-shaped part of a disc brake assembly, upon which the brake pads bear; also called, brake disc. 2. The device mounted atop the distributor shaft, which passes current to the distributor cap tower contacts.

SECONDARY CIRCUIT: The high voltage side of the ignition system, usually above 20,000 volts. The secondary includes the ignition coil, coil wire, distributor cap and rotor, spark plug wires and spark plugs.

SENDING UNIT: A mechanical, electrical, hydraulic or electro-magnetic device which transmits information to a gauge.

SENSOR: Any device designed to measure engine operating conditions or ambient pressures and temperatures. Usually electronic in nature and designed to send a voltage signal to an on-board computer, some sensors may operate as a simple on/off switch or they may provide a variable voltage signal (like a potentiometer) as conditions or measured parameters change.

SHIM: Spacers of precise, predetermined thickness used between parts to establish a proper working relationship.

SLAVE CYLINDER: In automotive use, a device in the hydraulic clutch system which is activated by hydraulic force, disengaging the clutch.

SOLENOID: A coil used to produce a magnetic field, the effect of which is to produce work.

SPARK PLUG: A device screwed into the combustion chamber of a spark ignition engine. The basic construction is a conductive core inside of a ceramic insulator, mounted in an outer conductive base. An electrical charge from the spark plug wire travels along the conductive core and jumps a preset air gap to a grounding point or points at the end of the conductive base. The resultant spark ignites the fuel/air mixture in the combustion chamber.

SPLINES: Ridges machined or cast onto the outer diameter of a shaft or inner diameter of a bore to enable parts to mate without rotation.

TACHOMETER: A device used to measure the rotary speed of an engine, shaft, gear, etc., usually in rotations per minute.

THERMOSTAT: A valve, located in the cooling system of an engine, which is closed when cold and opens gradually in response to engine heating, controlling the temperature of the coolant and rate of coolant flow.

TOP DEAD CENTER (TDC): The point at which the piston reaches the top of its travel on the compression stroke.

TORQUE: The twisting force applied to an object.

TORQUE CONVERTER: A turbine used to transmit power from a driving member to a driven member via hydraulic action, providing changes in drive ratio and torque. In automotive use, it links the driveplate at the rear of the engine to the automatic transmission.

TRANSDUCER: A device used to change a force into an electrical signal.

TRANSISTOR: A semi-conductor component which can be actuated by a small voltage to perform an electrical switching function.

TUNE-UP: A regular maintenance function, usually associated with the replacement and adjustment of parts and components in the electrical and fuel systems of a vehicle for the purpose of attaining optimum performance.

TURBOCHARGER: An exhaust driven pump which compresses intake air and forces it into the combustion chambers at higher than atmospheric pressures. The increased air pressure allows more fuel to be burned and results in increased horsepower being produced.

VACUUM ADVANCE: A device which advances the ignition timing in response to increased engine vacuum.

VACUUM GAUGE: An instrument used to measure the presence of vacuum in a chamber.

VALVE: A device which control the pressure, direction of flow or rate of flow of a liquid or gas.

VALVE CLEARANCE: The measured gap between the end of the valve stem and the rocker arm, cam lobe or follower that activates the valve.

VISCOSITY: The rating of a liquid's internal resistance to flow.

VOLTMETER: An instrument used for measuring electrical force in units called volts. Voltmeters are always connected parallel with the circuit being tested.

WHEEL CYLINDER: Found in the automotive drum brake assembly, it is a device, actuated by hydraulic pressure, which, through internal pistons, pushes the brake shoes outward against the drums.

PROFESSIONAL USED CAR INSPECTION

After you have made your own initial inspection, taken a test-drive, and then made a more detailed examination yourself, it's a good idea to ask the advice of a professional mechanic. It is possible there may be some nagging suspicions in one or two areas, and this is where the experienced hand/eye/ear of a mechanic can save you thousands of dollars in unwanted repairs. He has the background, training and specialized equipment to make more scientific, quantitative tests of most aspects of a car's condition.

Not every mechanic will make every test we have outlined here, and on the other hand, your mechanic may want to perform some tests we have not suggested. Hiring a mechanic to perform the complete list of tests could be an expensive check-out for a used car! Many of the tests would be done by the mechanic only after making a preliminary evaluation, listening to the engine and making a thorough visual examination. He may even want to take his own short test-drive. What he suspects from the above evaluation will prompt him to perform the necessary tests to eliminate or confirm potential trouble areas.

Who should make the tests? If you already have a favorite shop or mechanic, take the car there. Trust is an important factor, since you are banking on this evaluation for a purchase that make take you years to pay off. If you don't have a trusted mechanic, trust referrals from friends and relatives who have had good success with a shop or individual in your area. Check the classified section in your local newspaper or the yellow pages in your telephone book. You may find ads for mobile mechanics, who work out of a van or truck performing tune-ups and light mechanical work at any location, even your own driveway. Some even specialize in used car inspections. They may not have every diagnostic tool on hand on their truck, but they may be able to actually meet you at a car lot or private-party location to examine a vehicle. This may be an important factor when purchasing from a private party who doesn't want to let you take the vehicle away for diagnostic testing.

In many large cities you will find independent diagnostic centers whose main business is inspection and diagnosis for a fee. You may be able to source out a trustworthy site through your local Better Business Bureau, Bureau of Automotive Repair, State Department of Consumer Affairs, or through the local auto club. The AAA (American Automobile Association) in your area may have a list of approved local diagnostic centers. Generally, their recommendations are consistently updated and trustworthy.

All this preparation and leg work may seem like a lot of trouble, but if you have ever had a friend or acquaintance who has experienced major problems after buying a used car, you'll realize the inconvenience is well worth it. Remember that the best protection against fraud, misleading appearances or hidden problems is a thorough pre-purchase examination. While we are on the subject of misleading appearances, don't assume self-righteously that if you discover a serious defect or problem with the vehicle you are inspecting, the seller is consciously trying to deceive you. Your thoroughness may have uncovered problems the seller probably wasn't aware of. In fact, if a private party or dealer seems reluctant to have you make a thorough examination and have the vehicle further tested by a mechanic, assure them that they may have a copy of any checklists or reports on the vehicle's condition. A printed report, prepared at your expense, might prove of benefit to the seller in remedying apparent problems and making their car more appealing. The cost of having a full diagnostic check made by a professional is relatively inexpensive compared to the potential costs of buying a defective vehicle. Because of the expense, we recommend you proceed with this last step in the inspection process only after you have made your own inspection and test-drive, and are fairly certain this is the right car at the right price for you going in.

Be aware that a mechanic who's looking for work may be motivated to encourage the purchase, even when the vehicle has problems. Remember that the actual purchase decision must be yours. The mechanic is simply providing technical information and a cost estimate to repair the vehicle, which is the information you need to ultimately negotiate the purchase price of the vehicle.

We have included a photo sequence of a professional mechanic performing many of the tests and inspections we have described. As stated earlier, it may not be necessary for your mechanic to perform all of these tests, you and your mechanic will decide which tests may be excluded.

PROFESSIONAL CHECK

DESCRIPTION OF PROFESSIONAL TESTS

Underhood checks

CHECK THE FLUIDS AND FLUID LEVELS

Basically these are the same checks we have suggested making in Chapter 1, but the professional mechanic can make such checks quicker and with an experienced eye. He is looking for any fluid leaks and checking the "quality" of the fluids, looking at the color, smell and content of the car's fluids, anything that might hint to a possible problem area.

Tip
If you have reason to suspect the mileage shown on the odometer may not be accurate, ask the mechanic to also give his assessment - professionals know tell-tale signs to look for that can indicate fraudulent mileage readings.

CHECK THE BELTS, HOSES AND FILTERS

Although you probably have checked these items, an experienced mechanic is better qualified to inspect the sometimes confusing array of emission system hoses found on today's modern automobile. Often emissions system hoses are disconnected or missing and in many States must be brought back to factory specifications before the vehicle can be registered.

LISTEN FOR ANY UNUSUAL NOISES

Your mechanic is familiar with the sounds associated with good and bad engines. He can distinguish the difference between lifter noise and connecting-rod knock. He knows the difference between belt squeal from a worn-out, glazed drivebelt and an equivalent noise a defective power-steering pump, air conditioning compressor or alternator might make. He may be able to inform you, just from listening to the engine, of possible defects.

CHECK THE TIMING BELT

If the vehicle is approaching the 60,000-mile mark (this point varies with the make and model), it is probably due for a new timing belt. The mechanic can

The mechanic will start with a visual inspection, much like you have made, except that experience has taught him just what to look for, like finding this plugged vacuum hose (arrow)

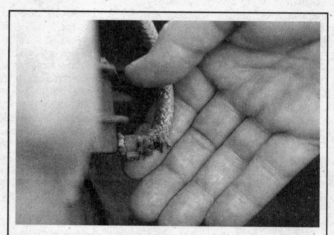

By bending and squeezing various vacuum, fuel, water and other hoses, the pro can turn up hidden problems like this splitting, cloth-covered European-style vacuum hose

While the average person might have missed this, our mechanic didn't - this disconnected heater hose was tucked under other components, to disguise the fact that the heater core had been blocked off and was probably defective

Only a sharp-eyed pro would spot that this accelerator/cruise control bracket (arrow) is missing its bottom leg and its mounting bolts

A quick check of the air filter element and the cleanliness of the air filter housing can tell the mechanic something about the maintenance of the vehicle

A mechanic's stethoscope is used to pinpoint the exact location of a particular engine noise

Tip

On many vehicles a failed timing belt can lead to serious engine damage due to valve-to-piston interference. Any timing belt in marginal condition must be replaced!

confirm this by removing one or more of the timing belt covers to inspect the belt for cracks and wear.

Engine diagnostic checks

ENGINE ANALYZER TESTS

By connecting a Diagnostic Engine Analyzer to the engine's electrical system, a mechanic can tell a great deal in a short time about the condition of the ignition system, charging system, timing and engine internal performance.

While the engine is running on an analyzer the mechanic can perform a

If in doubt about the condition of a timing belt merely based on indicated mileage, a mechanic may remove the upper belt cover for a close inspection

Power balance test in which he selectively cancels each cylinder, one at a time. He watches the rpm drop when each cylinder is canceled, and if one cylinder has less rpm drop when canceled than the others, it means that cylinder is

A quick check with a timing light can confirm whether an engine is currently in tune

Even without a large, sophisticated analysis machine, a technician can use smaller instruments like this one to check volts, ohms, point dwell and engine speed

The mechanic uses an ohmmeter to check the actual resistance of each plug wire, which will tell him if any wire is out-of-specifications

A state smog test isn't designed to give you a report on a used car, but a pro with the emissions-testing equipment can learn a lot about an engine's condition and state-of-tune

> **Tip**
>
> In some states, an emissions check will be required before you can register the vehicle in your name. If not provided by the seller, it may be wise to get the required state certification at this time.

(other emissions can be tested with more sophisticated analyzers, but these two reveal a great deal). He will check the engine at idle and at higher rpm, comparing the results to specs for that specific make and model of vehicle. A good test means that the engine's carburetion/fuel injection is working efficiently. Engine mechanical problems such as worn rings, valves, and valve guides can also be detected through an emissions test.

acting "weak", either from an ignition problem, which the scope could pinpoint, or from a mechanical problem (valves, rings, etc.), which would lead the mechanic to further tests to determine the cause.

The mechanic will also perform an **Ignition system primary and secondary circuit test**. By watching the patterns on the oscilloscope, the condition of coil, rotor, cap, spark plugs and spark plug wires can be checked. If any of these components are suspected of defects, they can be tested with smaller hand-held pieces of test equipment.

TEST THE CHARGING SYSTEM AND STARTER DRAW

In this test, a charging and starting system analyzer is connected to the alternator and battery. With the engine running, the output and regulation of the charging system is checked with the meters.

The condition of the starter is tested while the engine is cranked for 10 to 15 seconds. This test shows how many amps the starter is drawing, and is compared to specifications. Too much amperage draw could indicate a bad starter.

The battery condition is checked by performing a load test. A defective battery can further be diagnosed by sampling the electrolyte in the cells. The battery date code will also be checked.

CHECK THE SENSORS AND PULL COMPUTER CODES

On computer-managed engines (most cars from 1980 on), problems with various components and systems are recorded in the computer in the form of codes. With a "scan" tool, a mechanic can recall any codes that indicate problem areas. New-car dealerships have the most sophisticated equipment for this test, but many independent shops also have scan tools now.

TEST THE EXHAUST EMISSIONS

The vehicle may also be connected to an exhaust-gas-analyzer by inserting a probe into the tailpipe. With the car running in Neutral, the mechanic can check the amount of carbon monoxide (CO) and hydrocarbons (HC) in the exhaust

While in the shop's bay, a mechanic can quickly check the condition of the charging and starting systems

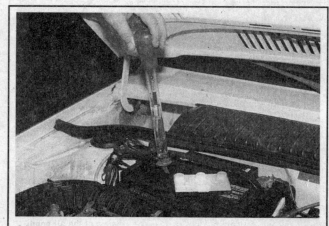

A battery hydrometer is used to check the state-of-charge of the battery

On computer-managed engines, a shop can hook up a code scanner that will read any maintenance or component fault codes that the computer is storing

Tip

On many vehicles, trouble codes can be displayed without any special tools – see the Haynes Computer Codes book for details.

PRESSURE-CHECK THE COOLING SYSTEM

The cooling system is pressurized with a small hand-pump connected in place of the vehicle's radiator cap. The radiator, hoses, gaskets and any other potential areas of leakage are then inspected. Any leaks or problem areas in the cooling system will immediately be located by the presence of antifreeze.

TEST THE COOLANT/ANTIFREEZE

Sampling the coolant from the radiator with a hydrometer will reveal the amount of freezing/corrosion protection (ratio of antifreeze to water) in the coolant.

By connecting a set of air conditioning system test gauges your mechanic will be able to evaluate the performance of the air conditioning system

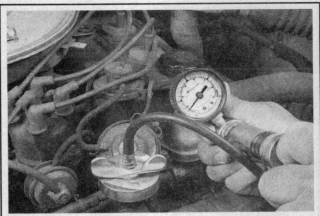

Attaching this tool to the radiator filler neck allows the mechanic to pressurize the cooling system, checking for possible leaks

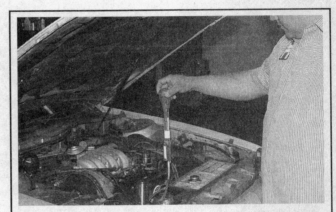

The amount and condition of antifreeze can easily and quickly be checked with a coolant hydrometer

CHECK THE AIR CONDITIONING SYSTEM

You may have noted in your detailed inspection that the air conditioning system was inoperative. Your mechanic can check the system with a set of gauges to determine the extent of repairs. If a low refrigerant charge is found, have him perform a refrigerant leak check to determine the point of escaping refrigerant.

An electronic leak-detector can quickly test an air conditioning system for the presence of escaping refrigerant

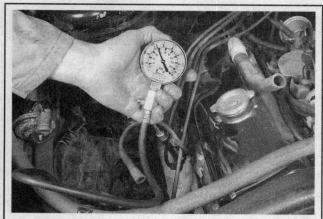

A cylinder compression check is performed with a gauge threaded into the spark plug hole - your mechanic will test all the cylinders, looking for one or more with low compression, indicating major mechanical problems

A tester like this takes a sample from the radiator, and if there are any combustion gasses present (signs of an engine internal problem), the test fluid changes from blue to yellow

CHECK THE CYLINDER COMPRESSION

If the cylinder balance test indicated there might be an internal mechanical problem, the spark plugs are removed and a pressure gauge is inserted into each spark plug hole, one cylinder at a time. When the engine is cranked for a few seconds, the gauge registers the compression developed, and can precisely indicate weak cylinders in terms of leaky valves, worn rings or a blown head gasket.

TEST FOR COMBUSTION GAS IN THE COOLANT

Not every shop has this particular test device (although almost all radiator shops do), but if the balance test and compression test indicated a problem, this test might be called for. A device samples coolant from the radiator with the engine running at high idle, and a test liquid changes color if there are combustion gasses present. If so, it indicates either a crack in the block or head(s), or a blown head gasket.

CHECK FOR TSB'S

If the vehicle is being checked out at a new-car dealership of the same make, The service department will run the original warranty card through their computer to check the car's record for recall notices. They can determine if these

Tip
Federal law requires auto manufacturers to make TSB's public, although dealerships often try to avoid giving them out for obvious reasons. Don't let them intimidate you. The registered owner of a vehicle has the right to demand to see all relevant TSB's.

recall "fixes" have actually been performed. They can also check their records for Technical Service Bulletins, which the manufacturers issue regularly to update mechanics on potential problem areas to look at on specific models. Some independent shops have access to these TSB's on their computer. They could, for instance, tell you that the transmission for that model had a lot of recalls or TSB's, and it may not be a good used-car buy in terms of reliability.

Undercar checks

Having access to a hoist is one of the key reasons you are bringing the vehicle to a professional for an inspection. A great deal can be examined when inspecting from underneath.

Besides the expensive test equipment he can utilize, the second reason for letting a mechanic check out your car prospect is that he has access to a hoist, where inspection of the underside can be much more thorough

Here the mechanic is pointing out an aftermarket suspension modification that has been made to this Sable - this modification makes rear wheel-alignment much easier and is a "plus point" for the vehicle

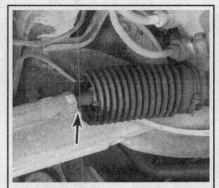

The torn boot (arrow) on this rack-and-pinion steering gear wasn't visible from looking under the front end, but was immediately noticed by a mechanic with a lift

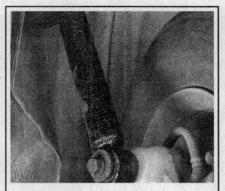

This oil-soaked shock absorber represents a repair of several hundred dollars (for all four coil-over shocks and struts), a major bargaining chip for you

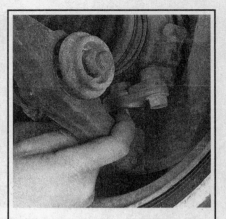

With a lift, these balljoint boots can be easily checked for damage

With the vehicle raised up, the mechanic can put a block under one front wheel and lower the chassis to where there is only half a load on the spring, and then check the wear/movement of the balljoints with a prybar

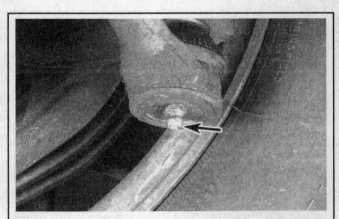

Many older vehicles have balljoint wear indicators - a close inspection reveals whether the grease fittings (arrow) have receded, indicating wear

CHECK THE SUSPENSION AND STEERING SYSTEMS

Besides the visual examination, he will check the suspension and steering components front and rear, looking for wear, collision damage and evidence of proper lubrication and maintenance. A mechanic equipped with a hoist can check the balljoints for wear, which can be unsafe if worn excessively. Ask your mechanic for his opinion of the tires. If there's any abnormal tread wear present, he'll give you his evaluation.

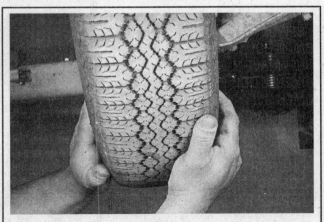

By moving the tire/wheel in and out at the bottom, the condition of the wheel bearings and other suspension elements can be determined

Your mechanic is well-equipped to inspect tires and diagnose what may have caused a particular pattern of uneven wear

The experienced pro can remove all four of the vehicle's wheels for a thorough inspection of calipers, hoses and other brake components

Flexible brake hoses should always be given close scrutiny - this cracked hose must be replaced

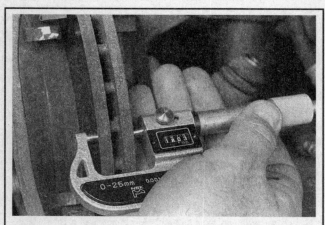

By checking the rotor thickness with a micrometer and comparing this to specifications, an approximation of the useful life left in the rotors can be made

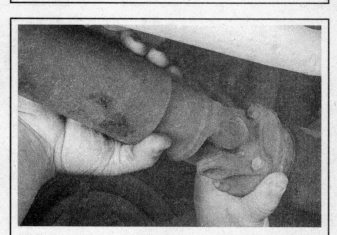

During his inspection of the driveline, the mechanic can check the U-joints by twisting each side in opposite directions to check for play - he'll also check the pinion-shaft play and pinion seal

CHECK THE BRAKING SYSTEM

Have your mechanic remove all four wheels, allowing him to carefully inspect the front and rear brakes, pad/shoe thickness, rotor thickness, wheel cylinder/caliper condition and emergency-brake linkages. In minutes, he can tell you approximately how much life is left in the current brake materials before needing a brake job.

CHECK THE DRIVELINE/DRIVEAXLES

Your mechanic should inspect the driveshaft and rear axle on rear-wheel drive vehicles. He'll be looking for defective U-joints and rear axle seal leaks. On front-wheel drive vehicles the driveaxle boots and constant-velocity joints will be inspected.

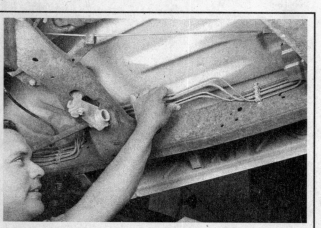

While on the hoist, it only takes a minute to check the full length of hoses and lines along the chassis

Tip
Exhaust system components are usually the first components on a car to rust through. Since exhaust gas is poisonous, you should always immediately replace any exhaust system components that are rusted through.

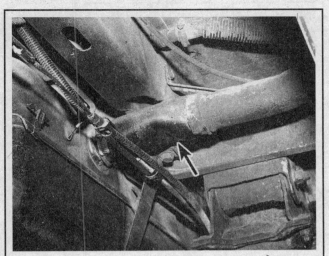

The wet spot on this fuel filler hose (arrow) indicated a potentially dangerous gasoline leak

CHECK FOR FLUID LEAKS

With the vehicle raised on a hoist its any easy matter to thoroughly inspect the undercarriage for any leaking components. Automobiles are notorious for leaking oil and fluids. Your mechanic will advise you on the seriousness of any leaks found. Minor leaks may be acceptable on a used car while major oil leaks and any fuel leaks should be repaired immediately.

CHECK THE EXHAUST SYSTEM

An exhaust system check will be performed, paying special attention to the catalytic converter and muffler. Also ask your mechanic to note any exhaust leaks. Some vehicles are notorious for cracking exhaust manifolds, which can be an expensive repair.

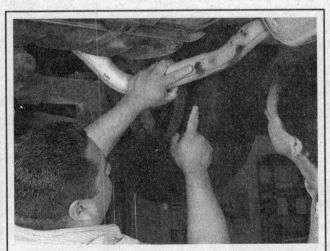

Besides pointing out defects like these exhaust system holes, the pro can tell you the priorities - which items need immediate attention and the relative costs of fixing various components and systems

Weeping transmission fluid here (arrow) implies that the transmission rear seal needs replacing

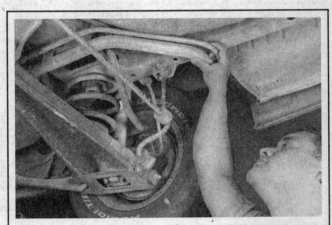

The fuel tank filler pipe/hose and vent line should both be checked for damage or restrictions

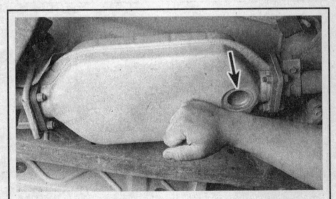

The emissions test will tell if the catalytic converter is working properly, and on older GM-type converters, the mechanic may hit the converter to see if the pellets rattle (they should) - only those converters that have a drain plug (arrow) have pellets

Professional Mechanic's Used Car Checklist

Underhood checks

- [ ] Check the fluids and fluid levels
- [ ] Check the belts, hoses and filters
- [ ] Listen for any unusual noises
- [ ] Check the timing belt

Engine diagnostic checks

- [ ] Engine analyzer tests
- [ ] Test the exhaust emissions
- [ ] Test the charging system and starter draw
- [ ] Check the sensors and pull computer codes
- [ ] Pressure-check the cooling system
- [ ] Test the coolant/antifreeze
- [ ] Check the air conditioning system
- [ ] Check the cylinder compression
- [ ] Test for combustion gas in coolant
- [ ] Check for TSBs

Undercar checks

- [ ] Check the suspension and steering systems
- [ ] Check the braking system
- [ ] Check the driveline/driveaxles
- [ ] Check for fluid leaks
- [ ] Check the exhaust system

MASTER
INDEX